Assessment Guide

Grade 1

Visit *The Learning Site!*
www.harcourtschool.com

Printed in the United States of America

ISBN 13: 978-0-15-356822-0
ISBN 10: 0-15-356822-4

1 2 3 4 5 6 7 8 9 10 054 16 15 14 13 12 11 10 09 08 07

Contents

MULTIPLE CHOICE TESTS

FREE RESPONSE TESTS

Introduction

Assessment in *HSP Math*

HSP Math provides a wide range of assessment tools to measure student achievement before, during, and after instruction. These tools include:

Entry Level Assessment

Progress Monitoring

Summative Evaluation

Test Preparation

Assessment Technology

Entry Level Assessment

Inventory Test—These tests should be administered at the beginning of the school year to assess mastery of content from the previous grade level.

Show What You Know—This feature appears at the beginning of every chapter in the *HSP Math* Student Edition. It may be used before chapter instruction begins to determine whether students possess crucial prerequisite skills. Tools for intervention are provided.

Pretests—The Beginning of Year Test, and Unit Benchmark Pretests, Form A (multiple choice) or Form B (free response), and Chapter Pretests, Form A (multiple choice), may be used to measure what students may already have mastered before instruction begins. These tests are provided in this *Assessment Guide.*

Progress Monitoring

Daily Assessment—These point-of-use strategies allow you to continually adjust instruction so that all students are constantly progressing toward mastery of the grade-level objectives. These strategies appear in every lesson of the *HSP Math* Teacher's Edition, and include the Quick Review, Mixed Review and Test Prep, and the Close section of the lesson plan.

Intervention—While monitoring student's progress, you may determine that intervention is needed. The Differentiated Instruction page for each lesson in the Teacher's Edition suggests several options for meeting individual needs.

Student Self-Assessment—Students evaluate their own work through checklists, surveys, and portfolios. Three self-assessment tools are provided. The *Group Checklist* is designed to help students assess the group's achievement and interaction with one another. The *Individual Checklist* helps the student recognize areas of strength and weakness regarding collaborating with others toward solving problems. The *Individual End of Chapter Survey* leads students to reflect on what they have learned and how they learned it. It is designed to help students learn more about their own capabilities and to develop confidence. Discuss directions for completing each checklist or survey with the students. Tell them there are no "right" responses to the questions.

Summative Evaluation

Formal Assessment—Several options are provided to help determine whether students have achieved the goals defined by the objectives. These options are provided at the end of each chapter and unit, and at the end of the year. They include:

Student Edition
Chapter Review/Test
Standardized Test Prep
Unit Review/Test

Assessment Guide
Chapter Posttests
Unit Benchmark Posttests
End of Year Test

Test Preparation

Mixed Review and Test Prep—At the end of most lessons, there are practice items.

Standardized Test Prep—At the end of each chapter in the *Student Edition,* these pages provide practice in solving problems.

Assessment Technology

Online Assessment

Online assessment offers assessment flexibility. With the option to electronically assign entire tests from the *Assessment Guide* or easily build your own test using a bank of questions, displayed by lesson objective, you can individualize assessment for each student. Upon student completion of a test, the test is automatically scored, providing you and the student instant feedback. Additionally, prescriptive suggestions are given to differentiate any necessary follow-up instruction.

ExamView

The ExamView Test Generator presents a unique way to administer a printed test. Using the ExamView CD-Rom, you can quickly print tests found in the *Assessment Guide,* create a custom test from a bank of questions, or author your own questions. The final page of the test supplies the answer key.

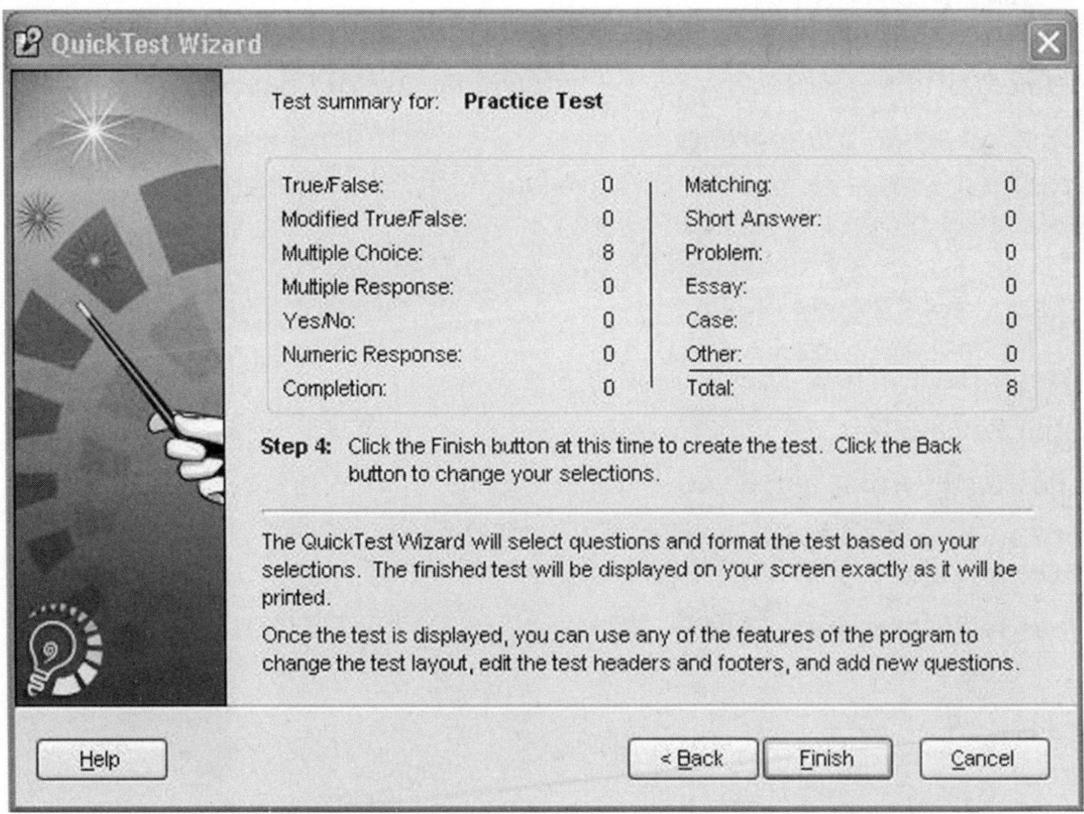

ASSESSMENT OPTIONS AT A GLANCE

ASSESSING PRIOR KNOWLEDGE

Show What You Know, *SE*

Inventory Test, Form A, *AG*

Beginning of Year Test, Form A and B, *AG*

Chapter Pretest, Form A, *AG*

Unit Benchmark Pretest, Form A and B, *AG*

TEST PREPARATION

Mixed Review and Test Prep, *SE*

Standardized Test Prep, *SE*

Unit Review/Test, *SE*

DAILY ASSESSMENT

Quick Review, *SE*

Mixed Review and Test Prep, *SE*

Problem of the Day, *TE*

Lesson Quiz, *on lesson transparency*

STUDENT SELF-ASSESSMENT

Group Checklist, *AG*

Individual Checklist, *AG*

Individual End of Chapter Survey, *AG*

Portfolio Guide, *AG*

FORMAL ASSESSMENT

Chapter Review/Test, *SE*

Unit Review/Test, *SE*

Chapter Posttest, Form A and B, *AG*

Unit Benchmark Posttest, Form A and B, *AG*

End of Year Test, Form A and B, *AG*

Key: SE = *Student Edition,* TE = *Teacher's Edition,* AG = *Assessment Guide*

OVERVIEW OF THE *ASSESSMENT GUIDE*

Management Forms

Individual Record Form—This management form contains all of the lesson objectives for the grade level. After each lesson objective are correlations to the test items in Form A and Form B format of the Chapter Posttests, Unit Benchmark Posttests, and the End of Year Test. Criterion scores for each lesson objective are given. The form provides a place to enter a single student's scores and to indicate the lesson objective he or she has met. Prescriptions to multiple resources are also included. These options include lessons in the *Student Edition* and *Teacher's Edition* and activities in the following workbooks: *Reteach Workbook, Practice Workbook,* and the *Problem Solving and Reading Strategies Workbook.* Additionally, there are *Mega Math* activities listed.

Class Record Form—This form makes it possible to record the test(s) scores of an entire class on a single form.

Tests

Inventory Test—This test assesses how well students have mastered the objectives from the previous grade level. Test results provide information about the kinds of review students may need to be successful in mathematics at the new grade level. The teacher should use the Inventory Test at the beginning of the school year or when a new student arrives in class.

Beginning of Year Test—This test assesses current grade-level content. There is a Form A and a Form B available. Test results provide helpful information on how to guide instruction, so it builds upon student's prior knowledge.

Chapter Pretests—These tests are available in Form A format. There is a pretest for each chapter, which can be given to assess prior knowledge of the skills and concepts to be taught in the upcoming chapter. Test results can help individualize instruction.

Unit Benchmark Pretest—These tests are available in Form A and Form B formats. There is a pretest for each unit, which can be given to assess prior knowledge of the skills and concepts to be taught in the upcoming unit. Test results can help individualize instruction.

Chapter Posttests—These tests are available in Form A and Form B formats. There is a posttest for each chapter, which can be given to measure student mastery of skills and concepts taught in that chapter. The free-response format (Form B) can be especially helpful in diagnosing specific errors in problem solutions.

Unit Benchmark Posttests—These tests are also available in Form A and Form B formats. There is a posttest for each unit, which can be given to measure student mastery of skills and concepts taught in that unit. The free-response format (Form B) can be especially helpful in diagnosing specific errors in problem solutions.

End of Year Test—This test assesses how well students have mastered the objectives in the grade level. There is a Form A and a Form B available. Test results may provide help in recommending a summer review program.

Answer Key

Answer Key—The answer key provides reduced replications of the tests with answers.

Project Name ______________________ Date __________

Group Members ____________________________________

GROUP CHECKLIST

How Did Our Group Do?

Ask your group these questions. Then circle the number of stars your group thinks it earned.

How well did our group	**Great Job**	**Good Job**	**Could Do Better**
1. share ideas?	★★★	★★	★
2. plan what to do?	★★★	★★	★
3. share the work?	★★★	★★	★
4. solve group problems without asking for help?	★★★	★★	★
5. show and check our work?	★★★	★★	★

Total __________

Write your group's answer to each question.

1. What did our group do best?

____

____

2. How can we help our group do better?

____

____

Project Name ______________________ Date __________

Name ____

INDIVIDUAL CHECKLIST

How Well Did I Work in My Group?

Circle ☺ if you agree. Circle ☹ if you disagree.

1. I shared ideas with my group.	☺	☹
2. I listened to the ideas of others in my group.	☺	☹
3. I was able to ask questions of my group.	☺	☹
4. I helped others in my group to share their ideas.	☺	☹
5. I was able to disagree with my group without any problems.	☺	☹
6. I helped my group plan.	☺	☹
7. I did my fair share of the group's work.	☺	☹
8. I understood the problem my group worked on.	☺	☹
9. I understood the solution to the problem my group worked on.	☺	☹
10. I can explain to others the problem my group worked on and its solution.	☺	☹

Name _______________ Date _________

INDIVIDUAL END OF CHAPTER SURVEY

Chapter _______________

How Did I Do?

Complete each sentence.

1. I thought the lessons in this chapter were

____

2. The lesson I liked the most was

____

3. Something that I still need to work on is

____

4. One thing that I think I did a great job on was

____

5. I would like to learn more about

____

6. Something I understand now that I did not understand before these lessons is

____

7. I think I might use the math I learned in these lessons to

____

8. The amount of effort I put into these lessons was

____

(very little some a lot)

PORTFOLIO ASSESSMENT

A portfolio is a collection of each student's work gathered over an extended period of time. A portfolio illustrates the growth, talents, achievements, and reflections of the learner and provides a means for you to assess the student's performance and progress.

Building a Portfolio

There are many opportunities to collect student's work throughout the year as you use *HSP Math*. Suggested portfolio items are found throughout the *Teacher's Edition.* Give students the opportunity to select some work samples to be included in the portfolio.

- Provide a folder for each student with the student's name clearly marked.
- Explain to students that throughout the year they will save some of their work in the folder. Sometimes it will be their individual work; sometimes it will be group reports and projects or completed checklists.
- Have students complete "A Guide to My Math Portfolio" several times during the year.

Evaluating a Portfolio

The following points made with regular portfolio evaluation will encourage growth in self-evaluation:

- Discuss the contents of the portfolio as you examine it with each student.
- Encourage and reward students by emphasizing growth, original thinking, and completion of tasks.
- Reinforce and adjust instruction of the broad goals you want to accomplish as you evaluate the portfolios.
- Examine each portfolio on the basis of individual growth rather than in comparison with other portfolios.
- Use the Portfolio Evaluation sheet for your comments.
- Share the portfolios with families during conferences or send the portfolio, including the Family Response form, home with the students.

Name ____________________

Date ____________________

A Guide to My Math Portfolio

What is in My Portfolio	What I Learned
1.	
2.	
3.	
4.	
5.	

I organized my portfolio this way because ____________________

____

____

Name ______________________

Date ______________________

Evaluating Performance	Evidence and Comments
1. What mathematical understandings are demonstrated?	
2. What skills are demonstrated?	
3. What approaches to problem solving and critical thinking are evident?	
4. What work habits and attitudes are demonstrated?	

Summary of Portfolio Assessment

For This Review			Since Last Review		
Excellent	Good	Fair	Improving	About the Same	Not as Good

Date ______________________

Dear Family,

This is your child's math portfolio. It contains work samples that your child and I have selected to show how his or her abilities in math have grown. Your child can explain what each sample shows.

Please look over the portfolio with your child and write a few comments in the blank space at the bottom of this sheet about what you have seen. Your child has been asked to bring the portfolio with your comments included back to school.

Thank you for helping your child evaluate his or her portfolio and for taking pride in the work he or she has done. Your interest and support is important to your child's success in school.

Sincerely,

____

(Teacher)

- -

Response to Portfolio:

____

(Family member)

Name ______________________

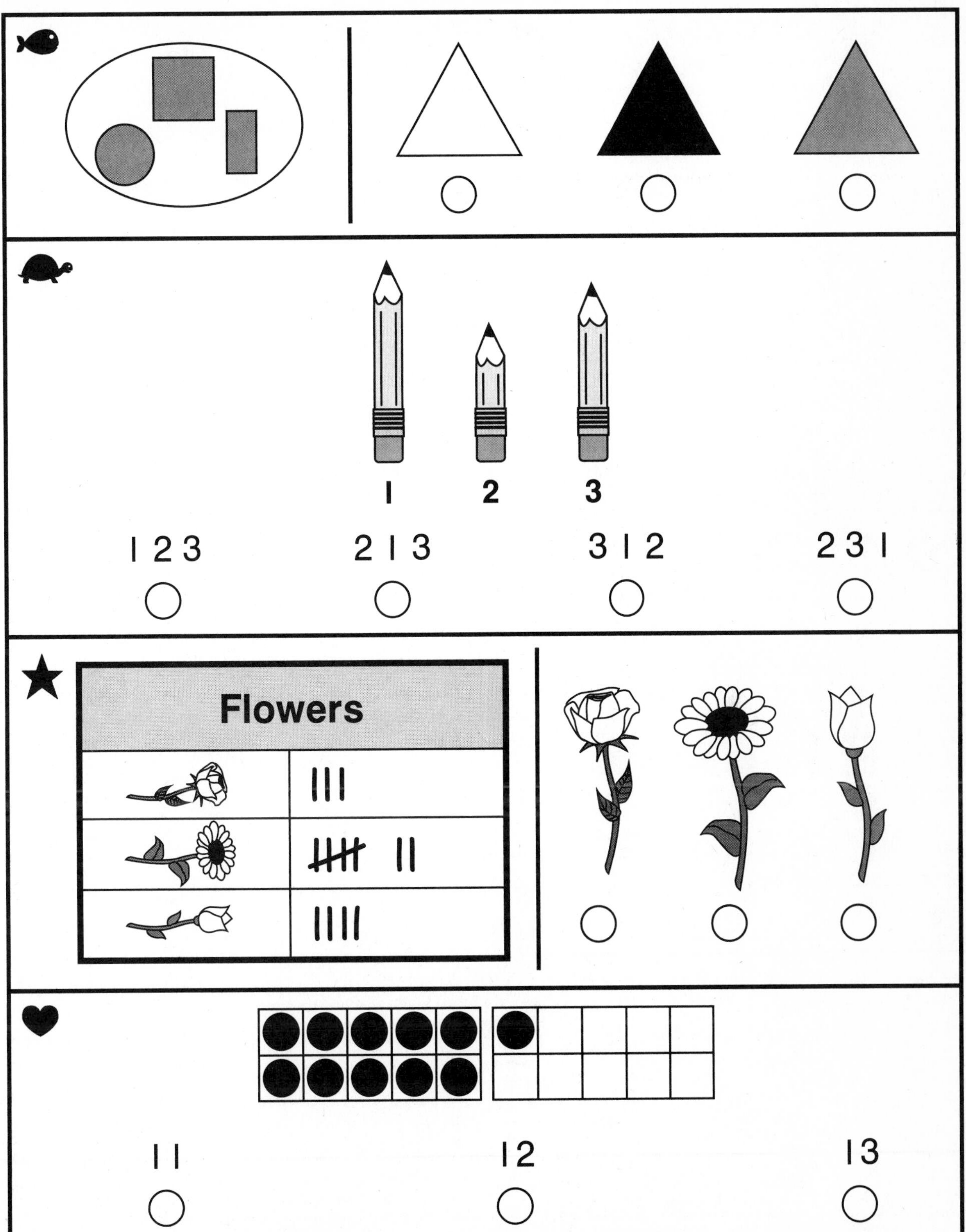

Look at the group of figures at the beginning of the row. Mark under the shape that belongs in the group.
Mark under the numbers that show the pencils in order from shortest to longest.
★ Read the table. Mark under the kind of flower there are the most of in this table.
♥ Mark under the number that tells how many counters there are in the ten frame.

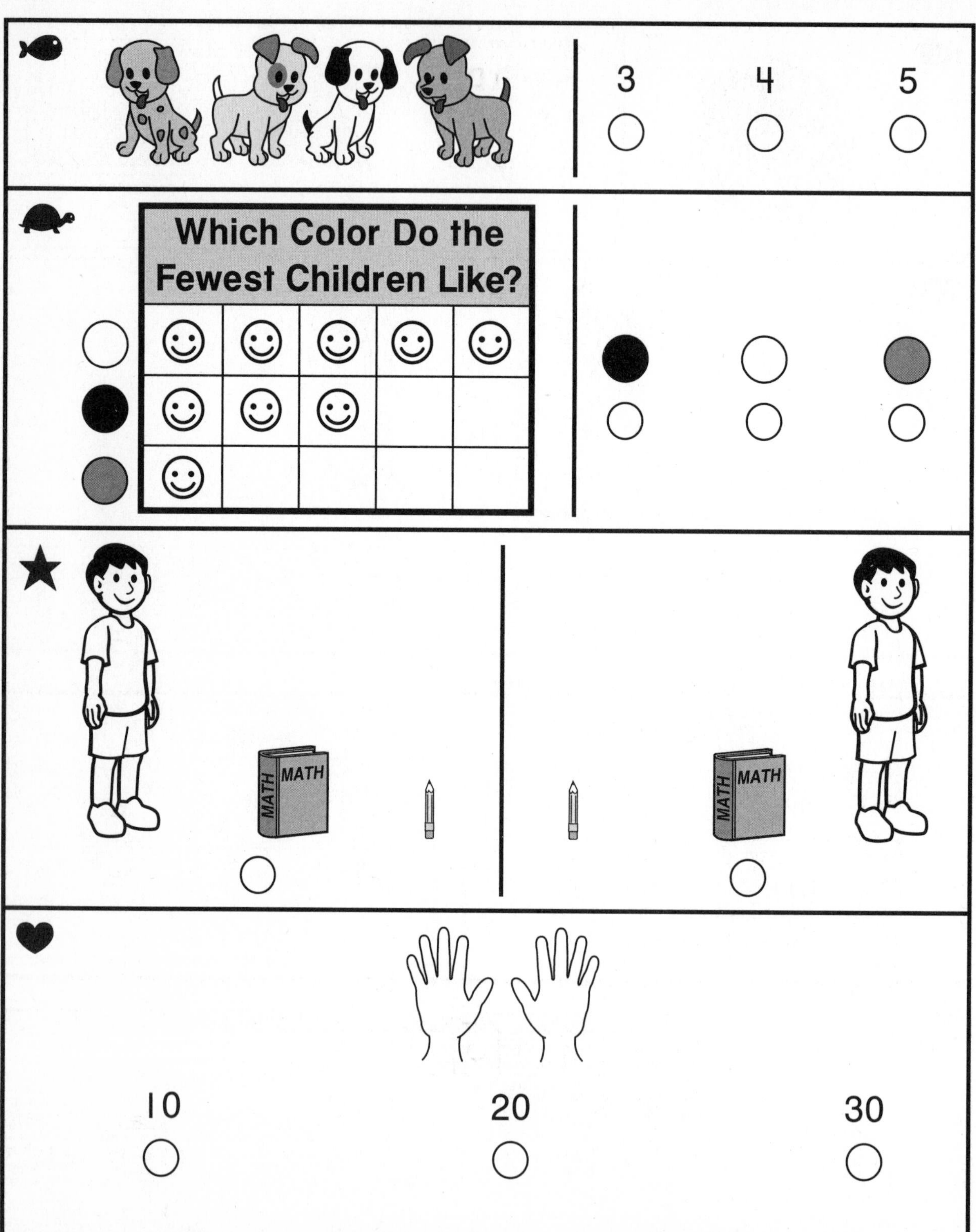

Draw an X on each puppy in the set as you count. Mark under the number that tells how many puppies there are in the picture.

Read the graph. Mark under the color the fewest children like.

★ Mark under the group of objects that are in order from lightest to heaviest.

♥ Count by tens. Mark under the number that tells how many fingers there are in the picture.

Name ____________________

○ ○ ○

4 + 5 = 9 ○   5 + 4 = 9 ○   5 + 5 = 10 ○   4 + 6 = 10 ○

2 ○   3 ○   4 ○   5 ○

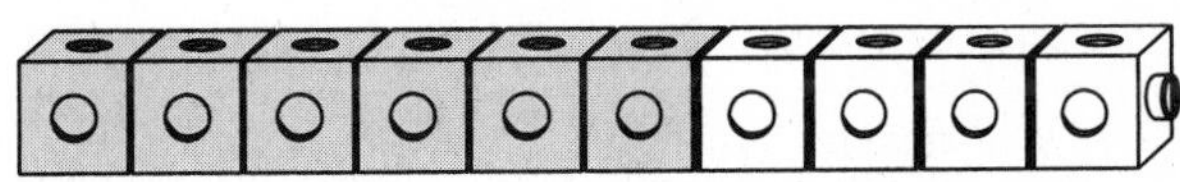

4 + 6 = 10 ○   6 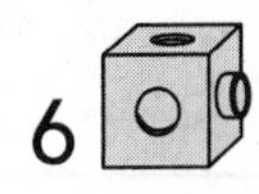 + 4 = 10 ○

Look at the figure at the beginning of the row. Mark under the object that is the same shape.

Look at the bees. Mark under the addition sentence that tells about the bees.

★ Look at the figure at the beginning of the row. Mark under the number that tells how many equal parts are shown in the figure.

♥ Mark under the addition sentence for the model.

Name ______________________________ INVENTORY TEST

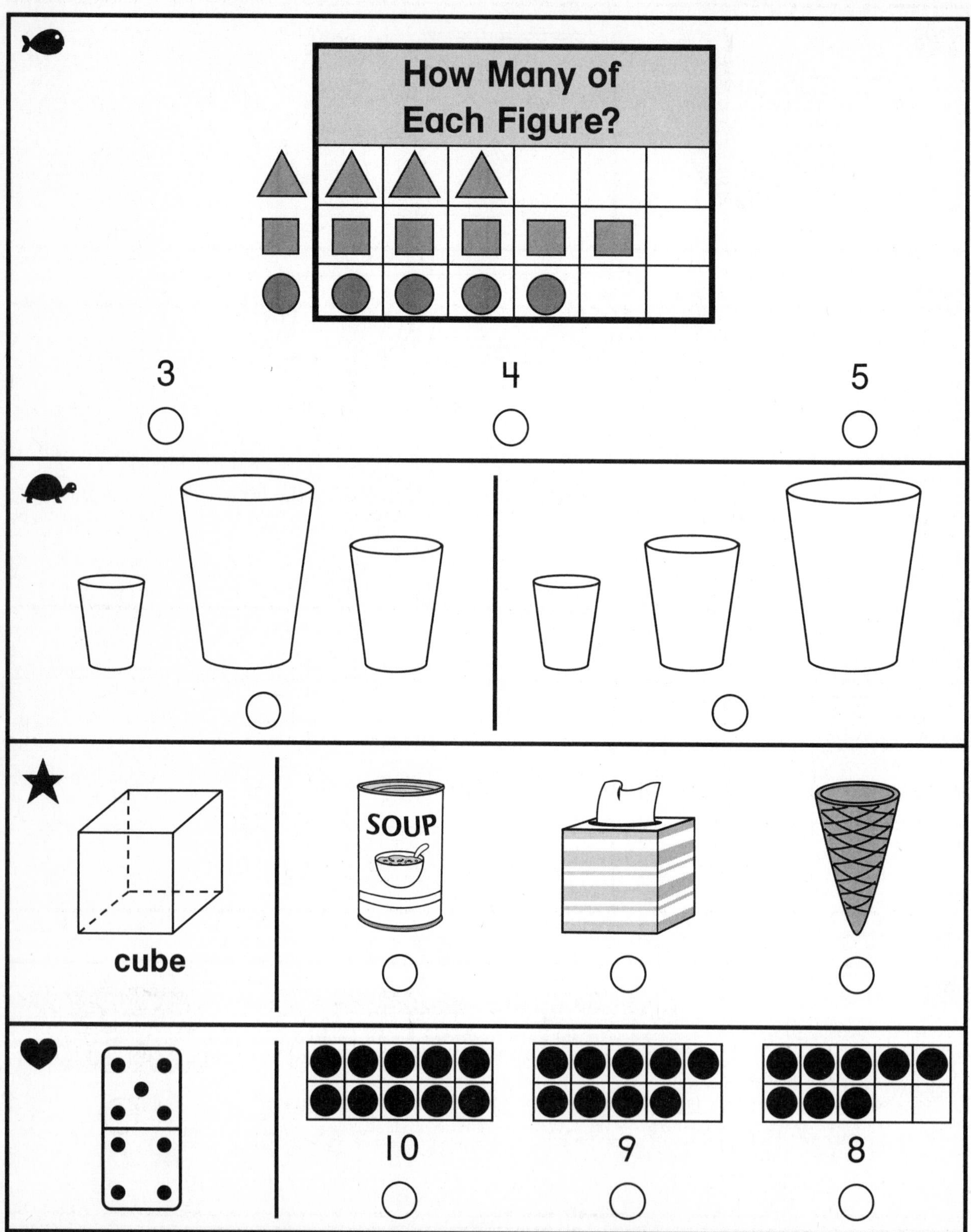

Read the graph. Mark under the number that tells how many squares there are in the graph.
Mark under the cups that are in order, beginning with the cup that holds the least amount of sand.
Mark under the object that is shaped like the solid figure.
…ok at the picture at the beginning of the row. Mark under the number that tells how many there are.

Name ______________________

INVENTORY TEST

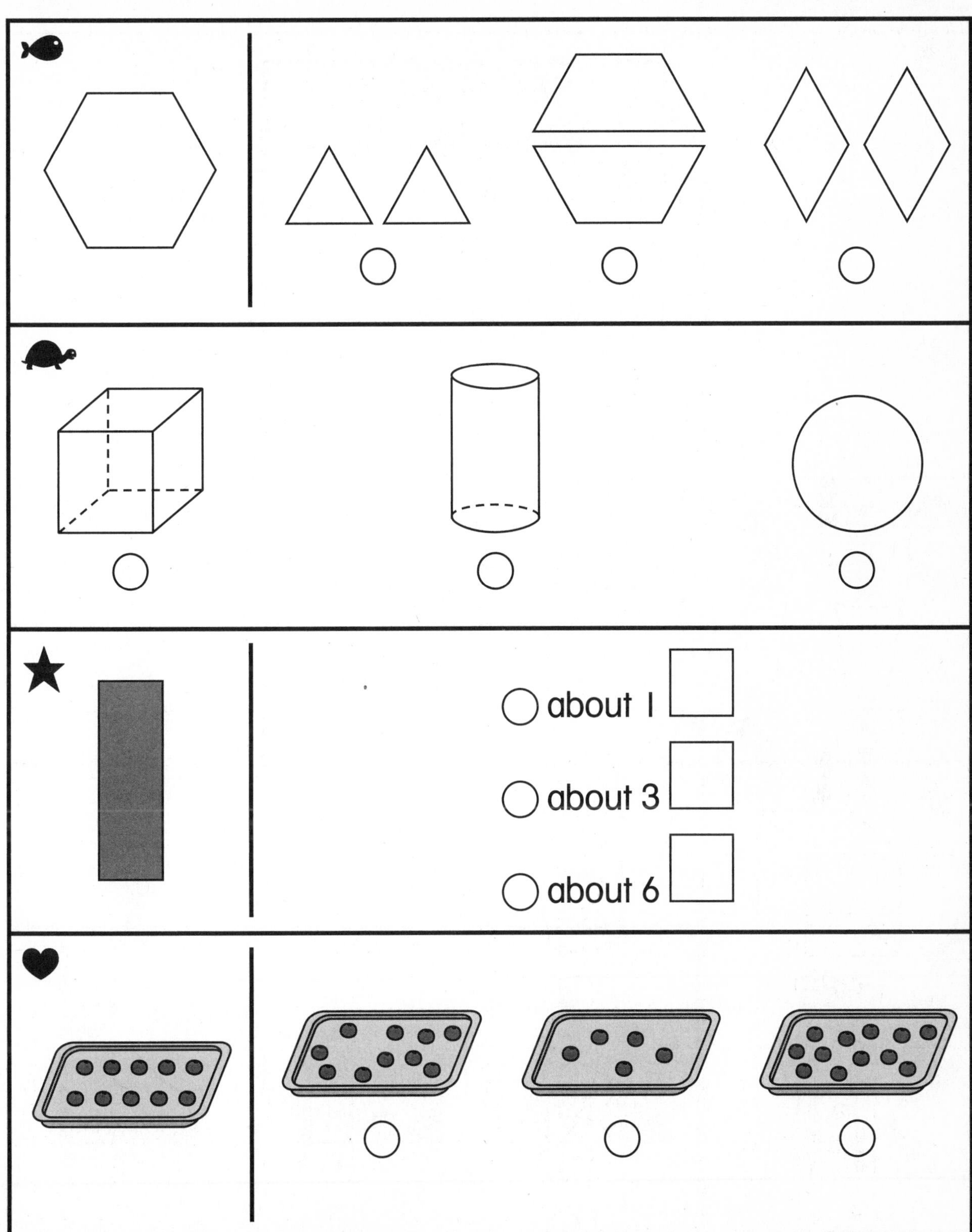

- Mark under the figures you can use to cover the outline of the figure at the beginning of the row.
- Mark under the figure that does not roll.
- ★ Estimate about how many tiles it will take to cover the area of the rectangle. Mark next to the estimate.
- ♥ Look at the picture at the beginning of the row. Without counting, mark under the tray that has fewer than 10 blueberries.

Name ______________________

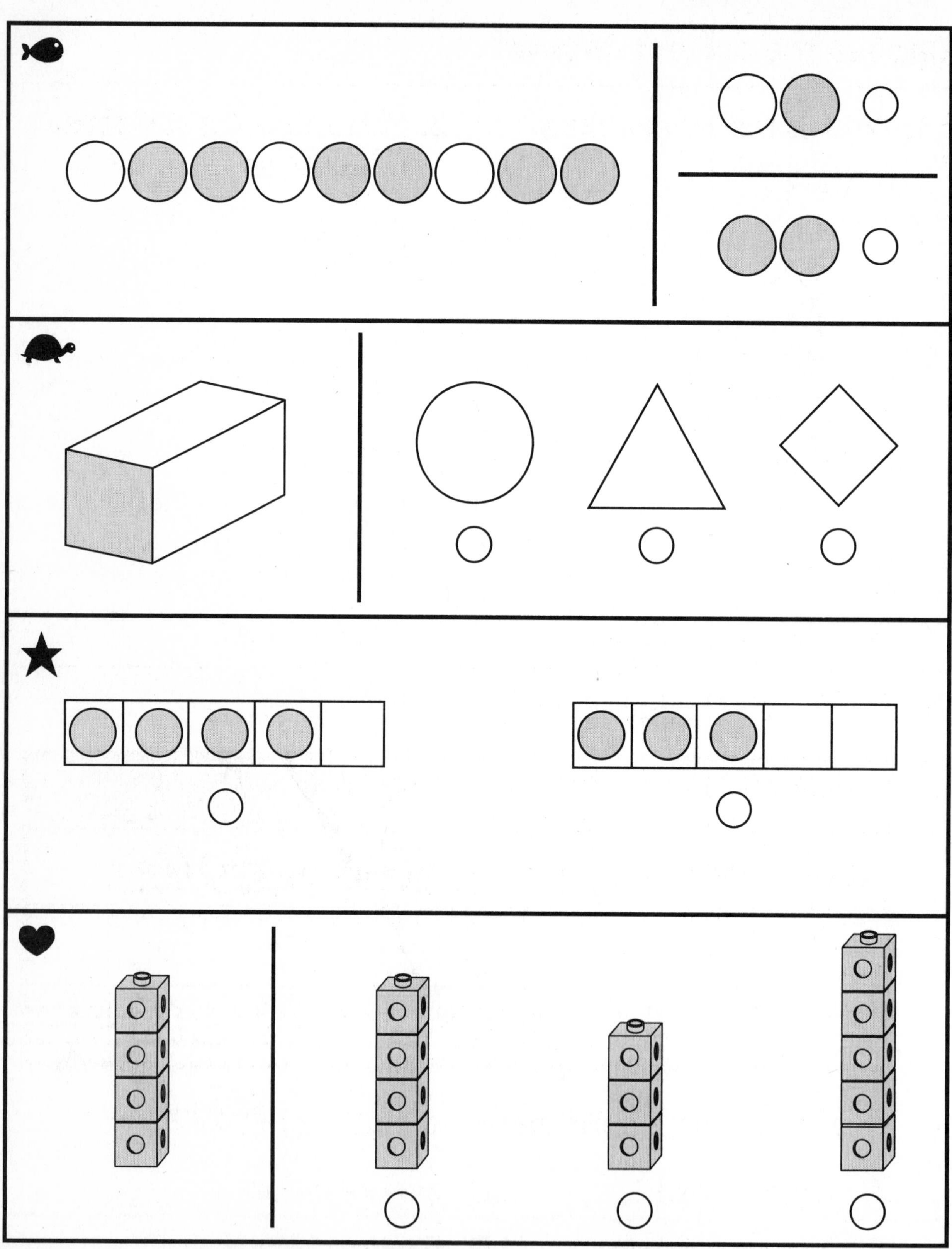

Mark next to the circles that most likely come next in the pattern.

Mark under the plane figure that matches the shape of the surface of the solid figure.

Mark under the counters that show 4.

at the cube train at the beginning of the row. Mark under the cube train that is the same length.

Name ______________________________

Choose the correct answer.

1. What is the temperature?

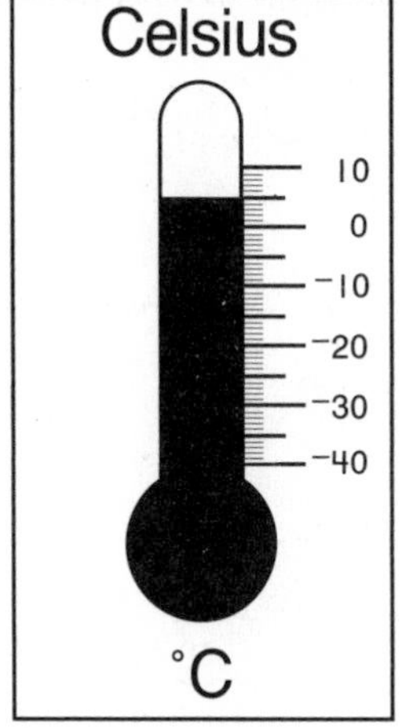

A 5°C **C** 15°C

B 10°C **D** 50°C

2. How many flat surfaces does the solid have?

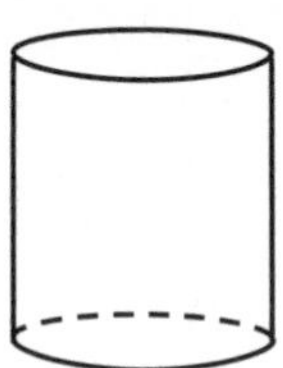

A 4

B 3

C 2

D 1

3. Use the picture graph to answer question 3.

Games We Like							
checkers							
4 **go fish**	4	4	4				
dominos							

How many more children chose [domino] than [checker]?

A 1 more child **C** 3 more children

B 2 more children **D** 5 more children

Go On

Choose the correct answer.

4. Which (bear) belongs in the group?

A  **B**  **C**  **D** 

5. What is the sum?

30 + 40 = ____

A 50

B 60

C 70

D 80

6. Which tells how many?

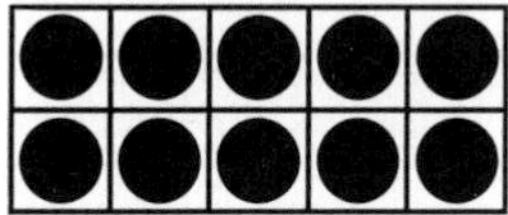 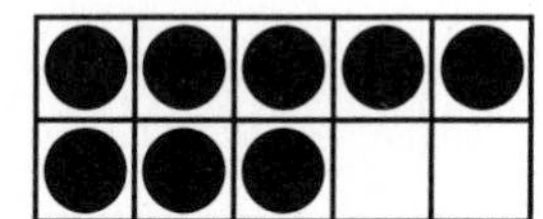

A nineteen

B eighteen

C seventeen

D thirteen

7. Which shows a pair of related subtraction facts?

A $\begin{array}{r} 12 \\ -\ 3 \\ \hline 9 \end{array}$ $\begin{array}{r} 9 \\ -3 \\ \hline 6 \end{array}$ **B** $\begin{array}{r} 10 \\ -\ 4 \\ \hline 6 \end{array}$ $\begin{array}{r} 12 \\ -\ 6 \\ \hline 6 \end{array}$ **C** $\begin{array}{r} 11 \\ -\ 3 \\ \hline 8 \end{array}$ $\begin{array}{r} 8 \\ -3 \\ \hline 5 \end{array}$ **D** $\begin{array}{r} 11 \\ -\ 5 \\ \hline 6 \end{array}$ $\begin{array}{r} 11 \\ -\ 6 \\ \hline 5 \end{array}$

Go On

Name ______________________________

Choose the correct answer.

8. Which type of move is shown?

A flip

B slide

C turn

D symmetry

9. Which tool will you use to measure how much the mug holds?

A

C 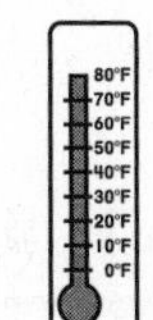

B 

D 

10. How many more leaves are there than birds?

$$\begin{array}{r} 12 \\ -\ 4 \\ \hline \end{array}$$

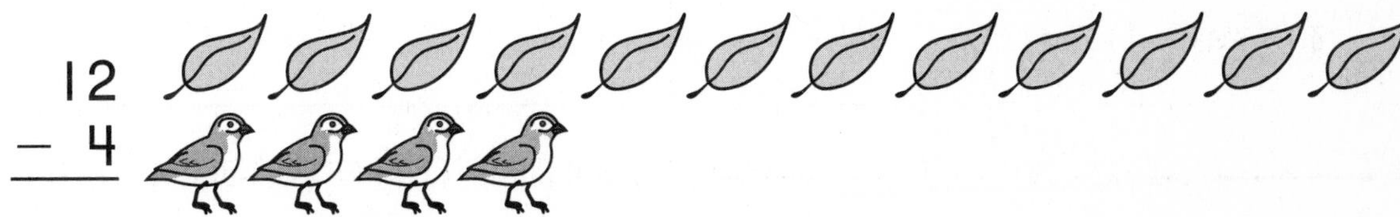

A 16 more leaves

B 9 more leaves

C 8 more leaves

D 6 more leaves

Go On

Name ____

Choose the correct answer.

11. Use the tally chart to answer the question.

Pets We Like	
dog	𝍸 |
cat	||||
fish	𝍸 |||

How many children chose the dog?

A 2 children

B 4 children

C 6 children

D 8 children

12. What time does the clock show?

A 12:00

B 7:30

C 8:00

D 7:00

13. Which symbol can you use to compare the amounts?

_____ ¢ ◯ _____ ¢

A < **B** > **C** =

Go On

Name ______________________________

Choose the correct answer.

14. Which number is missing?

3 1 2 3 1 __?__ 3 1 2

A 1 **B** 2 **C** 3 **D** 4

15. How many corners does this plane figure have?

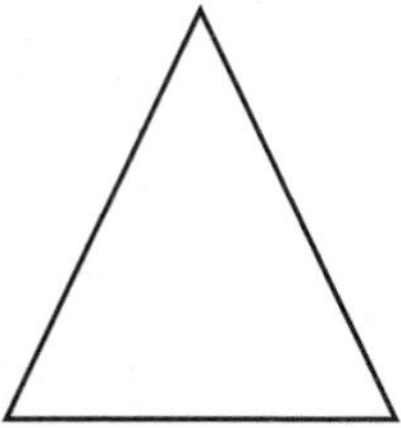

A 3

B 4

C 5

D 6

16. Count how many tens and ones. Which shows the number in a different way?

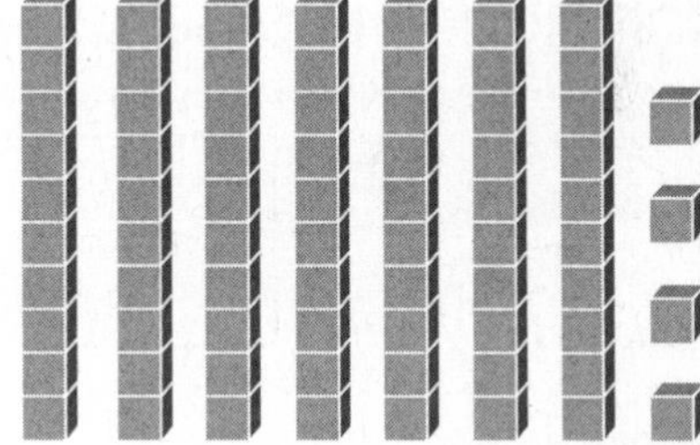

A 40 + 7

B 70 + 40

C 70 + 4

D 7 + 4

17. What is the difference?

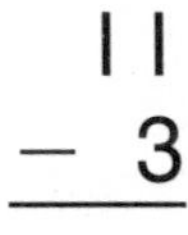

$$\begin{array}{r} 11 \\ -\ 3 \\ \hline \end{array}$$

A 14 **C** 9

B 10 **D** 8

18. Which number is between 54 and 56?

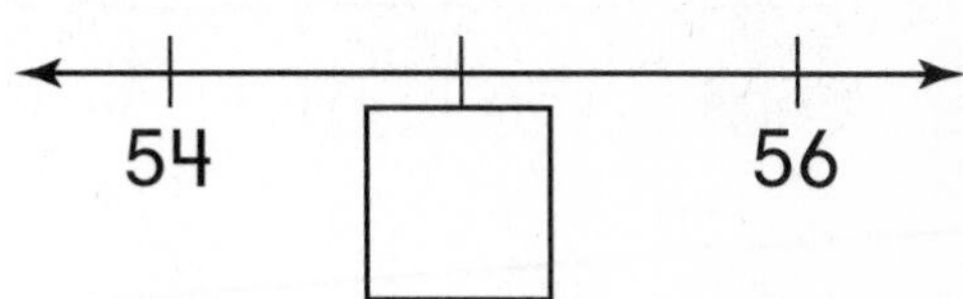

A 53 **C** 57

B 55 **D** 60

Go On

Name ____________________

Choose the correct answer.

19. Which comes next?

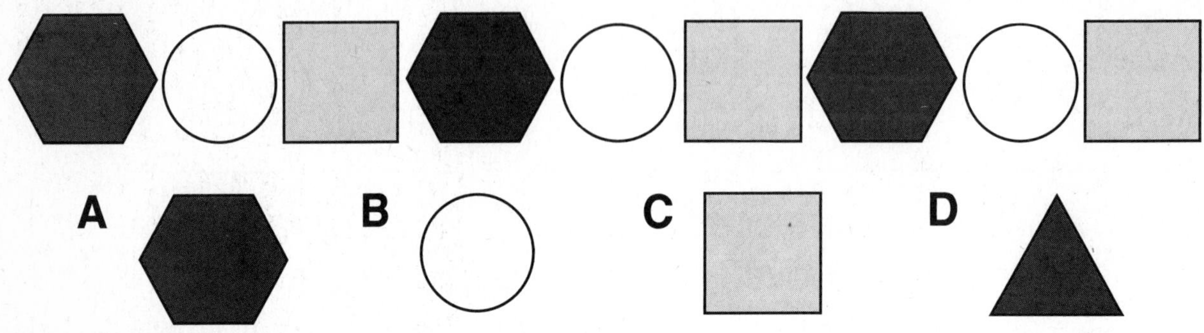

20. Which figure is a square?

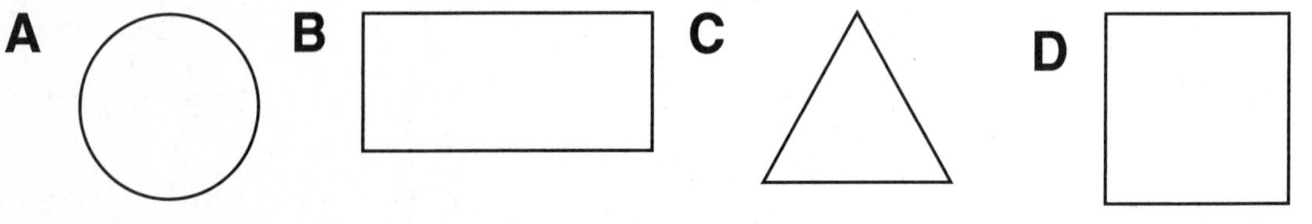

21. About how many paper clips long is the object?

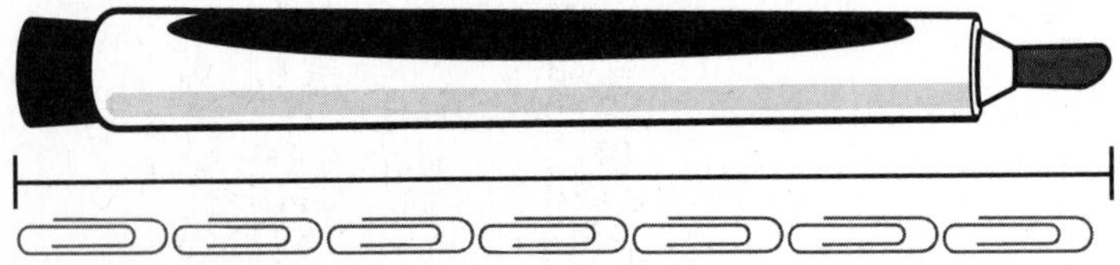

A about 6 paper clips

B about 7 paper clips

C about 8 paper clips

D about 9 paper clips

22. What is the sum?

$$\begin{array}{r} 6 \\ +3 \\ \hline \end{array}$$

A 3 C 9

B 8 D 10

23. What is the difference?

$$\begin{array}{r} 8 \\ -2 \\ \hline \end{array}$$

A 5 C 7

B 6 D 10

Go On

Choose the correct answer.

24. Which figure belongs in group C?

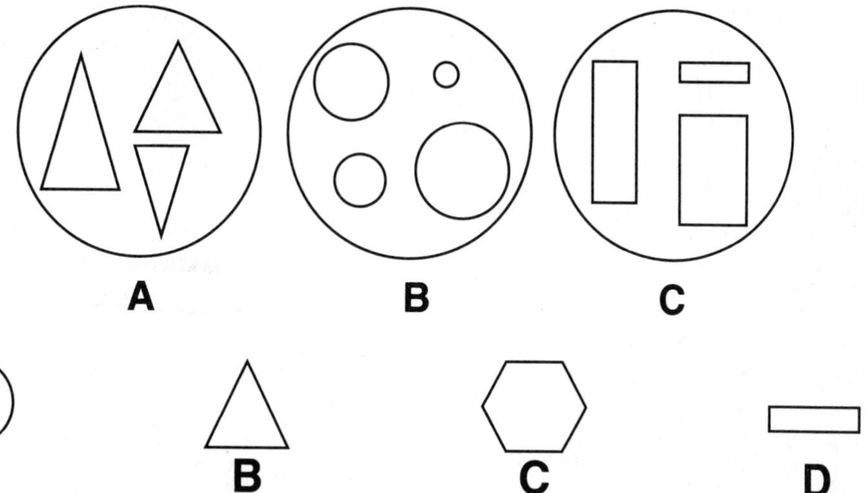

A B C D

25. From **Start**, go right 2. Go down 3. Go left 1. Where are you?

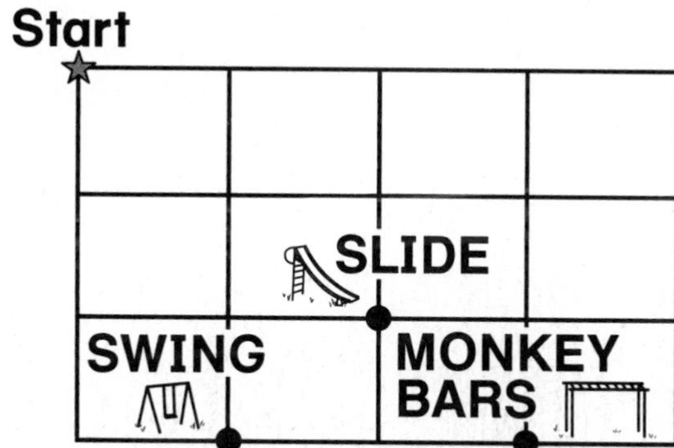

A swing

B slide

C monkey bars

26. What is the sum?

$$\begin{array}{r} 9 \\ +4 \\ \hline \end{array}$$

A 14 **C** 12

B 13 **D** 5

27. Which is a related subtraction fact?

$4 + 2 = 6$

A $4 - 2 = 2$

B $10 - 4 = 6$

C $6 - 4 = 2$

Go On

Name ____________________

Choose the correct answer.

28. From which box is it **impossible** to pull a gray cube?

A 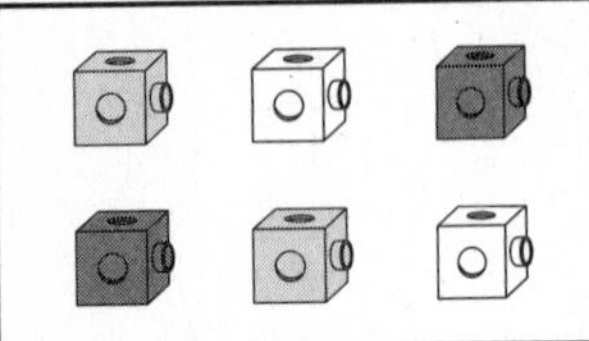

B 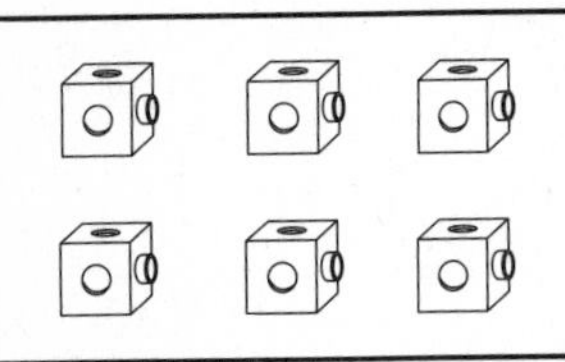

C 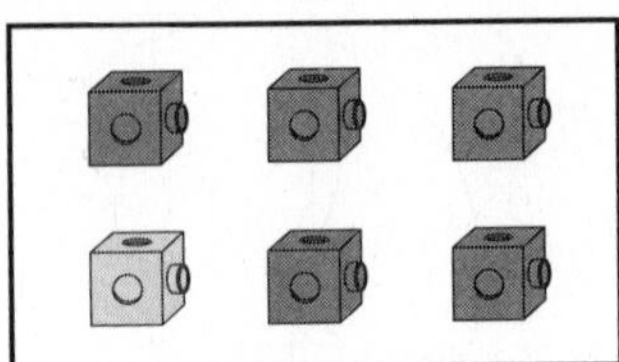

D 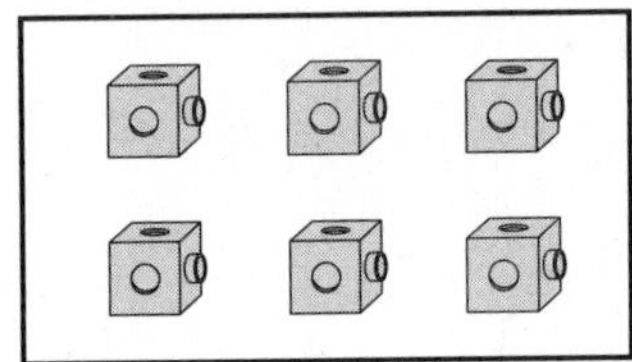

29. Which object is heaviest?

A 

B 

C 

D 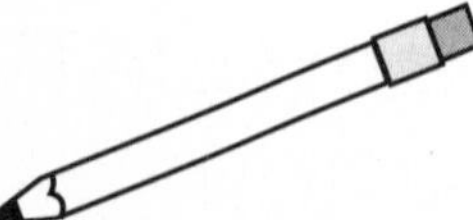

30. What is the difference?

	tens	ones
	3	8
−	1	5

Workmat

Tens	Ones

A 43

B 33

C 28

D 23

Go On

Name ________________________________

Choose the correct answer.

31. What is the time of day?

A morning

B afternoon

C evening

32. How many in all?

2 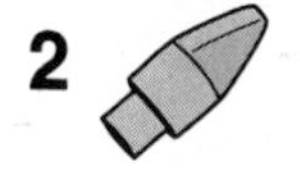 4

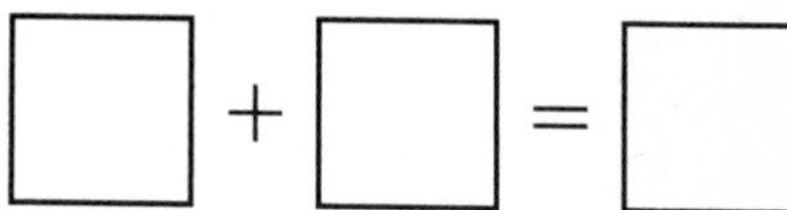

part part whole

A 6 in all

B 5 in all

C 4 in all

D 2 in all

33. Which solid figure has only flat surfaces?

A 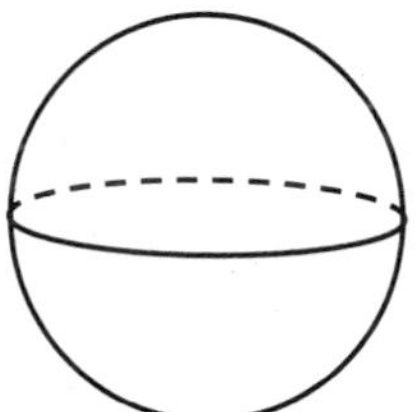

B 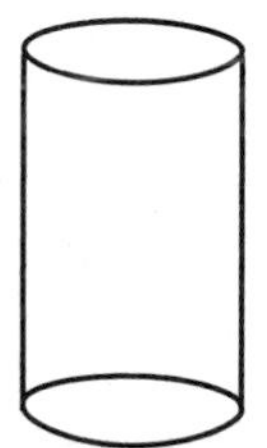

C 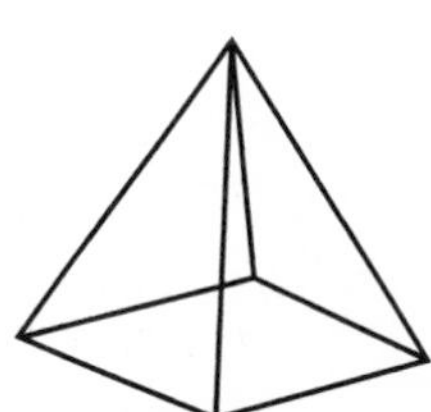

D 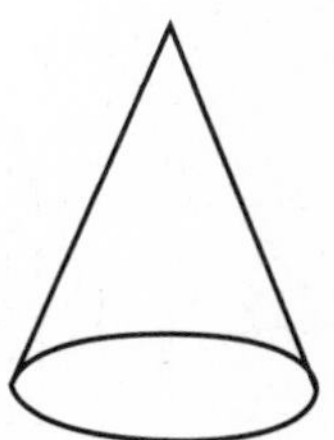

34. Which comes next?

A 

B 

C 

D 

Go On

Name ____________________

Choose the correct answer.

Use the bar graph to answer questions 35 and 36.

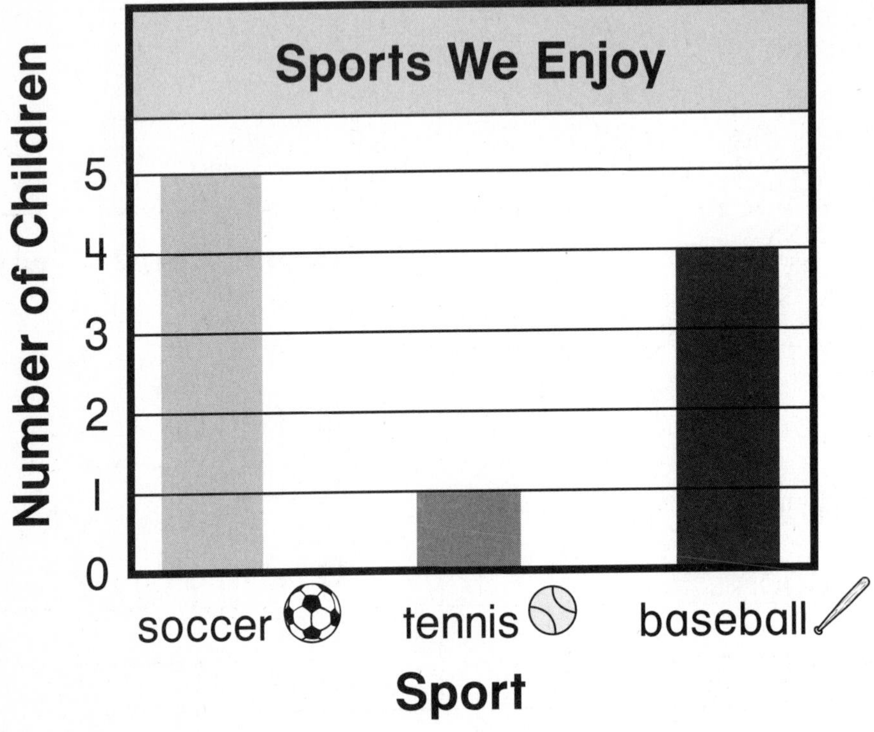

35. Which sport did the fewest children choose?

A    **B**    **C**

36. How many children chose ?

A 1 child   **B** 3 children   **C** 4 children   **D** 5 children

37. Which clock matches the time shown?

A    **B**    **C**    **D** 

Go On

Choose the correct answer.

38. Which figures show the same pattern?

39. About how many pounds is the object?

A about 100 pounds

B about 20 pounds

C about 10 pounds

D about 1 pound

40. Which shows $\frac{1}{4}$ shaded?

A 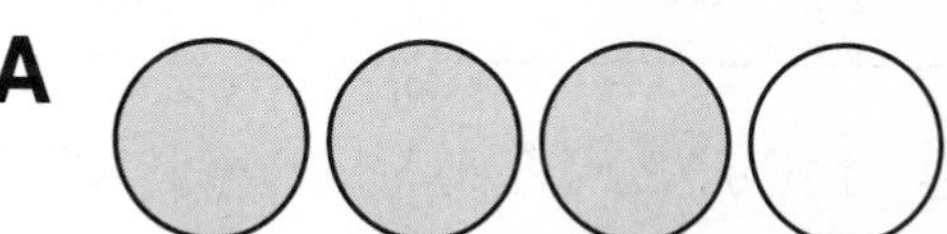

B 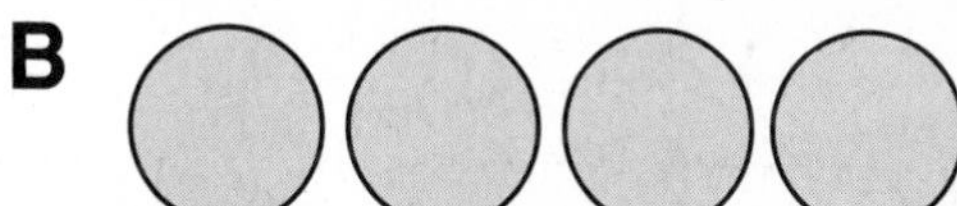

C 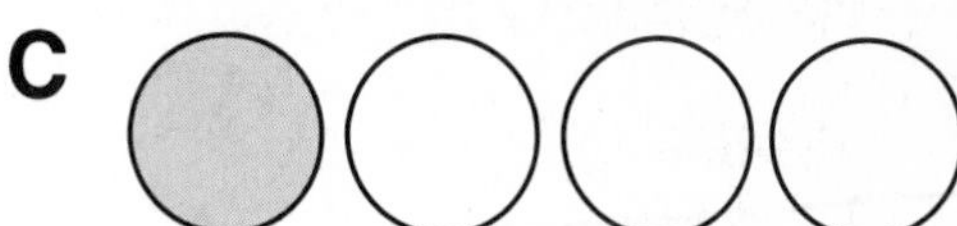

D 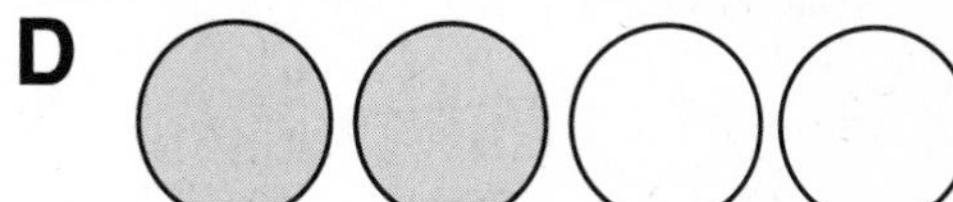

Go On

Choose the correct answer.

41. Which shows a line of symmetry?

A 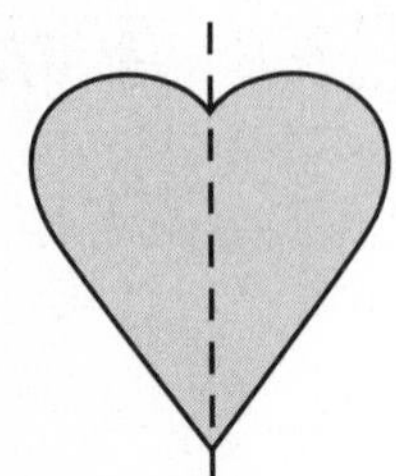
B 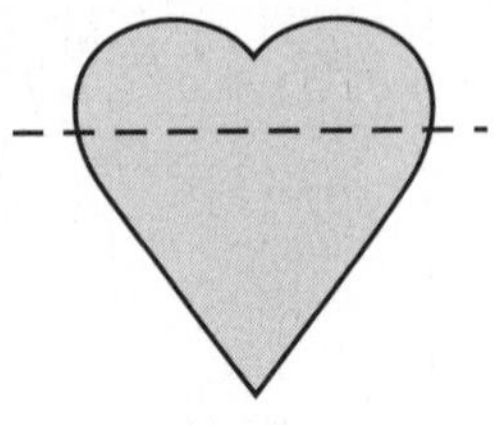
C 
D 

42. Which bear are you more likely to pull from the ?

A 
B
C 

43. How long is the object?

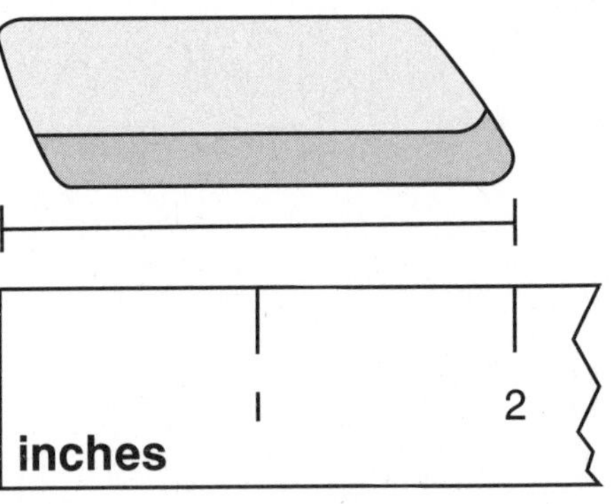

A about 1 inch
B about 2 inches
C about 3 inches
D about 20 inches

44. Which symbol should be used to compare the numbers?

46 ◯ 43

A >
B <
C =

Stop

Name ______________________________

Choose the correct answer.

1. Which is correct?

A 11 is less than 7.

B 12 is greater than 18.

C 13 is less than 11.

D 15 is greater than 13.

2. Which tells how many?

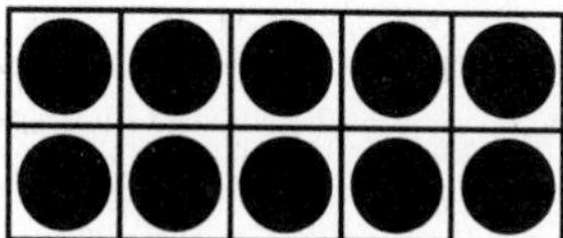
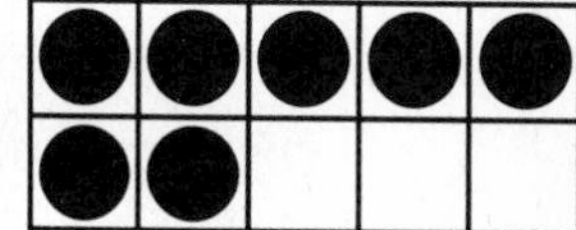

A twelve

B seventeen

C eighteen

D nineteen

3. Which shows the numbers in order from least to greatest?

A 9, 10, 12

B 9, 12, 10

C 12, 10, 9

D 10, 12, 9

4. Which is correct?

A 8 is less than 5.

B 14 is less than 20.

C 16 is greater than 18.

D 7 is greater than 9.

5. Which bear is sixth?

first

A 

B 

C 

D 

Go On

Name ____________________

Choose the correct answer.

6. Which is a way to show 8?

A 

B 

C seven

D 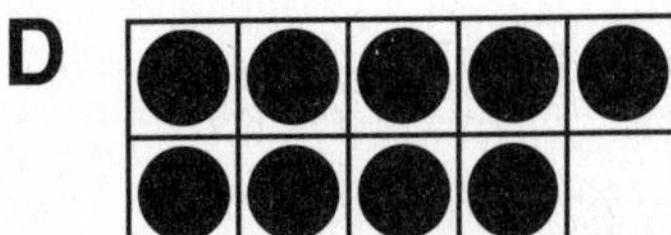

7. Draw lines to match.
Which shows how many more ?

A 5 more

B 4 more

C 3 more

D 2 more

Use the picture graph to answer questions 8 and 9.

8. Which way to travel has the least number?

A 

C 

B 

9. How many ?

A 4

C 6

B 5

D 7

Stop

Name ____________________

Choose the correct answer.

1. Which addition sentence does the picture show?

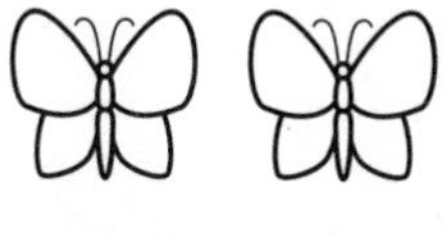

A $4 + 2 = 6$

B $2 + 2 = 4$

C $5 + 1 = 6$

D $3 + 3 = 6$

2. Which addition sentences use the same addends?

A $4 + 1 = 5$ and $1 + 4 = 5$

B $3 + 2 = 5$ and $3 + 3 = 6$

C $0 + 5 = 5$ and $1 + 4 = 5$

D $2 + 3 = 5$ and $0 + 4 = 4$

3. Draw circles to show each number. What is the sum?

$4 + 0 =$ ____

A 40

B 4

C 2

D 0

4. What is the sum?

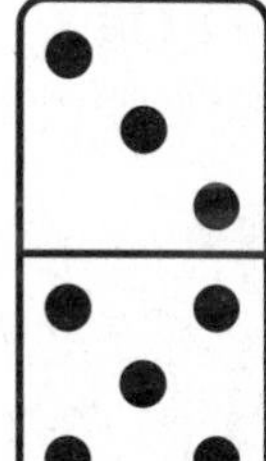

$$\begin{array}{r} 3 \\ +\ 5 \\ \hline \end{array}$$

A 2

B 4

C 7

D 8

Go On

Name ____________________

Choose the correct answer.

5. Which is a way to make 8?

A 5 + 4

B 6 + 2

C 3 + 4

D 7 + 2

6. How many in all?

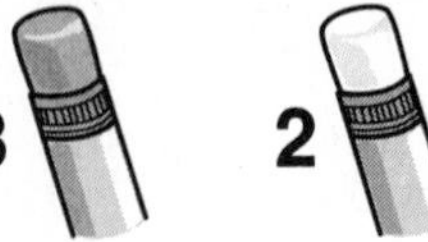

☐ + ☐ = ☐

part part whole

A 1 in all

B 4 in all

C 5 in all

D 6 in all

7. How many birds in all?

A 2 birds in all

B 3 birds in all

C 4 birds in all

D 5 birds in all

8. There are 4 children playing. The same number of children join them. How many children are there?

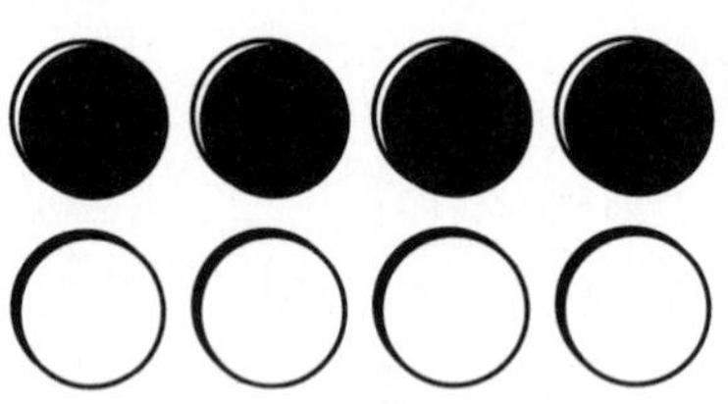

A 0 children

B 5 children

C 6 children

D 8 children

Stop

Name ______________________

Choose the correct answer.

1. What is the difference?

$$\begin{array}{r} 7 \\ -\ 2 \\ \hline \end{array}$$

A 4

B 5

C 6

D 9

2. What is the difference?

5 − 0 = ______

A 0

B 3

C 5

D 50

3. Which subtraction sentence is shown by the cube?

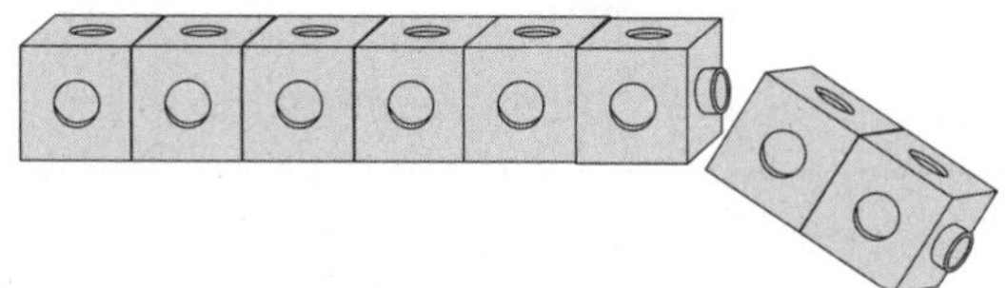

A 8 − 2 = 6

B 8 − 4 = 4

C 6 − 2 = 4

D 7 − 2 = 5

4. Which subtraction sentence does the picture show?

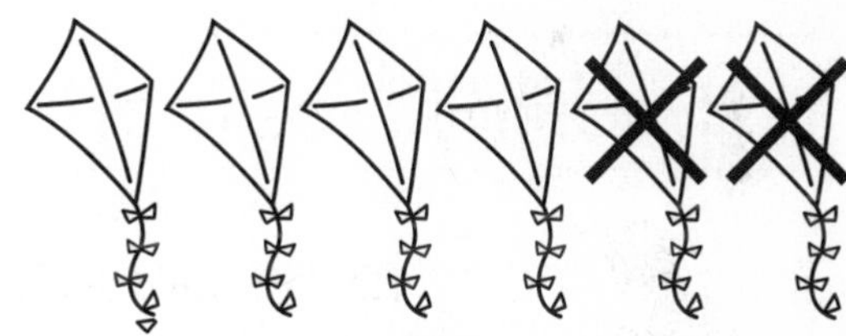

A 6 − 3 = 3

B 4 − 2 = 2

C 4 + 2 = 6

D 6 − 2 = 4

Go On

Name ____________________

Choose the correct answer.

5. How many fewer 🪣?

A 5 fewer

B 4 fewer

C 3 fewer

D 2 fewer

6. Which number completes the subtraction sentence?

8 − 5 = ☐

whole **part** **part**

A 2

B 3

C 4

D 5

7. How many frogs are left?

4 frogs **3 frogs hop away**

A 1 frog is left

B 2 frogs are left

C 3 frogs are left

D 5 frogs are left

8. There are 6 ladybugs and 2 bumblebees. How many fewer bumblebees are there?

A 8 fewer bumblebees

B 7 fewer bumblebees

C 5 fewer bumblebees

D 4 fewer bumblebees

Stop

Name

Choose the correct answer.

1. Which number sentences match the picture?

A 4 + 2 = 6
6 − 3 = 3

B 2 + 2 = 4
4 − 2 = 2

C 4 + 2 = 6
4 − 2 = 2

D 4 + 2 = 6
6 − 2 = 4

2. Which number sentence matches the picture?

A 4 − 3 = 1

B 7 − 3 = 4

C 3 + 1 = 4

D 4 + 3 = 7

3. Which is a related subtraction fact?

2 + 3 = 5

A 5 − 3 = 2

B 8 − 5 = 3

C 3 − 2 = 1

D 5 − 0 = 5

4. How many ants are there in all?

A 4

B 7

C 8

D 10

Go On

Choose the correct answer.

5. Which is a related addition fact?

5 − 5 = 0

A 0 + 5 = 5

B 5 + 5 = 10

C 2 + 3 = 5

D 4 + 1 = 5

6. Which number sentence matches the picture?

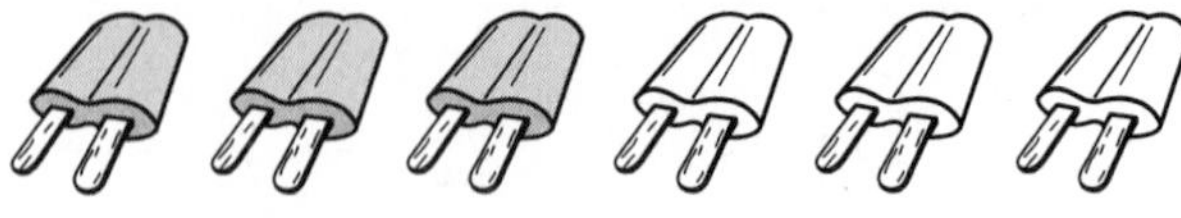

A 4 + 2 = 6

B 3 + 3 = 6

C 6 − 3 = 3

D 6 − 2 = 4

7. How many frogs hop away?

A 1 **B** 5 **C** 7 **D** 8

8. There are 6 soccer balls. The coach brings 2 more soccer balls. How many soccer balls are there now?

A 4

B 6

C 8

D 10

9. There are 5 school buses. 2 school buses leave. How many school buses are left?

A 3

B 5

C 7

D 8

Stop

Choose the correct answer.

1. Which shows the numbers in order from least to greatest?

A 7, 5, 8
B 8, 7, 5
C 5, 7, 8
D 8, 5, 7

2. Which is the difference?

$6 - 6 = \_\_\_\_$

A 0
B 3
C 6
D 66

3. Which addition sentences use the same addends?

A $3 + 4 = 7$ and $3 + 5 = 8$
B $2 + 4 = 6$ and $2 + 3 = 5$
C $0 + 2 = 2$ and $1 + 2 = 3$
D $1 + 3 = 4$ and $3 + 1 = 4$

4. There are 6 fire trucks. 3 fire trucks leave. Which number sentence matches the words?

A $9 - 3 = 6$
B $6 - 3 = 3$
C $3 + 6 = 9$
D $9 + 3 = 12$

5. Which is correct?

A 5 is less than 10.
B 12 is less than 8.
C 14 is greater than 17.
D 9 is greater than 12.

6. Which is a related subtraction fact?

$5 + 2 = 7$

A $5 - 2 = 3$
B $9 - 7 = 2$
C $7 - 2 = 5$
D $7 - 0 = 7$

Go On

Choose the correct answer.

7. Use the cube below. There are 5 grasshoppers and 3 beetles. How many fewer beetles are there?

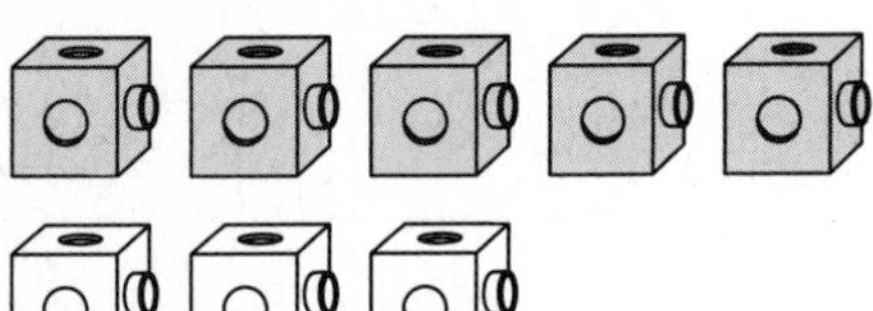

A 4 beetles

B 3 beetles

C 2 beetles

D 1 beetles

8. Which number sentence matches the picture?

A 8 − 3 = 5

B 5 − 3 = 2

C 3 + 5 = 8

D 2 + 3 = 5

9. Draw circles to show each number. What is the sum?

3 + 0 = ____

A 30

B 3

C 1

D 0

10. Which number completes the subtraction sentence?

6	−	4	=	
whole		part		part

A 1

B 2

C 3

D 4

Go On

Choose the correct answer.

11. Which is a way to make 5?

A 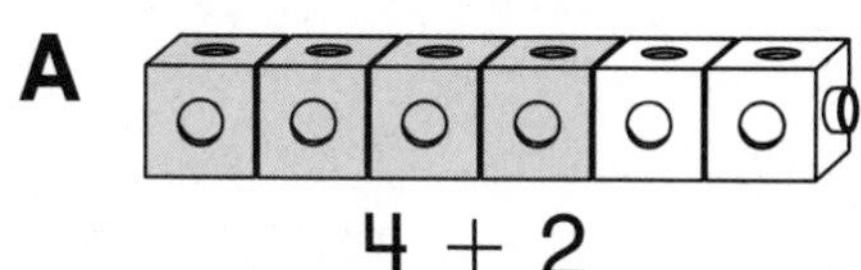
4 + 2

B 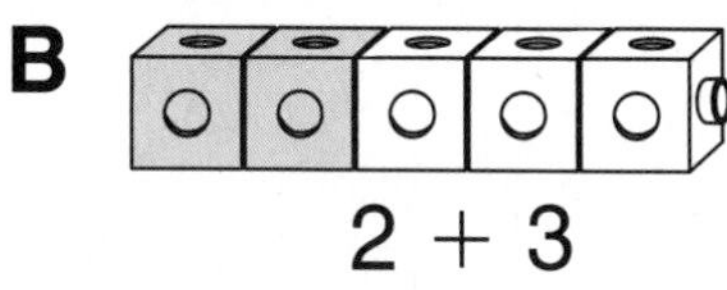
2 + 3

C 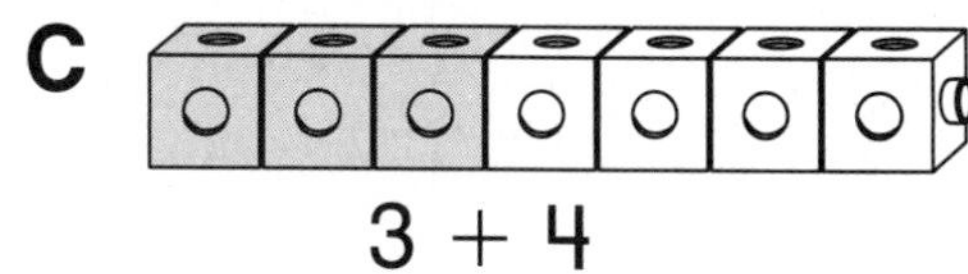
3 + 4

D 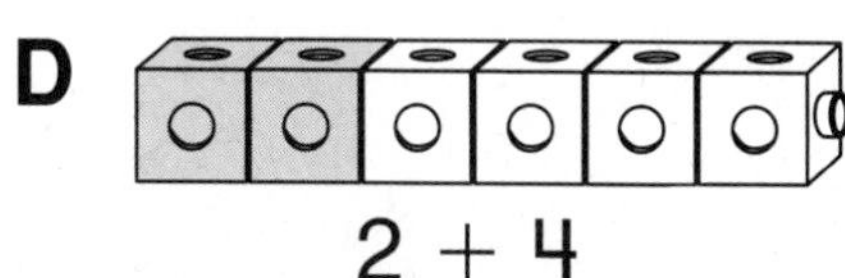
2 + 4

12. Draw lines to match. Which shows how many more 🎾?

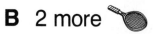

A 1 more

B 2 more

C 3 more

D 4 more

13. How many birds are left?

3 birds **2 birds fly away**

A 1 bird is left

B 2 birds are left

C 3 birds are left

D 5 birds are left

14. Which addition sentence does the picture show?

A 1 + 2 = 3

B 2 + 2 = 4

C 3 + 1 = 4

D 1 + 4 = 5

Go On

Name ______________________________________

Choose the correct answer.

15. Which number sentences match the picture?

A $6 + 3 = 9$
$9 - 6 = 3$

B $2 + 3 = 5$
$5 - 2 = 3$

C $5 + 4 = 9$
$9 - 4 = 5$

D $5 + 4 = 9$
$5 - 4 = 1$

16. Which is a way to show 6?

A 

B 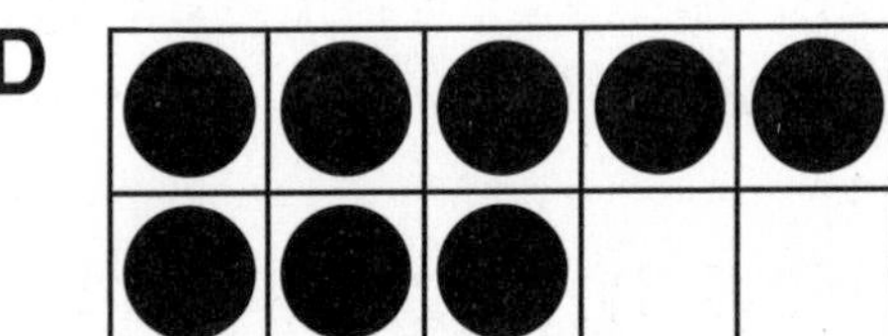

C five

D

●	●	●	●	●
●	●	●		

17. Which doll is third?

A 

B 

C 

D 

Go On

Choose the correct answer.

18. How many worms are there in all?

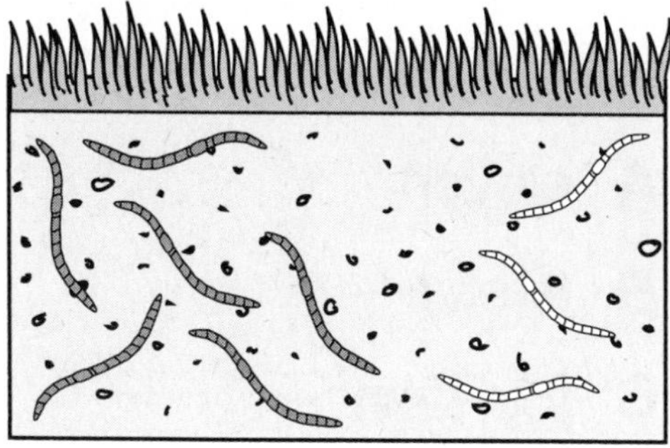

A 3

B 7

C 9

D 10

19. Which is the sum?

$$\begin{array}{r} 2 \\ +4 \\ \hline \end{array}$$

A 2

B 4

C 6

D 8

20. Which subtraction sentence is shown by the cube?

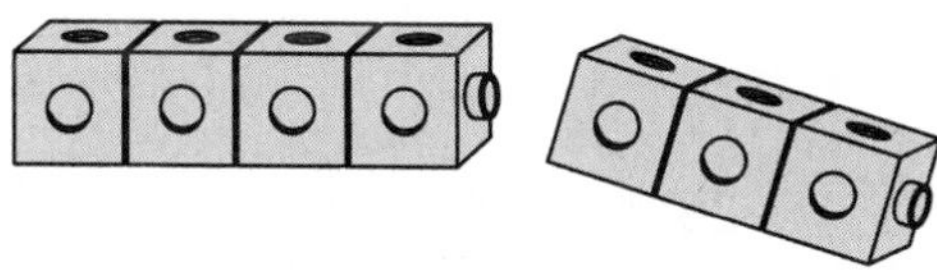

A $7 - 3 = 4$

B $7 - 5 = 2$

C $4 - 3 = 1$

D $6 - 3 = 3$

21. There are 3 dogs at a park. The same number of dogs join them. How many dogs are there at the park?

A 0 dogs

B 4 dogs

C 5 dogs

D 6 dogs

Go On

Name ______________________

Choose the correct answer.

22. What is the difference?

$$\begin{array}{r} 8 \\ -3 \\ \hline \end{array}$$

A 4

B 5

C 6

D 7

23. Which tells how many?

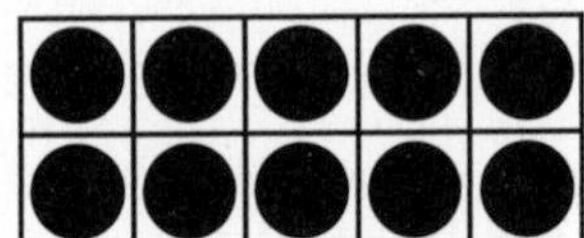

A eleven

B twelve

C fourteen

D fifteen

24. How many in all?

4  1 

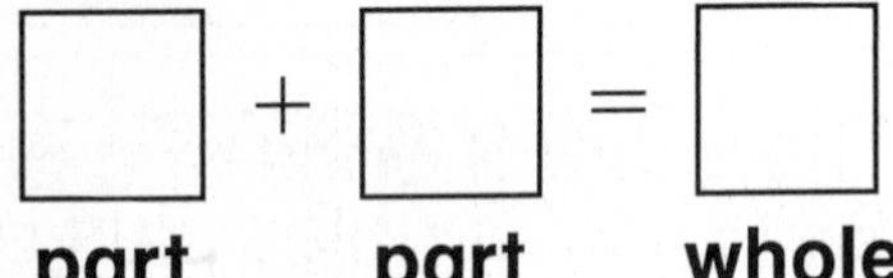

A 1 in all

B 2 in all

C 5 in all

D 6 in all

25. How many fewer ?

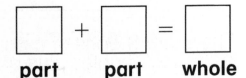

6 − 2 = ____

A 1 fewer

B 2 fewer

C 3 fewer

D 4 fewer

Stop

Choose the correct answer.

Use the number line to answer questions 1 and 2.

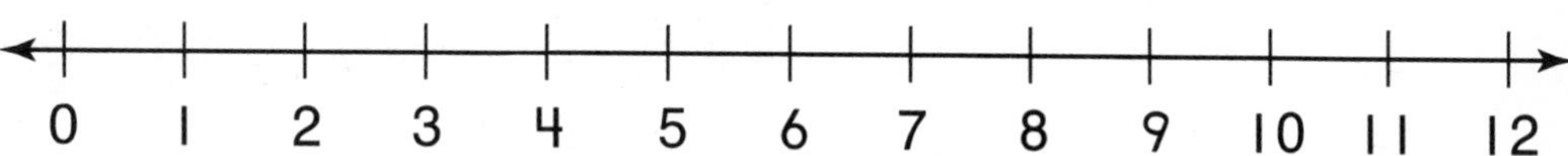

1. What is the sum?

$$\begin{array}{r} 8 \\ +\ 3 \\ \hline \end{array}$$

A 5

B 10

C 11

D 12

2. What is the sum?

$$\begin{array}{r} 7 \\ +\ 2 \\ \hline \end{array}$$

A 8

B 9

C 10

D 11

3. Which addition sentence shows the doubles fact?

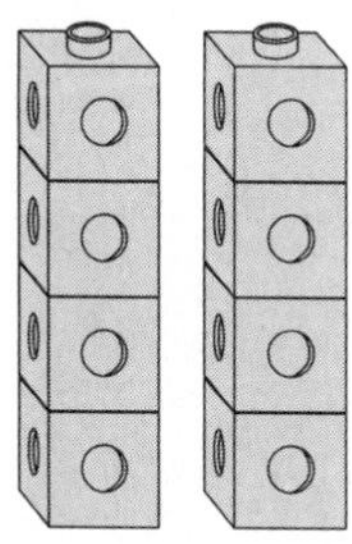

A $3 + 3 = 6$

B $4 + 2 = 6$

C $3 + 5 = 8$

D $4 + 4 = 8$

4. Which addition sentence shows the doubles plus one fact?

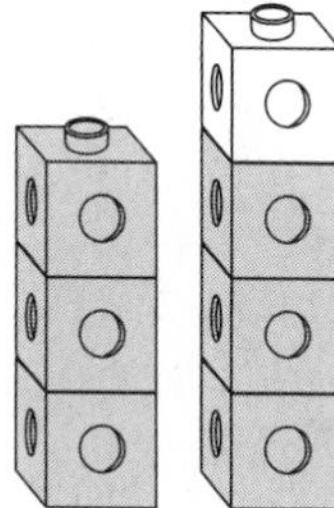

A $3 + 4 = 7$

B $4 + 4 = 8$

C $2 + 5 = 7$

D $3 + 3 = 6$

Go On

Choose the correct answer.

5. Count on. What is the sum?

$$\begin{array}{r} 7 \\ +\ 3 \\ \hline \end{array}$$

A 10 **C** 12

B 11 **D** 13

6. What is the sum?

5 + 4 = ____

A 7 **C** 9

B 8 **D** 10

7. Count on. What is the sum?

9 + 1 = ____

A 8 **B** 10 **C** 11 **D** 91

8. Draw a picture to solve. There are 11 marbles in all. 3 marbles are gray. The other marbles are white. How many marbles are white?

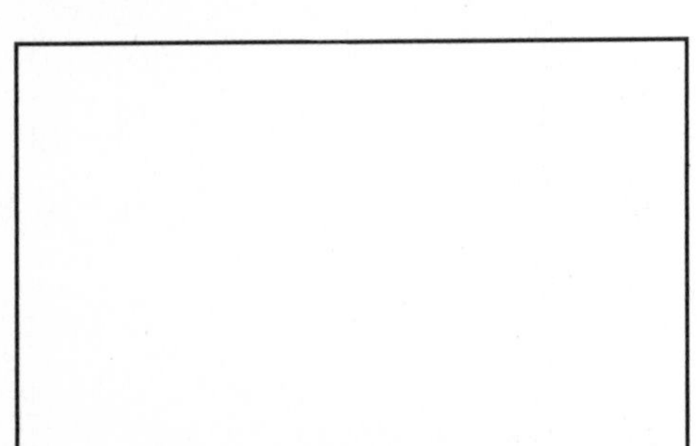

A 7 marbles

B 8 marbles

C 9 marbles

D 14 marbles

9. Draw a picture to solve. There are 10 fish in all. 4 fish are yellow. The other fish are red. How many fish are red?

A 14 fish

B 9 fish

C 7 fish

D 6 fish

Stop

Name________________________________

Choose the correct answer.

Use the number line to answer questions 1 through 4.

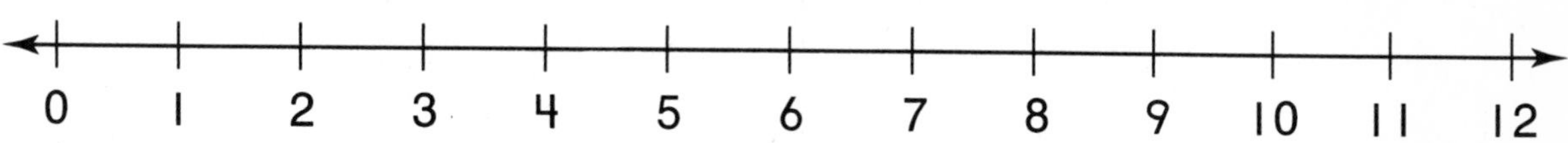

1. What is the difference?

$$\begin{array}{r} 10 \\ -\ 1 \\ \hline \end{array}$$

A 7

B 8

C 9

D 11

2. What is the difference?

11 − 3 = ____

A 8

B 9

C 10

D 14

3. What is the difference?

____ = 9 − 3

A 11

B 10

C 7

D 6

4. What is the difference?

$$\begin{array}{r} 8 \\ -\ 2 \\ \hline \end{array}$$

A 5

B 6

C 7

D 10

Go On

Name ______________________________________

Choose the correct answer.

5. What is the difference?

$$\begin{array}{r} 12 \\ -\ 6 \\ \hline \end{array}$$

A 3 **C** 10

B 6 **D** 18

6. What is the difference?

$$\begin{array}{r} 11 \\ -\ 2 \\ \hline \end{array}$$

A 13 **C** 9

B 10 **D** 8

7. Use ▢ and ▢ to add.

$$\begin{array}{r} 4 \\ +4 \\ \hline \end{array}$$

A 9 **C** 1

B 8 **D** 0

8. Use ▢ and ☒ to subtract.

$$\begin{array}{r} 6 \\ -2 \\ \hline \end{array}$$

A 8 **C** 4

B 7 **D** 3

9. Which number sentence matches the story?

There are 7 seals. 2 seals swim away. How many seals are there now?

A $5 + 2 = 7$

B $7 - 2 = 5$

C $9 - 2 = 7$

D $7 + 2 = 9$

10. Which number sentence matches the story?

There are 10 blue crabs. There are 3 red crabs. How many more blue crabs are there than red crabs?

A $10 - 3 = 7$

B $10 + 3 = 13$

C $7 - 3 = 4$

D $7 + 3 = 10$

Stop

Choose the correct answer.

1. Which numbers are in the fact family?

$8 + 4 = 12$ $12 - 4 = 8$

$4 + 8 = 12$ $12 - 8 = 4$

A 4, 8, 12

B 4, 12, 16

C 8, 12, 20

D 4, 4, 8

2. Which is a way to make 11?

A $12 - 3$

B $10 - 2$

C $7 + 5$

D $8 + 3$

3. Which shows the related addition fact?

$$\begin{array}{r} 5 \\ +7 \\ \hline \square \end{array}$$

A $\begin{array}{r} 4 \\ +8 \\ \hline 12 \end{array}$

B $\begin{array}{r} 7 \\ +5 \\ \hline 12 \end{array}$

C $\begin{array}{r} 6 \\ +6 \\ \hline 12 \end{array}$

D $\begin{array}{r} 9 \\ +3 \\ \hline 12 \end{array}$

4. Which number sentence shows how many fish there are?

4 gray fish

6 white fish

A $10 - 4 = 6$

B $6 - 4 = 2$

C $4 + 6 = 10$

D $10 + 4 = 14$

Go On

Choose the correct answer.

5. Which number completes the fact family?

5 + □ = 11   11 − □ = 5

□ + 5 = 11   11 − 5 = □

A 6   **C** 12

B 8   **D** 16

6. Follow the rule. Which number completes the table?

Subtract 2	
6	4
8	
10	8

A 5   **B** 6   **C** 7   **D** 8

7. Which shows a pair of related subtraction facts?

A $\begin{array}{r} 10 \\ -\ 3 \\ \hline 7 \end{array}$ $\begin{array}{r} 10 \\ -\ 7 \\ \hline 3 \end{array}$ **B** $\begin{array}{r} 12 \\ -\ 4 \\ \hline 8 \end{array}$ $\begin{array}{r} 12 \\ -\ 5 \\ \hline 7 \end{array}$ **C** $\begin{array}{r} 11 \\ -\ 6 \\ \hline 5 \end{array}$ $\begin{array}{r} 9 \\ -\ 4 \\ \hline 5 \end{array}$ **D** $\begin{array}{r} 8 \\ -\ 5 \\ \hline 3 \end{array}$ $\begin{array}{r} 8 \\ -\ 2 \\ \hline 6 \end{array}$

8. Draw a picture to solve. There are 10 hawks. Some hawks fly away. There are 7 hawks left. How many hawks flew away?

A 1 hawk   **C** 3 hawks

B 2 hawks   **D** 4 hawks

9. Draw a picture to solve. There are 12 skunks. Some skunks walk away. There are 8 skunks left. How many skunks walked away?

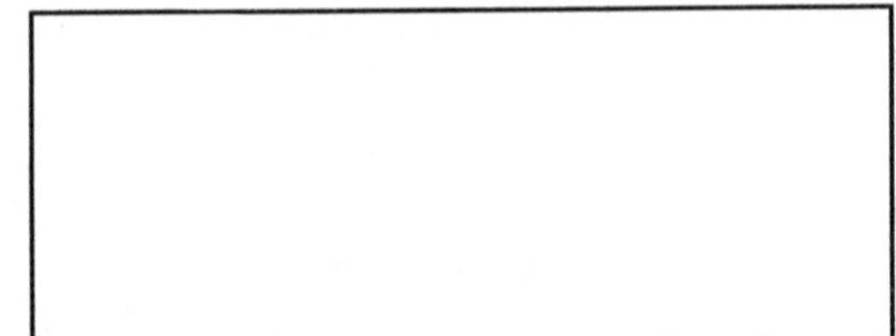

A 10 skunks   **C** 5 skunks

B 6 skunks   **D** 4 skunks

Stop

Choose the correct answer.

1. Which addition sentence shows the doubles fact?

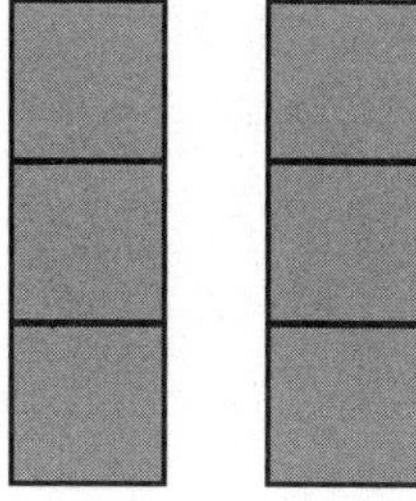

A 2 + 2 = 4

B 3 + 3 = 6

C 3 + 2 = 5

D 4 + 3 = 78

2. Draw a picture to solve. There are 10 deer. Some deer walk away. There are 6 deer left. How many deer walked away?

A 10 deer

B 8 deer

C 6 deer

D 4 deer

3. Follow the rule. Which number completes the table?

Subtract 2	
5	3
6	
7	5

A 6 **C** 4

B 5 **D** 3

4. Which numbers are in the fact family?

5 + 6 = 11 11 − 6 = 5

6 + 5 = 11 11 − 5 = 6

A 5, 6, 11

B 5, 11, 17

C 6, 11, 16

D 5, 5, 11

Go On

Name ____________________

Choose the correct answer.

Use the number line to answer questions 5 and 6.

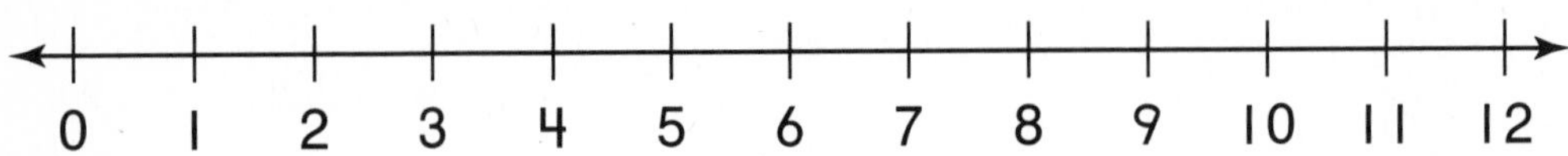

5. What is the sum?

$$\begin{array}{r} 4 \\ +2 \\ \hline \end{array}$$

A 5 **C** 7

B 6 **D** 8

6. What is the sum?

$$\begin{array}{r} 8 \\ +3 \\ \hline \end{array}$$

A 9 **C** 11

B 10 **D** 12

7. What is the difference?

$$\begin{array}{r} 11 \\ -\ 7 \\ \hline \end{array}$$

A 4 **C** 2

B 3 **D** 1

8. Use ▢ and ▢ to add.

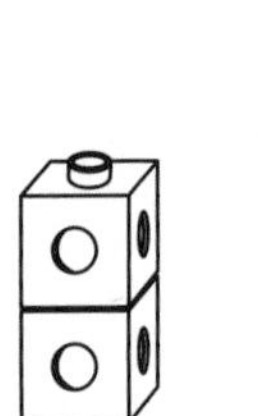

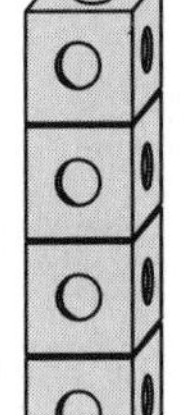

$$\begin{array}{r} 2 \\ +4 \\ \hline \end{array}$$

A 6 **C** 8

B 7 **D** 9

9. Which shows a pair of related subtraction facts?

A $\begin{array}{r} 7 \\ -2 \\ \hline 5 \end{array}$ $\begin{array}{r} 7 \\ -4 \\ \hline 3 \end{array}$ **B** $\begin{array}{r} 12 \\ -\ 4 \\ \hline 8 \end{array}$ $\begin{array}{r} 12 \\ -\ 7 \\ \hline 5 \end{array}$ **C** $\begin{array}{r} 8 \\ -2 \\ \hline 6 \end{array}$ $\begin{array}{r} 8 \\ -5 \\ \hline 3 \end{array}$ **D** $\begin{array}{r} 9 \\ -3 \\ \hline 6 \end{array}$ $\begin{array}{r} 9 \\ -6 \\ \hline 3 \end{array}$

Go On

Choose the correct answer.

10. Count on. What is the sum?

10 + 2 = _____

A 11   B 12   C 21   D 22

11. Which number sentence matches the story?

There are 11 starfish.
There are 5 sand dollars.
How many more starfish are there than sand dollars?

A 6 − 5 = 1

B 11 + 5 = 16

C 11 − 5 = 6

D 5 + 6 = 11

12. Which shows the related addition fact?

$$\begin{array}{r} 8 \\ +5 \\ \hline \end{array}$$

A $\begin{array}{r} 8 \\ +\ 4 \\ \hline 12 \end{array}$

C $\begin{array}{r} 5 \\ +\ 8 \\ \hline 13 \end{array}$

B $\begin{array}{r} 7 \\ +\ 5 \\ \hline 12 \end{array}$

D $\begin{array}{r} 8 \\ +\ 3 \\ \hline 11 \end{array}$

13. Which is a way to make 10?

A 12 − 4

B 7 + 3

C 11 − 2

D 8 + 4

14. Count on. What is the sum?

$$\begin{array}{r} 4 \\ +1 \\ \hline \end{array}$$

A 5   C 7

B 6   D 8

Go On

Choose the correct answer.

Use the number line to answer questions 15 and 16.

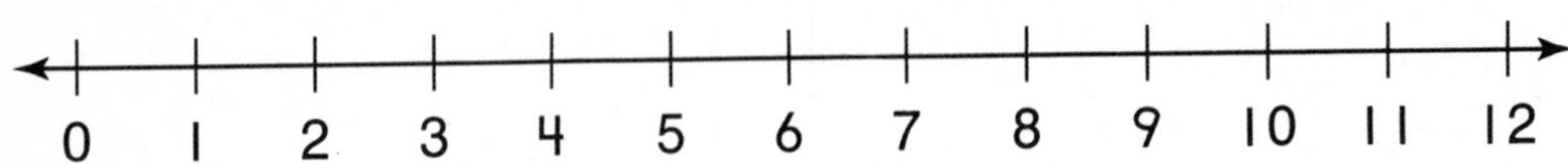

15. What is the difference?

$$\begin{array}{r} 8 \\ -\ 1 \\ \hline \end{array}$$

A 7

B 8

C 9

D 10

16. What is the difference?

12 − 3 = ______

A 8

B 9

C 10

D 11

17. Follow the rule. Which number completes the table?

Subtract 2	
10	8
9	
8	6

A 5

B 6

C 7

D 8

18. Which addition sentence shows the doubles plus one fact?

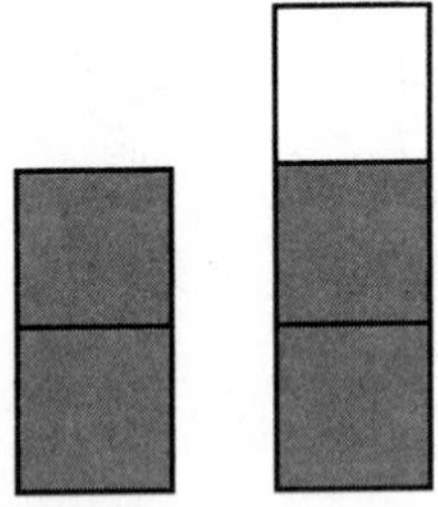

A 2 + 1 = 3

B 2 + 2 = 4

C 2 + 3 = 5

D 3 + 3 = 6

Go On

Choose the correct answer.

19. Which number completes the fact family?

8 + □ = 10   10 − □ = 8

□ + 8 = 10   10 − 8 = □

A 8

B 6

C 4

D 2

20. What is the sum?

6 + 5 = ______

A 9

B 10

C 11

D 12

21. Which number sentence shows how many rabbits there are?

_____ gray rabbits

_____ white rabbits

A 8 − 4 = 4

B 7 − 4 = 32

C 3 + 4 = 7

D 3 + 5 = 8

22. Which number sentence matches the story?

There are 9 fish. 3 fish swim away. How many fish are there now?

A 9 + 3 = 12

B 9 − 3 = 6

C 6 − 3 = 3

D 6 + 3 = 9

Go On

Name ______________________

Choose the correct answer.

23. Use ▢ and ▢ to subtract.

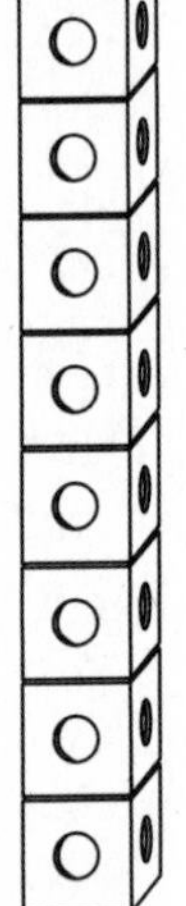

$$\begin{array}{r} 12 \\ -\ 4 \\ \hline \end{array}$$

A 4

B 5

C 6

D 8

24. Which numbers are in the fact family?

$6 + 4 = 10$ $10 - 4 = 6$

$4 + 6 = 10$ $10 - 6 = 4$

A 6, 8, 10

B 6, 10, 16

C 4, 8, 10

D 4, 6, 10

25. There are 12 bluebirds. Some bluebirds fly away. There are 9 bluebirds left. How many bluebirds flew away?

A 1 bluebird

B 2 bluebirds

C 3 bluebirds

D 4 bluebirds

26. There are 9 balls in all. 4 balls are green. The other balls are orange. How many balls are orange?

A 4 balls

B 5 balls

C 6 balls

D 7 balls

Stop

Choose the correct answer.

1. Which figure belongs in group A?

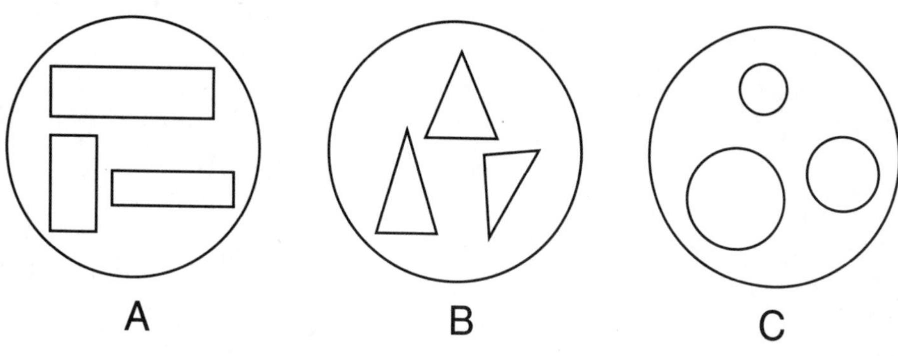

A 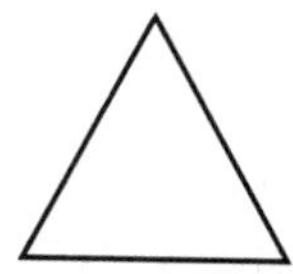

B 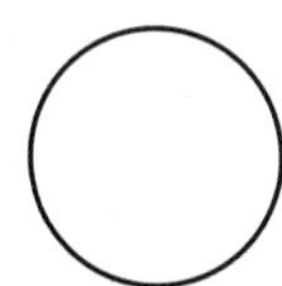

C 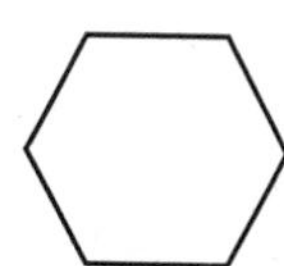

D 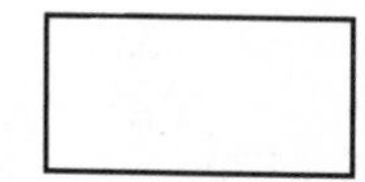

2. How many more children chose  than ?

Snacks We Like							
yogurt	Yogurt	Yogurt	Yogurt	Yogurt	Yogurt	Yogurt	Yogurt	
cracker								
fruit								

A 2 more children

B 3 more children

C 5 more children

D 7 more children

Go On

Name ______________________________

Choose the correct answer.

3. Which belongs in the group?

A 

B 

C 

D 

Use the picture graph to answer questions 5 and 6.

Plane Figures												
square	■	■	■	■	■	■	■	■	■			
triangle	△	△	△	△	△							
circle	●	●	●	●	●	●	●	●	●	●	●	

4. How many squares are there?

A 8 squares

B 9 squares

C 10 squares

D 11 squares

5. How many more circles are there than triangles?

A 8 more circles

B 7 more circles

C 6 more circles

D 5 more circles

Stop

Choose the correct answer.

1. Which bear are you more likely to pull from the bowl?

A 

B 

C 

2. Use the tally chart to answer the question.

Places We Like	
mountains	IIII
park	𝍸
zoo	𝍸 II

How many children chose the zoo?

A 4 children

B 5 children

C 6 children

D 7 children

3. From which box is it **impossible** to pull a gray cube?

A 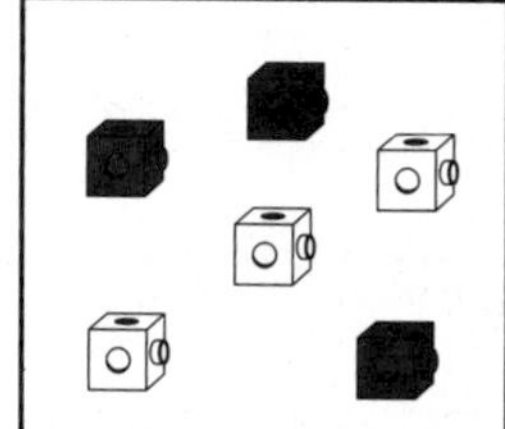

C 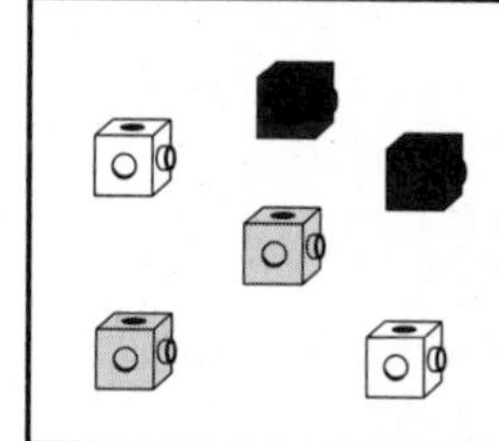

B 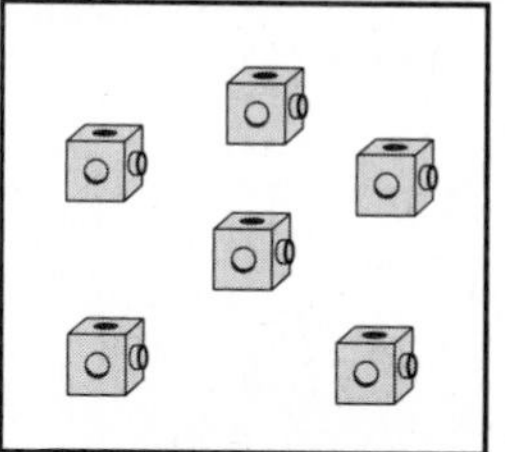

D 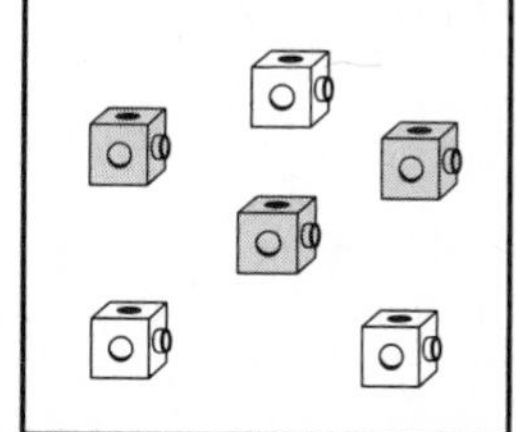

Go On

Name ______________________________

Choose the correct answer.

Use the bar graph to answer questions 4 and 5.

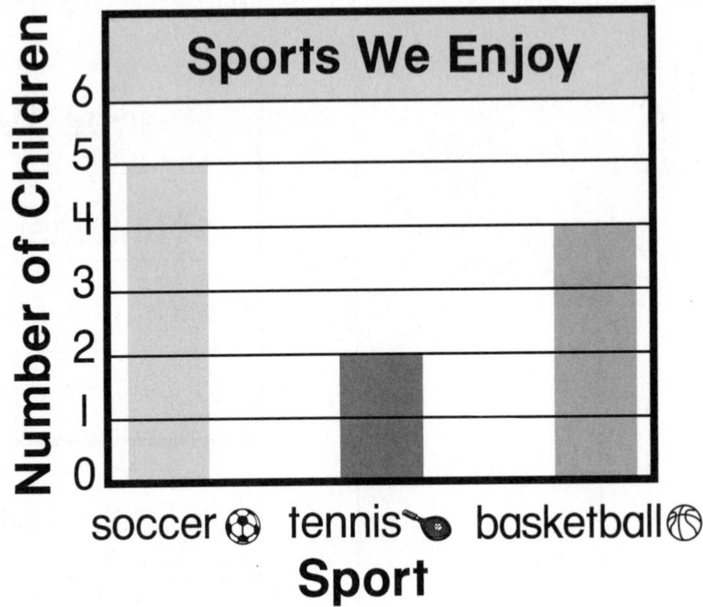

4. How many children chose ?

A 1 child **B** 2 children **C** 3 children **D** 4 children

5. Which sport did the most children choose?

A  **B**  **C** 

6. There are 4 and 7 in a bowl. Which color are you more likely to pull?

A

B

C

7. There are 8 and 5 in a bag. Which color are you more likely to pull?

A

B

C

Stop

Choose the correct answer.

1. Count how many tens and ones. What is the number?

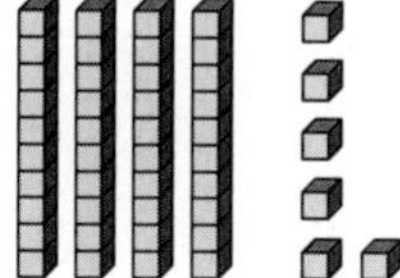

A 36
B 46
C 47
D 64

2. Count how many tens and ones. Which shows the number in a different way?

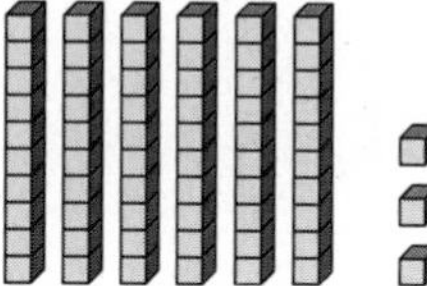

A 60 + 3
B 60 + 30
C 30 + 6
D 6 + 3

3. Count by tens. What number is shown?

5 tens 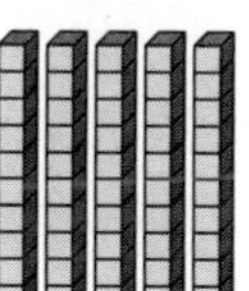

A 50
B 60
C 70
D 80

4. Which shows the number of tens and ones?

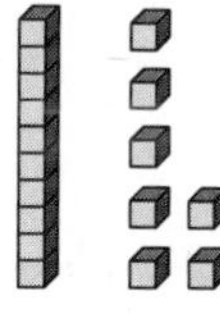

17 seventeen

A 0 tens 7 ones
B 10 tens 7 ones
C 7 tens 10 ones
D 1 ten 7 ones

Go On

Name ______________________

Choose the correct answer.

5. Count how many tens and ones. What is the number?

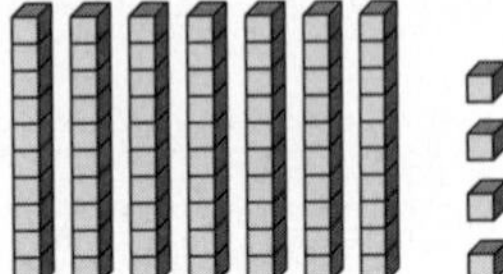

A 704

B 74

C 64

D 47

6. Count how many tens and ones. Which shows the number in a different way?

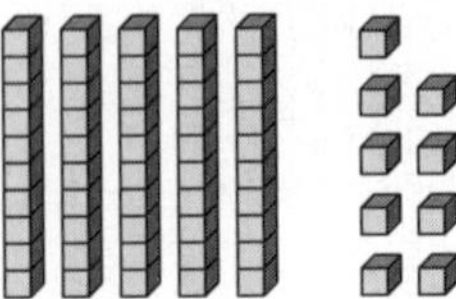

A 5 + 9

B 50 + 90

C 59 + 9

D 50 + 9

7. About how many [crayon] can you hold in one hand?

A about 5 [crayon]

B about 50 [crayon]

C about 500 [crayon]

8. About how many  would fill two cups?

A about 2 

B about 20 

C about 150 

Stop

Name ____________________

Choose the correct answer.

1. Which is true?

A 38 is greater than 32.

B 32 is greater than 38.

C 38 is equal to 32.

D 38 is less than 32.

2. Which number is between 61 and 63?

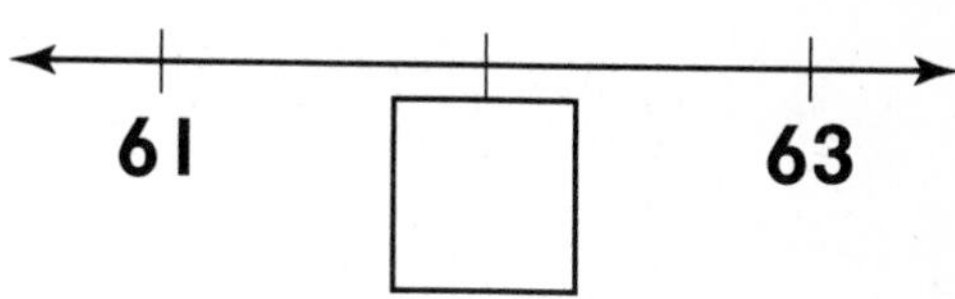

A 60

B 61

C 62

D 64

3. Which symbol can you use to compare the numbers?

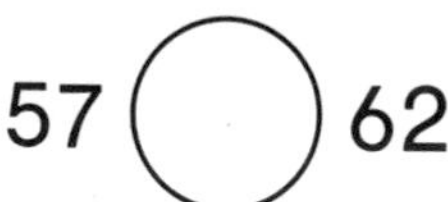

A >

B <

C =

4. Which shows the numbers in order from least to greatest?

55 74 51

A 74, 55, 51

B 51, 74, 55

C 55, 51, 74

D 51, 55, 74

5. Which number is one more than 46?

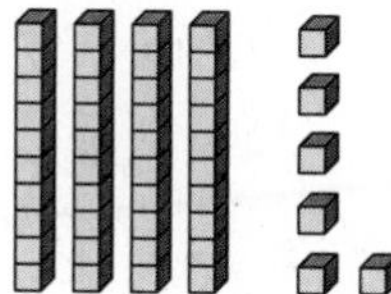

A 56 **B** 45 **C** 47 **D** 56

Go On

Name ____________________

Choose the correct answer.

6. Which is true?

A 88 is less than 84.

B 84 is less than 88.

C 88 is equal to 84.

D 84 is greater than 88.

7. Which number is ten less than 73?

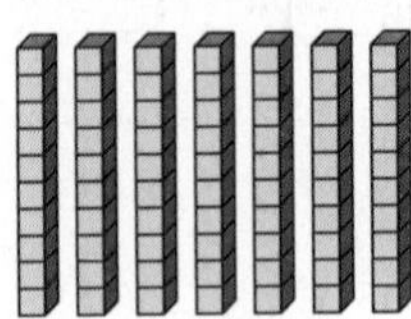

A 63

B 72

C 74

D 83

Use the table to answer questions 8 and 9.

Team	Points Scored
Bulldogs	56
Tigers	63
Panthers	48
Hawks	54

8. Which team scored more points?

A Hawks

B Tigers

9. Which team scored the least number of points?

A Bulldogs

B Tigers

C Panthers

D Hawks

Stop

Choose the correct answer.

Use the hundred chart for questions 1 and 2.

1	2	3	4	5	6	7	8	9	10
11	12	13	14	15	16	17	18	19	20
21	22	23	24	25	26	27	28	29	30
31	32	33	34	35	36	37	38	39	40
41	42	43	44	45	46	47	48	49	50
51	52	53	54	55	56	57	58	59	60

1. Count by twos. Which number comes next?

24, 26, 28, 30, 32, ____

A 33

B 34

C 37

D 42

2. Count by tens. Which numbers come next?

4, 14, 24, ____, ____, ____

A 25, 26, 27

B 30, 40, 50

C 29, 34, 39

D 34, 44, 54

3. Skip count. How many flowers are there?

A 5 **B** 6 **C** 30 **D** 60

Go On

Name____

Choose the correct answer.

4. Count forward. Which numbers come next?

46, 47, 48, ___, ___, ___

A 49, 50, 51

B 49, 40, 41

C 58, 68, 78

D 47, 46, 45

5. Find the pattern. What are the missing numbers?

20, 25, ___, 35, 40, ___

A 45, 50

B 30, 31

C 26, 26

D 30, 45

6. Which number is even?

A 11 **B** 13 **C** 14 **D** 15

7. There are 2 wings on a bird.
How many wings are there on 7 birds?

number of birds	1	2	3	4	5	6	7
number of wings	2	4					

A 6 wings

B 14 wings

C 35 wings

D 70 wings

Stop

Choose the correct answer.

1. Which number is between 55 and 57?

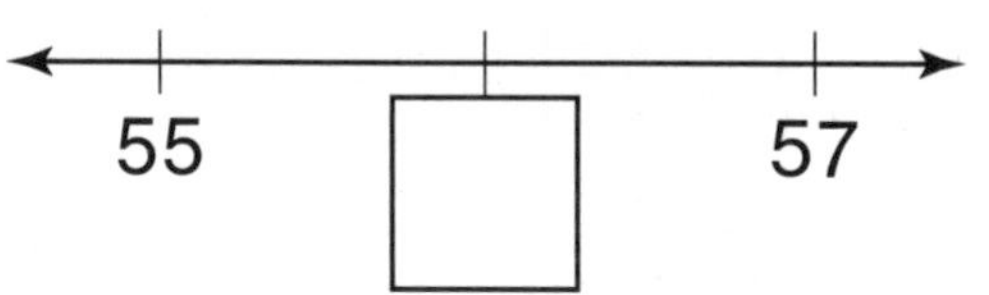

A 54

B 56

C 58

D 60

2. Count by tens. What number is shown?

4 tens 

A 20

B 30

C 40

D 50

3. How many children chose yellow?

Colors We Like	
purple	|||
yellow	~~||||~~ |
green	~~||||~~ |||

A 3 children

B 6 children

C 7 children

D 8 children

4. Count how many tens and ones. Which shows the number in a different way?

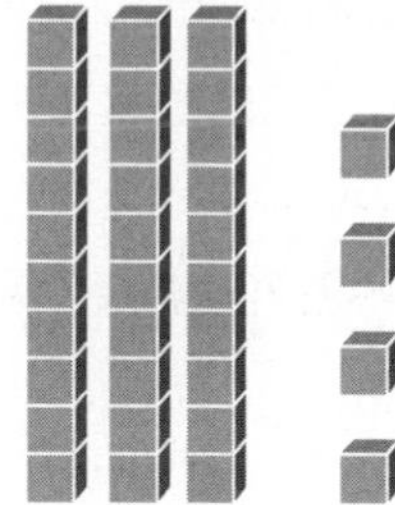

A $3 + 4$

B $30 + 40$

C $34 + 4$

D $30 + 4$

Go On

Name ____________________

Choose the correct answer.

Use the hundred chart for questions 5 and 6.

1	2	3	4	5	6	7	8	9	10
11	12	13	14	15	16	17	18	19	20
21	22	23	24	25	26	27	28	29	30
31	32	33	34	35	36	37	38	39	40
41	42	43	44	45	46	47	48	49	50
51	52	53	54	55	56	57	58	59	60
61	62	63	64	65	66	67	68	69	70
71	72	73	74	75	76	77	78	79	80
81	82	83	84	85	86	87	88	89	90
91	92	93	94	95	96	97	98	99	100

5. Count by fives. Which number comes next?

25, 30, 35, 40, 45, ____

A 47

B 50

C 55

D 60

6. Count by tens. Which numbers come next?

8, 18, 28, ____, ____, ____

A 38, 48, 58

B 33, 38, 43

C 30, 32, 34

D 29, 30, 31

Go On

Choose the correct answer.

7. Which  belongs in the group?

A  B  C  D 

8. From which box is it **possible** to pull a black cube?

A 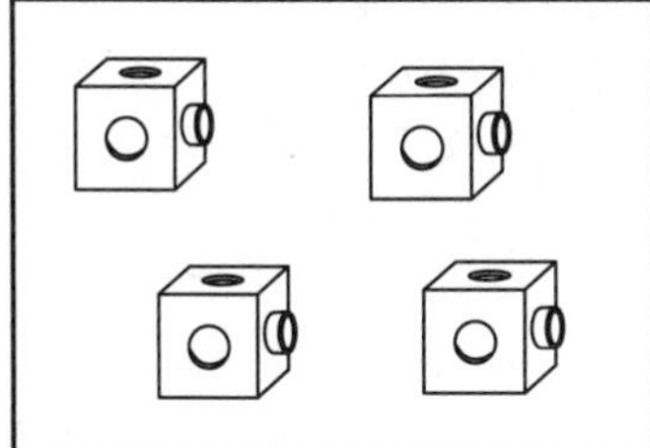

C 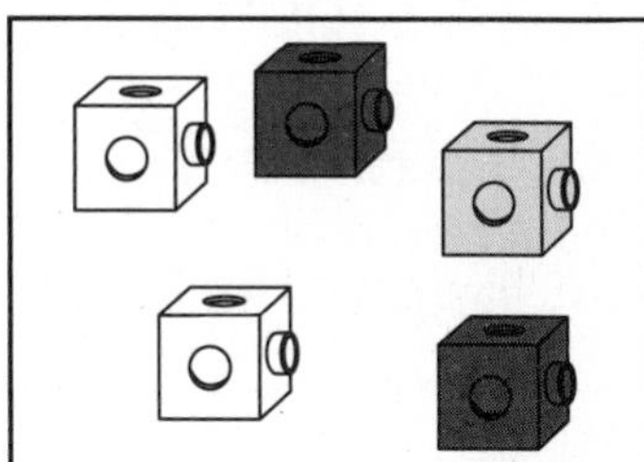

B 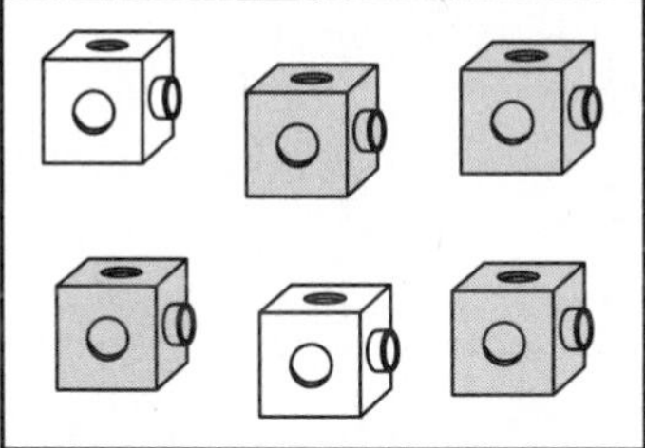

D 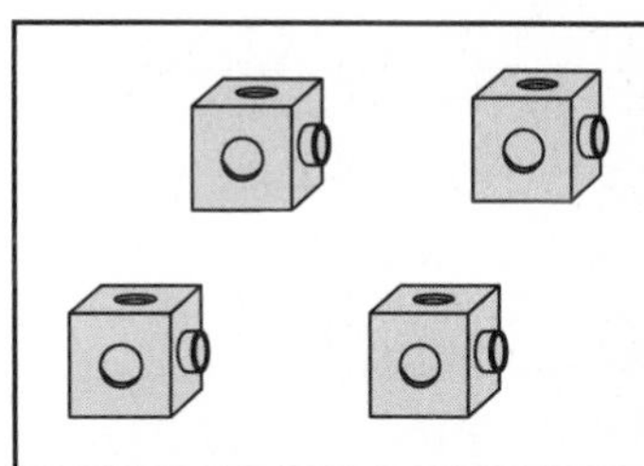

9. There are 2 wheels on a bicycle.
How many wheels are there on 6 bicycles?

number of bicycles	1	2	3	4	5	6
number of wheels	2	4				

A 6 wheels

B 8 wheels

C 10 wheels

D 12 wheels

Go On

Name ____________________

Choose the correct answer.

10. Which is true?

A 43 is greater than 47.

B 47 is less than 43.

C 43 is equal to 47.

D 43 is less than 47.

11. There are 6 and 7 in a bag. Which color are you more likely to pull?

A 

B 

C

Use the table to answer questions 12 and 13.

Game	Points Scored
First	62
Second	58
Third	47
Fourth	59

12. In which game did the team score the most points?

A First **C** Third

B Second **D** Fourth

13. In which game did the team score the least number of points?

A First **C** Third

B Second **D** Fourth

Go On

Choose the correct answer.

14. Which shows the number of tens and ones?

A 8 tens, 2 ones

B 2 tens, 8 ones

C 0 tens, 8 ones

D 1 ten, 8 ones

15. Count forward. Which numbers come next?

23, 24, 25, ___, ___, ___

A 26, 25, 24

B 30, 35, 40

C 27, 29, 31

D 26, 27, 28

16. Which symbol can you use to compare the numbers?

21 ◯ 32

A >

B <

C =

17. Which shows the numbers in order from least to greatest?

62 71 68

A 71, 68, 62

B 68, 62, 71

C 62, 68, 71

D 62, 71, 68

18. Which number is odd?

A 8 **B** 10 **C** 12 **D** 15

Go On

Name ____________________

Choose the correct answer.

19. Use the picture graph to answer question 19.

Fruits We Like								
grapes								
pears								
peaches								

How many more children chose than ?

A 8 more children

B 6 more children

C 4 more children

D 2 more children

20. Count how many tens and ones. What is the number?

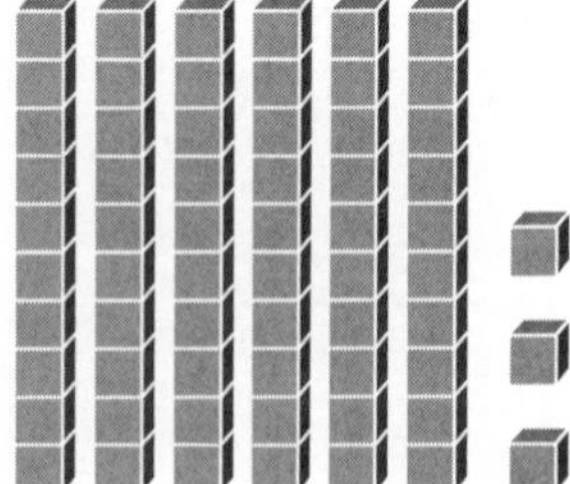

A 603

B 63

C 53

D 36

21. Which number is ten less than 54?

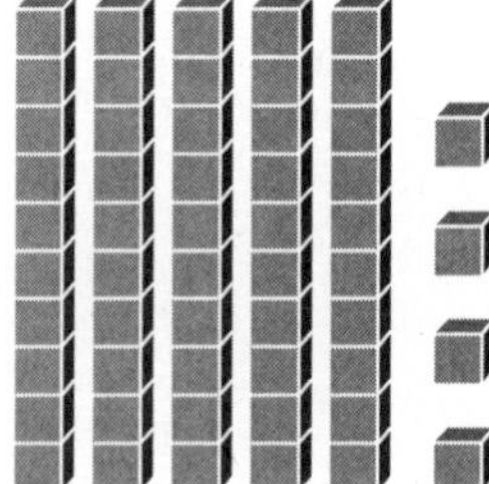

A 64

B 53

C 44

D 34

Stop

Name ____________________

Choose the correct answer.

1. Which object could you trace to make the figure?

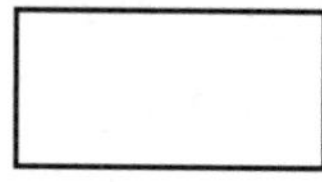

A 

B 

C 

D 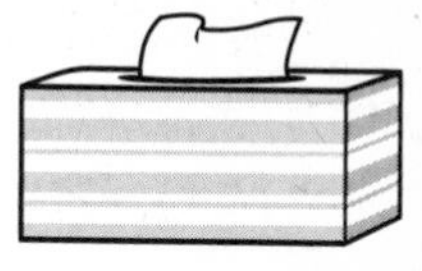

2. How many corners does the plane figure have?

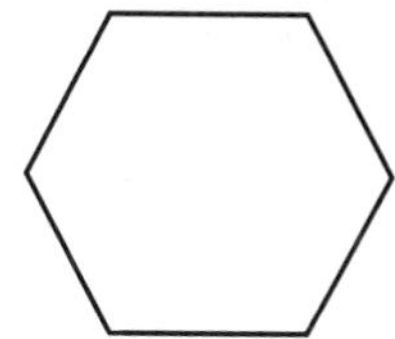

A 4

B 5

C 6

D 7

3. How many flat surfaces does the pyramid have?

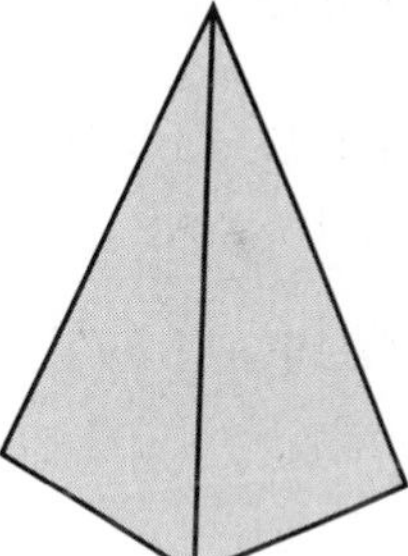

A 6

B 5

C 4

D 2

4. Which figure is a circle?

A 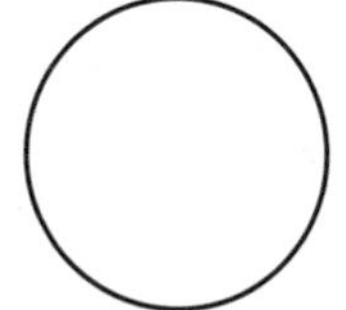

B 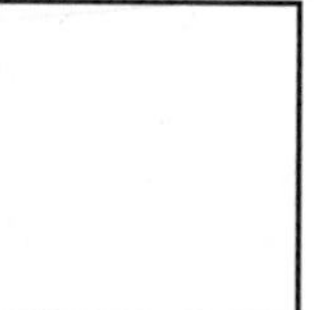

C 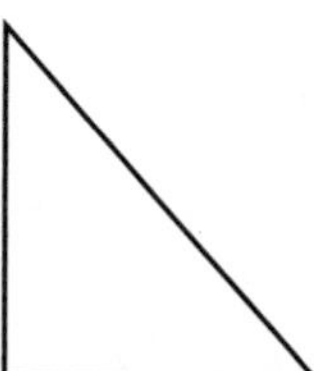

D 

Go On

Name ________________________________

Choose the correct answer.

5. Which solid figure has only flat surfaces?

A 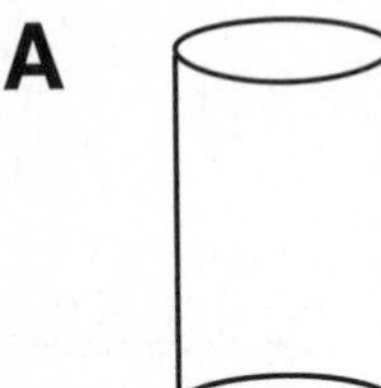 B 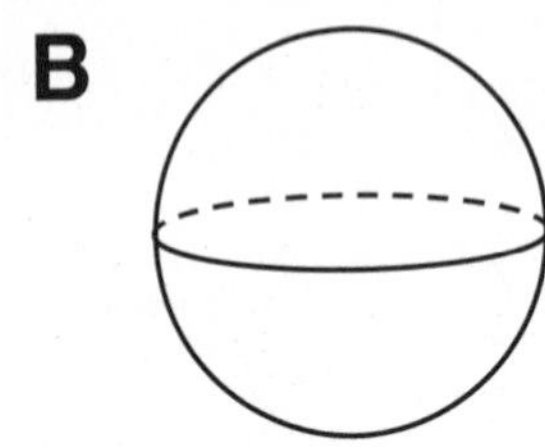 C 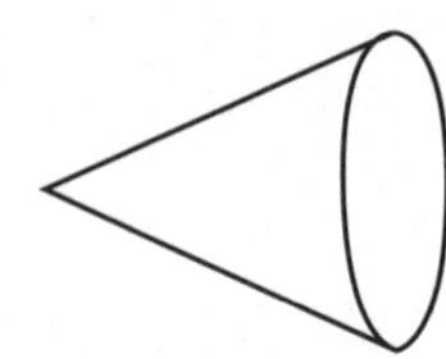 D 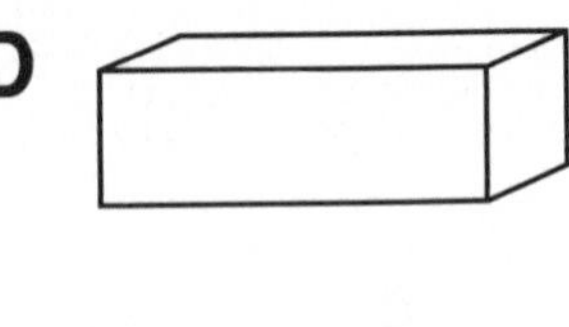

6. Which figure is a square?

A 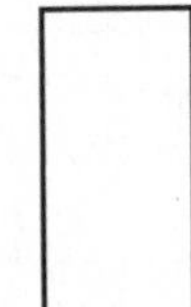 B 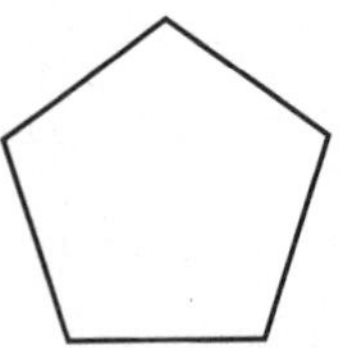 C 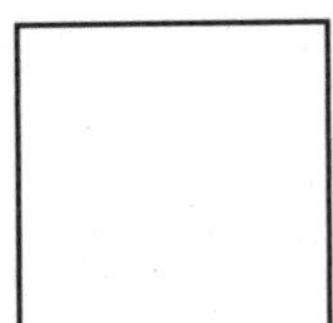 D 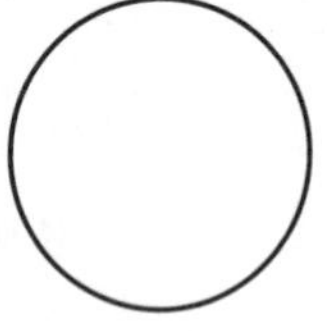

7. Which figure has a curved surface and flat surfaces with no corners?

A 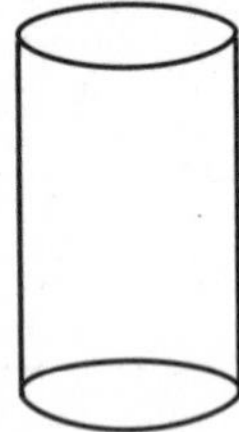 B 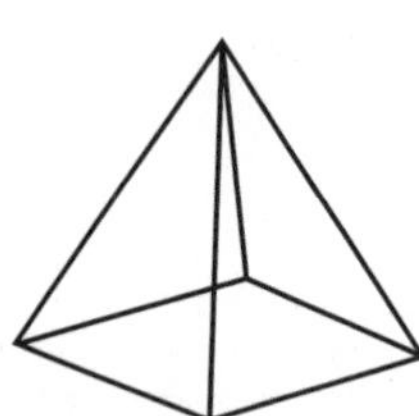 C 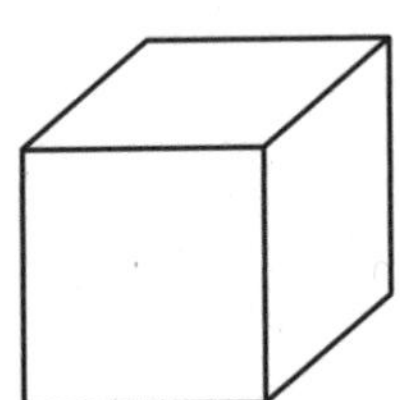 D 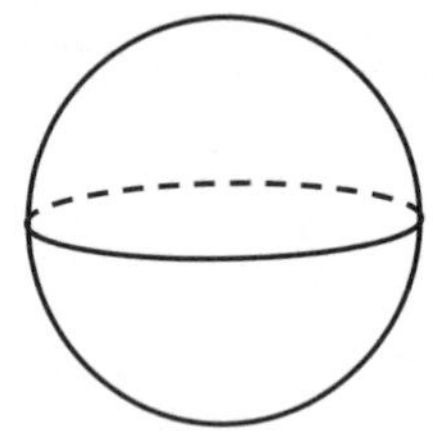

8. Which figure has fewer than 5 sides and more than 3 corners?

A 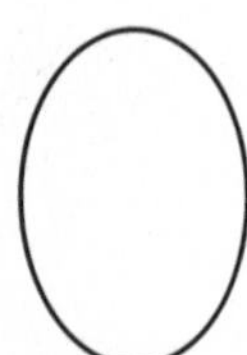 B 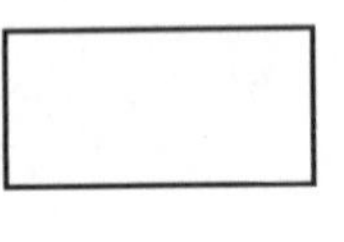 C  D 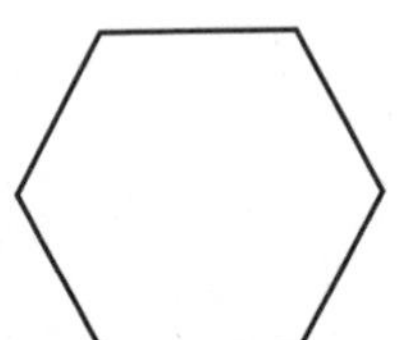

Stop

Name ____________________

Choose the correct answer.

1. Which comes next?

2. Which figures show the same pattern?

3. Which is the pattern unit?

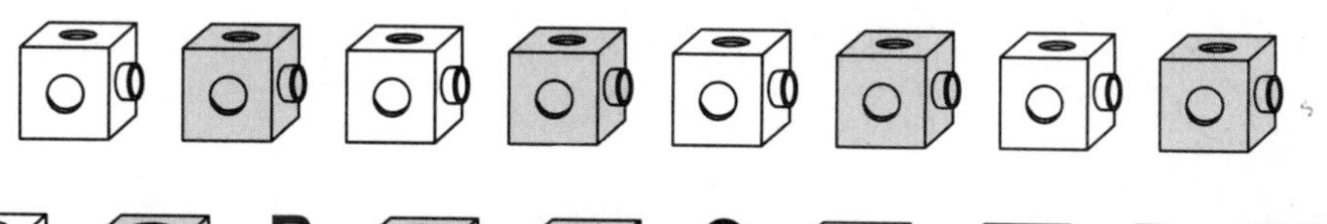

Go On

Name ____________________

Choose the correct answer.

4. Which number is missing?

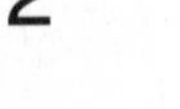

2 4 6 2 4 __?__ 2 4 6

A 2 B 4 C 5 D 6

5. Which figure comes next?

A B C D

6. Find the mistake in the pattern.
Which is the correct sticker?

A  B  C  D 

7. Find the mistake in the pattern.
Which is the correct bead?

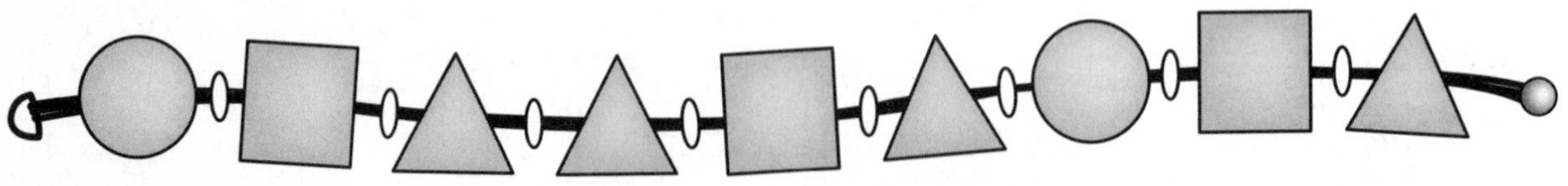

A 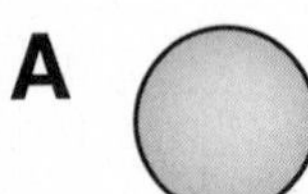 B 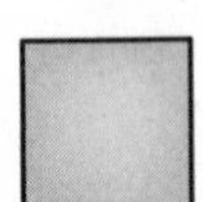 C 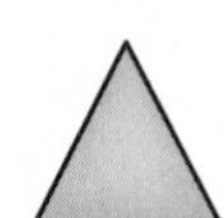 D 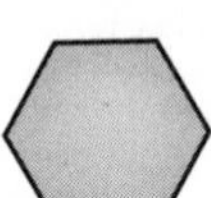

Stop

Name ________________________________

Choose the correct answer.

1. Which appears to show two congruent figures?

A 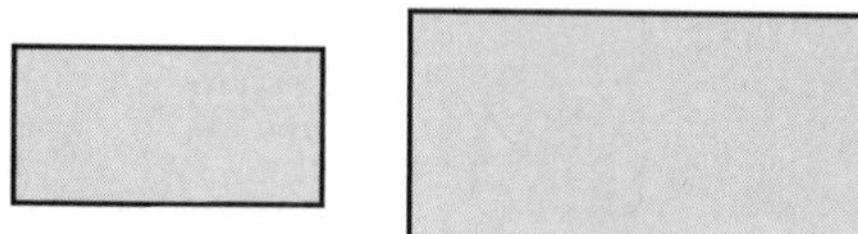

B 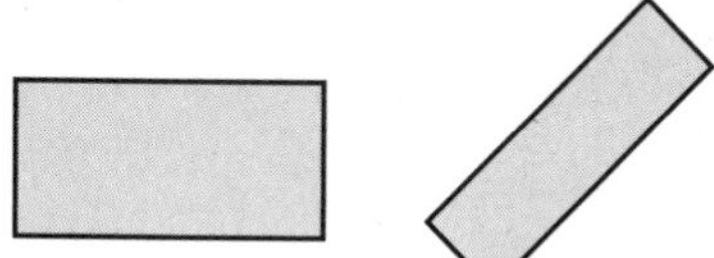

C 

D 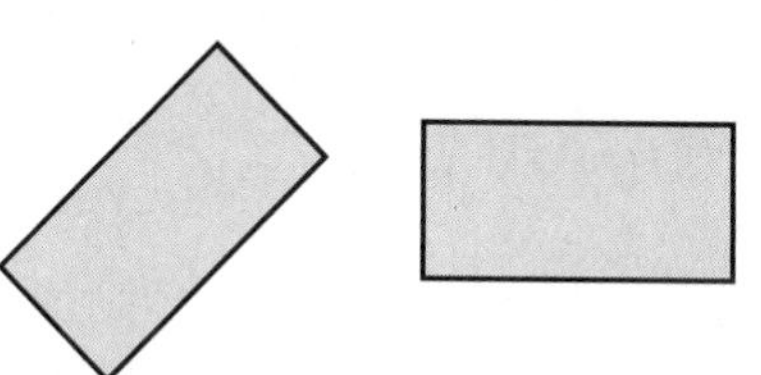

2. Which type of move is shown?

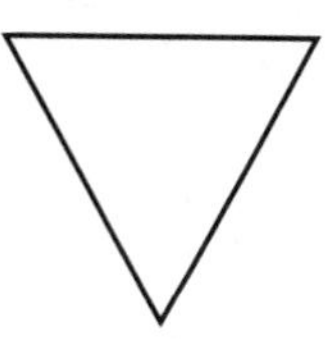

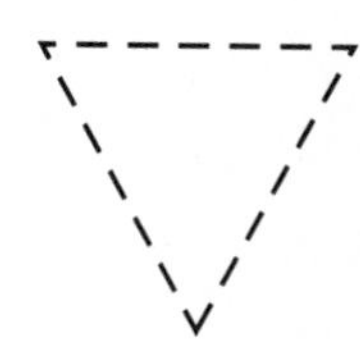

A slide

B flip

C turn

D symmetry

3. The [bird] is below the [cloud]. What is below the [kite]?

A 

B 

C 

D 

Go On

Name ______________________________

Choose the correct answer.

4. From **Start,** go right 2. Go down 1. Go left 1.
Where are you?

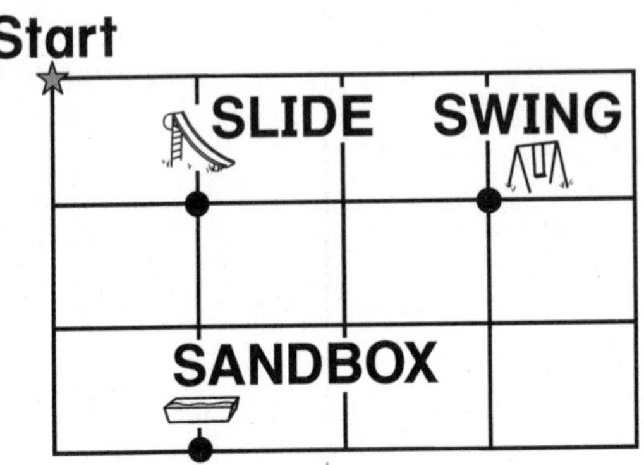

A slide **B** swing **C** sandbox

---

5. Which appears to show a line of symmetry?

A  **B** 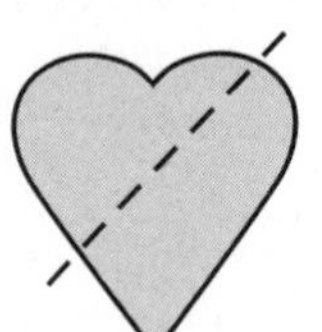 **C**  **D** 

---

6. Sam's toy is **above** a ▭. His toy has a **line of symmetry.** Which toy is Sam's?

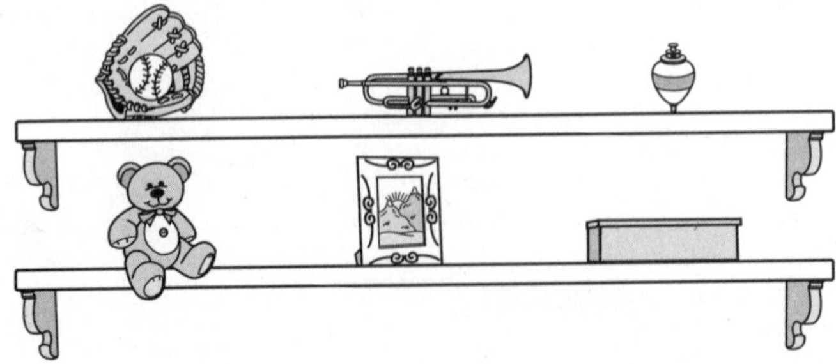

A  **B** **C**  **D** 

Stop

Name ______________________

Choose the correct answer.

1. Which figure is divided into two equal parts?

A 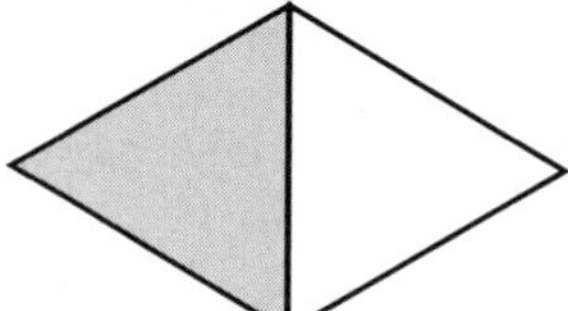

B 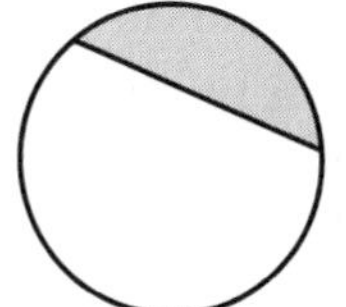

C 

D 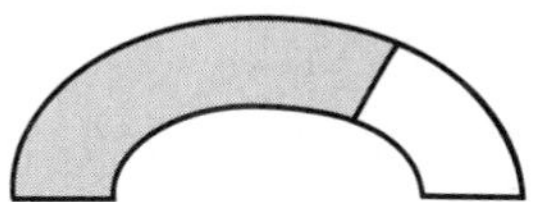

2. Which shows that 1 out of 3 🎈 are gray?

A 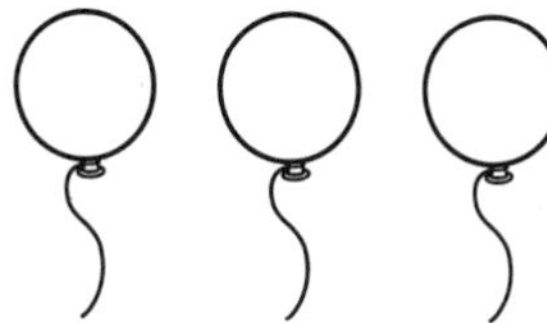

B 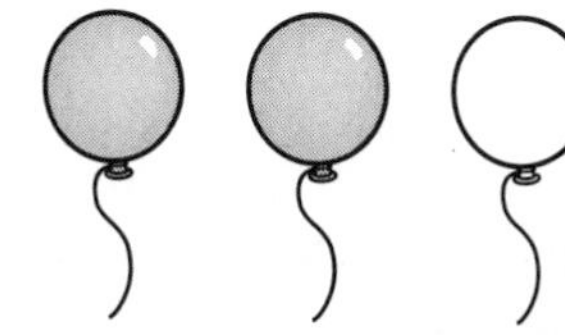

C 

D 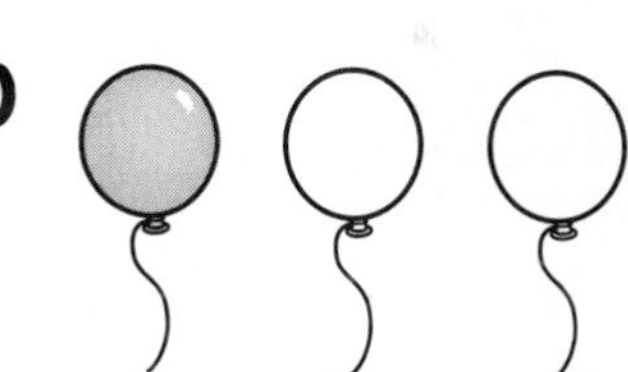

3. Which figure has equal parts?

A 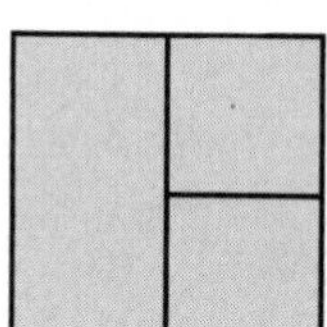

B 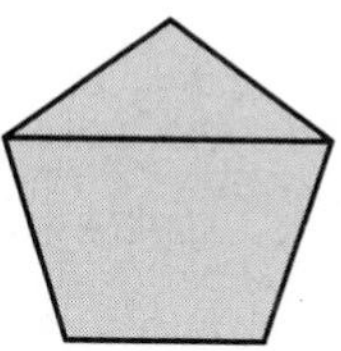

C 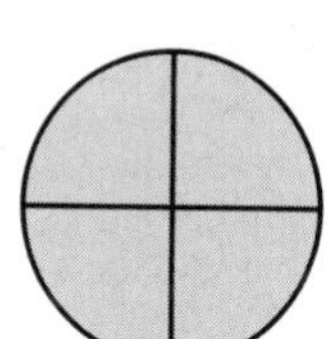

D 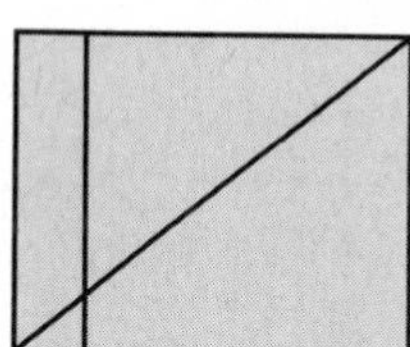

4. Which figure has $\frac{1}{4}$ shaded?

A 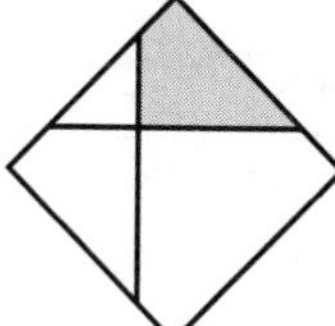

B 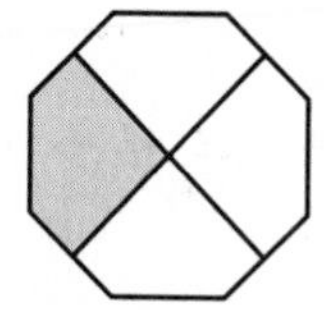

C 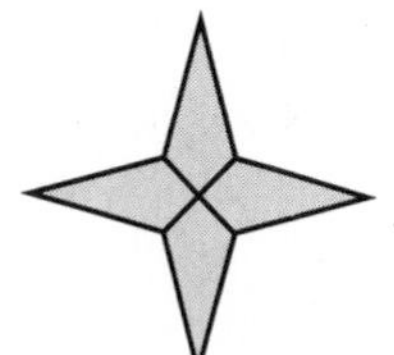

D 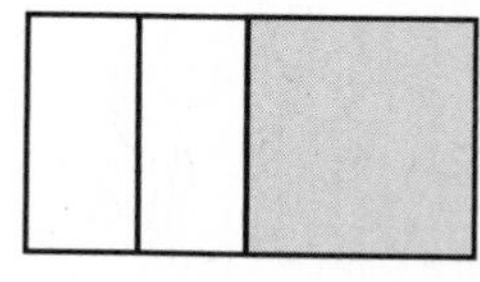

Go On

Name ____________________

Choose the correct answer.

5. Which figure has $\frac{1}{3}$ shaded?

A 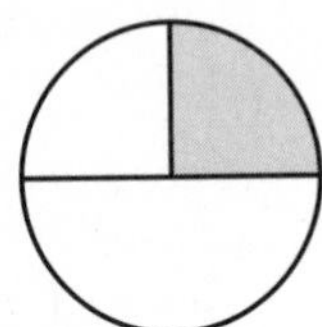

B 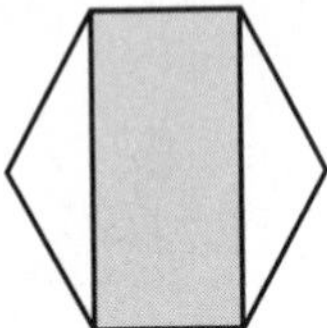

C 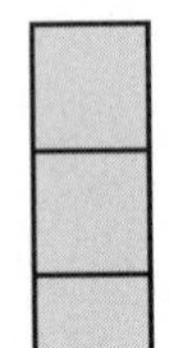

D 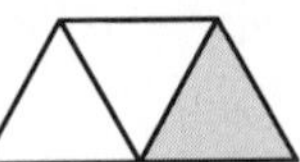

6. Tommy and 3 friends share a . Each gets an equal share. How would you cut the ?

A 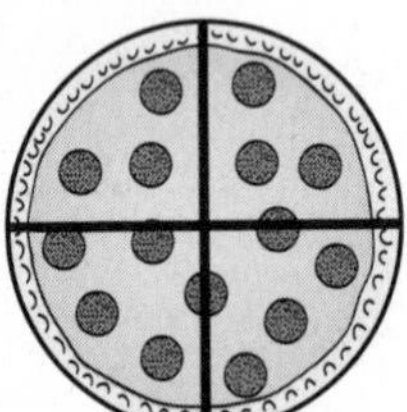

B 

C 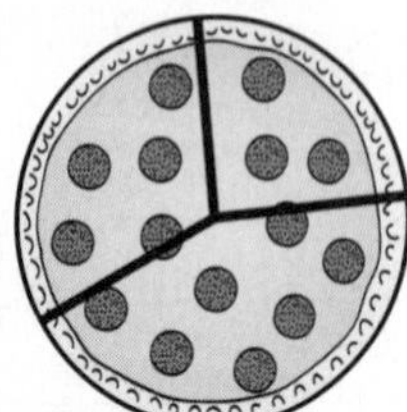

D 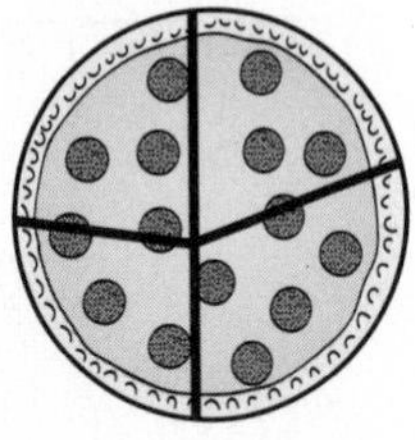

7. Gina and a friend share a . Each gets an equal share. How would you cut the ?

A 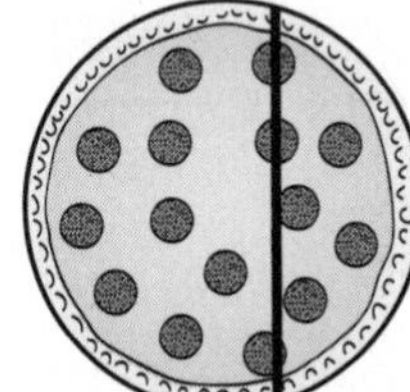

B 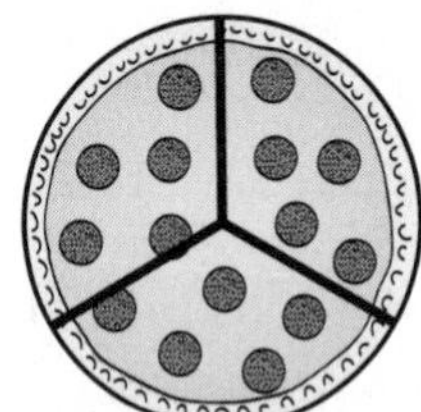

C 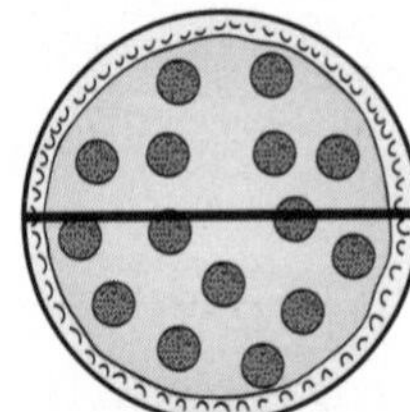

D 

Stop

Choose the correct answer.

1. How many corners does the plane figure have?

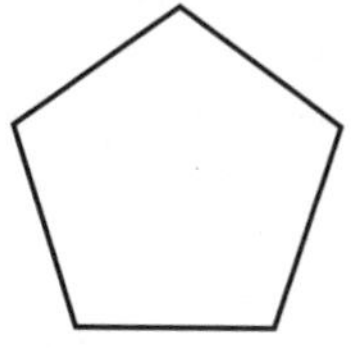

A 5

B 6

C 7

D 8

2. Which type of move is shown?

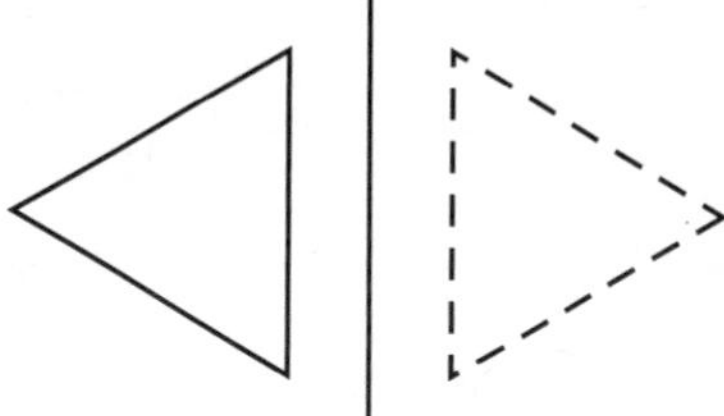

A turn

B flip

C slide

D symmetry

3. Which figure has equal parts?

A 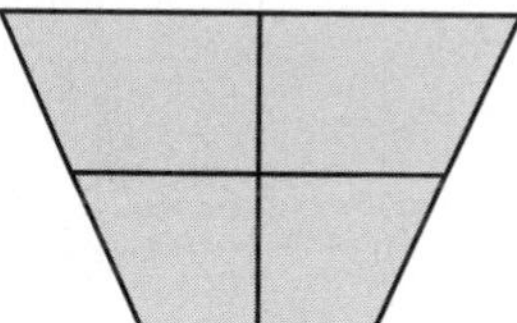 **B** 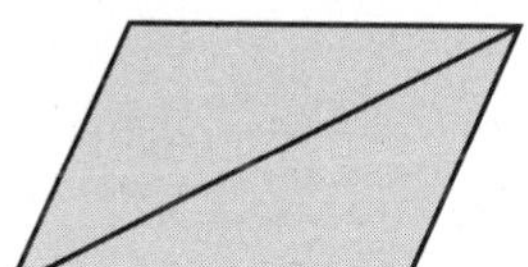 **C** 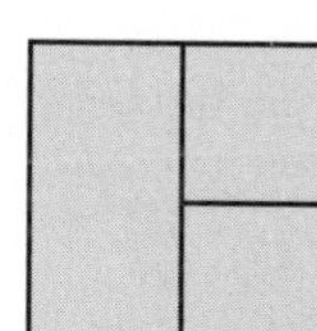 **D** 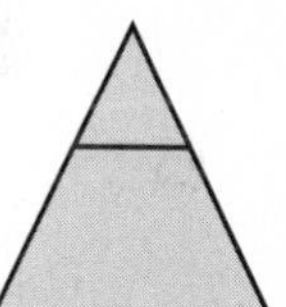

4. Which figure is a rectangle?

A 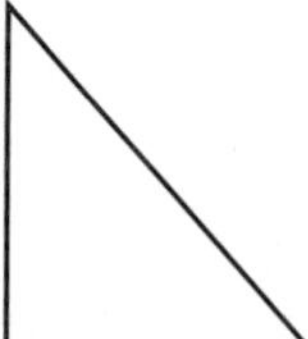 **B** 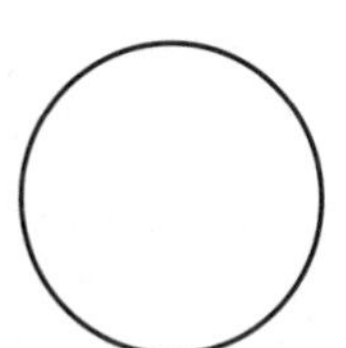 **C** 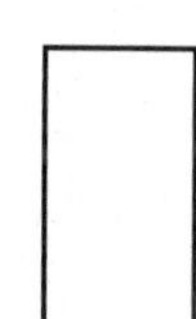 **D** 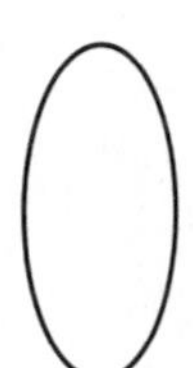

Go On

Choose the correct answer.

5. Which comes next?

A B C D

6. Which shows a line of symmetry?

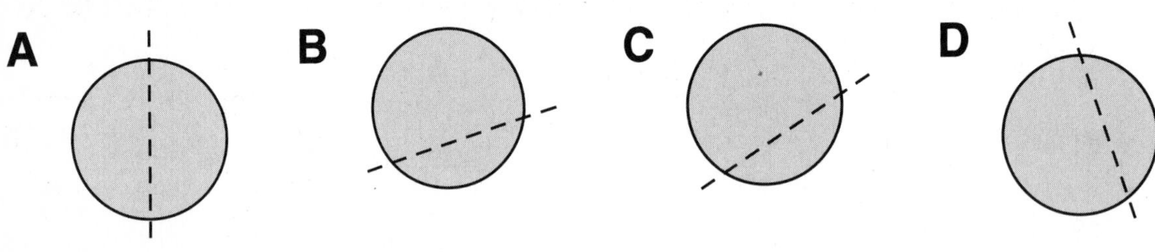

A B C D

7. Which figure has $\frac{1}{4}$ shaded?

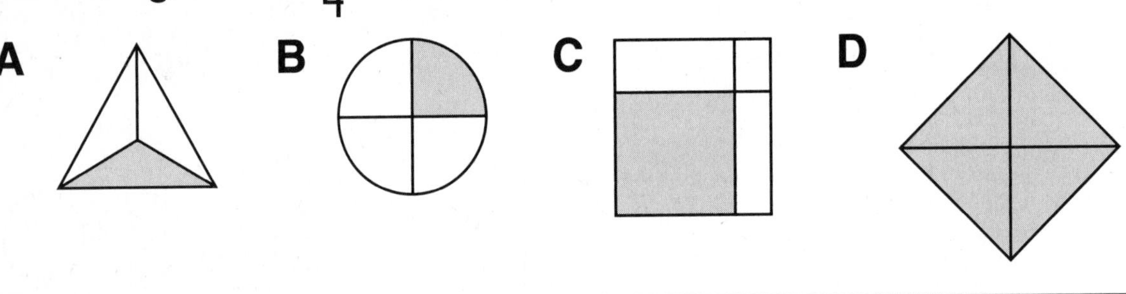

A B C D

8. Which object could you trace to make the figure?

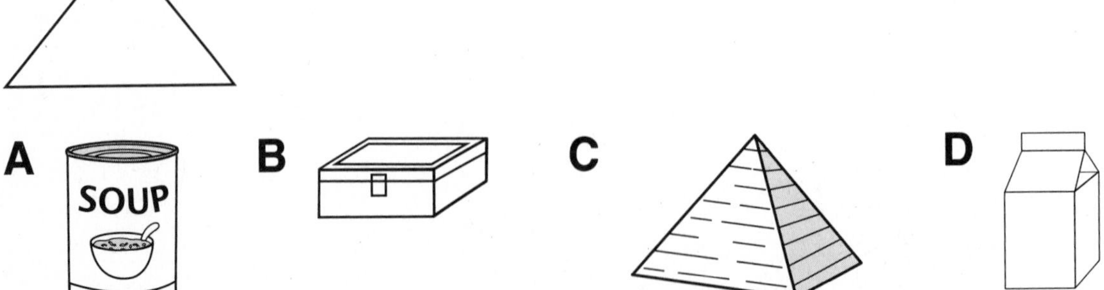

A B C D

Go On

Name ______________________

Choose the correct answer.

9. Which is the pattern unit?

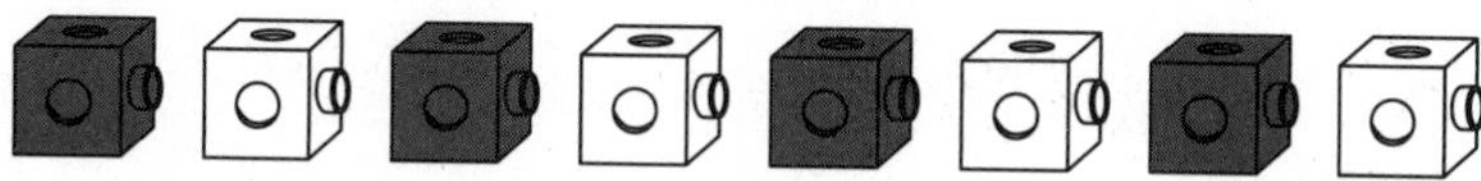

A  B 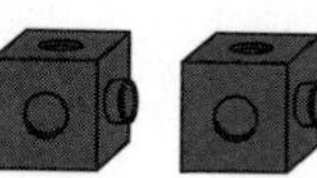    C    D  

10. 2 friends share a . Each gets an equal share. How would you cut the ?

A
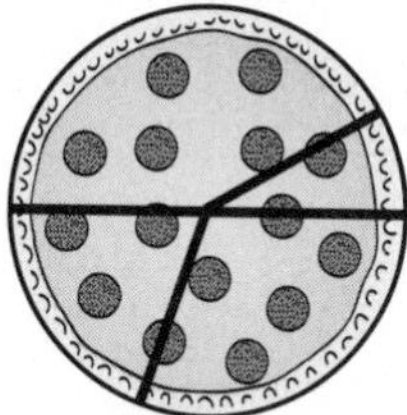

B
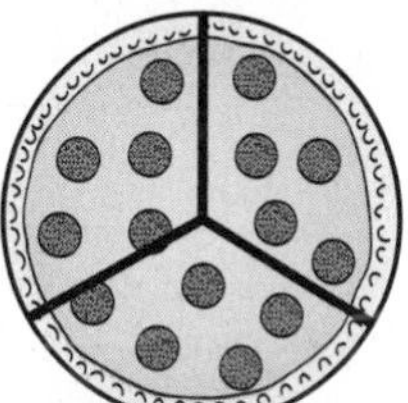

C
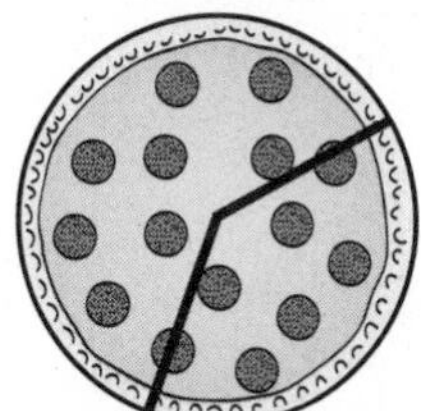

D
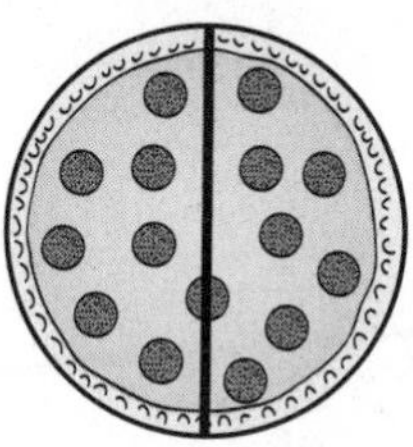

11. Which shows $\frac{1}{4}$ shaded?

A
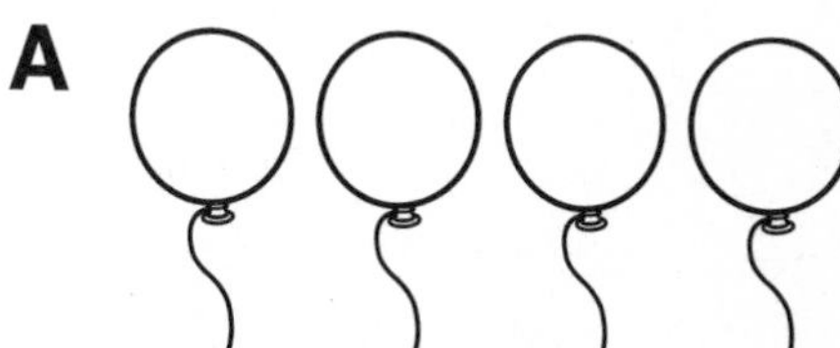

B
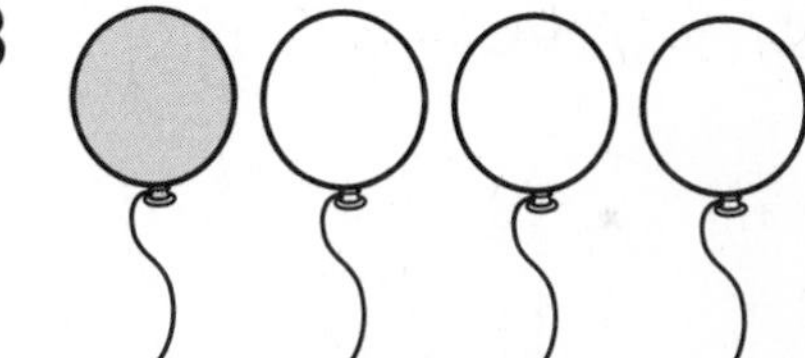

C

D
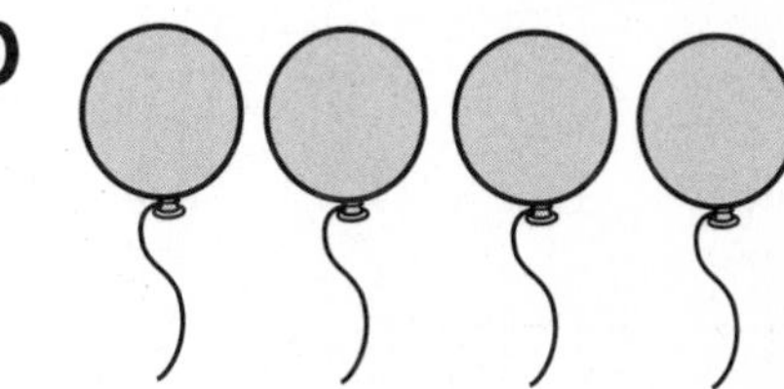

Go On

Choose the correct answer.

12. Which figure is a triangle?

A 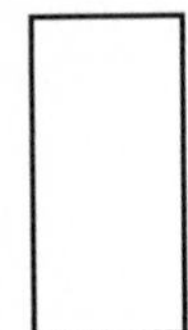 **B**  **C** 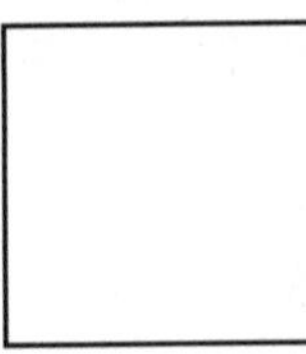 **D** 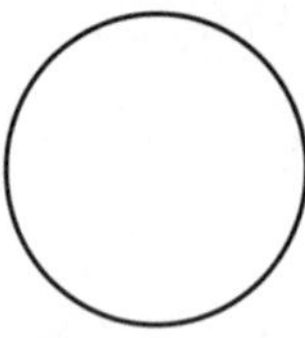

13. Which number is missing?

3 8 8 3 8 8 ? 8 8

A 3 **B** 6 **C** 8 **D** 9

14. Which solid figure has only one curved surface?

A 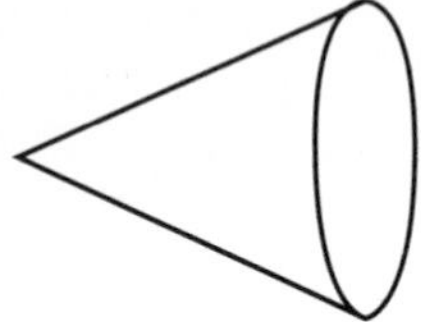 **B** 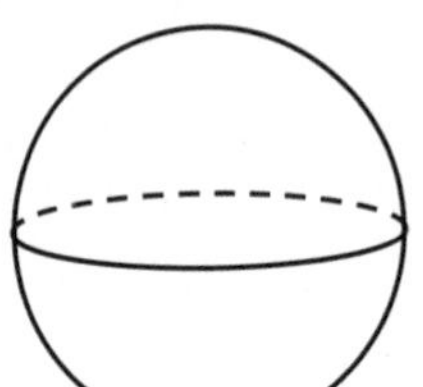 **C** 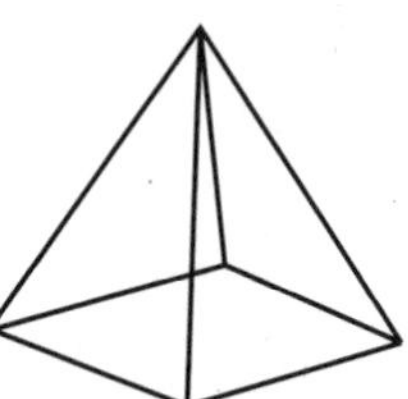 **D** 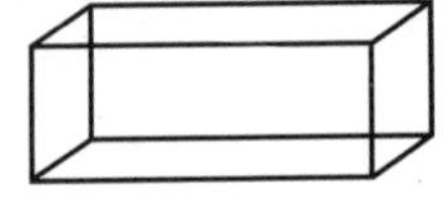

15. Which figures show the same pattern?

A 

B 

C 

Go On

Name ____________________

Choose the correct answer.

16. Which appears to show two congruent figures?

A 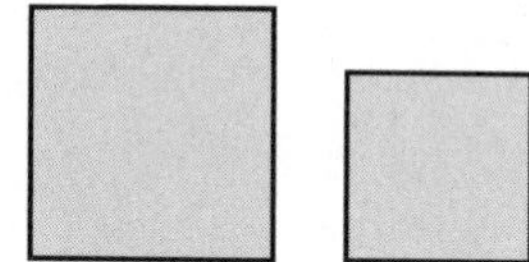

B 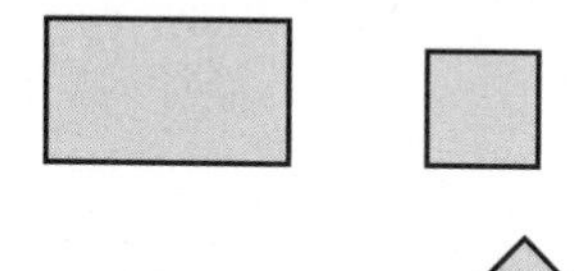

C 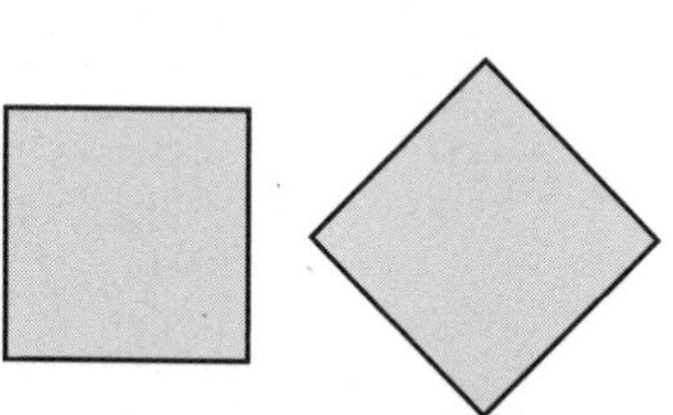

17. How many flat surfaces does the cube have?

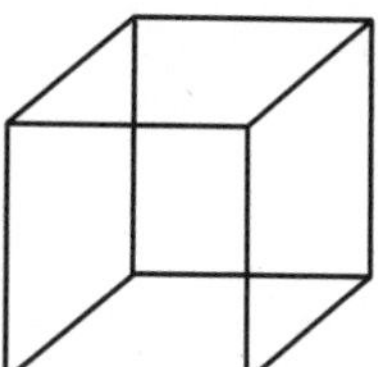

A 2

B 4

C 5

D 6

Use the picture for questions 18 and 19.

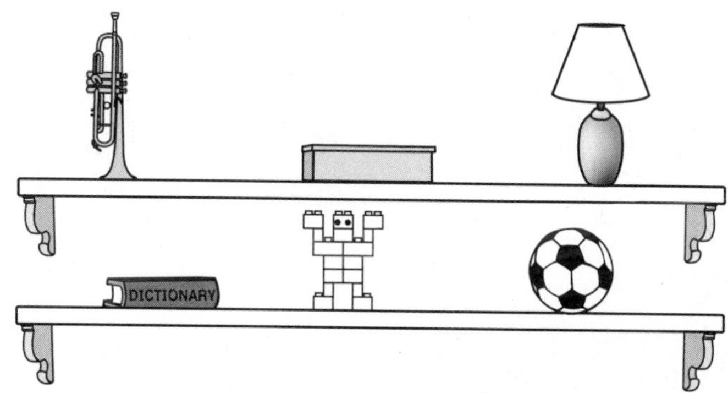

18. Chuck's toy is **above** the

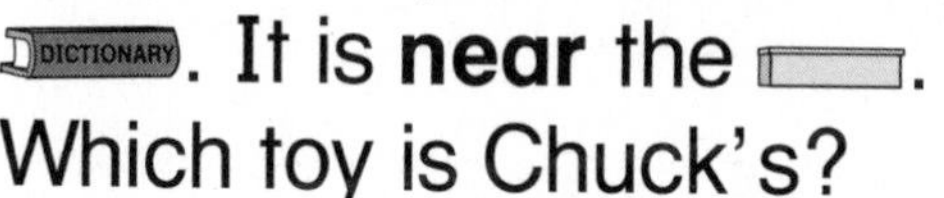

. It is **near** the . Which toy is Chuck's?

A 

B 

C 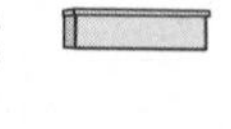

D

19. Tracy's toy is **below** the . Her toy has a **line of symmetry**. It is **near** the . Which toy is Tracy's?

A 

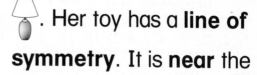

B  

C  

D 

Go On

Name ______________________

Choose the correct answer.

20. Find the mistake in the pattern. Which is the correct sticker?

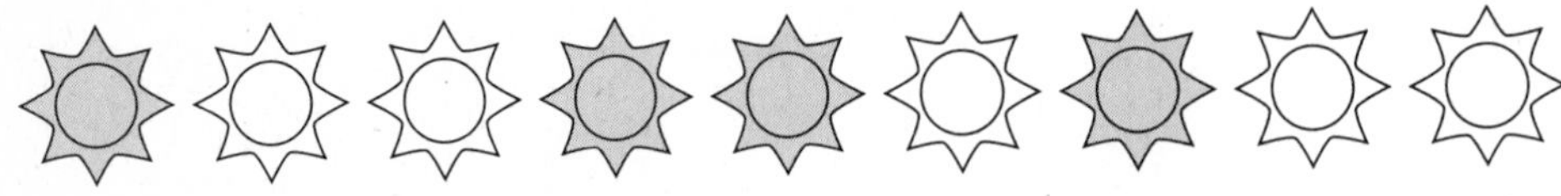

A  **B**  **C**  **D** 

21. Which figure has more than 4 corners and fewer than 6 sides?

A 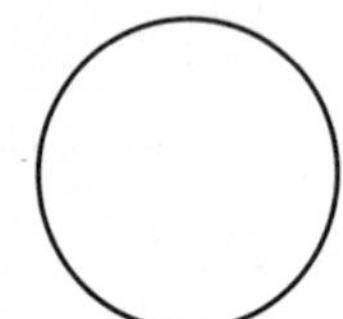 **B** 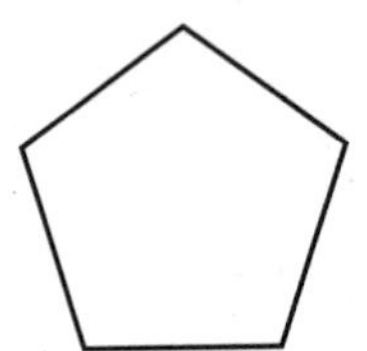 **C** 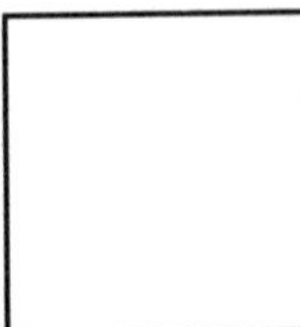 **D** 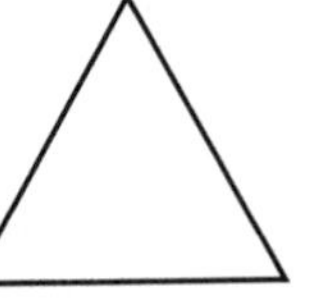

22. From **Start**, go right 2. Go down 2. Go right 1. Where are you?

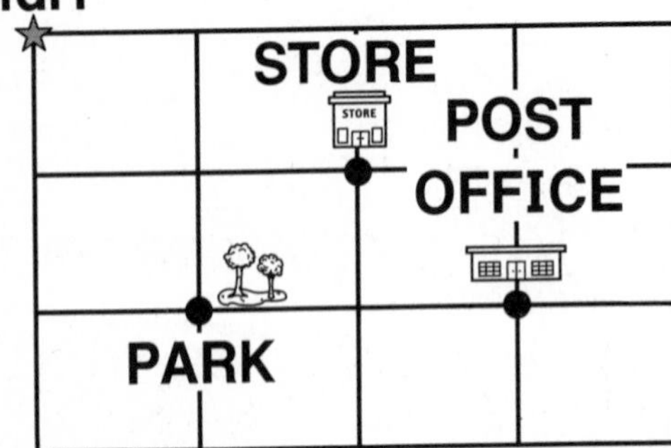

A store **B** post office **C** park

Stop

Name________________________________

Choose the correct answer.

1. What is the sum?

$$\begin{array}{r} 6 \\ +6 \\ \hline \end{array}$$

A 10

B 11

C 12

D 13

2. Make a ten and add. What is the sum?

$$\begin{array}{r} 8 \\ +7 \\ \hline \end{array}$$

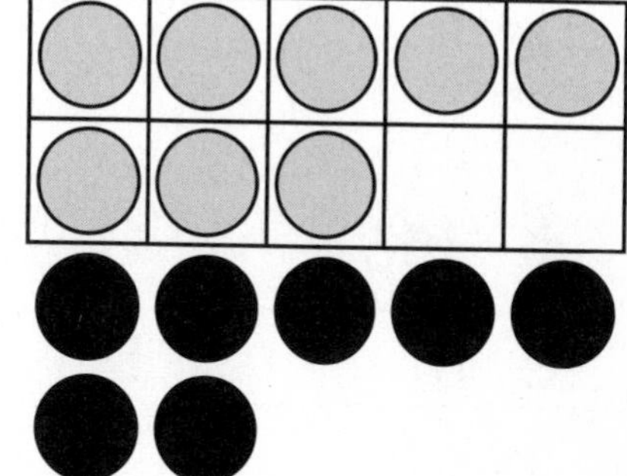

A 12

B 15

C 17

D 18

3. What is the sum?

$$\begin{array}{r} 8 \\ +4 \\ \hline \end{array}$$

A 16

B 14

C 13

D 12

4. What is the sum?

$$\begin{array}{r} 2 \\ 4 \\ +8 \\ \hline \end{array}$$

A 14

B 12

C 10

D 6

Go On

Name ____________________________

Choose the correct answer.

5. What is the sum?

$$\begin{array}{r} 10 \\ +\ 6 \\ \hline \end{array}$$

A 106 **C** 16

B 61 **D** 4

6. Make a ten and add. What is the sum?

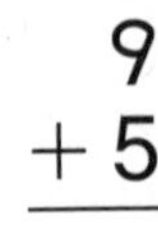

$$\begin{array}{r} 9 \\ +5 \\ \hline \end{array}$$

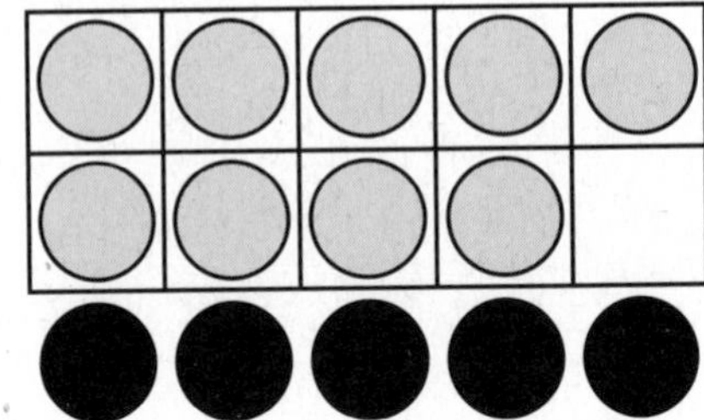

A 13 **C** 16

B 14 **D** 15

7. What is the sum?

4 + 4 = ____

A 88 **B** 80 **C** 40 **D** 8

8. Which number sentence matches the story? A mail carrier delivers 7 letters. Then she delivers 9 more letters. How many letters does the mail carrier deliver in all?

A 7 + 9 = 16

B 7 + 9 = 15

C 16 − 7 = 9

D 9 − 7 = 2

9. Which number sentence matches the story? 8 teachers are in the hallway. 8 more teachers join them. How many teachers are in the hallway?

A 8 − 8 = 0

B 8 + 8 = 14

C 8 + 8 = 16

D 16 − 6 = 8

Stop

Choose the correct answer.

Use the number line to answer questions 1 and 2.

1. What is the difference?

$$\begin{array}{r} 13 \\ -\ 5 \\ \hline \end{array}$$

A 7

B 8

C 9

D 18

2. What is the difference?

$$\begin{array}{r} 15 \\ -\ 6 \\ \hline \end{array}$$

A 9

B 8

C 7

D 1

3. How many more leaves are there than birds?

$$\begin{array}{r} 11 \\ -\ 4 \\ \hline \end{array}$$

A 15 more leaves

B 8 more leaves

C 7 more leaves

D 6 more leaves

4. What is the difference?

14 − 6 = ____

A 20 **B** 10 **C** 9 **D** 8

Go On

Name ____________________

Choose the correct answer.

5. Use the addition fact to help you subtract. What is the difference?

$$\begin{array}{r} 7 \\ +\ 5 \\ \hline \end{array} \qquad \begin{array}{r} 12 \\ -\ \ 5 \\ \hline \end{array}$$

A 6

B 7

C 9

D 17

6. What is the difference?

$$\begin{array}{r} 14 \\ -\ \ 9 \\ \hline \end{array}$$

A 5

B 6

C 7

D 8

7. How many fewer bees are there than flowers?

$$\begin{array}{r} 12 \\ -\ \ 8 \\ \hline \end{array}$$

A 20 fewer bees

B 8 fewer bees

C 4 fewer bees

D 3 fewer bees

8. There are 12 children playing on the playground. 3 more children join them. How many children are now playing on the playground?

A 9 children

B 12 children

C 14 children

D 15 children

9. There are 11 birds in a tree. 3 birds fly away. How many birds are in the tree now?

A 14 birds

B 12 birds

C 9 birds

D 8 birds

Stop

Choose the correct answer.

1. Which number is missing?

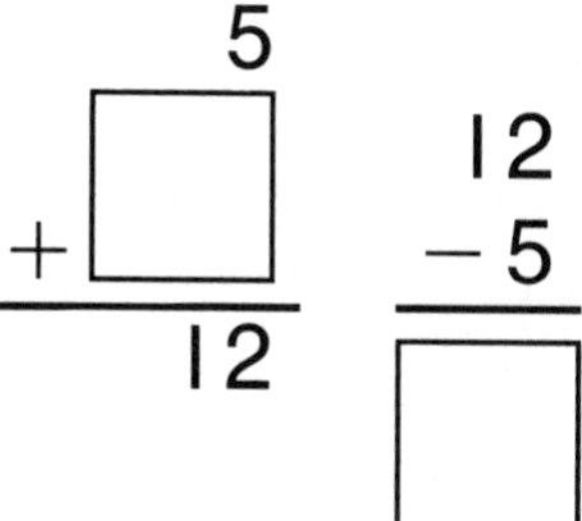

A 7 **C** 15

B 8 **D** 17

2. Which is a way to make 15?

A 13 − 8

B 17 − 5

C 9 + 8

D 2 + 5 + 8

3. Which number sentence shows how many umbrellas there are?

_____ gray umbrellas

_____ white umbrellas

A 9 − 8 = 1 **C** 8 + 9 = 17

B 12 + 5 = 17 **D** 17 − 9 = 8

4. Which number is missing?

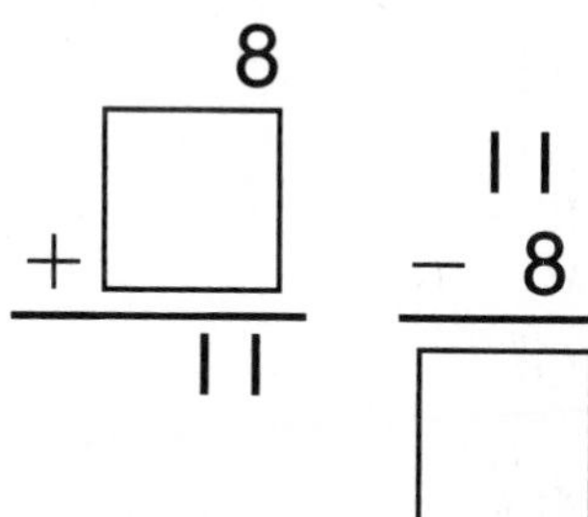

A 2 **B** 3 **C** 4 **D** 5

Go On

Choose the correct answer.

5. Which is a way to make 9?

A 4 + 3 + 4

B 6 + 4

C 12 − 5

D 15 − 6

6. Follow the rule. Which number completes the table?

Subtract 7	
12	5
14	7
16	
17	10

A 8 B 9 C 11 D 12

7. Which fact is part of the fact family?

$$\begin{array}{r} 9 \\ +4 \\ \hline 13 \end{array} \qquad \begin{array}{r} 4 \\ +9 \\ \hline 13 \end{array} \qquad \begin{array}{r} 13 \\ -\ 4 \\ \hline 9 \end{array}$$

A $\begin{array}{r} 13 \\ -\ 9 \\ \hline 4 \end{array}$ B $\begin{array}{r} 13 \\ +\ 4 \\ \hline 17 \end{array}$ C $\begin{array}{r} 9 \\ -4 \\ \hline 5 \end{array}$ D $\begin{array}{r} 5 \\ +4 \\ \hline 9 \end{array}$

8. Kara has 7 peaches. Henry brings 9 more peaches. How many peaches are there now?

A 2 peaches

B 14 peaches

C 15 peaches

D 16 peaches

9. Trevor buys 14 apples. He gives 7 apples away. How many apples does Trevor have now?

A 21 apples C 7 apples

B 8 apples D 6 apples

Stop

Name ______________________________

Choose the correct answer.

1. Which shows the amount of money in a different way?

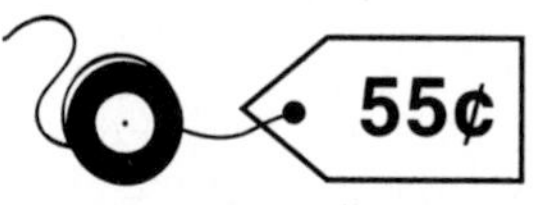

A 

B 

C 

D 

2. Which shows a way to make 1 dollar?

A 

B 

C 

D 

Go On

Choose the correct answer.

3. Which symbol can you use to compare the amounts?

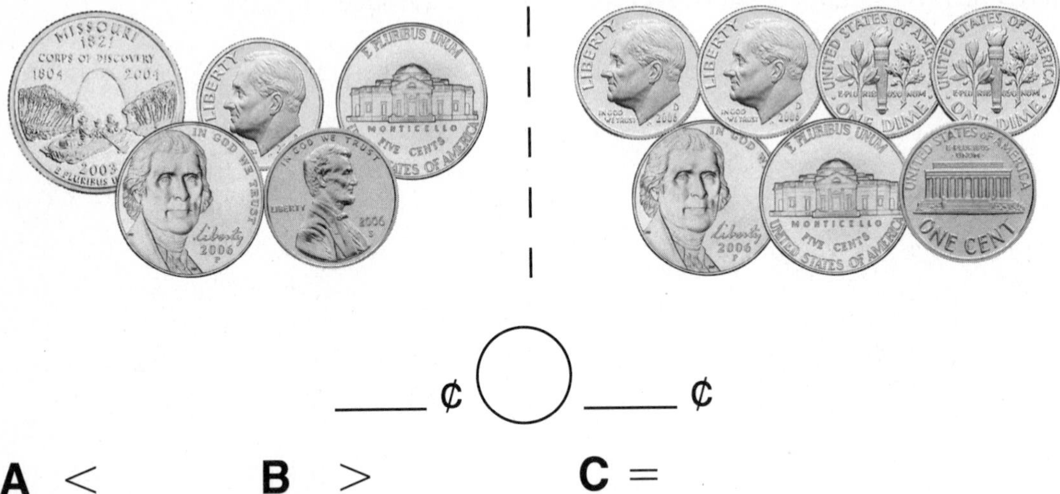

____ ¢ ◯ ____ ¢

A $<$ **B** $>$ **C** $=$

---

4. Jack buys a toy car for 75¢. He uses 3  .
Which shows the same amount in a different way?

A

B

C

D

Stop

Choose the correct answer.

1. What time does the clock show?

A 10:30

B 6:30

C 8:30

D 9:30

2. What time does the clock show?

A 12:00

B 2:00

C 2:30

D 11:00

3. Use the calendar. How many Mondays are in this month?

A 2

B 3

C 4

D 5

MAY						
Sunday	Monday	Tuesday	Wednesday	Thursday	Friday	Saturday
		1	2	3	4	5
6	7	8	9	10	11	12
13	14	15	16	17	18	19
20	21	22	23	24	25	26
27	28	29	30	31		

Go On

Name ______________________________

Choose the correct answer.

4. Which clock matches the time shown?

A 
B 
C 
D 

Use the table to answer questions 5 and 6.

Camp Sunrise		
Event	**Start**	**End**
crafts		
hiking		
soccer		

5. Which event starts at 3:30?

A crafts
B hiking
C soccer

6. Which event lasts the shortest time?

A crafts
B hiking
C soccer

Name____ UNIT 5 PRETEST

ChooseSheScorrectSanswer.

1. Use the calendar. How many Mondays are in June?

JUNE						
Sunday	Monday	Tuesday	Wednesday	Thursday	Friday	Saturday
					1	2
3	4	5	6	7	8	9
10	11	12	13	14	15	16
17	18	19	20	21	22	23
24	25	26	27	28	29	30

AS5 **C** 3

B S **D**

2. Use the addition fact to help you subtract. What is the difference?

$$\begin{array}{r} 8 \\ +5 \\ \hline \end{array} \qquad \begin{array}{r} 3 \\ -\ 5 \\ \hline \end{array}$$

AS

B S8

CS

DS

3. What is the sum?

$$\begin{array}{r} \\ + \\ \hline \end{array}$$

AS

BS 3

C S

DS 5

4. Follow the rule. Which number completes the table?

Subtract 8	
12	4
14	6
16	
17	9

AS 3 **C** 8

BS 0 **D**

Go On

Name ______________________________

Choose the correct answer.

5. How many more butterflies are there than flowers?

$$\begin{array}{r} 10 \\ -\ 3 \\ \hline \end{array}$$

A 13 more butterflies

B 8 more butterflies

C 7 more butterflies

D 6 more butterflies

6. Which number sentence shows how many umbrellas there are?

_____ gray umbrellas

_____ white umbrellas

A $8 - 7 = 1$

B $10 + 5 = 15$

C $15 - 7 = 8$

D $7 + 8 = 15$

7. What is the sum?

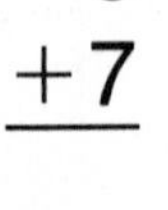

$$\begin{array}{r} 2 \\ 3 \\ +7 \\ \hline \end{array}$$

A 12

B 10

C 9

D 5

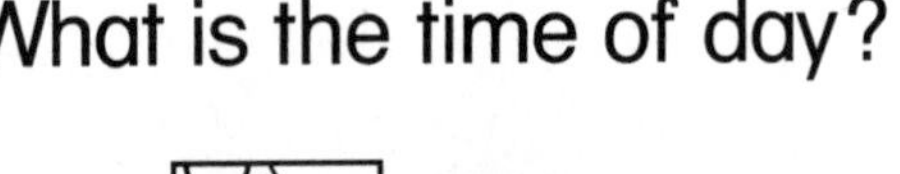

8. What is the time of day?

A morning

B afternoon

C evening

Go On

Name ____

Choose the correct answer.

9. Which shows the amount of money in a different way?

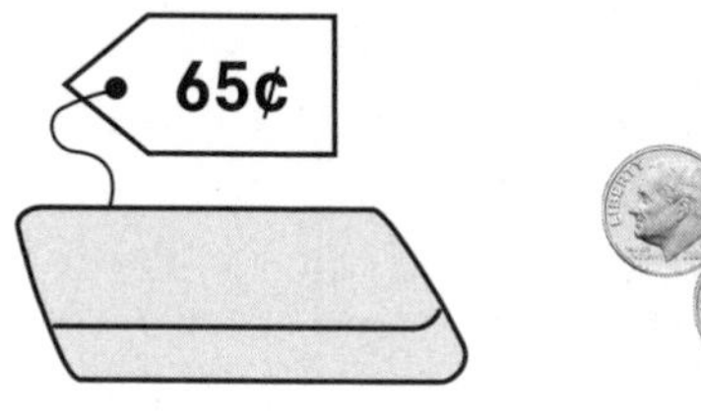

A

B

C

10. Which shows a way to make 1 dollar?

A

B

C

11. What is the difference?

$$\begin{array}{r} 15 \\ -\ 6 \\ \hline \end{array}$$

A 11 **B** 9 **C** 8 **D** 5

Go On

Name ______________________

Choose the correct answer.

12. Which number sentence matches the story?
A town has 5 buses. Then the town buys 7 more buses. How many buses does the town have in all?

A $5 + 7 = 13$

B $5 + 7 = 12$

C $15 - 7 = 8$

D $7 - 5 = 2$

13. Which number is missing?

$$\begin{array}{r} 8 \\ + \square \\ \hline 13 \end{array} \qquad \begin{array}{r} 13 \\ -\ 8 \\ \hline \square \end{array}$$

A 5

B 4

C 3

D 2

14. Make a ten and add. What is the sum?

$$\begin{array}{r} 7 \\ +6 \end{array}$$

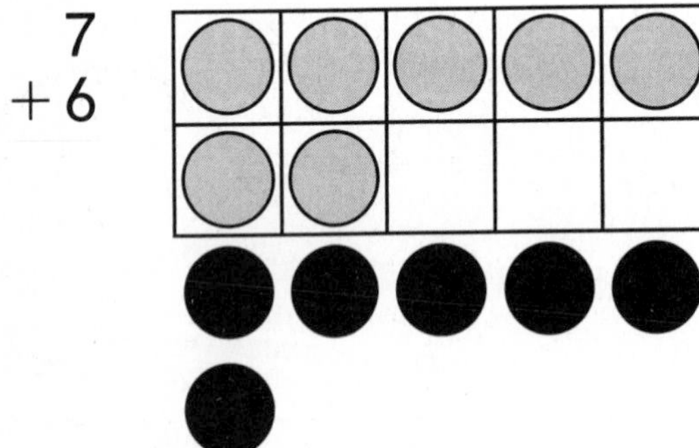

A 13

B 14

C 15

D 16

15. Rick has 4 bananas. Evan brings 7 more bananas. How many bananas are there in all?

A 11 bananas

B 10 bananas

C 9 bananas

D 3 bananas

Go On

Choose the correct answer.

16. Which symbol can you use to compare the amounts?

50 ¢ ◯ 40 ¢

A $<$ **B** $>$ **C** $=$

17. Which clock matches the time shown?

A

B

C

D

18. What is the sum?

9 + 8 = ____

A 77 **C** 7

B 17 **D** 1

19. What is the difference?

19 − 9 = ____

A 10 **C** 8

B 9 **D** 1

Go On

Name ____________________

UNIT 5 PRETEST

Choose the correct answer.

Use the table to answer question 20.

Community Center		
Event	Start	End
art class	11:00	11:30
game time	1:30	3:30
homework help	3:00	4:00

20. Which event starts at 3:00?

A art class **B** game time **C** homework help

21. Which fact is part of the fact family?

$\begin{array}{r} 6 \\ +7 \\ \hline 13 \end{array}$ $\begin{array}{r} 7 \\ +6 \\ \hline 13 \end{array}$ $\begin{array}{r} 13 \\ -\ 6 \\ \hline 7 \end{array}$

A $\begin{array}{r} 13 \\ +\ 3 \\ \hline 16 \end{array}$ **B** $\begin{array}{r} 13 \\ -\ 7 \\ \hline 6 \end{array}$ **C** $\begin{array}{r} 5 \\ +1 \\ \hline 6 \end{array}$ **D** $\begin{array}{r} 6 \\ -5 \\ \hline 1 \end{array}$

Stop

Choose the correct answer.

1. What is the temperature?

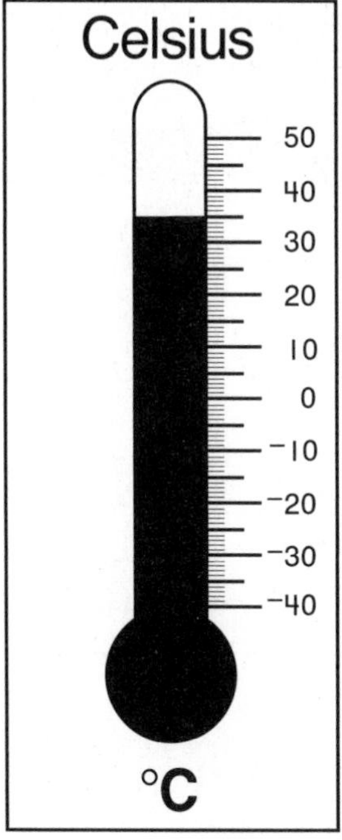

A 3°C
B 30°C
C 35°C
D 40°C

2. How long is the object?

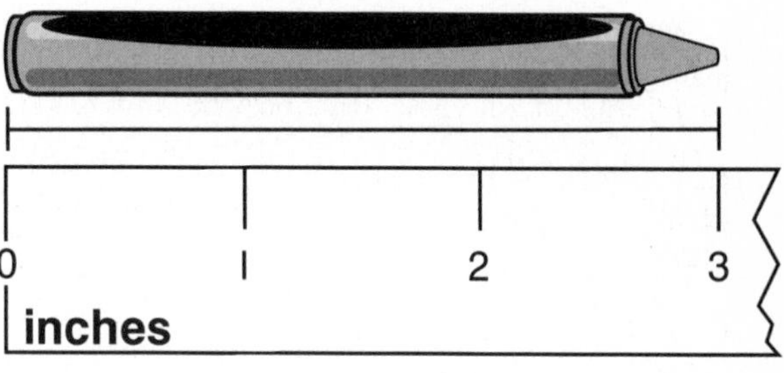

A about 2 inches
B about 3 inches
C about 4 inches
D about 5 inches

3. About how many paper clips long is the object?

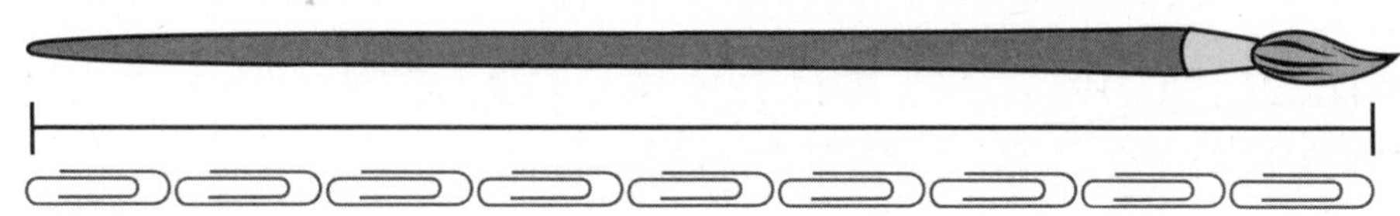

A about 6 paper clips
B about 7 paper clips
C about 8 paper clips
D about 9 paper clips

Go On

Name ______________________________

Choose the correct answer.

4. Which shows the ribbons in order from shortest to longest?

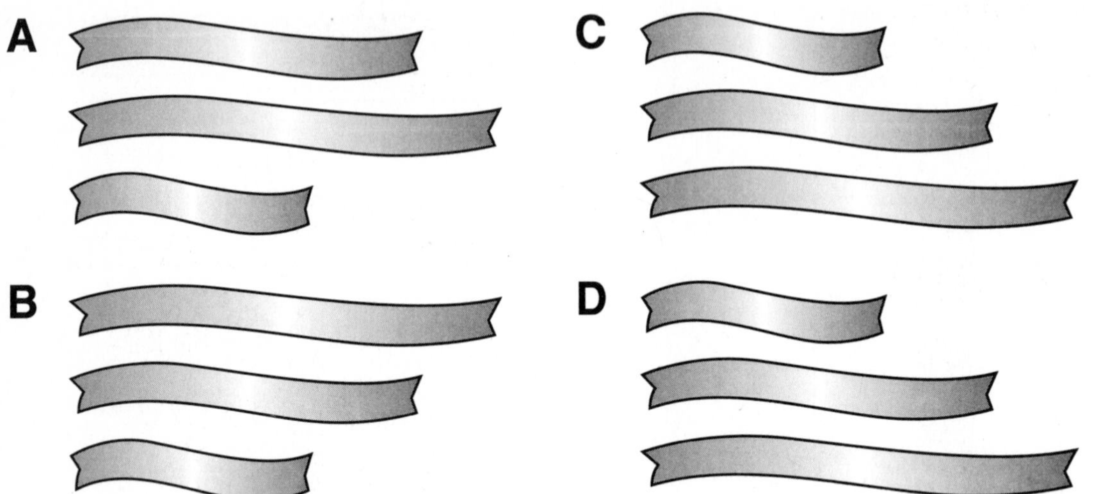

5. About how many (paper clips) long is the object?

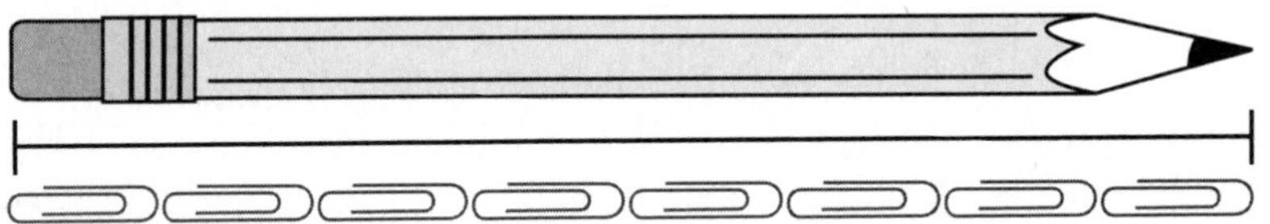

A about 2 (paper clips)

B about 4 (paper clips)

C about 6 (paper clips)

D about 8 (paper clips)

6. About how many (paper clips) long is the object?

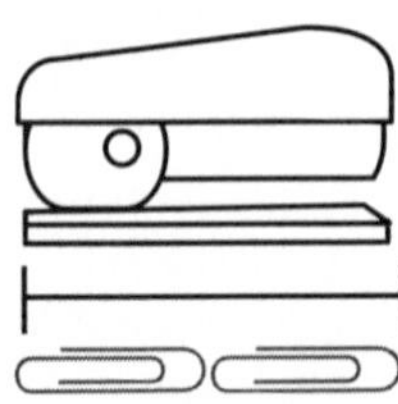

A about 1 (paper clips)

B about 2 (paper clips)

C about 3 (paper clips)

D about 4 (paper clips)

Stop

Name ____________________

Choose the correct answer.

1. Which object is the heaviest?

A 

B 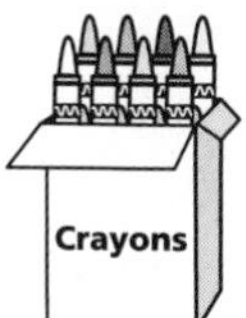

C 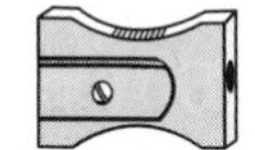

D

2. Which container holds the least?

A 

B 

C 

D 

3. About how many cups will the container hold?

A about 1 cup

B about 2 cups

C about 4 cups

D about 7 cups

4. About how many pounds is the object?

A about 100 pounds

B about 20 pounds

C about 10 pounds

D about 1 pound

Go On

Name ______________________________

Choose the correct answer.

5. Which tool will you use to measure how much the bowl holds?

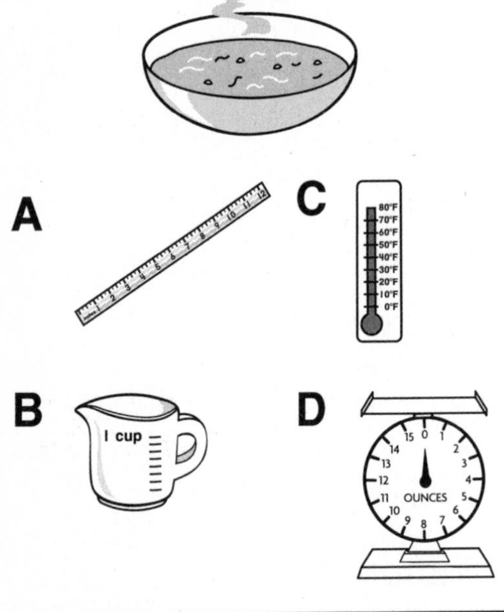

6. Which tool will you use to measure how heavy the apple is?

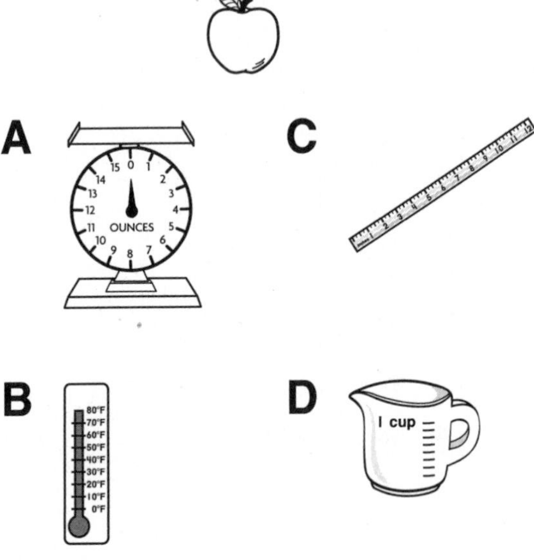

7. How many more cups do you need to fill the container to the top? This pitcher has I cup of juice in it.

A about 2 cups

B about 3 cups

C about 5 cups

8. How many more cups do you need to fill the container to the top? This bowl has I cup of soup in it.

A about 4 cups

B about 3 cups

C about 2 cups

D about I cup

Stop

Name ____________________

Choose the correct answer.

1. What is the difference?

90 − 60 = ____

A 20

B 30

C 40

D 50

2. What is the sum?

50 + 20 = ____

A 30

B 40

C 60

D 70

3. What is the difference?

	tens	ones
	3	9
−		5

Workmat

Tens | Ones

A 36

B 35

C 34

D 33

4. What is the sum?

	tens	ones
	2	2
+		4

Workmat

Tens | Ones

A 26

B 25

C 24

D 23

Go On

Name ______________________

Choose the correct answer.

5. What is the sum?

	tens	ones
	3	1
+	2	5

Workmat

Tens	Ones
3 tens	1 one
2 tens	5 ones

A 14

B 54

C 56

D 66

6. What is the difference?

	tens	ones
	3	7
−	1	3

Workmat

Tens	Ones
3 tens	7 ones

A 50

B 24

C 20

D 14

7. There are 52 birds in the trees. 9 of the birds fly away. About how many birds are left?

A about 4 birds

B about 40 birds

C about 100 birds

D about 400 birds

8. Laura counts 46 trees. Then she counts 50 more trees. About how many trees does Laura count in all?

A about 1 tree

B about 10 trees

C about 30 trees

D about 100 trees

Stop

Name ______________________

Choose the correct answer.

1. What is the sum?

	tens	ones
	3	4
+		3

Workmat

tens	ones

A 31

B 36

C 37

D 47

2. Which container holds the least amount of water?

A 

B 

C 

D 

3. About how many paper clips long is the object?

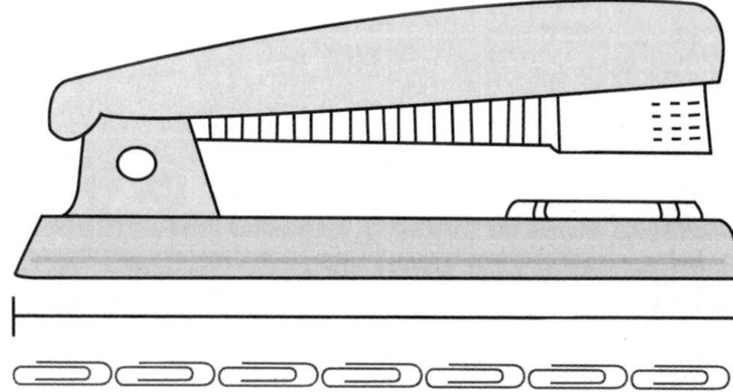

A about 5 paper clips

B about 6 paper clips

C about 7 paper clips

D about 8 paper clips

Go On

Name ______________________________

Choose the correct answer.

4. About how many pounds is the object?

A about 1 pound

B about 10 pounds

C about 20 pounds

D about 100 pounds

5. What is the temperature?

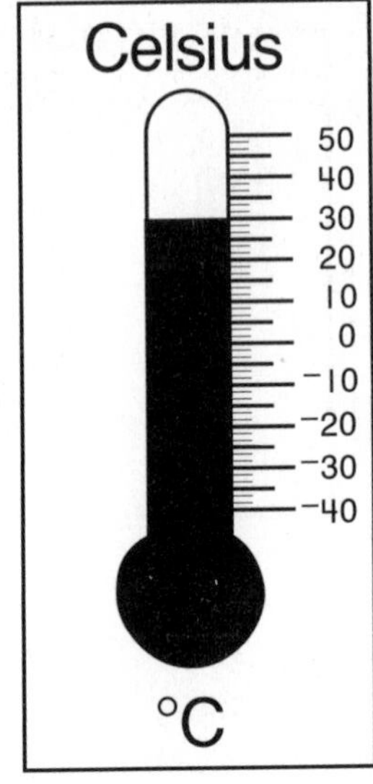

A 3°C

B 20°C

C 25°C

D 30°C

6. What is the difference?

80 − 20 = ______

A 40

B 60

C 70

D 100

7. About how many cups will the container hold?

A about 4 cups

B about 3 cups

C about 2 cups

D about 1 cup

Go On

Name ______________________________

Choose the correct answer.

8. What is the difference?

	tens	ones
	3	6
−	1	4

Workmat

tens	ones

A 50

B 38

C 32

D 22

9. How long is the object?

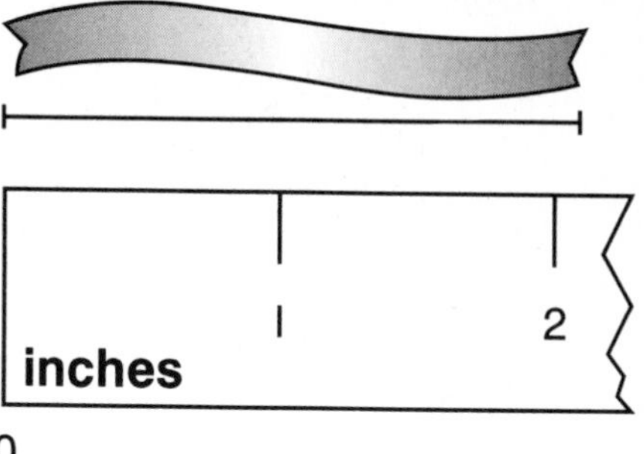

A about 2 inches

B about 3 inches

C about 4 inches

D about 5 inches

10. Which shows the ribbons in order from shortest to longest?

A

C

B

D

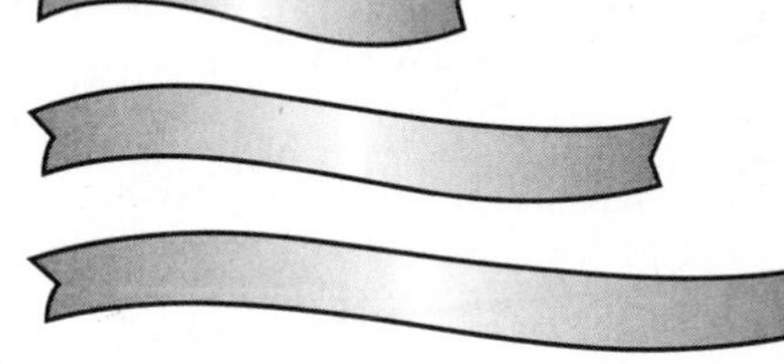

Go On

Name ______________________________

Choose the correct answer.

11. Which tool will you use to measure how much the mug holds?

A

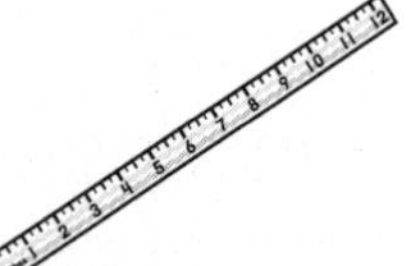

C

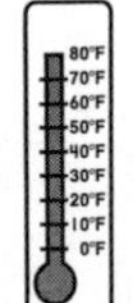

B

D

12. What is the sum?

	tens	ones
	2	3
+	2	5

Workmat

tens	ones

A 22

B 38

C 42

D 48

13. There are 41 birds in the trees. 8 of them fly away. About how many birds are left?

A about 3 birds

B about 30 birds

C about 100 birds

D about 300 birds

14. How many cups do you need to fill the container to the top?

This bowl has 1 cup of water in it.

A about 1 cup

B about 2 cups

C about 3 cups

D about 6 cups

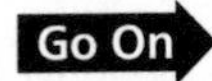

Name ____________________

Choose the correct answer.

15. How long is the object?

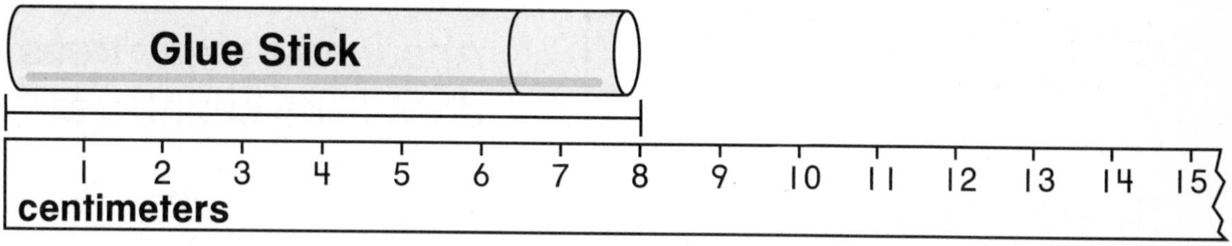

A about 6 centimeters

B about 7 centimeters

C about 8 centimeters

D about 9 centimeters

16. Which object is heaviest?

A 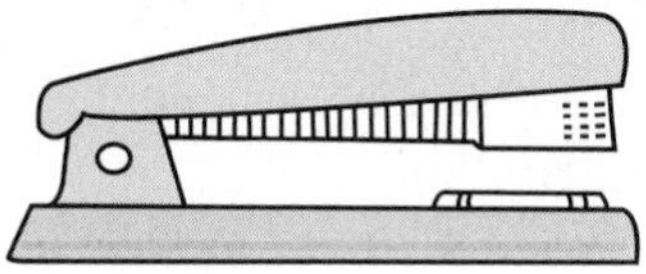

B 

C 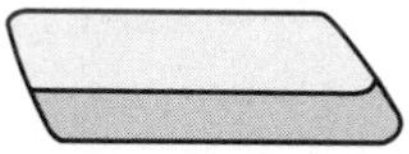

D 

17. What is the difference?

	tens	ones
	3	8
−		6

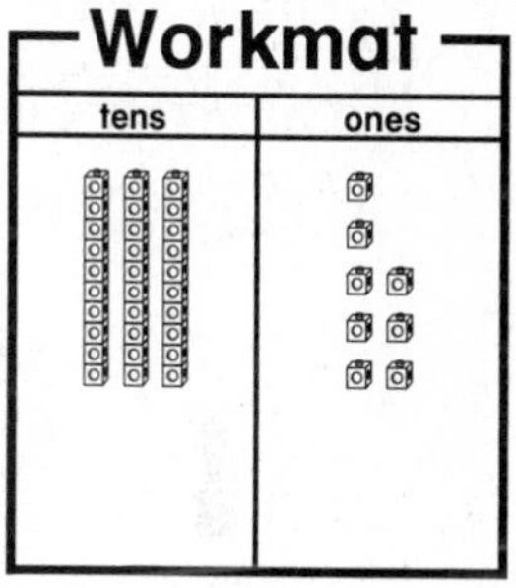

A 44

B 34

C 32

D 22

18. About how many paper clips long is the object?

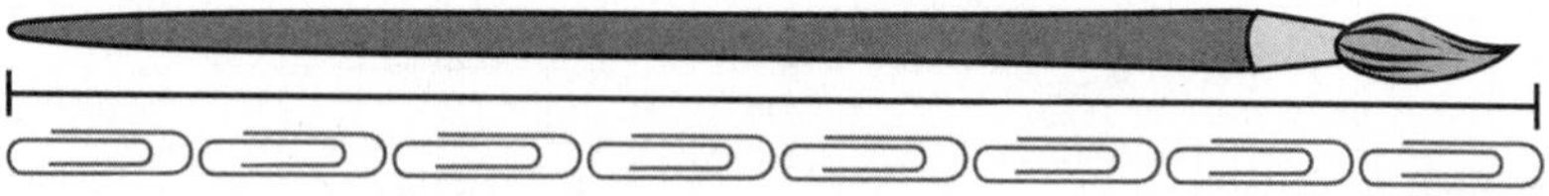

A about 2 paper clips

B about 4 paper clips

C about 6 paper clips

D about 8 paper clips

Go On

Name ____________________

Choose the correct answer.

19. What is the sum?

60 + 30 = ____

A 30

B 70

C 80

D 90

20. Gina counts 19 trees. Then she counts 80 more trees. About how many trees does Gina count in all?

A about 6 trees

B about 10 trees

C about 60 trees

D about 100 trees

21. Which tool will you use to measure how heavy the grapes are?

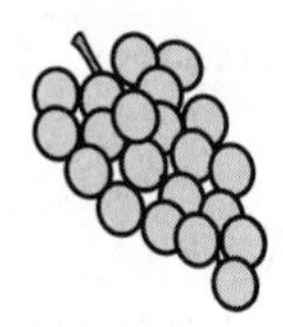

A

C

B

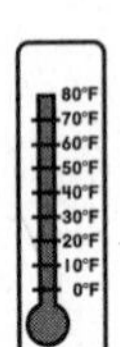

D

22. What is the temperature?

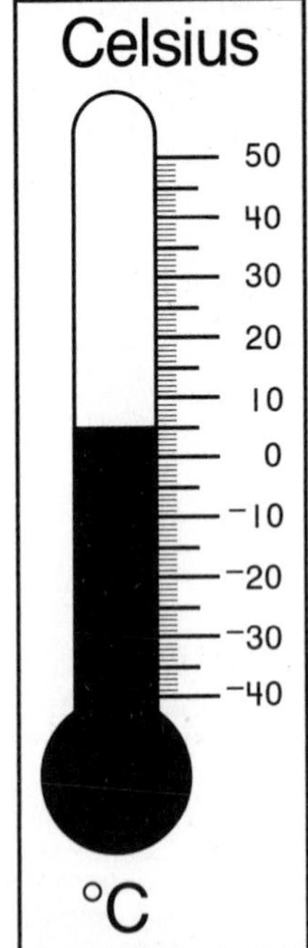

A 5°C

B 10°C

C 15°C

D 20°C

Stop

Choose the correct answer.

1. Which is correct?

A 15 is greater than 13.

B 14 is greater than 17.

C 12 is less than 9.

D 13 is less than 11.

2. Which tells how many?

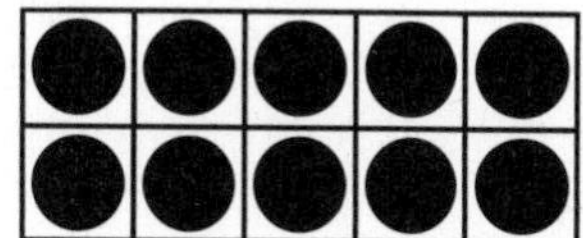
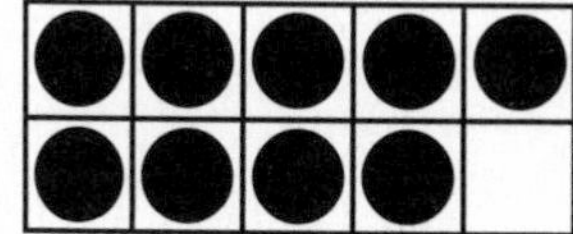

A nine

B fourteen

C eighteen

D nineteen

3. Which shows the numbers in order from least to greatest?

A 13, 12, 15

B 12, 13, 15

C 12, 15, 13

D 15, 13, 12

4. Which is correct?

A 11 is greater than 14.

B 17 is less than 15.

C 16 is less than 19.

D 14 is less than 12.

5. Which bunny is fifth?

first

A 

B 

C 

D 

Go On

Choose the correct answer.

6. Which is a way to show 6?

A eight

B 

C 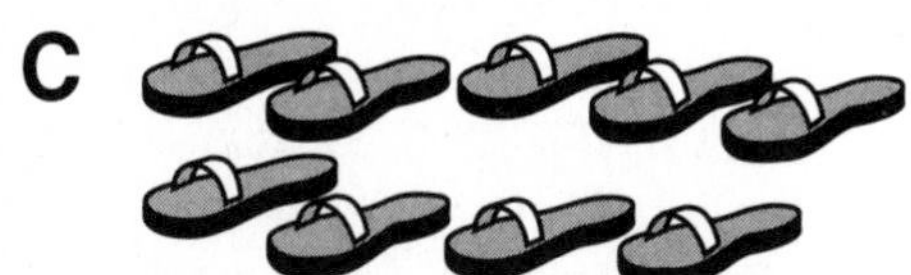

D

7. Draw lines to match. Which shows how many fewer ?

A 5 fewer

B 4 fewer

C 3 fewer

D 2 fewer

Use the picture graph to answer questions 8 and 9.

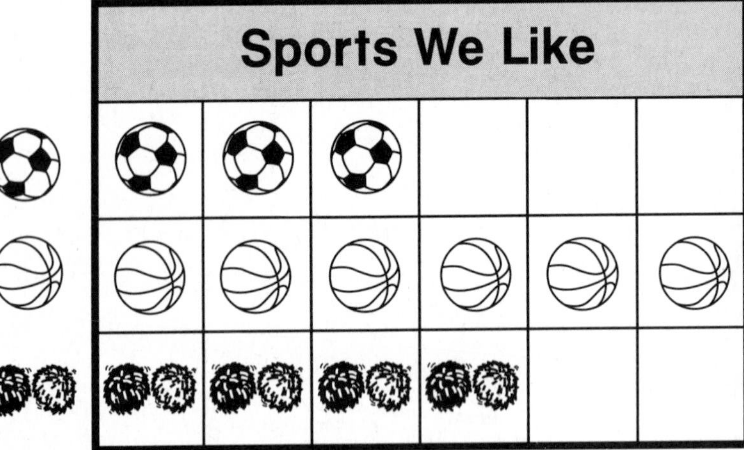

8. Which sport has the greatest number?

A  **B**  **C** 

9. How many ?

A 6 

B 5

C 4

D 3

Stop

Choose the correct answer.

1. Which addition sentence does the picture show?

A $3 + 2 = 5$

B $2 + 2 = 4$

C $3 + 3 = 6$

D $4 + 1 = 5$

2. Which addition sentences use the same addends?

A $4 + 1 = 5$ and $1 + 3 = 4$

B $1 + 4 = 5$ and $3 + 2 = 5$

C $2 + 2 = 4$ and $4 + 1 = 4$

D $3 + 1 = 4$ and $1 + 3 = 4$

3. Draw circles to show each number. What is the sum?

$0 + 6 =$ ____

A 60 **C** 3

B 6 **D** 0

4. Which is the sum?

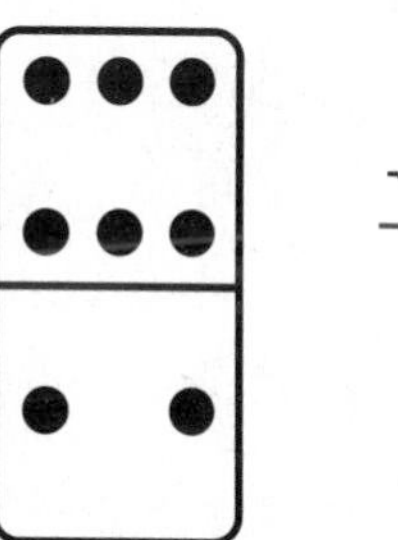

$$\begin{array}{r} 6 \\ +\ 2 \\ \hline \end{array}$$

A 4

B 7

C 8

D 9

Go On

Name ____________________

Choose the correct answer.

5. Which is a way to make 8?

A 2 + 6

B 4 + 3

C 2 + 7

D 6 + 1

6. How many in all?

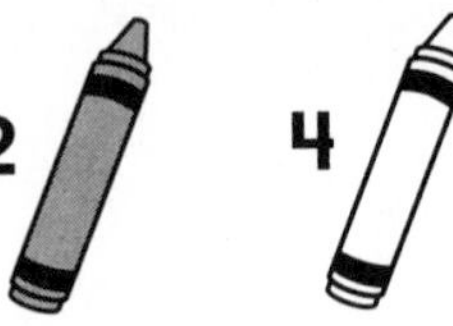

☐ + ☐ = ☐

part part whole

A 1 in all

B 4 in all

C 5 in all

D 6 in all

7. How many puppies in all?

2 puppies 2 more puppies

A 2 puppies in all

B 3 puppies in all

C 4 puppies in all

D 5 puppies in all

8. Glenn sees 3 flowers on a plant. He sees the same number of flowers on another plant. How many flowers does Glenn see in all?

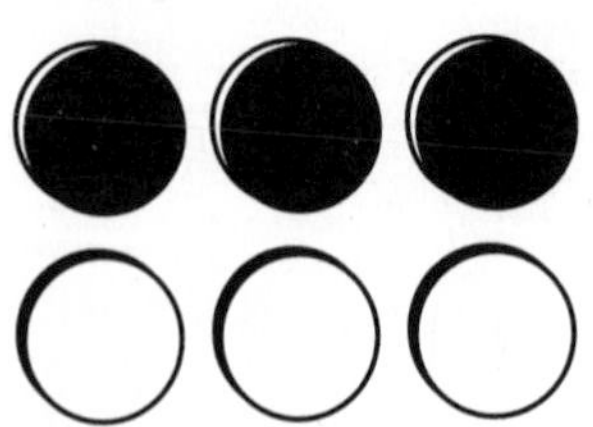

A 1 flower

B 6 flowers

C 7 flowers

D 8 flowers

Stop

Choose the correct answer.

1. What is the difference?

$$\begin{array}{r} 7 \\ -\ 4 \\ \hline \end{array}$$

A 2

B 3

C 4

D 5

2. What is the difference?

6 − 0 = ____

A 0

B 3

C 6

D 60

3. Which subtraction sentence is shown by the cube?

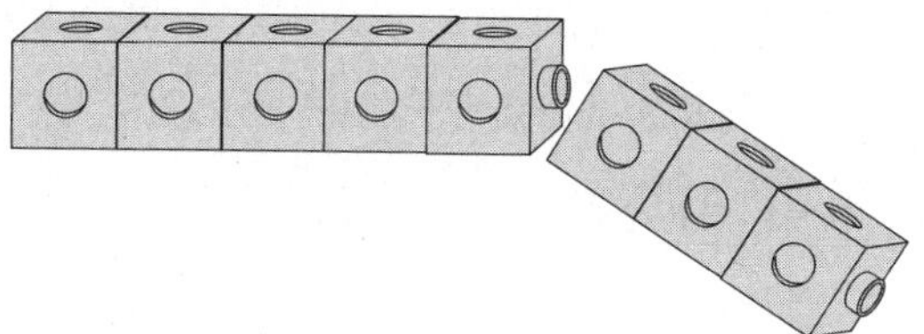

A 8 − 4 = 4

B 5 − 3 = 2

C 8 − 2 = 6

D 8 − 3 = 5

4. Which subtraction sentence does the picture show?

A 5 − 3 = 2

B 2 + 3 = 5

C 8 − 3 = 5

D 5 − 4 = 1

Go On

Name ____________________

Choose the correct answer.

5. How many fewer ?

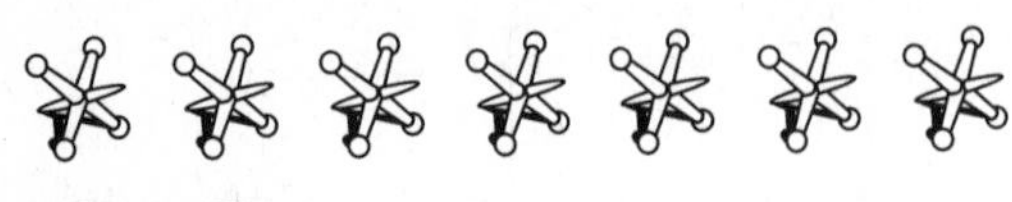

A 5 fewer

B 4 fewer

C 3 fewer

D 2 fewer

6. Which number completes the subtraction sentence?

6	−	4	=	
whole		**part**		**part**

A 10

B 5

C 3

D 2

7. How many boys are left?

3 boys **2 boys walk away**

A 0 boys are left

B 1 boy is left

C 2 boys are left

D 3 boys are left

8. There are 6 gray birds and 3 white birds in a tree. How many fewer white birds are there?

A 1 fewer white bird

B 2 fewer white birds

C 3 fewer white birds

D 9 fewer white birds

Stop

Choose the correct answer.

1. Which number sentences match the picture?

A 5 + 3 = 8
8 − 3 = 5

B 3 + 2 = 5
5 − 2 = 3

C 6 + 3 = 9
5 − 3 = 2

D 8 + 3 = 11
8 − 5 = 3

2. Which number sentence matches the picture?

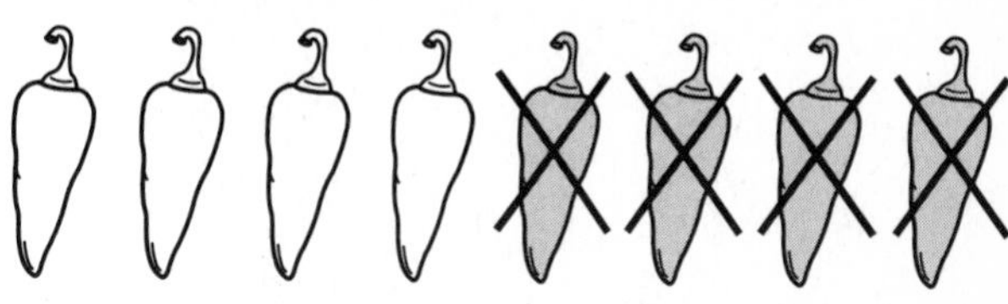

A 2 + 2 = 4

B 8 − 4 = 4

C 8 − 3 = 5

D 4 + 4 = 8

3. Which is a related subtraction fact?

1 + 6 = 7

A 6 + 1 = 5

B 8 − 7 = 1

C 7 − 5 = 2

D 7 − 6 = 1

4. How many butterflies are there in all?

A 1

B 6

C 7

D 8

Go On

Choose the correct answer.

5. Which is a related addition fact?

$6 - 2 = 4$

A $4 + 2 = 6$

B $6 + 2 = 8$

C $6 + 4 = 10$

D $3 + 3 = 6$

6. Which number sentence matches the picture?

A $4 + 3 = 7$

B $7 - 3 = 4$

C $5 - 2 = 3$

D $2 + 5 = 7$

7. How many birds fly away?

A 1 **B** 2 **C** 3 **D** 8

8. There are 6 markers. Carol brings 1 more marker. How many markers are there now?

A 5

B 7

C 8

D 9

9. There are 8 books. Jack takes 3 books away. How many books are left?

A 11

B 8

C 5

D 2

Stop

Name ________________________________

Choose the correct answer.

1. Which shows the numbers in order from least to greatest?

   A 13, 12, 7
   B 7, 12, 13
   C 12, 13, 7
   D 7, 13, 12

2. Which is the difference?

   $8 - 0 = \_\_\_\_$

   A 0
   B 4
   C 8
   D 88

3. Which addition sentences use the same addends?

   A $2 + 6 = 8$ and $6 + 2 = 8$
   B $6 + 2 = 8$ and $6 + 3 = 9$
   C $2 + 3 = 5$ and $1 + 4 = 5$
   D $4 + 2 = 6$ and $3 + 3 = 6$

4. There are 5 cars. 1 car leaves. Which number sentence matches the words?

   A $5 - 1 = 4$
   B $6 - 1 = 5$
   C $5 + 1 = 6$
   D $6 + 1 = 7$

5. Which is correct?

   A 9 is less than 7.
   B 18 is less than 8.
   C 6 is greater than 5.
   D 10 is greater than 13.

6. Which is a related subtraction fact?

   $4 + 5 = 9$

   A $5 - 2 = 3$
   B $9 - 3 = 6$
   C $5 - 4 = 1$
   D $9 - 5 = 4$

Go On

Name ______________________________

Choose the correct answer.

7. Use the cube below.
There are 6 beavers and 2 raccoons. How many fewer raccoons are there?

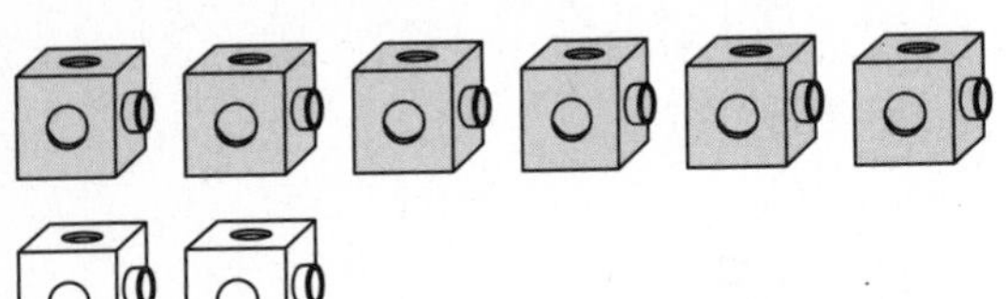

A 1 raccoon

B 2 raccoons

C 3 raccoons

D 4 raccoons

8. Which number sentence matches the picture?

A $7 - 5 = 2$

B $7 - 2 = 5$

C $7 + 2 = 9$

D $5 + 1 = 6$

9. Draw circles to show each number. Which is the sum?

$6 + 0 =$ ____

A 60

B 6

C 1

D 0

10. Which number completes the subtraction sentence?

8	−	3	=	
whole		**part**		**part**

A 5

B 4

C 3

D 2

Go On

Name ____________________

Choose the correct answer.

11. Which is a way to make 7?

A 4 + 4

B 2 + 6

C 3 + 4

D 1 + 3

12. Draw lines to match. Which shows how many more ?

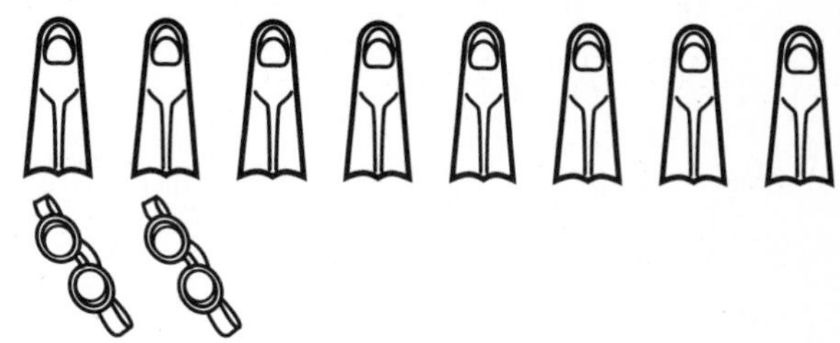

A 6 more

B 5 more

C 4 more

D 3 more

13. How many bats are left?

2 bats **1 bat flies away**

A 1 bat is left

B 2 bats are left

C 3 bats are left

D 4 bats are left

14. Which addition sentence does the picture show?

A 4 + 1 = 5

B 5 + 2 = 7

C 3 + 1 = 4

D 3 + 2 = 5

Go On

Choose the correct answer.

15. Which number sentences match the picture?

A $4 + 5 = 9$
$9 - 5 = 4$

B $6 + 3 = 9$
$9 - 6 = 3$

C $5 + 3 = 8$
$8 - 5 = 3$

D $4 + 3 = 7$
$7 - 4 = 3$

16. Which is a way to show 9?

A 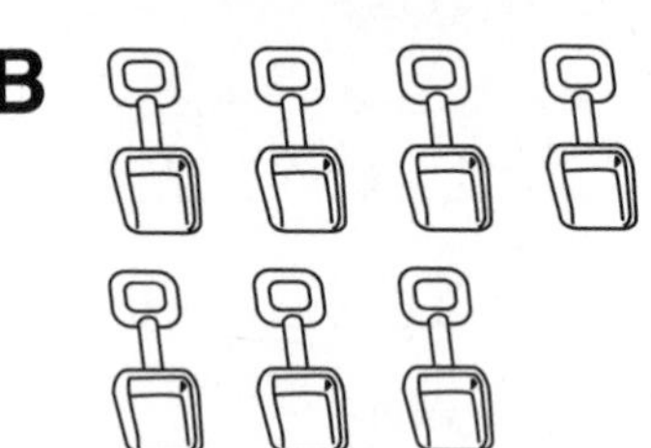

B

C eight

D

17. Which kitten is second?

A 

B 

C 

D 

Go On

Choose the correct answer.

18. How many mice are there in all?

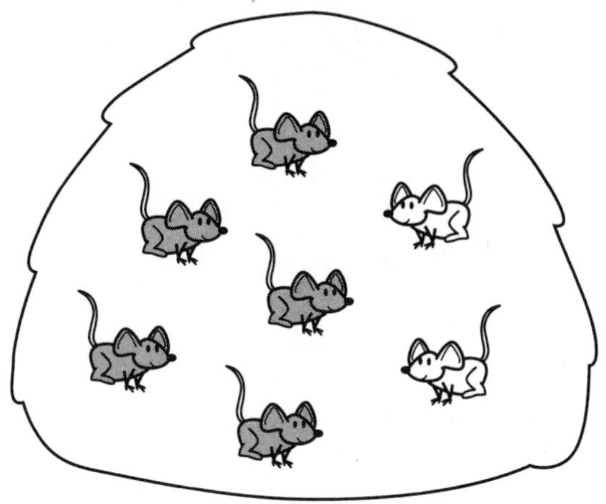

A 9
B 7
C 5
D 2

19. Which is the sum?

$$\begin{array}{r} 2 \\ -7 \\ \hline \end{array}$$

A 6
B 7
C 8
D 9

20. Which subtraction sentence is shown by the cube?

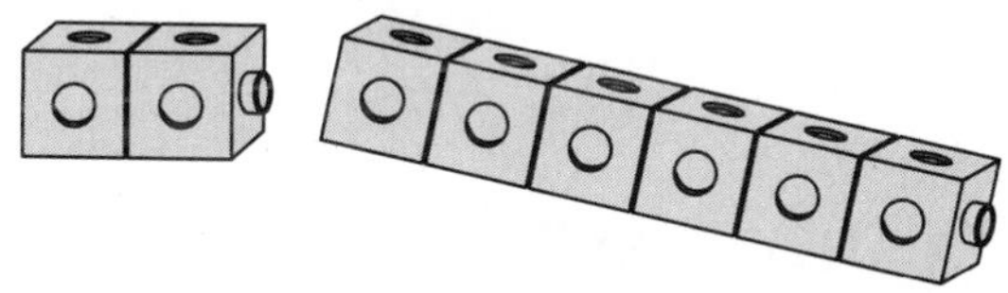

A 9 − 6 = 3
B 8 − 5 = 3
C 8 − 6 = 2
D 7 − 6 = 1

21. There are 2 children playing ball. The same number of children join them. How many children are there playing ball?

A 0 children
B 2 children
C 4 children
D 6 children

Go On

Choose the correct answer.

22. Which is the difference?

$$\begin{array}{r} 5 \\ -\ 1 \\ \hline \end{array}$$

A 1

B 2

C 3

D 4

23. Which tells how many?

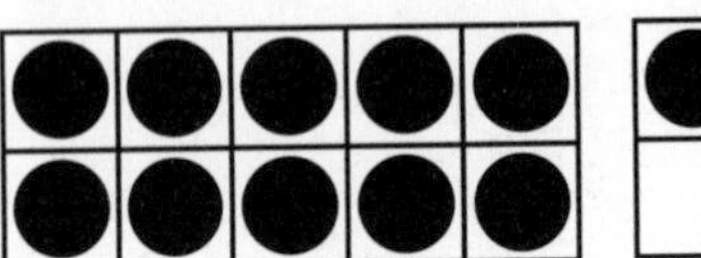

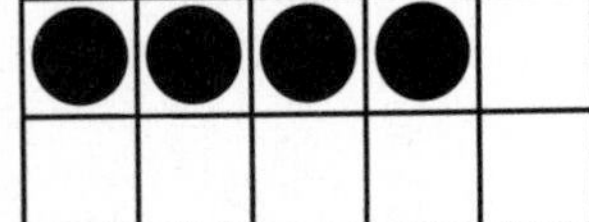

A fourteen

B fifteen

C eighteen

D nineteen

24. How many in all?

A 4 in all

B 5 in all

C 6 in all

D 7 in all

25. How many fewer ?

$9 - 3 =$ ____

A 7 fewer

B 6 fewer

C 5 fewer

D 4 fewer

Stop

Choose the correct answer.

Use the number line to answer questions 1 and 2.

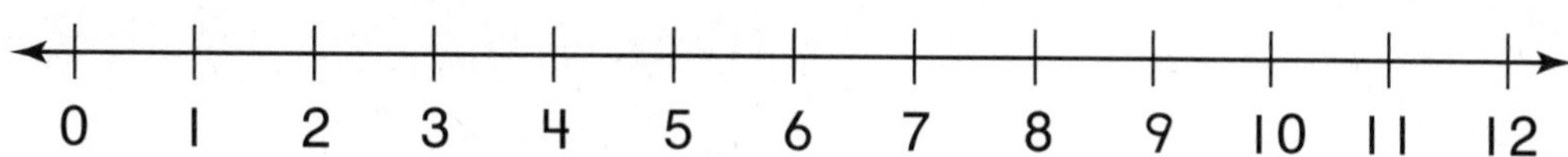

1. What is the sum?

$$\begin{array}{r} 6 \\ +\ 3 \\ \hline \end{array}$$

A 3

B 8

C 9

D 10

2. What is the sum?

$$\begin{array}{r} 8 \\ +\ 2 \\ \hline \end{array}$$

A 6

B 10

C 11

D 12

3. Which addition sentence shows the doubles fact?

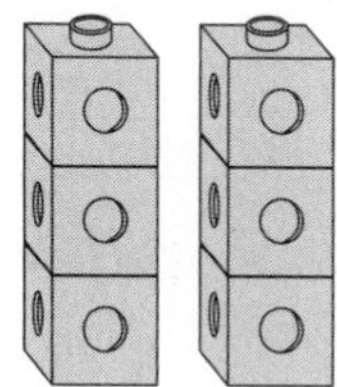

A $3 + 3 = 6$

B $2 + 4 = 6$

C $4 + 4 = 8$

D $3 + 2 = 5$

4. Which addition sentence shows the doubles plus one fact?

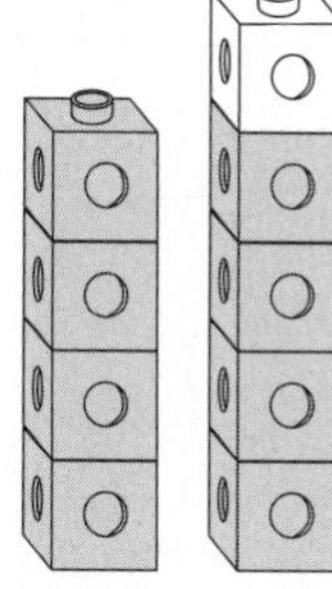

A $4 + 4 = 8$

B $3 + 4 = 7$

C $5 + 5 = 10$

D $4 + 5 = 9$

Go On

Name ____________________

Choose the correct answer.

5. Count on. What is the sum?

$$\begin{array}{r} 3 \\ +\ 8 \\ \hline \end{array}$$

A 11 **C** 9

B 10 **D** 5

6. What is the sum?

$9 + 3 =$ ____

A 6 **C** 11

B 10 **D** 12

7. Count on. What is the sum?

$7 + 2 =$ ____

A 8 **B** 9 **C** 10 **D** 11

8. Draw a picture to solve. There are 10 turtles in all. 5 turtles are brown. The other turtles are green. How many turtles are green?

A 5 turtles

B 7 turtles

C 8 turtles

D 15 turtles

9. Draw a picture to solve. There are 9 birds in all. 3 birds are blue. The other birds are red. How many birds are red?

A 12 birds

B 8 birds

C 6 birds

D 4 birds

Choose the correct answer.

Use the number line to answer questions 1 through 4.

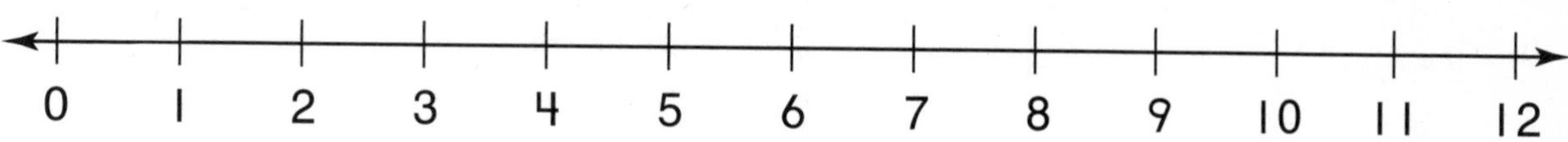

1. What is the difference?

$$\begin{array}{r} 9 \\ -\ 2 \\ \hline \end{array}$$

A 7

B 8

C 9

D 12

2. What is the difference?

10 − 3 = ____

A 6

B 7

C 8

D 9

3. What is the difference?

____ = 12 − 3

A 14

B 11

C 10

D 9

4. What is the difference?

$$\begin{array}{r} 9 \\ -\ 1 \\ \hline \end{array}$$

A 5

B 6

C 7

D 8

Go On

Choose the correct answer.

5. What is the difference?

$$\begin{array}{r} 12 \\ -\ 3 \\ \hline \end{array}$$

A 10 **C** 8

B 9 **D** 7

6. What is the difference?

$$\begin{array}{r} 7 \\ -\ 3 \\ \hline \end{array}$$

A 6 **C** 4

B 5 **D** 3

7. Use and to add.

$$\begin{array}{r} 6 \\ +\ 6 \\ \hline \end{array}$$

A 12 **C** 1

B 11 **D** 0

8. Use and to subtract.

$$\begin{array}{r} 5 \\ -\ 2 \\ \hline \end{array}$$

A 7 **C** 4

B 6 **D** 3

9. Which number sentence matches the story?

There are 9 seashells. 4 seashells are washed away. How many seashells are there now?

A 9 + 4 = 13

B 13 − 9 = 4

C 9 − 4 = 5

D 4 − 5 = 9

10. Which number sentence matches the story?

There are 11 fish. 3 fish swim away. How many fish are there now?

A 11 − 3 = 8

B 8 − 3 = 5

C 11 + 3 = 14

D 8 + 3 = 11

Stop

Name ______________________________

Choose the correct answer.

1. Which numbers are in the fact family?

$7 + 3 = 10$ $10 - 3 = 7$

$3 + 7 = 10$ $10 - 7 = 3$

A 3, 4, 7

B 3, 7, 10

C 3, 10, 13

D 7, 10, 17

2. Which is a way to make 12?

A $8 + 4$

B $12 - 1$

C $10 - 2$

D $9 + 2$

3. Which shows the related addition fact?

$$\begin{array}{r} 6 \\ +3 \\ \hline \square \end{array}$$

A $\begin{array}{r} 2 \\ +7 \\ \hline 9 \end{array}$

B $\begin{array}{r} 3 \\ +3 \\ \hline 6 \end{array}$

C $\begin{array}{r} 5 \\ +4 \\ \hline 9 \end{array}$

D $\begin{array}{r} 3 \\ +6 \\ \hline 9 \end{array}$

4. Which number sentence shows how many bugs there are?

__5__ gray bugs

__6__ white bugs

A $5 + 1 = 6$

B $6 - 5 = 1$

C $5 + 6 = 11$

D $11 - 6 = 5$

Go On

Choose the correct answer.

5. Which number completes the fact family?

4 + □ = 10 10 − □ = 4

□ + 4 = 10 10 − 4 = □

A 6 **C** 12

B 8 **D** 14

6. Follow the rule. Which number completes the table?

Subtract 3	
5	2
7	
9	6

A 3 **B** 4 **C** 5 **D** 10

7. Which shows a pair of related subtraction facts?

A $\begin{array}{r} 11 \\ -\ 4 \\ \hline 7 \end{array}$ $\begin{array}{r} 11 \\ -\ 5 \\ \hline 6 \end{array}$ **B** $\begin{array}{r} 10 \\ -\ 4 \\ \hline 6 \end{array}$ $\begin{array}{r} 12 \\ -\ 6 \\ \hline 6 \end{array}$ **C** $\begin{array}{r} 12 \\ -\ 3 \\ \hline 9 \end{array}$ $\begin{array}{r} 12 \\ -\ 5 \\ \hline 7 \end{array}$ **D** $\begin{array}{r} 10 \\ -\ 6 \\ \hline 4 \end{array}$ $\begin{array}{r} 10 \\ -\ 4 \\ \hline 6 \end{array}$

8. Draw a picture to solve. There are 11 owls. Some owls fly away. There are 6 owls left. How many owls flew away?

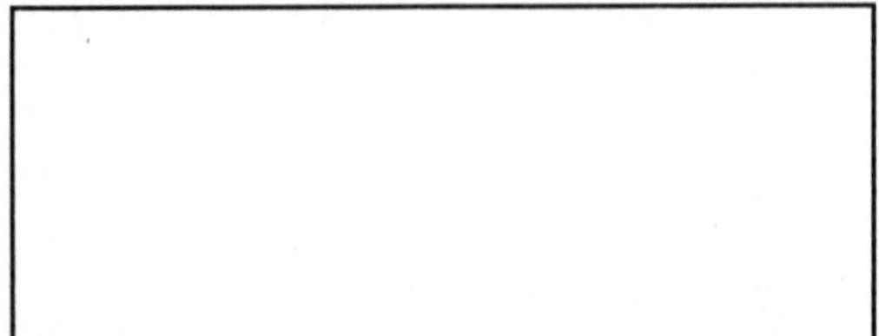

A 3 owls **C** 5 owls

B 4 owls **D** 6 owls

9. Draw a picture to solve. There are 12 rabbits. Some rabbits hop away. There are 7 rabbits left. How many rabbits hopped away?

A 6 rabbits **C** 4 rabbits

B 5 rabbits **D** 3 rabbits

Stop

Name ____________________

Choose the correct answer.

1. Which addition sentence shows the doubles fact?

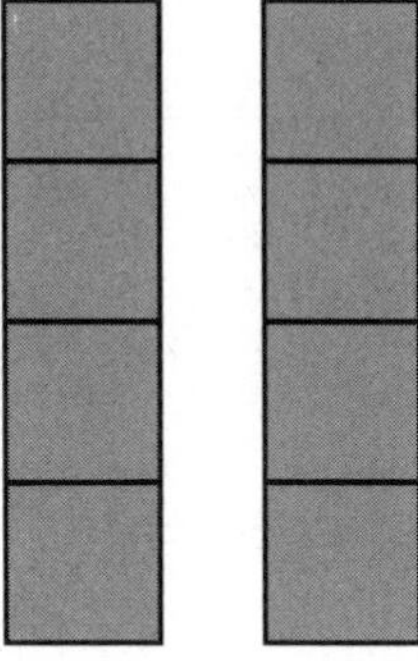

A $2 + 2 = 4$

B $3 + 3 = 6$

C $4 + 4 = 8$

D $4 + 3 = 7$

2. Draw a picture to solve. There are 6 zebras. Some zebras walk away. There are 4 zebras left. How many zebras walked away?

A 2 zebras

B 4 zebras

C 6 zebras

D 8 zebras

3. Follow the rule. Which number completes the table?

Subtract 3	
10	7
9	
8	5

A 3

B 4

C 5

D 6

4. Which numbers are in the fact family?

$7 + 3 = 10$ $10 - 3 = 7$

$3 + 7 = 10$ $10 - 7 = 3$

A 3, 7, 13

B 3, 10, 13

C 3, 7, 10

D 3, 10, 17

Go On

Choose the correct answer.

Use the number line to answer questions 5 and 6.

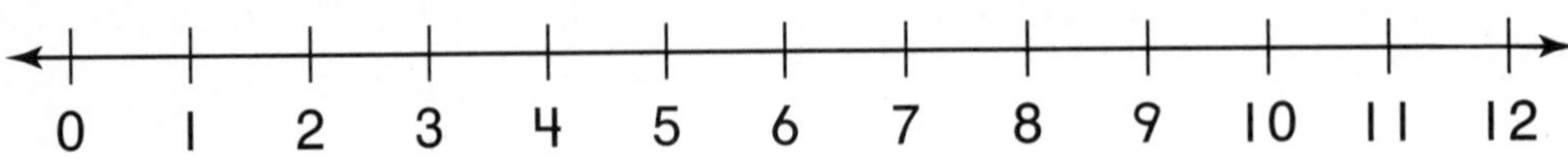

5. What is the sum?

$$\begin{array}{r} 9 \\ +1 \\ \hline \end{array}$$

A 8 **C** 10

B 9 **D** 11

6. What is the sum?

$$\begin{array}{r} 6 \\ +3 \\ \hline \end{array}$$

A 9 **C** 11

B 10 **D** 12

7. What is the difference?

$$\begin{array}{r} 12 \\ -\ 4 \\ \hline \end{array}$$

A 5 **C** 7

B 6 **D** 8

8. Use 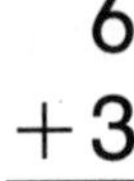 and to add.

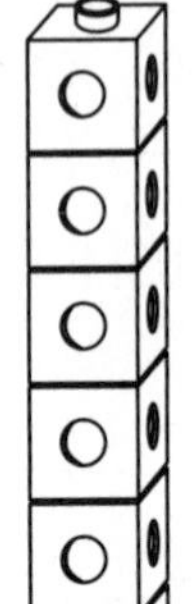
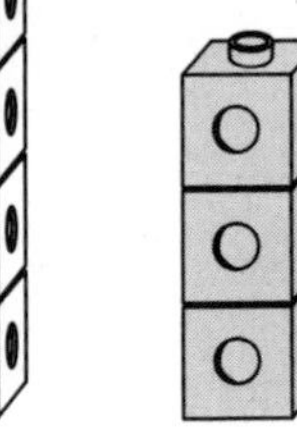

$$\begin{array}{r} 6 \\ +3 \\ \hline \end{array}$$

A 9 **C** 7

B 8 **D** 6

9. Which shows a pair of related subtraction facts?

A $\begin{array}{r} 9 \\ -2 \\ \hline 7 \end{array}$ $\begin{array}{r} 9 \\ -3 \\ \hline 6 \end{array}$ **B** $\begin{array}{r} 10 \\ -\ 3 \\ \hline 7 \end{array}$ $\begin{array}{r} 10 \\ -\ 7 \\ \hline 3 \end{array}$ **C** $\begin{array}{r} 5 \\ -3 \\ \hline 2 \end{array}$ $\begin{array}{r} 6 \\ -3 \\ \hline 3 \end{array}$ **D** $\begin{array}{r} 11 \\ -\ 5 \\ \hline 6 \end{array}$ $\begin{array}{r} 11 \\ -\ 7 \\ \hline 4 \end{array}$

Go On

Choose the correct answer.

10. Count on. What is the sum?

$7 + 1 = \_\_\_\_$

A 8 **B** 9 **C** 18 **D** 71

11. Which number sentence matches the story?

There are 10 sheep.
There are 4 goats.
How many more sheep are there than goats?

A $10 - 4 = 6$

B $10 + 6 = 16$

C $10 - 5 = 5$

D $4 + 5 = 9$

12. Which shows the related addition fact?

$$\begin{array}{r} 6 \\ +3 \\ \hline \end{array}$$

A $\begin{array}{r} 6 \\ +2 \\ \hline 8 \end{array}$

B $\begin{array}{r} 3 \\ +4 \\ \hline 7 \end{array}$

C $\begin{array}{r} 3 \\ +3 \\ \hline 6 \end{array}$

D $\begin{array}{r} 3 \\ +6 \\ \hline 9 \end{array}$

13. Which is a way to make 8?

A $12 - 5$

B $7 + 3$

C $11 - 3$

D $8 + 3$

14. Count on. What is the sum?

$$\begin{array}{r} 7 \\ +2 \\ \hline \end{array}$$

A 10 **C** 8

B 9 **D** 7

Go On

Choose the correct answer.

Use the number line to answer questions 15 and 16.

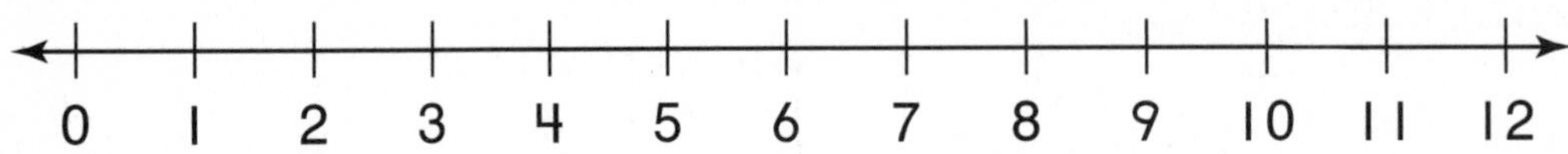

15. What is the difference?

$$\begin{array}{r} 7 \\ -2 \\ \hline \end{array}$$

A 7 **C** 5

B 6 **D** 4

16. What is the difference?

$10 - 2 =$ ____

A 8 **C** 6

B 7 **D** 5

17. Follow the rule. Which number completes the table?

Subtract 3	
6	3
5	
4	1

A 2 **C** 4

B 3 **D** 5

18. Which addition sentence shows the doubles plus one fact?

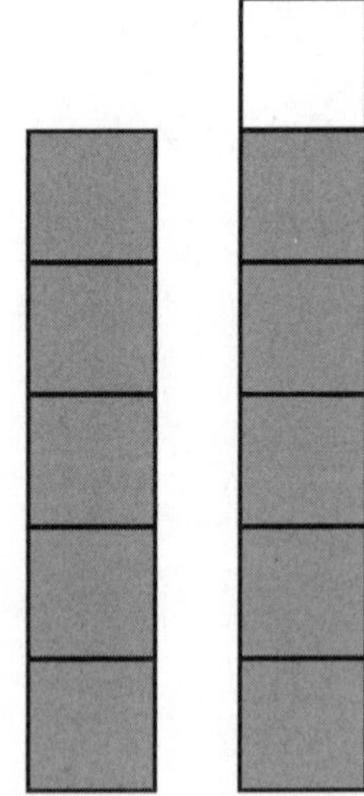

A $2 + 3 = 5$ **C** $4 + 5 = 9$

B $3 + 4 = 7$ **D** $5 + 6 = 11$

Go On

Name ____________________

Choose the correct answer.

19. Which number completes the fact family?

$4 + \square = 6 \quad 6 - \square = 4$

$\square + 4 = 6 \quad 6 - 4 = \square$

A 1

B 2

C 3

D 4

20. What is the sum?

$3 + 3 =$ ____

A 6

B 7

C 8

D 9

21. Which number sentence shows how many ducks there are?

____ gray ducks

____ white ducks

A $11 - 3 = 8$

B $12 - 3 = 9$

C $8 + 4 = 12$

D $8 + 3 = 11$

22. Which number sentence matches the story?

There are 9 horses.
5 horses trot away.
How many horses are there now?

A $9 + 5 = 14$

B $9 - 3 = 6$

C $9 - 5 = 4$

D $9 + 4 = 13$

Go On

Name ______________________________

Choose the correct answer.

23. Use [cube] and [cube] to subtract.

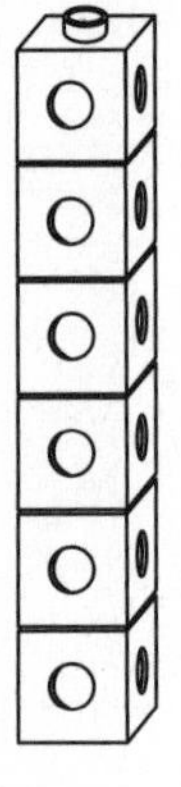
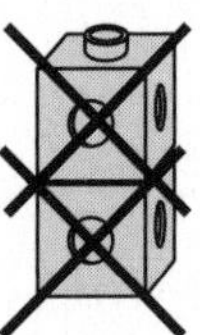

$$\begin{array}{r} 8 \\ -2 \\ \hline \end{array}$$

A 3 **C** 5

B 4 **D** 6

24. Which numbers are in the fact family?

$6 + 2 = 8$ $8 - 2 = 6$

$2 + 6 = 8$ $8 - 6 = 2$

A 2, 6, 14

B 2, 8, 10

C 2, 6, 8

D 6, 8, 14

25. There are 7 children. Some children walk away. There are 3 children left. How many children walked away?

A 1 children

B 2 children

C 3 children

D 4 children

26. There are 6 hats in all. 3 hats are red. The other hats are blue. How many hats are blue?

A 3 hats

B 4 hats

C 5 hats

D 6 hats

Stop

Name ____________________

Choose the correct answer.

1. Which figure belongs in group B?

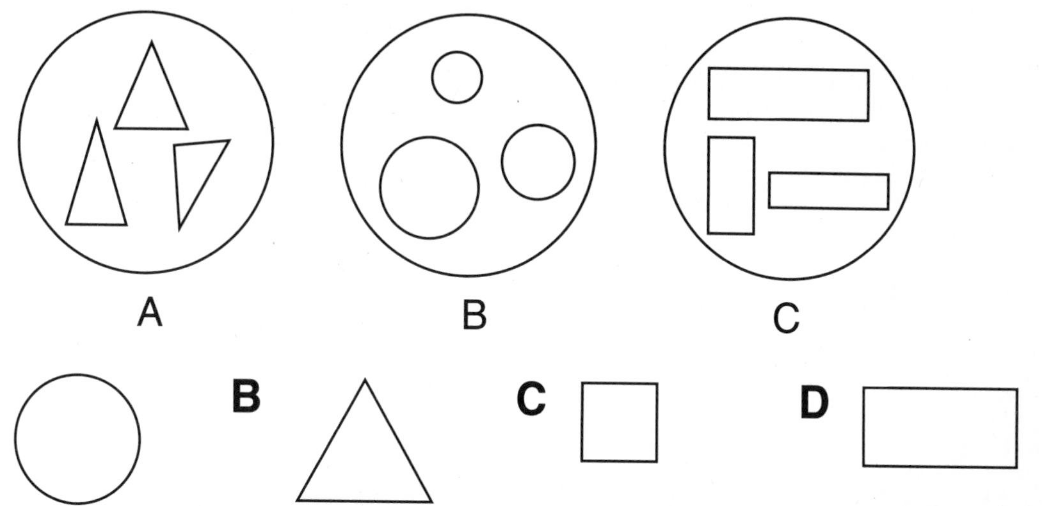

A   **B**   **C**   **D**

2. How many more children chose [dog] than [fish]?

Animals We Like								
fish								
cat								
dog								

A 1 more child

B 2 more children

C 3 more children

D 5 more children

Go On

Name ____________________

Choose the correct answer.

3. Which bear belongs in the group?

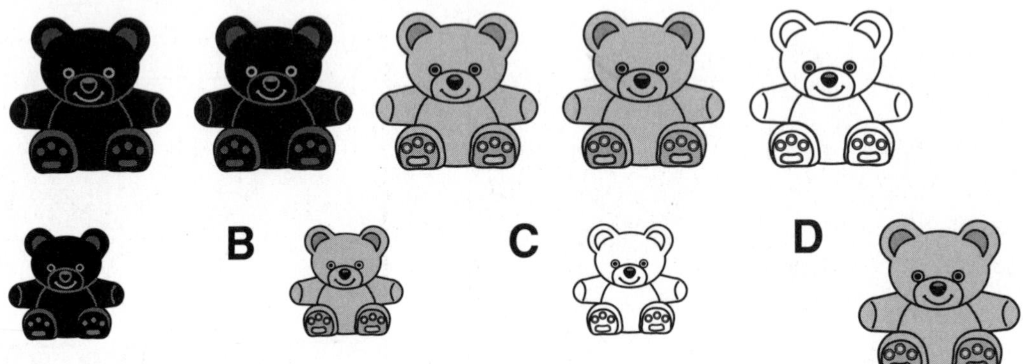

A   **B**   **C**   **D**

Use the picture graph to answer questions 5 and 6.

Kinds of Sport Balls
football
soccer ball
basketball

4. How many footballs are there?

A 7 footballs

B 8 footballs

C 9 footballs

D 11 footballs

5. How many fewer basketballs are there than soccer balls?

A 5 fewer basketballs

B 4 fewer basketballs

C 3 fewer basketballs

D 2 fewer basketballs

Stop

Choose the correct answer.

1. Which bear are you more likely to pull from the [bowl]?

A

B

C

2. Use the tally chart to answer the question.

Animals We Like	
fish	𝍸𝍷𝍷𝍷𝍷
turtle	𝍷𝍷
gerbil	𝍸𝍷

How many children chose the gerbil?

A 5 children

B 6 children

C 7 children

D 9 children

3. From which box is it **impossible** to pull a white cube?

A
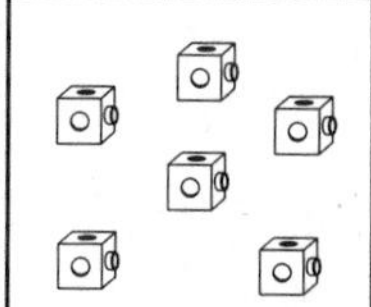

B
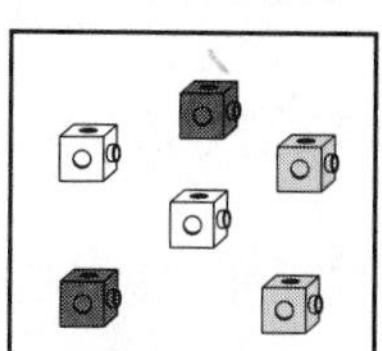

C
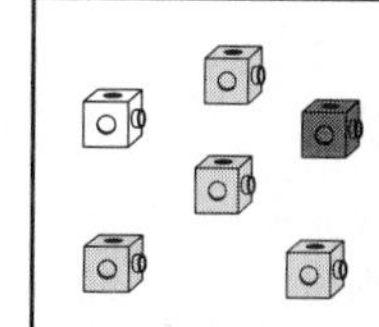

D
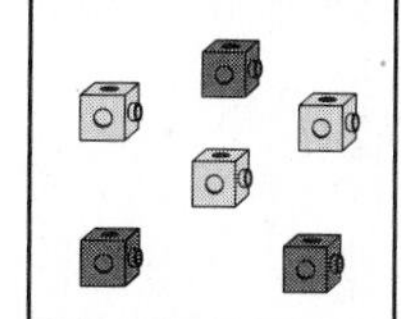

Go On

Name ______________________________

Choose the correct answer.

Use the bar graph to answer questions 4 and 5.

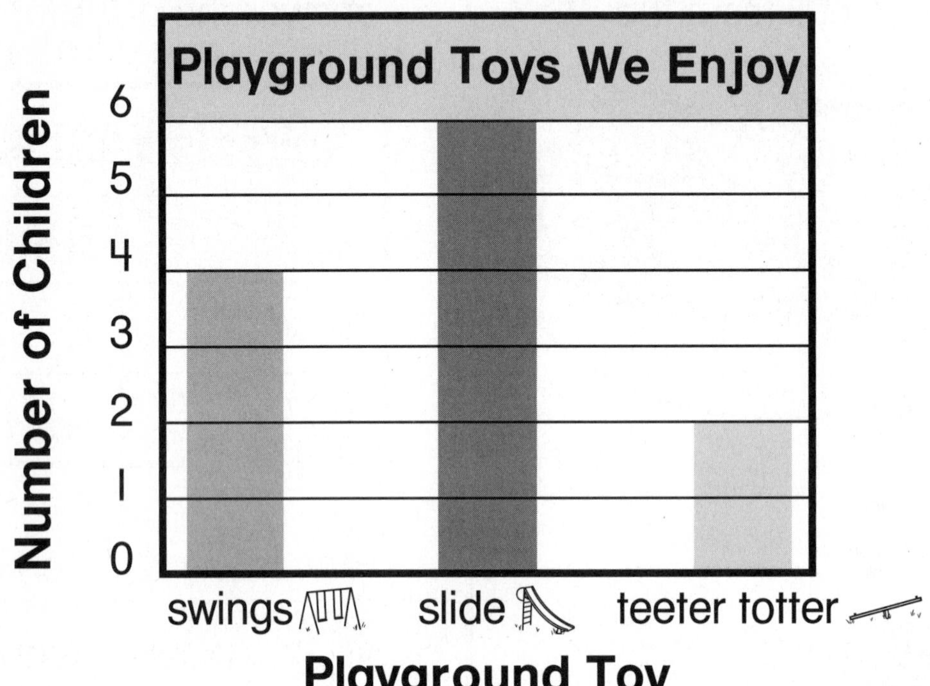

4. How many children chose slide?

A 2 children

B 4 children

C 5 children

D 6 children

5. Which playground toy did the fewest children choose?

A swings

B slide

C teeter totter

6. There are 9 white cubes and 2 gray cubes in a bowl. Which color are you more likely to pull?

A white

B gray

C black

7. There are 3 black cubes and 6 gray cubes in a bag. Which color are you more likely to pull?

A white

B gray

C black

Choose the correct answer.

1. Count how many tens and ones. What is the number?

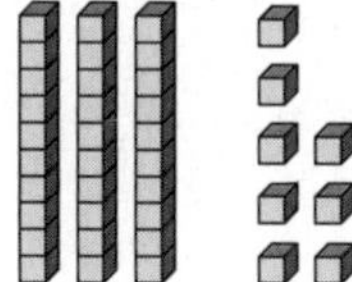

A 33

B 35

C 38

D 83

2. Count how many tens and ones. Which shows the number in a different way?

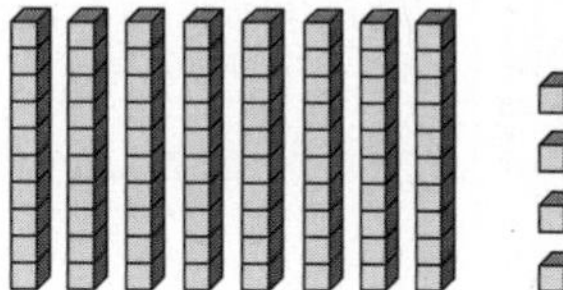

A 80 + 4

B 80 + 40

C 40 + 8

D 8 + 4

3. Count by tens. What number is shown?

6 tens 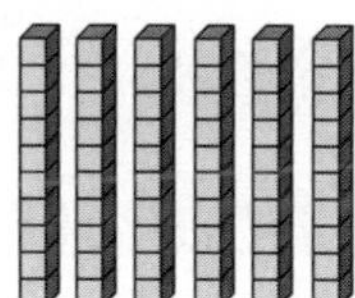

A 5

B 50

C 55

D 60

4. Which shows the number of tens and ones?

19 nineteen

A 0 tens 9 ones

B 10 tens 9 ones

C 9 tens 10 ones

D 1 ten 9 ones

Go On

Name ____________________

Choose the correct answer.

5. Count how many tens and ones. What is the number?

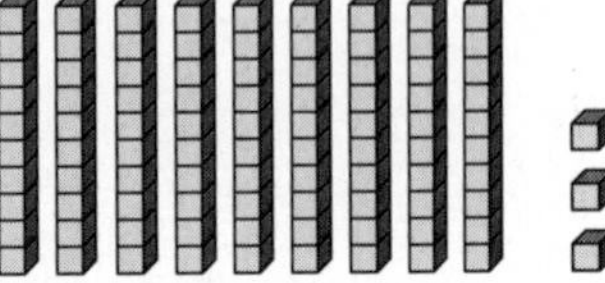

A 39

B 83

C 93

D 903

6. Count how many tens and ones. Which shows the number in a different way?

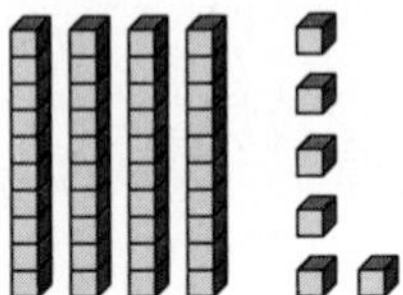

A 4 + 6

B 60 + 4

C 40 + 60

D 40 + 6

7. About how many (paper clip) can you hold in one hand?

A about 3 (paper clip)

B about 30 (paper clip)

C about 300 (paper clip)

8. About how many (MATH book) would cover your desk?

A about 6 (MATH book)

B about 60 (MATH book)

C about 600 (MATH book)

Stop

Name ______________________________

Choose the correct answer.

1. Which is true?

A 43 is greater than 47.

B 47 is greater than 43.

C 47 is equal to 43.

D 47 is less than 43.

2. Which number is between 56 and 58?

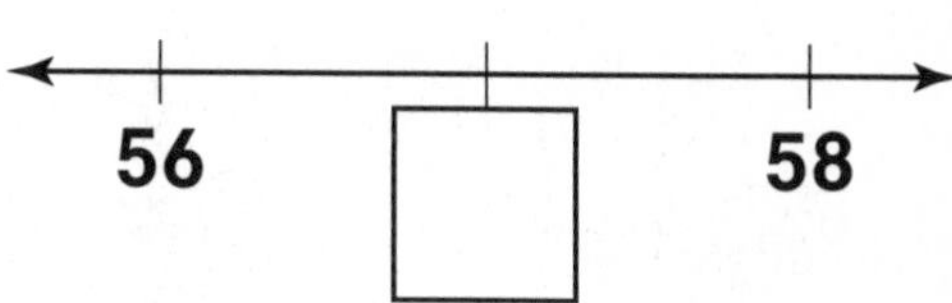

A 50

B 55

C 57

D 59

3. Which symbol can you use to compare the numbers?

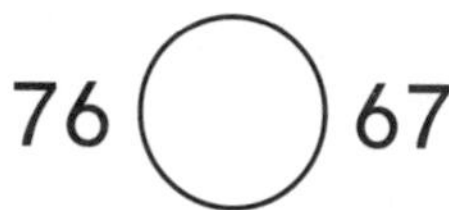

A $>$

B $<$

C $=$

4. Which shows the numbers in order from least to greatest?

48 29 25

A 48, 29, 25

B 29, 25, 48

C 25, 48, 29

D 25, 29, 48

5. Which number is one less than 63?

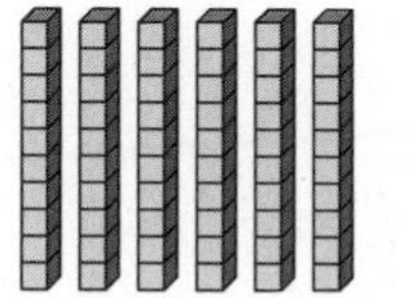

A 53 **B** 62 **C** 64 **D** 73

Go On

Choose the correct answer.

6. Which is true?

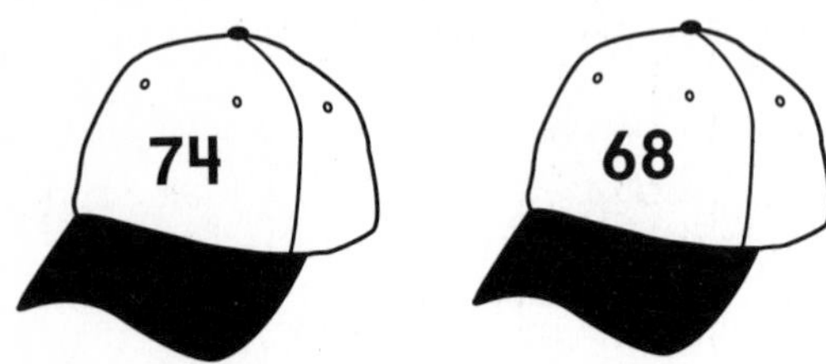

A 74 is less than 68.

B 68 is less than 74.

C 74 is equal to 68.

D 68 is greater than 74.

7. Which number is ten more than 54?

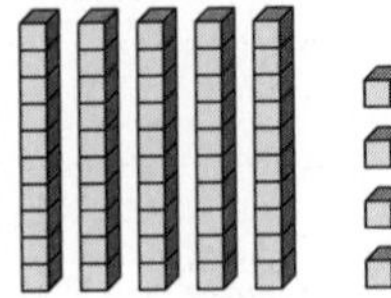

A 44

B 53

C 55

D 64

Use the table to answer questions 8 and 9.

Season	Sunny Days
spring	81
summer	87
fall	71
winter	78

8. Which season had more sunny days?

A spring

B fall

9. Which season had the least number of sunny days?

A spring

B summer

C fall

D winter

Stop

Choose the correct answer.

Use the hundred chart for questions 1 and 2.

1	2	3	4	5	6	7	8	9	10
11	12	13	14	15	16	17	18	19	20
21	22	23	24	25	26	27	28	29	30
31	32	33	34	35	36	37	38	39	40
41	42	43	44	45	46	47	48	49	50
51	52	53	54	55	56	57	58	59	60
61	62	63	64	65	66	67	68	69	70
71	72	73	74	75	76	77	78	79	80
81	82	83	84	85	86	87	88	89	90
91	92	93	94	95	96	97	98	99	100

1. Count by twos. Which number comes next?

36, 38, 40, 42, 44, ____

A 43

B 45

C 46

D 50

2. Count by tens. Which numbers come next?

7, 17, 27, ____, ____, ____

A 30, 40, 50

B 37, 47, 57

C 29, 31, 33

D 32, 37, 42

3. Skip count. How many fingers are there?

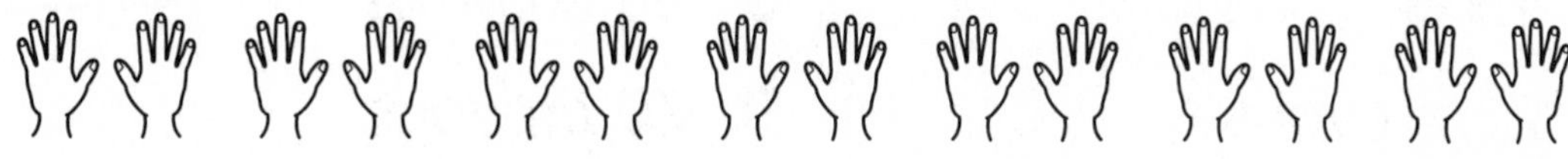

A 7 **B** 14 **C** 35 **D** 70

Go On

Choose the correct answer.

4. Count forward. Which numbers come next?

93, 94, 95, ___, ___, ___

A 100, 105, 110

B 96, 97, 98

C 97, 98, 99

D 96, 98, 100

5. Find the pattern. What are the missing numbers?

48, 50, ___, 54, 56, ___

A 51, 53

B 58, 60

C 51, 52

D 52, 58

6. Which number is even?

A 12 **B** 13 **C** 15 **D** 17

7. There are 10 crayons in a box.
How many crayons are there in 7 boxes?

number of boxes	1	2	3	4	5	6	7
number of crayons	10	20					

A 14 crayons

B 25 crayons

C 35 crayons

D 70 crayons

Stop

Choose the correct answer.

1. Which number is between 42 and 44?

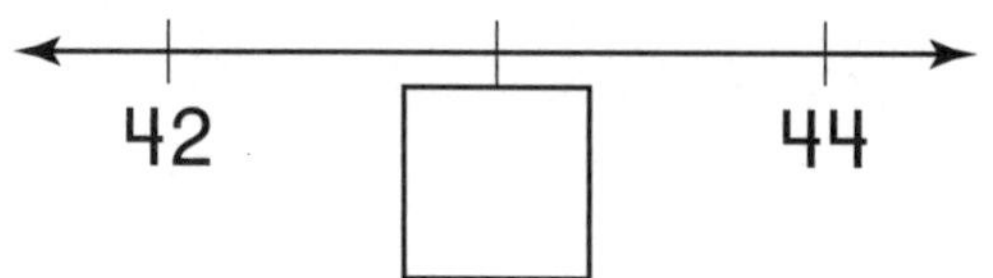

A 34 **C** 43

B 40 **D** 45

2. Count by tens. What number is shown?

5 tens 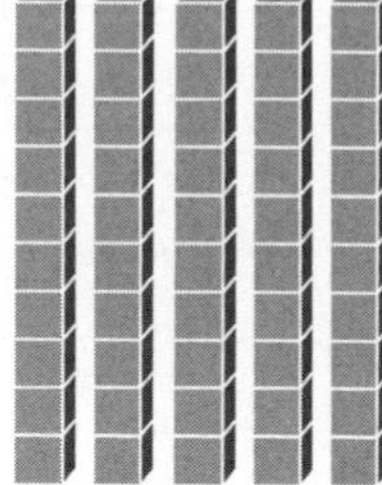

A 20 **C** 40

B 30 **D** 50

3. Use the tally chart to answer the question.

Snacks We Like	
popcorn	||||
fruit	~~||||~~ |
cheese	~~||||~~

How many children chose fruit?

A 4 children

B 5 children

C 6 children

D 7 children

4. Count how many tens and ones. Which shows the number in a different way?

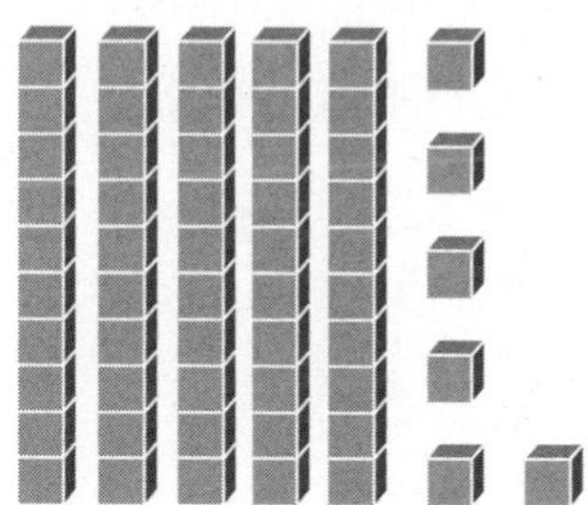

A 5 + 6

B 50 + 6

C 56 + 6

D 50 + 60

Go On

Name ______________________________

Choose the correct answer.

Use the hundred chart for questions 5 and 6.

1	2	3	4	5	6	7	8	9	10
11	12	13	14	15	16	17	18	19	20
21	22	23	24	25	26	27	28	29	30
31	32	33	34	35	36	37	38	39	40
41	42	43	44	45	46	47	48	49	50
51	52	53	54	55	56	57	58	59	60
61	62	63	64	65	66	67	68	69	70
71	72	73	74	75	76	77	78	79	80
81	82	83	84	85	86	87	88	89	90
91	92	93	94	95	96	97	98	99	100

5. Count by tens. Which number comes next?

40, 50, 60, 70, 80, ___

A 90

B 80

C 70

D 60

6. Count by twos. Which numbers come next?

22, 24, 26, ___, ___, ___

A 36, 46, 56

B 28, 29, 30

C 31, 36, 41

D 28, 30, 32

Go On

Name ______________________________

Choose the correct answer.

7. Which dog belongs in the group?

A 

B 

C 

D 

8. From which box is it **impossible** to pull a gray cube?

A 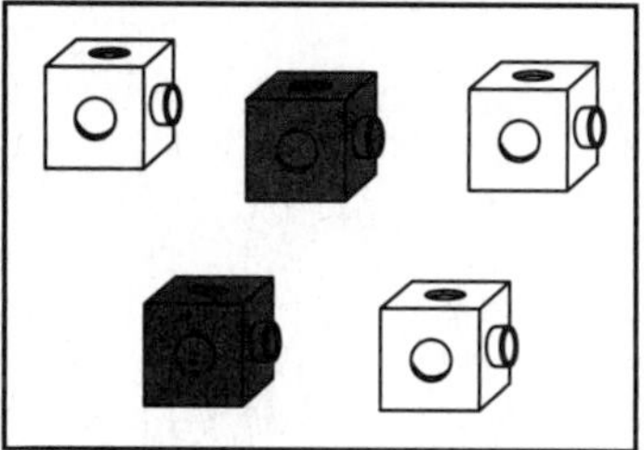

C 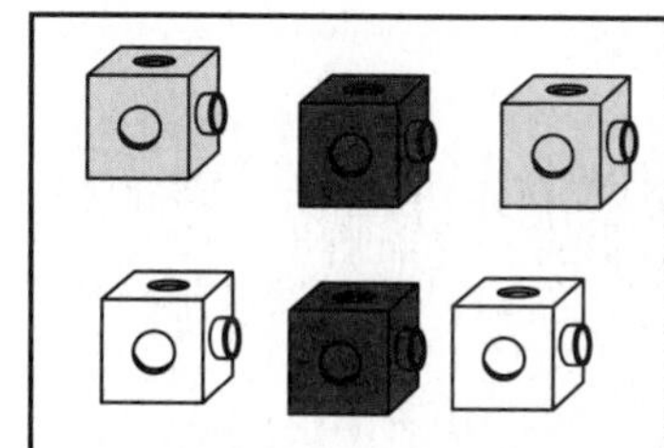

B 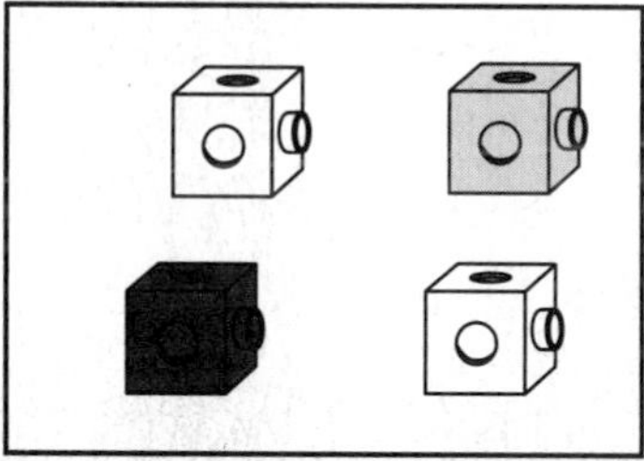

D 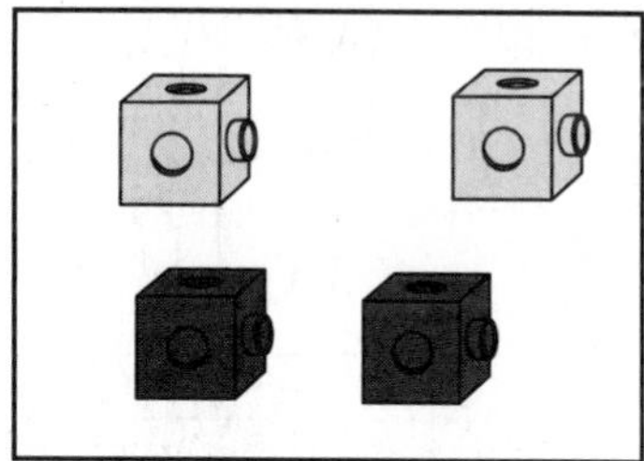

9. There are 10 oranges in a bag.
How many oranges are there in 7 bags?

number of bags	1	2	3	4	5	6	7
number of oranges	10	20					

A 7 oranges

B 8 oranges

C 70 oranges

D 80 oranges

Go On

Name ______________________________

Choose the correct answer.

10. Which is true?

A 36 is greater than 46.

B 36 is less than 46.

C 36 is equal to 46.

D 46 is less than 36.

11. There are 8 and 3 in a bag. Which color are you more likely to pull?

A

C 

B

Use the table to answer questions 12 and 13.

Month	Windy Days
December	12
January	15
February	10
March	16

12. Which month had the most number of windy days?

A December

B January

C February

D March

13. Which month had the least number of windy days?

A December

B January

C February

D March

Choose the correct answer.

14. Which shows the number of tens and ones?

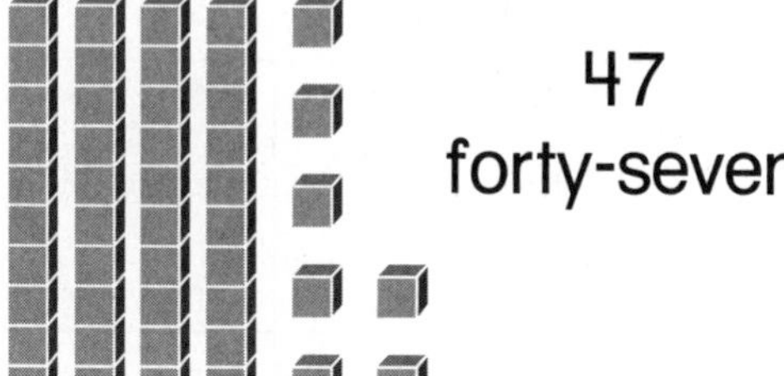

47
forty-seven

A 4 tens, 7 ones

B 0 tens, 4 ones

C 7 tens, 4 ones

D 1 ten, 7 ones

15. Count forward. Which numbers come next?

39, 40, 41, ___, ___, ___

A 42, 44, 46

B 42, 43, 44

C 43, 44, 45

D 43, 45, 47

16. Which symbol can you use to compare the numbers?

16 ◯ 16

A >

B <

C =

17. Which shows the numbers in order from least to greatest?

31 36 29

A 29, 36, 31

B 31, 36, 29

C 36, 31, 29

D 29, 31, 36

18. Which number is even?

A 13 B 14 C 15 D 17

Go On

Choose the correct answer.

19. Use the picture graph to answer question 19.

Berries We Like								
strawberries	🍓	🍓	🍓	🍓	🍓	🍓	🍓	
raspberries	●	●	●					
blueberries	●	●	●	●	●	●	●	●

How many more children chose blueberries than raspberries?

A 2 more children

B 3 more children

C 4 more children

D 5 more children

20. Count how many tens and ones. What is the number?

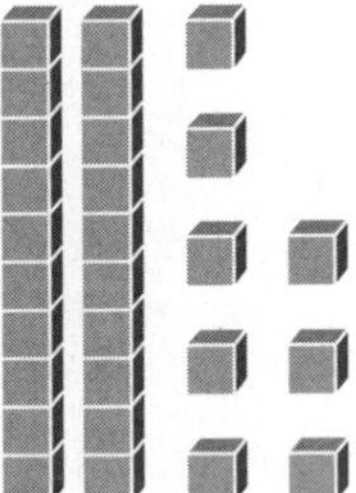

A 280

B 28

C 25

D 18

21. Which number is ten less than 49?

A 39

B 38

C 37

D 36

Stop

Name ______________________________

Choose the correct answer.

1. Which object could you trace to make the figure?

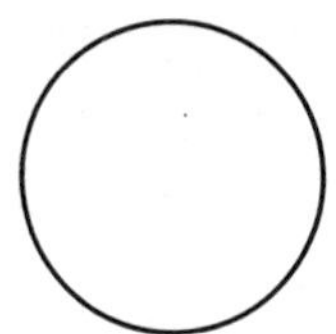

A 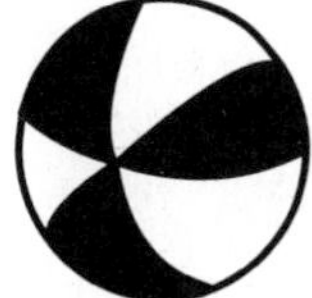

B 

C 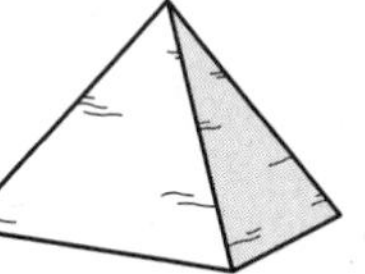

D 

2. How many straight sides does the plane figure have?

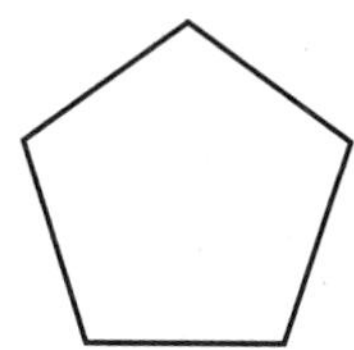

A 3

B 4

C 5

D 6

3. How many corners does the cube have?

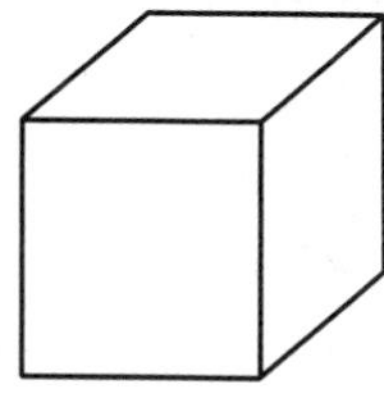

A 4

B 6

C 7

D 8

4. Which figure is a triangle?

A 

B 

C 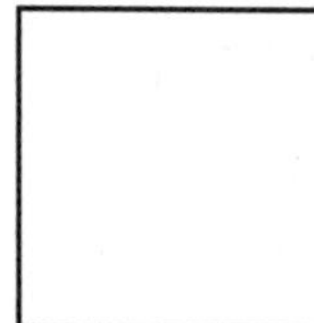

D 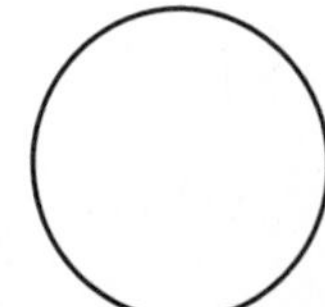

Go On

Name ______________________

Choose the correct answer.

5. Which solid figure has both curved and flat surfaces?

A 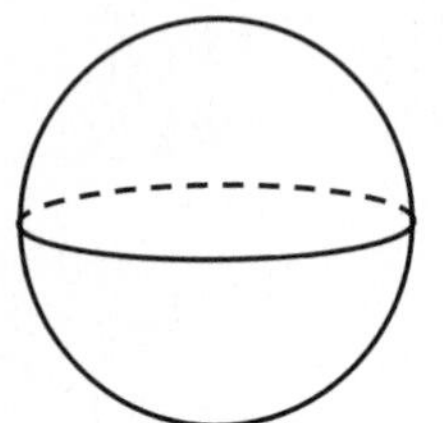 B 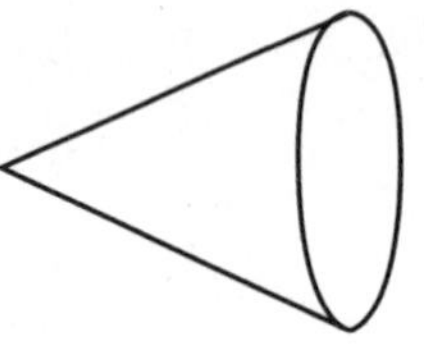 C 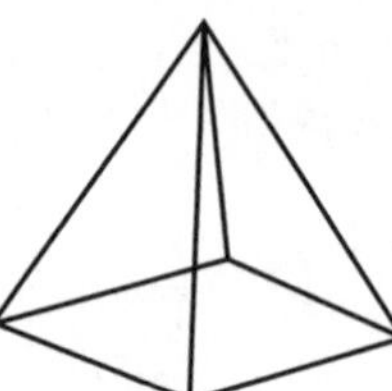 D 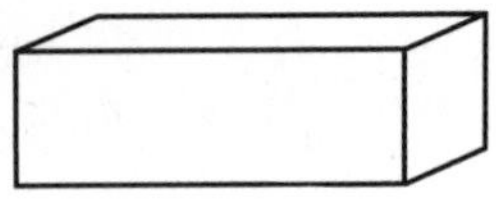

6. Which figure is a rectangle?

A 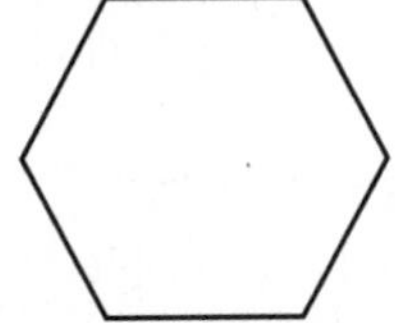 B 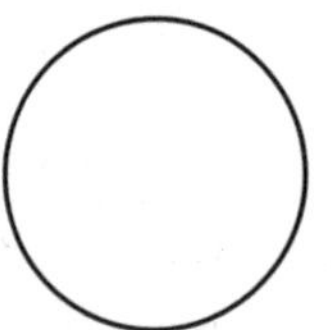 C 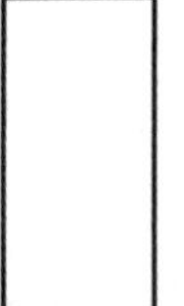 D 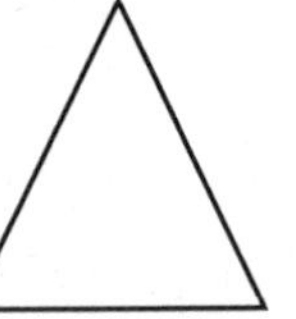

7. Which figure has a curved surface and two flat surfaces with no corners?

A 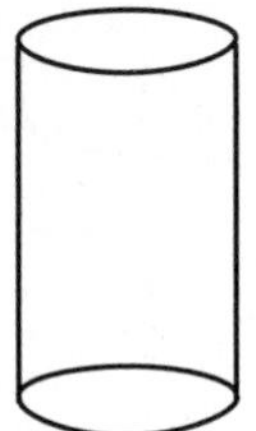 B 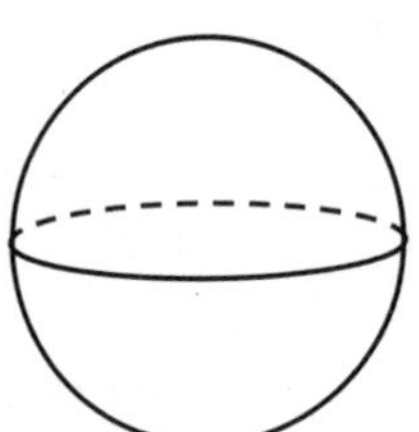 C 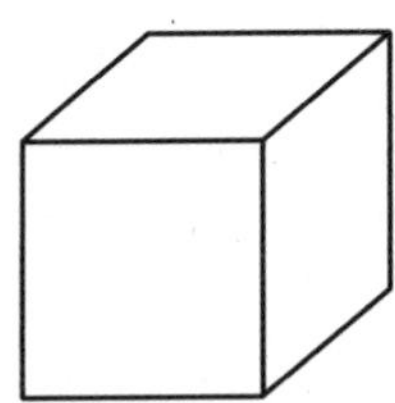 D 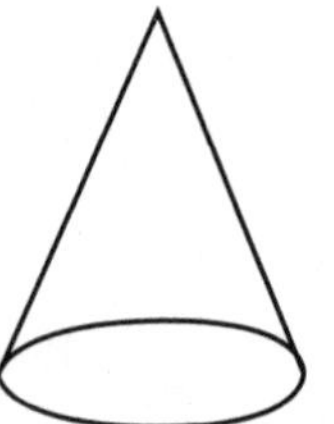

8. Which figure has fewer than 5 sides and only 4 corners?

A 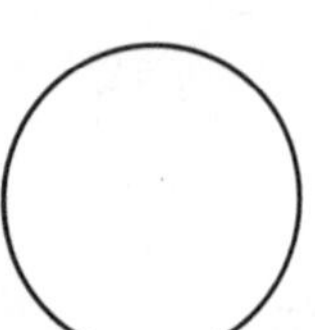 B 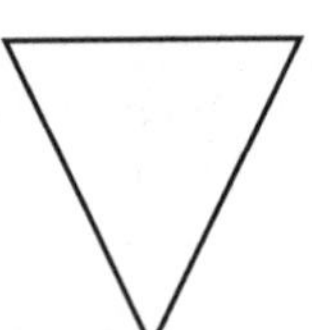 C 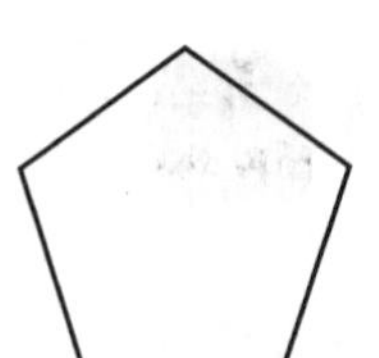 D 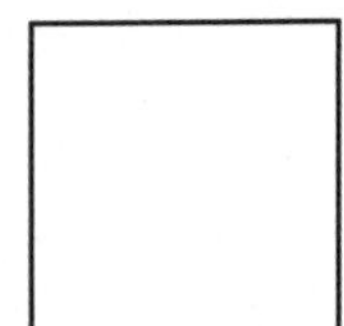

Stop

Name ____________________

Choose the correct answer.

1. Which comes next?

A  **B** **C** 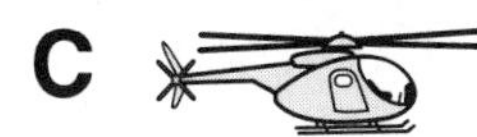 **D** 

2. Which figures show the same pattern?

3. Which is the pattern unit?

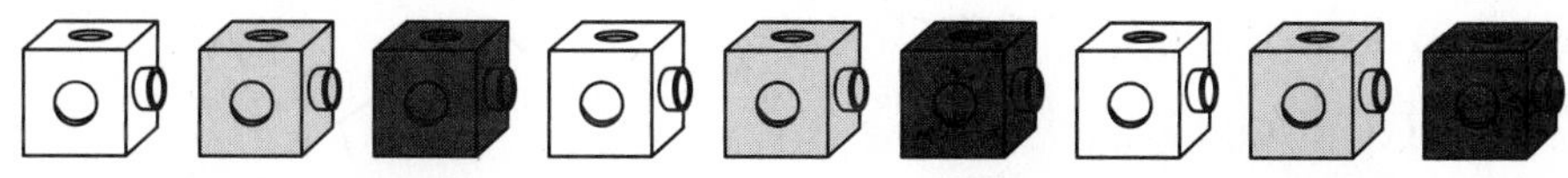

A 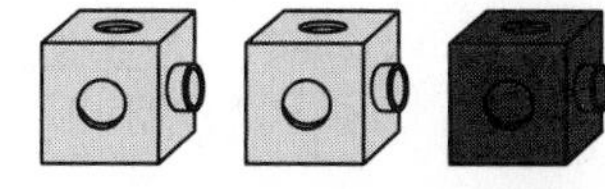

C 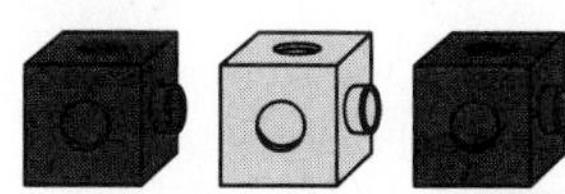

B 

D 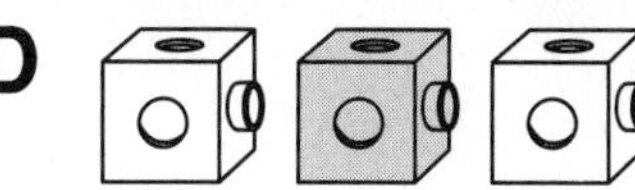

Go On

Choose the correct answer.

4. Which number is missing?

5 1 4 5 1 __?__ 5 1 4

A 1 **B** 2 **C** 3 **D** 4

5. Which figure comes next?

A 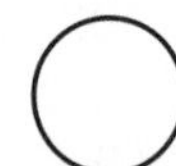 **B**  **C**  **D** 

6. Find the mistake in the pattern.
Which is the correct sticker?

A  **B**  **C**  **D** 

7. Find the mistake in the pattern.
Which is the correct bead?

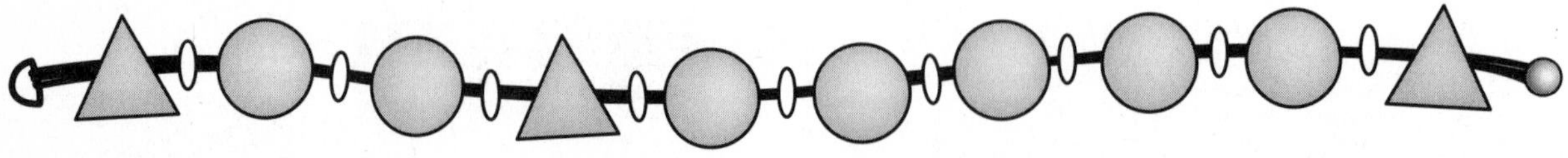

A **B**  **C**  **D** 

Stop

Name ____________________

Choose the correct answer.

1. Which appears to show two congruent figures?

A 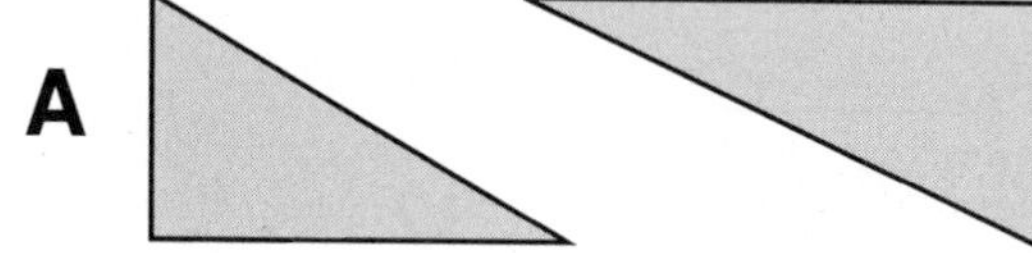

B 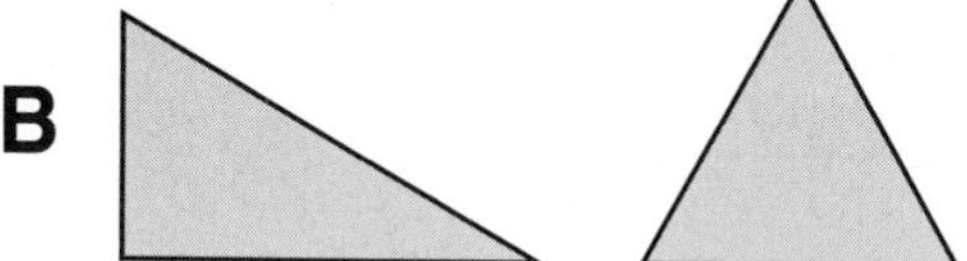

C 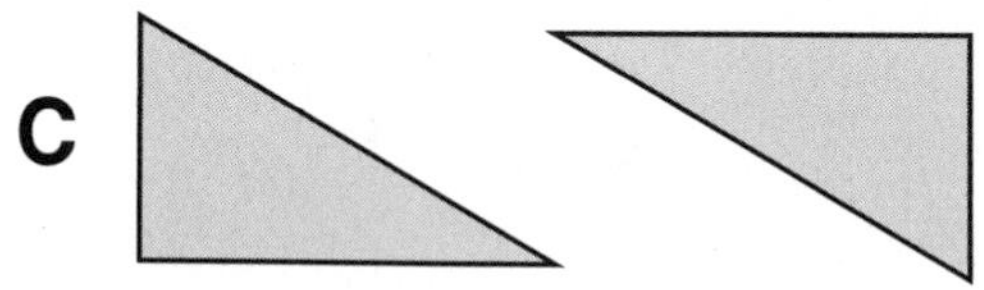

D 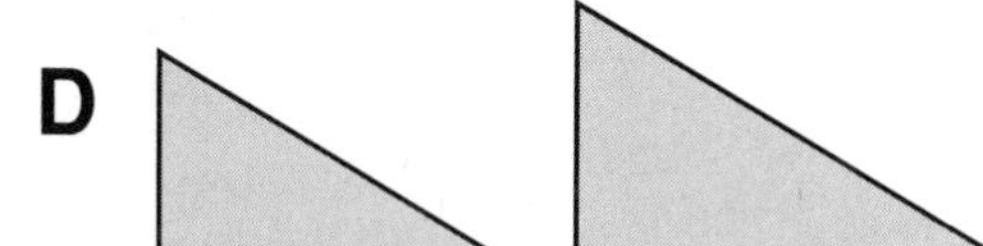

2. Which type of move is shown?

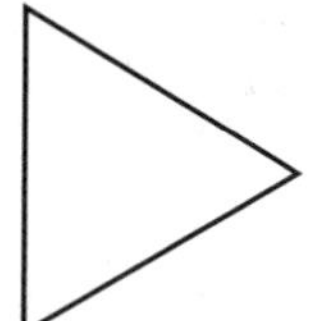
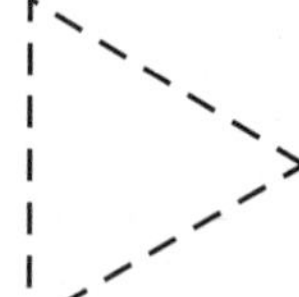

A flip

B slide

C turn

D symmetry

3. The is beside the 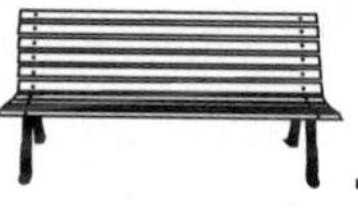. What is beside the ?

A 

B 

C 

D 

Go On

Name ________________________________

Choose the correct answer.

4. From **Start**, go right 1. Go down 2. Go left 1. Where are you?

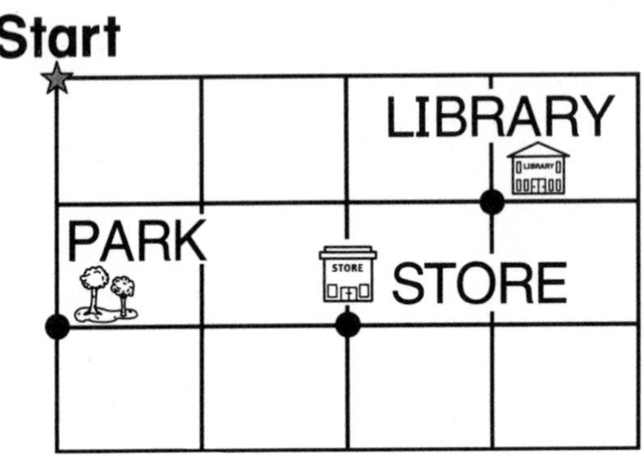

A park　　**B** store　　**C** library

5. Which appears to show a line of symmetry?

A 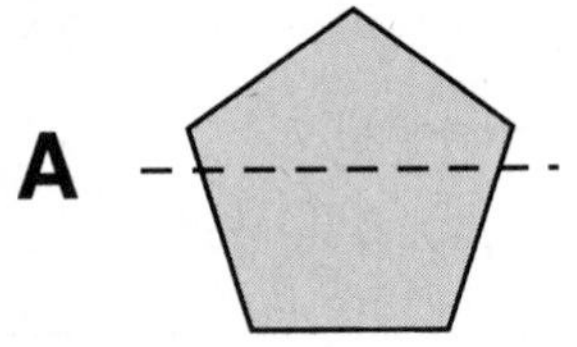　　**B** 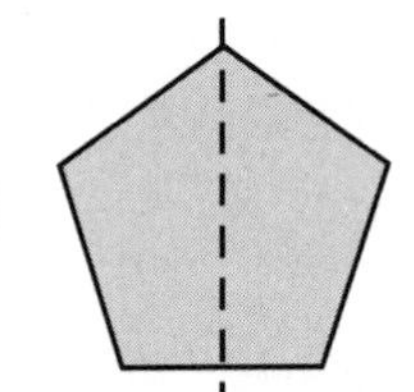　　**C** 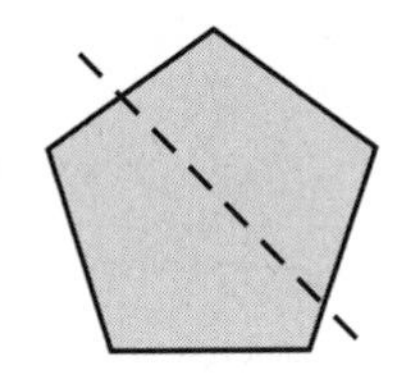　　**D** 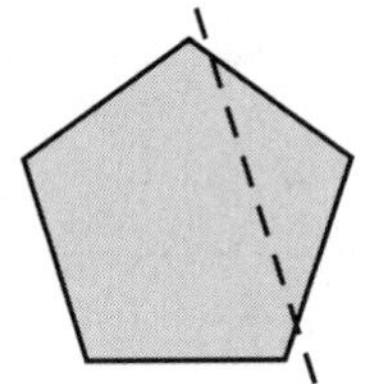

6. Jack's toy is **above** a [glove]. It is **near** the [GAME]. Which toy is Jack's?

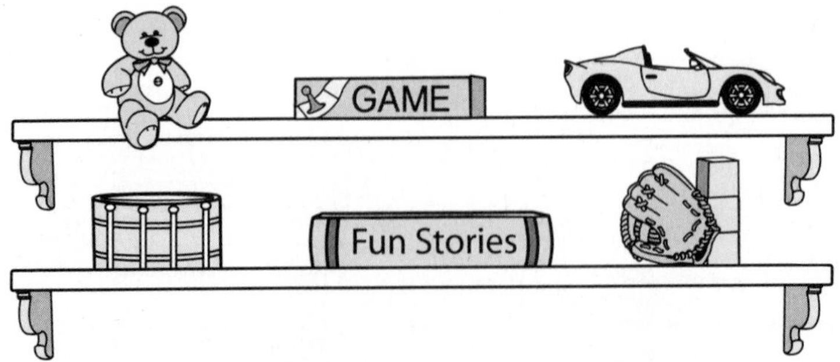

A 　　**B** 　　**C** 　　**D** 

Stop

Choose the correct answer.

1. Which figure is divided into two equal parts?

A 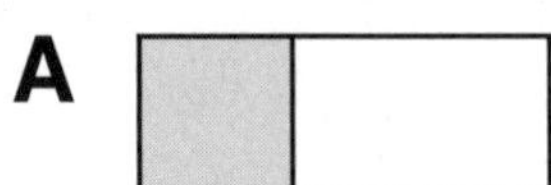

B 

C 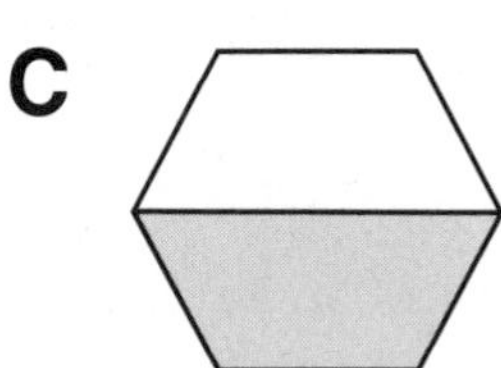

D 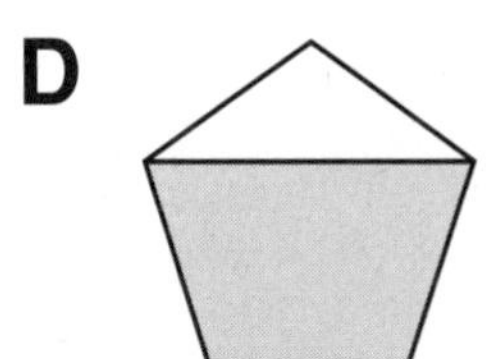

2. Which shows that 1 out of 4 cars are gray?

A 

B 

C 

D

3. Which figure has equal parts?

A

B 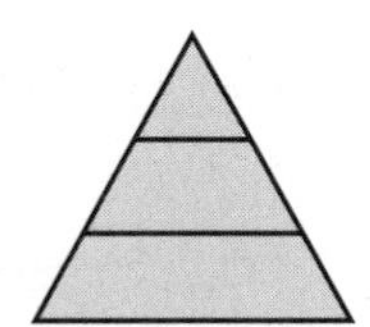

C 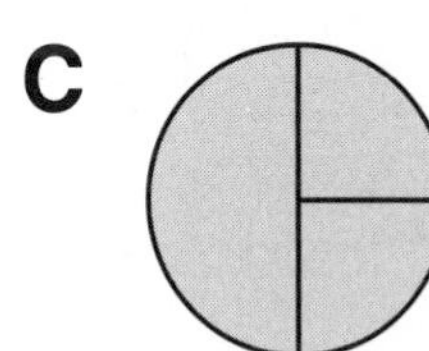

D 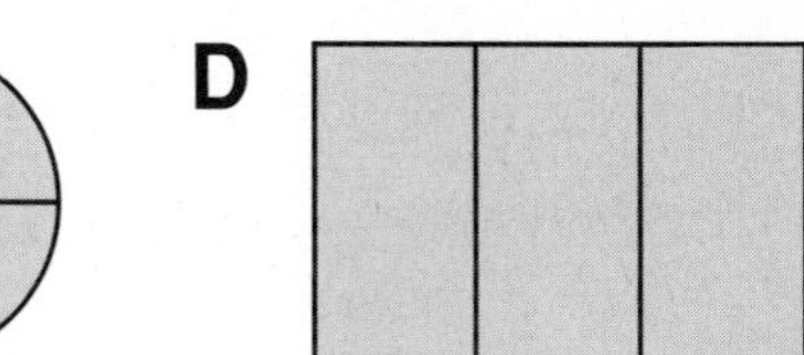

4. Which figure has $\frac{1}{4}$ shaded?

A

B 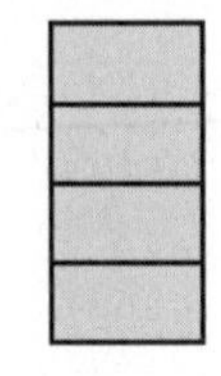

C 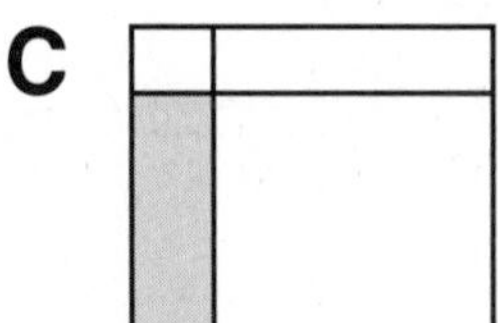

D 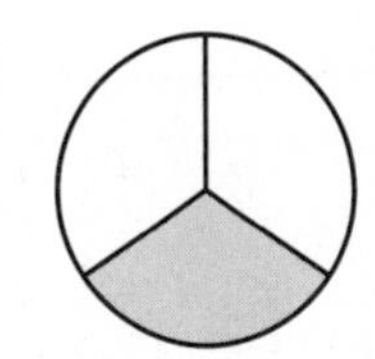

Go On

Choose the correct answer.

5. Which figure has $\frac{1}{3}$ shaded?

A 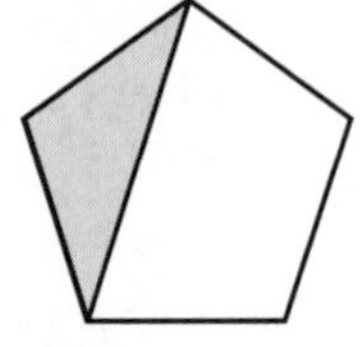

B 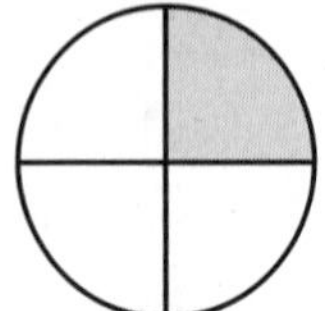

C 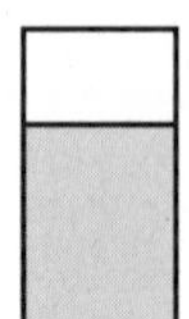

D 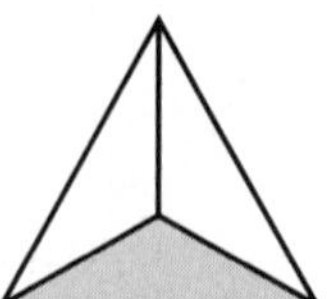

6. Sarah, Kelly, and Em share a pizza. Each gets an equal share. How would you cut the pizza?

A 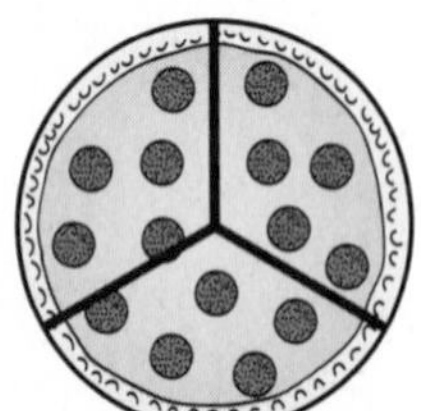

B 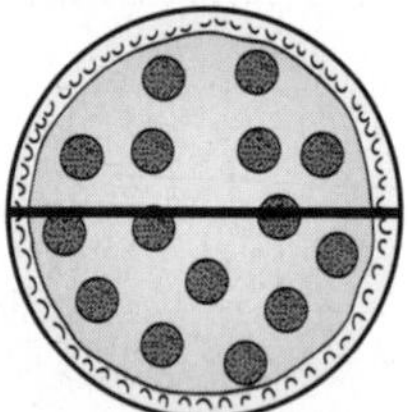

C 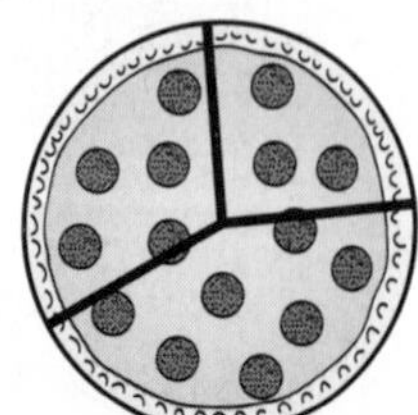

D 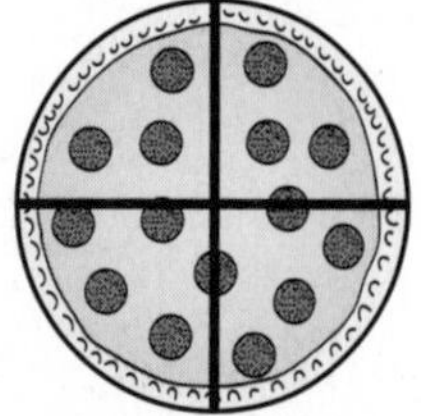

7. There are 4 friends who share a pizza. Each gets an equal share. How would you cut the pizza?

A 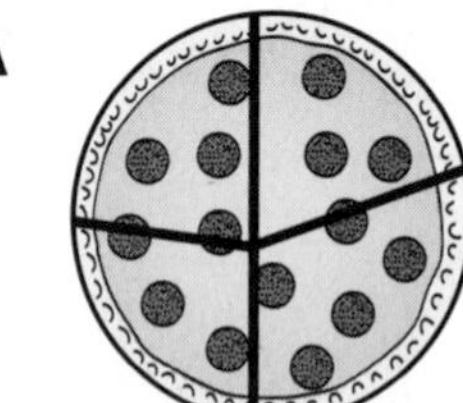

B 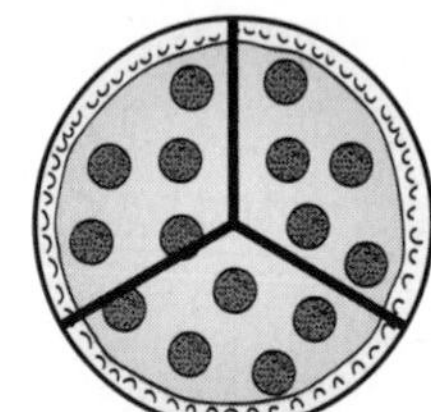

C 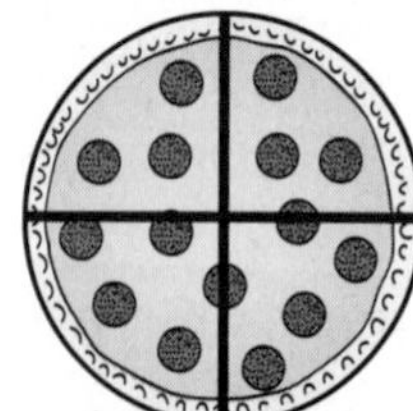

D 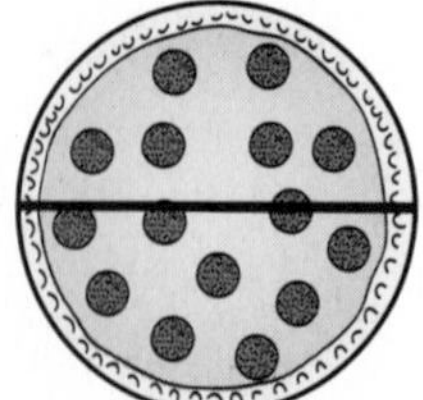

Stop

Name ____________________

Choose the correct answer.

1. How many sides does the plane figure have?

A 2

B 4

C 5

D 6

2. Which type of move is shown?

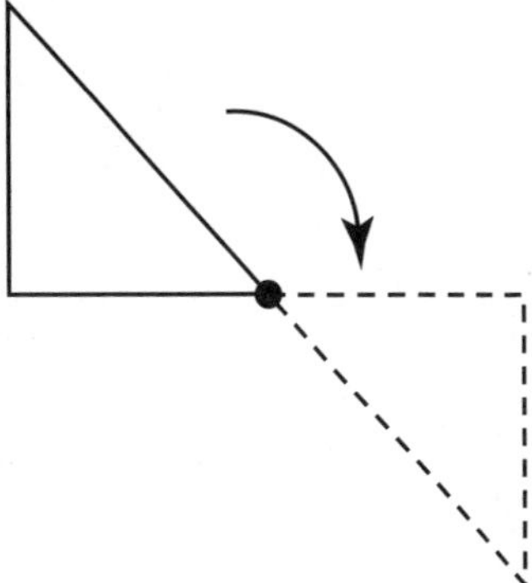

A turn

B symmetry

C slide

D flip

3. Which figure has equal parts?

A 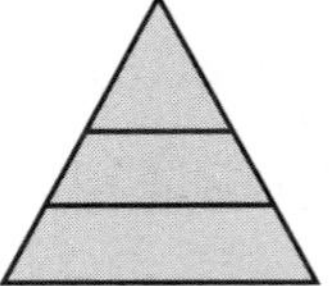

B 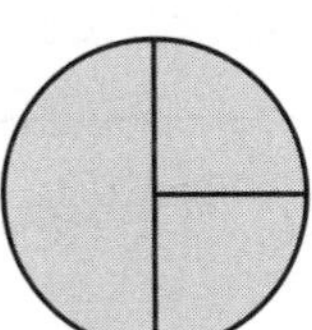

C 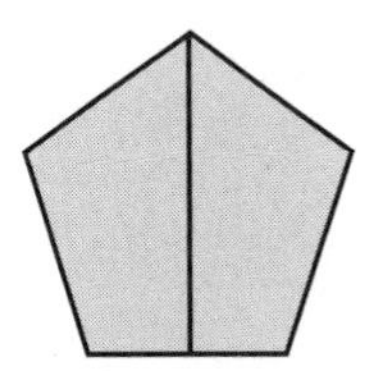

D 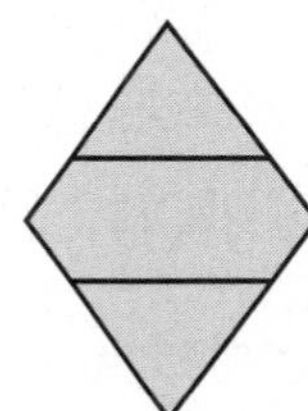

4. Which figure is a square?

A 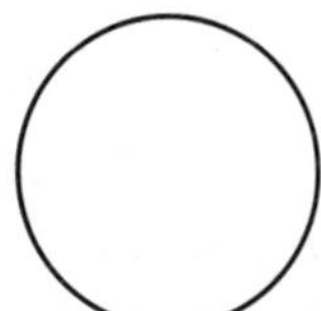

B 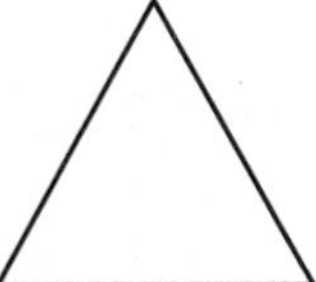

C 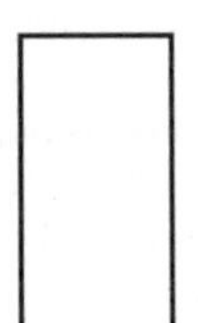

D 

Go On

Choose the correct answer.

5. Which comes next?

A  **B** **C** **D**

6. Which shows a line of symmetry?

A  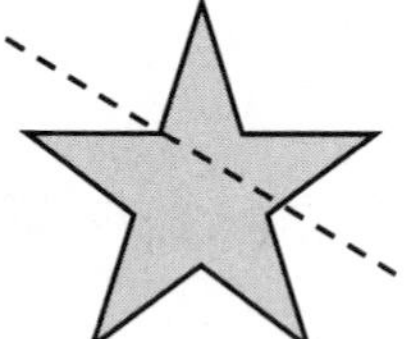 **B** 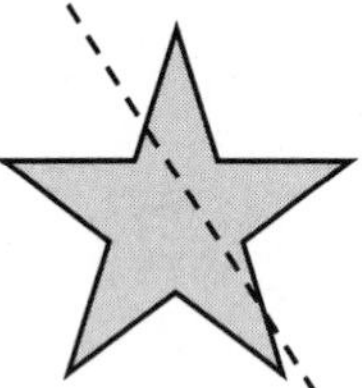 **C**  **D** 

7. Which figure has $\frac{1}{4}$ shaded?

A 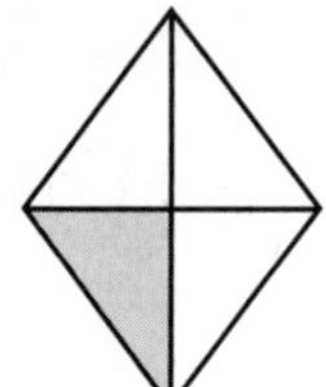 **B** 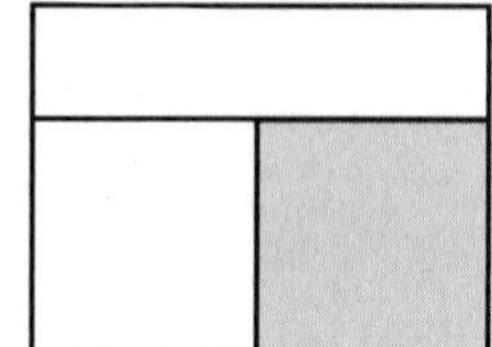 **C** 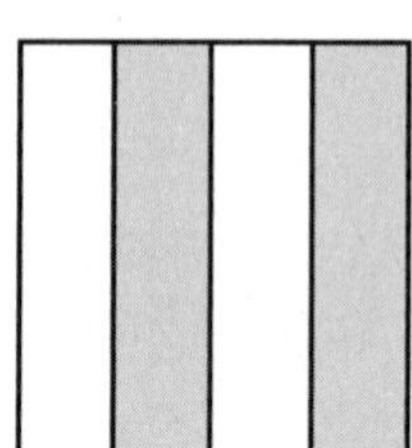 **D** 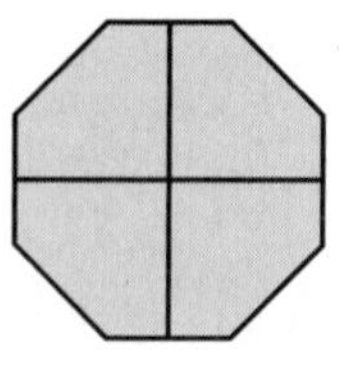

8. Which object could you trace to make the figure?

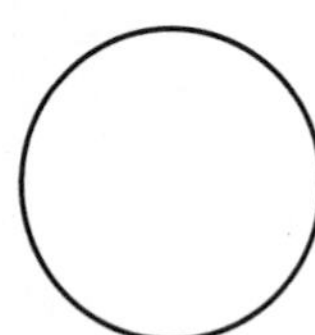

A 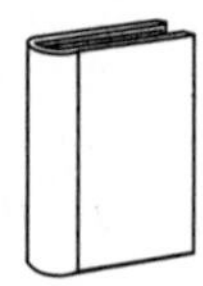 **B** 

C 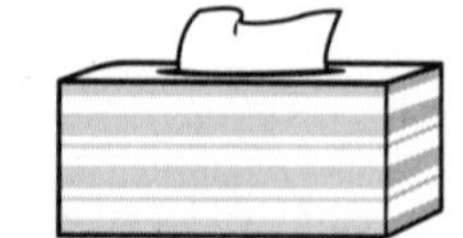 **D** 

Go On

Choose the correct answer.

9. Which is the pattern unit?

A 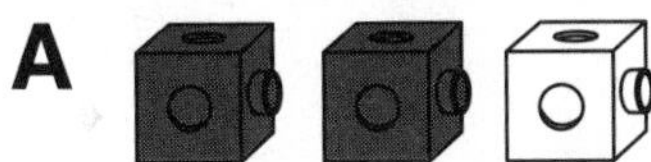

C 

B 

D 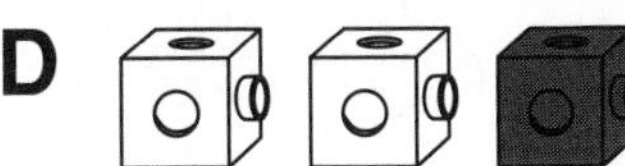

10. 4 friends share a pizza. Each gets an equal share. How would you cut the pizza?

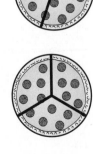

A 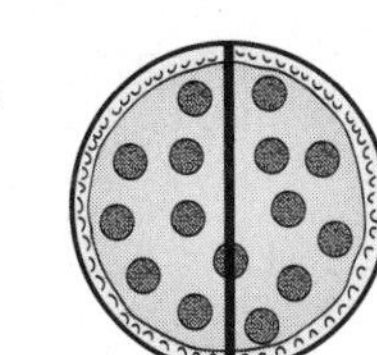

B 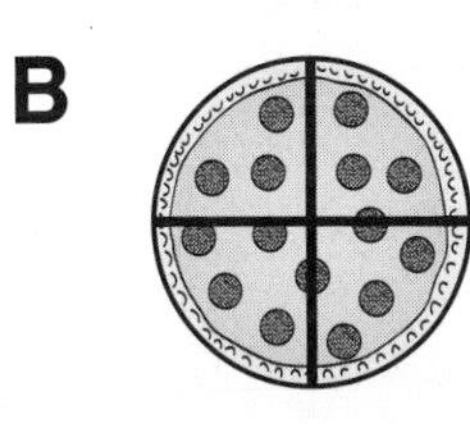

C 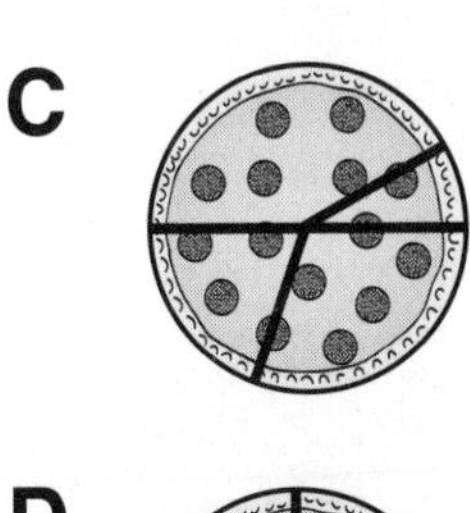

D

11. Which shows $\frac{1}{3}$ shaded?

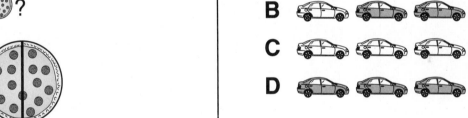

A 

B 

C

D

Go On

Name ____________________ **UNIT 4 POSTTEST**

Choose the correct answer.

12. Which figure is a circle?

A 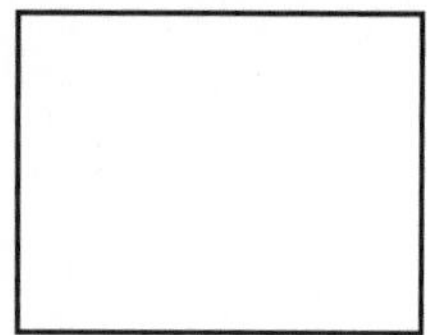 **B** 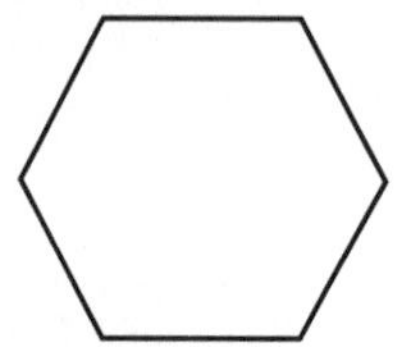 **C**  **D** 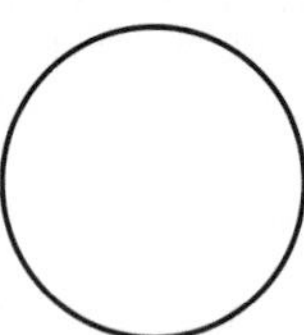

13. Which number is missing?

1 7 9 1 7 9 ? 7 9

A 9 **B** 7 **C** 5 **D** 1

14. Which solid figure has a curved surface and 2 flat surfaces with no corners?

A 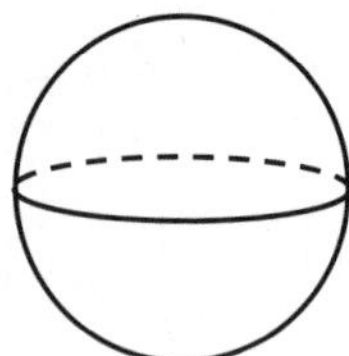 **B** 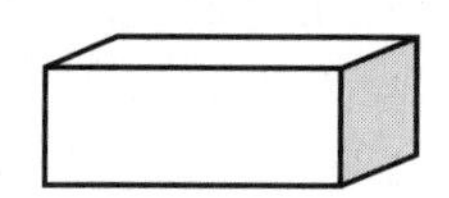 **C** 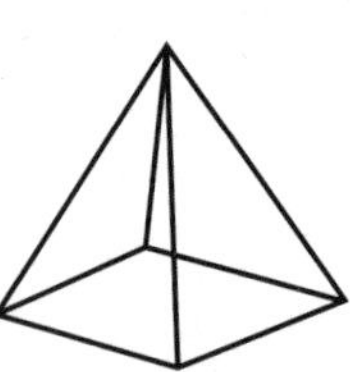 **D** 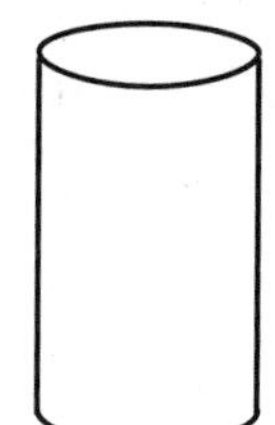

15. Which figures show the same pattern?

A

B 

C

Go On

Name ______________________________

Choose the correct answer.

16. Which shows two congruent figures?

A

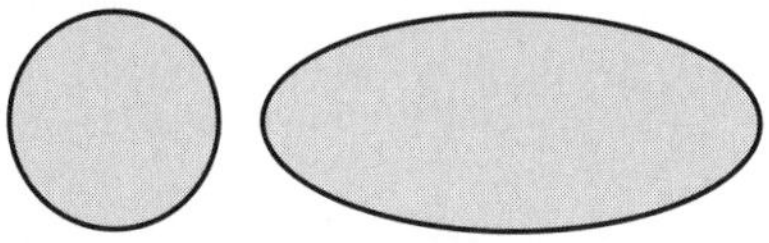

B 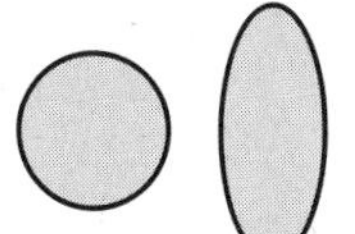

C 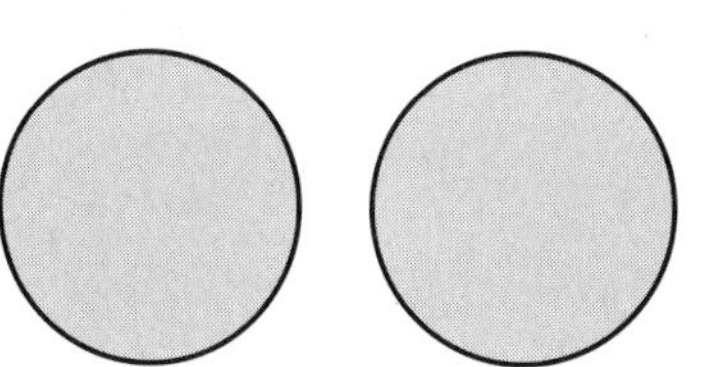

17. How many corners does the pyramid have?

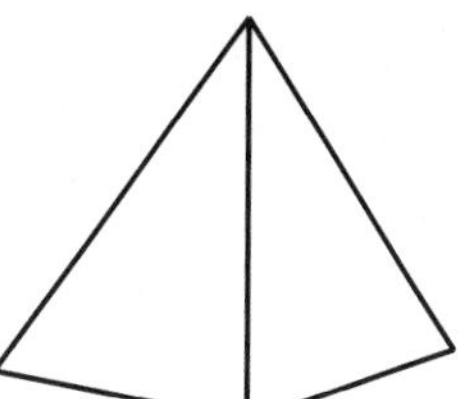

A 6 **C** 4

B 5 **D** 3

Use the picture for questions 18 and 19.

18. Samira's toy is **below** the doll. Her toy has a **line of symmetry**. It is **near** the dinosaur. Which toy is Samira's?

A **C**

B 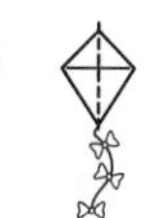 **D** 

19. Sandy's toy is **above** the horse. It is **near** the doll. Which toy is Sandy's?

A **C** 

B  **D** 

Go On

Choose the correct answer.

20. Find the mistake in the pattern.
Which is the correct bead?

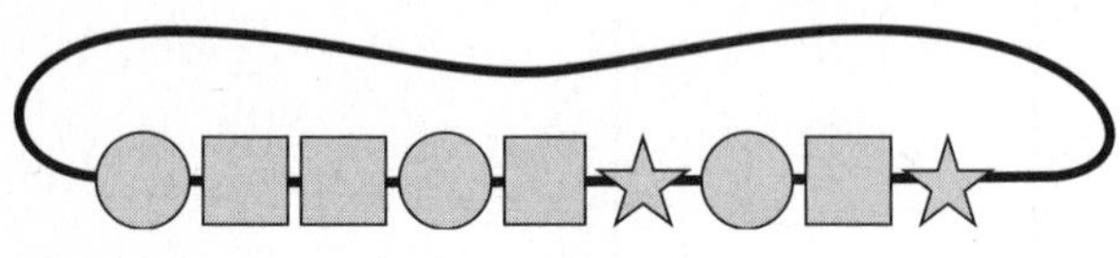

A  **B**  **C** ☆ **D** 

21. Which figure has a curved surface and one flat surface?

A 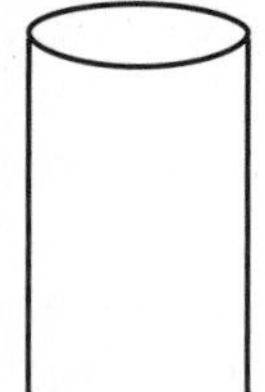 **B** 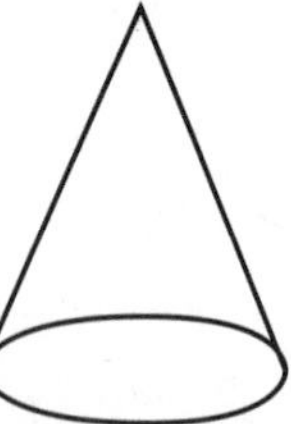 **C** 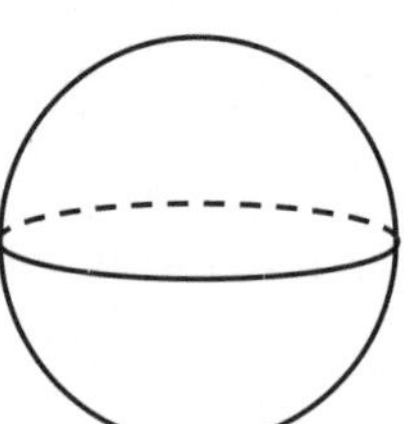 **D** 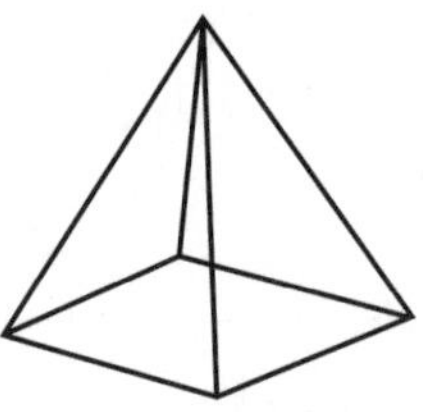

22. From **Start**, go down 1. Go right 3.
Where are you?

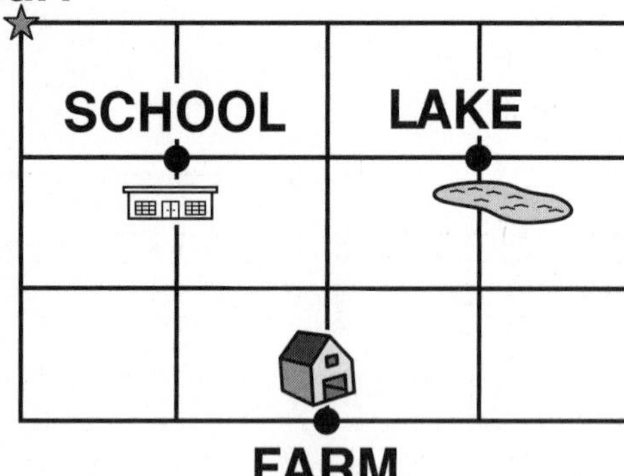

A lake **B** school **C** farm

Stop

Name ____________________

Choose the correct answer.

1. What is the sum?

$$\begin{array}{r} 9 \\ +9 \\ \hline \end{array}$$

A 14

B 16

C 18

D 88

2. Make a ten and add. What is the sum?

$$\begin{array}{r} 6 \\ +5 \\ \hline \end{array}$$

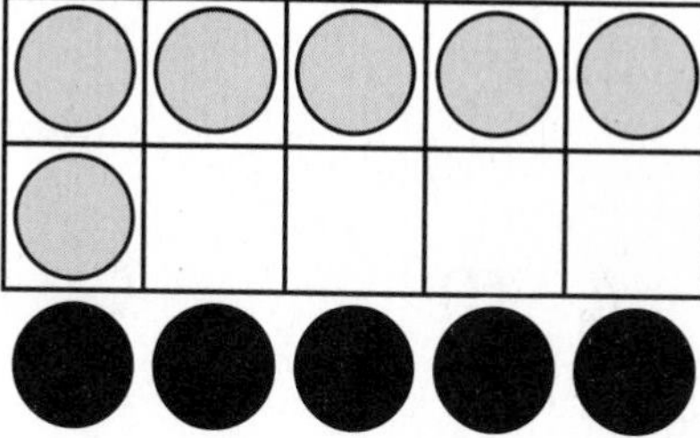

A 3

B 11

C 14

D 15

3. What is the sum?

$$\begin{array}{r} 7 \\ +6 \\ \hline \end{array}$$

A 13

B 14

C 15

D 16

4. What is the sum?

$$\begin{array}{r} 3 \\ 6 \\ +3 \\ \hline \end{array}$$

A 6

B 9

C 12

D 15

Go On

Name ______________________________

Choose the correct answer.

5. What is the sum?

$$\begin{array}{r} 10 \\ +\ 4 \\ \hline \end{array}$$

A 104
B 41
C 14
D 4

6. Make a ten and add. What is the sum?

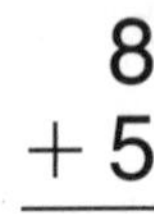

$$\begin{array}{r} 8 \\ +\ 5 \\ \hline \end{array}$$

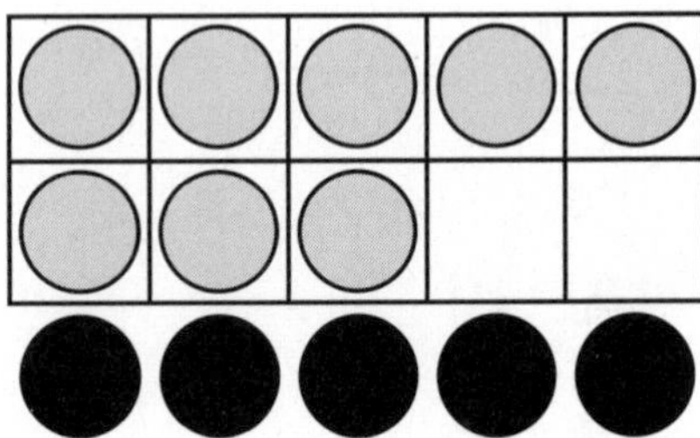

A 12
B 13
C 14
D 18

7. What is the sum?

$10 + 10 =$ ____

A 1010
B 21
C 20
D 11

8. Which number sentence matches the story?
7 firefighters arrive at a fire. 5 more firefighters join them. How many firefighters are at the fire now?

A $7 + 5 = 12$
B $7 - 5 = 2$
C $2 + 5 = 7$
D $12 - 7 = 5$

9. Which number sentence matches the story? A town has 5 police cars. Then the town buys 6 more police cars. How many police cars does the town have altogether?

A $11 - 5 = 6$
B $6 - 5 = 1$
C $11 + 5 = 16$
D $5 + 6 = 11$

Stop

Name ______________________________

Choose the correct answer.

Use the number line to answer questions 1 and 2.

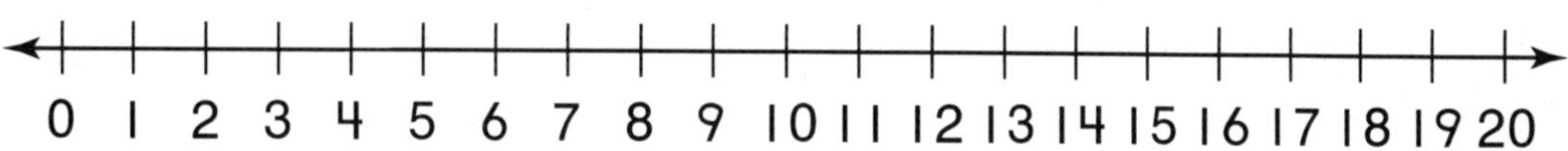

1. What is the difference?

$$\begin{array}{r} 14 \\ -\ 5 \\ \hline \end{array}$$

A 7

B 8

C 9

D 19

2. What is the difference?

$$\begin{array}{r} 13 \\ -\ 7 \\ \hline \end{array}$$

A 8

B 6

C 5

D 4

3. How many more birds are there than nests?

$$\begin{array}{r} 12 \\ -\ 3 \\ \hline \end{array}$$

A 15 more birds

B 11 more birds

C 10 more birds

D 9 more birds

4. What is the difference?

14 − 8 = ____

A 6 **B** 7 **C** 9 **D** 22

Go On

Name ____________________

Choose the correct answer.

5. Use the addition fact to help you subtract. What is the difference?

$$\begin{array}{r} 7 \\ +9 \\ \hline \end{array} \qquad \begin{array}{r} 16 \\ -\ 9 \\ \hline \end{array}$$

A 7
B 8
C 13
D 25

6. What is the difference?

$$\begin{array}{r} 15 \\ -\ 6 \\ \hline \end{array}$$

A 7
B 8
C 9
D 11

7. How many more butterflies are there than flowers?

$$\begin{array}{r} 13 \\ -\ 8 \\ \hline \end{array}$$

A 21 more butterflies
B 7 more butterflies
C 6 more butterflies
D 5 more butterflies

8. There are 16 children playing on the playground. 8 children go home. How many children are now playing on the playground?

A 12 children
B 8 children
C 6 children
D 2 children

9. Sarah counted trees in her backyard. She counted 7 oak trees and 9 elm trees. How many trees did Sara count in all?

A 2 trees
B 12 trees
C 16 trees
D 79 trees

Stop

Name ______________________

Choose the correct answer.

1. Which number is missing?

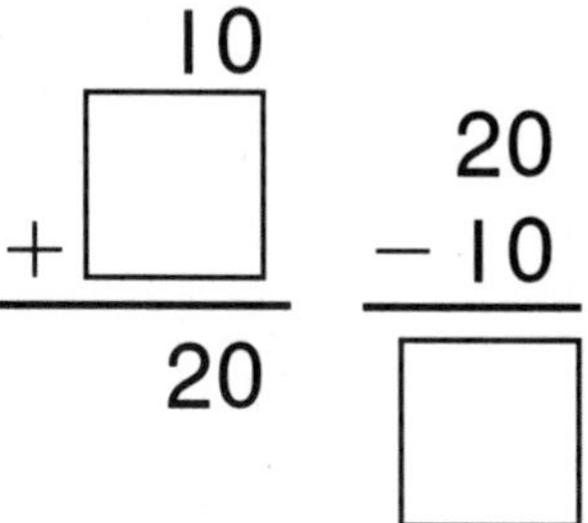

$$\begin{array}{r} 10 \\ + \square \\ \hline 20 \end{array} \qquad \begin{array}{r} 20 \\ - 10 \\ \hline \square \end{array}$$

A 5 **C** 12

B 10 **D** 21

2. Which is a way to make 14?

A 18 − 5

B 8 + 8

C 15 − 2

D 3 + 7 + 4

3. Which number sentence shows how many kites there are?

____ gray kites

____ white kites

A 7 + 8 = 15 **C** 8 − 7 = 1

B 15 − 7 = 8 **D** 9 + 6 = 15

4. Which number is missing?

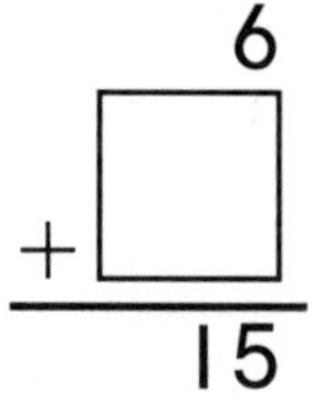

$$\begin{array}{r} 6 \\ + \square \\ \hline 15 \end{array} \qquad \begin{array}{r} 15 \\ - 6 \\ \hline \square \end{array}$$

A 7 **B** 8 **C** 9 **D** 11

Choose the correct answer.

5. Which is a way to make 7?

A 1 + 5

B 16 − 7

C 15 − 8

D 2 + 2 + 4

6. Follow the rule. Which number completes the table?

Subtract 8	
12	4
14	
16	8
17	9

A 5 **B** 6 **C** 7 **D** 10

7. Which fact is part of the fact family?

$$\begin{array}{r} 6 \\ +7 \\ \hline 13 \end{array} \qquad \begin{array}{r} 7 \\ +6 \\ \hline 13 \end{array} \qquad \begin{array}{r} 13 \\ -6 \\ \hline 7 \end{array}$$

A $\begin{array}{r} 13 \\ -7 \\ \hline 6 \end{array}$ **B** $\begin{array}{r} 13 \\ +6 \\ \hline 19 \end{array}$ **C** $\begin{array}{r} 7 \\ -6 \\ \hline 1 \end{array}$ **D** $\begin{array}{r} 8 \\ +5 \\ \hline 13 \end{array}$

8. Michelle has 5 apples. Zack brings 9 more apples. How many apples are there now?

A 4 apples **C** 14 apples

B 13 apples **D** 15 apples

9. Andy buys 14 pears. He gives 6 pears away. How many pears does Andy have now?

A 20 pears **C** 9 pears

B 12 pears **D** 8 pears

Stop

Name ____________________

Choose the correct answer.

1. Which shows the amount of money in a different way?

A 

B 

C 

D 

2. Which shows a way to make 1 dollar?

A 

B 

C 

D 

Go On

Name ____________________

Choose the correct answer.

3. Which symbol can you use to compare the amounts?

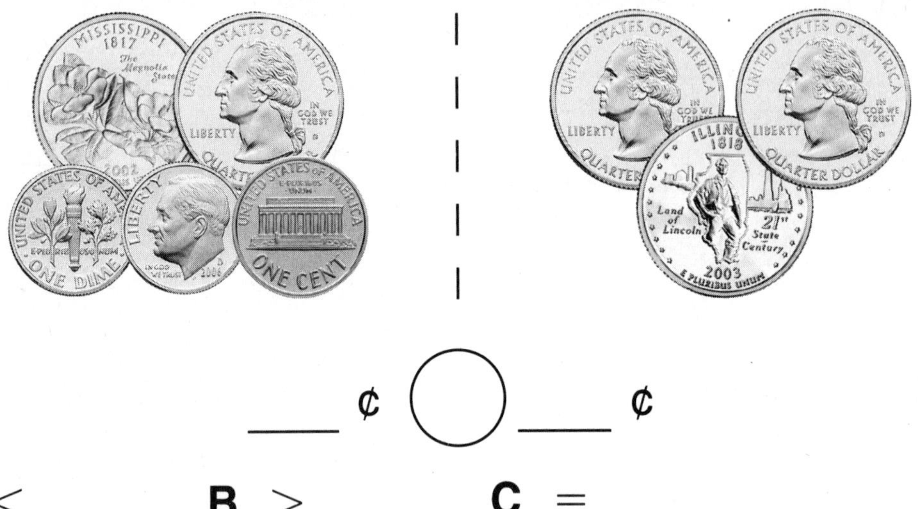

____ ¢ ◯ ____ ¢

A < **B** > **C** =

4. Max buys a toy boat for 55¢. He uses

2  and 1 . Which shows the

same amount in a different way?

A 

C 

B 

D 

Stop

Name ____________________

Choose the correct answer.

1. What time does the clock show?

A 3:30

B 4:30

C 4:00

D 6:30

2. What time does the clock show?

A 8:00

B 12:00

C 8:30

D 9:00

3. Use the calendar. How many Mondays are in this month?

A 2

B 3

C 4

D 5

OCTOBER						
Sunday	Monday	Tuesday	Wednesday	Thursday	Friday	Saturday
	1	2	3	4	5	6
7	8	9	10	11	12	13
14	15	16	17	18	19	20
21	22	23	24	25	26	27
28	29	30	31			

Go On

Name ______________________________________

Choose the correct answer.

4. Which clock matches the time shown?

A  **B**  **C**  **D** 

Use the table to answer questions 5 and 6.

Sports Camp		
Event	**Start**	**End**
 tennis lessons		
 soccer practice		
 swim class		

5. Which event starts at 1:00?

A tennis lessons

B soccer practice

C swim class

6. Which event lasts the longest time?

A tennis lessons

B soccer practice

C swim class

Stop

Name ______________________________

Choose the correct answer.

1. Use the calendar. How many days are in this month?

October						
Sunday	Monday	Tuesday	Wednesday	Thursday	Friday	Saturday
	1	2	3	4	5	6
7	8	9	10	11	12	13
14	15	16	17	18	19	20
21	22	23	24	25	26	27
28	29	30	31			

A 7 **C** 21

B 17 **D** 31

2. Use the addition fact to help you subtract. What is the difference?

$$\begin{array}{r} 4 \\ +\ 9 \\ \hline \end{array} \qquad \begin{array}{r} 13 \\ -\ 9 \\ \hline \end{array}$$

A 16

B 9

C 6

D 4

3. What is the sum?

$$\begin{array}{r} 9 \\ +\ 9 \\ \hline \end{array}$$

A 19

B 18

C 11

D 9

4. Follow the rule. Which number completes the table?

Add 6	
4	10
6	12
8	
9	15

A 13 **C** 17

B 14 **D** 19

Go On

Choose the correct answer.

5. How many fewer bees are there than flowers?

$$\begin{array}{r} 14 \\ -\ 8 \\ \hline \end{array}$$

A 4 fewer bees

B 6 fewer bees

C 8 fewer bees

D 9 fewer bees

6. Which number sentence shows how many umbrellas are gray?

______ umbrellas in all

______ white umbrellas

A $12 - 5 = 7$

B $12 - 6 = 6$

C $7 + 5 = 12$

D $12 - 7 = 5$

7. What is the sum?

$$\begin{array}{r} 4 \\ 3 \\ +6 \\ \hline \end{array}$$

A 7

B 10

C 13

D 15

8. What is the time of day?

A morning

B afternoon

C evening

Go On

Name______________________________________

Choose the correct answer.

9. Which shows the amount of money in a different way?

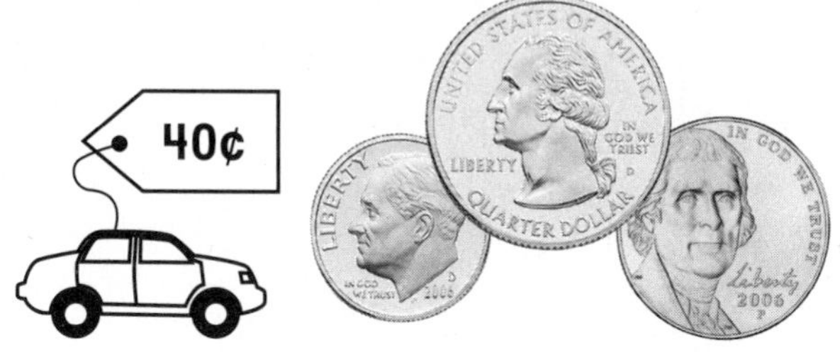

A

B

C

D

10. Which shows a way to make 1 dollar?

A

B

C

11. What is the difference?

$$\begin{array}{r} 18 \\ -\ 9 \\ \hline \end{array}$$

A 9 **C** 11

B 10 **D** 12

Go On

Choose the correct answer.

12. Which number sentence matches the story?

A man buys 6 daisies. Then he buys 4 roses. How many flowers does the man buy in all?

A $6 - 2 = 4$

B $14 - 6 = 8$

C $6 + 4 = 10$

D $16 + 4 = 20$

13. Which number is missing?

$$\begin{array}{r} 9 \\ + \square \\ \hline 12 \end{array} \qquad \begin{array}{r} 12 \\ - 9 \\ \hline \square \end{array}$$

A 2

B 3

C 4

D 5

14. Make a ten and add. What is the sum?

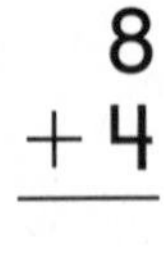

$$\begin{array}{r} 8 \\ + 4 \\ \hline \end{array}$$

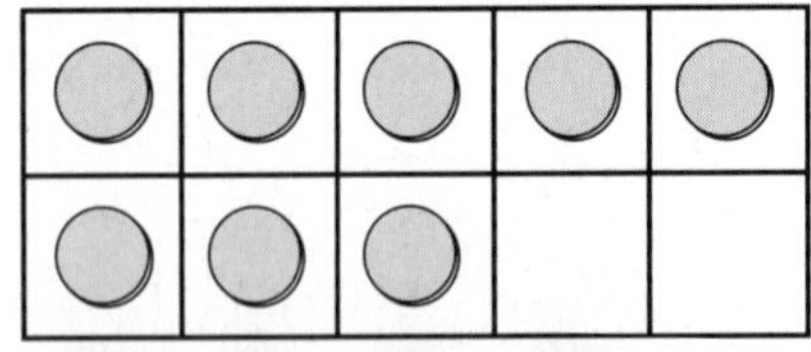

A 10

B 12

C 14

D 16

15. Albert has 16 oranges. He gives 7 oranges to his mother. How many oranges does Albert have now?

A 6 oranges

B 7 oranges

C 8 oranges

D 9 oranges

Go On

Choose the correct answer.

16. Which symbol can you use to compare the amounts?

40 ¢ ◯ 50 ¢

A < **B** > **C** =

17. Which clock matches the time shown?

A 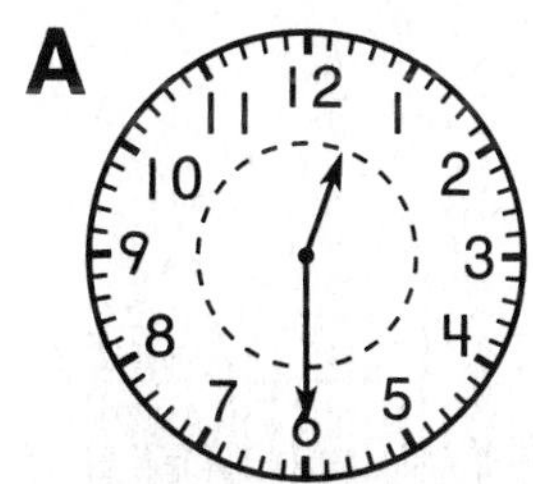

B

C 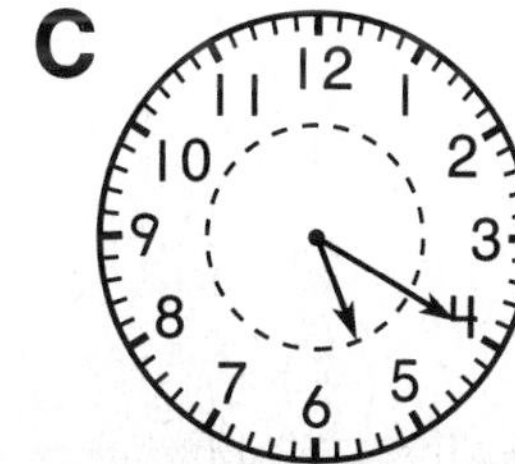

D 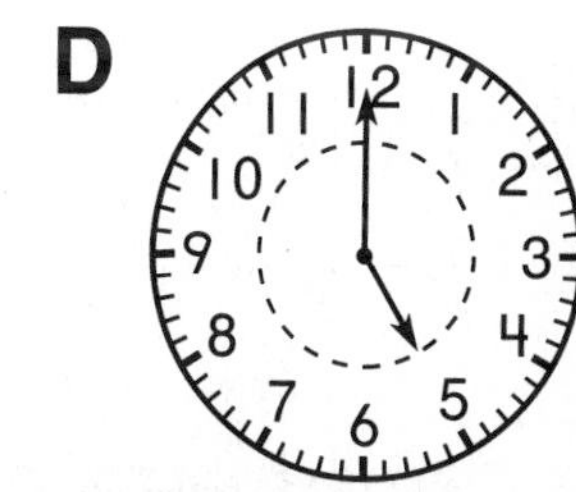

18. What is the sum?

5 + 6 = ____

A 7 **C** 16

B 11 **D** 56

19. What is the difference?

12 − 3 = ____

A 7 **C** 9

B 8 **D** 15

Go On

Name ______________________________________ **UNIT 5 POSTTEST**

Choose the correct answer.

Use the table to answer question 20.

Ms. Clark's Class		
Event	**Start**	**End**
 rest time		
 lunch		
 recess		

20. Which event starts at 12:00?

A rest time **B** lunch **C** recess

---

21. Which fact is part of the fact family?

$$\begin{array}{r} 8 \\ +9 \\ \hline 17 \end{array} \quad \begin{array}{r} 17 \\ -\ 9 \\ \hline 8 \end{array} \quad \begin{array}{r} 17 \\ -\ 8 \\ \hline 9 \end{array}$$

A $\begin{array}{r} 17 \\ -\ 6 \\ \hline 11 \end{array}$ **B** $\begin{array}{r} 10 \\ +\ 7 \\ \hline 17 \end{array}$ **C** $\begin{array}{r} 9 \\ +8 \\ \hline 17 \end{array}$ **D** $\begin{array}{r} 20 \\ -\ 3 \\ \hline 17 \end{array}$

Stop

Choose the correct answer.

1. What is the temperature?

A 0°C
B 5°C
C 10°C
D 50°C

2. How long is the object?

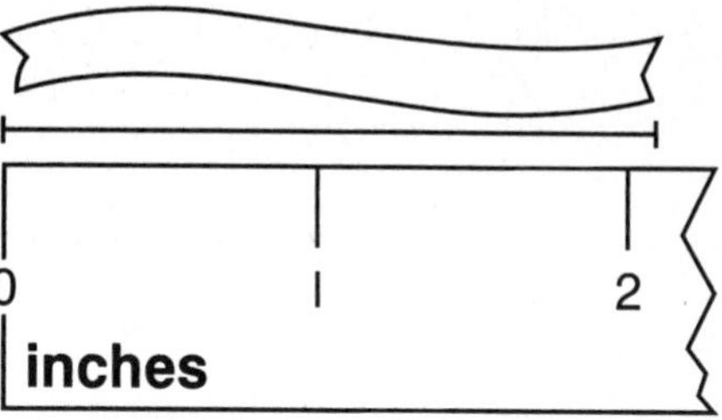

A about 1 inch
B about 2 inches
C about 3 inches
D about 4 inches

3. About how many [paper clip] long is the object?

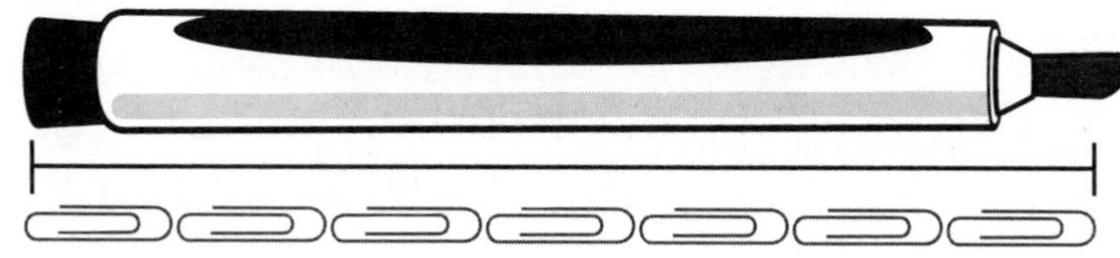

A about 5 [paper clip]
B about 6 [paper clip]
C about 7 [paper clip]
D about 8 [paper clip]

Go On

Name ____________________

Choose the correct answer.

4. Which shows the crayons in order from longest to shortest?

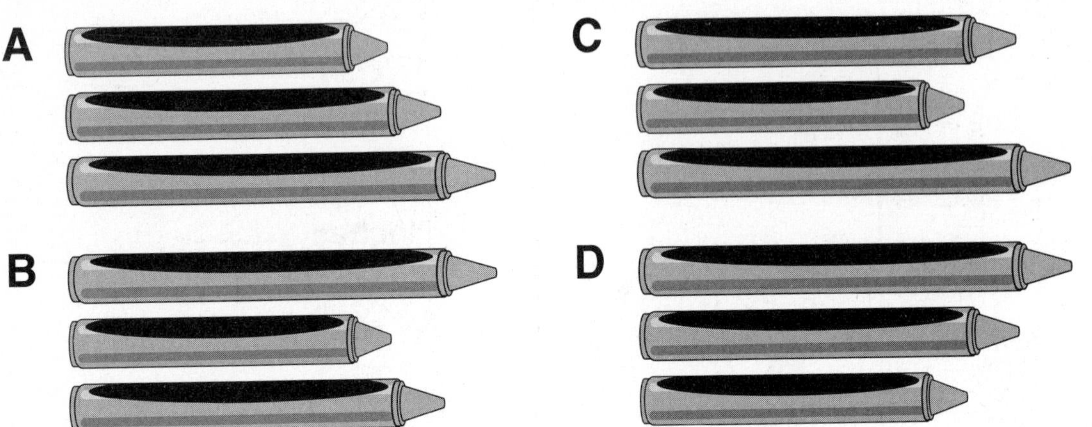

5. About how many (paper clips) long is the object?

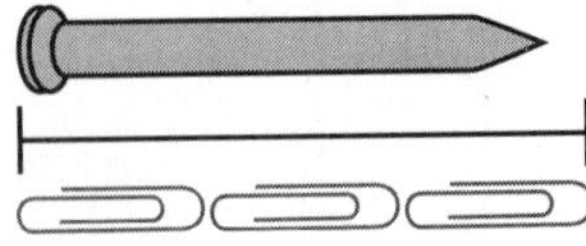

A about 4 (paper clips)

B about 3 (paper clips)

C about 2 (paper clips)

D about 1 (paper clip)

6. About how many (paper clips) long is the object?

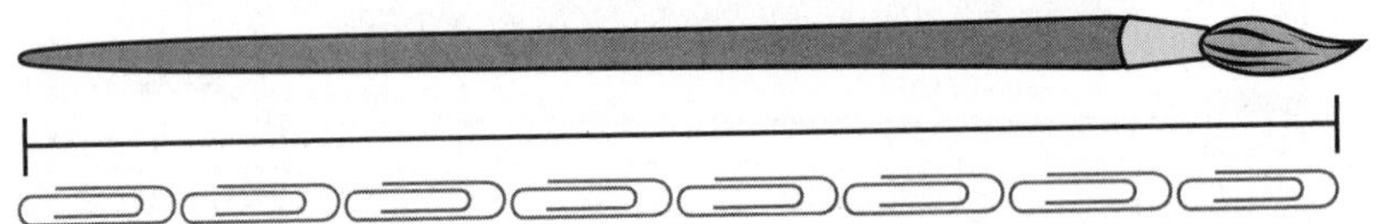

A about 8 (paper clips)

B about 7 (paper clips)

C about 6 (paper clips)

D about 5 (paper clips)

Stop

Name ____________________

Choose the correct answer.

1. Which object is the heaviest?

A 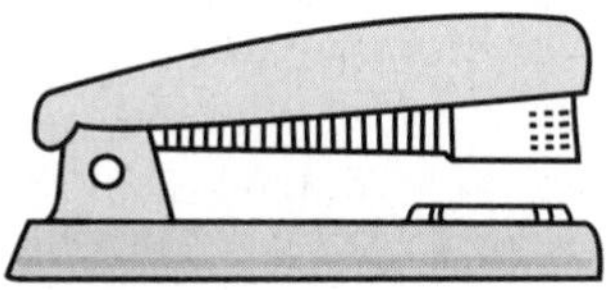

B 

C 

D 

2. Which container holds the least?

A 

B 

C 

D 

3. About how many cups will the container hold?

A about 1 cup

B about 2 cups

C about 3 cups

D about 4 cups

4. About how many pounds is the object?

A about 1 pound

B about 10 pounds

C about 50 pounds

D about 100 pounds

Go On

Choose the correct answer.

5. Which tool will you use to measure how hot the soup is?

A 

C 

B 

D 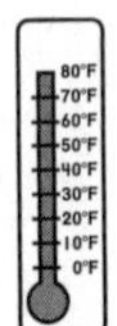

6. Which tool will you use to measure how tall the juice box is?

A 

C 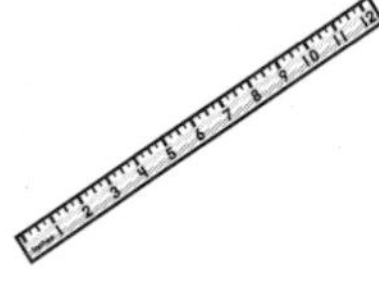

B 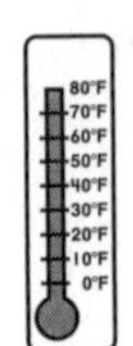

D 

7. How many more cups do you need to fill the container to the top? This glass has 1 cup of juice in it.

A about 1 cup

B about 2 cups

C about 3 cups

8. How many more cups do you need to fill the container to the top? This bowl has 2 cups of soup in it.

A about 1 cup

B about 2 cups

C about 3 cups

D about 4 cups

Stop

Name ____________________

Choose the correct answer.

1. What is the difference?

80 − 30 = ____

A 30
B 40
C 50
D 60

2. What is the sum?

70 + 20 = ____

A 50
B 60
C 80
D 90

3. What is the difference?

	tens	ones
	2	8
−		3

Workmat

Tens	Ones
2 tens	8 ones

A 22
B 25
C 26
D 31

4. What is the sum?

	tens	ones
	3	4
+		5

Workmat

Tens	Ones
3 tens	4 ones
	5 ones

A 39
B 37
C 33
D 31

Go On

Name ______________________________

Choose the correct answer.

5. What is the sum?

	tens	ones
	3	3
+	2	4

Workmat: Tens | Ones

A 17

B 51

C 57

D 67

6. What is the difference?

	tens	ones
	3	6
−	1	4

Workmat: Tens | Ones

A 42

B 22

C 20

D 12

8. There are 63 books on bugs. Julie checks out 8 of the books. About how many books are left?

A about 5 books

B about 50 books

C about 70 books

D about 500 books

9. Luke counts 56 birds. Then he counts 40 more birds. About how many birds does Luke count in all?

A about 1 bird

B about 10 birds

C about 20 birds

D about 100 birds

Stop

Choose the correct answer.

1. What is the sum?

	tens	ones
	2	3
+		5

Workmat

tens	ones

A 29

B 28

C 27

D 22

2. Which container holds the most milk?

A 

B 

C 

D 

3. About how many ⊂⊃ long is the object?

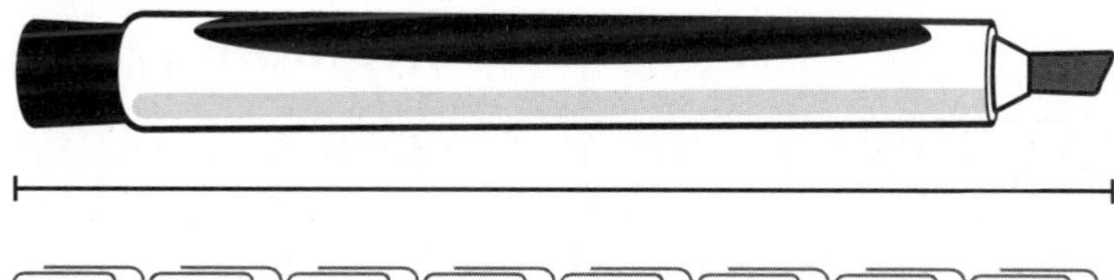

A about 6 ⊂⊃

B about 7 ⊂⊃

C about 8 ⊂⊃

D about 9 ⊂⊃

Go On

Choose the correct answer.

4. About how many pounds is the object?

A about 1 pound

B about 10 pounds

C about 20 pounds

D about 100 pounds

5. What is the temperature?

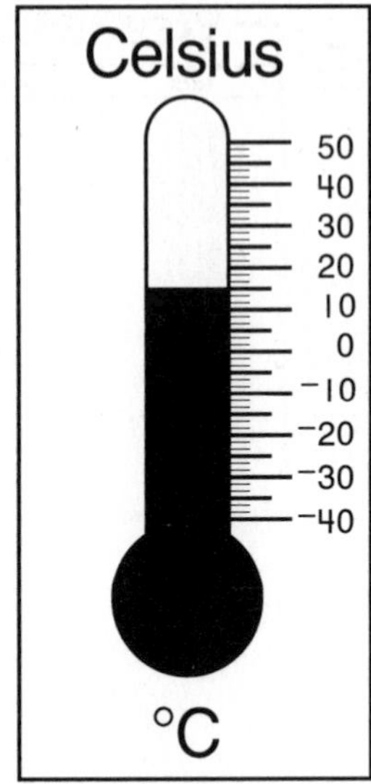

A 0°C

B 5°C

C 10°C

D 15°C

6. What is the difference?

90 − 40 = ____

A 70

B 60

C 50

D 40

7. About how many cups will the container hold?

A about 4 cups

B about 3 cups

C about 2 cups

D about 1 cup

Go On

Name ____________________

Choose the correct answer.

8. What is the difference?

	tens	ones
	3	5
−	2	1

Workmat

tens	ones

A 56

B 24

C 15

D 14

9. How long is the object?

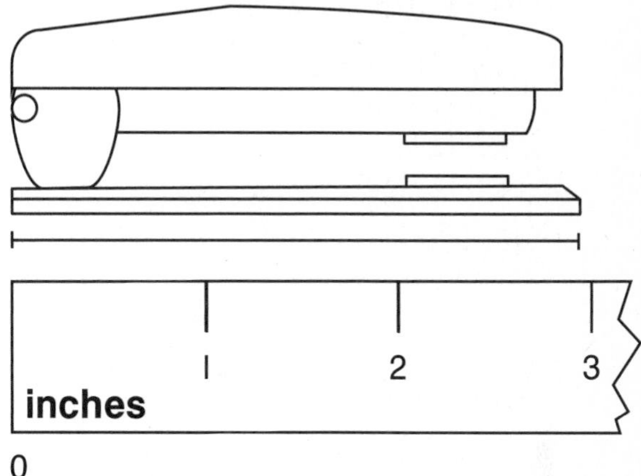

A about 2 inches

B about 3 inches

C about 4 inches

D about 5 inches

10. Which shows the crayons in order from longest to shortest?

A

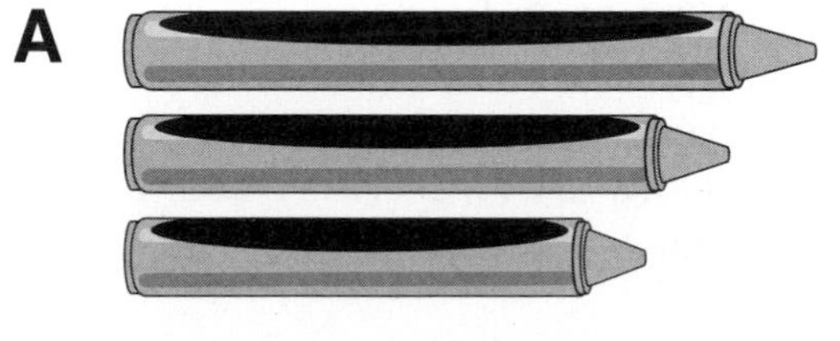

C

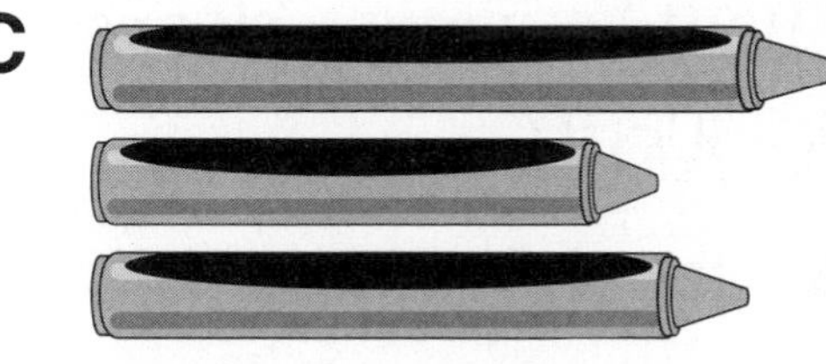

B

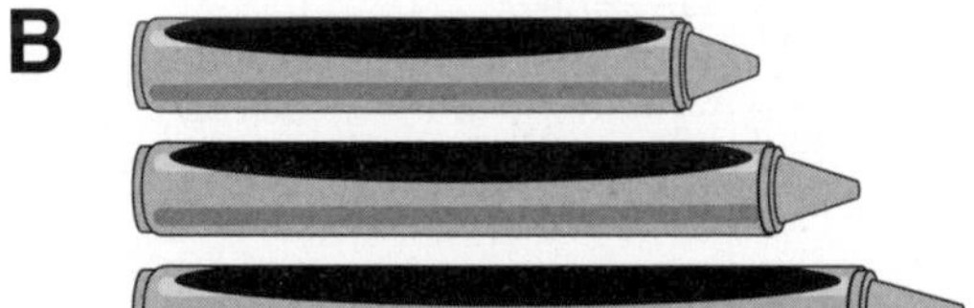

D

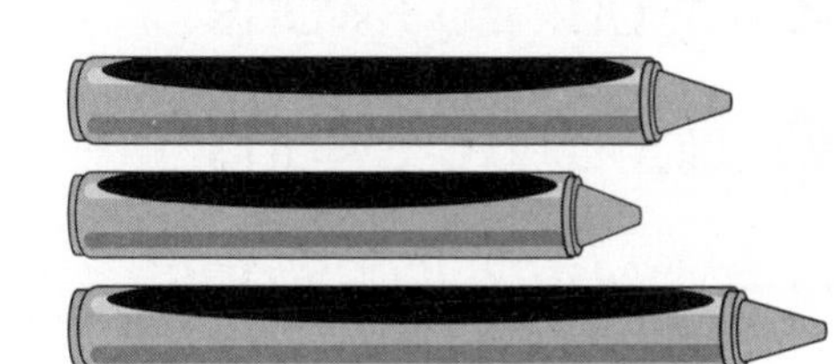

Go On

Name ______________________________

Choose the correct answer.

11. Which tool will you use to measure how warm the hot chocolate is?

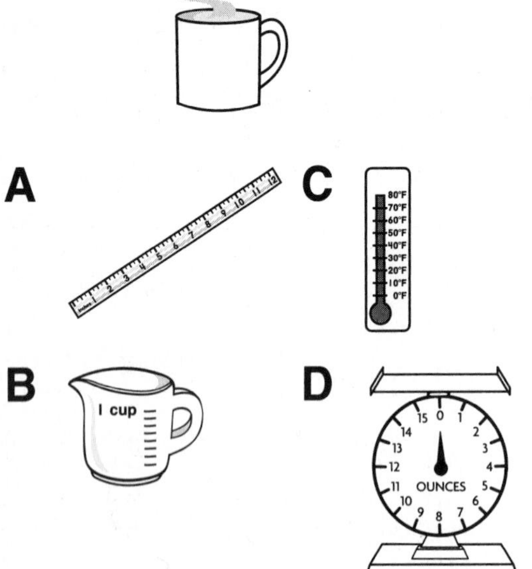

12. What is the sum?

	tens	ones
	3	4
+	2	3

Workmat

tens	ones

A 11

B 47

C 56

D 57

13. 53 ducks and swans are at the pond. 31 are ducks. About how many swans are there?

A about 2 swans

B about 20 swans

C about 80 swans

D about 200 swans

14. How many cups do you need to fill the container to the top?

This container has 1 cup of water in it.

A about 1 cup

B about 2 cups

C about 3 cups

D about 6 cups

Choose the correct answer.

15. How long is the object?

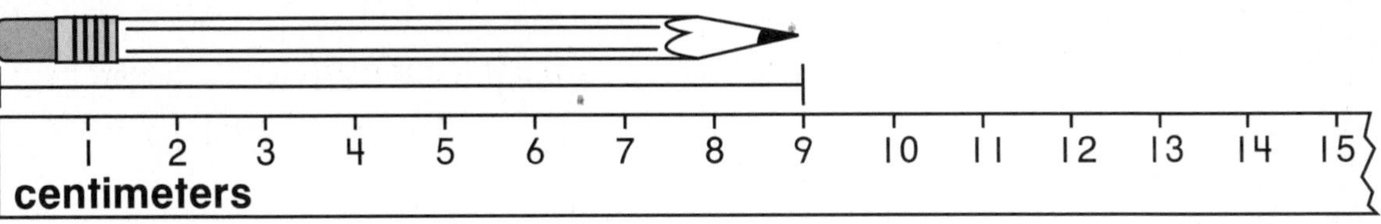

A about 9 centimeters
B about 8 centimeters
C about 7 centimeters
D about 6 centimeters

16. Which object is lightest?

A 

B 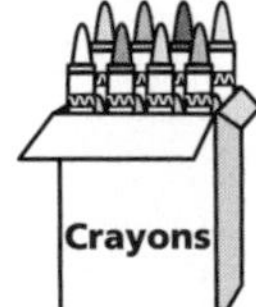

C 

D 

17. What is the difference?

	tens	ones
	2	6
−		3

Workmat: tens | ones

A 24
B 23
C 22
D 13

18. About how many paper clips long is the object?

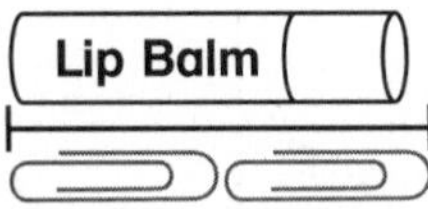

A about 8
B about 6
C about 4
D about 2

Go On

Name ____________________

Choose the correct answer.

19. What is the sum?

40 + 20 = ____

A 20

B 50

C 60

D 70

20. A bird eats 28 seeds. Then it eats 9 more seeds. About how many seeds does the bird eat in all?

A about 4 seeds

B about 20 seeds

C about 40 seeds

D about 400 seeds

21. Which tool will you use to measure how tall the juice box is?

A 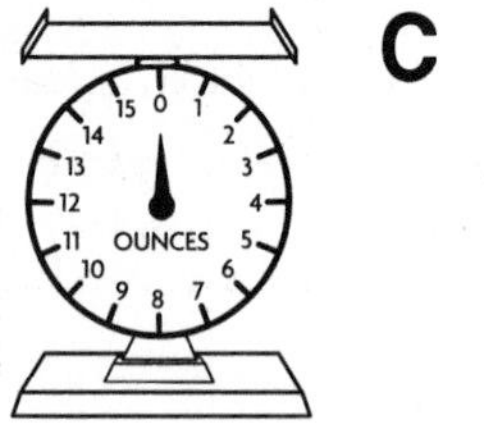

C 

B 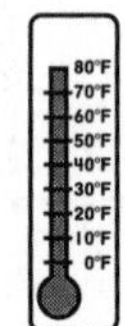

D 

22. What is the temperature?

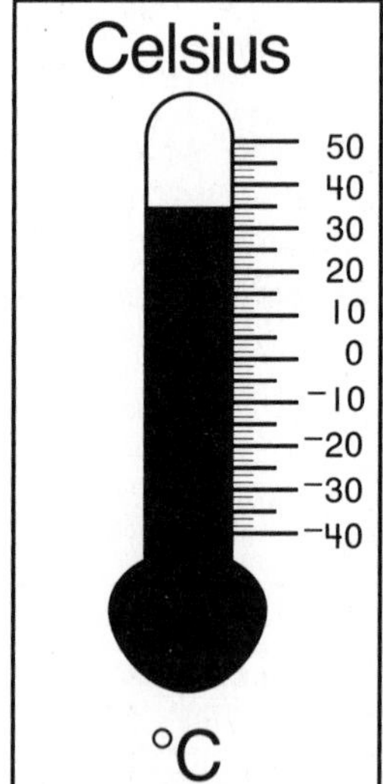

A 35°C

B 30°C

C 25°C

D 15°C

Stop

Name ____________________

Choose the correct answer.

1. What is the temperature?

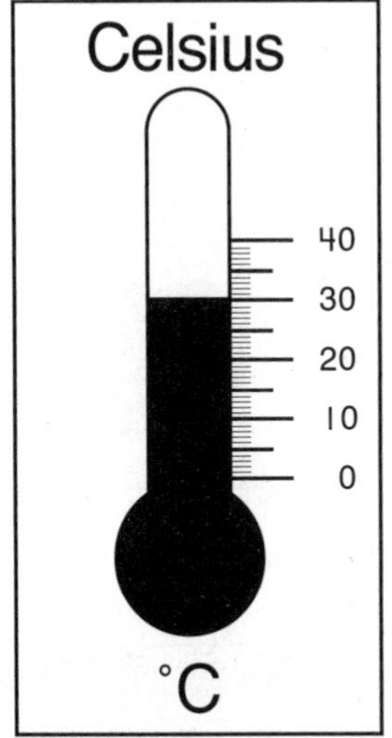

A 3°C
B 13°C
C 30°C
D 35°C

2. How many flat surfaces does the solid figure have?

A 1
B 2
C 3
D 4

3. Use the picture graph to answer question 3.

Sports We Like							
	baseball						
	soccer						
	football						

How many more children chose than ?

A 1 more child
B 2 more children
C 3 more children
D 5 more children

Go On

Choose the correct answer.

4. Which belongs in the group?

A 

B 

C 

D 

5. What is the sum?

$60 + 20 =$ ____

A 40

B 70

C 80

D 90

6. Which tells how many?

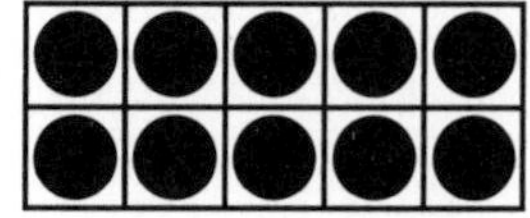 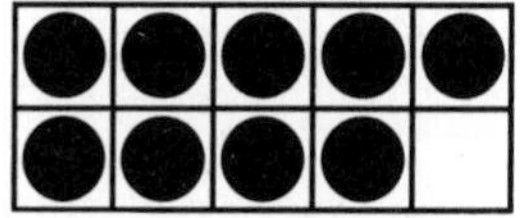

A nineteen

B eighteen

C sixteen

D fourteen

7. Which shows a pair of related subtraction facts?

A $\begin{array}{r}12\\-\ 4\\\hline 8\end{array}$ $\begin{array}{r}8\\-4\\\hline 4\end{array}$

B $\begin{array}{r}11\\-\ 3\\\hline 8\end{array}$ $\begin{array}{r}11\\-\ 8\\\hline 3\end{array}$

C $\begin{array}{r}10\\-\ 3\\\hline 7\end{array}$ $\begin{array}{r}11\\-\ 4\\\hline 7\end{array}$

D $\begin{array}{r}12\\-\ 5\\\hline 7\end{array}$ $\begin{array}{r}12\\-\ 6\\\hline 6\end{array}$

Go On

Choose the correct answer.

8. Which type of move is shown?

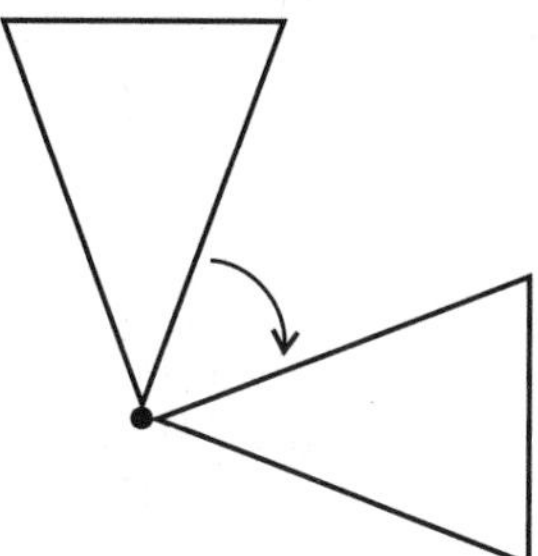

A flip

B slide

C turn

D symmetry

9. Which tool will you use to measure how tall the can is?

A

C

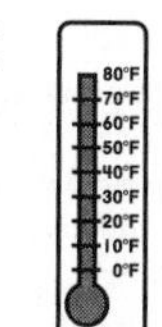

B

D

10. How many fewer bees are there than flowers?

$$\begin{array}{r} 11 \\ -\ 4 \\ \hline \end{array}$$

A 15 fewer bees

B 7 fewer bees

C 6 fewer bees

D 4 fewer bees

Go On

Name ______________________ END OF YEAR TEST

Choose the correct answer.

11. Use the tally chart to answer the question.

Snacks We Like	
cheese	III
yogurt	卌 I
pretzels	卌 III

How many children chose yogurt?

A 3 children

B 6 children

C 8 children

D 9 children

12. What time does the clock show?

A 1:00

B 12:30

C 1:30

D 12:00

13. Which symbol can you use to compare the amounts?

   |  

_____¢ ◯ _____¢

A < **B** > **C** =

Go On

Name ______________________________

Choose the correct answer.

14. Which number is missing?

8 5 3 8 5 ? 8 5 3

A 3 **B** 5 **C** 6 **D** 8

15. How many sides does the plane figure have?

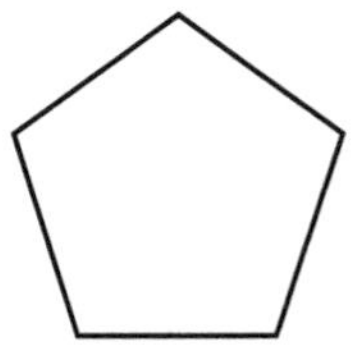

A 4

B 5

C 6

D 7

16. Count how many tens and ones. Which shows the number in a different way?

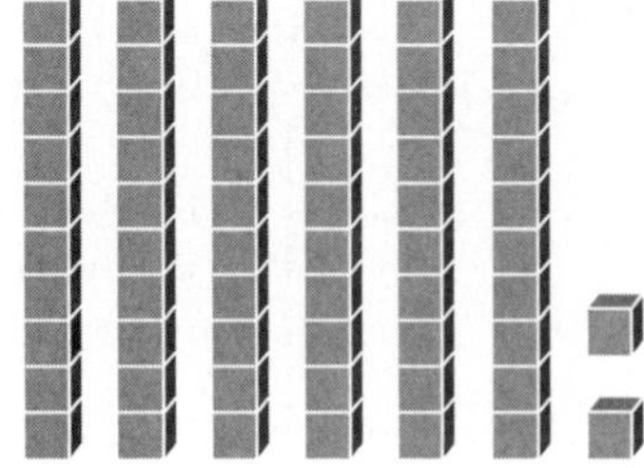

A 6 + 2

B 20 + 6

C 60 + 20

D 60 + 2

17. What is the difference?

$$\begin{array}{r} 12 \\ -\ 3 \\ \hline \end{array}$$

A 15 **C** 9

B 10 **D** 8

18. Which number is just after 36?

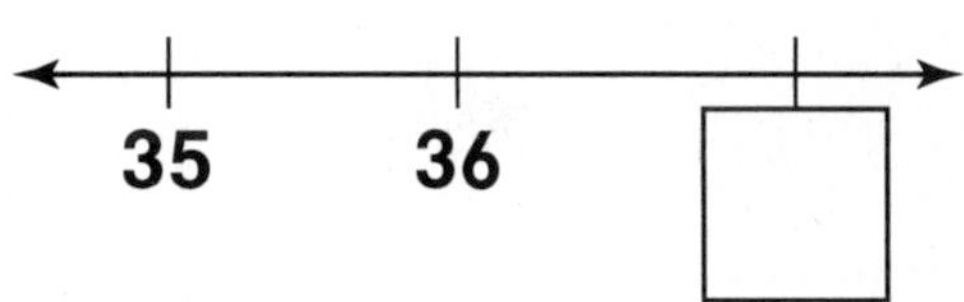

A 30 **C** 37

B 34 **D** 40

Go On

Name ____________________

Choose the correct answer.

19. Which comes next?

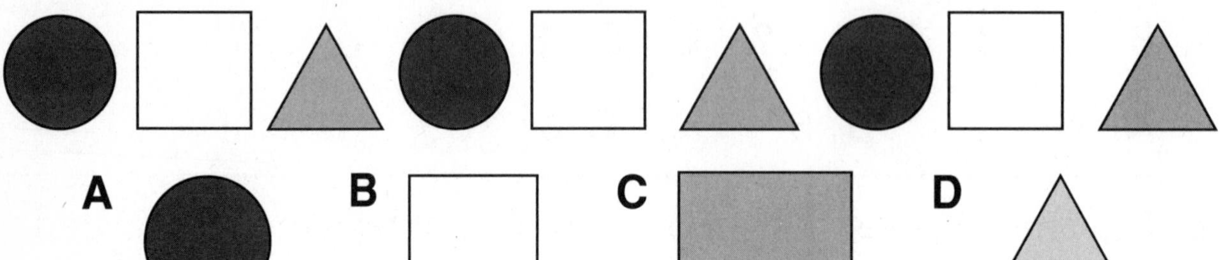

20. Which figure is a triangle?

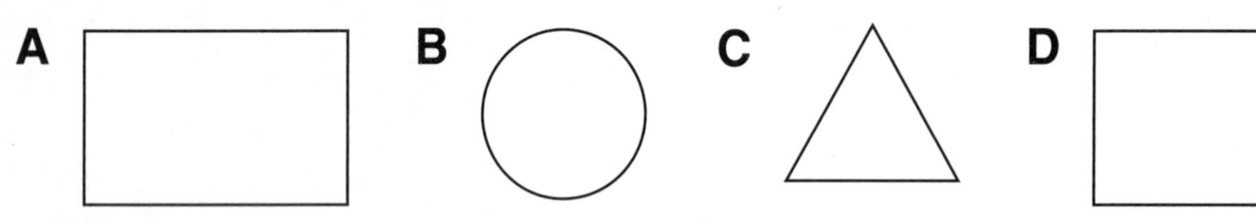

21. About how many paper clips long is the object?

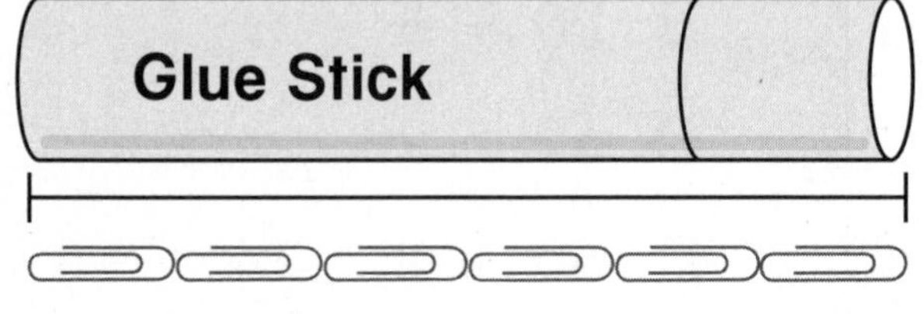

A about 5 paper clips

B about 6 paper clips

C about 7 paper clips

D about 8 paper clips

22. What is the sum?

$$\begin{array}{r} 8 \\ +2 \\ \hline \end{array}$$

A 6

B 7

C 9

D 10

23. What is the difference?

$$\begin{array}{r} 8 \\ -2 \\ \hline \end{array}$$

A 5

B 6

C 7

D 10

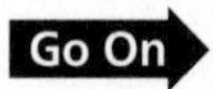

Name ________________________

Choose the correct answer.

24. Which figure belongs in group B?

A

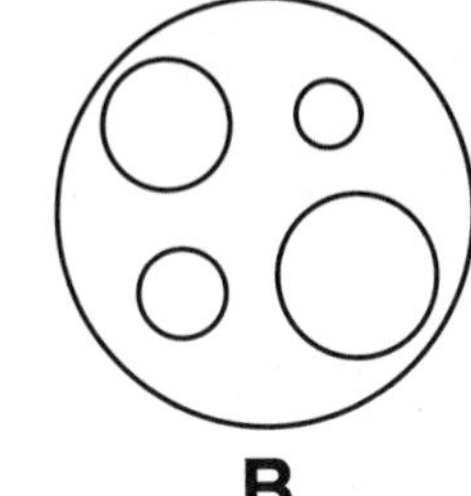
B

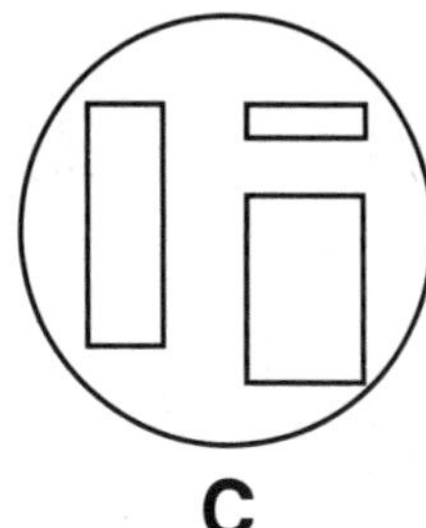
C

A 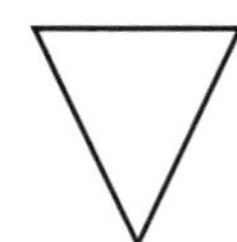 **B** 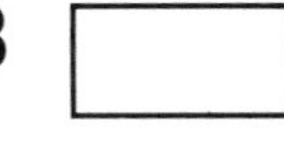 **C** 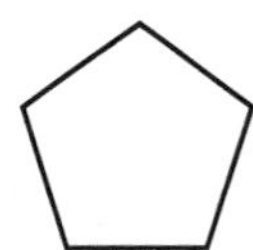 **D** 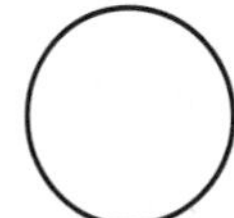

25. From **Start**, go right 3. Go down 1. Go left 2. Where are you?

A seal **B** lion **C** monkey

26. What is the sum?

$$\begin{array}{r} 8 \\ +4 \\ \hline \end{array}$$

A 14 **C** 12

B 13 **D** 4

27. Which is a related subtraction fact?

$5 + 3 = 8$

A $8 - 3 = 5$

B $12 - 4 = 8$

C $5 - 3 = 2$

Go On

Name ____________________

Choose the correct answer.

28. From which box is it **certain** to pull a black cube?

A 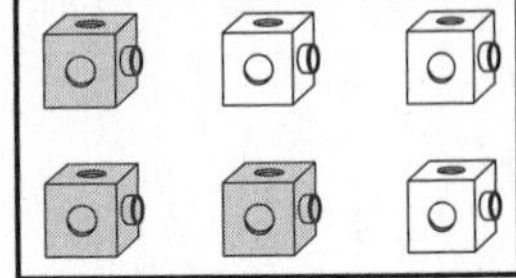

C 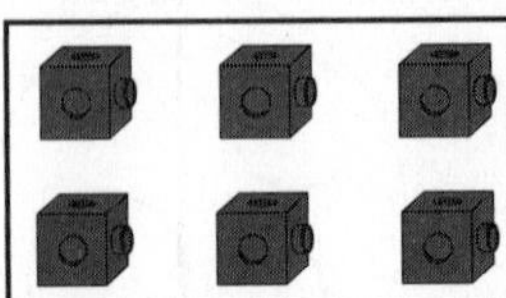

B 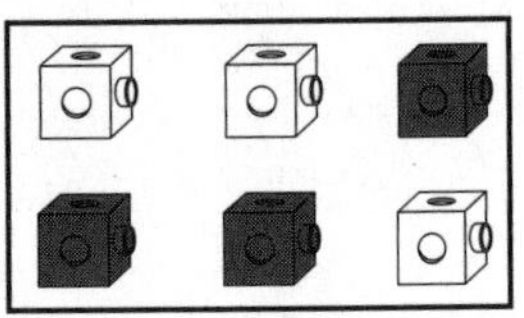

D 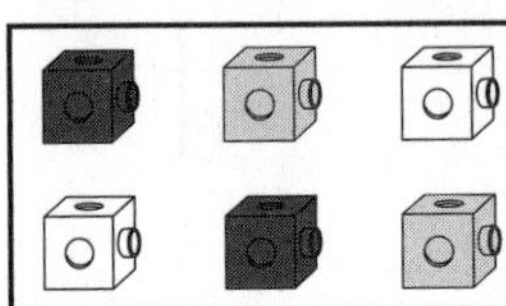

29. Which object is lightest?

A 

B 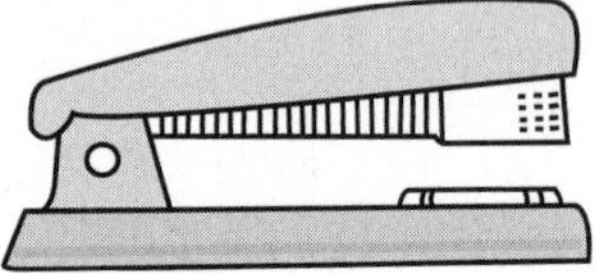

C 

D 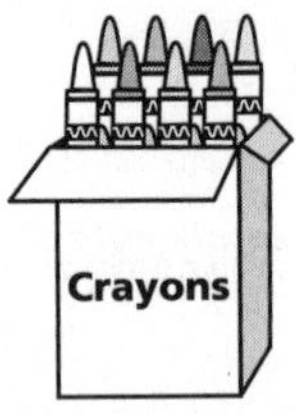

30. What is the difference?

	tens	ones
	3	4
−	1	2

tens	ones

A 12

B 22

C 32

D 46

Go On

Choose the correct answer.

31. What is the time of day?

A morning

B afternoon

C evening

32. How many in all?

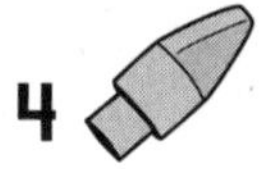

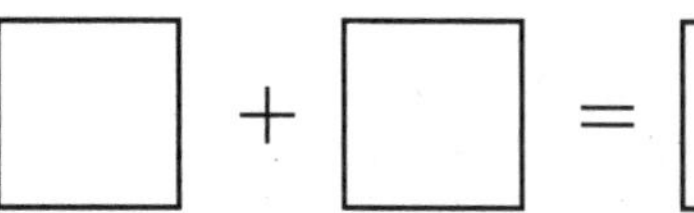

part part whole

A 7 in all

B 6 in all

C 5 in all

D 1 in all

33. Which solid figure has only a curved surface?

A 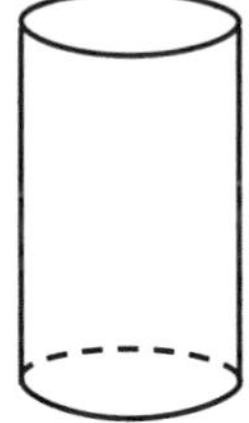

B 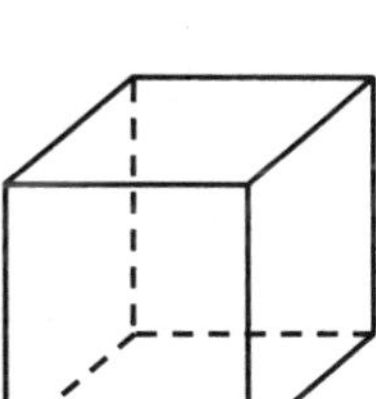

C 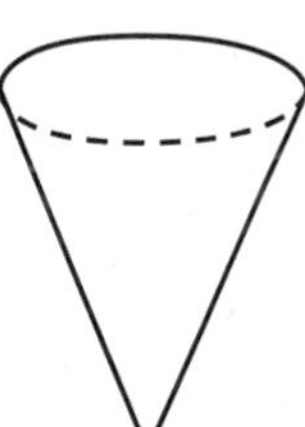

D 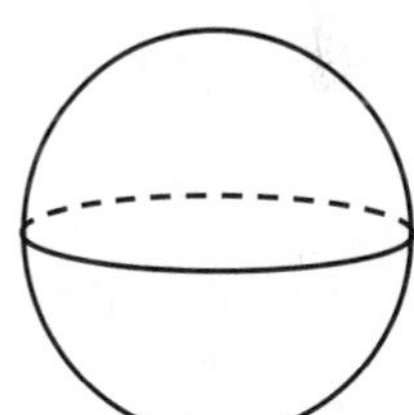

34. Which comes next?

A 

B 

C 

D

Go On

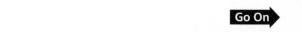

Name

Choose the correct answer.

Use the bar graph to answer questions 36 and 37.

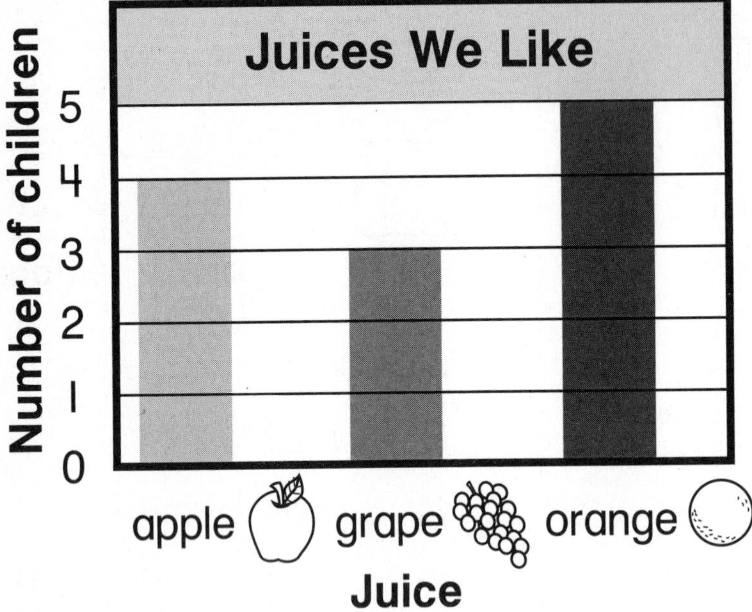

35. Which juice did the most children choose?

A  **B**  **C** 

36. How many children chose grape?

A 3 children **B** 4 children **C** 5 children **D** 6 children

37. Which clock matches the time shown?

A  **B**  **C**  **D** 

Go On

Name ______________________________

Choose the correct answer.

38. Which figures show the same pattern?

39. About how many pounds is the object?

A about 1 pound

B about 10 pounds

C about 50 pounds

D about 100 pounds

40. Which shows $\frac{1}{3}$ shaded?

A

B

C

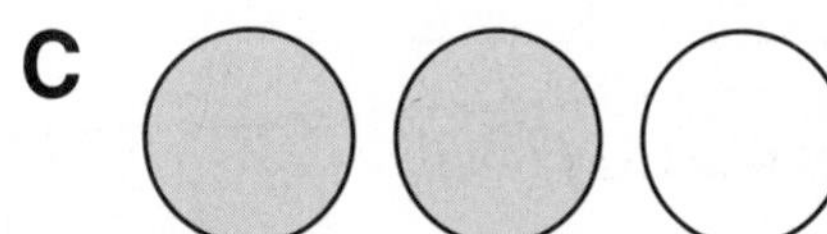

D

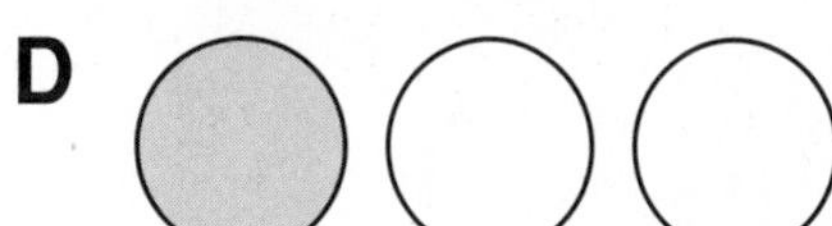

Go On

Choose the correct answer.

41. Which shows a line of symmetry?

A 
B 
C 
D 

42. Which bear are you more likely to pull from the ?

A 

B 

C 

43. How long is the object?

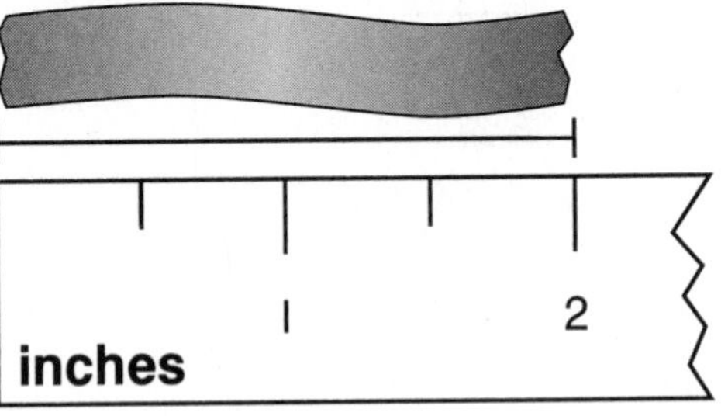

A about 1 inch

B about 2 inches

C about 3 inches

D about 30 inches

44. Which symbol can you use to compare the numbers?

83 ◯ 78

A > B < C =

Stop

Name ____________________

Write the correct answer.

1. Write the temperature.

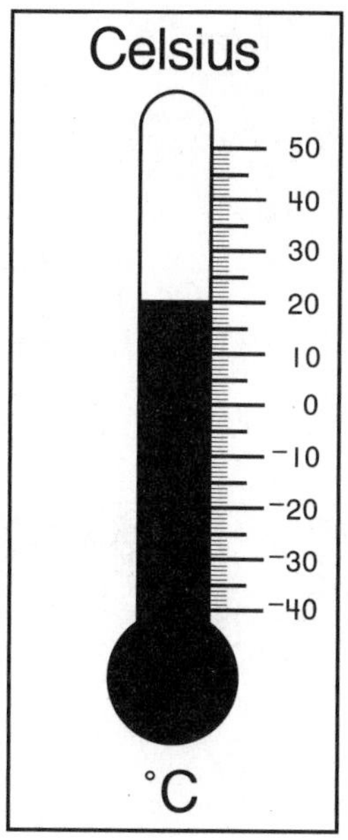

____ °C

2. Write how many corners the solid has.

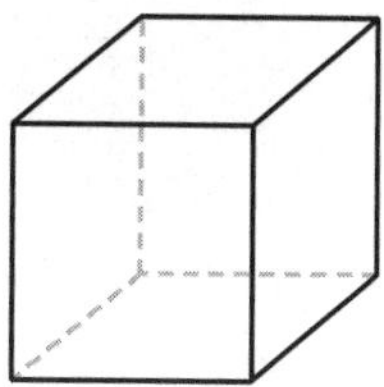

____ corners

3. Use the picture graph to answer question 3.

Snacks We Like								
pretzels								
yogurt								
crackers								

Write how many more children chose yogurt than crackers.

____ more children

Go On

Write the correct answer.

4. Circle which belongs in the group.

     |  

5. What is the sum?

50 + 30 = ____

6. Write the number word that tells how many.

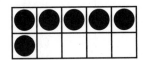

____

7. Circle the pair of related subtraction facts.

$$\begin{array}{r} 10 \\ -\ 3 \\ \hline 7 \end{array} \quad \begin{array}{r} 11 \\ -\ 4 \\ \hline 7 \end{array} \qquad \begin{array}{r} 11 \\ -\ 7 \\ \hline 4 \end{array} \quad \begin{array}{r} 11 \\ -\ 4 \\ \hline 7 \end{array} \qquad \begin{array}{r} 12 \\ -\ 3 \\ \hline 9 \end{array} \quad \begin{array}{r} 12 \\ -\ 5 \\ \hline 7 \end{array} \qquad \begin{array}{r} 10 \\ -\ 4 \\ \hline 6 \end{array} \quad \begin{array}{r} 6 \\ -4 \\ \hline 2 \end{array}$$

Go On

Write the correct answer.

8. Circle slide, flip, or turn to name the move.

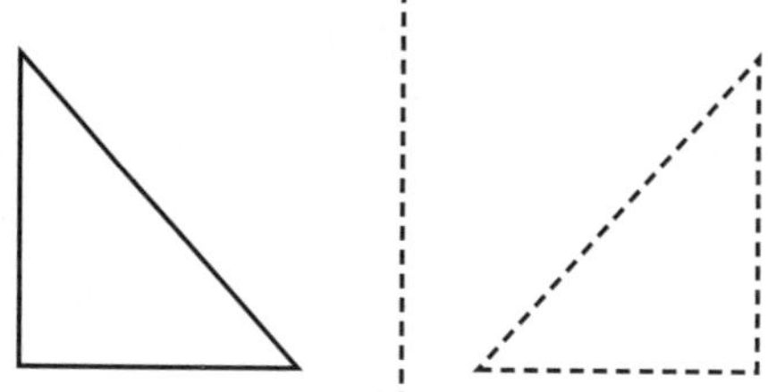

slide **flip** **turn**

9. Circle which tool you will use to measure how warm the water is.

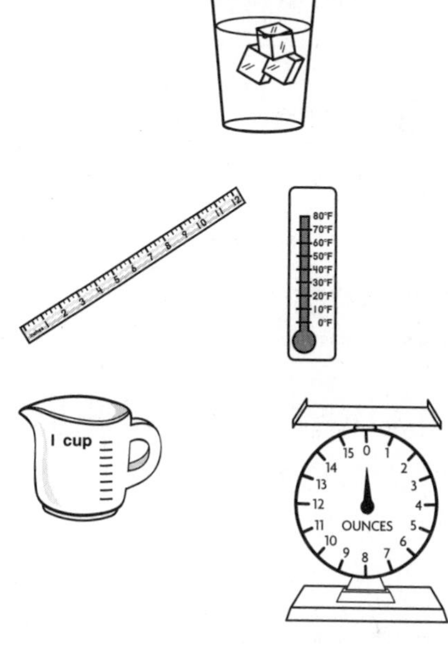

10. Write how more leaves there are than birds.

$$\begin{array}{r} 10 \\ -\ 3 \\ \hline \end{array}$$

______ more leaves

Go On

Write the correct answer.

11. Use the tally chart to answer the question.

Places We Like	
city	𝍸 II
park	IIII
mountains	𝍸

Write how many children chose the city.

_____ children

12. Write the time.

13. Count. Compare the amounts. Write <, >, or =.

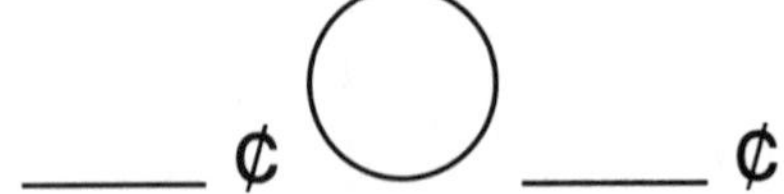

____ ¢ ◯ ____ ¢

Go On

Name ______________________

Write the correct answer.

14. Write the missing number.

2 4 1 2 4 ____ 2 4 1

15. Write how many sides this plane figure has.

______ sides

16. Count how many tens and ones. Write the number in a different way.

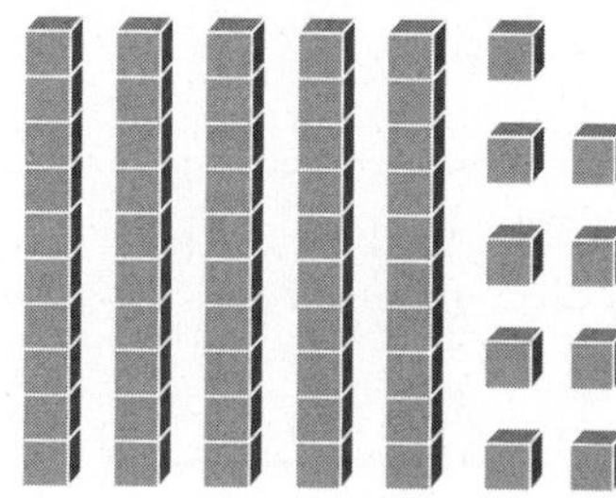

______ tens ______ ones

______ + ______

17. Write the difference.

$$\begin{array}{r} 12 \\ -\ 4 \\ \hline \end{array}$$

18. Write the number between 62 and 64.

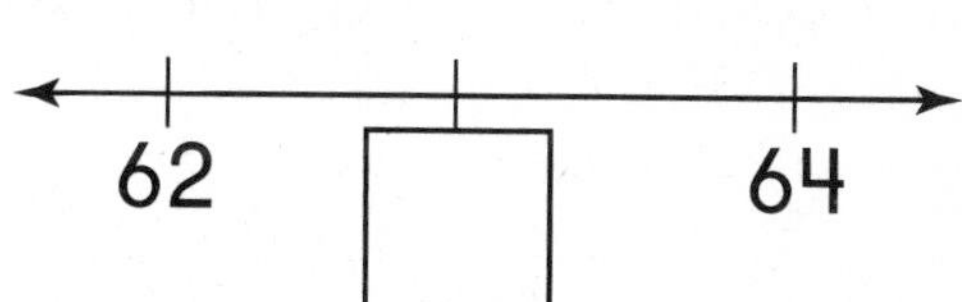

Go On

Name ______________________________

Write the correct answer.

19. Draw and color what comes next.

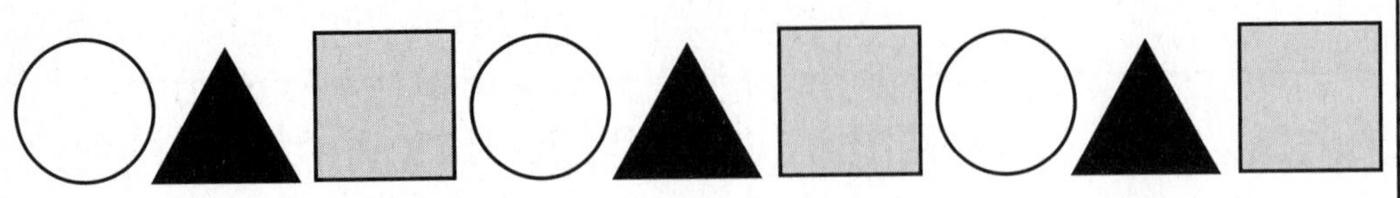

20. Color the circle RED.

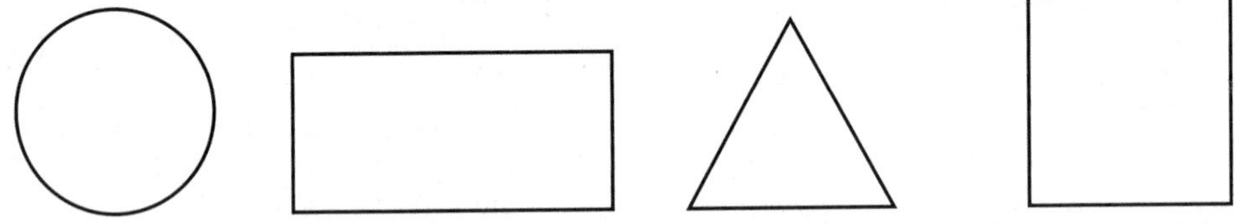

21. Write about how many paper clips long the object is.

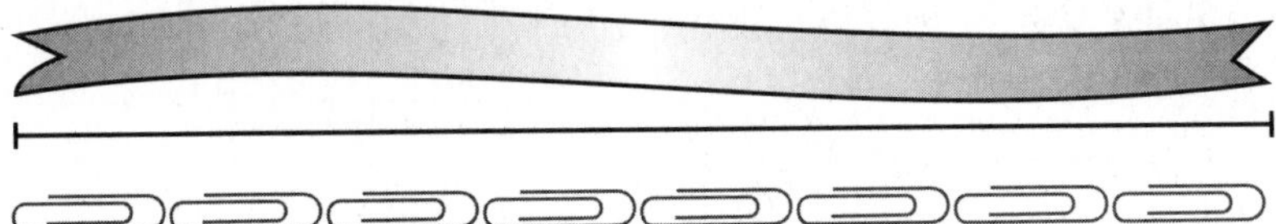

about ____ paper clips

22. Count on. Write the sum.

$$\begin{array}{r} 7 \\ +2 \\ \hline \end{array}$$

23. Write the difference.

$$\begin{array}{r} 6 \\ -4 \\ \hline \end{array}$$

Go On

Write the correct answer.

24. Write A, B, or C to show the group the figure belongs in.

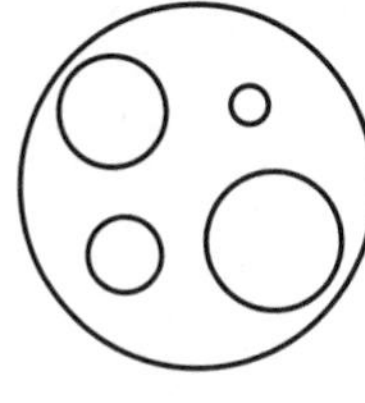

A B C

☐ ____

25. From **Start**, go right 3. Go down 2. Go left 1.
Write where you are.

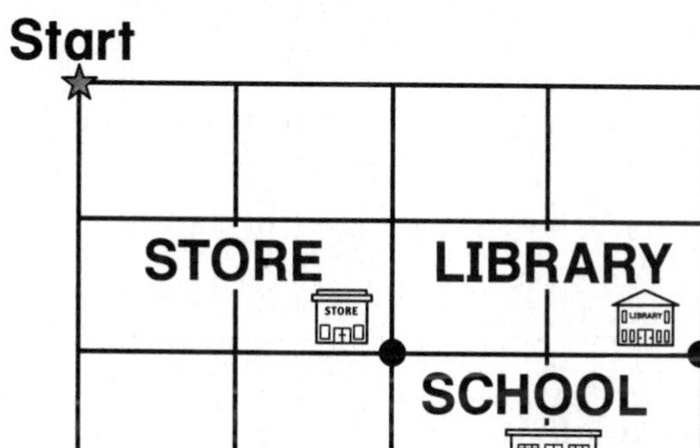

____

26. Write the sum.

$$\begin{array}{r} 9 \\ +3 \\ \hline \end{array}$$

27. Write a related subtraction fact.

4 + 2 = 6

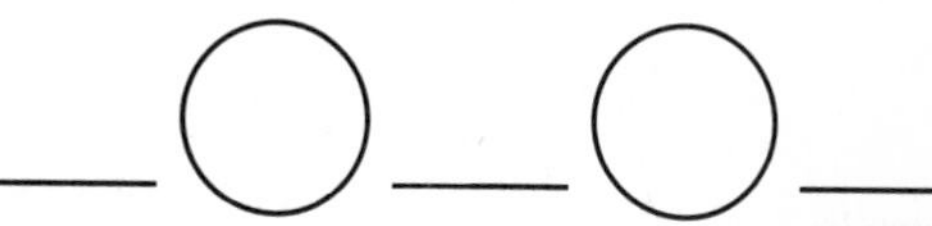

Go On

Name ______________________

Write the correct answer.

28. Color the cubes to make the sentence true.
It is **impossible** to pull a white cube.

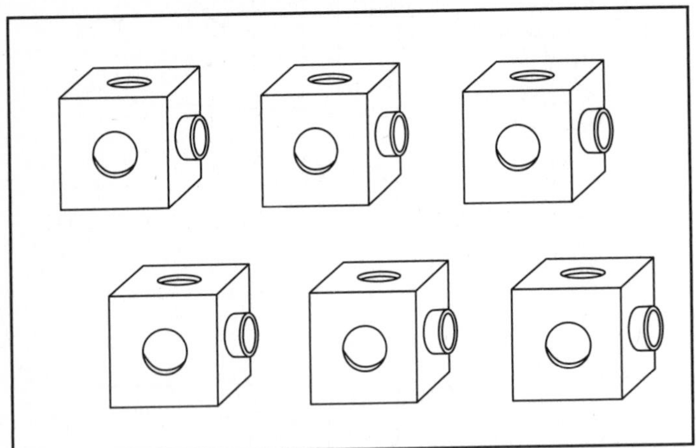

29. Circle the heaviest object.

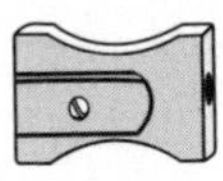

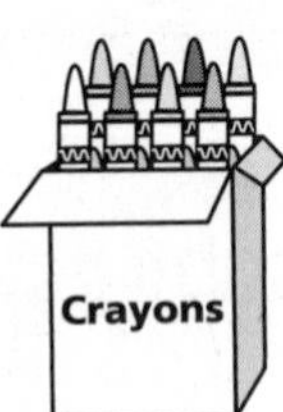

30. Write the difference.

	tens	ones
	3	6
−	1	2

Workmat

tens	ones

____

Go On

Name ______________________________

Write the correct answer.

31. Circle the time of day.

morning

afternoon

evening

32. Write how many in all.

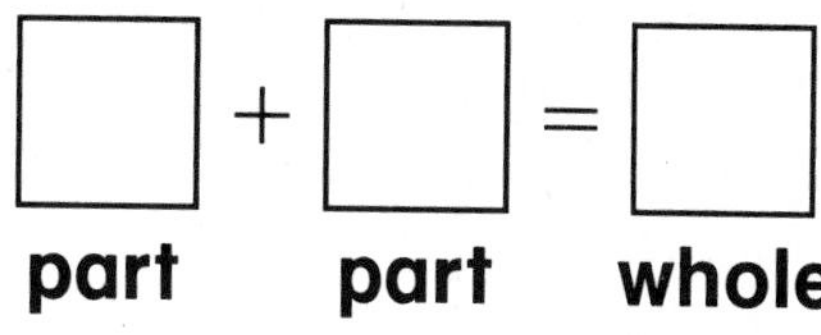

_____ in all

33. Circle the solid figure that has flat and curved surfaces.

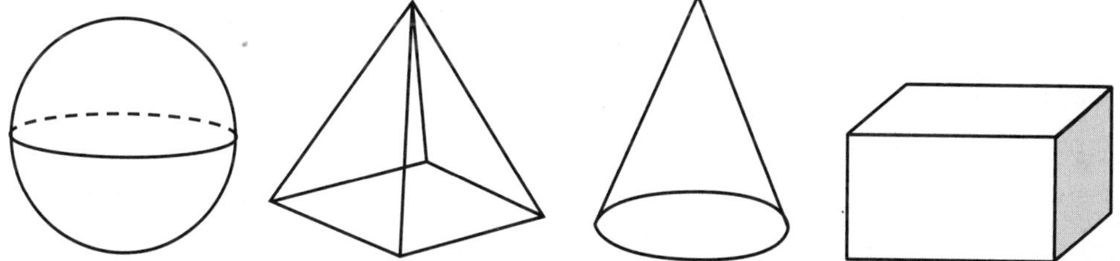

34. Circle which comes next.

Go On

Name ____________________

Write the correct answer.

Use the bar graph to answer questions 35 and 36.

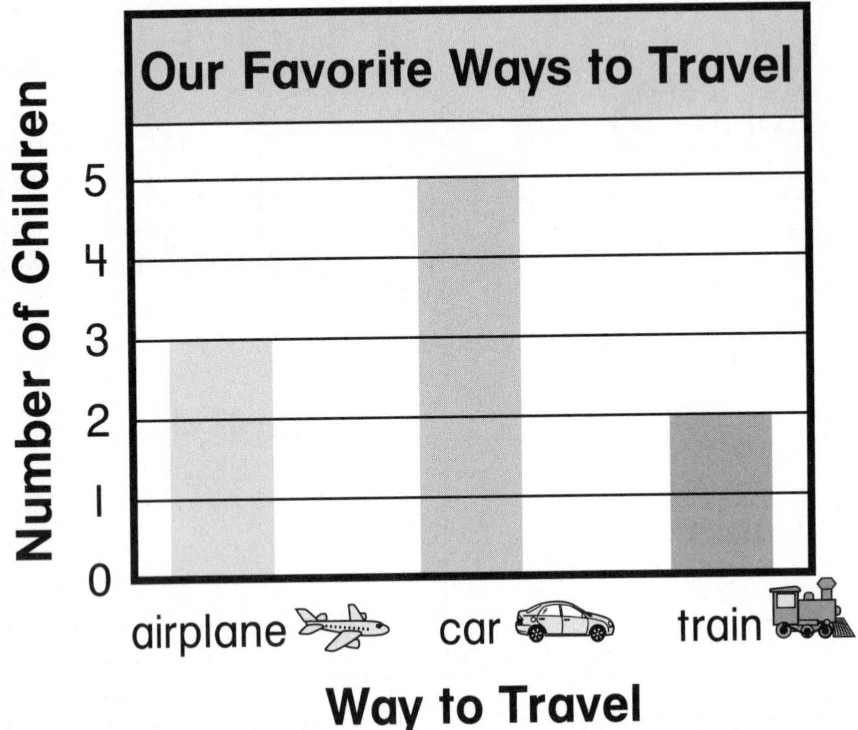

35. Circle the way of travel the most children chose.

36. Write how many children chose airplane.

_____ children

37. Draw the hour hand and minute hand to show the time.

Name ______________________________

Write the correct answer.

38. Use figures to show the same pattern.
Draw the figures.

39. Circle the better estimate.

about 1 pound

about 10 pounds

40. Use BLUE.

Color to show $\frac{1}{3}$. Complete the sentence.

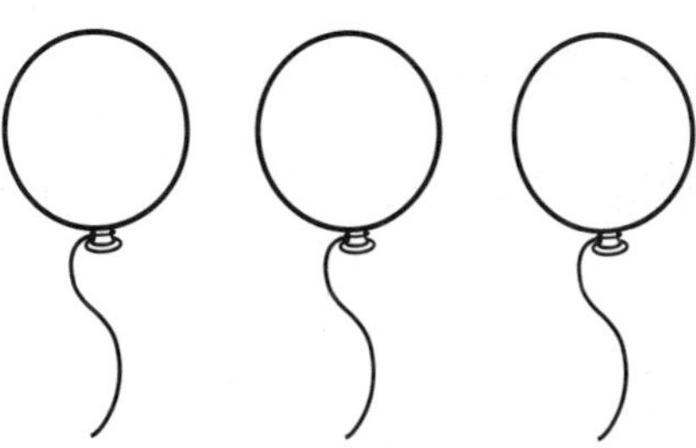

_____ out of _____ is blue.

Go On

Write the correct answer.

41. Draw a line of symmetry.

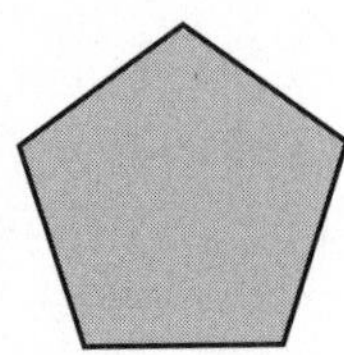

42. Circle which bear are you more likely to pull from the bowl.

43. Measure the object. Write the length.

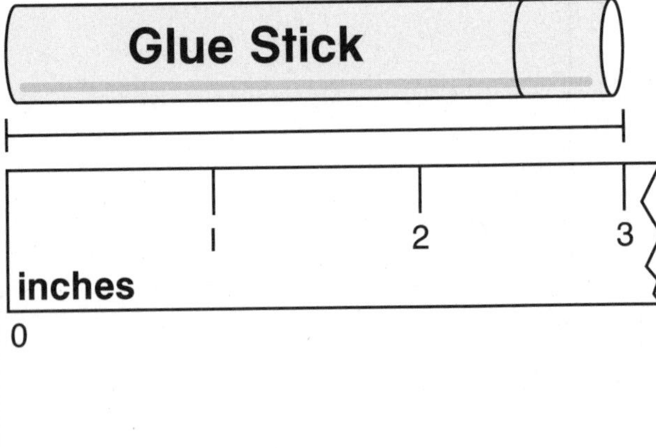

about _____ inches

44. Compare the numbers. Write $<$, $>$, or $=$.

72 ◯ 74

Stop

Name ____________________

Write the correct answer.

1. Write the numbers in order from least to greatest.

12, 10, 15

____ ____ ____

2. Write the difference.

8 − 0 = ____

3. Circle the addition sentences that use the same addends.

1 + 8 = 9

5 + 4 = 9

2 + 7 = 9

4 + 5 = 9

4. Write the number sentence.

There are 5 oranges.
Casey takes 3 oranges away.
How many oranges are left?

____ oranges

5. Write **is greater than** or **is less than** to make the sentence true.

12 ____________________ 13.

6. Circle the related subtraction fact.

3 + 4 = 7

6 + 2 = 8

7 − 4 = 3

9 − 3 = 6

Go On

Write the correct answer.

7. Use the cube below. Draw lines to match. There are 6 black cats and 3 white cats. How many fewer white cats are there?

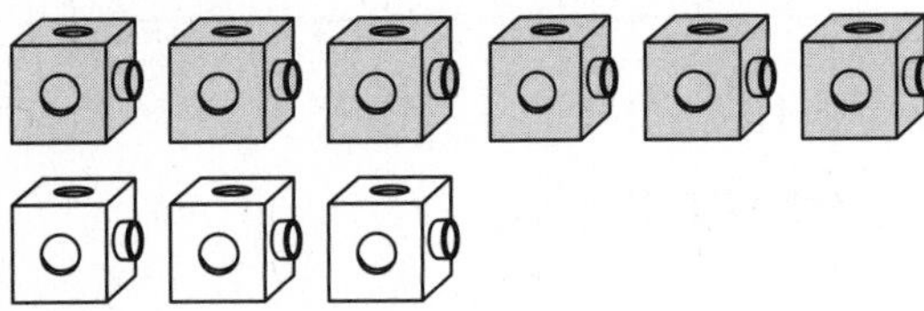

_____ white cats

8. Write a number sentence to match the picture.

_____ ◯ _____ ◯ _____

9. Draw circles to show each number. Write the sum.

0 + 7 = _____

10. Complete the subtraction sentence.

9	−	3	=	
whole		**part**		**part**

Go On

Write the correct answer.

11. Circle a way to make 7.

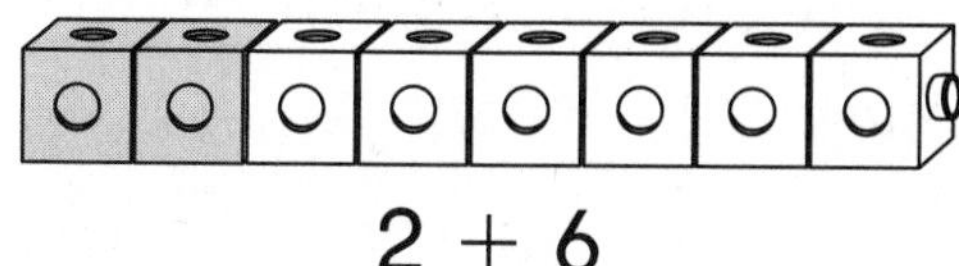

2 + 6

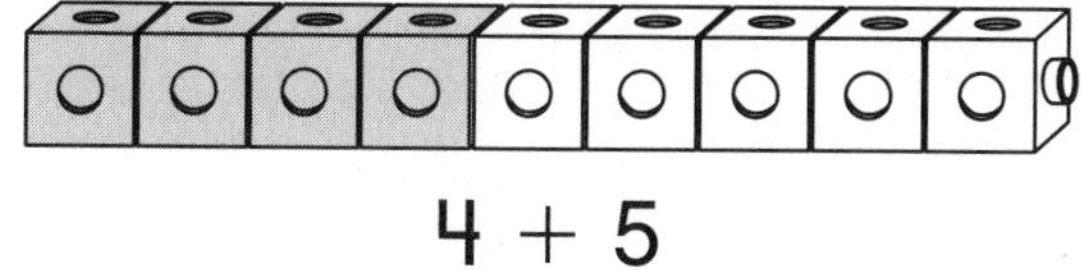

4 + 5

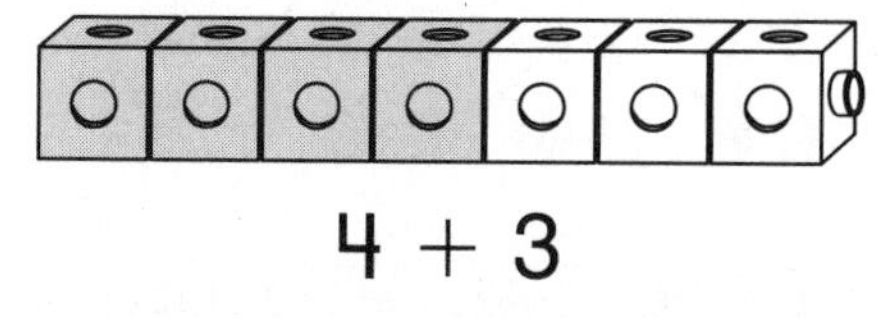

4 + 3

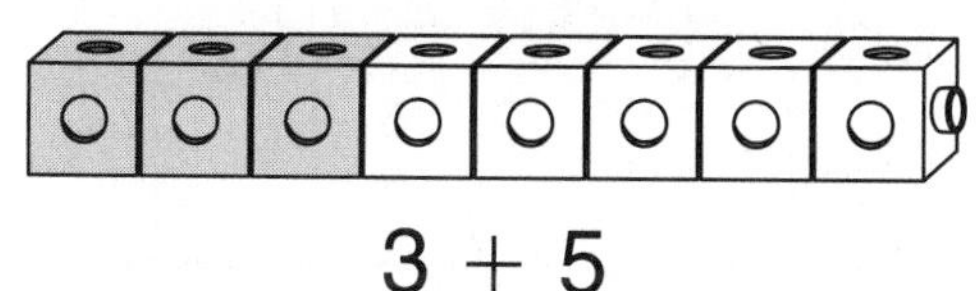

3 + 5

12. Draw lines to match. Which shows how many more ?

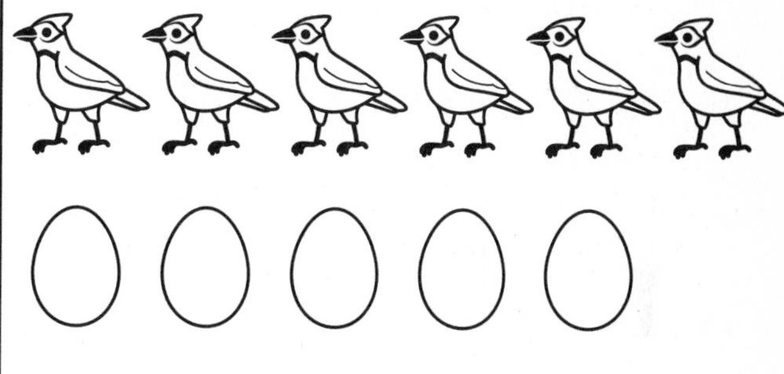

____ fewer

13. How many mice are left?

4 mice **2 mice run away**

____ mice are left

14. Use the picture to write the addition sentence.

____ ◯ ____ ◯ ____

Go On

Name ______________________

Write the correct answer.

15. Add. Then subtract.

8 + 2 = ____

10 − 2 = ____

16. Circle a way to show 5.

five

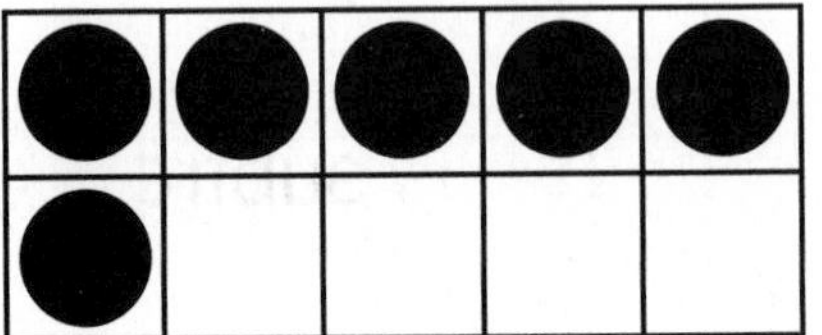

17. Circle the fifth lamb.

Go On

Name ____________________

Write the correct answer.

18. How many birds are there in all?

____

19. Write the sum.

$$\begin{array}{r} 1 \\ +6 \\ \hline \end{array}$$

____

20. Use the cube below. Complete the subtraction sentence.

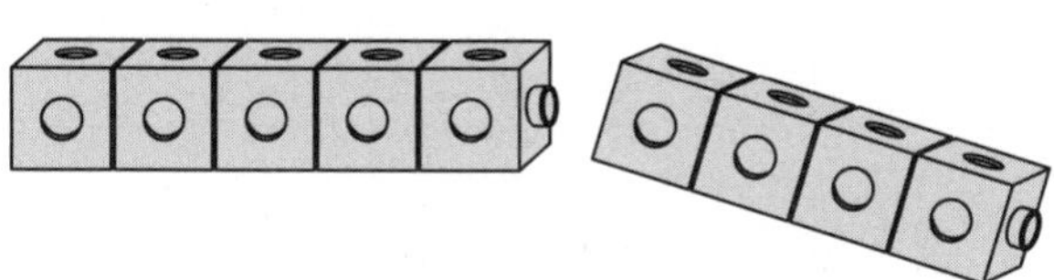

9 − ____ = ____

21. Write a number sentence.

Addie has 2 red crayons. She has the same number of green crayons. How many crayons does Addie have in all?

____ + ____ = ____

____ crayons

Go On

Name ____________________

Write the correct answer.

22. Write the difference.

$$\begin{array}{r} 9 \\ -2 \\ \hline \end{array}$$

____

23. Circle the number word that tells how many.

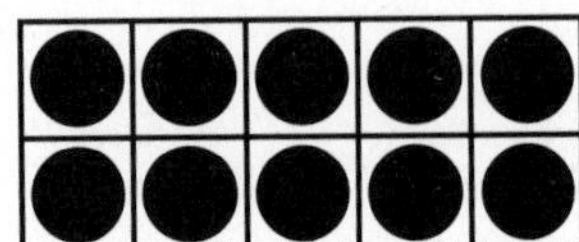
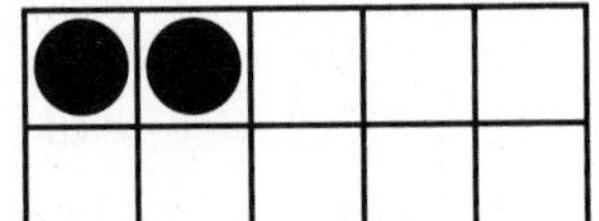

twelve thirteen

24. Write how many in all.

5 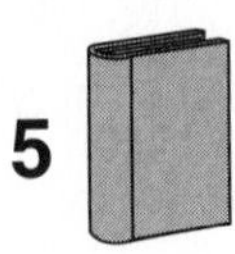 2 

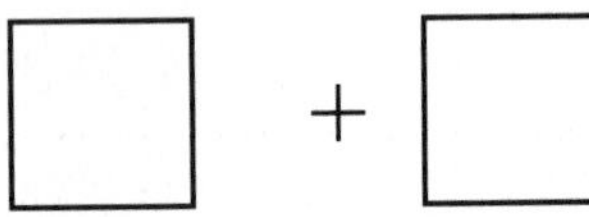

part + part = whole

____  in all

25. Draw lines to match. Write how many fewer ?

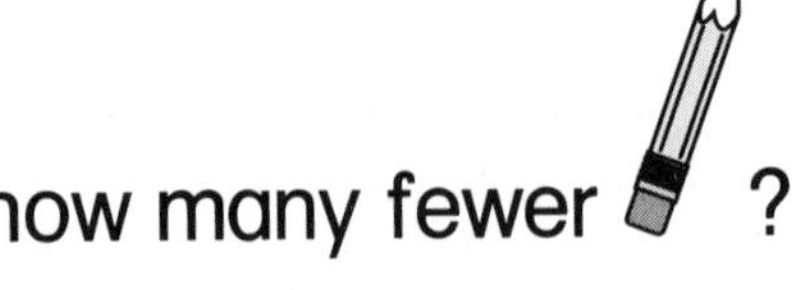

8 − 4 = ____

____ fewer

Stop

Name ______________________________

Write the correct answer.

1. Write the doubles fact.

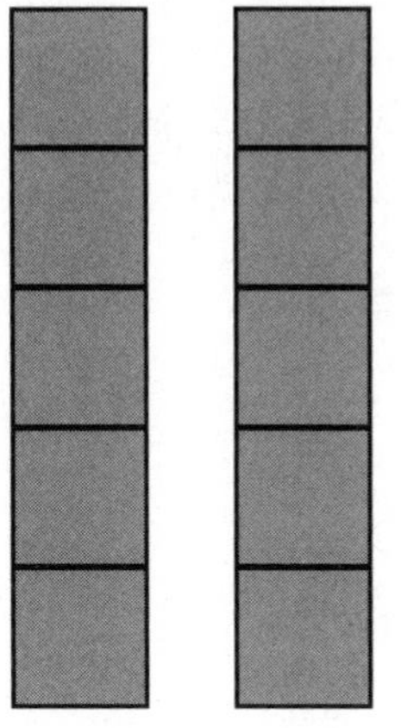

2. Draw a picture to solve. There are 7 prairie dogs. Some prairie dogs go underground. There are 3 prairie dogs left. How many prairie dogs went underground?

____ prairie dogs

3. Follow the rule to complete the table.

Subtract 3	
8	5
7	
6	3

4. Write the numbers in the fact family.

$2 + 3 = 5$ $5 - 3 = 2$

$3 + 2 = 5$ $5 - 2 = 3$

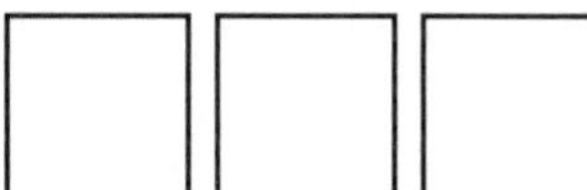

Go On

Name ____________________

Write the correct answer.

Use the number line to answer questions 5 and 6.

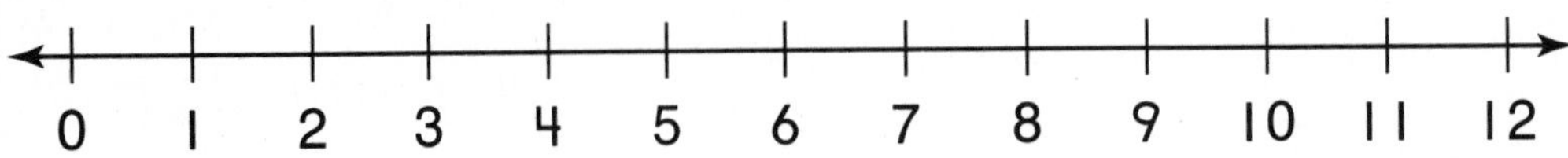

5. What is the sum?

$$\begin{array}{r} 5 \\ +3 \\ \hline \end{array}$$

6. What is the sum?

$$\begin{array}{r} 7 \\ +2 \\ \hline \end{array}$$

7. What is the difference?

$$\begin{array}{r} 11 \\ -\ 7 \\ \hline \end{array}$$

8. Use [cube] and [cube] to add.

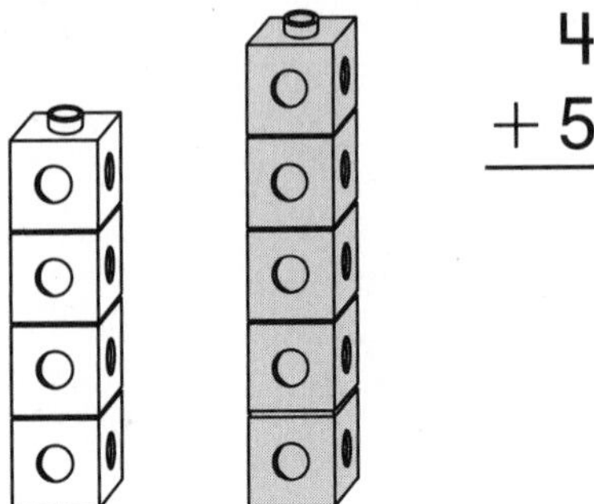

$$\begin{array}{r} 4 \\ +5 \\ \hline \end{array}$$

9. Circle the pair of related subtraction facts.

$$\begin{array}{r} 7 \\ -3 \\ \hline 4 \end{array} \quad \begin{array}{r} 7 \\ -5 \\ \hline 2 \end{array} \qquad \begin{array}{r} 11 \\ -\ 8 \\ \hline 3 \end{array} \quad \begin{array}{r} 11 \\ -\ 3 \\ \hline 8 \end{array} \qquad \begin{array}{r} 11 \\ -\ 4 \\ \hline 7 \end{array} \quad \begin{array}{r} 11 \\ -\ 5 \\ \hline 6 \end{array} \qquad \begin{array}{r} 8 \\ -4 \\ \hline 4 \end{array} \quad \begin{array}{r} 8 \\ -5 \\ \hline 3 \end{array}$$

Go On

Write the correct answer.

10. Count on. Write the sum.

7 + 2 = ____

11. Write a number sentence to match the story.

There are 12 black dogs.
There are 5 white dogs.
How many more black dogs are there than white dogs?

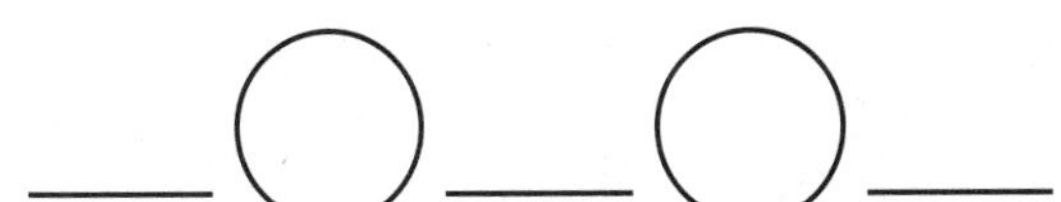

____ black dogs

12. Write the sum. Then write the related addition fact.

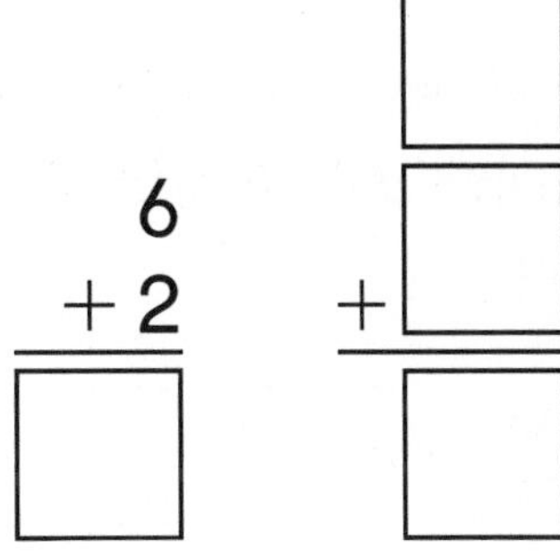

13. Circle the ways to make 9.

10 − 1

5 + 4

10 − 3

5 + 6

14. Count on. Write the sum.

$$\begin{array}{r} 8 \\ +2 \\ \hline \end{array}$$

Go On

Write the correct answer.

Use the number line to answer questions 15 and 16.

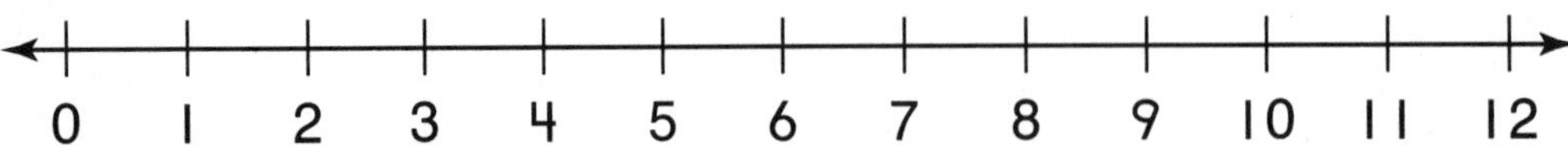

15. Write the difference.

$$\begin{array}{r} 9 \\ -\ 2 \\ \hline \end{array}$$

16. Write the difference.

5 − 3 = ____

17. Follow the rule to complete the table.

Subtract 2	
6	4
5	
4	2

18. Write the doubles plus one fact.

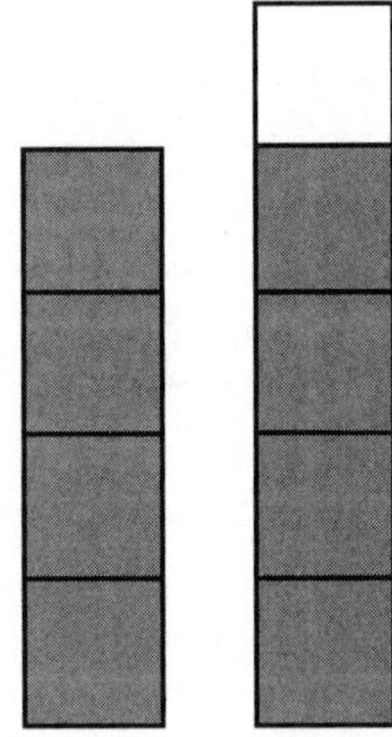

____ ◯ ____ ◯ ____

Go On

Name ______________________

Write the correct answer.

19. Complete the fact family.

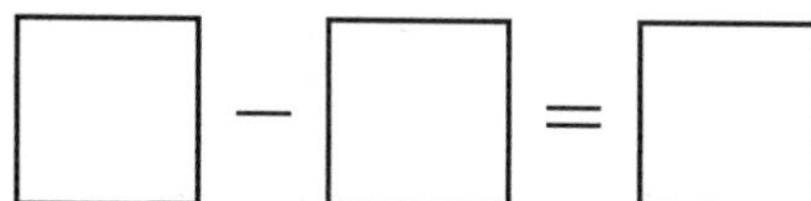

☐ + 5 = 11

5 + 6 = ☐

11 − ☐ = 6

☐ − ☐ = ☐

20. Write the sum.

9 + 1 = ____

21. Write the number sentence that shows how many buttons there are.

____ gray buttons

____ white buttons

22. Write the number sentence that matches the story.

There are 12 grasshoppers. 3 grasshoppers hop away. How many grasshoppers are there now?

____ grasshoppers

Go On

Name ________________________

Write the correct answer.

23. Use 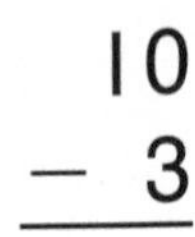 and to subtract.

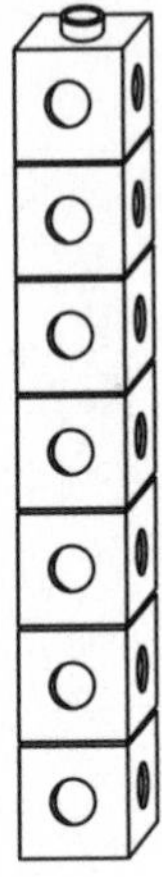

$$\begin{array}{r} 10 \\ -\ 3 \\ \hline \end{array}$$

24. Write the numbers in the fact family.

9 + 2 = 11   11 − 2 = 9

2 + 9 = 11   11 − 9 = 2

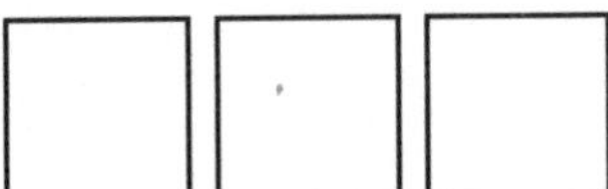

25. There are 10 ants. Some ants walk away. There are 7 ants left. How many ants walked away?

_____ ants

26. There are 8 mittens in all. 3 mittens are blue. The other mittens are yellow. How many mittens are yellow?

_____ mittens

Stop

Name ______________________________

UNIT 3 PRETEST

Write the correct answer.

1. Write the number that is between 38 and 40.

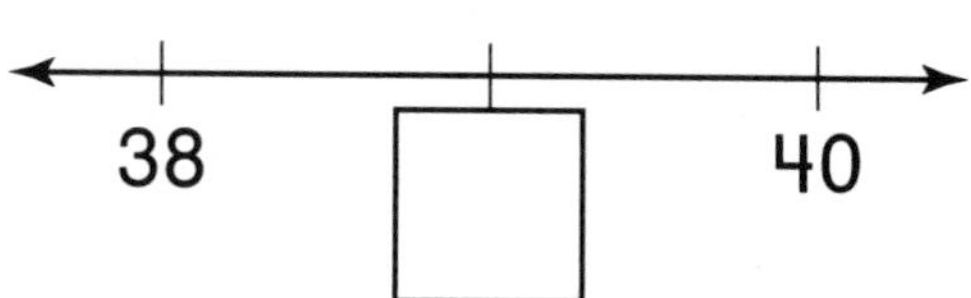

2. Count by tens. Write the number.

3 tens

____

3. Use the tally chart to answer the question.

Drinks We Like	
milk	卌 I
juice	卌 III
water	IIII

Write how many children chose milk.

______ children

4. Count how many tens and ones. Write the number in a different way.

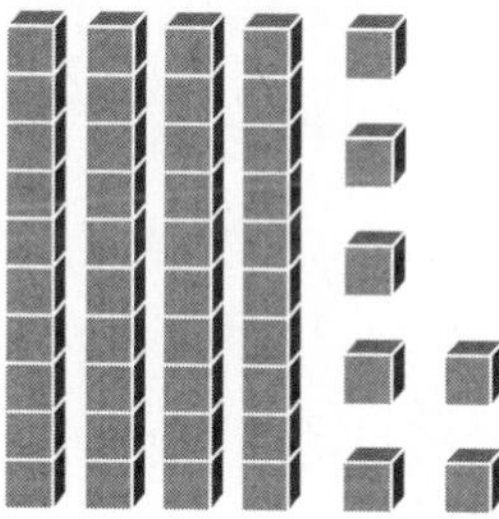

____ tens ____ ones

____ + ____

Go On

Name ____________________

Write the correct answer.

Use the hundred chart for questions 5 and 6.

1	2	3	4	5	6	7	8	9	10
11	12	13	14	15	16	17	18	19	20
21	22	23	24	25	26	27	28	29	30
31	32	33	34	35	36	37	38	39	40
41	42	43	44	45	46	47	48	49	50
51	52	53	54	55	56	57	58	59	60
61	62	63	64	65	66	67	68	69	70
71	72	73	74	75	76	77	78	79	80
81	82	83	84	85	86	87	88	89	90
91	92	93	94	95	96	97	98	99	100

5. Count by twos. Write the number that comes next.

12, 14, 16, 18, 20, ____

6. Count by fives. Write the numbers that come next.

34, 39, 44, ____, ____, ____

Go On

Name ___________________________________ UNIT 3 PRETEST

Write the correct answer.

7. Circle which belongs in the group.

8. Color the cubes to make the sentence true.
It is **impossible** to pull a white cube.

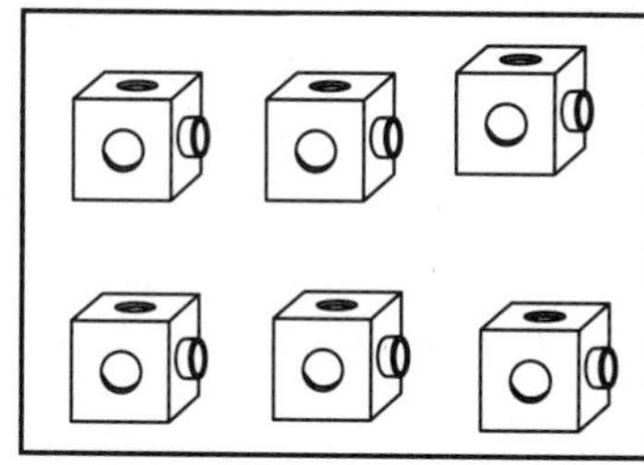

9. There are 5 pencils in a box.
Write how many pencils there are in 7 boxes.

number of boxes	1	2	3	4	5	6	7
number of pencils	5	10					

7 boxes have ____ pencils.

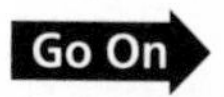

Name ______________________________

Write the correct answer.

10. Write the numbers.

_____ is less than _____.

_____ < _____

11. There are 9 [black cube] and 5 [white cube] in a bag. Circle which color you are more likely to pull.

Use the table to answer questions 12 and 13.

Month	Rainy Days
May	12
June	15
July	10
August	11

12. Write the month that had more rainy days.

_____ ◯ _____
May **June**

____

13. Write the month that had the least number of rainy days.

_____ _____ _____ _____
greatest **least**

____

Go On

Name____________________

Write the correct answer.

14. Write the number of tens and ones.

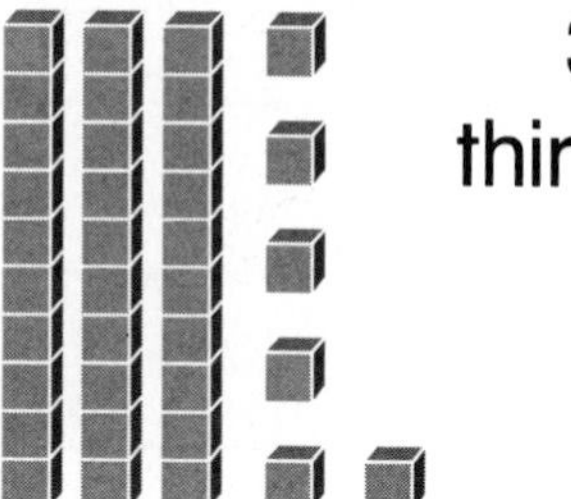

36
thirty-six

____ tens ____ ones

15. Count forward. Write the numbers that come next.

55, 56, 57, ____, ____, ____

16. Compare the numbers. Write $<$, $>$, or $=$.

67 ◯ 61

17. Write the numbers in order from least to greatest.

85 75 83

____ ____ ____

18. Circle even or odd.

18 even odd

Go On

Name ____________________

Write the correct answer.

19. Use the picture graph to answer question 19.

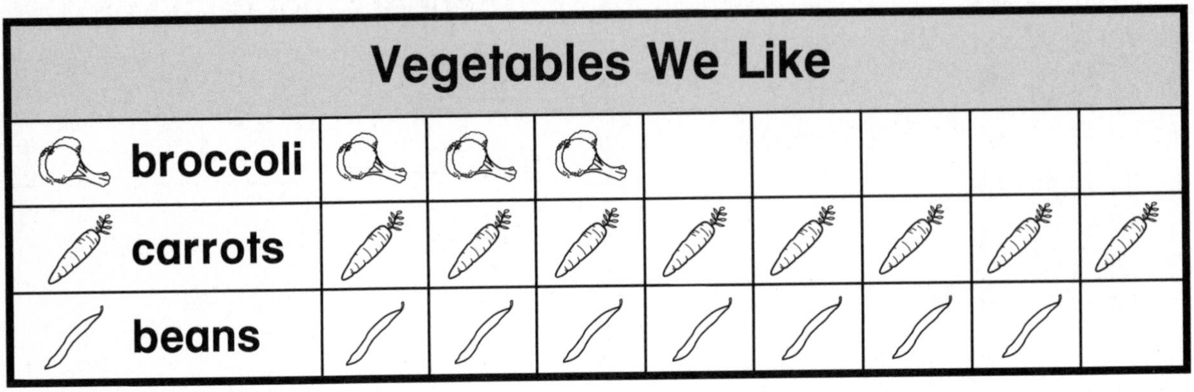

Vegetables We Like								
broccoli	broccoli	broccoli	broccoli					
carrots	carrot	carrot	carrot	carrot	carrot	carrot	carrot	carrot
beans	bean	bean	bean	bean	bean	bean	bean	

How many more children chose carrot than broccoli?

_____ more children

20. Count how many tens and ones. What is the number?

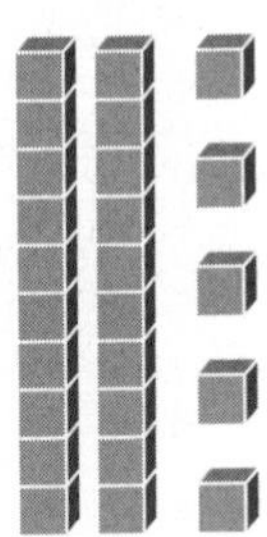

_____ tens _____ ones = _____

21. Write the number that is ten more than 43.

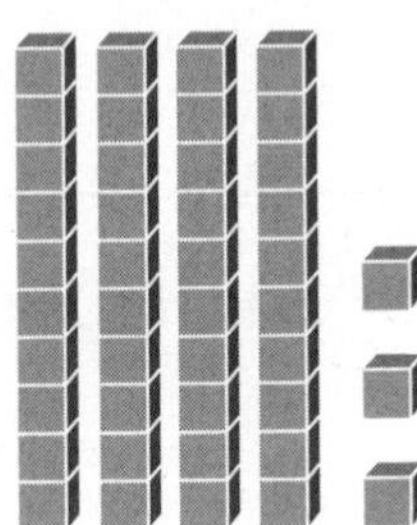

____

Stop

Name ______________________________

Write the correct answer.

1. Write the number of sides and corners the plane figure has.

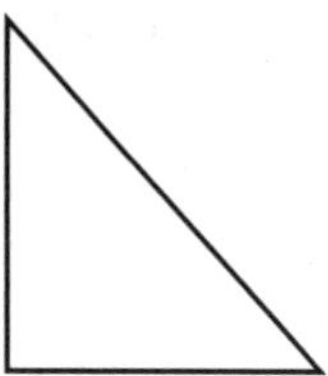

_____ sides

_____ corners

2. Circle slide, flip, or turn to name the move.

slide flip turn

3. Circle the figures with equal parts.
Cross out the figures with unequal parts.

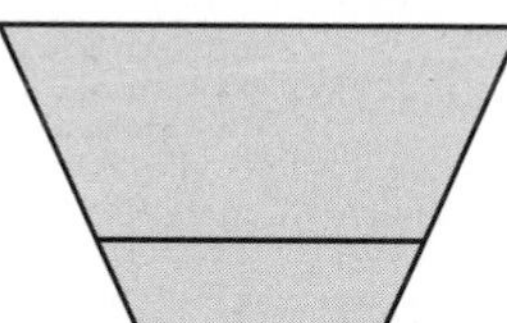

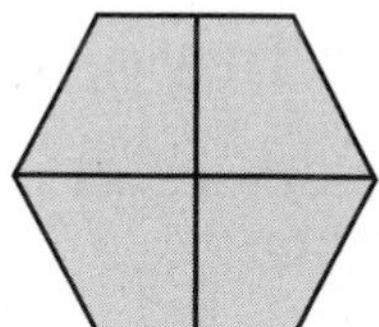

4. Color the circle GREEN.

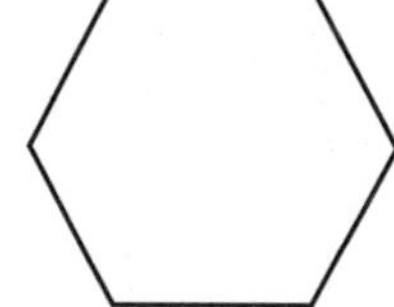

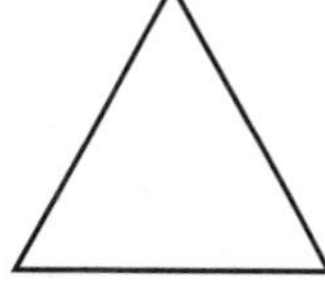

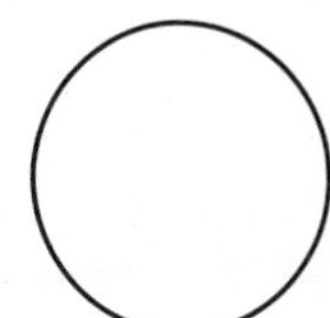

Go On

Name ____________________

Write the correct answer.

5. Circle which comes next.

6. Draw a line of symmetry to make two parts that match.

7. Find the figure that is divided into four equal parts.

Color $\frac{1}{4}$ of the figure.

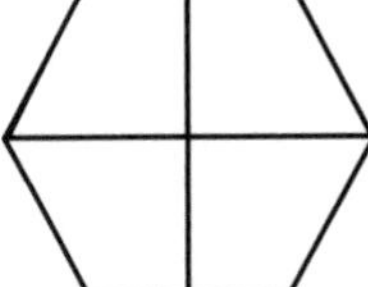

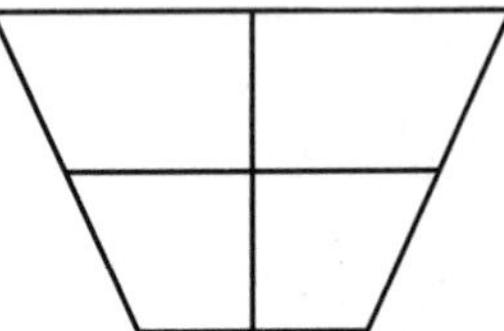

8. Circle the object you could trace to make the figure.

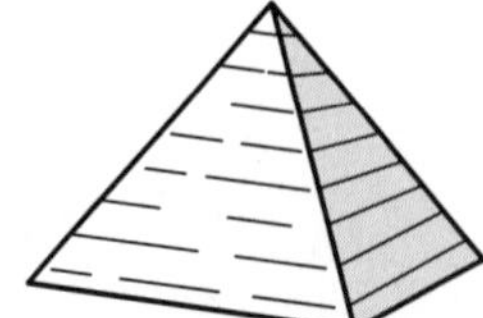

Go On

Write the correct answer.

9. Circle the pattern unit.

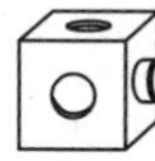  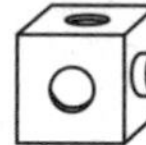  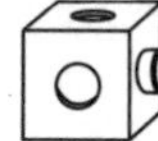   

10. Jon, Masha, and Jill share a pizza. Each gets an equal share. Circle how you would cut the pizza.

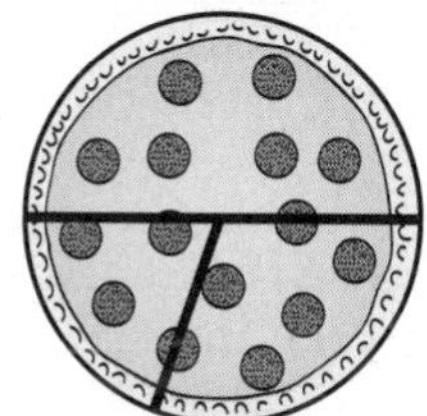

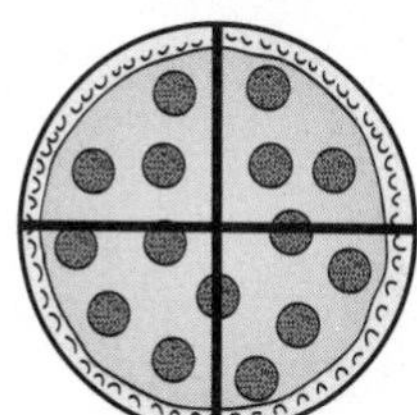

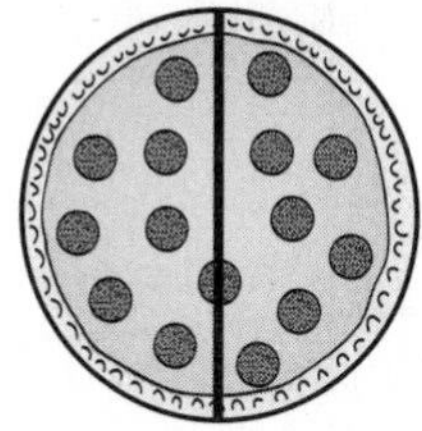

11. Use RED crayon.

Color to show $\frac{1}{2}$. Complete the sentence.

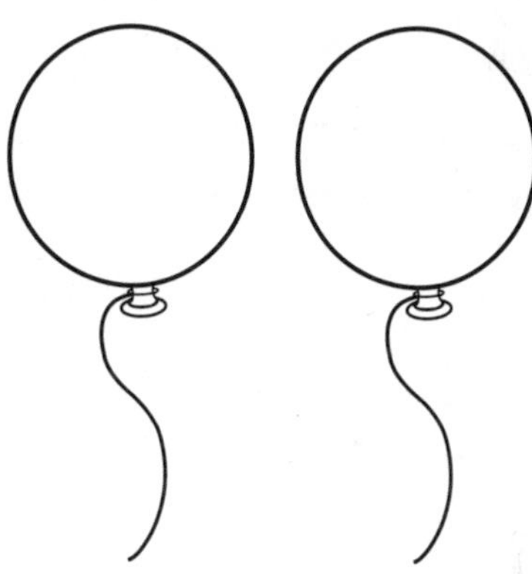

_____ out of _____ balloons is red.

Go On

Write the correct answer.

12. Color the square BLUE.

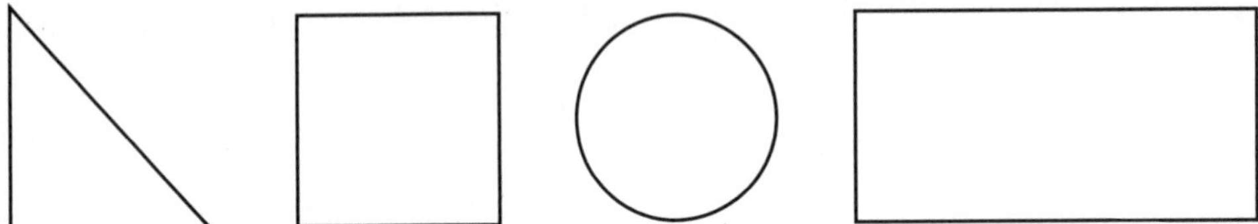

13. Write the missing number.

4 9 1 4 9 ____ 4 9 1

14. Circle the solid figure that has only flat surfaces.

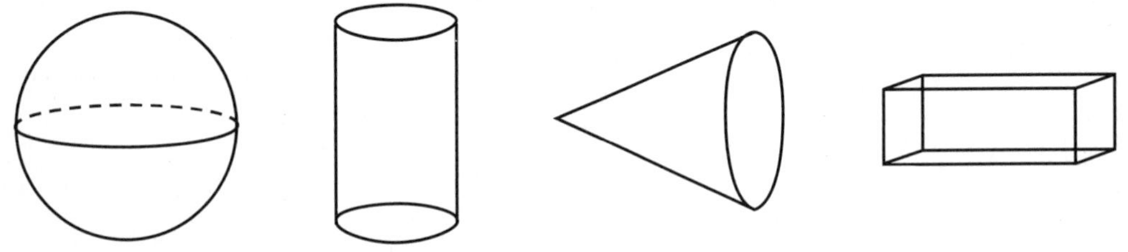

15. Use figures to show the same pattern. Draw the figures.

Go On

Write the correct answer.

16. Circle the two figures that appear to be congruent.

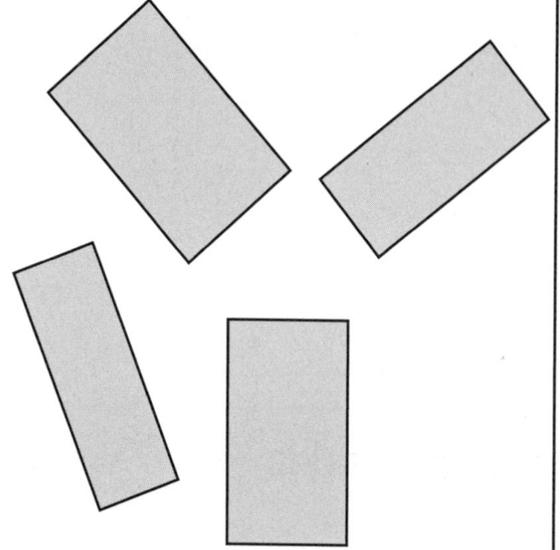

17. Write how corners the cube has.

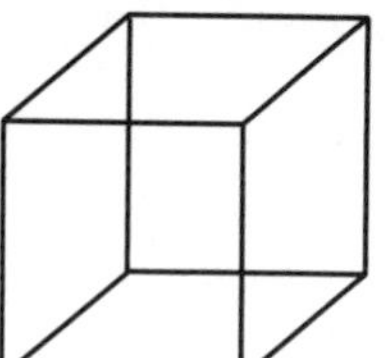

_________ corners

Use the picture for questions 18 and 19.

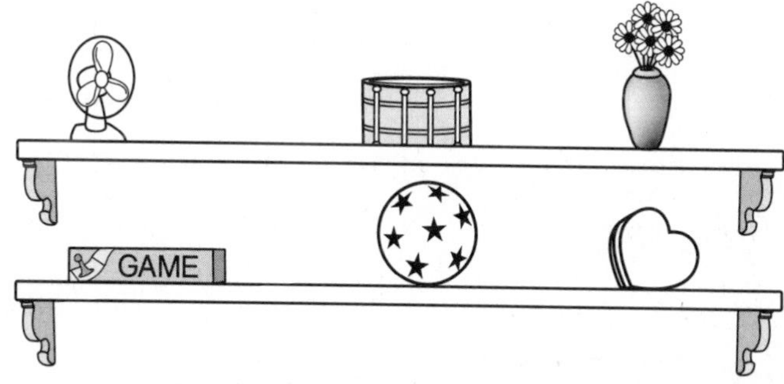

18. Dina's toy is to the **left** of the ball. It has **above** the GAME. Circle Dina's toy.

19. Pedro's toy is **near** the vase. It is to the **right** of the fan. Circle Pedro's toy.

Go On

Name ___________________________________ **UNIT 4 PRETEST**

Write the correct answer.

20. Circle the mistake in the pattern. Draw the correct pattern.

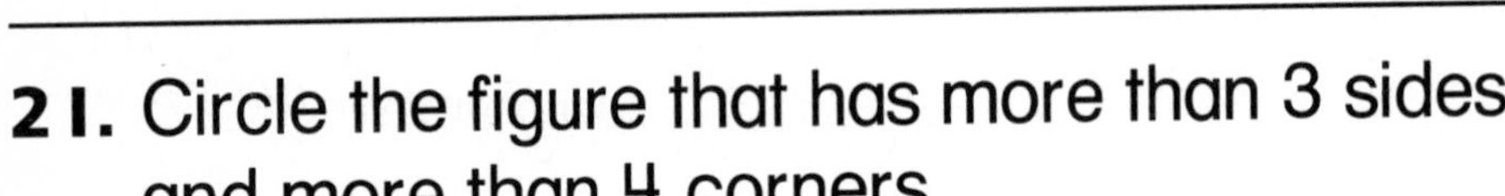

21. Circle the figure that has more than 3 sides and more than 4 corners.

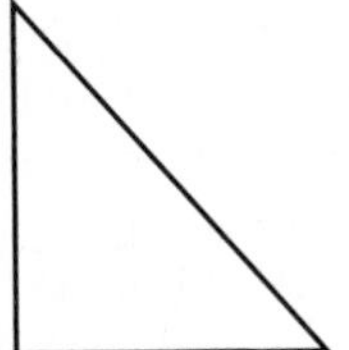

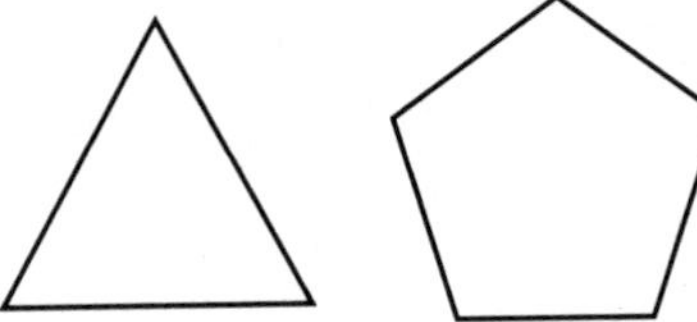

22. From **Start**, go right 3. Go down 2. Go right 1. Write where you are.

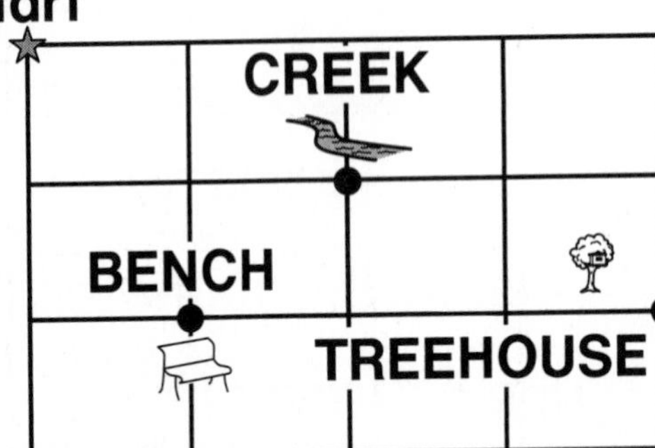

____

Stop

Name ______________________________

Write the correct answer.

1. Use the calendar. Write how many Mondays are in this month.

July						
Sunday	Monday	Tuesday	Wednesday	Thursday	Friday	Saturday
1	2	3	4	5	6	7
8	9	10	11	12	13	14
15	16	17	18	19	20	21
22	23	24	25	26	27	28
29	30	31				

____ Mondays

2. Use the addition fact to help you subtract. Write the sum. Then write the difference.

$$\begin{array}{r} 7 \\ +4 \\ \hline \end{array} \qquad \begin{array}{r} 11 \\ -4 \\ \hline \end{array}$$

3. Write the sum.

$$\begin{array}{r} 6 \\ +6 \\ \hline \end{array}$$

4. Follow the rule. Write the number that completes the table.

Subtract 7	
12	5
14	7
16	
17	10

Go On

Name ____________________

Write the correct answer.

5. Write how many more birds there are than nests.

$$\begin{array}{r} 15 \\ -\ 8 \\ \hline \end{array}$$

6. Use the picture to write the numbers.
Write a number sentence to show how many kites there are.

____ gray kites

____ white kites

____ ◯ ____ ◯ ____

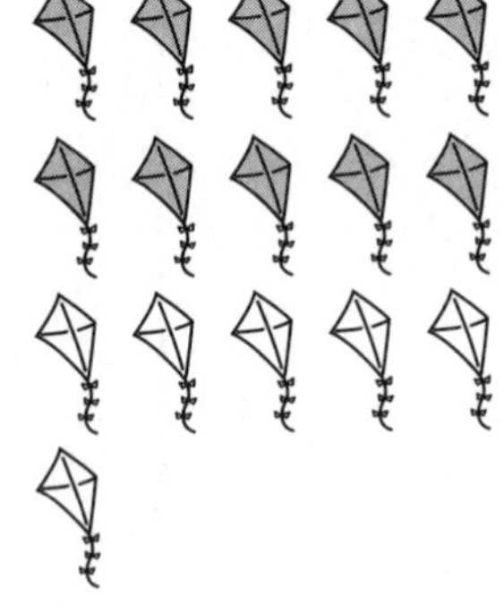

7. Write the sum.

$$\begin{array}{r} 4 \\ 5 \\ +6 \\ \hline \end{array}$$

8. Circle the time of day.

morning evening

afternoon

Go On

Name ______________________________

Write the correct answer.

9. Draw and label coins to show the amount a different way.

10. Draw and label coins to show a way to make 1 dollar. Use quarters and nickels.

11. Write the difference.

$$\begin{array}{r} 14 \\ -\ 5 \\ \hline \end{array}$$

Go On

Write the correct answer.

12. Write a number sentence to solve.

7 children are waiting for the bus. 6 more children join them. How many children are waiting for the bus now?

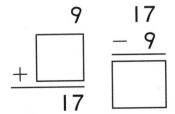

____ children

13. Write the missing numbers.

$$\begin{array}{r} 9 \\ + \square \\ \hline 17 \end{array} \qquad \begin{array}{r} 17 \\ -\ 9 \\ \hline \square \end{array}$$

14. Make a ten and add. Write the sum.

$$\begin{array}{r} 4 \\ +\ 9 \\ \hline \end{array}$$

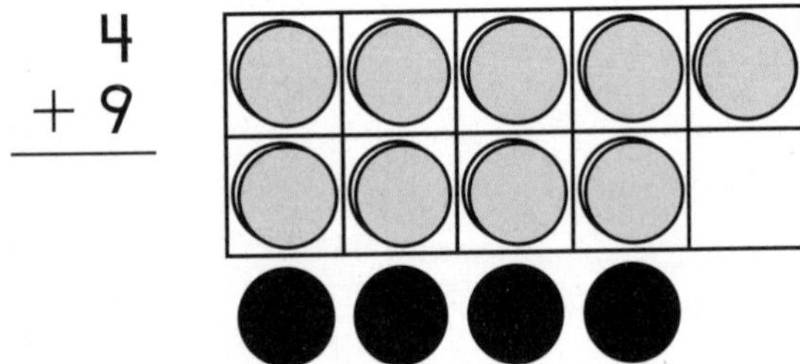

15. Write a number sentence to solve.

Daisy has 8 strawberries. Sally brings 4 more strawberries. How many strawberries are there in all?

____ ◯ ____ ◯ ____

____ strawberries

Go On

Name ______________________

Write the correct answer.

16. Count. Compare the amounts. Write <, >, or =.

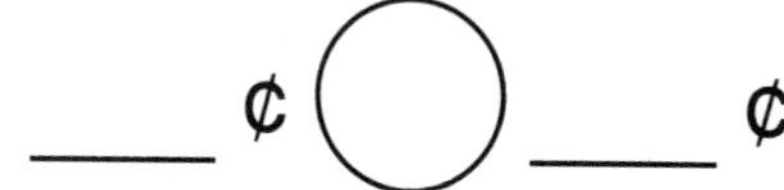

____ ¢ ◯ ____ ¢

17. Draw the hour hand and minute hand to show the time.

18. Write the sum.

10 + 10 = ____

19. Write the difference.

16 − 8 = ____

Go On

Name ___________________________________

Write the correct answer.

Use the table to answer question 20.

Festival Events		
Event	**Start**	**End**
picnic	12:00	7:00
music	7:30	8:00
fireworks	9:30	10:00

20. Which event starts at 9:30?

____

21. Write each sum or difference.
Circle the facts in the same fact family.

$$\begin{array}{r} 6 \\ +5 \\ \hline \end{array} \quad \begin{array}{r} 10 \\ -5 \\ \hline \end{array} \quad \begin{array}{r} 11 \\ -6 \\ \hline \end{array} \quad \begin{array}{r} 5 \\ +6 \\ \hline \end{array} \quad \begin{array}{r} 11 \\ -5 \\ \hline \end{array}$$

Stop

Name ______________________________

Write the correct answer.

1. Write the sum.

	tens	ones
	3	2
+		5

Workmat

tens	ones

2. Circle the container that holds the least amount of juice.

3. Write about how many long the object is.

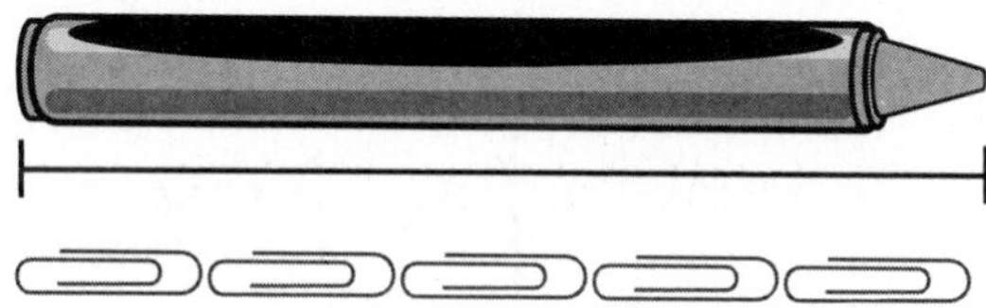

about ____

Go On

Write the correct answer.

4. Circle the better estimate.

about 1 pound

about 10 pounds

5. Write the temperature.

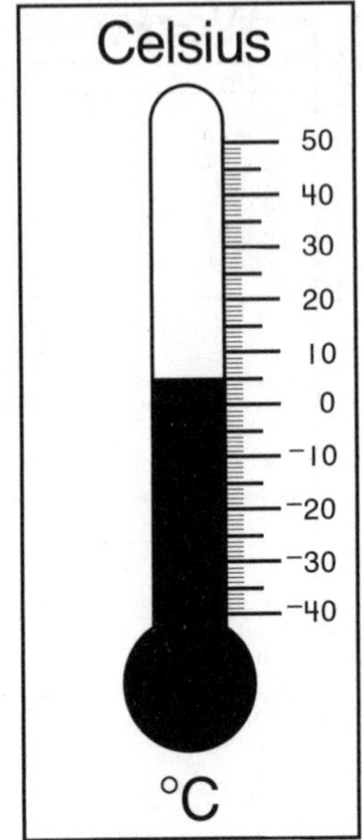

_____ °C

6. Write the difference.

80 − 10 = _____

7. Circle the size of the container.

pint   quart

Go On

Name ____________________

Write the correct answer.

8. Write the difference.

	tens	ones
	3	6
−	2	1

Workmat

tens	ones

9. Measure the object. Write the length.

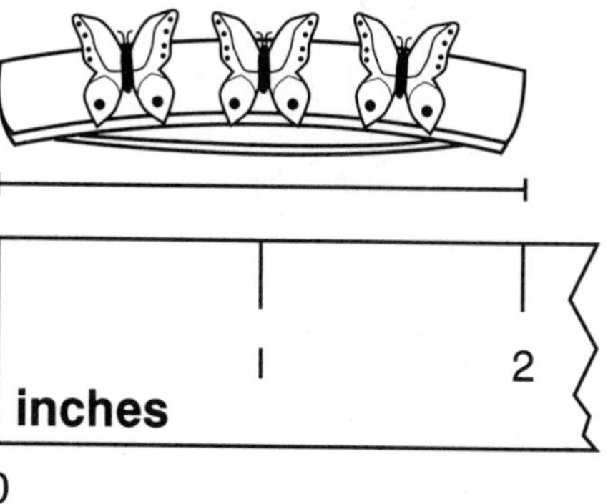

about ____ inches

10. Circle the ribbons that are in order from shortest to longest.

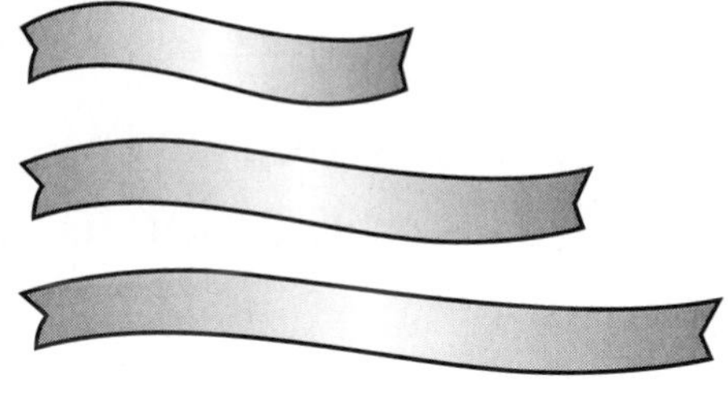

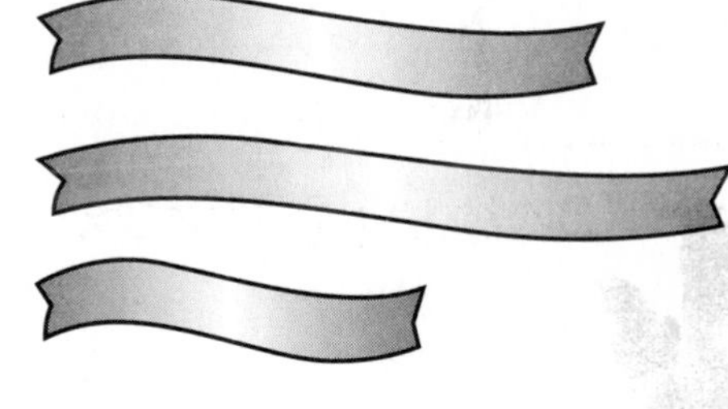

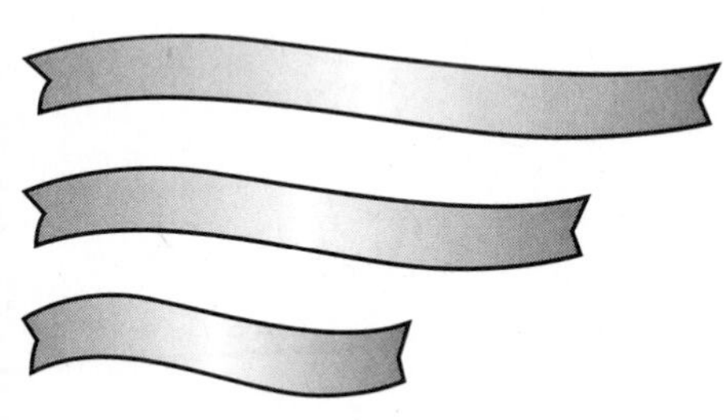

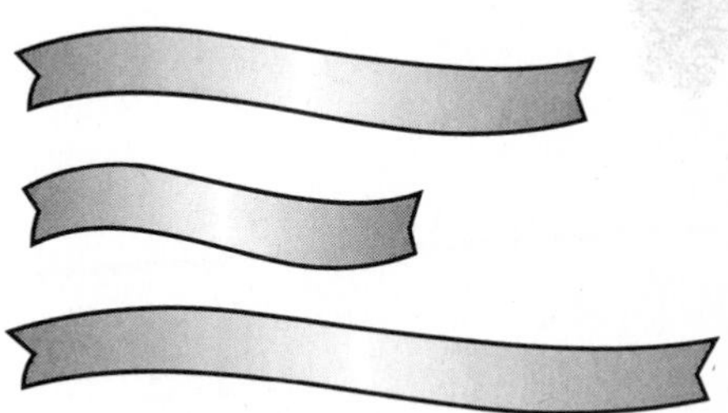

Go On

Write the correct answer.

11. Circle the tool you will use to measure how heavy the math book is.

12. Write the sum.

	tens	ones
	1	6
+	1	3

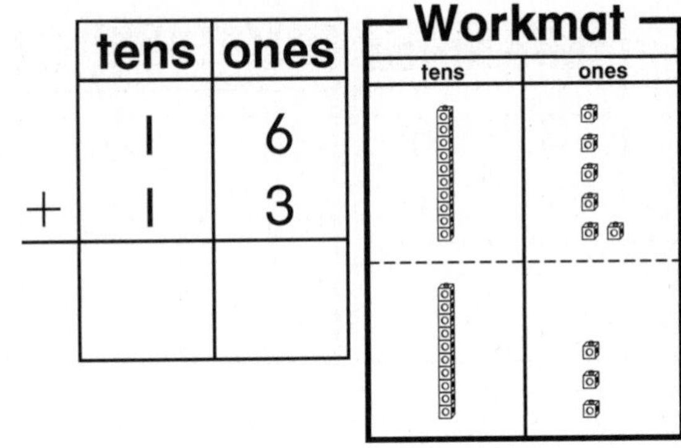

13. Without adding or subtracting, circle the best estimate.

There are 38 maple trees by a river. There are 3 oak trees. About how many trees are there in all?

about 4 trees

about 40 trees

about 400 trees

14. Circle how many cups you need to fill the container to the top.

This glass has 1 cup of juice in it.

1 cup 3 cups

2 cups

Go On

Name ______________________________

Write the correct answer.

15. Measure the object. Write the length.

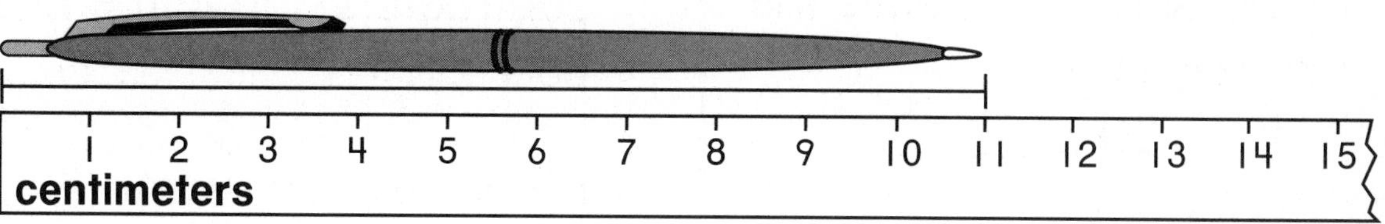

about _____centimeters

16. Circle the lightest object.

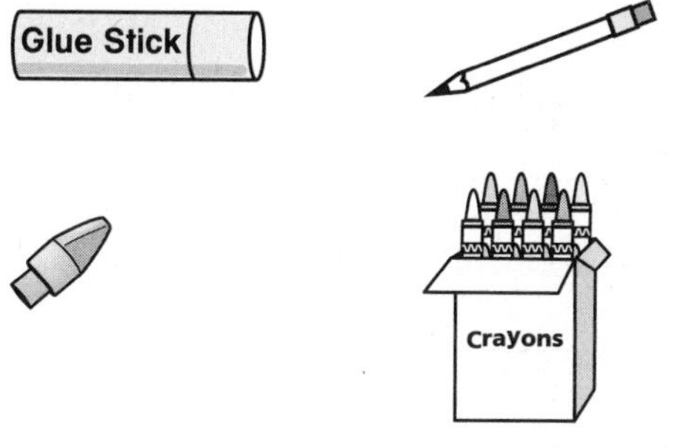

17. Write the difference.

	tens	ones
	2	7
−		4

Workmat

tens	ones

18. About how many paper clips long is the object? Circle the estimate that makes sense.

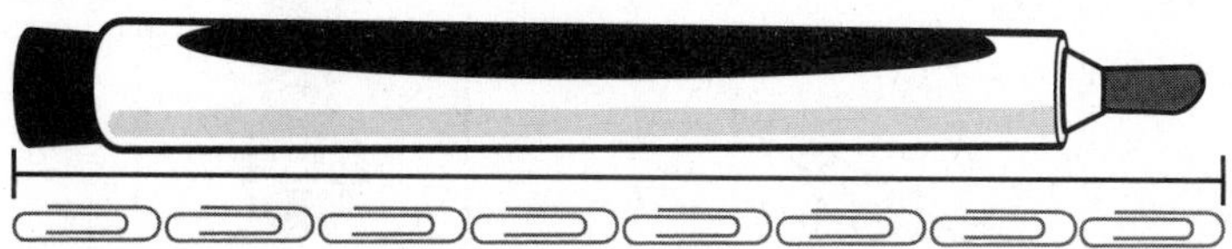

about 7 paper clips

about 8 paper clips

Go On

Name ____________________

Write the correct answer.

19. Write the sum.

40 + 30 = ______

20. Without adding or subtracting, circle the best estimate.

82 birds are in a tree. 9 of the birds fly away. About how many birds are left?

about 7 birds

about 70 birds

about 700 birds

21. Circle the tool you will use to measure how long the notebook is.

22. Write the temperature.

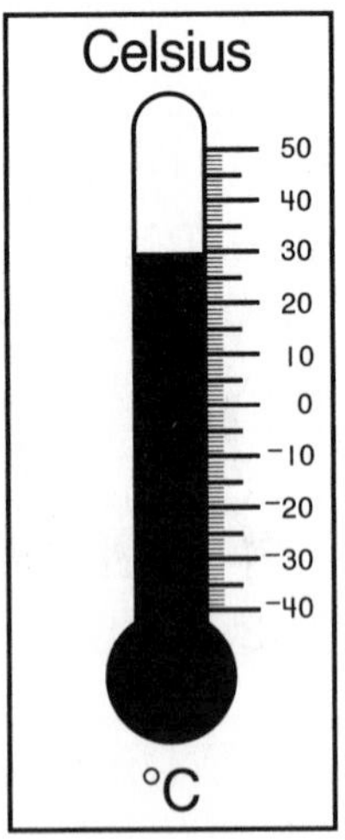

____°C

Stop

Name ________________________________

Write the correct answer.

1. Write **is greater than** or **is less than**.

19 ______________________ 12.

2. Circle the number word that tells how many.

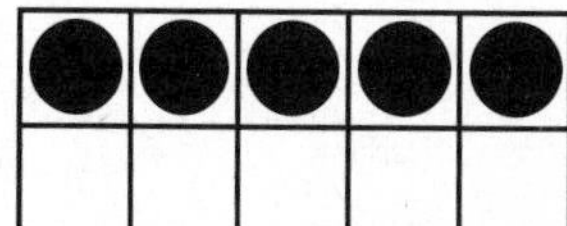

fifteen sixteen

fourteen thirteen

3. Write the numbers in order from least to greatest.

15, 18, 11

____ ____ ____

4. Write **is greater than** or **is less than**.

11 ______________________ 17.

5. Circle the second bunny.

first

Go On

Name ______________________________

Write the correct answer.

6. Circle a way to show 8.

eight

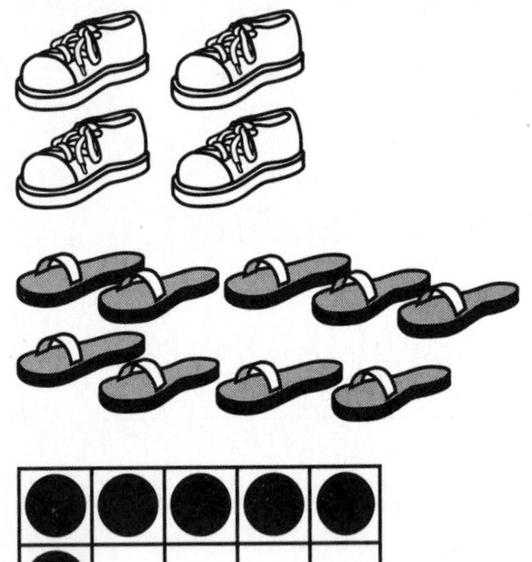

7. Draw lines to match. Write how many fewer.

_______ fewer

Use the picture graph to answer questions 8 and 9.

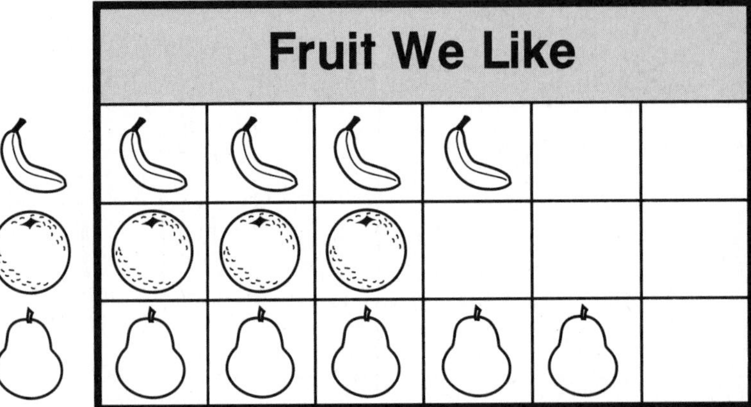

8. Circle the fruit that has the greatest number?

9. Write how many?

____

Stop

Name ____________________

Write the correct answer.

1. Use the picture to write the addition sentence.

2 puppies **2 more puppies**

2. Circle the addition sentences that use the same addends.

1 + 5 = 6

2 + 3 = 5

5 + 1 = 6

3 + 3 = 6

3. Draw circles to show each number. Write the sum.

0 + 4 = ____

4. Write the sum.

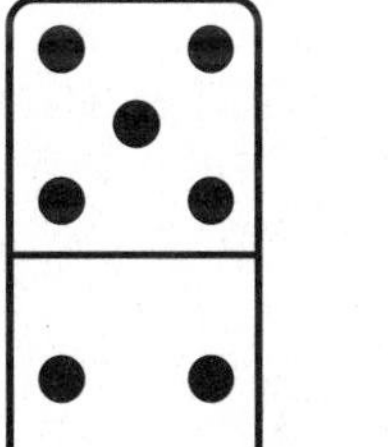

$$\begin{array}{r} 5 \\ +\ 2 \\ \hline \end{array}$$

Go On

Name ______________________________

Write the correct answer.

5. Circle a way to make 8.

2 + 6

4 + 3

2 + 7

6 + 1

6. Write how many in all.

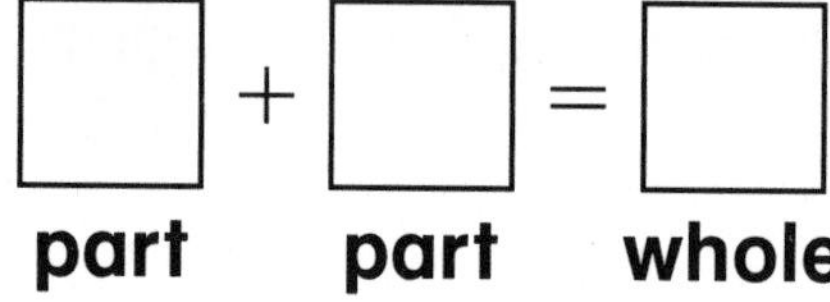

_____ in all

7. Write how many chicks in all.

2 chicks **1 more chick**

_____ chicks in all

8. Write the number sentence.

Tori sees 4 red pens. She sees the same number of blue pens. How many pens does Tori see in all?

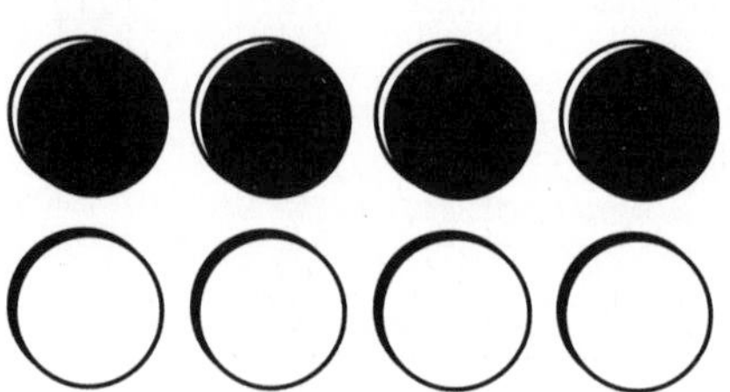

_____ + _____ = _____

_____ pens

Stop

Write the correct answer.

1. Write the difference.

$$\begin{array}{r} 7 \\ -\ 3 \\ \hline \end{array}$$

2. Write the difference.

3 − 0 = ____

3. Use the cube below. Complete the subtraction sentence.

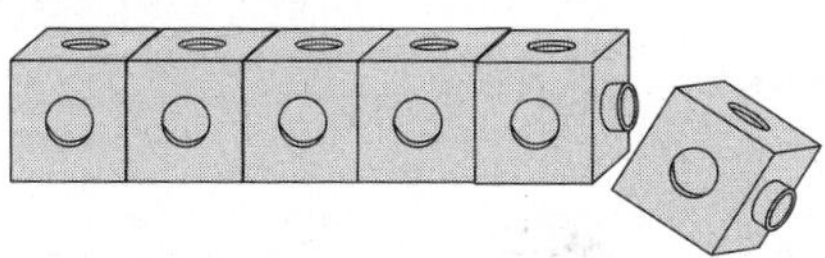

6 − ____ = ____

4. Use the picture. Write the subtraction sentence.

____ ◯ ____ ◯ ____

Go On

Write the correct answer.

5. Draw lines to match. Write how many fewer ✏.

____ fewer ✏

6. Complete the subtraction sentence.

7	−	3	=	
whole		**part**		**part**

7. Write how many girls are left.

2 girls **1 girl walks away**

____ girl is left

8. There are 5 brown bats and 2 fruit bats. How many fewer fruit bats are there?

____ fewer fruit bats

Stop

Name ____________________

Write the correct answer.

1. Add. Then subtract.

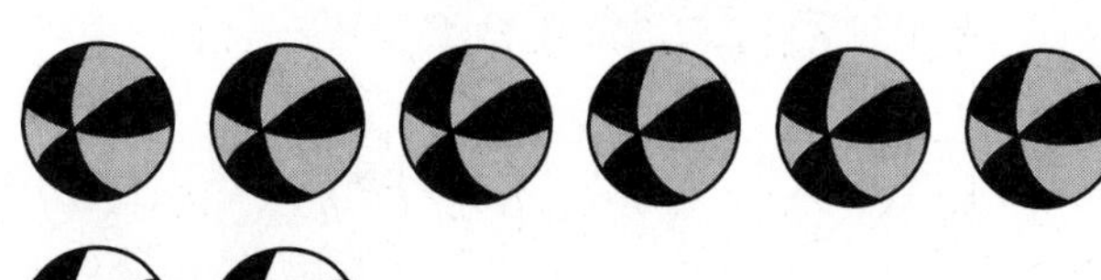

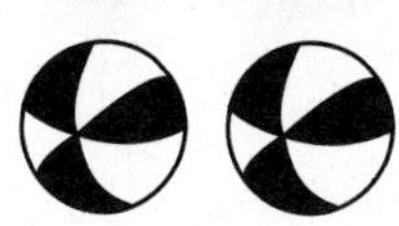

6 + 2 = ____

8 − 2 = ____

2. Write a number sentence to match the picture.

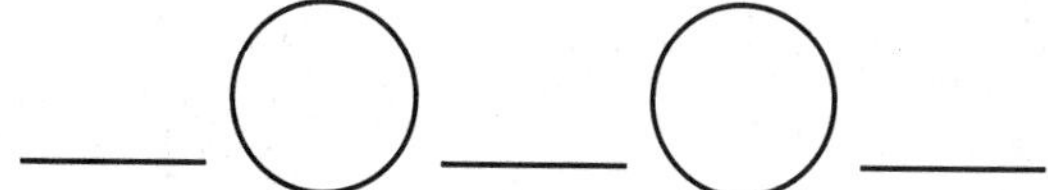

3. Circle the related subtraction fact.

6 + 3 = 9

6 + 3 = 9

9 − 3 = 6

8 − 6 = 2

8 − 4 = 4

4. How many ladybugs are there in all?

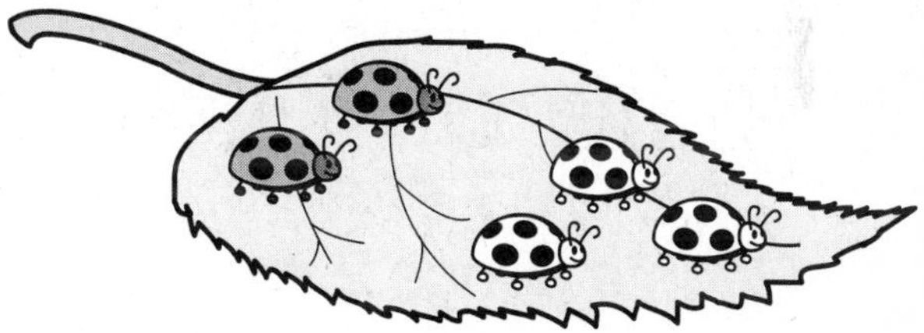

____

Go On

Name ____________________

Write the correct answer.

5. Circle the related addition fact.

$2 - 0 = 2$

$4 - 0 = 4$ $0 + 3 = 3$

$0 + 2 = 2$ $2 + 2 = 4$

6. Write a number sentence to match the picture.

7. How many squirrels run away?

____

8. Write the number sentence. There are 7 erasers. Chante brings 2 more erasers. How many erasers are there now?

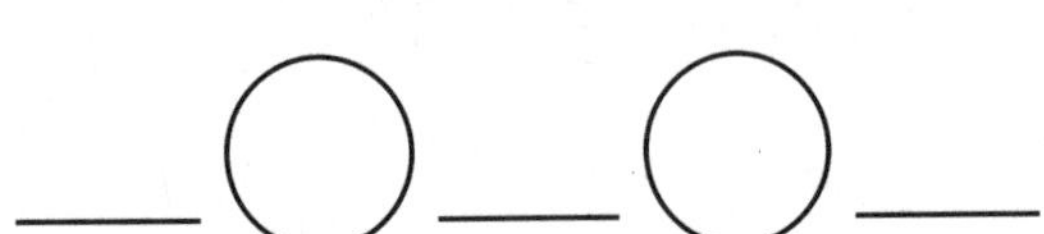

____ erasers

9. Write the number sentence. There are 6 blocks. Paige takes 2 blocks away. How many blocks are left?

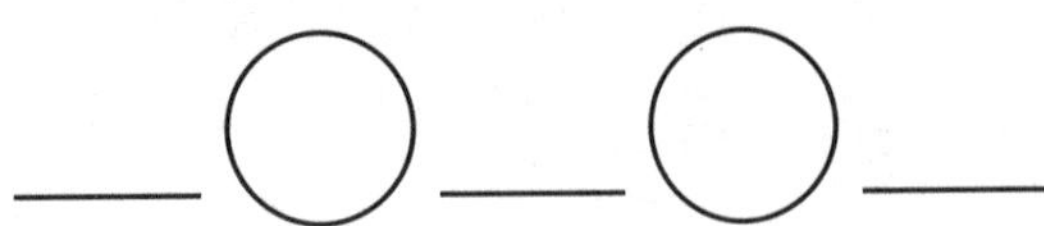

____ blocks

Stop

Name ______________________

Write the correct answer.

1. Write the numbers in order from least to greatest.

9, 14, 11

____ ____ ____

2. Write the difference.

3 − 0 = ____

3. Circle the addition sentences that use the same addends.

1 + 3 = 4

4 + 1 = 5

2 + 3 = 5

3 + 1 = 4

4. Write the number sentence.

There are 8 grapes.
Sadie takes 6 grapes away.
How many grapes are left?

____ grapes

5. Write **is greater than** or **is less than** to make the sentence true.

17 ______________________ 11.

6. Circle the related subtraction fact.

2 + 3 = 5

2 + 2 = 4

3 − 2 = 1

5 − 3 = 2

Go On

Name ________________________________

Write the correct answer.

7. Use the [cube] below.
There are 5 gray blocks and 1 white block. How many fewer white blocks are there?

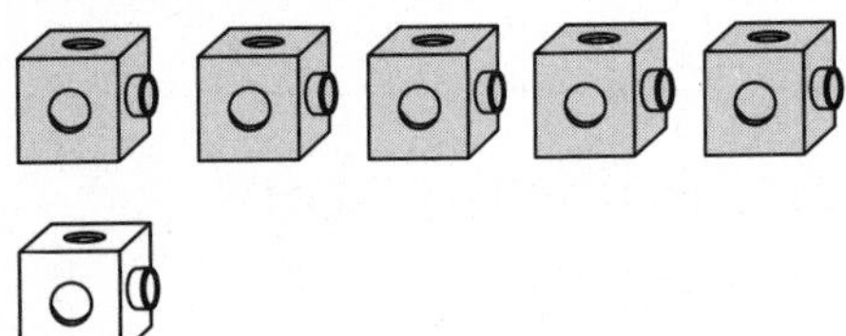

____ white blocks

8. Write a number sentence to match the picture.

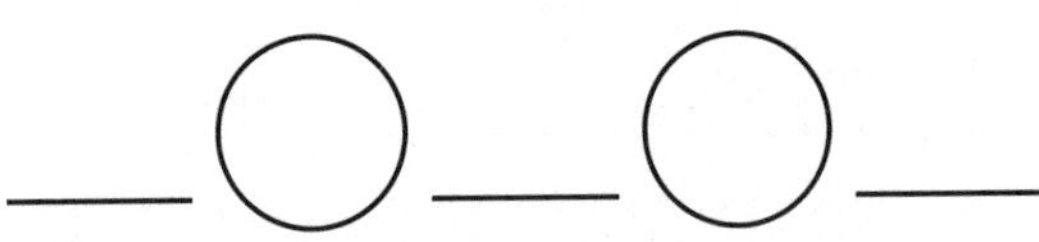

9. Draw circles to show each number. Write the sum.

0 + 3 = ____

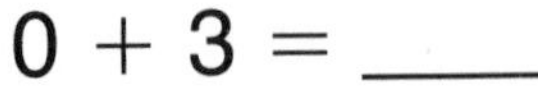

10. Complete the subtraction sentence.

7	−	4	=	
whole		**part**		**part**

Go On

Name ____________________

Write the correct answer.

11. Circle a way to make 5.

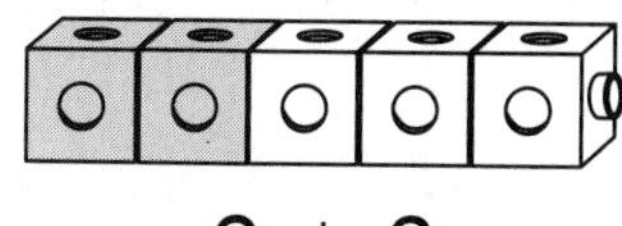

2 + 3

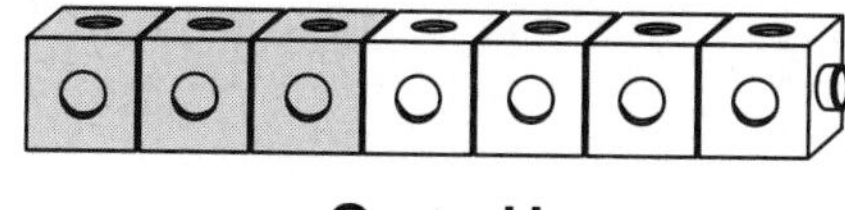

3 + 4

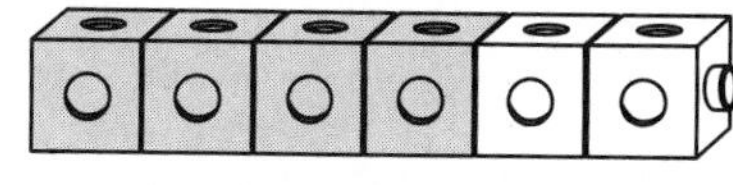

4 + 2

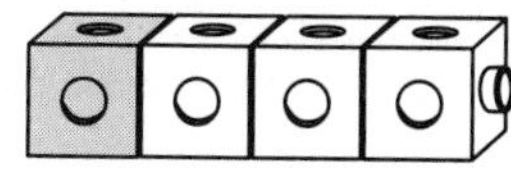

1 + 3

12. Draw lines to match. Which shows how many more ?

____ more

13. How many fish are left?

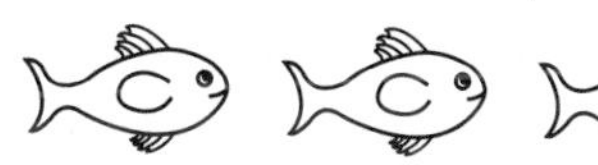

4 fish **1 fish swims away**

____ fish are left

14. Use the picture to write the addition sentence.

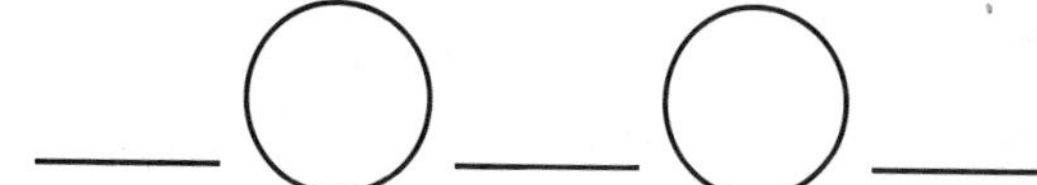

Go On

Name ____________________

Write the correct answer.

15. Add. Then subtract.

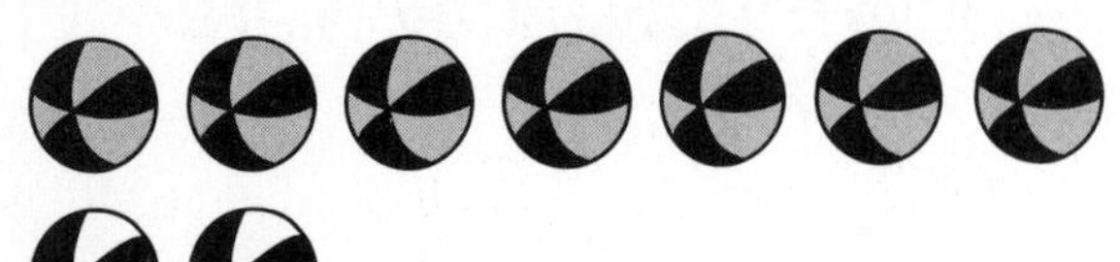

$7 + 2 =$ ____

$9 - 2 =$ ____

16. Circle a way to show 3.

four

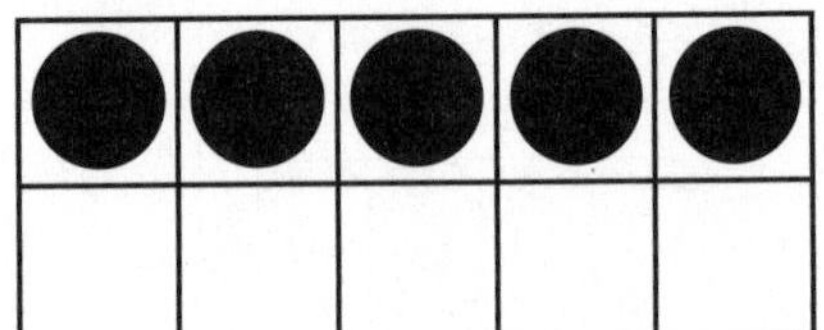

17. Circle the fourth puppy.

first

Go On

Write the correct answer.

18. How many hamsters are there in all?

____

19. Write the sum.

$$\begin{array}{r} 4 \\ +5 \\ \hline \end{array}$$

20. Use the [cube] below. Complete the subtraction sentence.

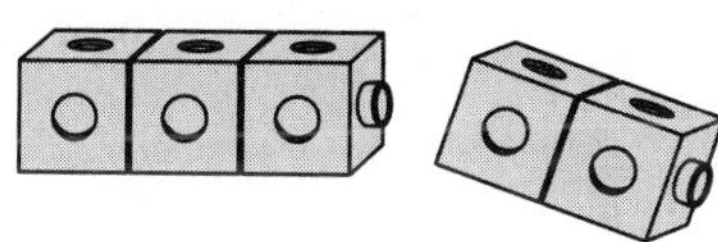

5 − ____ = ____

21. Write a number sentence.

There are 4 children in a pool. The same number of children join them. How many children are there in all?

____ children

Go On

Write the correct answer.

22. Write the difference.

$$\begin{array}{r} 9 \\ -\ 1 \\ \hline \end{array}$$

23. Circle the number word that tells how many.

fourteen eighteen

24. Write how many in all.

2  7

☐ + ☐ = ☐

part **part** **whole**

____ in all

25. Draw lines to match. Write how many fewer ?

6 − 4 = ____

____ fewer

Stop

Write the correct answer.

Use the number line to answer questions 1 and 2.

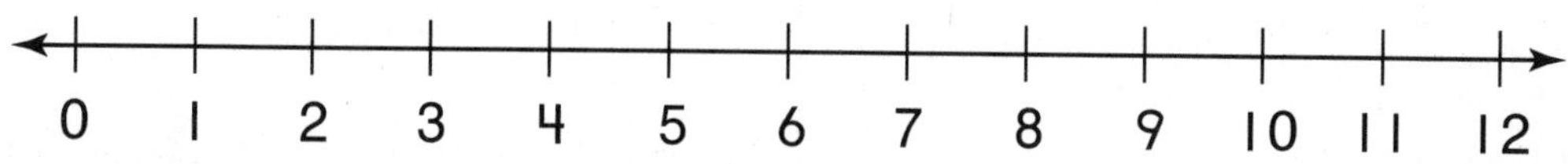

1. What is the sum?

$$\begin{array}{r} 3 \\ +3 \\ \hline \end{array}$$

2. What is the sum?

$$\begin{array}{r} 4 \\ +2 \\ \hline \end{array}$$

3. Write the doubles fact.

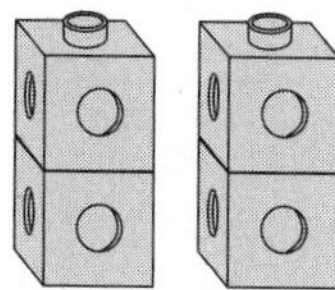

4. Write the double plus one fact.

Go On

Write the correct answer.

5. Count on. Write the sum.

$$\begin{array}{r} 2 \\ +9 \\ \hline \end{array}$$

6. Write the sum.

$6 + 3 =$ ______

7. Count on. Write the sum.

$5 + 3 =$ ______

8. Draw a picture to solve. There are 9 flowers in all. 4 flowers are red. The other flowers are yellow. Write how many flowers are yellow.

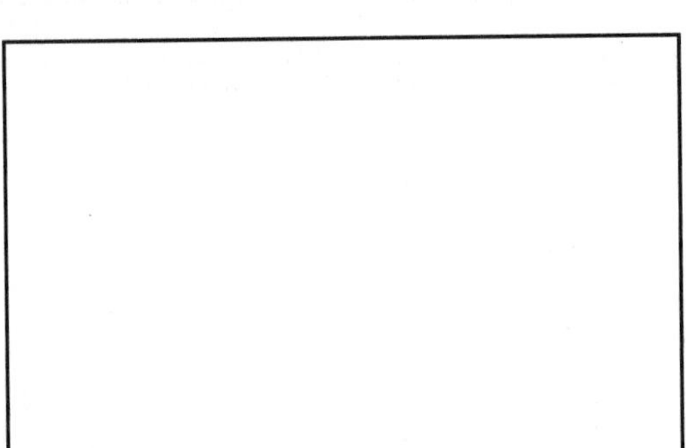

______ yellow flowers

9. Draw a picture to solve. There are 4 bananas in all. 2 bananas are yellow. The other bananas are green. Write how many bananas are green.

______ green bananas

Stop

Name ____________________

Write the correct answer.

Use the number line to answer questions 1 through 4.

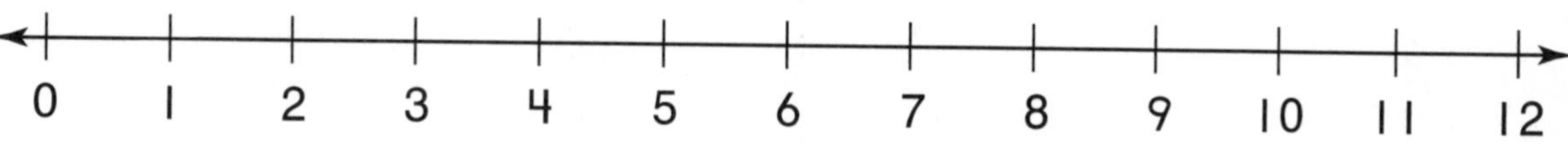

1. Write the difference.

$$\begin{array}{r} 10 \\ -\ 2 \\ \hline \end{array}$$

2. Write the difference.

$9 - 3 =$ ______

3. Write the difference.

______ $= 11 - 3$

4. Write the difference.

$$\begin{array}{r} 8 \\ -\ 1 \\ \hline \end{array}$$

Go On

Name ______________________________

Write the correct answer.

5. Write the difference.

$$\begin{array}{r} 12 \\ -\ 2 \\ \hline \end{array}$$

6. Write the difference.

$$\begin{array}{r} 10 \\ -\ 3 \\ \hline \end{array}$$

7. Use ▢ and ▢ to add.

$$\begin{array}{r} 5 \\ +5 \\ \hline \end{array}$$

8. Use ▢ and ☒ to subtract.

$$\begin{array}{r} 6 \\ -3 \\ \hline \end{array}$$

9. Write a number sentence to match the story.

There are 11 seashells. 3 seashells are washed away. How many seashells are there now?

_____ seashells

10. Write a number sentence to match the story.

There are 10 fish. 1 fish swims away. How many fish are there now?

_____ fish

Stop

Name ______________________________

Write the correct answer.

1. Write the numbers in the fact family.

7 + 3 = 10   10 − 3 = 7

3 + 7 = 10   10 − 7 = 3

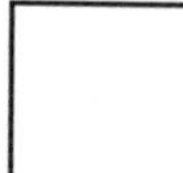  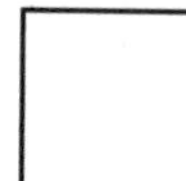

2. Circle the ways to make 11.

8 + 4

3 + 8

10 − 2

12 − 1

3. Write the sum. Then write the related addition fact.

$$\begin{array}{r} 7 \\ +\,3 \\ \hline \square \end{array}$$

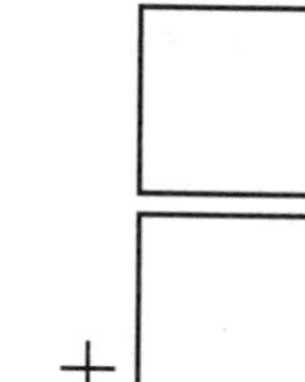

4. Write the numbers and a number sentence to show how many flowers there are.

____ gray flowers

____ white flowers

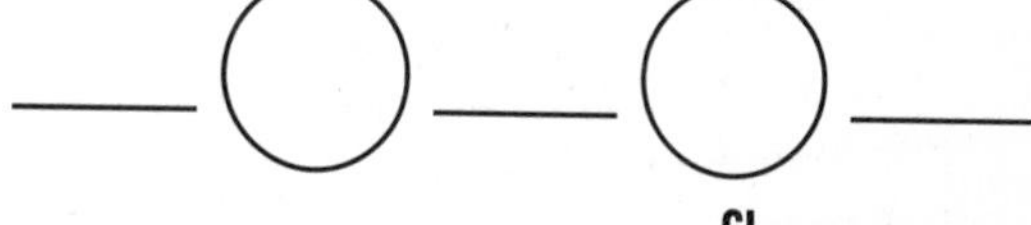

flowers

Go On

Name ____________________

Write the correct answer.

5. Complete the fact family.

□ + 5 = 12

5 + 7 = □

12 − □ = 7

□ − □ = □

6. Follow the rule to complete the table.

Subtract 3	
11	8
10	
8	5

7. Circle the pair of related subtraction facts?

$\begin{array}{r} 11 \\ -\ 3 \\ \hline 8 \end{array}$ $\begin{array}{r} 11 \\ -\ 3 \\ \hline 7 \end{array}$ $\begin{array}{r} 12 \\ -\ 3 \\ \hline 6 \end{array}$ $\begin{array}{r} 12 \\ -\ 3 \\ \hline 6 \end{array}$ $\begin{array}{r} 10 \\ -\ 3 \\ \hline 7 \end{array}$ $\begin{array}{r} 10 \\ -\ 7 \\ \hline 3 \end{array}$ $\begin{array}{r} 12 \\ -\ 5 \\ \hline 7 \end{array}$ $\begin{array}{r} 11 \\ -\ 4 \\ \hline 7 \end{array}$

8. Draw a picture to solve.

There are 12 blue jays. Some blue jays fly away. There are 4 blue jays left. How many blue jays flew away?

_____ blue jays

9. Draw a picture to solve.

There are 11 frogs. Some frogs hop away. There are 5 frogs left. How many frogs hopped away?

_____ frogs

Stop

Write the correct answer.

1. Write the doubles fact.

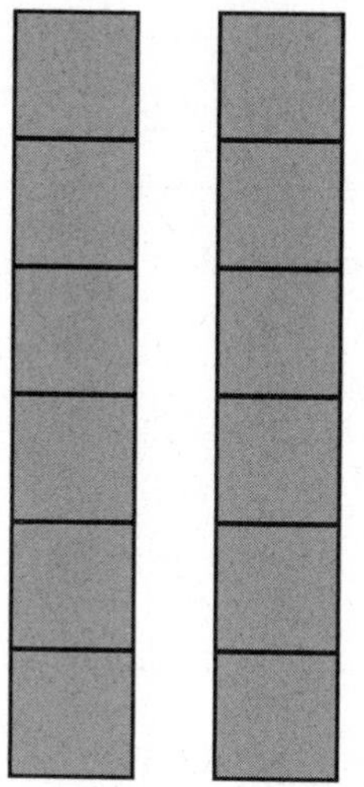

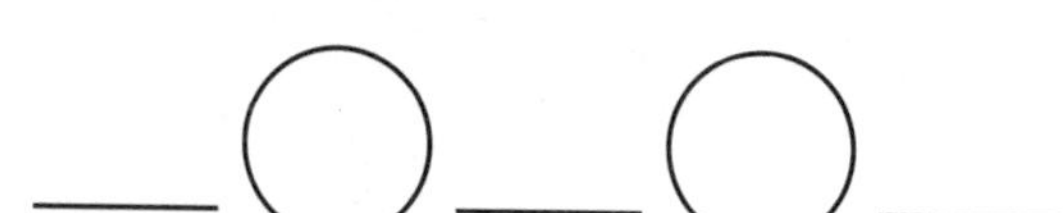

2. Draw a picture to solve.
There are 7 dolphins.
Some dolphins swim away.
There are 4 dolphins left.
How many dolphins swam away?

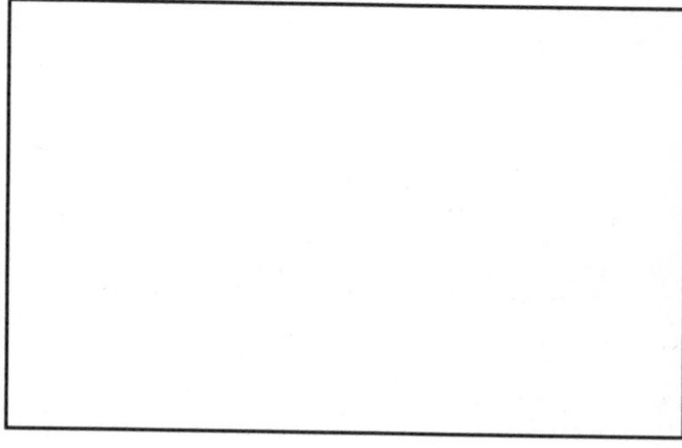

____ dolphins

3. Follow the rule to complete the table.

Subtract 2	
10	8
11	
12	10

4. Write the numbers in the fact family.

$4 + 7 = 11$ $11 - 7 = 4$

$7 + 4 = 11$ $11 - 4 = 7$

☐ ☐ ☐

Go On

Name ____________________

Write the correct answer.

Use the number line to answer questions 5 and 6.

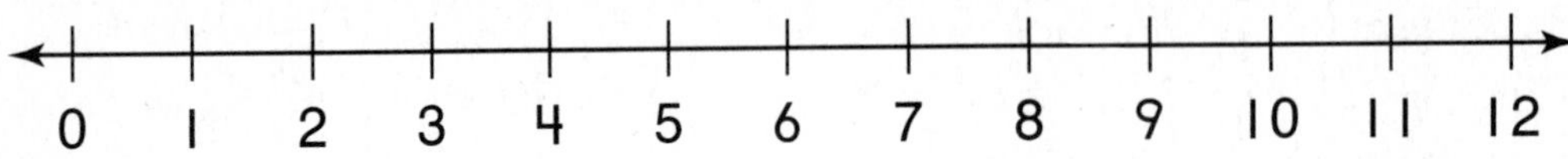

5. What is the sum?

$$\begin{array}{r} 9 \\ +3 \\ \hline \end{array}$$

6. What is the sum?

$$\begin{array}{r} 5 \\ +1 \\ \hline \end{array}$$

7. What is the difference?

$$\begin{array}{r} 9 \\ -4 \\ \hline \end{array}$$

8. Use 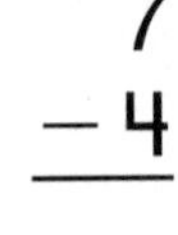 and 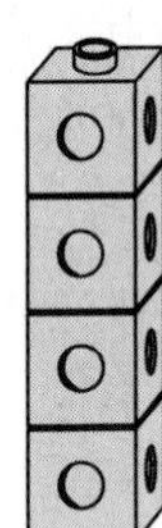 to add.

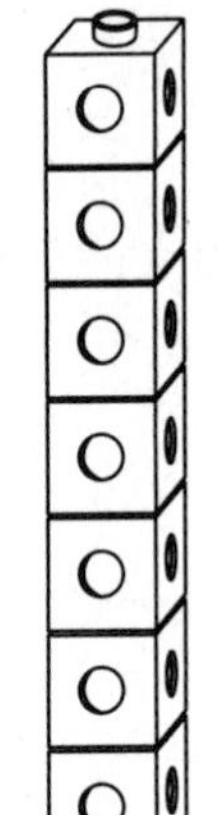

$$\begin{array}{r} 7 \\ -4 \\ \hline \end{array}$$

9. Circle the pair of related subtraction facts.

$$\begin{array}{r} 6 \\ -2 \\ \hline 4 \end{array} \quad \begin{array}{r} 6 \\ +4 \\ \hline 2 \end{array} \qquad \begin{array}{r} 10 \\ -6 \\ \hline 4 \end{array} \quad \begin{array}{r} 11 \\ -4 \\ \hline 7 \end{array} \qquad \begin{array}{r} 9 \\ -5 \\ \hline 4 \end{array} \quad \begin{array}{r} 9 \\ -6 \\ \hline 3 \end{array} \qquad \begin{array}{r} 7 \\ -3 \\ \hline 4 \end{array} \quad \begin{array}{r} 7 \\ -5 \\ \hline 2 \end{array}$$

Write the correct answer.

10. Count on. Write the sum.

5 + 1 = ____

11. Write a number sentence to match the story.

There are 10 green leaves. There are 6 orange leaves. How many more green leaves are there than orange leaves?

____ ◯ ____ ◯ ____

____ green leaves

12. Write the sum. Then write the related addition fact.

$$\begin{array}{r} 8 \\ +\ 4 \\ \hline \square \end{array} \qquad \begin{array}{r} \square \\ +\ \square \\ \hline \square \end{array}$$

13. Circle the ways to make 11.

12 − 1

5 + 5

11 − 1

5 + 6

14. Count on. Write the sum.

$$\begin{array}{r} 4 \\ +\ 3 \\ \hline \end{array}$$

Go On

Name ______________________

Write the correct answer.

Use the number line to answer questions 15 and 16.

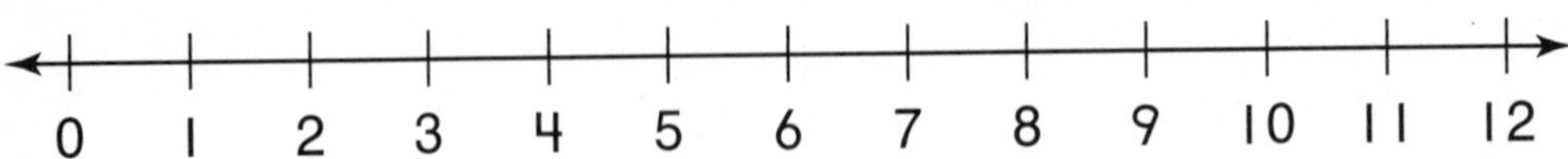

15. Write the difference.

$$\begin{array}{r} 11 \\ -\ 1 \\ \hline \end{array}$$

16. Write the difference.

9 − 3 = ____

17. Follow the rule to complete the table.

Subtract 3	
7	4
8	
9	6

18. Write the doubles plus one fact.

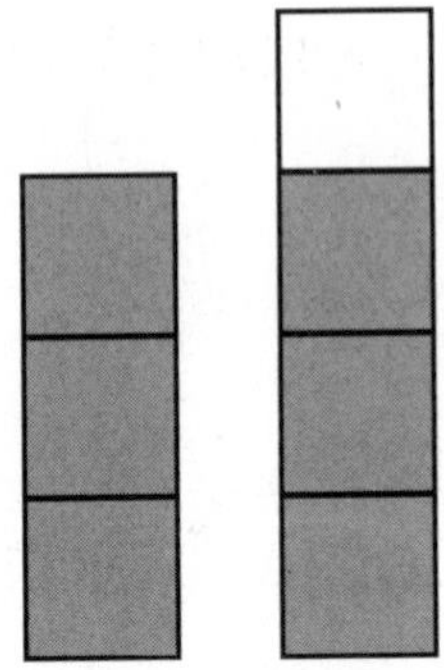

____ ◯ ____ ◯ ____

Go On

Write the correct answer.

19. Complete the fact family.

☐ + 5 = 12

5 + 7 = ☐

12 − ☐ = 7

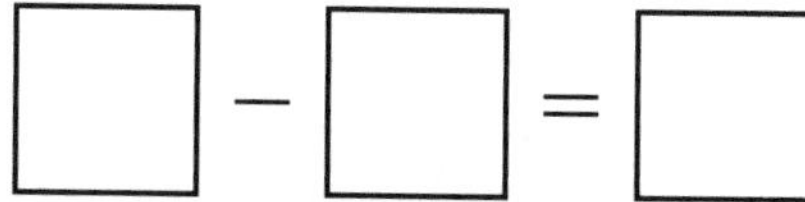

20. Write the sum.

4 + 5 = ____

21. Write the number sentence that shows how many bears there are.

____ gray bears

____ white bears

22. Write the number sentence that matches the story.

There are 10 ladybugs. 3 ladybugs fly away. How many ladybugs are there now?

____ ladybugs

Go On

Write the correct answer.

23. Use and to subtract.

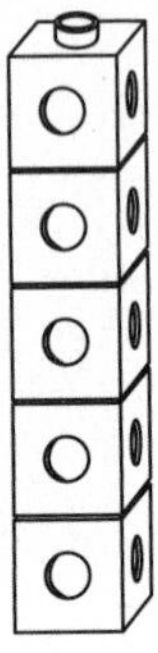

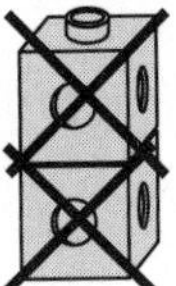

$$\begin{array}{r} 7 \\ -\ 2 \\ \hline \end{array}$$

24. Write the numbers in the fact family.

$5 + 4 = 9$ $9 - 4 = 5$

$4 + 5 = 9$ $9 - 5 = 4$

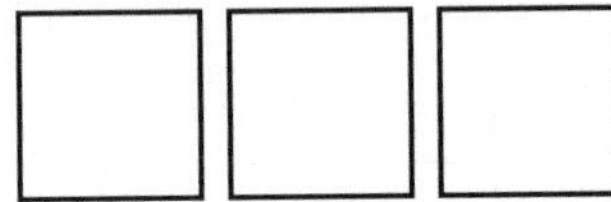

25. There are 8 seals. Some seals swim away. There are 6 seals left. How many seals swam away?

____ seals

26. There are 7 socks in all. 2 socks are green. The other socks are white. How many socks are white?

____ socks

Stop

Write the correct answer.

1. Write A, B, or C to show the group the figure belongs in.

A

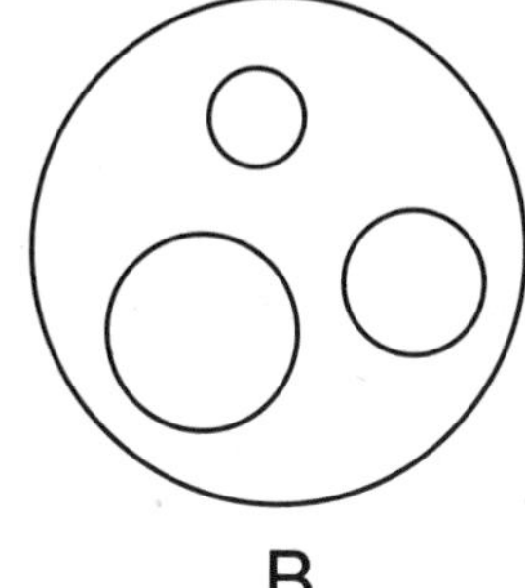

B

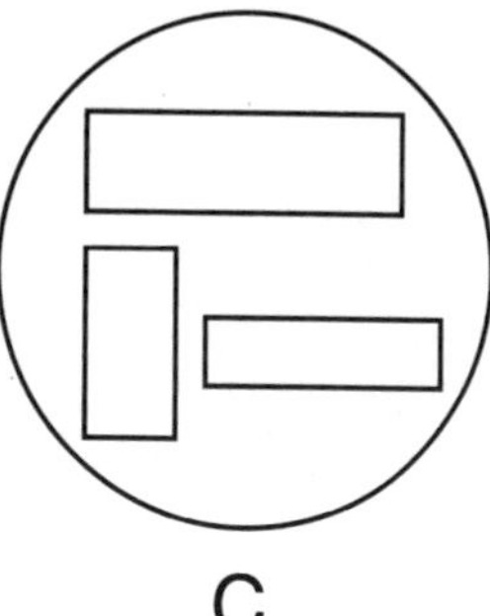

C

 ______

2. How many more children chose fish than turtle?

Animals We Like								
fish	fish	fish	fish	fish	fish	fish		
turtle	turtle	turtle	turtle	turtle				
cat	cat	cat	cat	cat	cat	cat	cat	cat

______ more children

Go On

Write the correct answer.

3. Circle which belongs in the group.

Use the picture graph to answer questions 5 and 6.

Kinds of Birds
hawk
peacock
blue bird

4. How many hawks are there?

______ hawks

5. How many fewer peacocks are there than blue birds?

______ fewer peacocks

Stop

Name ____________________

Write the correct answer.

1. Circle the bear you are more likely to pull from the bowl.

2. Use the tally chart to answer the question.

Pets We Like	
dog	~~IIII~~ III
cat	III
fish	~~IIII~~ II

Write how many children chose the fish.

_____ children

3. Color the cubes to make the sentence true.
It is **possible** to pull a gray cube.

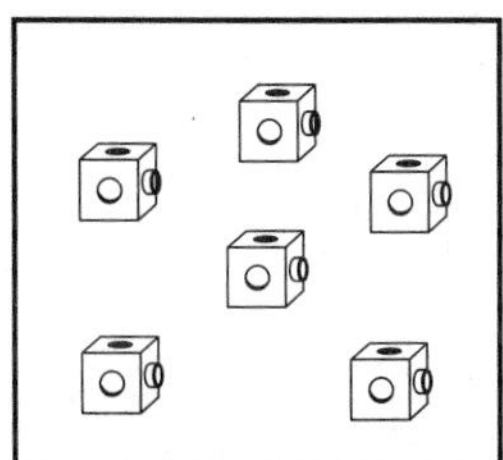

Go On

Name ______________________

Write the correct answer.

Use the bar graph to answer questions 4 and 5.

4. Write how many children chose .

_____ children

5. Circle which drink the most children chose.

6. There are 7 and 4 in a bowl. Circle the color you are more likely to pull.

7. There are 6 and 1 in a bag. Circle the color you are more likely to pull.

Stop

Name ______________________________

Write the correct answer.

1. Count how many tens and ones. Write the number.

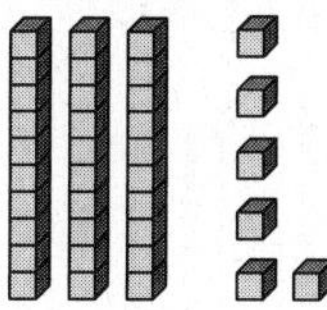

____ tens ____ ones

= ____

2. Count how many tens and ones. Write the number in a different way.

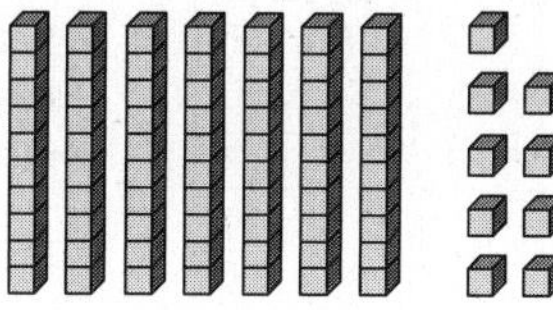

____ tens ____ ones

____ + ____

3. Count by tens. Write the number.

7 tens

____

4. Write the number of tens and ones.

18 eighteen

____ tens ____ ones

Go On

Write the correct answer.

5. Count how many tens and ones. Write the number.

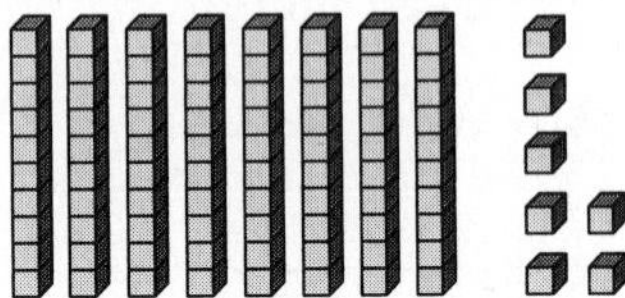

____ tens ____ ones

= ____

6. Count how many tens and ones. Write the number in a different way.

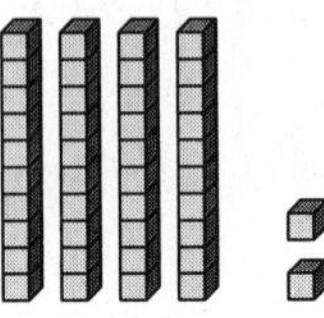

____ tens ____ ones

____ + ____

7. Circle the closest estimate.

About how many  can you hold in one hand?

about 9 

about 90 

about 900 

8. Circle the closest estimate.
About how many would fit in one cup?

about 3

about 30

about 300

Stop

Write the correct answer.

1. Write the numbers.

____ is greater than ____.

2. Write the number that is between 88 and 90.

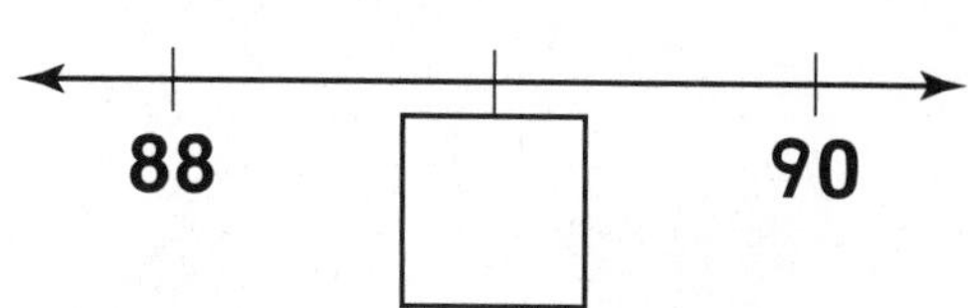

3. Compare the numbers. Write <, >, or =.

39 ◯ 34

4. Write the numbers in order from least to greatest.

38 63 36

____ ____ ____

5. Write the number that is one less than 74.

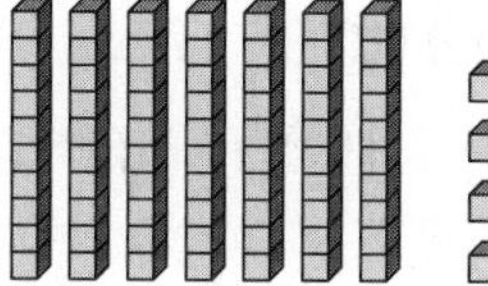

____

Go On

Write the correct answer.

6. Write the numbers.

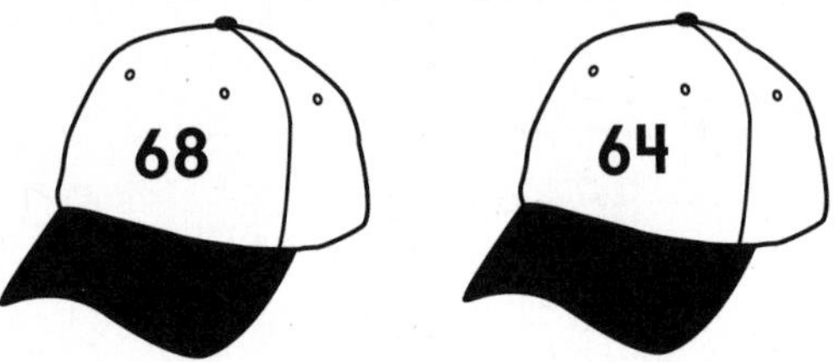

_____ is less than _____.

7. Write the number that is ten more than 62.

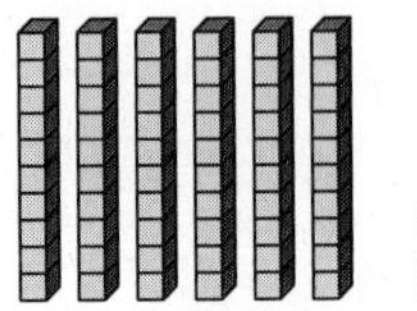

_____

Use the table to answer questions 8 and 9.

Month	Sunny Days
March	21
April	17
May	28
June	23

8. Compare the number of sunny days for the given months. Write the numbers.

_____ ◯ _____

March June

9. Write the number of sunny days in order from greatest to least.

_____ _____ _____ _____

Stop

Write the correct answer.

Use the hundred chart for questions 1 and 2.

1	2	3	4	5	6	7	8	9	10
11	12	13	14	15	16	17	18	19	20
21	22	23	24	25	26	27	28	29	30
31	32	33	34	35	36	37	38	39	40
41	42	43	44	45	46	47	48	49	50
51	52	53	54	55	56	57	58	59	60
61	62	63	64	65	66	67	68	69	70
71	72	73	74	75	76	77	78	79	80
81	82	83	84	85	86	87	88	89	90
91	92	93	94	95	96	97	98	99	100

1. Count by twos. Write the number that comes next.

56, 58, 60, 62, 64, ____

2. Count by tens. Write the numbers that come next.

6, 16, 26, ____, ____, ____

3. Skip count. Write how many toes there are.

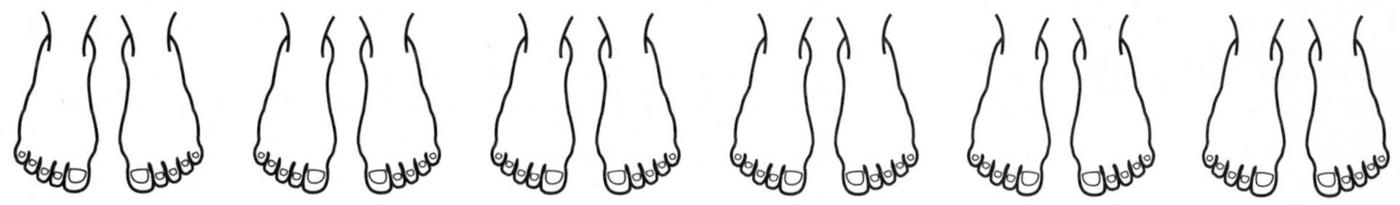

____ ____ ____ ____ ____ ____ toes

Go On

Write the correct answer.

4. Count forward. Write the numbers that come next.

82, 83, 84, ____, ____, ____

5. Find the pattern. Write the missing numbers.

34, 36, ____, 40, 42, ____

6. Is the number odd or even? Circle even or odd.

17 even odd

7. There are 2 wheels on a bicycle.
Write how many wheels there are on 7 bicycles.

number of bicycles	1	2	3	4	5	6	7
number of wheels	2	4					

__________ wheels

Stop

Name ______________________________

Write the correct answer.

1. Write the number that is between 71 and 73.

71 ☐ 73

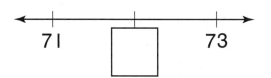

2. Count by tens. Write the number.

6 tens 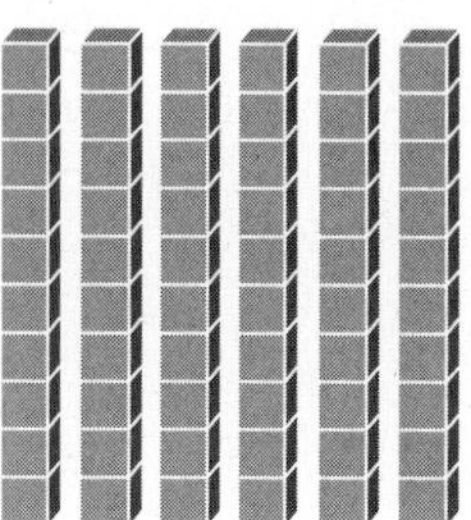

____

3. Use the tally chart to answer the question.

Sports We Like	
soccer	𝍸 I
baseball	𝍸 III
swimming	𝍸 IIII

Write how many children chose swimming.

____ children

4. Count how many tens and ones. Write the number in a different way.

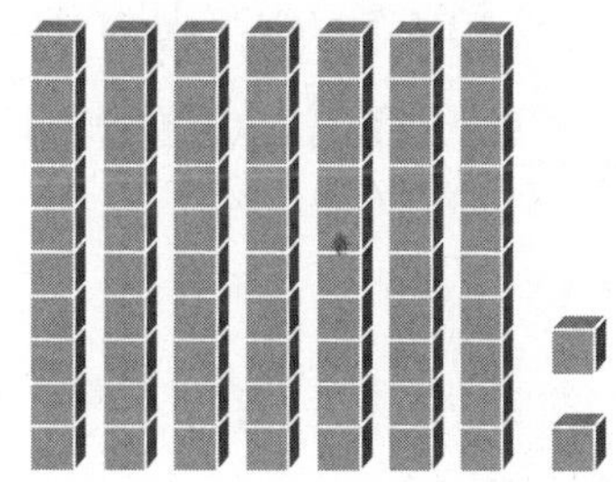

____ tens ____ ones

____ + ____

Go On

Write the correct answer.

Use the hundred chart for questions 5 and 6.

1	2	3	4	5	6	7	8	9	10
11	12	13	14	15	16	17	18	19	20
21	22	23	24	25	26	27	28	29	30
31	32	33	34	35	36	37	38	39	40
41	42	43	44	45	46	47	48	49	50
51	52	53	54	55	56	57	58	59	60
61	62	63	64	65	66	67	68	69	70
71	72	73	74	75	76	77	78	79	80
81	82	83	84	85	86	87	88	89	90
91	92	93	94	95	96	97	98	99	100

5. Count by fives. Write the number that comes next.

35, 40, 45, 50, 55, ____

6. Count by tens. Write the numbers that come next.

21, 31, 41, ____, ____, ____

Go On

Name ______________________________

Write the correct answer.

7. Circle which belongs in the group.

8. Color the cubes to make the sentence true. It is **possible** to pull a black cube.

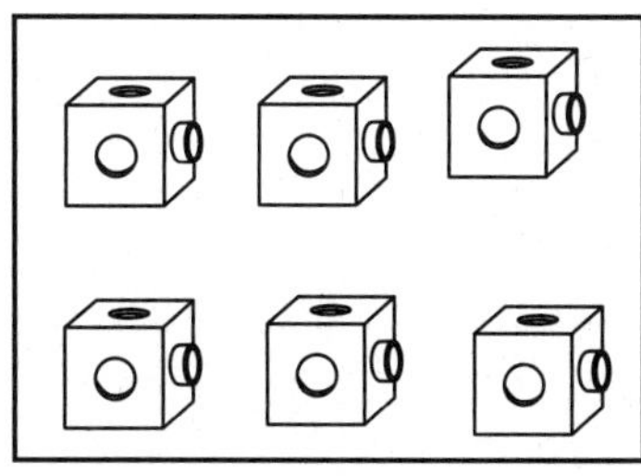

9. There are 2 wheels on a scooter.
Write how many wheels there are on 7 scooters.

number of scooters	1	2	3	4	5	6	7
number of wheels	2	4					

7 scooters have _____ wheels.

Go On

Write the correct answer.

10. Write the numbers.

____ is less than ____.

____ < ____

11. There are 2  and 6  in a bag. Circle which color you are more likely to pull.

Use the table to answer questions 12 and 13.

Team	Points Scored
Jays	55
Wolves	65
Lions	49
Mammoths	63

12. Write the team that scored more points.

____ ◯ ____

Jays Wolves

____

13. Write the team that scored the least number of points.

____ ____ ____ ____

greatest least

____

Go On

Name ____________________

Write the correct answer.

14. Write the number of tens and ones.

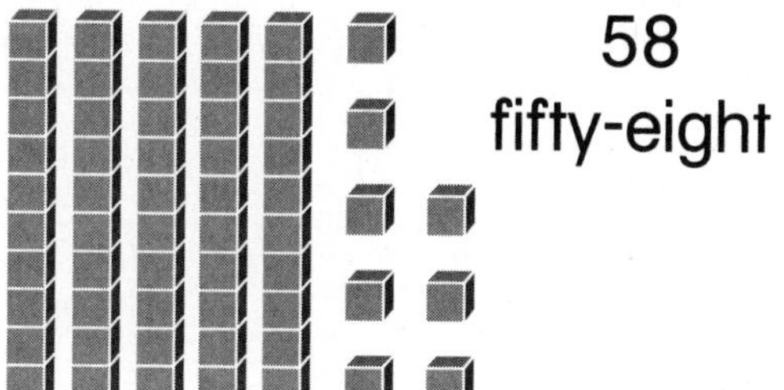

58
fifty-eight

____ tens ____ ones

15. Count forward. Write the numbers that come next.

76, 77, 78, ____, ____, ____

16. Compare the numbers. Write <, >, or =.

12 ◯ 15

17. Write the numbers in order from least to greatest.

40   29   34

____ ____ ____

18. Circle even or odd.

17   even   odd

Go On

Write the correct answer.

19. Use the picture graph to answer question 19.

Juices We Like								
apple	🍎	🍎	🍎	🍎	🍎	🍎		
orange	🍊	🍊	🍊	🍊	🍊			
grape	🍇	🍇	🍇	🍇	🍇	🍇	🍇	

How many more children chose grape than orange?

_____ more children

20. Count how many tens and ones. What is the number?

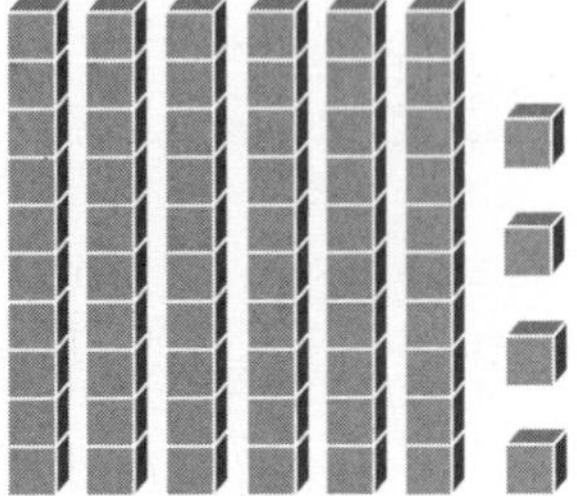

____ tens ____ ones = ____

21. Write the number that is ten more than 27.

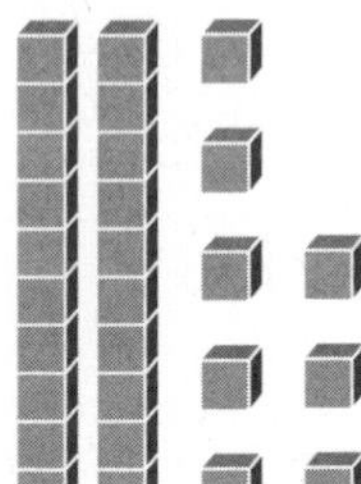

_____

Stop

Name ____________________ CHAPTER 13 POSTTEST

Write the correct answer.

1. Circle the object you could trace to make the figure.

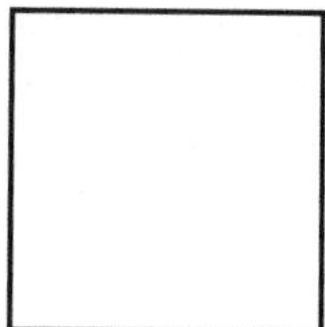

2. Write the number of sides and corners that the plane figure has.

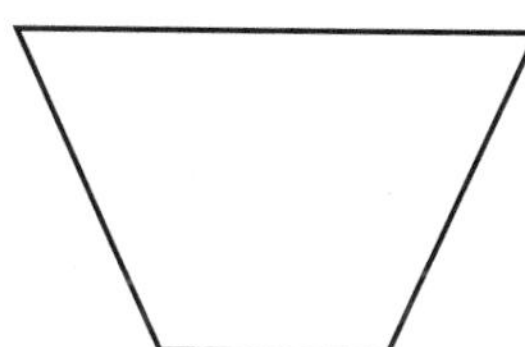

_____ sides

_____ corners

3. Write how many corners the rectangular prism has.

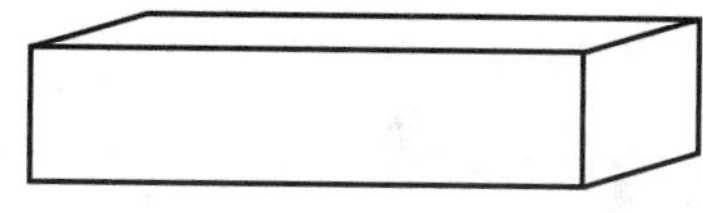

_____ corners

4. Color the square 

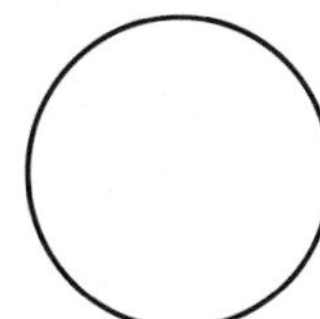

Go On

Name ______________________

Circle the correct answer.

5. Circle the solid figure with both curved and flat surfaces.

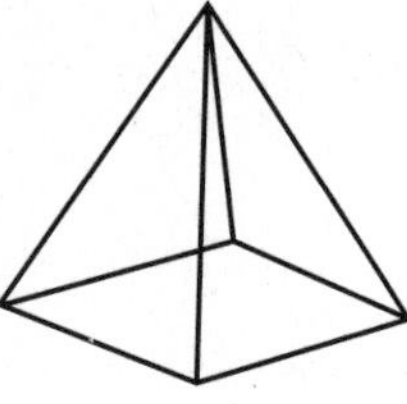
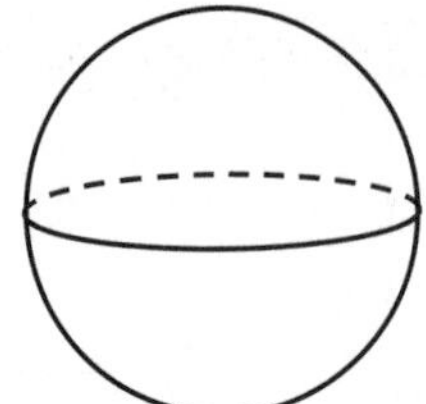
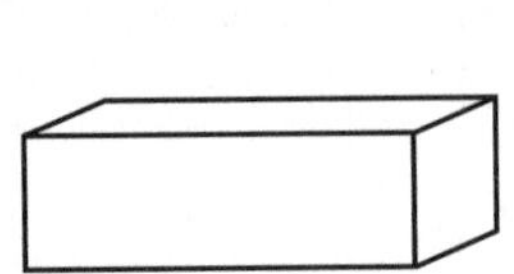

6. Color the triangle BLUE

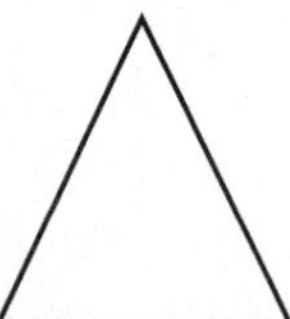
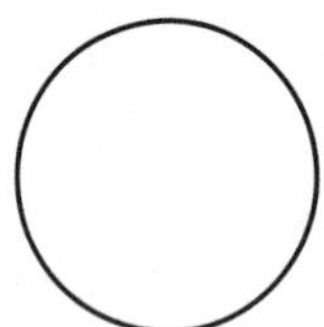
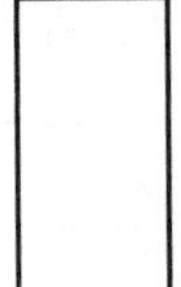
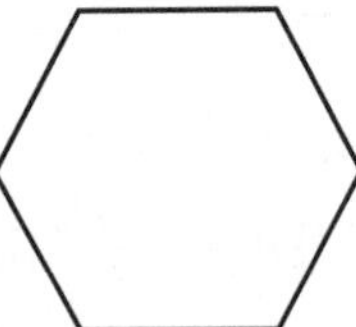

7. Circle the figure that has a curved surface and one flat surface with no corners.

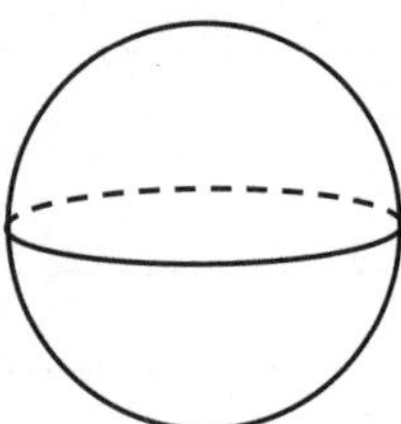
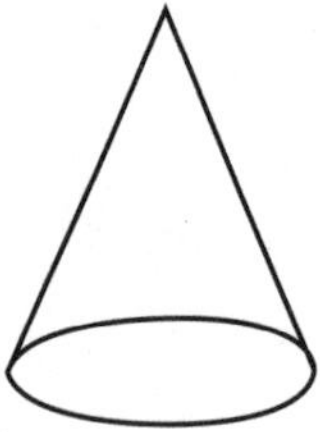
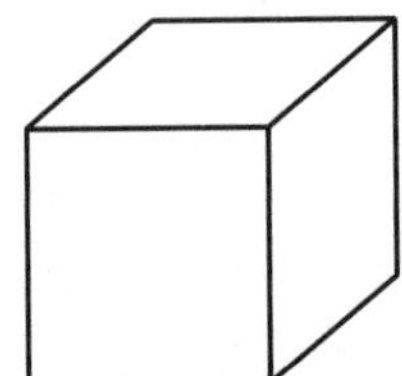
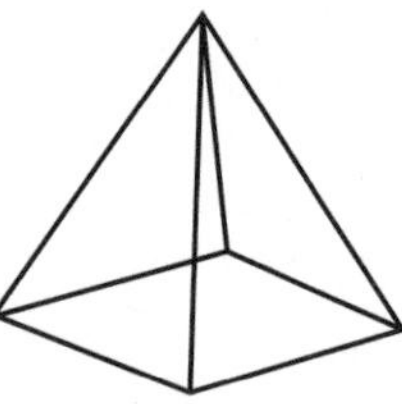

8. Circle the figure that has more than 4 sides and only 5 corners.

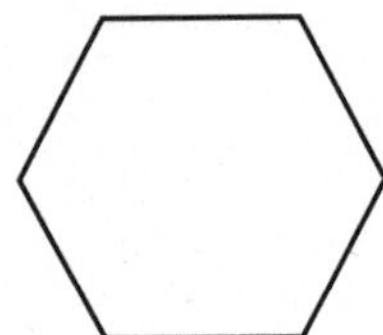
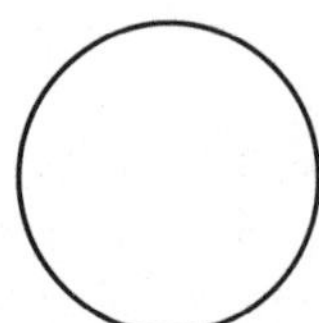
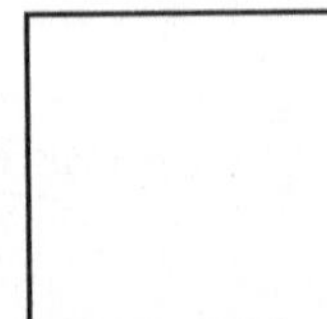
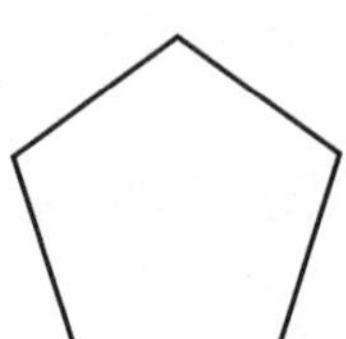

Stop

Name ______________________________

Write the correct answer.

1. Circle which comes next.

2. Use figures to show the same pattern.
Draw the figures.

3. Circle the pattern unit.

     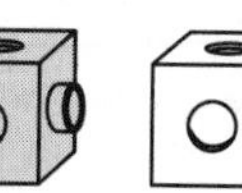    

Go On

Name ______________________________________

Write the correct answer.

4. Write the missing number.

3 3 4 3 3 _?_ 3 3 4

______

5. Draw and color what comes next.

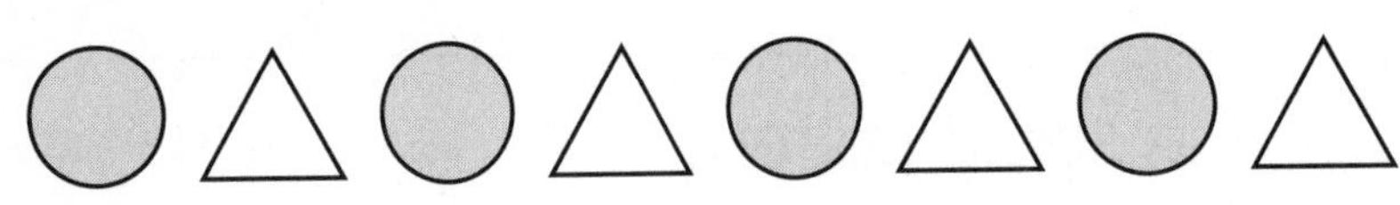

6. Circle the mistake in the pattern. Draw the correct pattern.

7. Circle the mistake in the pattern. Draw the correct pattern.

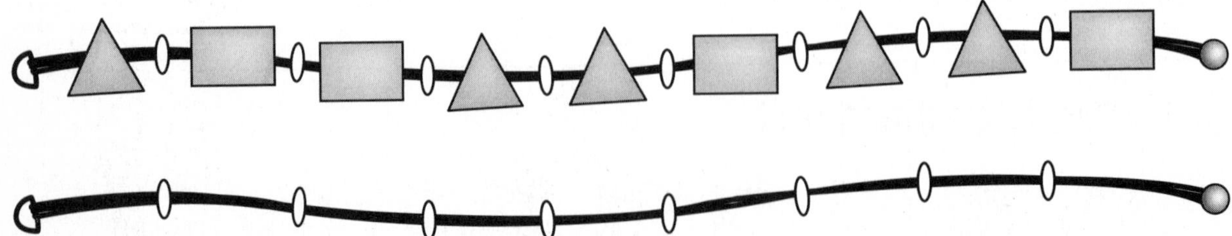

Stop

Choose the correct answer.

1. Circle the two figures that appear to be congruent.

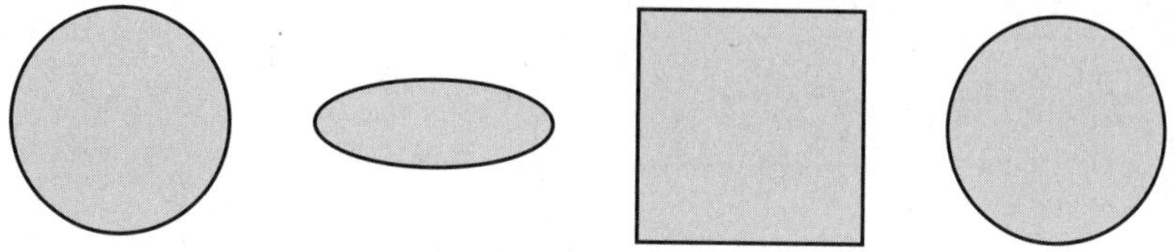

2. Circle slide, flip, or turn to name the move.

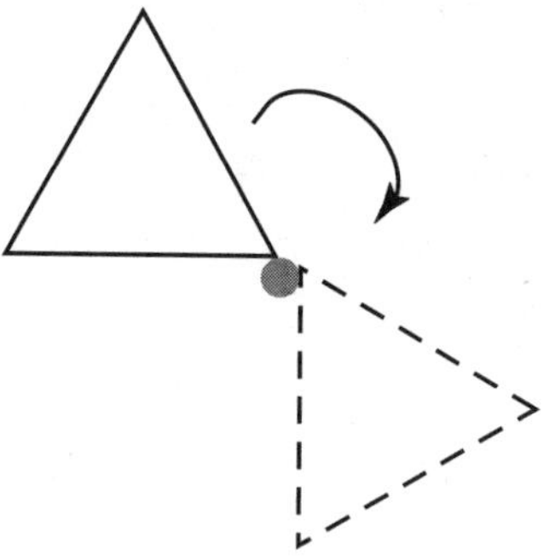

slide flip turn

3. The tent is next to the tree. Circle what is next to the girl.

Go On

Name ______________________________

Write the correct answer.

4. From **Start,** go right 2. Go down 2. Go left 1. Write where you are.

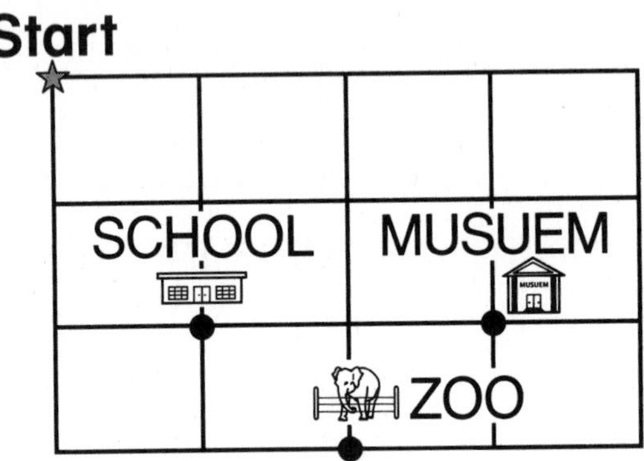

____

5. Draw a line of symmetry to make two parts that match.

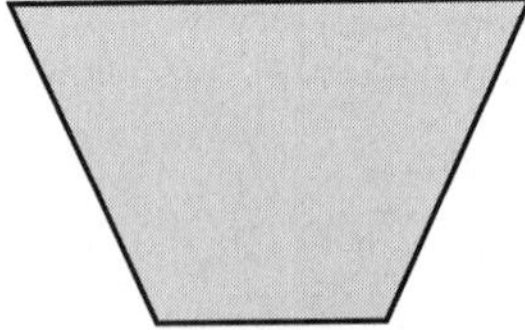

6. Jorge's toy is **above** the CATS DOGS Stories. It has a **line of symmetry**. Circle Jorge's toy.

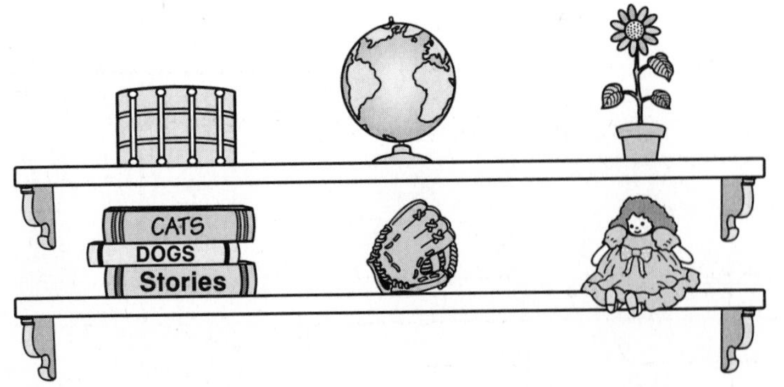

Stop

Write the correct answer.

1. Find the figure that is divided into two equal parts. Color $\frac{1}{2}$ of the figure.

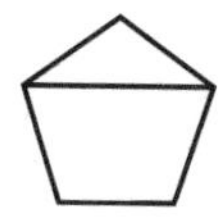
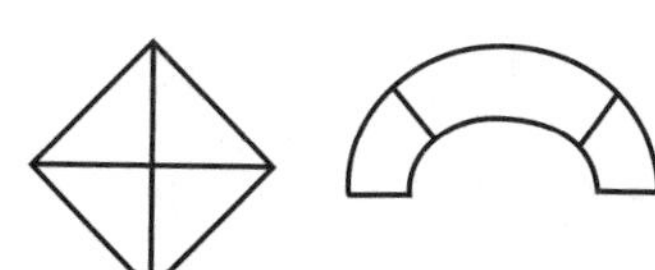

2. Use BLUE. Color to show $\frac{1}{4}$. Complete the sentence.

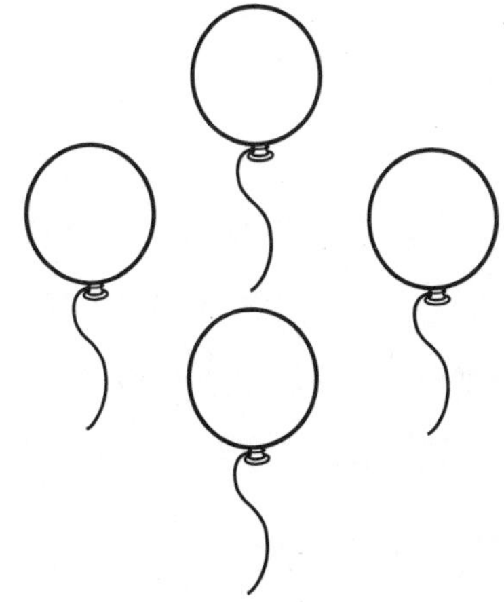

_____ out of _____ is blue.

3. Circle the figures with equal parts. Cross out the figures with unequal parts.

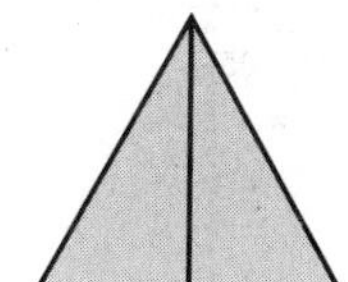
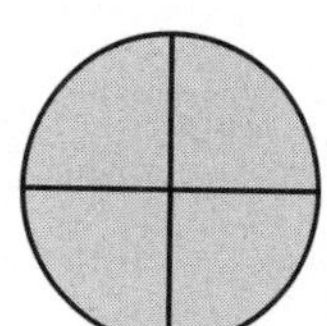

4. Find the figure that is divided into four equal parts. Color $\frac{1}{4}$ of the figure.

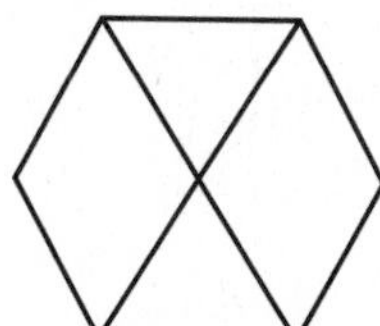
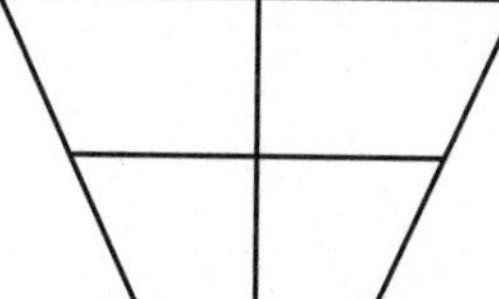

Go On

Write the correct answer.

5. Find the figure that is divided into three equal parts.

Color $\frac{1}{3}$ of the figure.

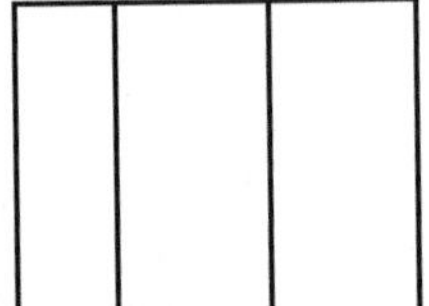

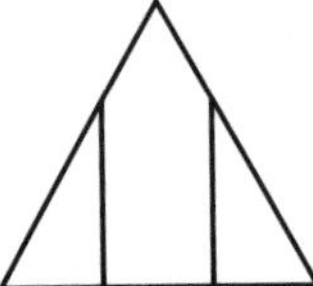
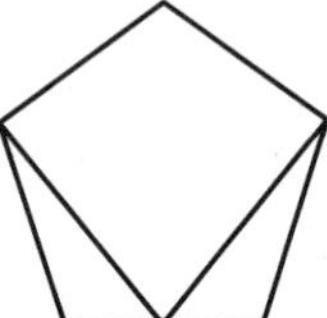

6. Jon and a friend share a . Each gets an equal share. Circle how you would cut the .

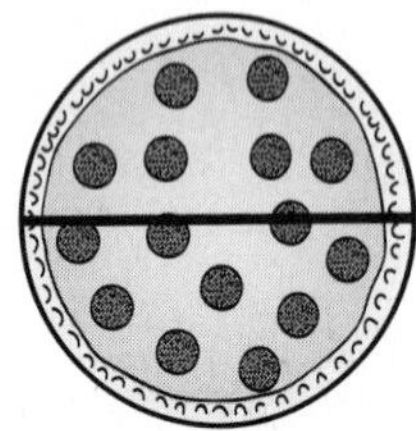
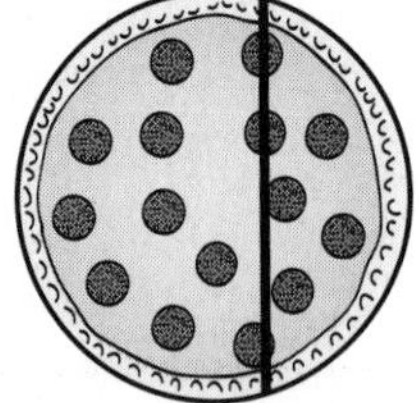
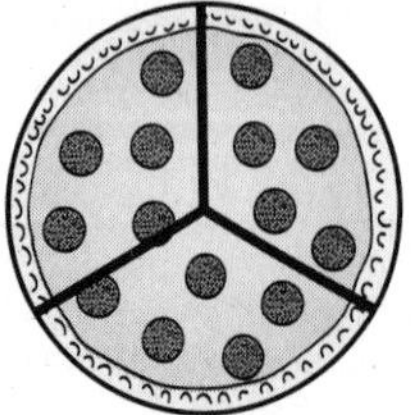

7. Ruby, Angie, and Sam share a . Each gets an equal share. Circle how you would cut the .

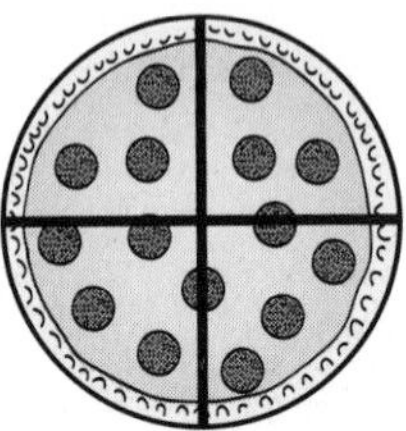
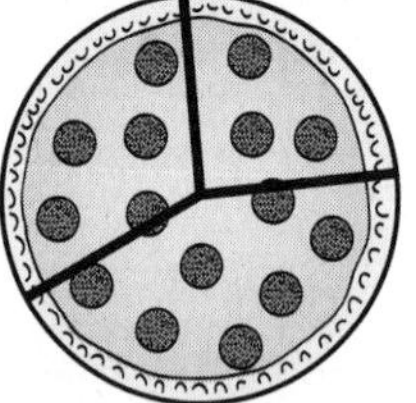
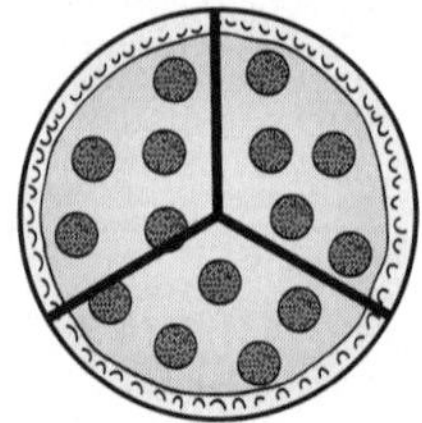

Stop

Name ______________________________

Write the correct answer.

1. Write the number of sides and corners the plane figure has.

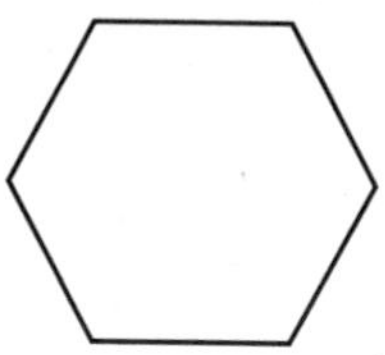

____ sides

____ corners

2. Circle slide, flip, or turn to name the move.

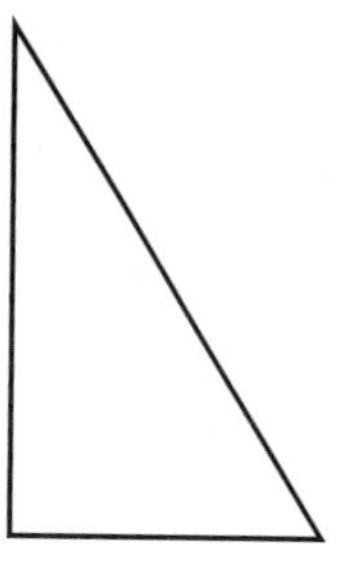

slide flip turn

3. Circle the figures with equal parts. Cross out the figures with unequal parts.

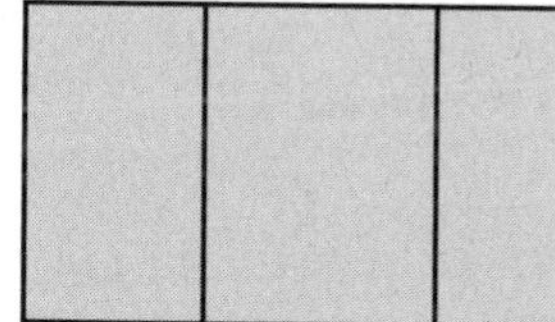 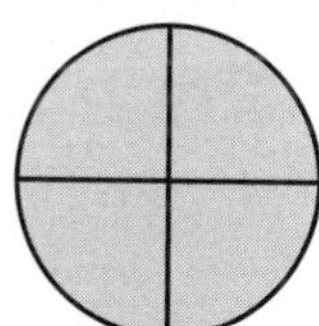 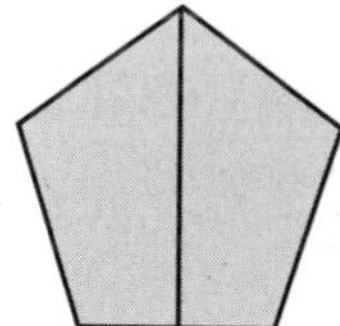

4. Color the triangle RED.

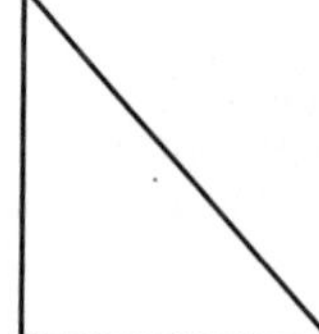 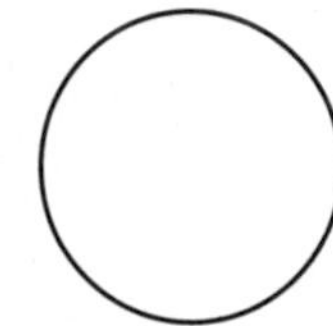  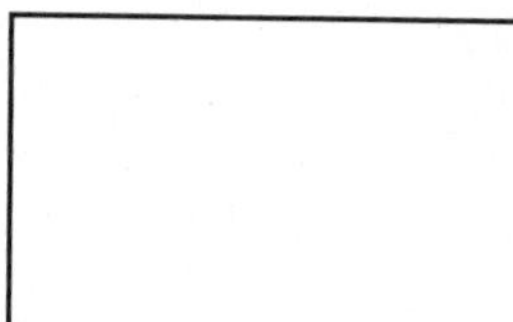

Go On

Write the correct answer.

5. Circle which comes next.

6. Draw a line of symmetry to make two parts that match.

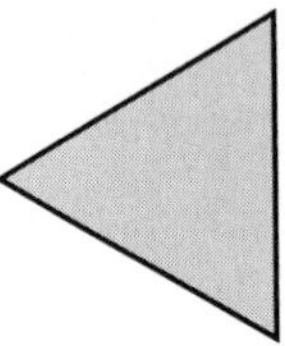

7. Find the figure that is divided into four equal parts.

Color $\frac{1}{4}$ of the figure.

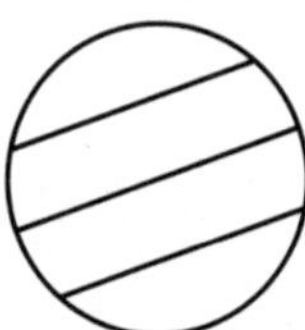

8. Circle the object you could trace to make the figure.

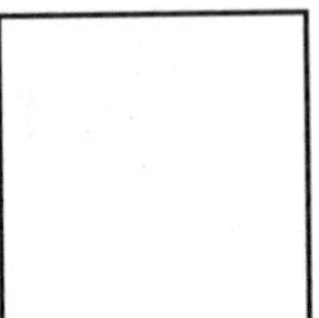

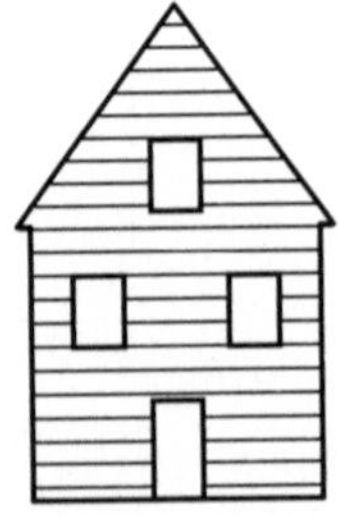
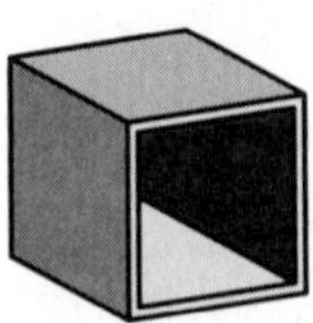

Go On

Name ____________________

Write the correct answer.

9. Circle the pattern unit.

  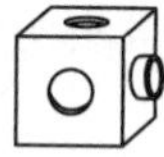   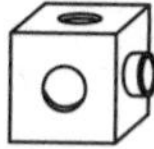   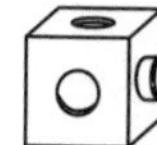

10. Chi and Lucy share a pizza. Each gets an equal share. Circle how you would cut the pizza.

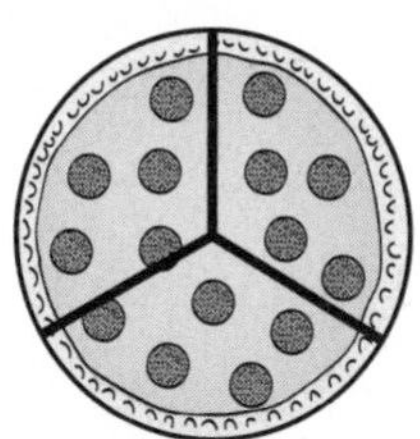

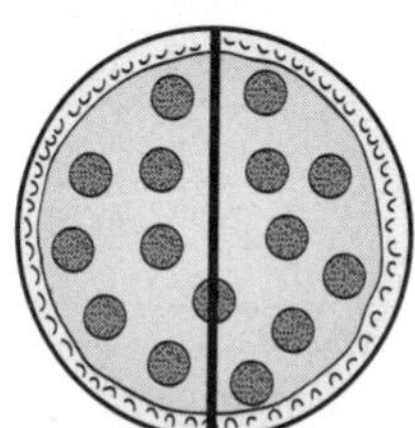

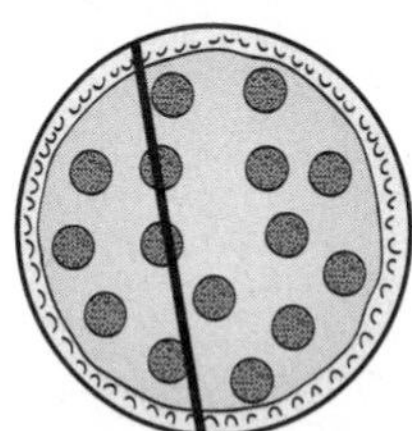

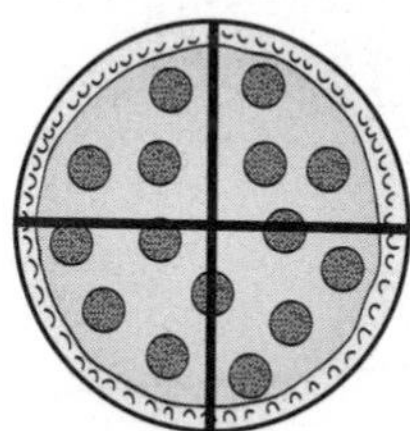

11. Use BLUE crayon.

Color to show $\frac{1}{3}$. Complete the sentence.

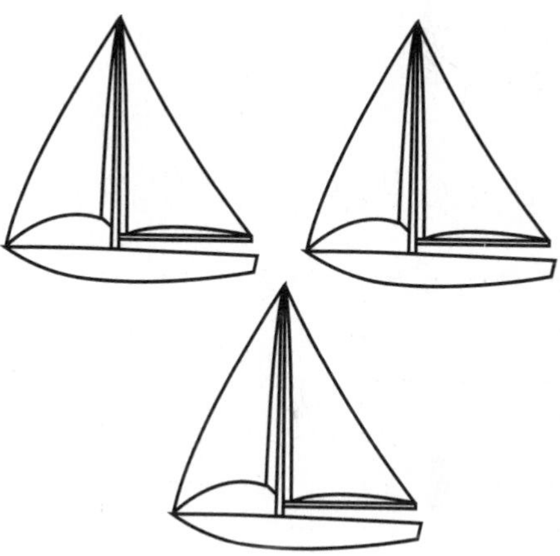

_____ out of _____ sailboats is blue.

Go On

Write the correct answer.

12. Color the rectangle YELLOW.

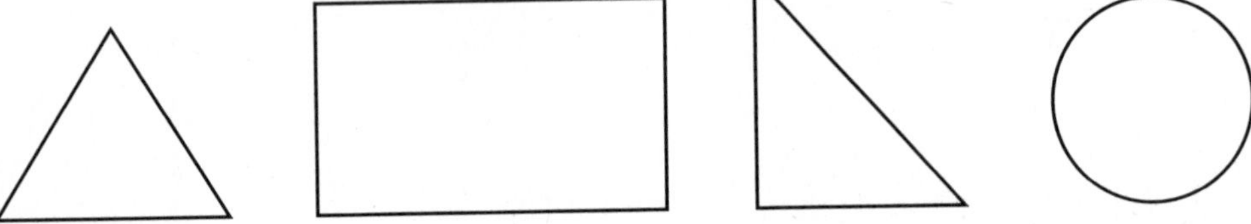

13. Write the missing number.

2 6 ___ 2 6 6 2 6 6

14. Circle the solid figure with both curved and flat surfaces.

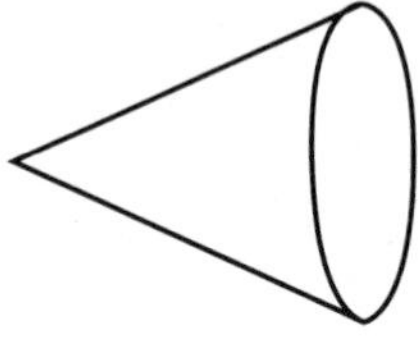
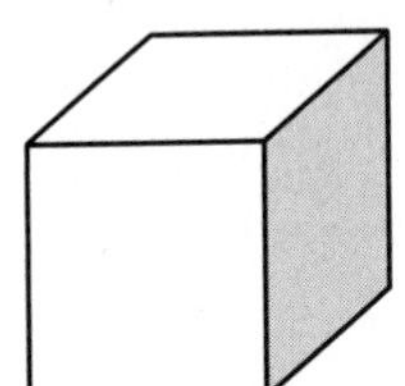
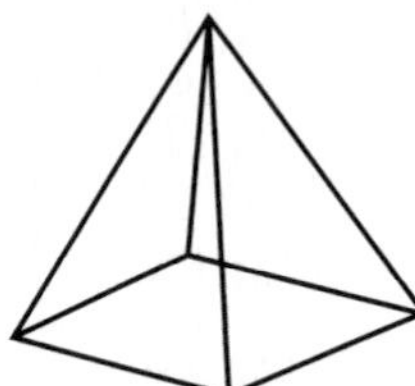
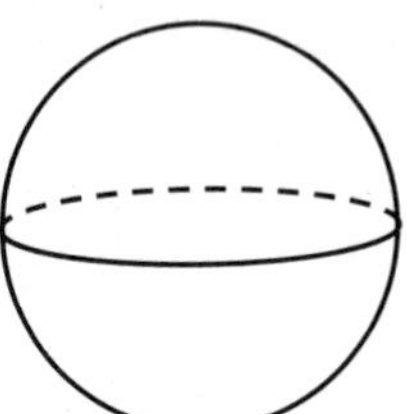

15. Use figures to show the same pattern.
Draw the figures.

Go On

Write the correct answer.

16. Circle the two figures that appear to be congruent.

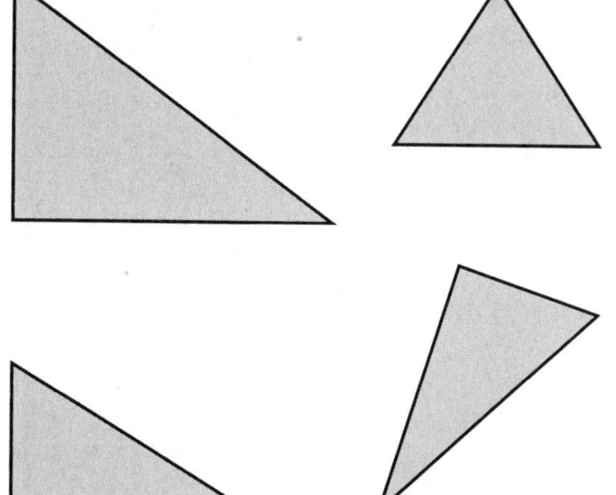

17. Write how many flat sides the pyramid has.

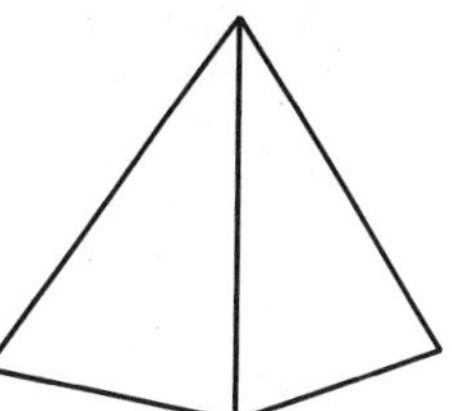

_____ flat sides

Use the picture for questions 18 and 19.

18. Rachel's toy is **near** the [books]. It has a **line of symmetry.** Circle Rachel's toy.

19. Doug's toy is **near** the [clock]. It is **above** the [picture]. Circle Doug's toy.

Go On

Write the correct answer.

20. Circle the mistake in the pattern.
Draw the correct pattern.

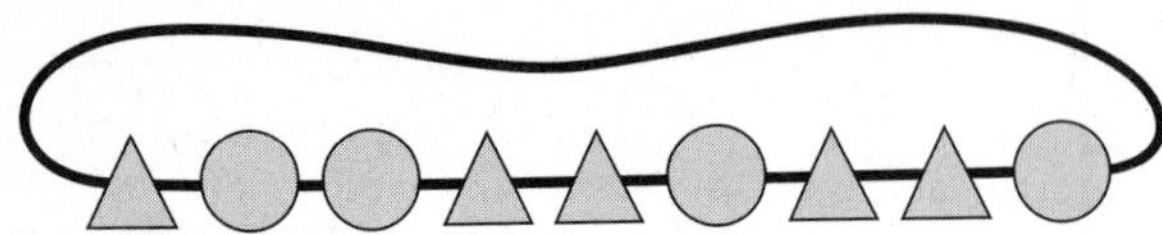

21. Circle the figure that has only flat surfaces.

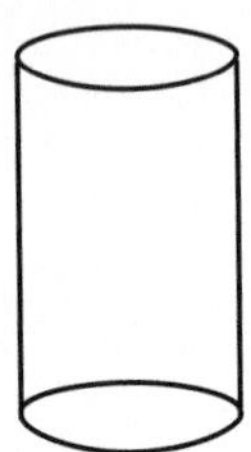 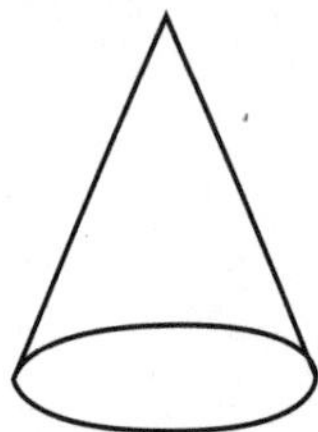 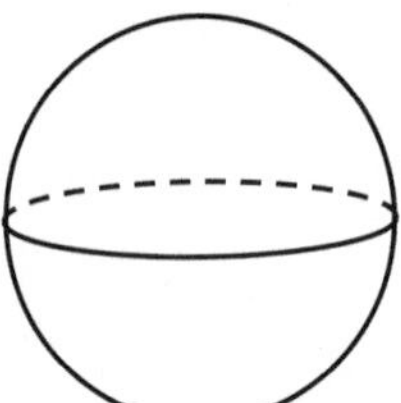 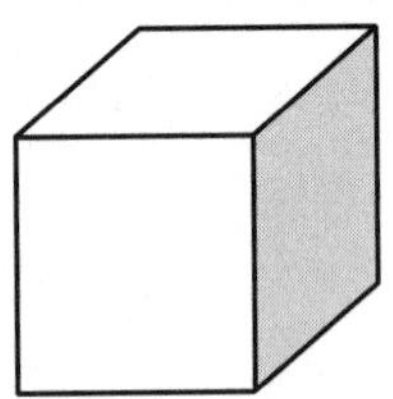

22. From **Start,** go right 1. Go down 3. Go left 1.
Write where you are.

Start

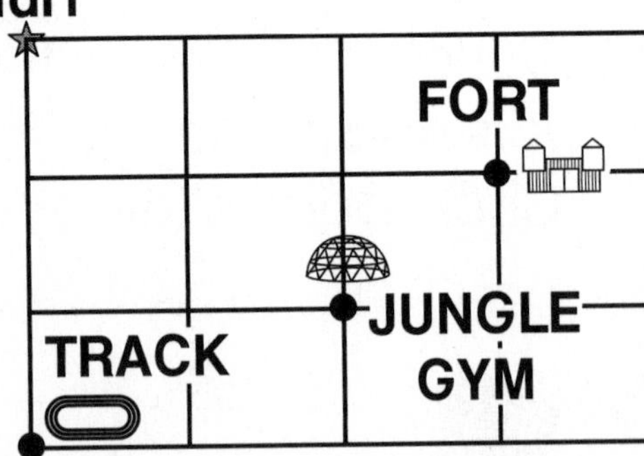

____

Stop

Write the correct answer.

1. Write the sum.

$$\begin{array}{r} 7 \\ +7 \\ \hline \end{array}$$

____

2. Make a ten and add. Write the sum.

$$\begin{array}{r} 8 \\ +6 \\ \hline \end{array}$$

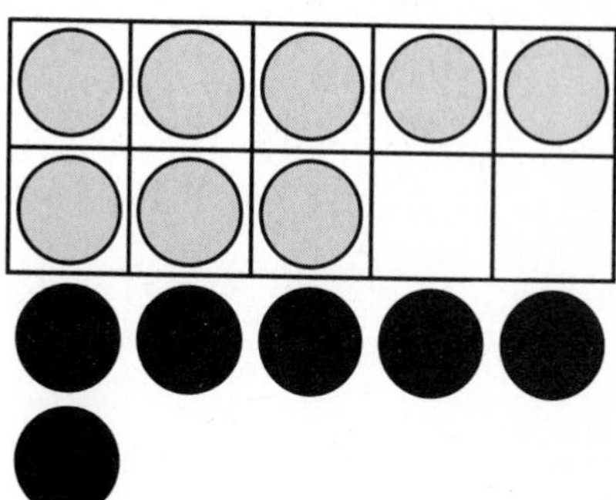

____

3. Write the sum.

$$\begin{array}{r} 8 \\ +9 \\ \hline \end{array}$$

____

4. Write the sum.

$$\begin{array}{r} 2 \\ 3 \\ +8 \\ \hline \end{array}$$

____

Go On

Name ____________________

Write the correct answer.

5. Write the sum.

$$\begin{array}{r} 10 \\ +5 \\ \hline \end{array}$$

____

6. Make a ten and add. Write the sum.

$$\begin{array}{r} 9 \\ +6 \\ \hline \end{array}$$

____

7. Write the sum.

$8 + 8 =$ ____

8. Write a number sentence to solve.
8 firefighters arrive at a fire. 4 more firefighters join them. How many firefighters are at the fire now?

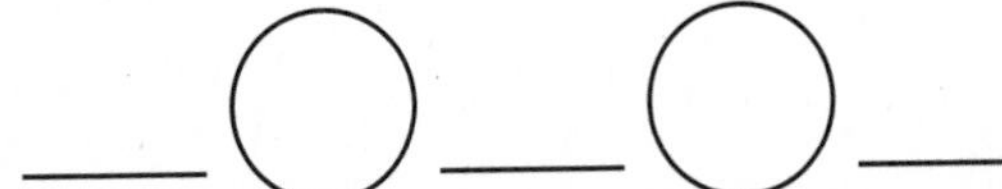

____ firefighters

9. Write a number sentence to solve.
A mail carrier delivers 7 letters. Then he delivers 6 more letters. How many letters does the mail carrier deliver in all?

____ letters

Stop

Write the correct answer.

Use the number line to answer questions 1 and 2.

1. Write the difference.

$$\begin{array}{r} 15 \\ -\ 7 \\ \hline \end{array}$$

2. Write the difference.

$$\begin{array}{r} 13 \\ -\ 6 \\ \hline \end{array}$$

3. Write how many more birds there are than nests.

$$\begin{array}{r} 14 \\ -\ 7 \\ \hline \end{array}$$

4. Write the difference.

17 − 8 = ____

Go On

Name ___________________________

Write the correct answer.

5. Use the addition fact to help you subtract. Write the sum. Then write the difference.

$$\begin{array}{r} 9 \\ +\ 6 \\ \hline \end{array} \qquad \begin{array}{r} 15 \\ -\ 6 \\ \hline \end{array}$$

6. Write the difference.

$$\begin{array}{r} 13 \\ -\ 8 \\ \hline \end{array}$$

7. Write how many fewer butterflies there are than flowers.

$$\begin{array}{r} 14 \\ -\ 8 \\ \hline \end{array}$$

8. There are 14 children playing on the playground. 6 children go home. Write how many children are playing on the playground now.

_____ children

9. Peter counted birds at the park. He counted 8 wrens and 9 robins. Write how many birds Peter counted in all.

_____ birds

Stop

Write the correct answer.

1. Write the missing number.

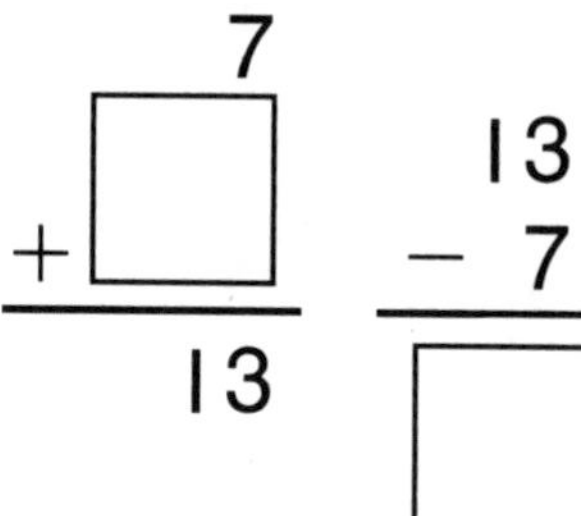

2. Write a way to make 15.

____ + ____ + ____

3. Use the picture to write the numbers. Write a number sentence to show how many kites there are.

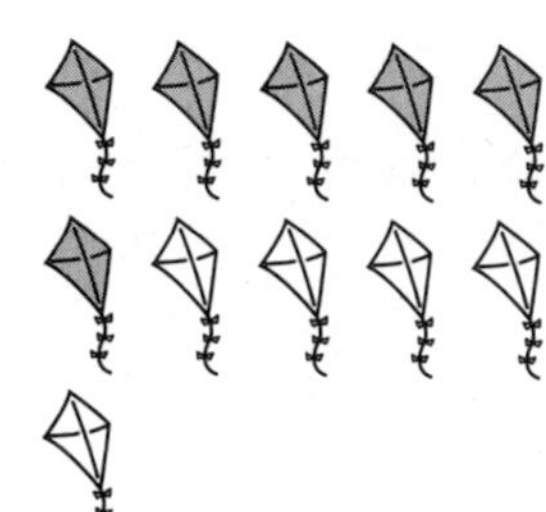

____ gray kites

____ white kites

____ ◯ ____ ◯ ____

4. Write the missing numbers.

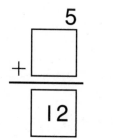

$$\begin{array}{r} 5 \\ + \square \\ \hline \boxed{12} \end{array} \qquad \begin{array}{r} 12 \\ - \ 5 \\ \hline \square \end{array}$$

Go On

Write the correct answer.

5. Write a way to make 9.

____ – ____

6. Follow the rule. Write the number that completes the table.

Subtract 9	
12	3
14	5
16	
17	8

7. Write each sum or difference.
Circle the facts in the same fact family.

$$\begin{array}{r} 8 \\ +7 \\ \hline \end{array} \quad \begin{array}{r} 15 \\ -7 \\ \hline \end{array} \quad \begin{array}{r} 13 \\ -7 \\ \hline \end{array} \quad \begin{array}{r} 7 \\ +8 \\ \hline \end{array} \quad \begin{array}{r} 15 \\ -8 \\ \hline \end{array}$$

8. Write a number sentence to solve.
Jamie has 7 peppers. Aidan brings 7 more peppers. How many peppers are there in all?

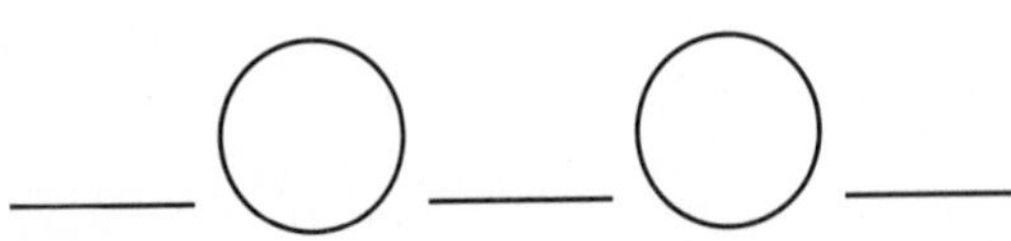

____ peppers

9. Write a number sentence to solve.
A store has 15 watermelons. Gina buys 8 of them. How many watermelons are still at the store?

____ watermelons

Stop

Name ____________________

Write the correct answer.

1. Draw and label coins to show the amount in a different way.

2. Use quarters and dimes. Draw and label coins to show a way to make 1 dollar.

Go On

Write the correct answer.

3. Count. Compare the amounts. Write <, >, or =.

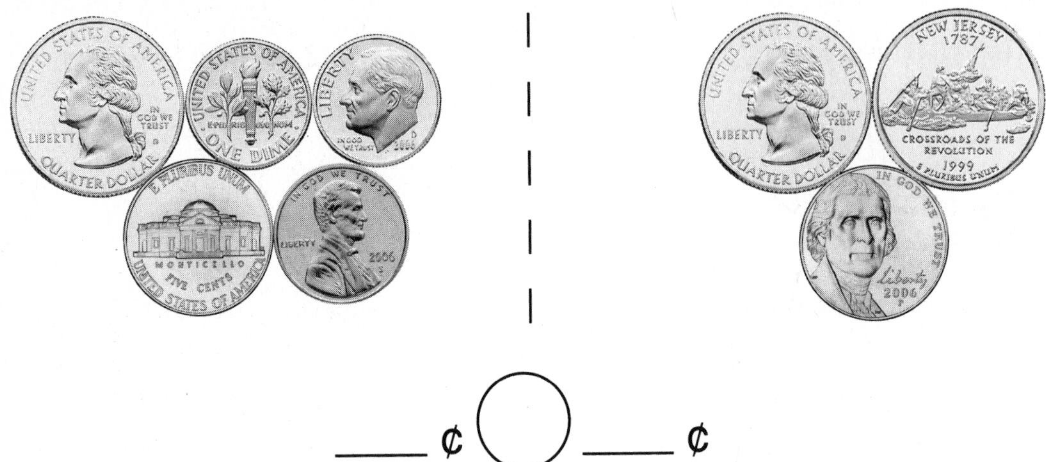

____ ¢ ◯ ____ ¢

4. Charlie buys a teddy bear for 50¢. He uses 2 .
Draw and label coins to show the same amount in a different way.

Stop

Name____

Write the correct answer.

1. Write the time.

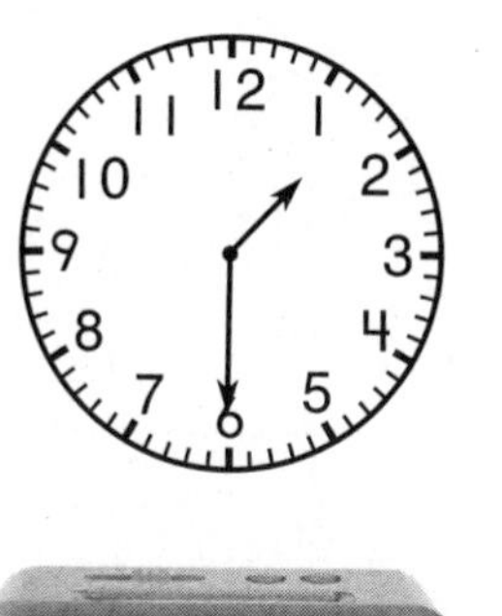

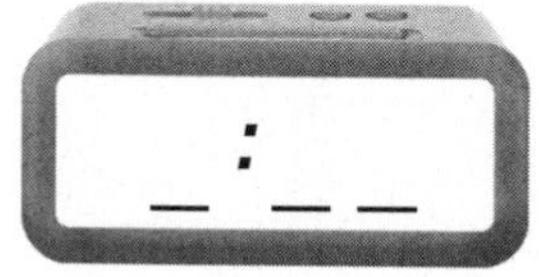

2. Write the time.

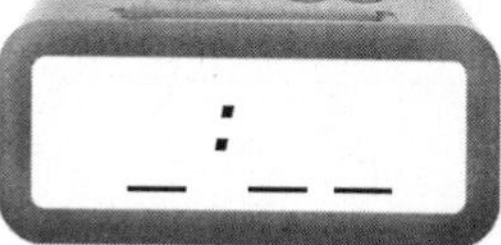

3. Use the calendar. Write how many days are in this month.

JUNE						
Sunday	Monday	Tuesday	Wednesday	Thursday	Friday	Saturday
					1	2
3	4	5	6	7	8	9
10	11	12	13	14	15	16
17	18	19	20	21	22	23
24	25	26	27	28	29	30

____ days

Go On

Name ________________________________

Write the correct answer.

4. Draw the hour hand and minute hand to show the time.

Use the table to answer questions 5 and 6.

Field Day		
Event	**Start**	**End**
 sack race		
 relay race		
 tug-of-war		

5. Which event starts at 10:30?

____

6. Which event lasts the shortest time?

____

Stop

Write the correct answer.

1. Use the calendar. Write how many days are in this month.

March						
Sunday	Monday	Tuesday	Wednesday	Thursday	Friday	Saturday
						1
2	3	4	5	6	7	8
9	10	11	12	13	14	15
16	17	18	19	20	21	22
23	24	25	26	27	28	29
30	31					

_____ days

2. Use the addition fact to help you subtract. Write the sum. Then write the difference.

$$\begin{array}{r} 6 \\ +\ 8 \\ \hline \end{array} \qquad \begin{array}{r} 14 \\ -\ 8 \\ \hline \end{array}$$

3. Write the sum.

$$\begin{array}{r} 8 \\ +\ 8 \\ \hline \end{array}$$

4. Follow the rule. Write the number that completes the table.

Add 5	
6	11
8	13
9	
10	15

Go On

Name ____________________

Write the correct answer.

5. Write how many fewer birds are there than leaves.

$$\begin{array}{r} 12 \\ -\ 6 \\ \hline \end{array}$$

6. Use the picture to write the numbers. Write a number sentence to show how many kites are white.

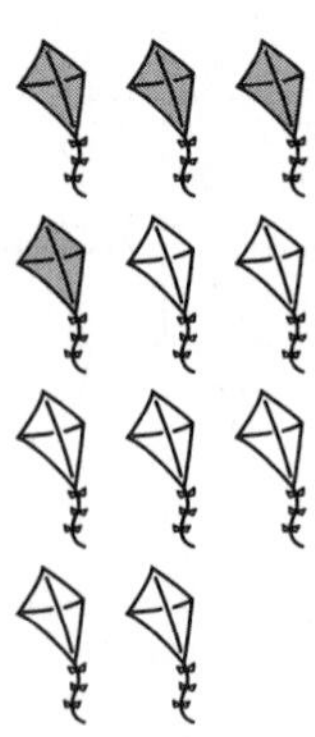

_____ kites in all

_____ gray kites

7. Write the sum.

$$\begin{array}{r} 2 \\ 3 \\ +\ 8 \\ \hline \end{array}$$

8. Circle the time of day.

morning evening

afternoon

Go On

Write the correct answer.

9. Draw and label coins to show the amount a different way.

10. Draw and label coins to show a way to make 1 dollar.
Use dimes and nickels.

11. Write the difference.

$$\begin{array}{r} 17 \\ -\ 9 \\ \hline \end{array}$$

Go On

Name ______________________________

Write the correct answer.

12. Write a number sentence to solve.

A woman buys 3 books. Then she buys 9 more books. How many books does the woman buy in all?

____ books

13. Write the missing numbers.

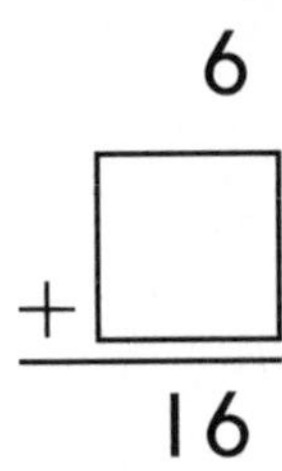

$$\begin{array}{r} 6 \\ +\square \\ \hline 16 \end{array}$$

$$\begin{array}{r} 16 \\ -\ 6 \\ \hline \square \end{array}$$

14. Make a ten and add. Write the sum.

$$\begin{array}{r} 8 \\ +\ 7 \\ \hline \end{array}$$

15. Write a number sentence to solve.

Pablo has 14 apples. He gives 9 apples away. How many apples does Pablo have now?

____ ○ ____ ○ ____

____ apples

Go On

Name ____________________________________

Write the correct answer.

16. Count. Compare the amounts. Write <, >, or =.

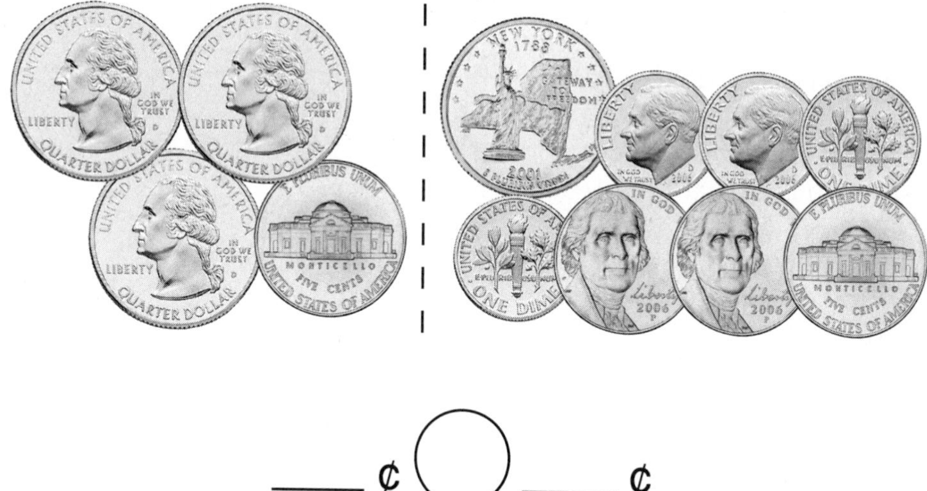

____ ¢ ◯ ____ ¢

17. Draw the hour hand and minute hand to show the time.

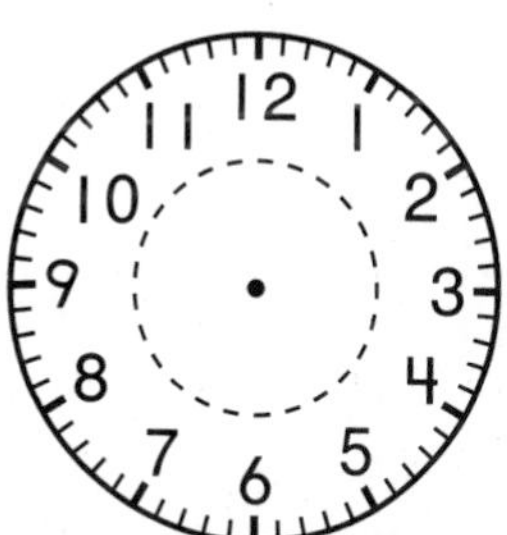

18. Write the sum.

$4 + 5 =$ ____

19. Write the difference.

$10 - 8 =$ ____

Go On

Name ____________________

Write the correct answer.

Use the table to answer question 20.

Aquarium		
Event	**Start**	**End**
tour		
feed turtles		
dolphin show		

20. Which event starts at 11:00?

____

21. Write each sum or difference.
Circle the facts in the same fact family.

$$\begin{array}{r} 14 \\ -\ 5 \\ \hline \end{array} \quad \begin{array}{r} 14 \\ -\ 9 \\ \hline \end{array} \quad \begin{array}{r} 9 \\ +5 \\ \hline \end{array} \quad \begin{array}{r} 5 \\ +9 \\ \hline \end{array} \quad \begin{array}{r} 19 \\ -\ 5 \\ \hline \end{array}$$

Stop

Name ______________________________

Write the correct answer.

1. Write the temperature.

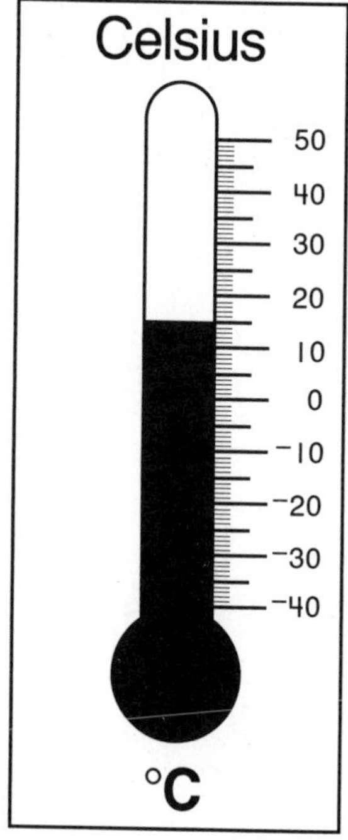

____ °C

2. Measure the object. Write the length.

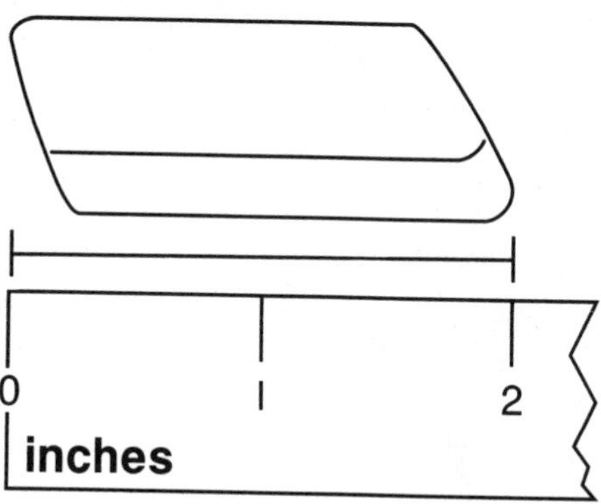

about ____ inches

3. Write about how many [paper clip] long the object is.

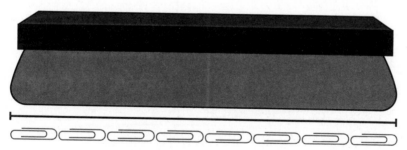

about ____ [paper clip]

Go On

Write the correct answer.

4. Circle the ribbons that are in order from longest to shortest.

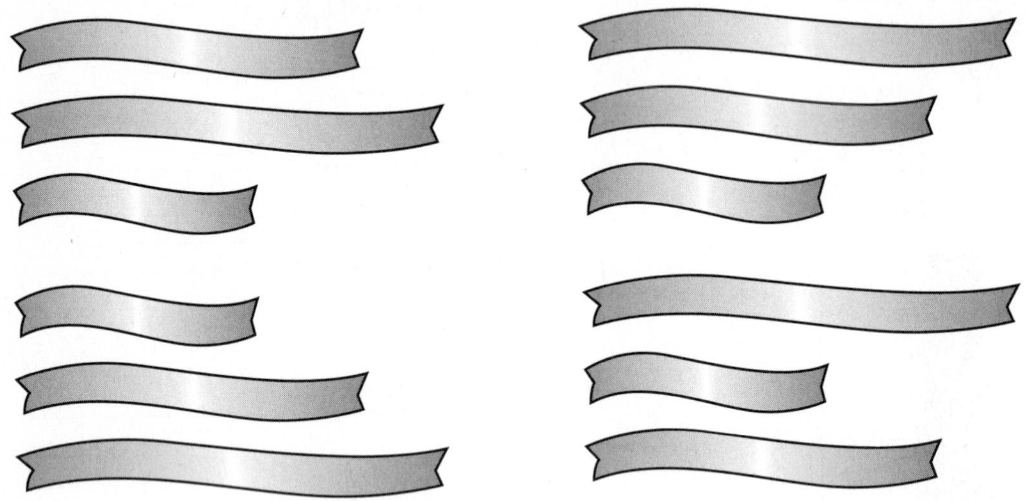

5. About how many ⊂⊃ long is the object? Circle the estimate that makes sense.

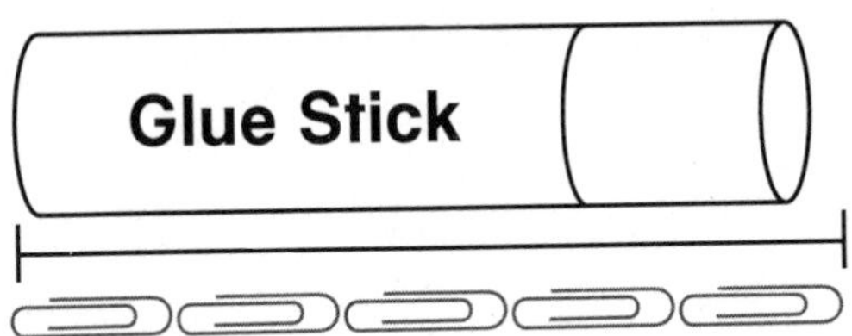

about 5 ⊂⊃ about 6 ⊂⊃

6. About how many ⊂⊃ long is the object? Circle the estimate that makes sense.

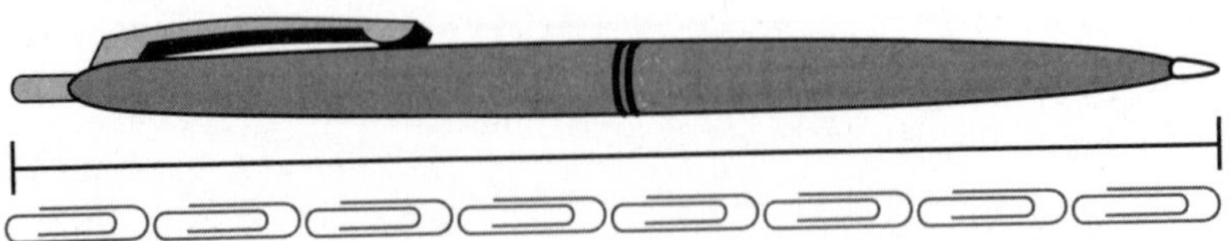

about 6 ⊂⊃ about 8 ⊂⊃

Stop

Choose the correct answer.

1. Circle the heaviest object.

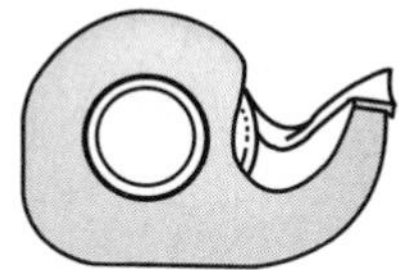

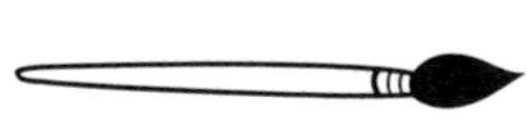

2. Circle the container that holds the most.

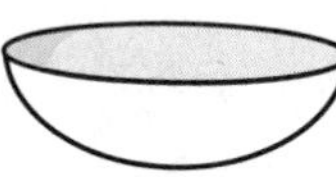

3. Circle the size of the container.

pint

quart

4. Circle the better estimate for the weight of the object.

about 1 pound

about 10 pounds

Go On

Name ____________________

Choose the correct answer.

5. Circle the tool you will use to measure how tall the juice container is.

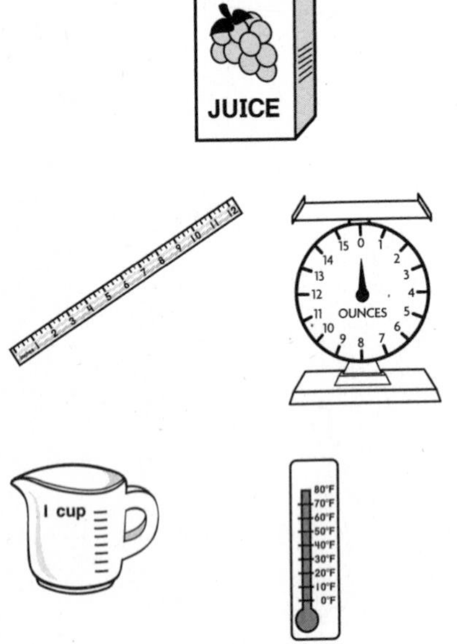

6. Circle the tool you will use to measure how heavy the pear is.

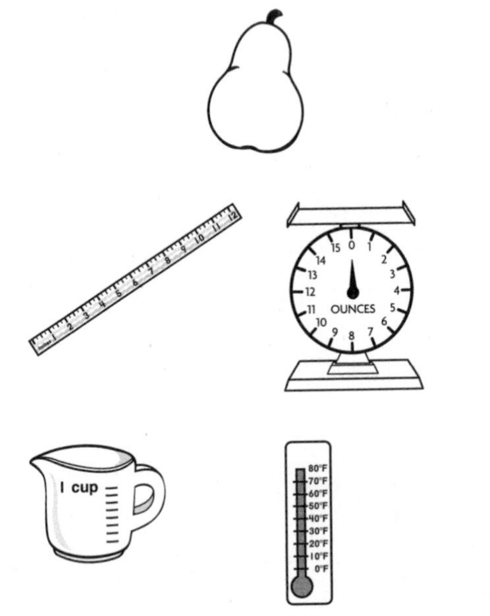

7. Circle how many more cups you need to fill the container to the top.

This glass has I cup of juice in it.

I cup   3 cups

2 cups

8. Circle how many more cups you need to fill the container to the top.

This bowl has 2 cups of soup in it.

I cup   3 cups

2 cups

Stop

Name ______________________________

Write the correct answer.

1. Write the difference.

70 − 40 = ____

2. Write the sum.

30 + 50 = ____

3. Write the difference.

	tens	ones
	3	6
−		4

Workmat

Tens	Ones

4. Write the sum.

	tens	ones
	2	3
+		6

Workmat

Tens	Ones

Go On

Name ____________________

Write the correct answer.

5. Write the sum.

	tens	ones
	2	4
+	1	5

Workmat

Tens	Ones

6. Write the difference.

	tens	ones
	2	7
−	1	4

Workmat

Tens	Ones

8. Circle the best estimate. There are 51 birds at the lake. 9 of the birds fly away. About how many birds are left?

about 4 birds

about 40 birds

about 400 birds

9. Circle the best estimate. Brett has 41 stickers in his collection. Anna has 28 stickers in her collection. About how many stickers do they both have?

about 7 stickers

about 70 stickers

about 700 stickers

Stop

Name ______________________________

Write the correct answer.

1. Write the sum.

	tens	ones
	2	3
+		6

Workmat

tens	ones

____

2. Circle the container that holds the most water.

3. Write about how many long the object is.

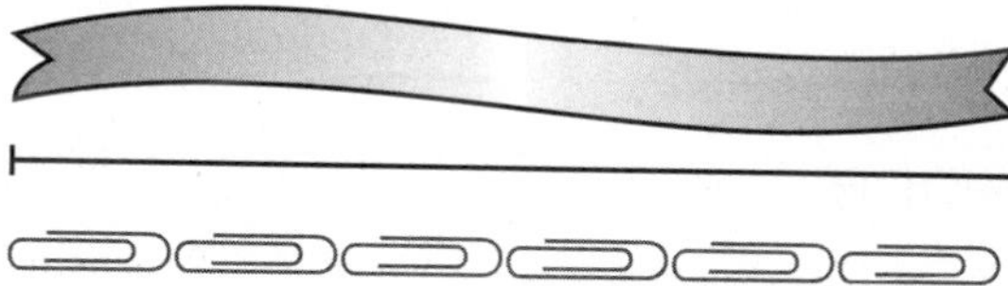

about ____

Go On

Name ____________________

Write the correct answer.

4. Circle the better estimate.

about 1 pound

about 10 pounds

5. Write the temperature.

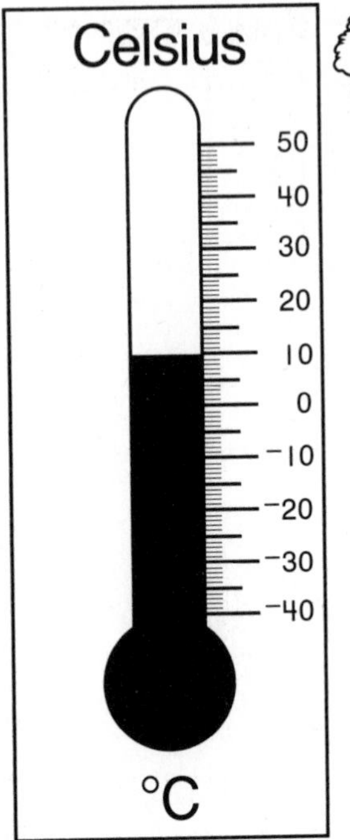

____°C

6. Write the difference.

70 − 30 = ____

7. Circle the size of the container.

pint quart

Go On

Name ______________________________

Choose the correct answer.

8. Write the difference.

	tens	ones
	3	4
−	1	2

Workmat

tens	ones

____

9. Measure the object. Write the length.

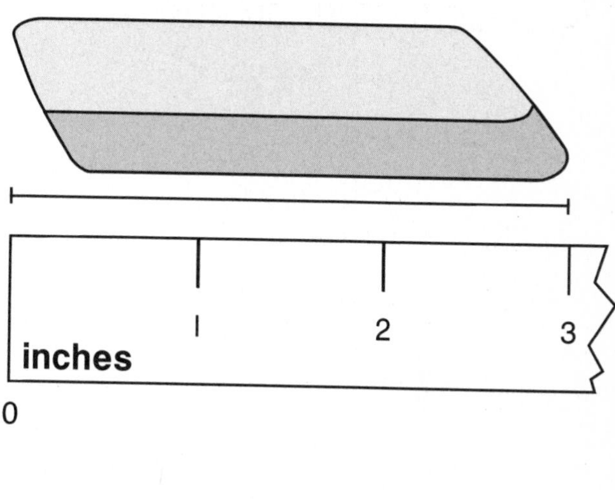

about ____ inches

10. Circle the pencils that are in order from longest to shortest.

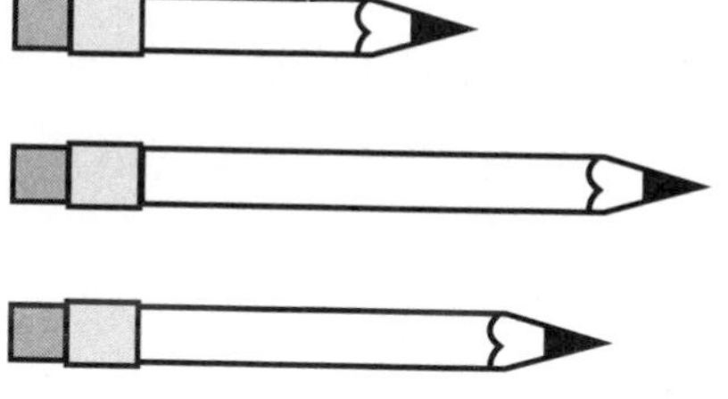

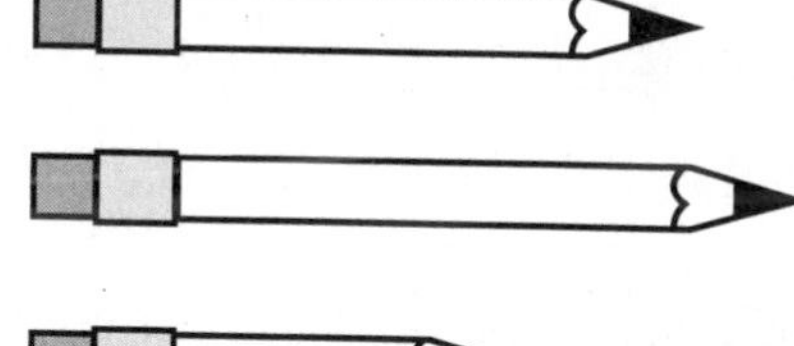

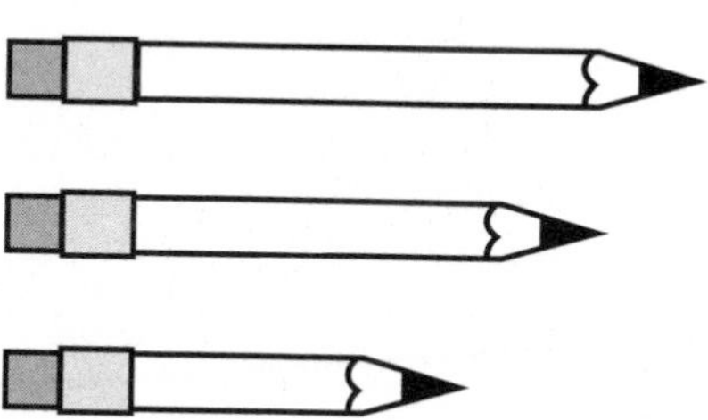

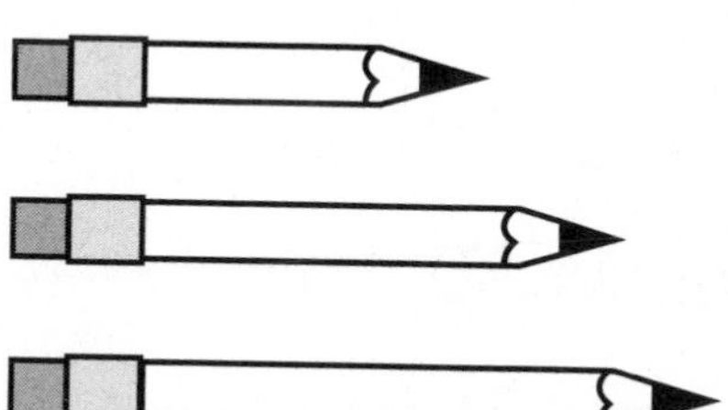

Go On

Name ______________________________

Choose the correct answer.

11. Circle the tool you will use to measure how much juice the punch bowl holds.

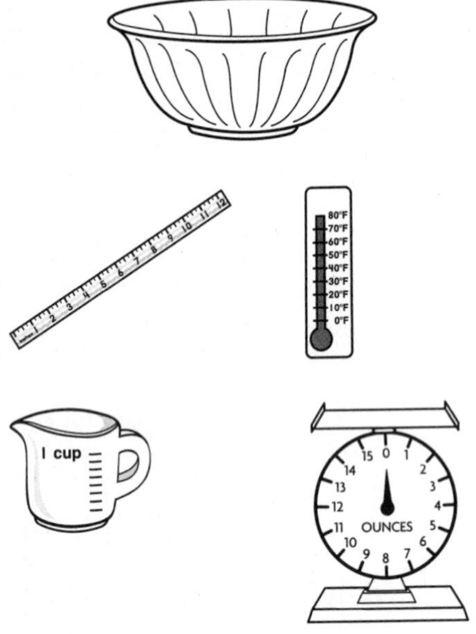

12. Write the sum.

	tens	ones
	2	7
+	I	2

Workmat

tens	ones

____

13. Without adding or subtracting, circle the best estimate.

There are 72 birds at the lake. 8 of the birds fly away. About how many birds are left?

about 6 birds

about 60 birds

about 600 birds

14. Circle how many cups you need to fill the container to the top.

This glass has I cup of juice in it.

I cup

2 cups

3 cups

Go On

Name ____________________

Write the correct answer.

15. Measure the object. Write the length.

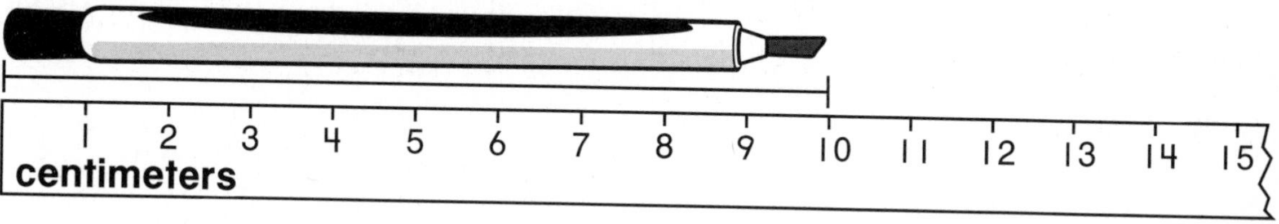

about ____ centimeters

16. Circle the heaviest object.

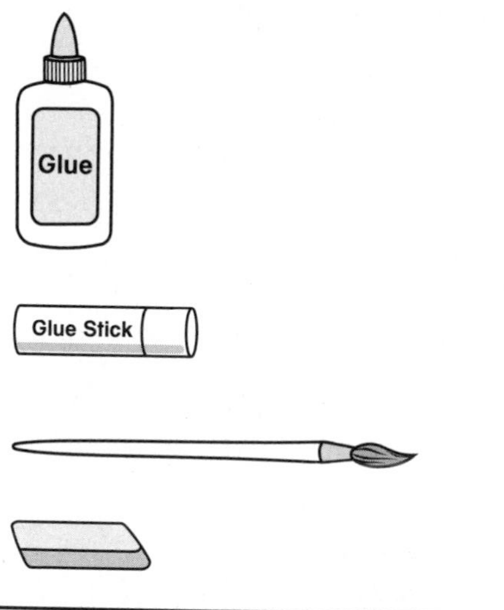

17. Write the difference.

	tens	ones
	3	9
−		4

Workmat

tens	tnes

____

18. About how many (paper clips) long is the object? Circle the estimate that makes sense.

about 5 (paper clips)   about 6 (paper clips)

Go On

Name ________________________________

Write the correct answer.

19. Write the sum.

50 + 20 = ____

20. Without adding or subtracting, circle the best estimate.

Jeremy counts 63 birds. Anna counts 35 birds. About how many birds do they count in all?

about 1 birds

about 10 birds

about 100 birds

21. Circle the tool you will use to measure how warm the soup is.

22. Write the temperature.

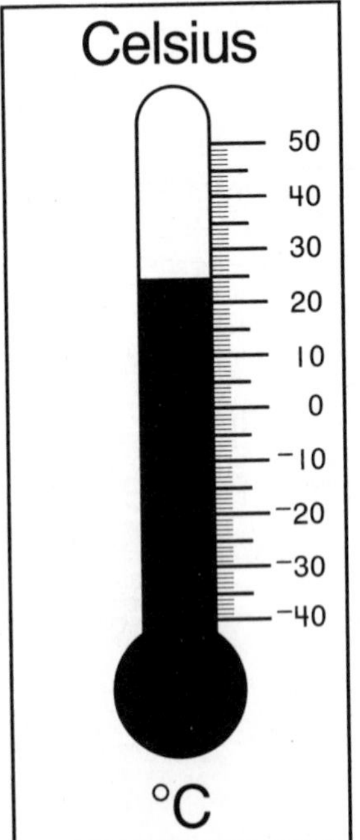

____ °C

Stop

Name ____________________

END OF YEAR TEST

Write the correct answer.

1. Write the temperature.

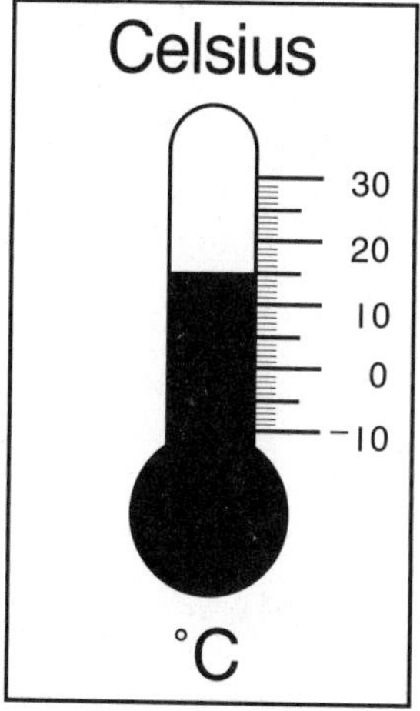

_____ °C

2. Write how many flat surfaces the solid figure has.

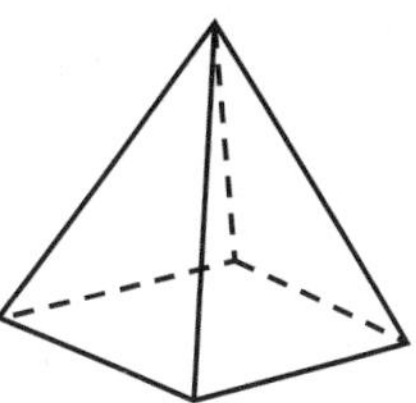

_____ flat surfaces

3. Use the picture graph to answer question 3.

Special Classes We Like									
(tambourine)	music	(tambourine)	(tambourine)	(tambourine)	(tambourine)	(tambourine)	(tambourine)		
(palette)	art	(palette)	(palette)	(palette)	(palette)	(palette)	(palette)	(palette)	
(shoe)	gym	(shoe)	(shoe)	(shoe)	(shoe)				

Write how many more children chose (tambourine) than (shoe).

_____ more children

Go On

Name ____________________

Write the correct answer.

4. Circle which belongs in the group.

     |  

5. Write the sum.

20 + 70 = ______

6. Write the number word that tells how many.

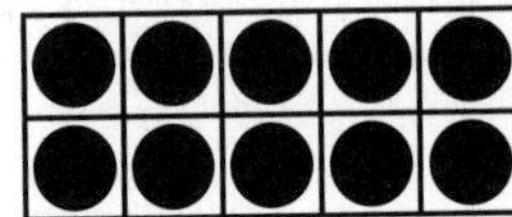

____

7. Circle the pair of related subtraction facts.

11 − 2 = 9	11 − 9 = 2
10 − 3 = 7	11 − 4 = 7
12 − 4 = 8	8 − 4 = 4
12 − 5 = 7	12 − 3 = 9

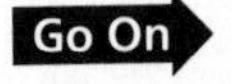

Write the correct answer.

8. Circle slide, flip, or turn to name the move.

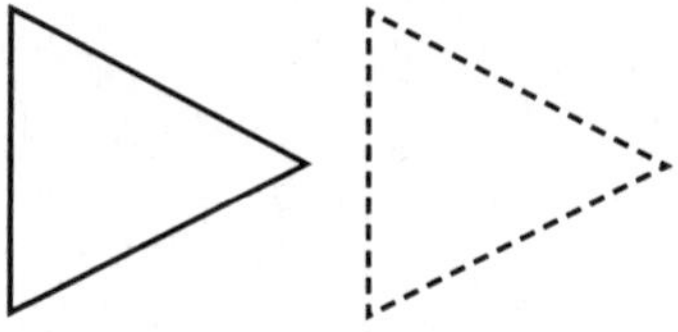

slide flip turn

9. Circle which tool you will use to measure how much water the bucket holds.

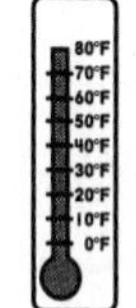

10. Write how more nests there are than birds.

$$\begin{array}{r} 12 \\ -\ 3 \\ \hline \end{array}$$

______ more nests

Go On

Name ______________________________

Write the correct answer.

11. Use the tally chart to answer the question.

Music We Like	
country	𝍸 I
pop	𝍸 IIII
classical	II

Write how many children chose country music.

______ children

12. Write the time.

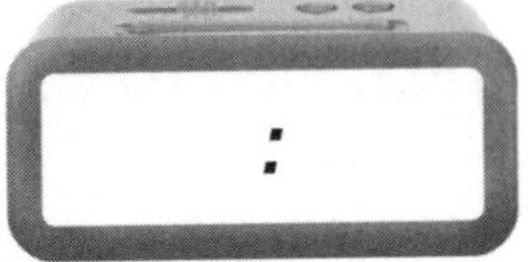

13. Count. Compare the amounts. Write <, >, or =.

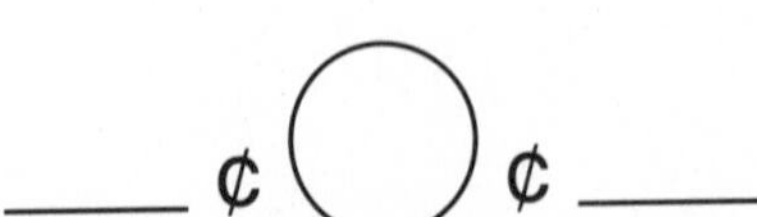

Name ______________________________

Write the correct answer.

14. Write the missing number.

2 4 7 2 4 ______ 2 4 7

15. Write how many corners the plane figure has.

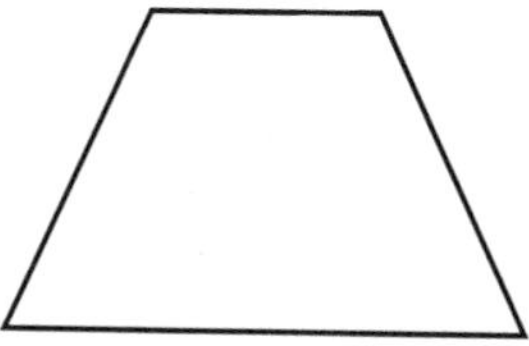

______ corners

16. Count how many tens and ones. Write the number in a different way.

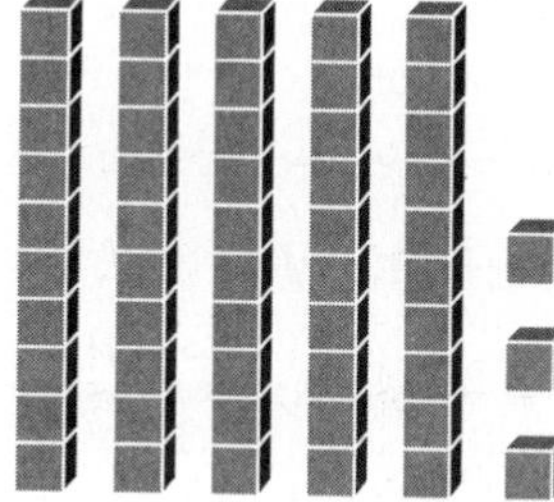

______ tens ______ ones

______ + ______

17. Write the difference.

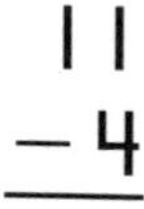

$$\begin{array}{r} 11 \\ -\ 4 \\ \hline \end{array}$$

18. Write the number just after 38.

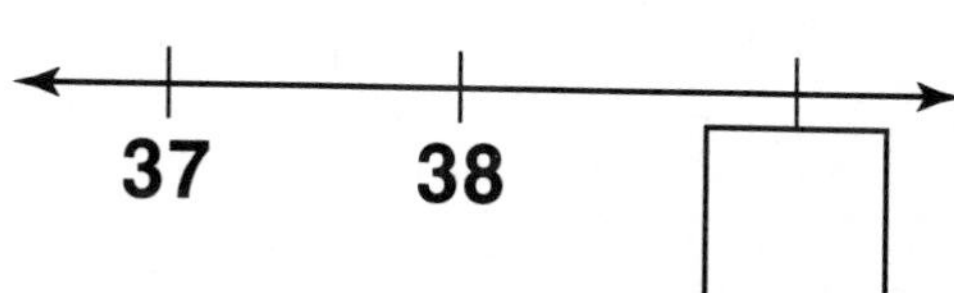

Go On

Name ____________________

Write the correct answer.

19. Draw and color what comes next.

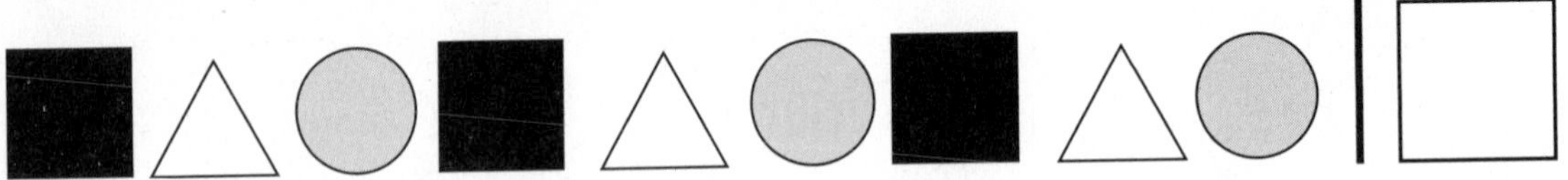

20. Color the triangle RED.

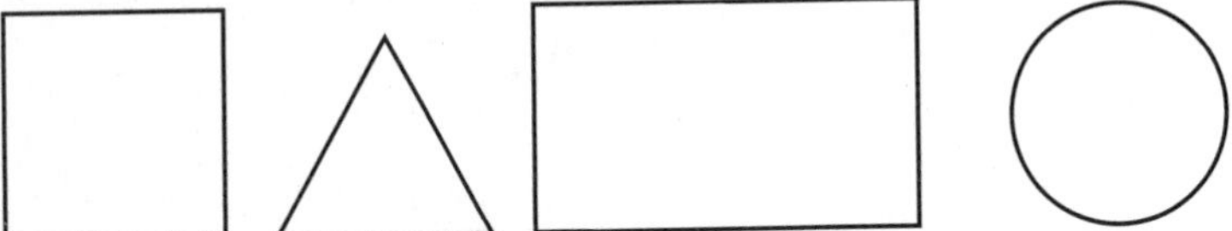

21. Write about how many paper clips long the object is.

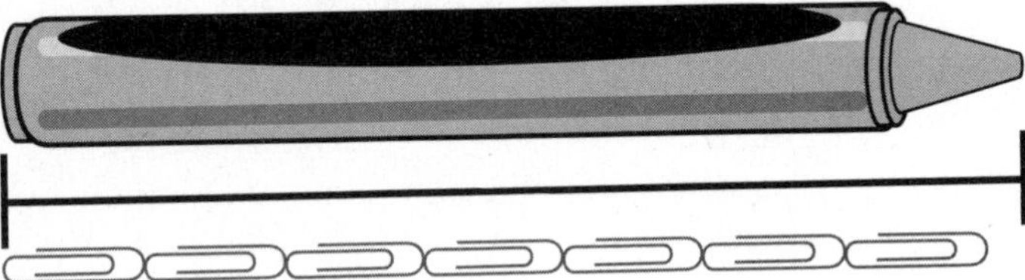

about ______ paper clips

22. Write the sum.

$$\begin{array}{r} 4 \\ +3 \\ \hline \end{array}$$

23. Write the difference.

$$\begin{array}{r} 7 \\ -2 \\ \hline \end{array}$$

Go On

Write the correct answer.

24. Write A, B, or C to show the group the figure belongs in.

A

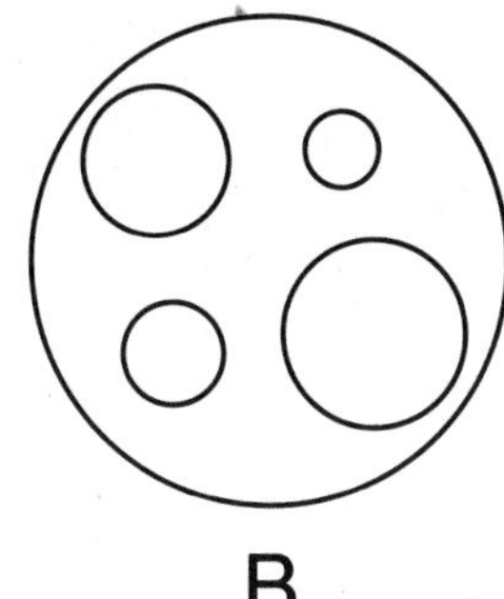

B

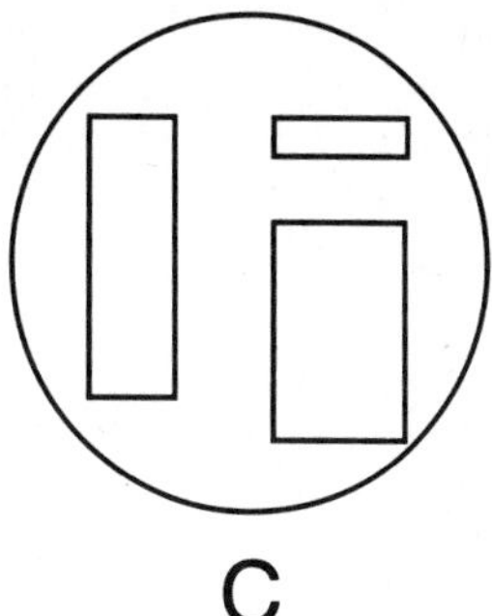

C

◯ ____

25. From **Start,** go right 2. Go down 3. Go left 1.
Write where you are.

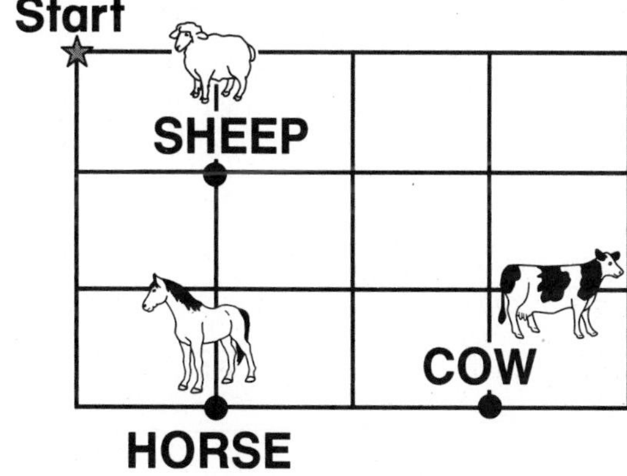

____

26. Write the sum.

$$\begin{array}{r} 8 \\ +3 \\ \hline \end{array}$$

27. Write a related subtraction fact.

1 + 4 = 5

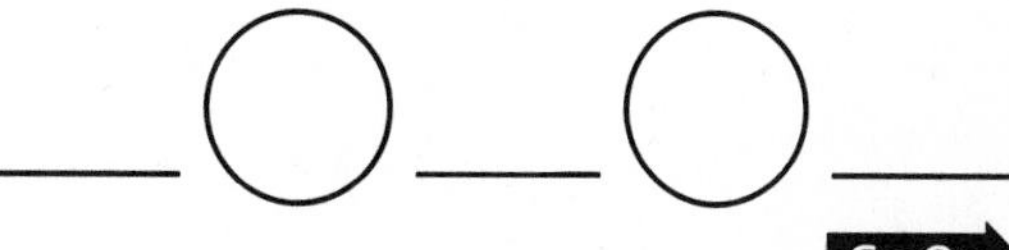

Go On

Write the correct answer.

28. Color the cubes to make the sentence true.
It is **certain** to pull a gray cube.

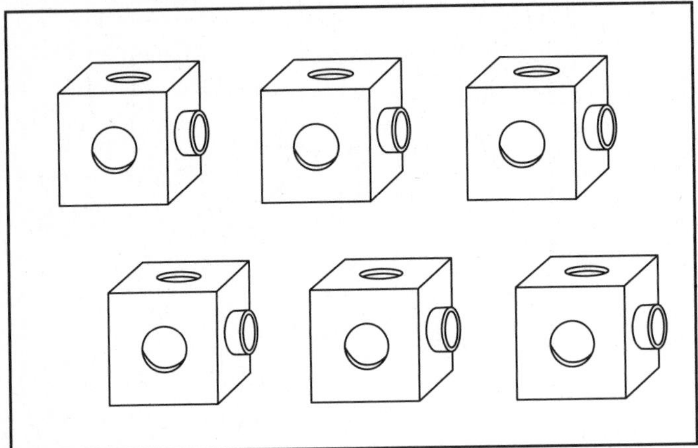

29. Circle the heaviest object.

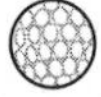

30. Write the difference.

	tens	ones
	2	5
−	1	4

Tens	Ones

Go On

Name ______________________________________

Write the correct answer.

31. Circle the time of day.

morning

afternoon

evening

32. Write how many in all.

5 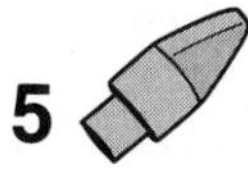 2

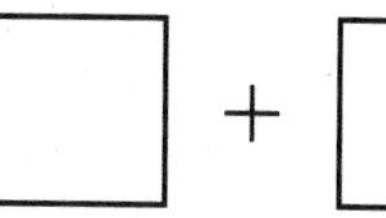

☐ + ☐ = ☐

part   part   whole

_____ in all

33. Circle the solid figure with only flat surfaces.

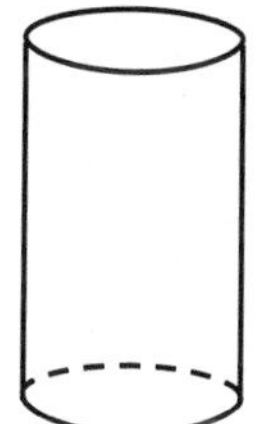 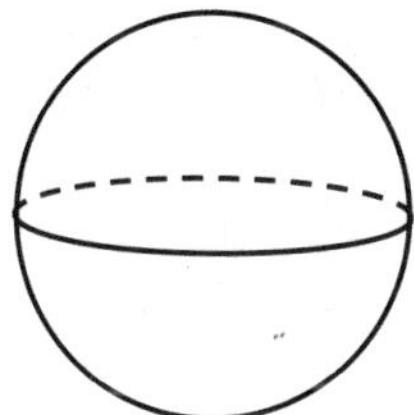 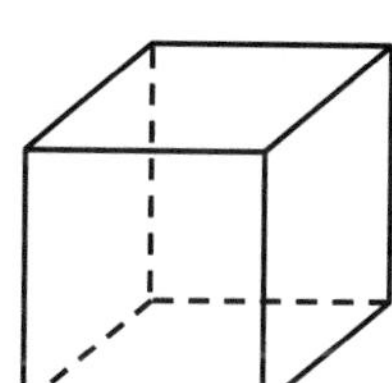 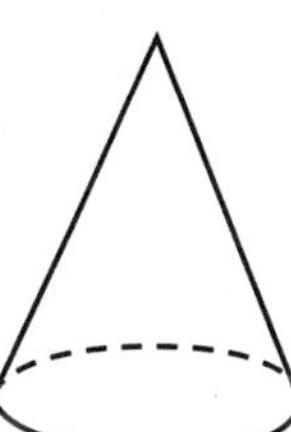

34. Circle which comes next.

     | 

Go On

Name ______________________

Write the correct answer.

Use the bar graph to answer questions 35 and 36.

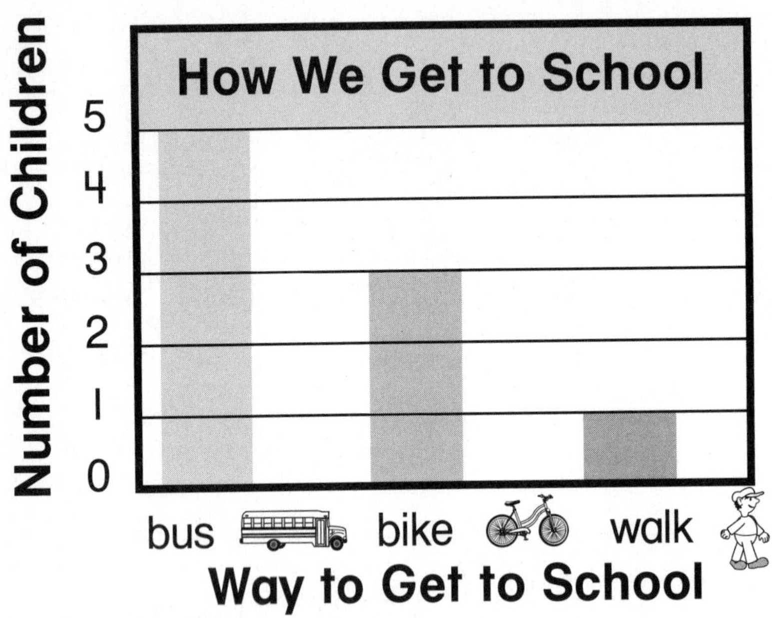

35. Circle the way of travel the fewest children chose.

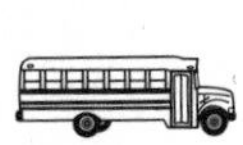  

36. Write how many children chose bus.

_____ in all

37. Draw the hour hand and minute hand to show the time.

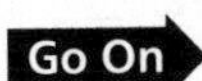

Name ______________________________

Write the correct answer.

38. Use figures to show the same pattern.
Draw the figures.

39. Circle the better estimate.

about 1 pound

about 10 pounds

40. Use BLUE. Color to show $\frac{1}{4}$. Complete the sentence.

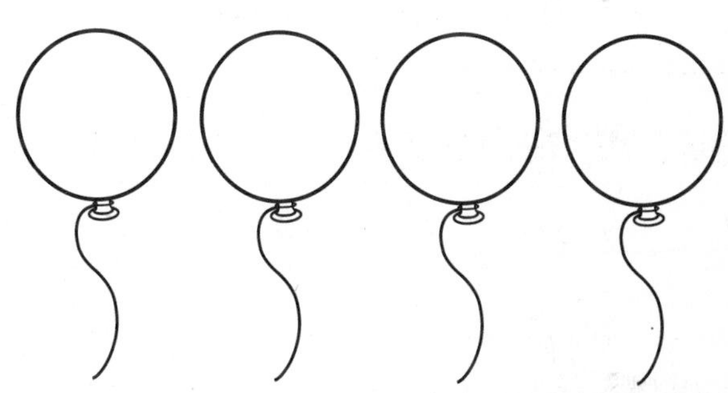

____ out of ____ is blue.

Go On

Name ____________________

Write the correct answer.

41. Draw a line of symmetry to make two parts that match.

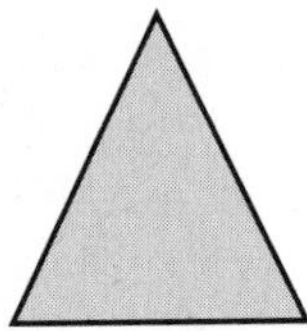

42. Circle the bear you are less likely to pull from the .

43. Measure the object. Write the length.

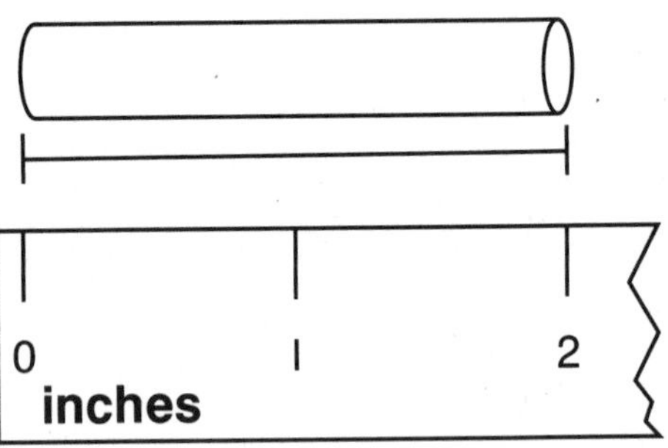

about ____ inches

44. Compare the numbers. Write <, >, or =.

Stop

Name________________________ INVENTORY TEST

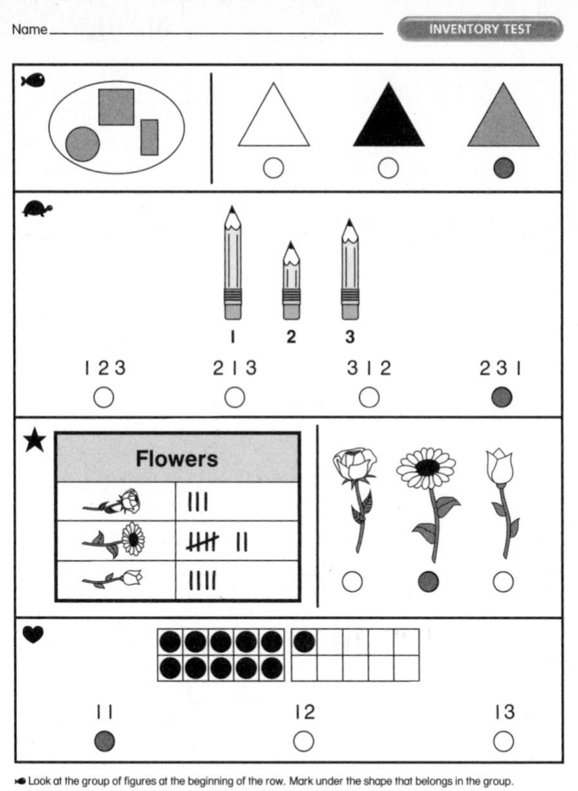

- Look at the group of figures at the beginning of the row. Mark under the shape that belongs in the group.
- Mark under the numbers that show the pencils in order from shortest to longest.
- ★ Read the table. Mark under the kind of flower there are the most of in this table.
- ♥ Mark under the number that tells how many counters there are in the ten frame.

Name________________________ INVENTORY TEST

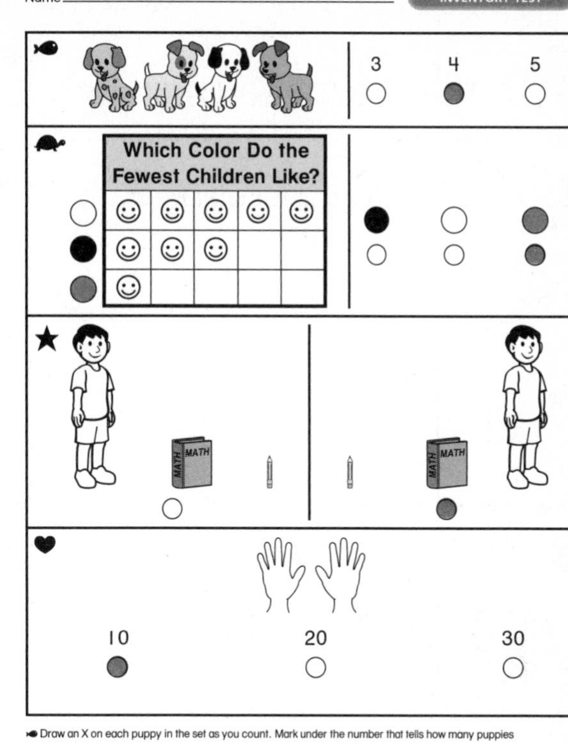

- Draw an X on each puppy in the set as you count. Mark under the number that tells how many puppies there are in the picture.
- Read the graph. Mark under the color the fewest children like.
- ★ Mark under the group of objects that are in order from lightest to heaviest.
- ♥ Count by tens. Mark under the number that tells how many fingers there are in the picture.

Name________________________ INVENTORY TEST

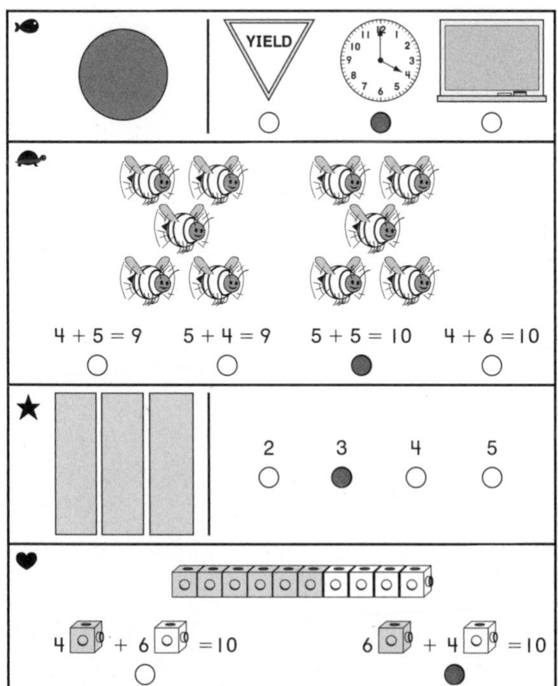

- Look at the figure at the beginning of the row. Mark under the object that is the same shape.
- Look at the bees. Mark under the addition sentence that tells about the bees.
- ★ Look at the figure at the beginning of the row. Mark under the number that tells how many equal parts are shown in the figure.
- ♥ Mark under the addition sentence for the model.

Name________________________ INVENTORY TEST

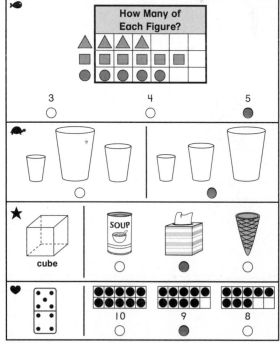

How Many of Each Figure?

3 4 5

cube

SOUP

10 9 8

- Read the graph. Mark under the number that tells how many squares there are in the graph.
- Mark under the cups that are in order, beginning with the cup that holds the least amount of sand.
- ★ Mark under the object that is shaped like the solid figure.
- ♥ Look at the picture at the beginning of the row. Mark under the number that tells how many there are.

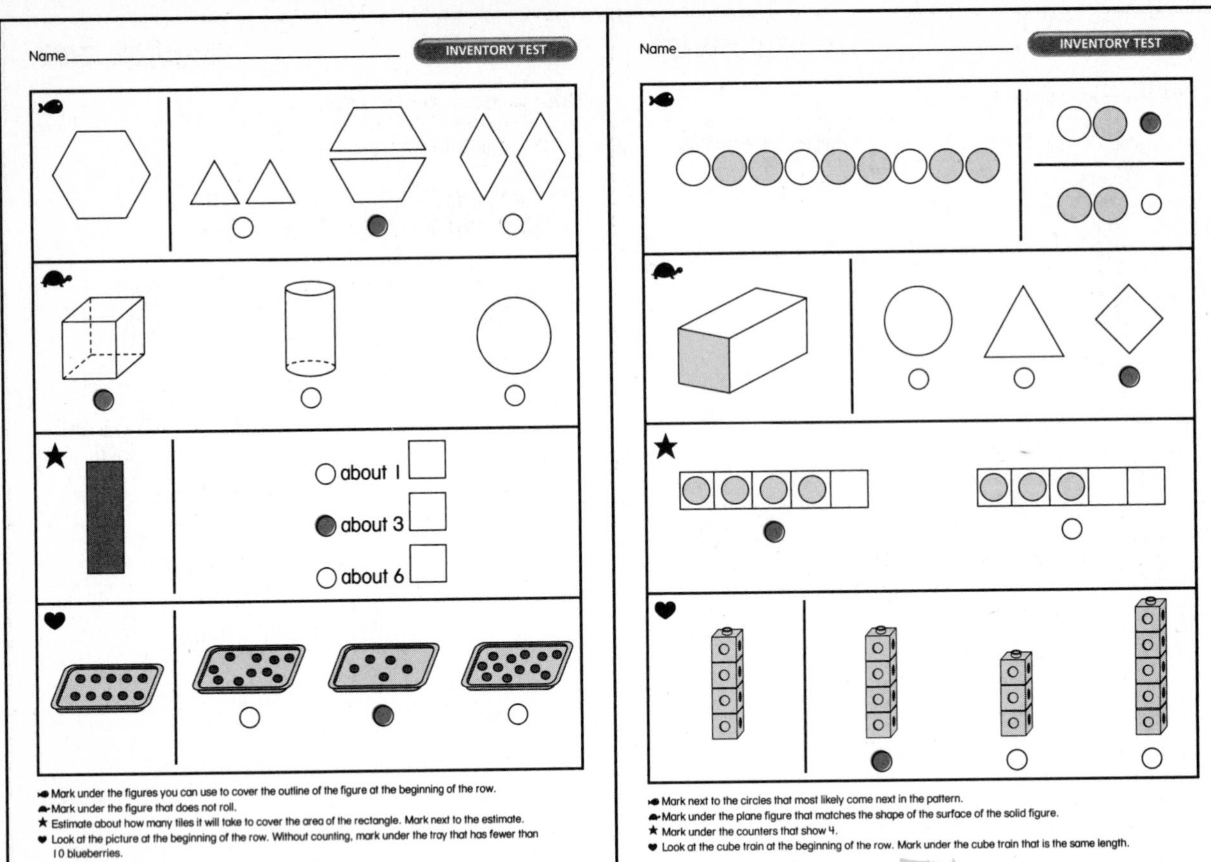

Name ______________________ INVENTORY TEST

○ about 1
○ about 3
○ about 6

Mark under the figures you can use to cover the outline of the figure at the beginning of the row.
Mark under the figure that does not roll.
★ Estimate about how many tiles it will take to cover the area of the rectangle. Mark next to the estimate.
♥ Look at the picture at the beginning of the row. Without counting, mark under the tray that has fewer than 10 blueberries.

Inventory Test IN5 Assessment Guide
© Harcourt • Grade 1

Name ______________________ INVENTORY TEST

Mark next to the circles that most likely come next in the pattern.
Mark under the plane figure that matches the shape of the surface of the solid figure.
★ Mark under the counters that show 4.
♥ Look at the cube train at the beginning of the row. Mark under the cube train that is the same length.

Assessment Guide IN6 Inventory Test
© Harcourt • Grade 1

Name

BEGINNING OF YEAR TEST

Choose the correct answer.

1. What is the temperature?

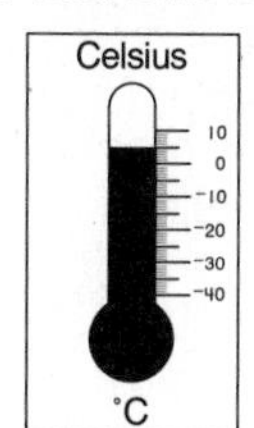

(A) 5°C
B 10°C
C 15°C
D 50°C

2. How many flat surfaces does the solid have?

A 4
B 3
(C) 2
D 1

3. Use the picture graph to answer question 3.

Games We Like							
checkers	★	★	★	★	★	★	
go fish	4	4	4				
dominos	⁞	⁞	⁞	⁞	⁞	⁞	⁞

How many more children chose  than ★?

(A) 1 more child
B 2 more children
C 3 more children
D 5 more children

Go On

Name

BEGINNING OF YEAR TEST

Choose the correct answer.

4. Which  belongs in the group?

(A) 
B 
C 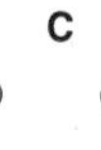
D 

5. What is the sum?

30 + 40 = ____

A 50
B 60
(C) 70
D 80

6. Which tells how many?

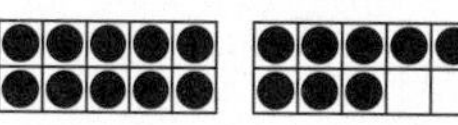

A nineteen
(B) eighteen
C seventeen
D thirteen

7. Which shows a pair of related subtraction facts?

A $12 - 3 = 9$, $9 - 3 = 6$
B $10 - 4 = 6$, $12 - 6 = 6$
C $11 - 3 = 8$, $8 - 3 = 5$
(D) $11 - 5 = 6$, $11 - 6 = 5$

Go On

Name

BEGINNING OF YEAR TEST

Choose the correct answer.

8. Which type of move is shown?

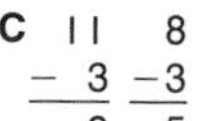
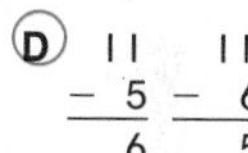

A flip
(B) slide
C turn
D symmetry

9. Which tool will you use to measure how much the mug holds?

A 
C 
(B) 

D 

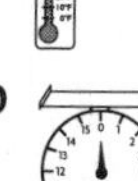

10. How many more leaves are there than birds?

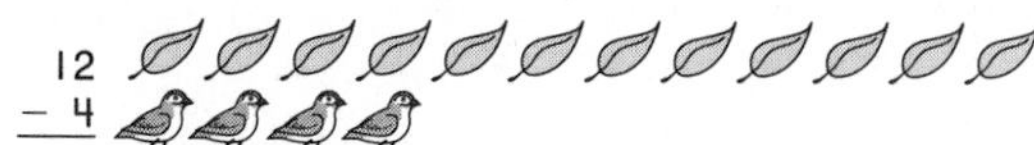

$$\begin{array}{r} 12 \\ -\ 4 \\ \hline \end{array}$$

A 16 more leaves
B 9 more leaves
(C) 8 more leaves
D 6 more leaves

Go On

Name

BEGINNING OF YEAR TEST

Choose the correct answer.

11. Use the tally chart to answer the question.

Pets We Like	
dog	𝍸 I
cat	IIII
fish	𝍸 III

How many children chose the dog?

A 2 children
B 4 children
(C) 6 children
D 8 children

12. What time does the clock show?

A 12:00
B 7:30
C 8:00
(D) 7:00

13. Which symbol can you use to compare the amounts?

____ ¢ ◯ ____ ¢

A <
B >
(C) =

Go On

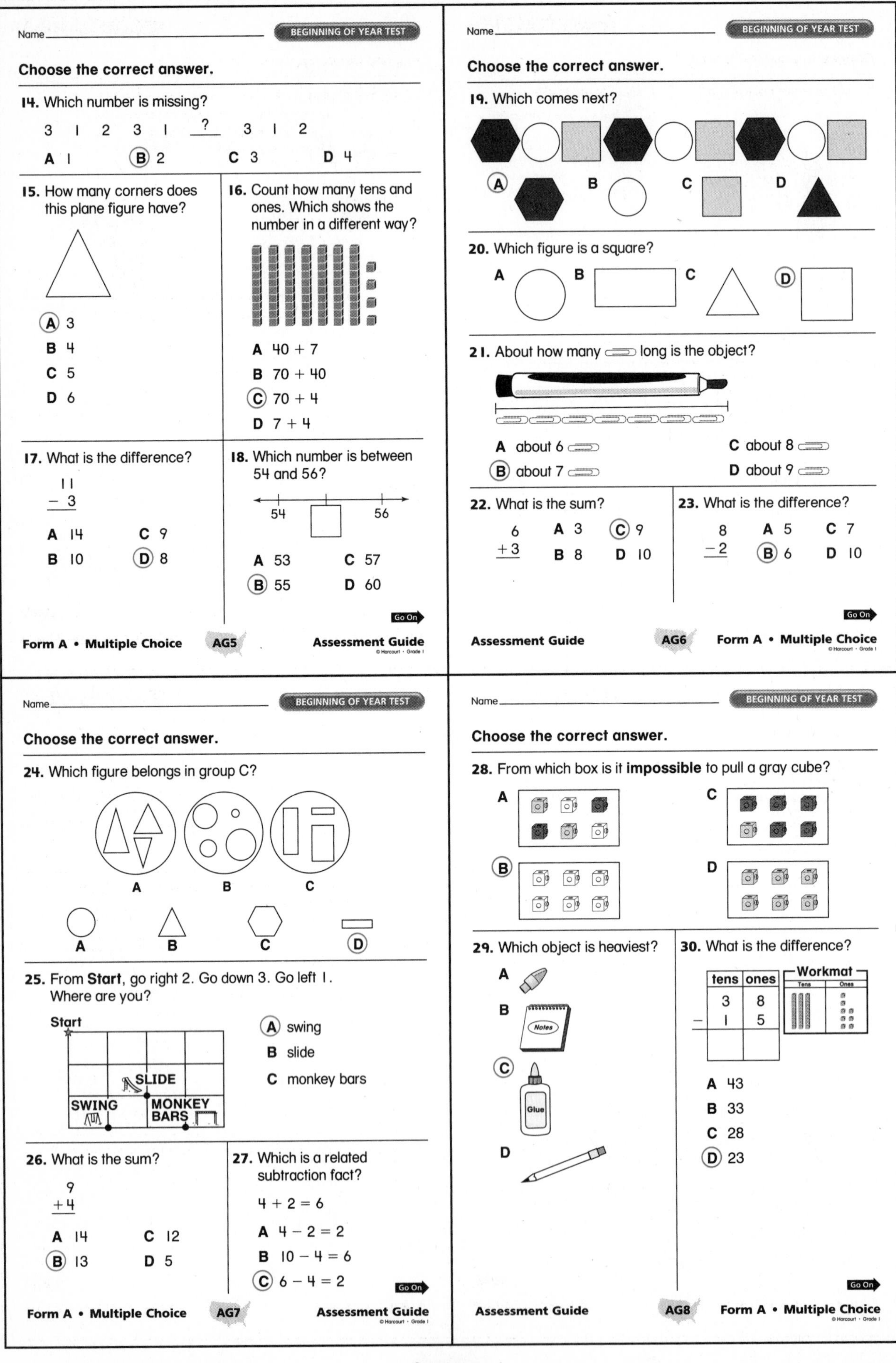

Name_______________ BEGINNING OF YEAR TEST

Choose the correct answer.

14. Which number is missing?

3 1 2 3 1 ? 3 1 2

A 1 (B) 2 C 3 D 4

15. How many corners does this plane figure have?

(A) 3
B 4
C 5
D 6

16. Count how many tens and ones. Which shows the number in a different way?

A 40 + 7
B 70 + 40
(C) 70 + 4
D 7 + 4

17. What is the difference?

$$\begin{array}{r} 11 \\ -\ 3 \\ \hline \end{array}$$

A 14 C 9
B 10 (D) 8

18. Which number is between 54 and 56?

54 56

A 53 C 57
(B) 55 D 60

Go On

Form A • Multiple Choice AG5 Assessment Guide © Harcourt • Grade 1

Name_______________ BEGINNING OF YEAR TEST

Choose the correct answer.

19. Which comes next?

(A) B C D

20. Which figure is a square?

A B C (D)

21. About how many long is the object?

A about 6 C about 8
(B) about 7 D about 9

22. What is the sum?

$$\begin{array}{r} 6 \\ +3 \\ \hline \end{array}$$

A 3 (C) 9
B 8 D 10

23. What is the difference?

$$\begin{array}{r} 8 \\ -2 \\ \hline \end{array}$$

A 5 C 7
(B) 6 D 10

Go On

Assessment Guide AG6 Form A • Multiple Choice © Harcourt • Grade 1

Name_______________ BEGINNING OF YEAR TEST

Choose the correct answer.

24. Which figure belongs in group C?

A B C

A B C (D)

25. From **Start**, go right 2. Go down 3. Go left 1. Where are you?

Start
SLIDE
SWING
MONKEY BARS

(A) swing
B slide
C monkey bars

26. What is the sum?

$$\begin{array}{r} 9 \\ +4 \\ \hline \end{array}$$

A 14 C 12
(B) 13 D 5

27. Which is a related subtraction fact?

4 + 2 = 6

A 4 − 2 = 2
B 10 − 4 = 6
(C) 6 − 4 = 2

Go On

Form A • Multiple Choice AG7 Assessment Guide © Harcourt • Grade 1

Name_______________ BEGINNING OF YEAR TEST

Choose the correct answer.

28. From which box is it **impossible** to pull a gray cube?

A C
(B) D

29. Which object is heaviest?

A
B Notes
(C) Glue
D

30. What is the difference?

	tens	ones
	3	8
−	1	5

Workmat
Tens Ones

A 43
B 33
C 28
(D) 23

Go On

Assessment Guide AG8 Form A • Multiple Choice © Harcourt • Grade 1

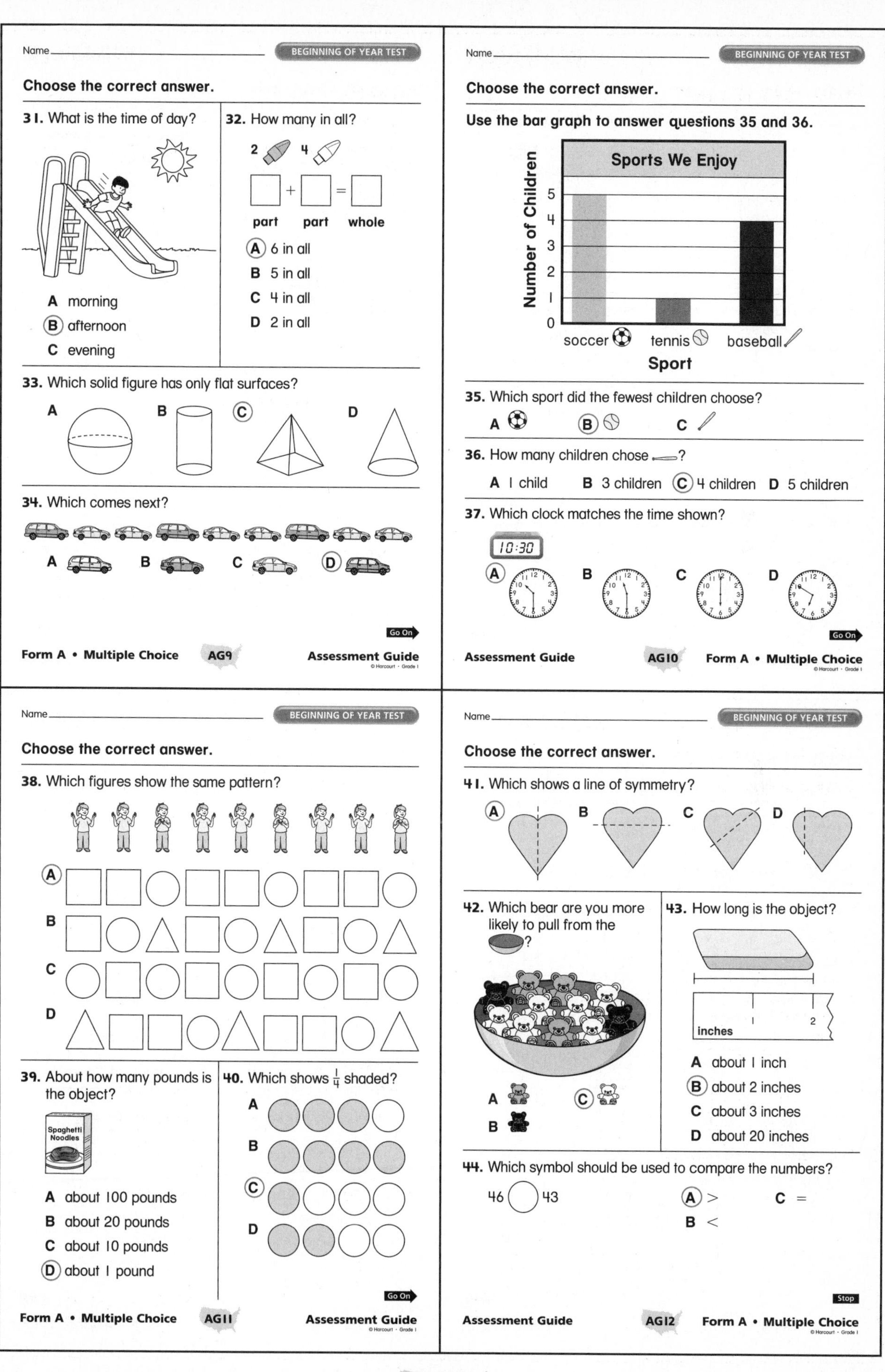

Name ____________ BEGINNING OF YEAR TEST

Choose the correct answer.

31. What is the time of day?

A morning
(B) afternoon
C evening

32. How many in all?

2 4

☐ + ☐ = ☐

part part whole

(A) 6 in all
B 5 in all
C 4 in all
D 2 in all

33. Which solid figure has only flat surfaces?

A B (C) D

34. Which comes next?

A B C (D)

Go On

Form A • Multiple Choice AG9 Assessment Guide

© Harcourt • Grade 1

Name ____________ BEGINNING OF YEAR TEST

Choose the correct answer.

Use the bar graph to answer questions 35 and 36.

35. Which sport did the fewest children choose?

A (B) C

36. How many children chose ?

A 1 child B 3 children (C) 4 children D 5 children

37. Which clock matches the time shown?

10:30

(A) B C D

Go On

Assessment Guide AG10 Form A • Multiple Choice

© Harcourt • Grade 1

Name ____________ BEGINNING OF YEAR TEST

Choose the correct answer.

38. Which figures show the same pattern?

(A)
B
C
D

39. About how many pounds is the object?

A about 100 pounds
B about 20 pounds
C about 10 pounds
(D) about 1 pound

40. Which shows $\frac{1}{4}$ shaded?

A
B
(C)
D

Go On

Form A • Multiple Choice AG11 Assessment Guide

© Harcourt • Grade 1

Name ____________ BEGINNING OF YEAR TEST

Choose the correct answer.

41. Which shows a line of symmetry?

(A) B C D

42. Which bear are you more likely to pull from the ?

A (C)
B

43. How long is the object?

A about 1 inch
(B) about 2 inches
C about 3 inches
D about 20 inches

44. Which symbol should be used to compare the numbers?

46 ◯ 43

(A) > C =
B <

Stop

Assessment Guide AG12 Form A • Multiple Choice

© Harcourt • Grade 1

Name________________ CHAPTER 1 PRETEST

Choose the correct answer.

1. Which is correct?

- A 11 is less than 7.
- B 12 is greater than 18.
- C 13 is less than 11.
- (D) 15 is greater than 13.

2. Which tells how many?

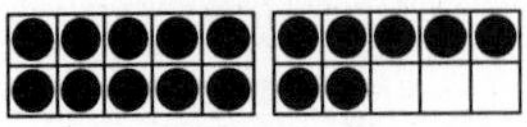

- A twelve
- (B) seventeen
- C eighteen
- D nineteen

3. Which shows the numbers in order from least to greatest?

- (A) 9, 10, 12
- B 9, 12, 10
- C 12, 10, 9
- D 10, 12, 9

4. Which is correct?

- A 8 is less than 5.
- (B) 14 is less than 20.
- C 16 is greater than 18.
- D 7 is greater than 9.

5. Which bear is sixth?

first

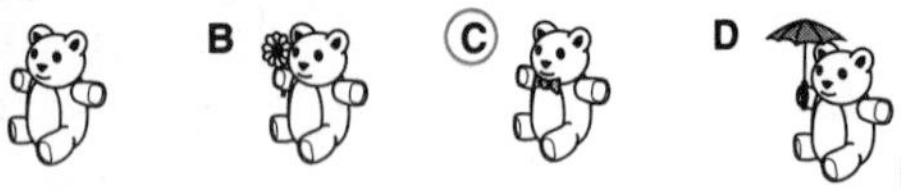

A B (C) D

Go On

Name________________ CHAPTER 1 PRETEST

Choose the correct answer.

6. Which is a way to show 8?

- (A) 
- B 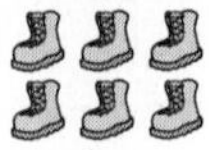
- C seven
- D

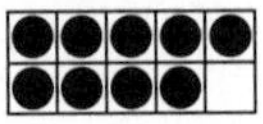

7. Draw lines to match. Which shows how many more?

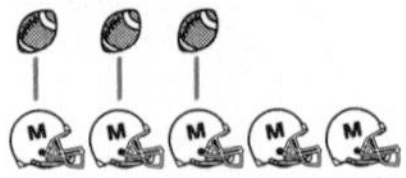

- A 5 more
- B 4 more
- C 3 more
- (D) 2 more

Use the picture graph to answer questions 8 and 9.

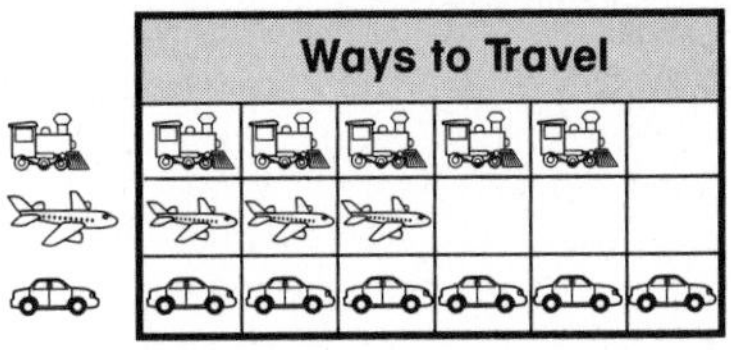

Ways to Travel

8. Which way to travel has the least number?

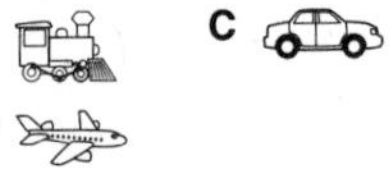

- A
- (B)
- C

9. How many?

- A 4
- B 5
- (C) 6
- D 7

Stop

Name________________ CHAPTER 2 PRETEST

Choose the correct answer.

1. Which addition sentence does the picture show?

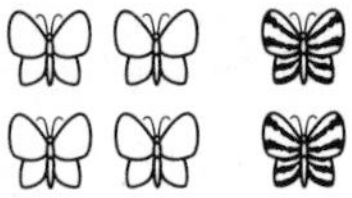

- (A) 4 + 2 = 6
- B 2 + 2 = 4
- C 5 + 1 = 6
- D 3 + 3 = 6

2. Which addition sentences use the same addends?

- (A) 4 + 1 = 5 and 1 + 4 = 5
- B 3 + 2 = 5 and 3 + 3 = 6
- C 0 + 5 = 5 and 1 + 4 = 5
- D 2 + 3 = 5 and 0 + 4 = 4

3. Draw circles to show each number. What is the sum?

4 + 0 = ____

- A 40
- (B) 4
- C 2
- D 0

4. What is the sum?

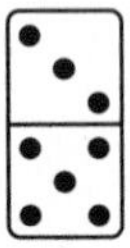

$$\begin{array}{r} 3 \\ +\ 5 \\ \hline \end{array}$$

- A 2
- B 4
- C 7
- (D) 8

Go On

Name________________ CHAPTER 2 PRETEST

Choose the correct answer.

5. Which is a way to make 8?

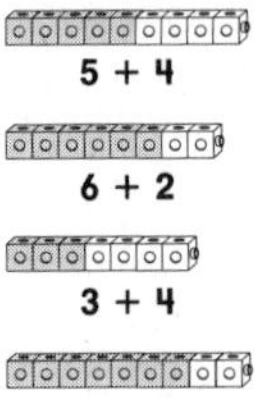

- A 5 + 4
- (B) 6 + 2
- C 3 + 4
- D 7 + 2

6. How many in all?

3 2

☐ + ☐ = ☐

part part whole

- A 1 in all
- B 4 in all
- (C) 5 in all
- D 6 in all

7. How many birds in all?

1 bird 3 more birds

- A 2 birds in all
- B 3 birds in all
- (C) 4 birds in all
- D 5 birds in all

8. There are 4 children playing. The same number of children join them. How many children are there?

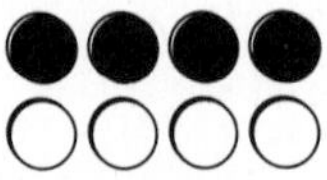

- A 0 children
- B 5 children
- C 6 children
- (D) 8 children

Stop

Name________________________ CHAPTER 3 PRETEST

Choose the correct answer.

1. What is the difference?

$$\begin{array}{r} 7 \\ -\,2 \\ \hline \end{array}$$

A 4
(B) 5
C 6
D 9

2. What is the difference?

5 − 0 = ______

A 0
B 3
(C) 5
D 50

3. Which subtraction sentence is shown by the cube?

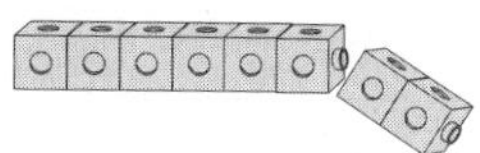

(A) 8 − 2 = 6
B 8 − 4 = 4
C 6 − 2 = 4
D 7 − 2 = 5

4. Which subtraction sentence does the picture show?

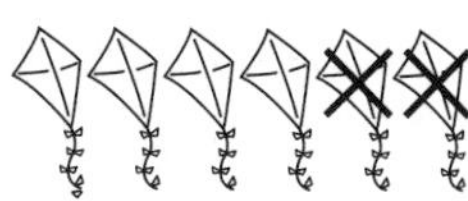

A 6 − 3 = 3
B 4 − 2 = 2
C 4 + 2 = 6
(D) 6 − 2 = 4

Go On

Name________________________ CHAPTER 3 PRETEST

Choose the correct answer.

5. How many fewer shovels?

A 5 fewer
B 4 fewer
(C) 3 fewer
D 2 fewer

6. Which number completes the subtraction sentence?

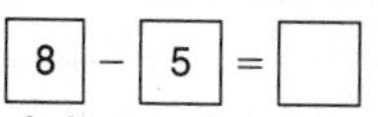

8	−	5	=	
whole		part		part

A 2
(B) 3
C 4
D 5

7. How many frogs are left?

(A) 1 frog is left
B 2 frogs are left
C 3 frogs are left
D 5 frogs are left

8. There are 6 ladybugs and 2 bumblebees. How many fewer bumblebees are there?

A 8 fewer bumblebees
B 7 fewer bumblebees
C 5 fewer bumblebees
(D) 4 fewer bumblebees

Stop

Name________________________ CHAPTER 4 PRETEST

Choose the correct answer.

1. Which number sentences match the picture?

A 4 + 2 = 6
6 − 3 = 3
B 2 + 2 = 4
4 − 2 = 2
C 4 + 2 = 6
4 − 2 = 2
(D) 4 + 2 = 6
6 − 2 = 4

2. Which number sentence matches the picture?

A 4 − 3 = 1
(B) 7 − 3 = 4
C 3 + 1 = 4
D 4 + 3 = 7

3. Which is a related subtraction fact?

2 + 3 = 5

(A) 5 − 3 = 2
B 8 − 5 = 3
C 3 − 2 = 1
D 5 − 0 = 5

4. How many ants are there in all?

A 4
B 7
(C) 8
D 10

Go On

Name________________________ CHAPTER 4 PRETEST

Choose the correct answer.

5. Which is a related addition fact?

5 − 5 = 0

(A) 0 + 5 = 5
B 5 + 5 = 10
C 2 + 3 = 5
D 4 + 1 = 5

6. Which number sentence matches the picture?

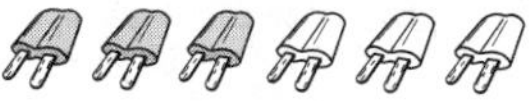

A 4 + 2 = 6
(B) 3 + 3 = 6
C 6 − 3 = 3
D 6 − 2 = 4

7. How many frogs hop away?

A 1 B 5 (C) 7 D 8

8. There are 6 soccer balls. The coach brings 2 more soccer balls. How many soccer balls are there now?

A 4
B 6
(C) 8
D 10

9. There are 5 school buses. 2 school buses leave. How many school buses are left?

(A) 3
B 5
C 7
D 8

Stop

Name

UNIT 1 PRETEST

Choose the correct answer.

1. Which shows the numbers in order from least to greatest?

A 7, 5, 8 (C) 5, 7, 8
B 8, 7, 5 D 8, 5, 7

2. Which is the difference?

6 − 6 = ____

(A) 0 C 6
B 3 D 66

3. Which addition sentences use the same addends?

A 3 + 4 = 7 and 3 + 5 = 8
B 2 + 4 = 6 and 2 + 3 = 5
C 0 + 2 = 2 and 1 + 2 = 3
(D) 1 + 3 = 4 and 3 + 1 = 4

4. There are 6 fire trucks. 3 fire trucks leave. Which number sentence matches the words?

A 9 − 3 = 6
(B) 6 − 3 = 3
C 3 + 6 = 9
D 9 + 3 = 12

5. Which is correct?

(A) 5 is less than 10.
B 12 is less than 8.
C 14 is greater than 17.
D 9 is greater than 12.

6. Which is a related subtraction fact?

5 + 2 = 7

A 5 − 2 = 3
B 9 − 7 = 2
(C) 7 − 2 = 5
D 7 − 0 = 7

Go On

Name

UNIT 1 PRETEST

Choose the correct answer.

7. Use the cube below. There are 5 grasshoppers and 3 beetles. How many fewer beetles are there?

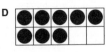

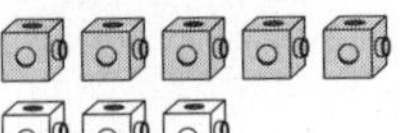

A 4 beetles
B 3 beetles
(C) 2 beetles
D 1 beetles

8. Which number sentence matches the picture?

(A) 8 − 3 = 5
B 5 − 3 = 2
C 3 + 5 = 8
D 2 + 3 = 5

9. Draw circles to show each number. What is the sum?

3 + 0 = ____

A 30
(B) 3
C 1
D 0

10. Which number completes the subtraction sentence?

6	−	4	=	
whole		part		part

A 1
(B) 2
C 3
D 4

Go On

Name

UNIT 1 PRETEST

Choose the correct answer.

11. Which is a way to make 5?

A 4 + 2

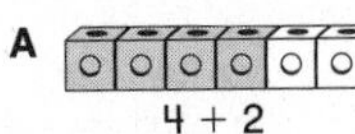

(B) 2 + 3

C 3 + 4

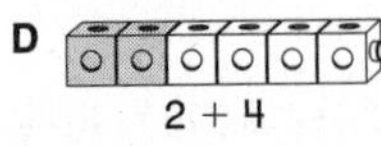

D 2 + 4

12. Draw lines to match. Which shows how many more ?

A 1 more
B 2 more
(C) 3 more
D 4 more

13. How many birds are left?

3 birds 2 birds fly away

(A) 1 bird is left
B 2 birds are left
C 3 birds are left
D 5 birds are left

14. Which addition sentence does the picture show?

A 1 + 2 = 3
(B) 2 + 2 = 4
C 3 + 1 = 4
D 1 + 4 = 5

Go On

Name

UNIT 1 PRETEST

Choose the correct answer.

15. Which number sentences match the picture?

A 6 + 3 = 9, 9 − 6 = 3
B 2 + 3 = 5, 5 − 2 = 3
(C) 5 + 4 = 9, 9 − 4 = 5
D 5 + 4 = 9, 5 − 4 = 1

16. Which is a way to show 6?

A

(B)

C five

D

17. Which doll is third?

first

A

B

C

(D)

Go On

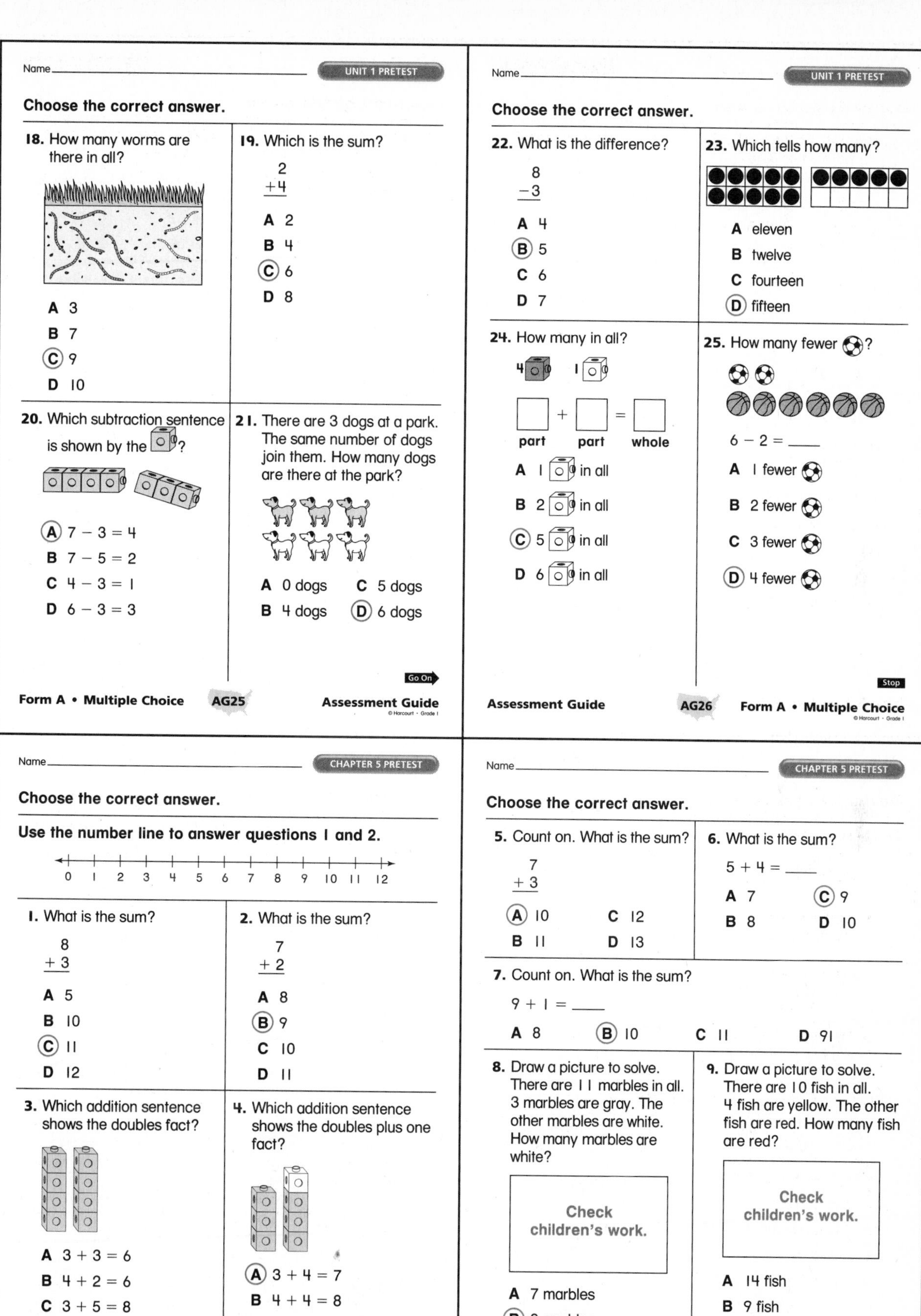

Name ______________________ UNIT 1 PRETEST

Choose the correct answer.

18. How many worms are there in all?

A 3
B 7
(C) 9
D 10

19. Which is the sum?

$$\begin{array}{r} 2 \\ +4 \\ \hline \end{array}$$

A 2
B 4
(C) 6
D 8

20. Which subtraction sentence is shown by the cubes?

(A) 7 − 3 = 4
B 7 − 5 = 2
C 4 − 3 = 1
D 6 − 3 = 3

21. There are 3 dogs at a park. The same number of dogs join them. How many dogs are there at the park?

A 0 dogs
B 4 dogs
C 5 dogs
(D) 6 dogs

Go On

Form A • Multiple Choice AG25 Assessment Guide © Harcourt • Grade 1

Name ______________________ UNIT 1 PRETEST

Choose the correct answer.

22. What is the difference?

$$\begin{array}{r} 8 \\ -3 \\ \hline \end{array}$$

A 4
(B) 5
C 6
D 7

23. Which tells how many?

A eleven
B twelve
C fourteen
(D) fifteen

24. How many in all?

4 cubes 1 cube

☐ + ☐ = ☐
part part whole

A 1 cube in all
B 2 cubes in all
(C) 5 cubes in all
D 6 cubes in all

25. How many fewer soccer balls?

6 − 2 = ____

A 1 fewer soccer ball
B 2 fewer soccer balls
C 3 fewer soccer balls
(D) 4 fewer soccer balls

Stop

Assessment Guide AG26 Form A • Multiple Choice © Harcourt • Grade 1

Name ______________________ CHAPTER 5 PRETEST

Choose the correct answer.

Use the number line to answer questions 1 and 2.

0 1 2 3 4 5 6 7 8 9 10 11 12

1. What is the sum?

$$\begin{array}{r} 8 \\ +3 \\ \hline \end{array}$$

A 5
B 10
(C) 11
D 12

2. What is the sum?

$$\begin{array}{r} 7 \\ +2 \\ \hline \end{array}$$

A 8
(B) 9
C 10
D 11

3. Which addition sentence shows the doubles fact?

A 3 + 3 = 6
B 4 + 2 = 6
C 3 + 5 = 8
(D) 4 + 4 = 8

4. Which addition sentence shows the doubles plus one fact?

(A) 3 + 4 = 7
B 4 + 4 = 8
C 2 + 5 = 7
D 3 + 3 = 6

Go On

Form A • Multiple Choice AG27 Assessment Guide © Harcourt • Grade 1

Name ______________________ CHAPTER 5 PRETEST

Choose the correct answer.

5. Count on. What is the sum?

$$\begin{array}{r} 7 \\ +3 \\ \hline \end{array}$$

(A) 10
B 11
C 12
D 13

6. What is the sum?

5 + 4 = ____

A 7
B 8
(C) 9
D 10

7. Count on. What is the sum?

9 + 1 = ____

A 8
(B) 10
C 11
D 91

8. Draw a picture to solve. There are 11 marbles in all. 3 marbles are gray. The other marbles are white. How many marbles are white?

Check children's work.

A 7 marbles
(B) 8 marbles
C 9 marbles
D 14 marbles

9. Draw a picture to solve. There are 10 fish in all. 4 fish are yellow. The other fish are red. How many fish are red?

Check children's work.

A 14 fish
B 9 fish
C 7 fish
(D) 6 fish

Stop

Assessment Guide AG28 Form A • Multiple Choice © Harcourt • Grade 1

Name ______________________ CHAPTER 6 PRETEST

Choose the correct answer.

Use the number line to answer questions 1 through 4.

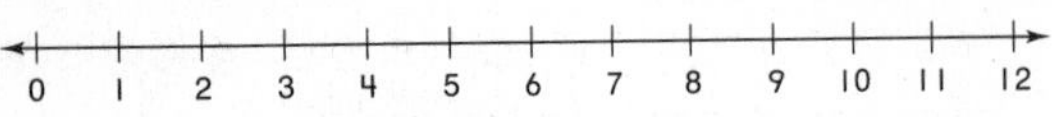

1. What is the difference?

$\begin{array}{r} 10 \\ -\ 1 \\ \hline \end{array}$

A 7
B 8
(C) 9
D 11

2. What is the difference?

11 − 3 = ____

(A) 8
B 9
C 10
D 14

3. What is the difference?

____ = 9 − 3

A 11
B 10
C 7
(D) 6

4. What is the difference?

$\begin{array}{r} 8 \\ -\ 2 \\ \hline \end{array}$

A 5
(B) 6
C 7
D 10

Go On

Name ______________________ CHAPTER 6 PRETEST

Choose the correct answer.

5. What is the difference?

$\begin{array}{r} 12 \\ -\ 6 \\ \hline \end{array}$

A 3 C 10
(B) 6 D 18

6. What is the difference?

$\begin{array}{r} 11 \\ -\ 2 \\ \hline \end{array}$

A 13 (C) 9
B 10 D 8

7. Use and to add.

$\begin{array}{r} 4 \\ +\ 4 \\ \hline \end{array}$

A 9 C 1
(B) 8 D 0

8. Use and to subtract.

$\begin{array}{r} 6 \\ -\ 2 \\ \hline \end{array}$

A 8 (C) 4
B 7 D 3

9. Which number sentence matches the story?

There are 7 seals. 2 seals swim away. How many seals are there now?

A 5 + 2 = 7
(B) 7 − 2 = 5
C 9 − 2 = 7
D 7 + 2 = 9

10. Which number sentence matches the story?

There are 10 blue crabs. There are 3 red crabs. How many more blue crabs are there than red crabs?

(A) 10 − 3 = 7
B 10 + 3 = 13
C 7 − 3 = 4
D 7 + 3 = 10

Stop

Name ______________________ CHAPTER 7 PRETEST

Choose the correct answer.

1. Which numbers are in the fact family?

8 + 4 = 12 12 − 4 = 8
4 + 8 = 12 12 − 8 = 4

(A) 4, 8, 12
B 4, 12, 16
C 8, 12, 20
D 4, 4, 8

2. Which is a way to make 11?

A 12 − 3
B 10 − 2
C 7 + 5
(D) 8 + 3

3. Which shows the related addition fact?

$\begin{array}{r} 5 \\ +\ 7 \\ \hline \square \end{array}$

A $\begin{array}{r} 4 \\ +\ 8 \\ \hline 12 \end{array}$ C $\begin{array}{r} 6 \\ +\ 6 \\ \hline 12 \end{array}$

(B) $\begin{array}{r} 7 \\ +\ 5 \\ \hline 12 \end{array}$ D $\begin{array}{r} 9 \\ +\ 3 \\ \hline 12 \end{array}$

4. Which number sentence shows how many fish there are?

4 gray fish

6 white fish

A 10 − 4 = 6
B 6 − 4 = 2
(C) 4 + 6 = 10
D 10 + 4 = 14

Go On

Name ______________________ CHAPTER 7 PRETEST

Choose the correct answer.

5. Which number completes the fact family?

5 + □ = 11 11 − □ = 5
□ + 5 = 11 11 − 5 = □

(A) 6 C 12
B 8 D 16

6. Follow the rule. Which number completes the table?

Subtract 2	
6	4
8	
10	8

A 5 (B) 6 C 7 D 8

7. Which shows a pair of related subtraction facts?

(A) $\begin{array}{r} 10 \\ -\ 3 \\ \hline 7 \end{array}$ $\begin{array}{r} 10 \\ -\ 7 \\ \hline 3 \end{array}$ B $\begin{array}{r} 12 \\ -\ 4 \\ \hline 8 \end{array}$ $\begin{array}{r} 12 \\ -\ 5 \\ \hline 7 \end{array}$ C $\begin{array}{r} 11 \\ -\ 6 \\ \hline 5 \end{array}$ $\begin{array}{r} 9 \\ -\ 4 \\ \hline 5 \end{array}$ D $\begin{array}{r} 8 \\ -\ 5 \\ \hline 3 \end{array}$ $\begin{array}{r} 8 \\ -\ 2 \\ \hline 6 \end{array}$

8. Draw a picture to solve. There are 10 hawks. Some hawks fly away. There are 7 hawks left. How many hawks flew away?

Check children's work.

A 1 hawk (C) 3 hawks
B 2 hawks D 4 hawks

9. Draw a picture to solve. There are 12 skunks. Some skunks walk away. There are 8 skunks left. How many skunks walked away?

Check children's work.

A 10 skunks C 5 skunks
B 6 skunks (D) 4 skunks

Stop

Name ______________________ UNIT 2 PRETEST

Choose the correct answer.

1. Which addition sentence shows the doubles fact?

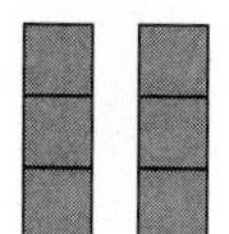

A $2 + 2 = 4$
(B) $3 + 3 = 6$
C $3 + 2 = 5$
D $4 + 3 = 78$

2. Draw a picture to solve. There are 10 deer. Some deer walk away. There are 6 deer left. How many deer walked away?

Check children's work.

A 10 deer
B 8 deer
C 6 deer
(D) 4 deer

3. Follow the rule. Which number completes the table?

Subtract 2	
5	3
6	
7	5

A 6
B 5
(C) 4
D 3

4. Which numbers are in the fact family?

$5 + 6 = 11$ $\quad 11 - 6 = 5$
$6 + 5 = 11$ $\quad 11 - 5 = 6$

(A) 5, 6, 11
B 5, 11, 17
C 6, 11, 16
D 5, 5, 11

Go On

Name ______________________ UNIT 2 PRETEST

Choose the correct answer.

Use the number line to answer questions 5 and 6.

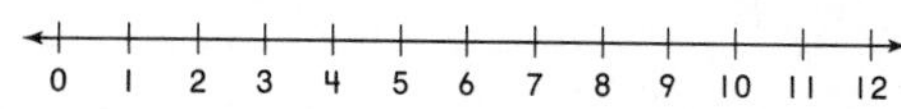

5. What is the sum?

$$\begin{array}{r} 4 \\ +2 \\ \hline \end{array}$$

A 5
(B) 6
C 7
D 8

6. What is the sum?

$$\begin{array}{r} 8 \\ +3 \\ \hline \end{array}$$

A 9
B 10
(C) 11
D 12

7. What is the difference?

$$\begin{array}{r} 11 \\ -7 \\ \hline \end{array}$$

(A) 4
B 3
C 2
D 1

8. Use 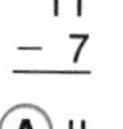 and to add.

$$\begin{array}{r} 2 \\ +4 \\ \hline \end{array}$$

(A) 6
B 7
C 8
D 9

9. Which shows a pair of related subtraction facts?

A $7 - 2 = 5$, $7 - 4 = 3$
B $12 - 4 = 8$, $12 - 7 = 5$
C $8 - 2 = 6$, $8 - 5 = 3$
(D) $9 - 3 = 6$, $9 - 6 = 3$

Go On

Name ______________________ UNIT 2 PRETEST

Choose the correct answer.

10. Count on. What is the sum?

$10 + 2 =$ ____

A 11
(B) 12
C 21
D 22

11. Which number sentence matches the story?

There are 11 starfish. There are 5 sand dollars. How many more starfish are there than sand dollars?

A $6 - 5 = 1$
B $11 + 5 = 16$
(C) $11 - 5 = 6$
D $5 + 6 = 11$

12. Which shows the related addition fact?

$$\begin{array}{r} 8 \\ +5 \\ \hline \end{array}$$

A $8 + 4 = 12$
(C) $5 + 8 = 13$
B $7 + 5 = 12$
D $8 + 3 = 11$

13. Which is a way to make 10?

A $12 - 4$
(B) $7 + 3$
C $11 - 2$
D $8 + 4$

14. Count on. What is the sum?

$$\begin{array}{r} 4 \\ +1 \\ \hline \end{array}$$

(A) 5
B 6
C 7
D 8

Go On

Name ______________________ UNIT 2 PRETEST

Choose the correct answer.

Use the number line to answer questions 15 and 16.

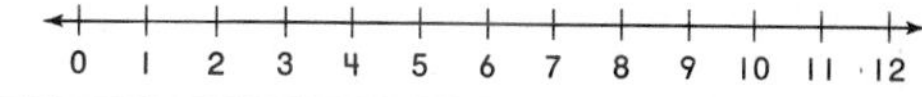

15. What is the difference?

$$\begin{array}{r} 8 \\ -1 \\ \hline \end{array}$$

(A) 7
B 8
C 9
D 10

16. What is the difference?

$12 - 3 =$ ____

A 8
(B) 9
C 10
D 11

17. Follow the rule. Which number completes the table?

Subtract 2	
10	8
9	
8	6

A 5
B 6
(C) 7
D 8

18. Which addition sentence shows the doubles plus one fact?

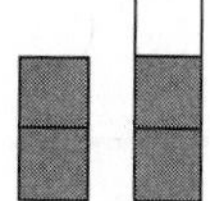

A $2 + 1 = 3$
B $2 + 2 = 4$
(C) $2 + 3 = 5$
D $3 + 3 = 6$

Go On

Name

UNIT 2 PRETEST

Choose the correct answer.

19. Which number completes the fact family?

8 + □ = 10   10 − □ = 8

□ + 8 = 10   10 − 8 = □

A 8
B 6
C 4
(D) 2

20. What is the sum?

6 + 5 = ____

A 9
B 10
(C) 11
D 12

21. Which number sentence shows how many rabbits there are?

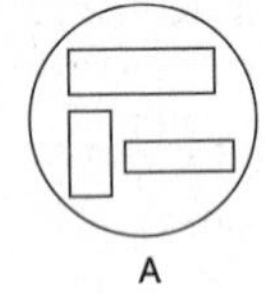

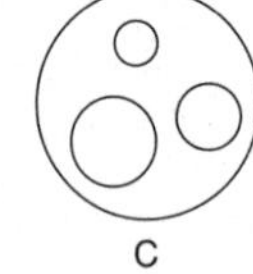
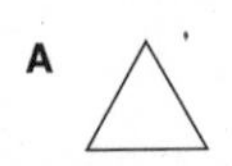
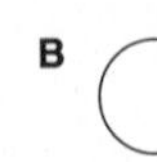
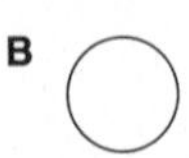

____ gray rabbits
____ white rabbits

A 8 − 4 = 4
B 7 − 4 = 32
C 3 + 4 = 7
(D) 3 + 5 = 8

22. Which number sentence matches the story?

There are 9 fish. 3 fish swim away. How many fish are there now?

A 9 + 3 = 12
(B) 9 − 3 = 6
C 6 − 3 = 3
D 6 + 3 = 9

Go On

Name

UNIT 2 PRETEST

Choose the correct answer.

23. Use and to subtract.

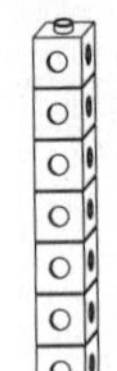

$\begin{array}{r} 12 \\ -\ 4 \\ \hline \end{array}$

A 4
B 5
C 6
(D) 8

24. Which numbers are in the fact family?

6 + 4 = 10   10 − 4 = 6

4 + 6 = 10   10 − 6 = 4

A 6, 8, 10
B 6, 10, 16
C 4, 8, 10
(D) 4, 6, 10

25. There are 12 bluebirds. Some bluebirds fly away. There are 9 bluebirds left. How many bluebirds flew away?

A 1 bluebird
B 2 bluebirds
(C) 3 bluebirds
D 4 bluebirds

26. There are 9 balls in all. 4 balls are green. The other balls are orange. How many balls are orange?

A 4 balls
(B) 5 balls
C 6 balls
D 7 balls

Stop

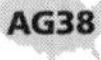

Name

CHAPTER 8 PRETEST

Choose the correct answer.

1. Which figure belongs in group A?

A B C

A B C (D)

2. How many more children chose than ?

Snacks We Like								
yogurt	●	●	●	●	●	●	●	
cracker	●	●	●	●	●			
fruit	●	●	●	●	●	●		

(A) 2 more children
B 3 more children
C 5 more children
D 7 more children

Go On

Name

CHAPTER 8 PRETEST

Choose the correct answer.

3. Which belongs in the group?

A 
B 
C 
(D) 

Use the picture graph to answer questions 5 and 6.

Plane Figures											
square	■	■	■	■	■	■	■	■	■		
triangle	▲	▲	▲	▲	▲						
circle	●	●	●	●	●	●	●	●	●	●	●

4. How many squares are there?

A 8 squares
(B) 9 squares
C 10 squares
D 11 squares

5. How many more circles are there than triangles?

A 8 more circles
B 7 more circles
(C) 6 more circles
D 5 more circles

Stop

Name ______ CHAPTER 9 PRETEST

Choose the correct answer.

1. Which bear are you more likely to pull from the bowl?

A 

B 

(C) 

2. Use the tally chart to answer the question.

Places We Like	
mountains	IIII
park	~~IIII~~
zoo	~~IIII~~ II

How many children chose the zoo?

A 4 children
B 5 children
C 6 children
(D) 7 children

3. From which box is it **impossible** to pull a gray cube?

(A) 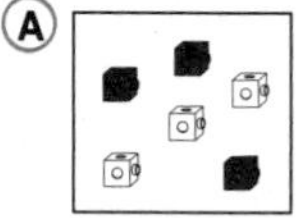

C 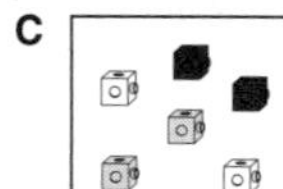

B 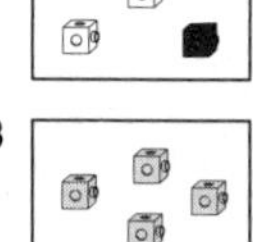

D 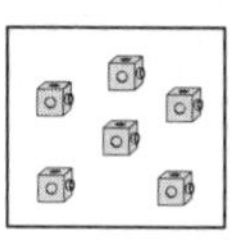 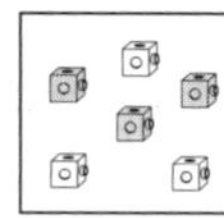

Go On

Form A • Multiple Choice AG41 **Assessment Guide**
© Harcourt • Grade 1

Name ______ CHAPTER 9 PRETEST

Choose the correct answer.

Use the bar graph to answer questions 4 and 5.

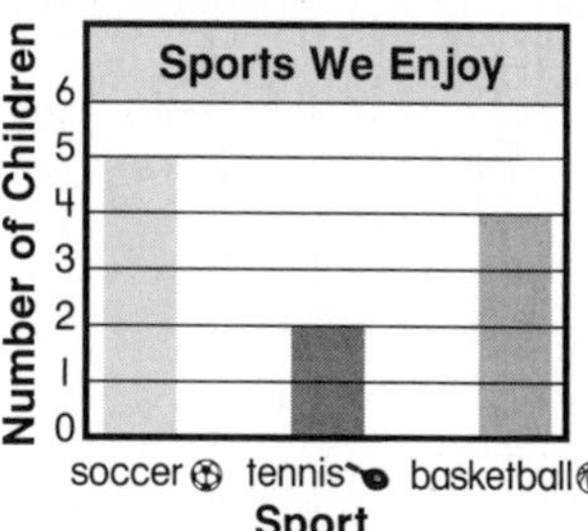

4. How many children chose tennis?

A 1 child (B) 2 children C 3 children D 4 children

5. Which sport did the most children choose?

(A) soccer B tennis C basketball

6. There are 4 gray cubes and 7 white cubes in a bowl. Which color are you more likely to pull?

A gray C black
(B) white

7. There are 8 black cubes and 5 white cubes in a bag. Which color are you more likely to pull?

A gray (C) black
B white

Stop

Assessment Guide AG42 **Form A • Multiple Choice**
© Harcourt • Grade 1

Name ______ CHAPTER 10 PRETEST

Choose the correct answer.

1. Count how many tens and ones. What is the number?

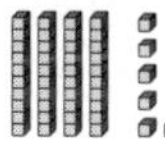

A 36
(B) 46
C 47
D 64

2. Count how many tens and ones. Which shows the number in a different way?

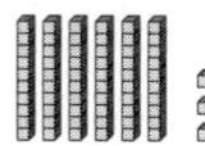

(A) 60 + 3
B 60 + 30
C 30 + 6
D 6 + 3

3. Count by tens. What number is shown?

5 tens 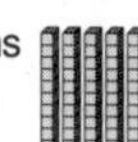

(A) 50
B 60
C 70
D 80

4. Which shows the number of tens and ones?

17 seventeen

A 0 tens 7 ones
B 10 tens 7 ones
C 7 tens 10 ones
(D) 1 ten 7 ones

Go On

Form A • Multiple Choice AG43 **Assessment Guide**
© Harcourt • Grade 1

Name ______ CHAPTER 10 PRETEST

Choose the correct answer.

5. Count how many tens and ones. What is the number?

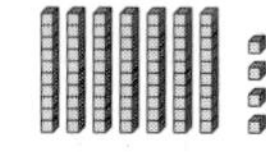
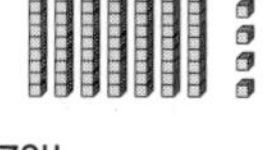

A 704
(B) 74
C 64
D 47

6. Count how many tens and ones. Which shows the number in a different way?

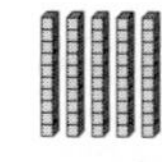

A 5 + 9
B 50 + 90
C 59 + 9
(D) 50 + 9

7. About how many crayons can you hold in one hand?

(A) about 5
B about 50
C about 500

8. About how many nickels would fill two cups?

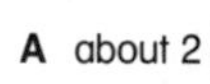

A about 2 

B about 20 

(C) about 150 

Stop

Assessment Guide AG44 **Form A • Multiple Choice**
© Harcourt • Grade 1

Name ____________________ CHAPTER 11 PRETEST

Choose the correct answer.

1. Which is true?

38 32

(A) 38 is greater than 32.
B 32 is greater than 38.
C 38 is equal to 32.
D 38 is less than 32.

2. Which number is between 61 and 63?

61 ☐ 63

A 60
B 61
(C) 62
D 64

3. Which symbol can you use to compare the numbers?

57 ◯ 62

A >
(B) <
C =

4. Which shows the numbers in order from least to greatest?

55 74 51

A 74, 55, 51
B 51, 74, 55
C 55, 51, 74
(D) 51, 55, 74

5. Which number is one more than 46?

A 56 **B** 45 (C) 47 **D** 56

Go On

Name ____________________ CHAPTER 11 PRETEST

Choose the correct answer.

6. Which is true?

88 84

A 88 is less than 84.
(B) 84 is less than 88.
C 88 is equal to 84.
D 84 is greater than 88.

7. Which number is ten less than 73?

(A) 63
B 72
C 74
D 83

Use the table to answer questions 8 and 9.

Team	Points Scored
Bulldogs	56
Tigers	63
Panthers	48
Hawks	54

8. Which team scored more points?

A Hawks
(B) Tigers

9. Which team scored the least number of points?

A Bulldogs
B Tigers
(C) Panthers
D Hawks

Stop

Name ____________________ CHAPTER 12 PRETEST

Choose the correct answer.

Use the hundred chart for questions 1 and 2.

1	2	3	4	5	6	7	8	9	10
11	12	13	14	15	16	17	18	19	20
21	22	23	24	25	26	27	28	29	30
31	32	33	34	35	36	37	38	39	40
41	42	43	44	45	46	47	48	49	50
51	52	53	54	55	56	57	58	59	60

1. Count by twos. Which number comes next?

24, 26, 28, 30, 32, ____

A 33
(B) 34
C 37
D 42

2. Count by tens. Which numbers come next?

4, 14, 24, ____, ____, ____

A 25, 26, 27
B 30, 40, 50
C 29, 34, 39
(D) 34, 44, 54

3. Skip count. How many flowers are there?

A 5 **B** 6 (C) 30 **D** 60

Go On

Name ____________________ CHAPTER 12 PRETEST

Choose the correct answer.

4. Count forward. Which numbers come next?

46, 47, 48, ____, ____, ____

(A) 49, 50, 51
B 49, 40, 41
C 58, 68, 78
D 47, 46, 45

5. Find the pattern. What are the missing numbers?

20, 25, ____, 35, 40, ____

A 45, 50
B 30, 31
C 26, 26
(D) 30, 45

6. Which number is even?

A 11 **B** 13 (C) 14 **D** 15

7. There are 2 wings on a bird.
How many wings are there on 7 birds?

number of birds	1	2	3	4	5	6	7
number of wings	2	4					

A 6 wings
(B) 14 wings
C 35 wings
D 70 wings

Stop

Name ____________________ UNIT 3 PRETEST

Choose the correct answer.

1. Which number is between 55 and 57?

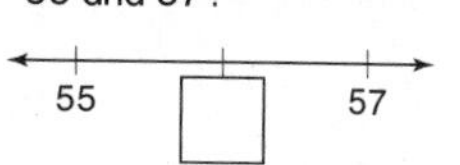

A 54 C 58
(B) 56 D 60

2. Count by tens. What number is shown?

4 tens 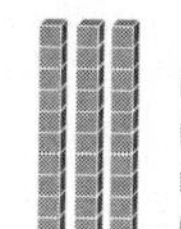

A 20 (C) 40
B 30 D 50

3. How many children chose yellow?

Colors We Like	
purple	ǀǀǀ
yellow	𝍸 ǀ
green	𝍸 ǀǀǀ

A 3 children
(B) 6 children
C 7 children
D 8 children

4. Count how many tens and ones. Which shows the number in a different way?

A 3 + 4
B 30 + 40
C 34 + 4
(D) 30 + 4

Go On

Name ____________________ UNIT 3 PRETEST

Choose the correct answer.

Use the hundred chart for questions 5 and 6.

1	2	3	4	5	6	7	8	9	10
11	12	13	14	15	16	17	18	19	20
21	22	23	24	25	26	27	28	29	30
31	32	33	34	35	36	37	38	39	40
41	42	43	44	45	46	47	48	49	50
51	52	53	54	55	56	57	58	59	60
61	62	63	64	65	66	67	68	69	70
71	72	73	74	75	76	77	78	79	80
81	82	83	84	85	86	87	88	89	90
91	92	93	94	95	96	97	98	99	100

5. Count by fives. Which number comes next?

25, 30, 35, 40, 45, ____

A 47
(B) 50
C 55
D 60

6. Count by tens. Which numbers come next?

8, 18, 28, ____, ____, ____

(A) 38, 48, 58
B 33, 38, 43
C 30, 32, 34
D 29, 30, 31

Go On

Name ____________________ UNIT 3 PRETEST

Choose the correct answer.

7. Which fish belongs in the group?

(A)  B   C  D 

8. From which box is it **possible** to pull a black cube?

A 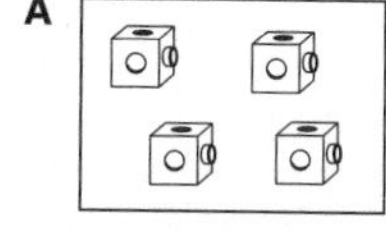

(C) 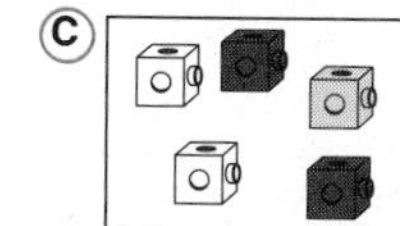

B 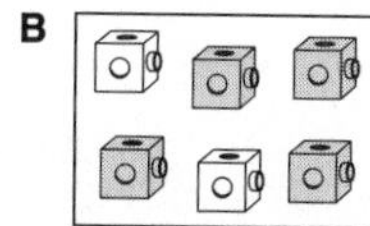

D 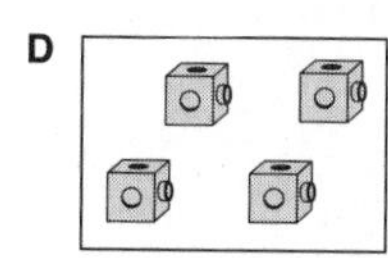

9. There are 2 wheels on a bicycle.
How many wheels are there on 6 bicycles?

number of bicycles	1	2	3	4	5	6
number of wheels	2	4				

A 6 wheels C 10 wheels
B 8 wheels (D) 12 wheels

Go On

Name ____________________ UNIT 3 PRETEST

Choose the correct answer.

10. Which is true?

A 43 is greater than 47.
B 47 is less than 43.
C 43 is equal to 47.
(D) 43 is less than 47.

11. There are 6 black cubes and 7 white cubes in a bag. Which color are you more likely to pull?

(A) white cube
B gray cube
C black cube

Use the table to answer questions 12 and 13.

Game	Points Scored
First	62
Second	58
Third	47
Fourth	59

12. In which game did the team score the most points?

(A) First C Third
B Second D Fourth

13. In which game did the team score the least number of points?

A First (C) Third
B Second D Fourth

Go On

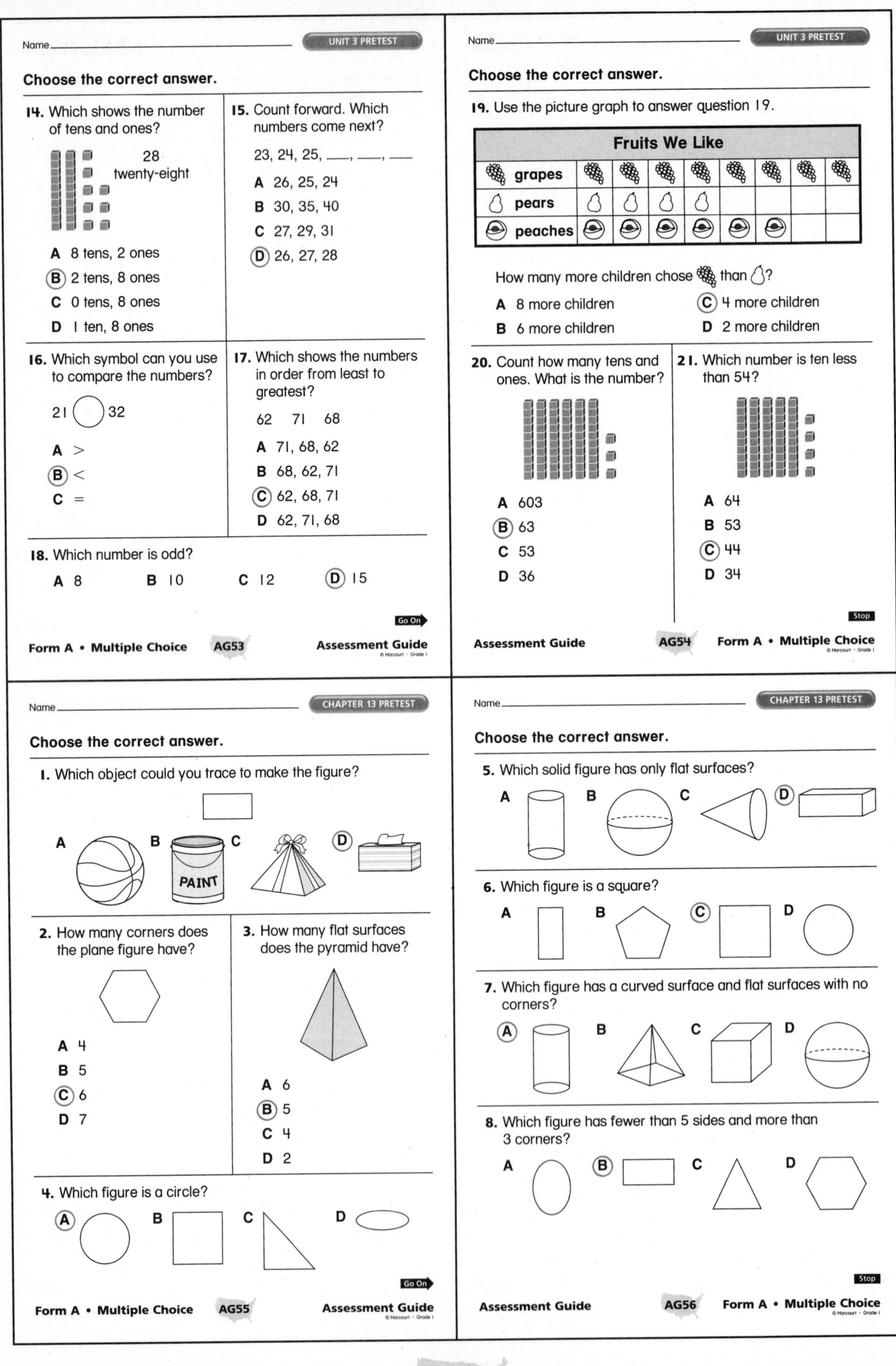

Name ______________________ UNIT 3 PRETEST

Choose the correct answer.

14. Which shows the number of tens and ones?

28
twenty-eight

A 8 tens, 2 ones
(B) 2 tens, 8 ones
C 0 tens, 8 ones
D 1 ten, 8 ones

15. Count forward. Which numbers come next?

23, 24, 25, ___, ___, ___

A 26, 25, 24
B 30, 35, 40
C 27, 29, 31
(D) 26, 27, 28

16. Which symbol can you use to compare the numbers?

21 ◯ 32

A >
(B) <
C =

17. Which shows the numbers in order from least to greatest?

62 71 68

A 71, 68, 62
B 68, 62, 71
(C) 62, 68, 71
D 62, 71, 68

18. Which number is odd?

A 8 B 10 C 12 (D) 15

Go On

Form A • Multiple Choice AG53 Assessment Guide
© Harcourt • Grade 1

Name ______________________ UNIT 3 PRETEST

Choose the correct answer.

19. Use the picture graph to answer question 19.

Fruits We Like								
🍇 grapes	🍇	🍇	🍇	🍇	🍇	🍇	🍇	🍇
🍐 pears	🍐	🍐	🍐	🍐				
🍑 peaches	🍑	🍑	🍑	🍑	🍑	🍑		

How many more children chose 🍇 than 🍐?

A 8 more children
B 6 more children
(C) 4 more children
D 2 more children

20. Count how many tens and ones. What is the number?

A 603
(B) 63
C 53
D 36

21. Which number is ten less than 54?

A 64
B 53
(C) 44
D 34

Stop

Assessment Guide AG54 Form A • Multiple Choice
© Harcourt • Grade 1

Name ______________________ CHAPTER 13 PRETEST

Choose the correct answer.

1. Which object could you trace to make the figure?

A B C (D)

PAINT

2. How many corners does the plane figure have?

A 4
B 5
(C) 6
D 7

3. How many flat surfaces does the pyramid have?

A 6
(B) 5
C 4
D 2

4. Which figure is a circle?

(A) B C D

Go On

Form A • Multiple Choice AG55 Assessment Guide
© Harcourt • Grade 1

Name ______________________ CHAPTER 13 PRETEST

Choose the correct answer.

5. Which solid figure has only flat surfaces?

A B C (D)

6. Which figure is a square?

A B (C) D

7. Which figure has a curved surface and flat surfaces with no corners?

(A) B C D

8. Which figure has fewer than 5 sides and more than 3 corners?

A (B) C D

Stop

Assessment Guide AG56 Form A • Multiple Choice
© Harcourt • Grade 1

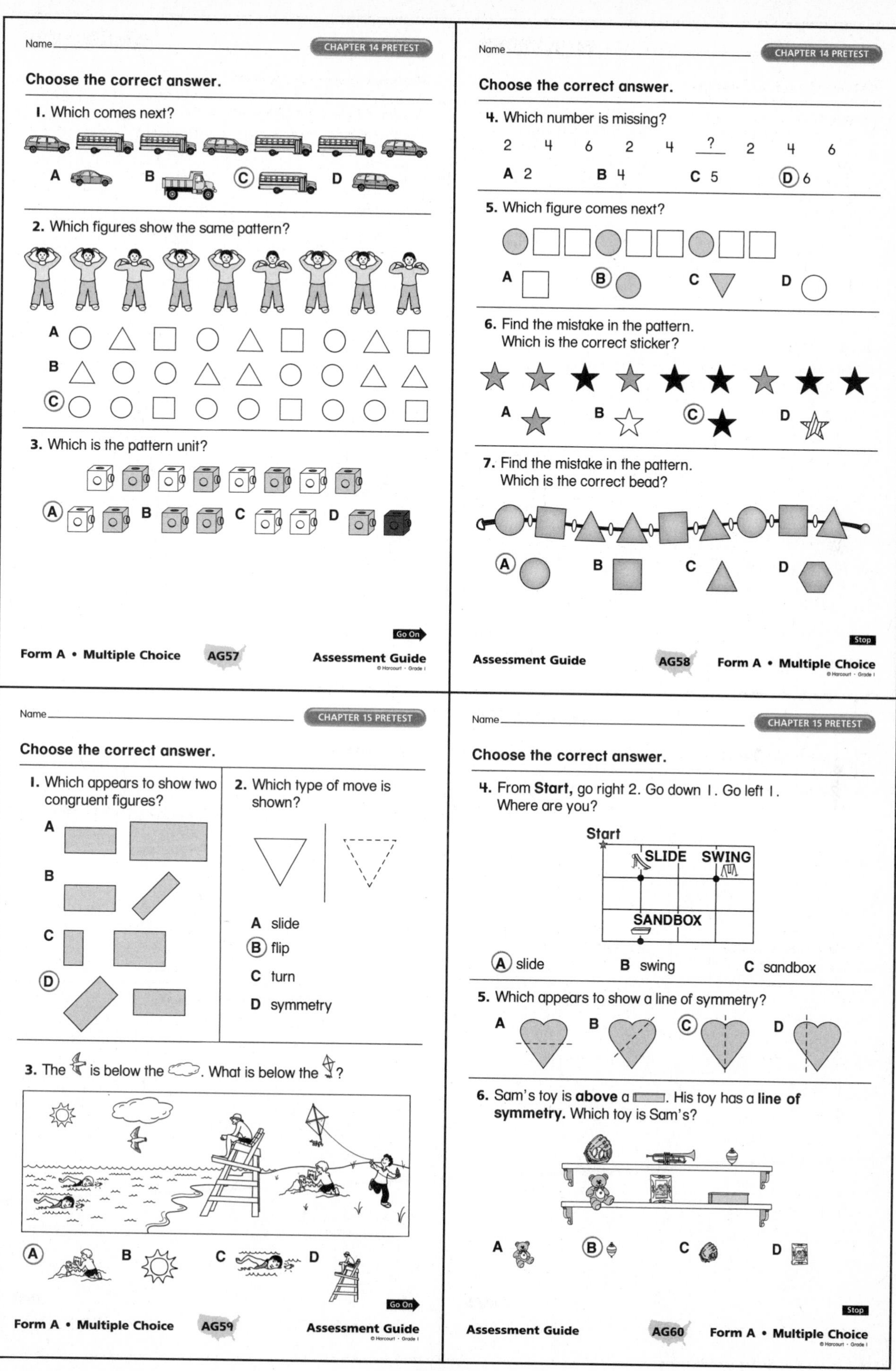

Name______________________ CHAPTER 14 PRETEST

Choose the correct answer.

1. Which comes next?

A B (C) D

2. Which figures show the same pattern?

A ○ △ □ ○ △ □ ○ △ □
B △ ○ ○ △ △ ○ ○ △ △
(C) ○ ○ □ ○ ○ □ ○ ○ □

3. Which is the pattern unit?

(A) B C D

Go On

Form A • Multiple Choice AG57 Assessment Guide
© Harcourt • Grade 1

Name______________________ CHAPTER 14 PRETEST

Choose the correct answer.

4. Which number is missing?

2 4 6 2 4 __?__ 2 4 6

A 2 B 4 C 5 (D) 6

5. Which figure comes next?

A B (B) C D

6. Find the mistake in the pattern. Which is the correct sticker?

A B (C) D

7. Find the mistake in the pattern. Which is the correct bead?

(A) B C D

Stop

Assessment Guide AG58 Form A • Multiple Choice
© Harcourt • Grade 1

Name______________________ CHAPTER 15 PRETEST

Choose the correct answer.

1. Which appears to show two congruent figures?

A B C (D)

2. Which type of move is shown?

A slide
(B) flip
C turn
D symmetry

3. The [bird] is below the [cloud]. What is below the [kite]?

(A) B C D

Go On

Form A • Multiple Choice AG59 Assessment Guide
© Harcourt • Grade 1

Name______________________ CHAPTER 15 PRETEST

Choose the correct answer.

4. From **Start,** go right 2. Go down 1. Go left 1. Where are you?

Start
SLIDE SWING
SANDBOX

(A) slide B swing C sandbox

5. Which appears to show a line of symmetry?

A B (C) D

6. Sam's toy is **above** a [block]. His toy has a **line of symmetry.** Which toy is Sam's?

A (B) C D

Stop

Assessment Guide AG60 Form A • Multiple Choice
© Harcourt • Grade 1

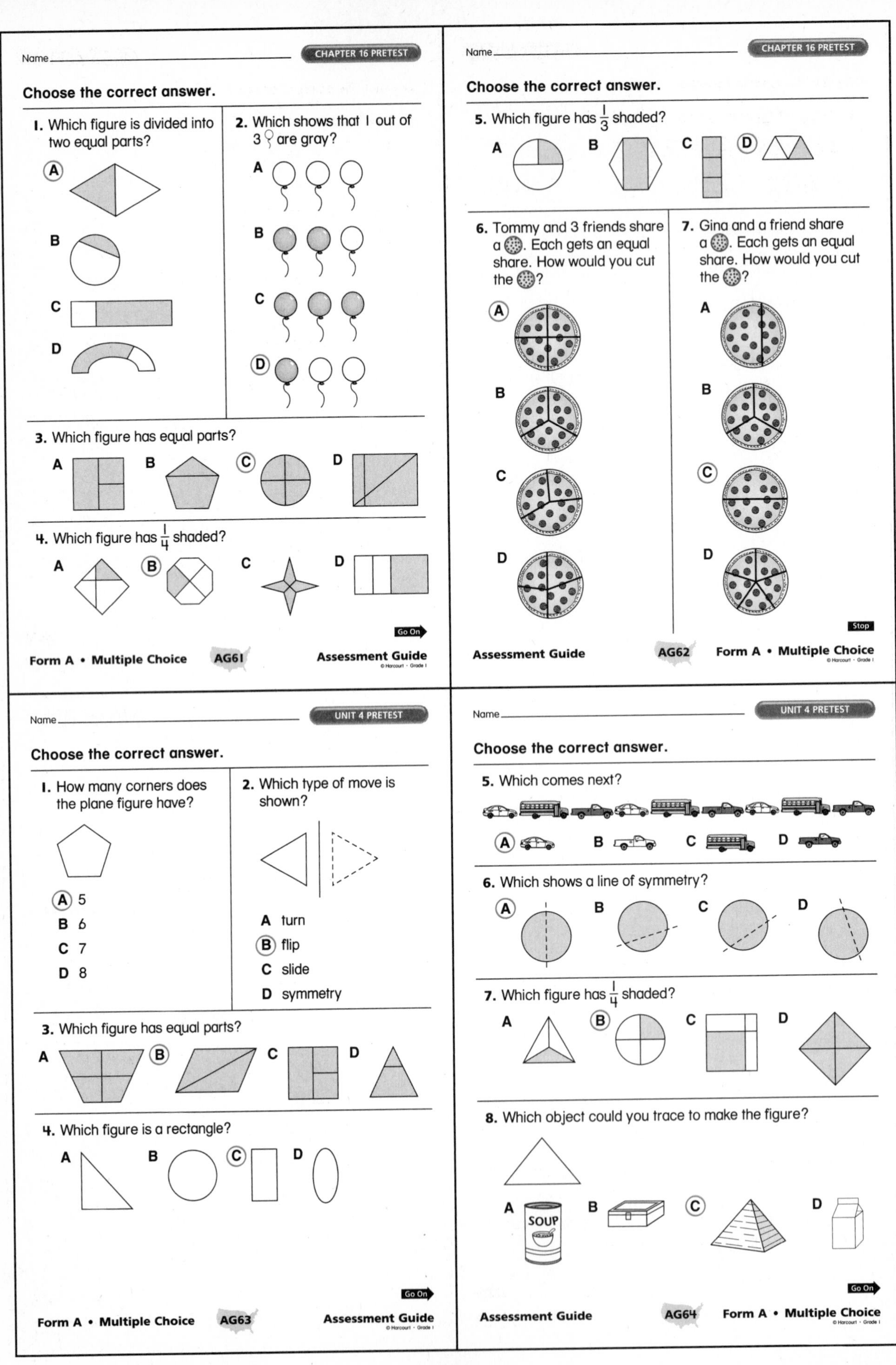

Name ______________________ CHAPTER 16 PRETEST

Choose the correct answer.

1. Which figure is divided into two equal parts?

(A) B C D

2. Which shows that 1 out of 3 balloons are gray?

A B C (D)

3. Which figure has equal parts?

A B (C) D

4. Which figure has $\frac{1}{4}$ shaded?

A (B) C D

Go On

Form A • Multiple Choice AG61 **Assessment Guide**

© Harcourt • Grade 1

Name ______________________ CHAPTER 16 PRETEST

Choose the correct answer.

5. Which figure has $\frac{1}{3}$ shaded?

A B C (D)

6. Tommy and 3 friends share a pizza. Each gets an equal share. How would you cut the pizza?

(A) B C D

7. Gina and a friend share a pizza. Each gets an equal share. How would you cut the pizza?

A B (C) D

Stop

Assessment Guide AG62 **Form A • Multiple Choice**

© Harcourt • Grade 1

Name ______________________ UNIT 4 PRETEST

Choose the correct answer.

1. How many corners does the plane figure have?

(A) 5
B 6
C 7
D 8

2. Which type of move is shown?

A turn
(B) flip
C slide
D symmetry

3. Which figure has equal parts?

A (B) C D

4. Which figure is a rectangle?

A B (C) D

Go On

Form A • Multiple Choice AG63 **Assessment Guide**

© Harcourt • Grade 1

Name ______________________ UNIT 4 PRETEST

Choose the correct answer.

5. Which comes next?

(A) B C D

6. Which shows a line of symmetry?

(A) B C D

7. Which figure has $\frac{1}{4}$ shaded?

A (B) C D

8. Which object could you trace to make the figure?

A SOUP B (C) D

Go On

Assessment Guide AG64 **Form A • Multiple Choice**

© Harcourt • Grade 1

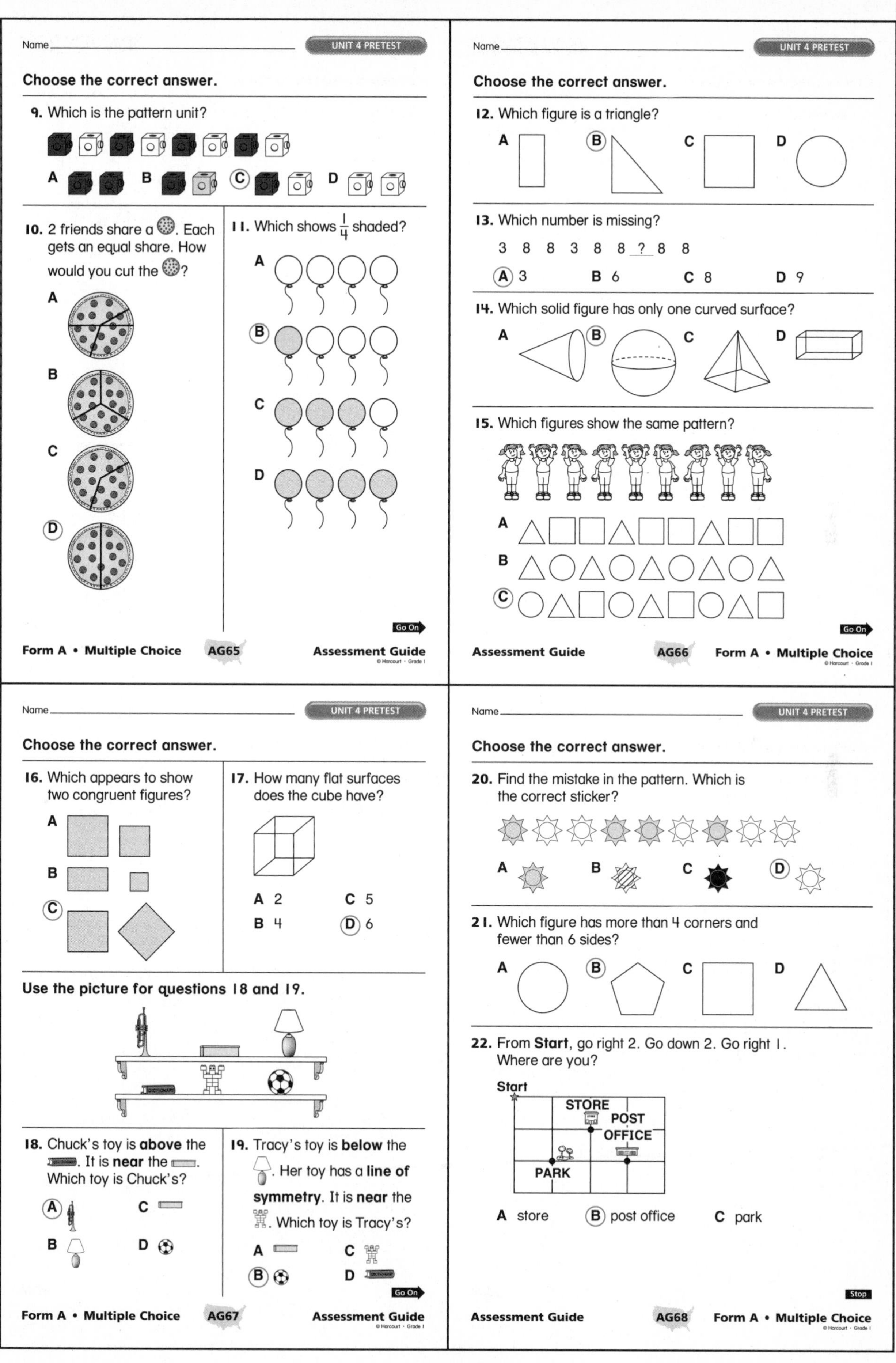

Name__________________________ UNIT 4 PRETEST

Choose the correct answer.

9. Which is the pattern unit?

A B (C) D

10. 2 friends share a pizza. Each gets an equal share. How would you cut the pizza?

A

B

C

(D)

11. Which shows $\frac{1}{4}$ shaded?

A

(B)

C

D

Go On

Form A • Multiple Choice AG65 Assessment Guide

© Harcourt · Grade 1

Name__________________________ UNIT 4 PRETEST

Choose the correct answer.

12. Which figure is a triangle?

A (B) C D

13. Which number is missing?

3 8 8 3 8 8 ? 8 8

(A) 3 B 6 C 8 D 9

14. Which solid figure has only one curved surface?

A (B) C D

15. Which figures show the same pattern?

A △□□△□□△□□

B △○△○△○△○△

(C) ○△□○△□○△□

Go On

Assessment Guide AG66 Form A • Multiple Choice

© Harcourt · Grade 1

Name__________________________ UNIT 4 PRETEST

Choose the correct answer.

16. Which appears to show two congruent figures?

A

B

(C)

17. How many flat surfaces does the cube have?

A 2 C 5

B 4 (D) 6

Use the picture for questions 18 and 19.

DICTIONARY

18. Chuck's toy is **above** the dictionary. It is **near** the box. Which toy is Chuck's?

(A) C

B D

19. Tracy's toy is **below** the lamp. Her toy has a **line of symmetry**. It is **near** the robot. Which toy is Tracy's?

A C

(B) D

Go On

Form A • Multiple Choice AG67 Assessment Guide

© Harcourt · Grade 1

Name__________________________ UNIT 4 PRETEST

Choose the correct answer.

20. Find the mistake in the pattern. Which is the correct sticker?

A B C (D)

21. Which figure has more than 4 corners and fewer than 6 sides?

A (B) C D

22. From **Start**, go right 2. Go down 2. Go right 1. Where are you?

Start

STORE

POST OFFICE

PARK

A store (B) post office C park

Stop

Assessment Guide AG68 Form A • Multiple Choice

© Harcourt · Grade 1

Name ____________________ CHAPTER 17 PRETEST

Choose the correct answer.

1. What is the sum?

$$\begin{array}{r} 6 \\ +6 \\ \hline \end{array}$$

A 10
B 11
(C) 12
D 13

2. Make a ten and add. What is the sum?

$$\begin{array}{r} 8 \\ +7 \\ \hline \end{array}$$

A 12
(B) 15
C 17
D 18

3. What is the sum?

$$\begin{array}{r} 8 \\ +4 \\ \hline \end{array}$$

A 16
B 14
C 13
(D) 12

4. What is the sum?

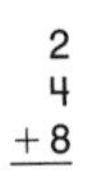

$$\begin{array}{r} 2 \\ 4 \\ +8 \\ \hline \end{array}$$

(A) 14
B 12
C 10
D 6

Go On

Name ____________________ CHAPTER 17 PRETEST

Choose the correct answer.

5. What is the sum?

$$\begin{array}{r} 10 \\ +6 \\ \hline \end{array}$$

A 106
B 61
(C) 16
D 4

6. Make a ten and add. What is the sum?

$$\begin{array}{r} 9 \\ +5 \\ \hline \end{array}$$

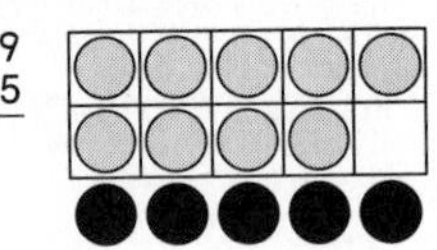

A 13
(B) 14
C 16
D 15

7. What is the sum?

4 + 4 = ____

A 88
B 80
C 40
(D) 8

8. Which number sentence matches the story? A mail carrier delivers 7 letters. Then she delivers 9 more letters. How many letters does the mail carrier deliver in all?

(A) 7 + 9 = 16
B 7 + 9 = 15
C 16 − 7 = 9
D 9 − 7 = 2

9. Which number sentence matches the story? 8 teachers are in the hallway. 8 more teachers join them. How many teachers are in the hallway?

A 8 − 8 = 0
B 8 + 8 = 14
(C) 8 + 8 = 16
D 16 − 6 = 8

Stop

Name ____________________ CHAPTER 18 PRETEST

Choose the correct answer.

Use the number line to answer questions 1 and 2.

1. What is the difference?

$$\begin{array}{r} 13 \\ -5 \\ \hline \end{array}$$

A 7
(B) 8
C 9
D 18

2. What is the difference?

$$\begin{array}{r} 15 \\ -6 \\ \hline \end{array}$$

(A) 9
B 8
C 7
D 1

3. How many more leaves are there than birds?

$$\begin{array}{r} 11 \\ -4 \\ \hline \end{array}$$

A 15 more leaves
B 8 more leaves
(C) 7 more leaves
D 6 more leaves

4. What is the difference?

14 − 6 = ____

A 20
B 10
C 9
(D) 8

Go On

Name ____________________ CHAPTER 18 PRETEST

Choose the correct answer.

5. Use the addition fact to help you subtract. What is the difference?

$$\begin{array}{r} 7 \\ +5 \\ \hline \end{array} \qquad \begin{array}{r} 12 \\ -5 \\ \hline \end{array}$$

A 6
(B) 7
C 9
D 17

6. What is the difference?

$$\begin{array}{r} 14 \\ -9 \\ \hline \end{array}$$

(A) 5
B 6
C 7
D 8

7. How many fewer bees are there than flowers?

$$\begin{array}{r} 12 \\ -8 \\ \hline \end{array}$$

A 20 fewer bees
B 8 fewer bees
(C) 4 fewer bees
D 3 fewer bees

8. There are 12 children playing on the playground. 3 more children join them. How many children are now playing on the playground?

A 9 children
B 12 children
C 14 children
(D) 15 children

9. There are 11 birds in a tree. 3 birds fly away. How many birds are in the tree now?

A 14 birds
B 12 birds
C 9 birds
(D) 8 birds

Stop

Name ______________________ CHAPTER 19 PRETEST

Choose the correct answer.

1. Which number is missing?

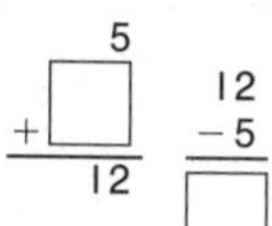

$$\begin{array}{r} 5 \\ +\square \\ \hline 12 \end{array} \qquad \begin{array}{r} 12 \\ -5 \\ \hline \square \end{array}$$

(A) 7 C 15

B 8 D 17

2. Which is a way to make 15?

A 13 − 8

B 17 − 5

C 9 + 8

(D) 2 + 5 + 8

3. Which number sentence shows how many umbrellas there are?

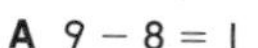

____ gray umbrellas

____ white umbrellas

A 9 − 8 = 1 (C) 8 + 9 = 17

B 12 + 5 = 17 D 17 − 9 = 8

4. Which number is missing?

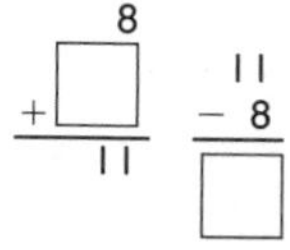

$$\begin{array}{r} 8 \\ +\square \\ \hline 11 \end{array} \qquad \begin{array}{r} 11 \\ -8 \\ \hline \square \end{array}$$

A 2 (B) 3 C 4 D 5

Go On

Name ______________________ CHAPTER 19 PRETEST

Choose the correct answer.

5. Which is a way to make 9?

A 4 + 3 + 4

B 6 + 4

C 12 − 5

(D) 15 − 6

6. Follow the rule. Which number completes the table?

Subtract 7	
12	5
14	7
16	
17	10

A 8 (B) 9 C 11 D 12

7. Which fact is part of the fact family?

$$\begin{array}{r} 9 \\ +4 \\ \hline 13 \end{array} \qquad \begin{array}{r} 4 \\ +9 \\ \hline 13 \end{array} \qquad \begin{array}{r} 13 \\ -4 \\ \hline 9 \end{array}$$

(A) $\begin{array}{r} 13 \\ -9 \\ \hline 4 \end{array}$ B $\begin{array}{r} 13 \\ +4 \\ \hline 17 \end{array}$ C $\begin{array}{r} 9 \\ -4 \\ \hline 5 \end{array}$ D $\begin{array}{r} 5 \\ +4 \\ \hline 9 \end{array}$

8. Kara has 7 peaches. Henry brings 9 more peaches. How many peaches are there now?

A 2 peaches

B 14 peaches

C 15 peaches

(D) 16 peaches

9. Trevor buys 14 apples. He gives 7 apples away. How many apples does Trevor have now?

A 21 apples (C) 7 apples

B 8 apples D 6 apples

Stop

Name ______________________ CHAPTER 20 PRETEST

Choose the correct answer.

1. Which shows the amount of money in a different way?

A

B

C

(D)

2. Which shows a way to make 1 dollar?

A

(B)

C

D

Go On

Name ______________________ CHAPTER 20 PRETEST

Choose the correct answer.

3. Which symbol can you use to compare the amounts?

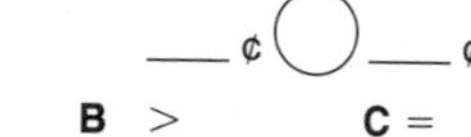

____ ¢ ◯ ____ ¢

(A) < B > C =

4. Jack buys a toy car for 75¢. He uses 3 . Which shows the same amount in a different way?

(A)

B

C

D

Stop

Name ____________________ CHAPTER 21 PRETEST

Choose the correct answer.

1. What time does the clock show?

A 10:30
B 6:30
C 8:30
(D) 9:30

2. What time does the clock show?

A 12:00
(B) 2:00
C 2:30
D 11:00

3. Use the calendar. How many Mondays are in this month?

MAY						
Sunday	Monday	Tuesday	Wednesday	Thursday	Friday	Saturday
		1	2	3	4	5
6	7	8	9	10	11	12
13	14	15	16	17	18	19
20	21	22	23	24	25	26
27	28	29	30	31		

A 2
B 3
(C) 4
D 5

Go On

Name ____________________ CHAPTER 21 PRETEST

Choose the correct answer.

4. Which clock matches the time shown?

4:30

A 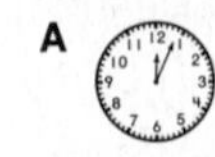
(B) 
C 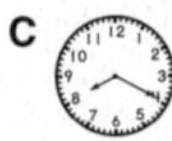
D 

Use the table to answer questions 5 and 6.

Camp Sunrise		
Event	Start	End
crafts		
hiking		
soccer		

5. Which event starts at 3:30?

A crafts
B hiking
(C) soccer

6. Which event lasts the shortest time?

(A) crafts
B hiking
C soccer

Stop

Name ____________________ UNIT 5 PRETEST

Choose the correct answer.

1. Use the calendar. How many Mondays are in June?

JUNE						
Sunday	Monday	Tuesday	Wednesday	Thursday	Friday	Saturday
					1	2
3	4	5	6	7	8	9
10	11	12	13	14	15	16
17	18	19	20	21	22	23
24	25	26	27	28	29	30

A 5
(B) 4
C 3
D 2

2. Use the addition fact to help you subtract. What is the difference?

$$\begin{array}{r} 8 \\ +5 \\ \hline \end{array} \qquad \begin{array}{r} 13 \\ -\ 5 \\ \hline \end{array}$$

A 9
(B) 8
C 7
D 6

3. What is the sum?

$$\begin{array}{r} 7 \\ +7 \\ \hline \end{array}$$

A 12
B 13
(C) 14
D 15

4. Follow the rule. Which number completes the table?

Subtract 8	
12	4
14	6
16	
17	9

A 13
B 10
(C) 8
D 7

Go On

Name ____________________ UNIT 5 PRETEST

Choose the correct answer.

5. How many more butterflies are there than flowers?

$$\begin{array}{r} 10 \\ -\ 3 \\ \hline \end{array}$$

A 13 more butterflies
B 8 more butterflies
(C) 7 more butterflies
D 6 more butterflies

6. Which number sentence shows how many umbrellas there are?

____ gray umbrellas

____ white umbrellas

A 8 − 7 = 1
B 10 + 5 = 15
C 15 − 7 = 8
(D) 7 + 8 = 15

7. What is the sum?

$$\begin{array}{r} 2 \\ 3 \\ +7 \\ \hline \end{array}$$

(A) 12
B 10
C 9
D 5

8. What is the time of day?

A morning
(B) afternoon
C evening

Go On

Name____________________

Choose the correct answer.

9. Which shows the amount of money in a different way?

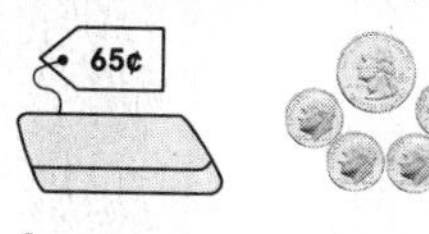

A

(B)

C

10. Which shows a way to make 1 dollar?

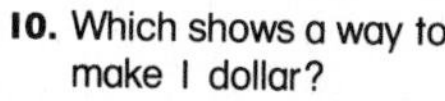

A

B

(C)

11. What is the difference?

$$\begin{array}{r} 15 \\ -\ 6 \\ \hline \end{array}$$

A 11 **(B)** 9 **C** 8 **D** 5

Go On

Name____________________

Choose the correct answer.

12. Which number sentence matches the story?
A town has 5 buses. Then the town buys 7 more buses. How many buses does the town have in all?

A 5 + 7 = 13

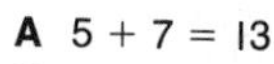

(B) 5 + 7 = 12

C 15 − 7 = 8

D 7 − 5 = 2

13. Which number is missing?

$$\begin{array}{r} 8 \\ +\square \\ \hline 13 \end{array} \qquad \begin{array}{r} 13 \\ -\ 8 \\ \hline \square \end{array}$$

(A) 5 **C** 3

B 4 **D** 2

14. Make a ten and add. What is the sum?

$$\begin{array}{r} 7 \\ +6 \\ \hline \end{array}$$

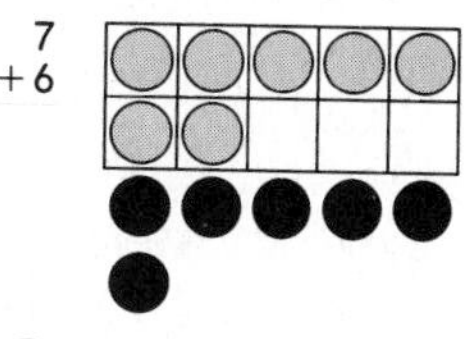

(A) 13 **C** 15

B 14 **D** 16

15. Rick has 4 bananas. Evan brings 7 more bananas. How many bananas are there in all?

(A) 11 bananas

B 10 bananas

C 9 bananas

D 3 bananas

Go On

Name____________________

Choose the correct answer.

16. Which symbol can you use to compare the amounts?

A < **(B)** > **C** =

17. Which clock matches the time shown?

A

B

C

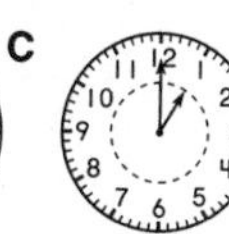

(D)

18. What is the sum?

9 + 8 = ____

A 77 **C** 7

(B) 17 **D** 1

19. What is the difference?

19 − 9 = ____

(A) 10 **C** 8

B 9 **D** 1

Go On

Name____________________

Choose the correct answer.

Use the table to answer question 20.

Community Center		
Event	**Start**	**End**
art class		
game time		
homework help		

20. Which event starts at 3:00?

A art class **B** game time **(C)** homework help

21. Which fact is part of the fact family?

$$\begin{array}{r} 6 \\ +7 \\ \hline 13 \end{array} \qquad \begin{array}{r} 7 \\ +6 \\ \hline 13 \end{array} \qquad \begin{array}{r} 13 \\ -\ 6 \\ \hline 7 \end{array}$$

A $\begin{array}{r} 13 \\ +\ 3 \\ \hline 16 \end{array}$ **(B)** $\begin{array}{r} 13 \\ -\ 7 \\ \hline 6 \end{array}$ **C** $\begin{array}{r} 5 \\ +1 \\ \hline 6 \end{array}$ **D** $\begin{array}{r} 6 \\ -5 \\ \hline 1 \end{array}$

Stop

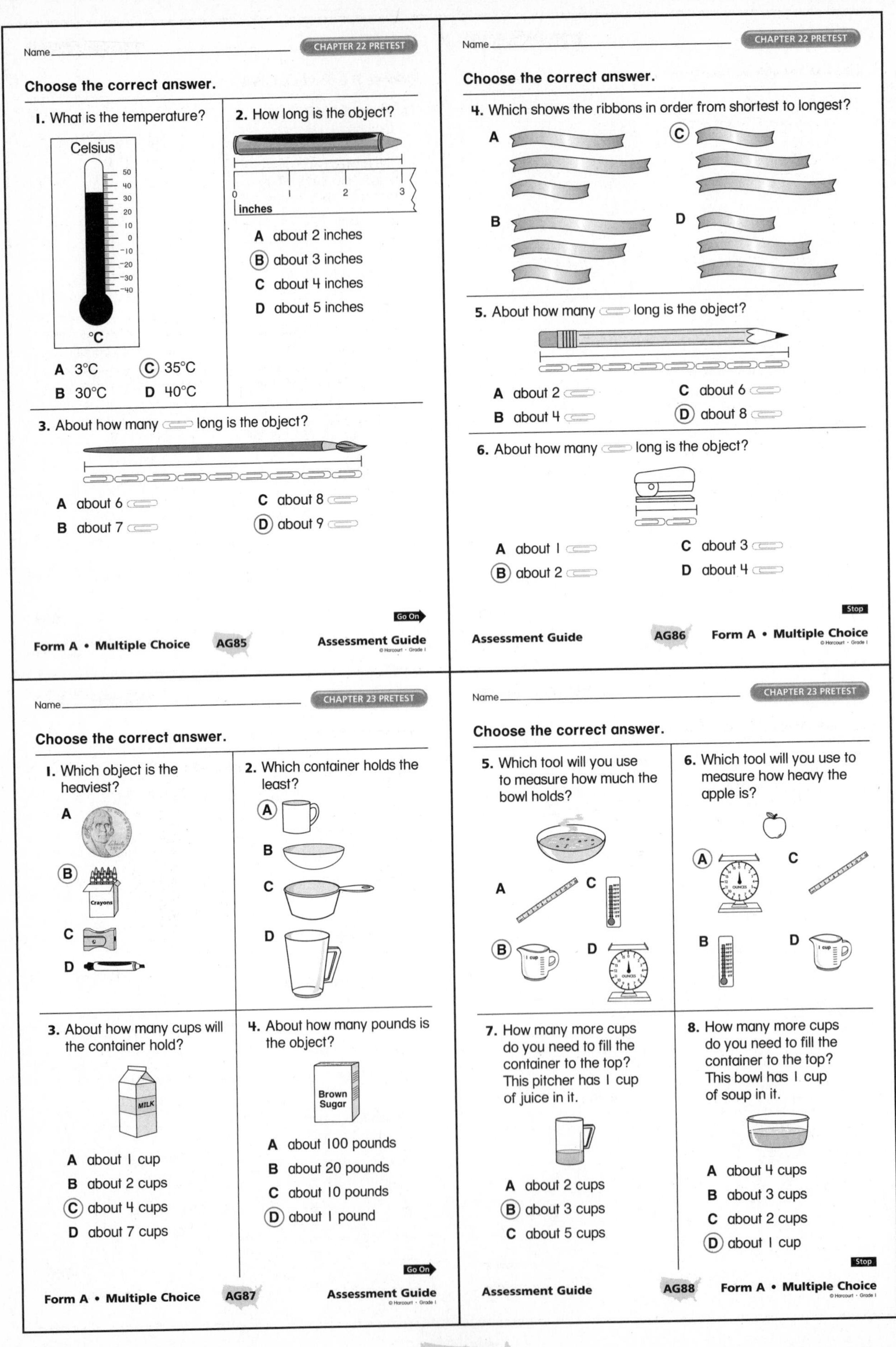

Name

CHAPTER 22 PRETEST

Choose the correct answer.

1. What is the temperature?

Celsius

50, 40, 30, 20, 10, 0, −10, −20, −30, −40

°C

A 3°C
B 30°C
(C) 35°C
D 40°C

2. How long is the object?

0, 1, 2, 3 inches

A about 2 inches
(B) about 3 inches
C about 4 inches
D about 5 inches

3. About how many ▭ long is the object?

A about 6 ▭
B about 7 ▭
C about 8 ▭
(D) about 9 ▭

Go On

Form A • Multiple Choice AG85 Assessment Guide © Harcourt • Grade 1

Name

CHAPTER 22 PRETEST

Choose the correct answer.

4. Which shows the ribbons in order from shortest to longest?

A
(C)
B
D

5. About how many ▭ long is the object?

A about 2 ▭
B about 4 ▭
C about 6 ▭
(D) about 8 ▭

6. About how many ▭ long is the object?

A about 1 ▭
(B) about 2 ▭
C about 3 ▭
D about 4 ▭

Stop

Assessment Guide AG86 Form A • Multiple Choice © Harcourt • Grade 1

Name

CHAPTER 23 PRETEST

Choose the correct answer.

1. Which object is the heaviest?

A
(B) Crayons
C
D

2. Which container holds the least?

(A)
B
C
D

3. About how many cups will the container hold?

MILK

A about 1 cup
B about 2 cups
(C) about 4 cups
D about 7 cups

4. About how many pounds is the object?

Brown Sugar

A about 100 pounds
B about 20 pounds
C about 10 pounds
(D) about 1 pound

Go On

Form A • Multiple Choice AG87 Assessment Guide © Harcourt • Grade 1

Name

CHAPTER 23 PRETEST

Choose the correct answer.

5. Which tool will you use to measure how much the bowl holds?

A
C
(B) 1 cup
D OUNCES

6. Which tool will you use to measure how heavy the apple is?

(A) OUNCES
C
B
D 1 cup

7. How many more cups do you need to fill the container to the top? This pitcher has 1 cup of juice in it.

A about 2 cups
(B) about 3 cups
C about 5 cups

8. How many more cups do you need to fill the container to the top? This bowl has 1 cup of soup in it.

A about 4 cups
B about 3 cups
C about 2 cups
(D) about 1 cup

Stop

Assessment Guide AG88 Form A • Multiple Choice © Harcourt • Grade 1

Name ______________________________ CHAPTER 24 PRETEST

Choose the correct answer.

1. What is the difference?

90 − 60 = ____

A 20
(B) 30
C 40
D 50

2. What is the sum?

50 + 20 = ____

A 30
B 40
C 60
(D) 70

3. What is the difference?

	tens	ones
	3	9
−		5

Workmat (Tens | Ones)

A 36
B 35
(C) 34
D 33

4. What is the sum?

	tens	ones
	2	2
+		4

Workmat (Tens | Ones)

(A) 26
B 25
C 24
D 23

Go On

Name ______________________________ CHAPTER 24 PRETEST

Choose the correct answer.

5. What is the sum?

	tens	ones
	3	1
+	2	5

Workmat (Tens | Ones)

A 14
B 54
(C) 56
D 66

6. What is the difference?

	tens	ones
	3	7
−	1	3

Workmat (Tens | Ones)

A 50
(B) 24
C 20
D 14

7. There are 52 birds in the trees. 9 of the birds fly away. About how many birds are left?

A about 4 birds
(B) about 40 birds
C about 100 birds
D about 400 birds

8. Laura counts 46 trees. Then she counts 50 more trees. About how many trees does Laura count in all?

A about 1 tree
B about 10 trees
C about 30 trees
(D) about 100 trees

Stop

Name ______________________________ UNIT 6 PRETEST

Choose the correct answer.

1. What is the sum?

	tens	ones
	3	4
+		3

Workmat (tens | ones)

A 31
B 36
(C) 37
D 47

2. Which container holds the least amount of water?

A
(B)
C
D

3. About how many ⊂⊃ long is the object?

A about 5 ⊂⊃
B about 6 ⊂⊃
(C) about 7 ⊂⊃
D about 8 ⊂⊃

Go On

Name ______________________________ UNIT 6 PRETEST

Choose the correct answer.

4. About how many pounds is the object?

Pasta

(A) about 1 pound
B about 10 pounds
C about 20 pounds
D about 100 pounds

5. What is the temperature?

Celsius
50 40 30 20 10 0 −10 −20 −30 −40
°C

A 3°C
B 20°C
C 25°C
(D) 30°C

6. What is the difference?

80 − 20 = ____

A 40
(B) 60
C 70
D 100

7. About how many cups will the container hold?

Milk

A about 4 cups
B about 3 cups
(C) about 2 cups
D about 1 cup

Go On

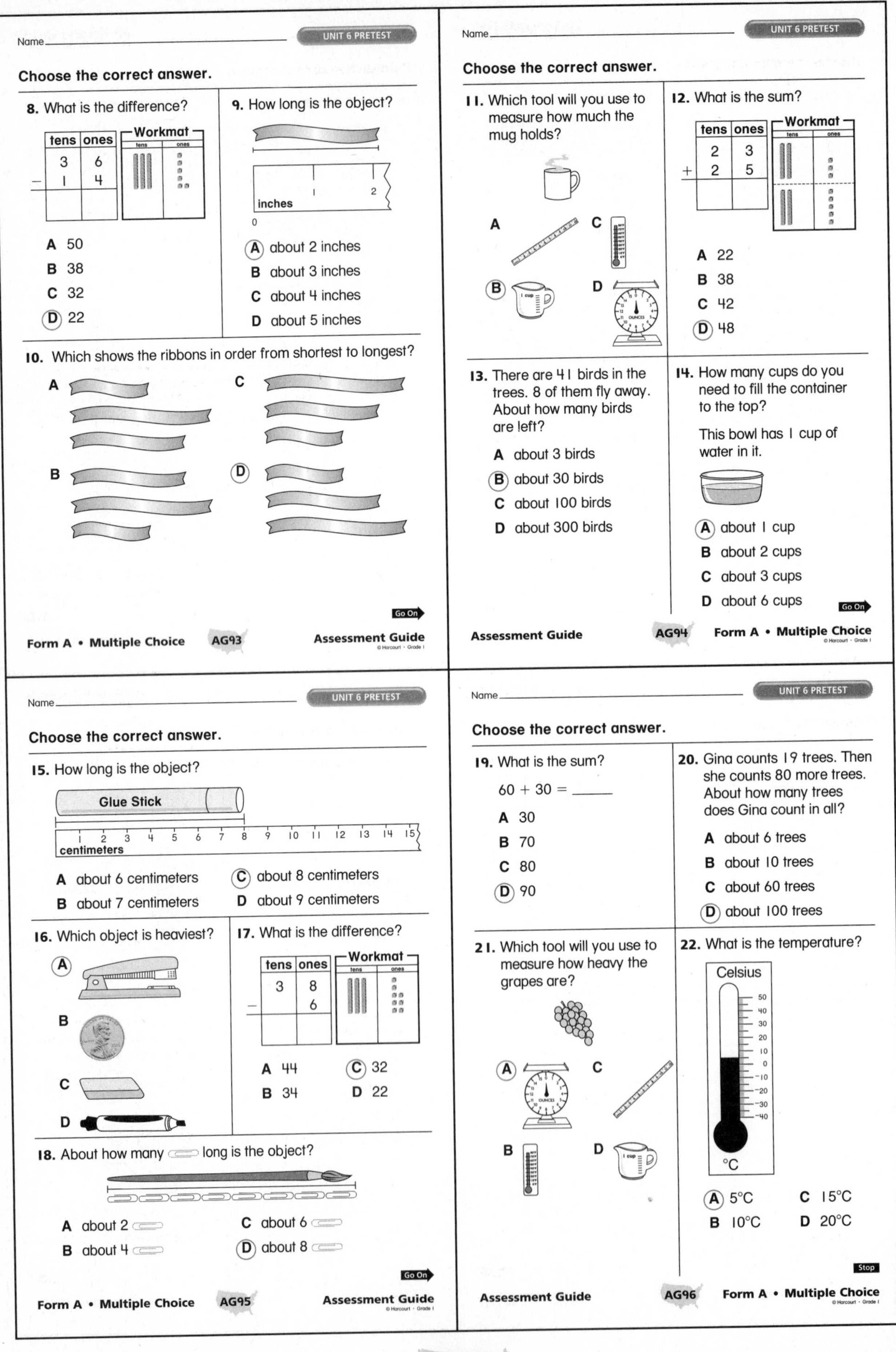

Name ______________________ UNIT 6 PRETEST

Choose the correct answer.

8. What is the difference?

	tens	ones
	3	6
−	1	4

Workmat (tens | ones)

A 50
B 38
C 32
(D) 22

9. How long is the object?

inches 0 1 2

(A) about 2 inches
B about 3 inches
C about 4 inches
D about 5 inches

10. Which shows the ribbons in order from shortest to longest?

A
B
C
(D)

Go On

Form A • Multiple Choice AG93 Assessment Guide
© Harcourt • Grade 1

Name ______________________ UNIT 6 PRETEST

Choose the correct answer.

11. Which tool will you use to measure how much the mug holds?

A
(B) 1 cup
C
D OUNCES

12. What is the sum?

	tens	ones
	2	3
+	2	5

Workmat (tens | ones)

A 22
B 38
C 42
(D) 48

13. There are 41 birds in the trees. 8 of them fly away. About how many birds are left?

A about 3 birds
(B) about 30 birds
C about 100 birds
D about 300 birds

14. How many cups do you need to fill the container to the top?

This bowl has 1 cup of water in it.

(A) about 1 cup
B about 2 cups
C about 3 cups
D about 6 cups

Go On

Assessment Guide AG94 Form A • Multiple Choice
© Harcourt • Grade 1

Name ______________________ UNIT 6 PRETEST

Choose the correct answer.

15. How long is the object?

Glue Stick

centimeters 1 2 3 4 5 6 7 8 9 10 11 12 13 14 15

A about 6 centimeters
B about 7 centimeters
(C) about 8 centimeters
D about 9 centimeters

16. Which object is heaviest?

(A)
B
C
D

17. What is the difference?

	tens	ones
	3	8
−		6

Workmat (tens | ones)

A 44
B 34
(C) 32
D 22

18. About how many (paper clips) long is the object?

A about 2
B about 4
C about 6
(D) about 8

Go On

Form A • Multiple Choice AG95 Assessment Guide
© Harcourt • Grade 1

Name ______________________ UNIT 6 PRETEST

Choose the correct answer.

19. What is the sum?

60 + 30 = ______

A 30
B 70
C 80
(D) 90

20. Gina counts 19 trees. Then she counts 80 more trees. About how many trees does Gina count in all?

A about 6 trees
B about 10 trees
C about 60 trees
(D) about 100 trees

21. Which tool will you use to measure how heavy the grapes are?

(A) OUNCES
B
C
D 1 cup

22. What is the temperature?

Celsius 50 40 30 20 10 0 −10 −20 −30 −40 °C

(A) 5°C
B 10°C
C 15°C
D 20°C

Stop

Assessment Guide AG96 Form A • Multiple Choice
© Harcourt • Grade 1

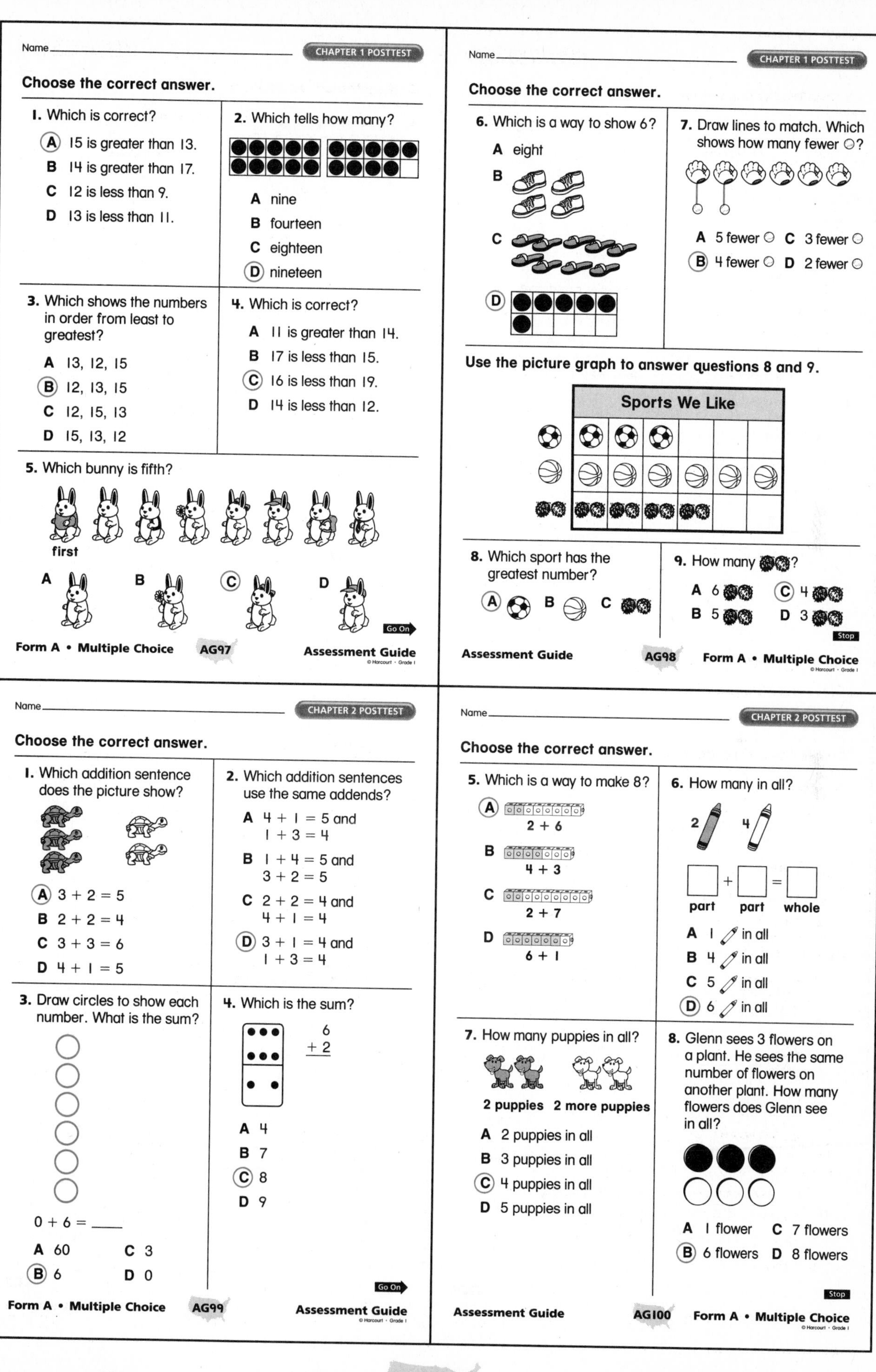

Name ____________ CHAPTER 1 POSTTEST

Choose the correct answer.

1. Which is correct?
   - (A) 15 is greater than 13.
   - B 14 is greater than 17.
   - C 12 is less than 9.
   - D 13 is less than 11.

2. Which tells how many?
   - A nine
   - B fourteen
   - C eighteen
   - (D) nineteen

3. Which shows the numbers in order from least to greatest?
   - A 13, 12, 15
   - (B) 12, 13, 15
   - C 12, 15, 13
   - D 15, 13, 12

4. Which is correct?
   - A 11 is greater than 14.
   - B 17 is less than 15.
   - (C) 16 is less than 19.
   - D 14 is less than 12.

5. Which bunny is fifth?

   first

   A B (C) D

Go On

Form A • Multiple Choice AG97 Assessment Guide © Harcourt • Grade 1

Name ____________ CHAPTER 1 POSTTEST

Choose the correct answer.

6. Which is a way to show 6?
   - A eight
   - B
   - C
   - (D)

7. Draw lines to match. Which shows how many fewer?
   - A 5 fewer
   - (B) 4 fewer
   - C 3 fewer
   - D 2 fewer

Use the picture graph to answer questions 8 and 9.

Sports We Like

8. Which sport has the greatest number?

   (A) B C

9. How many?
   - A 6
   - B 5
   - (C) 4
   - D 3

Stop

Assessment Guide AG98 Form A • Multiple Choice © Harcourt • Grade 1

Name ____________ CHAPTER 2 POSTTEST

Choose the correct answer.

1. Which addition sentence does the picture show?
   - (A) 3 + 2 = 5
   - B 2 + 2 = 4
   - C 3 + 3 = 6
   - D 4 + 1 = 5

2. Which addition sentences use the same addends?
   - A 4 + 1 = 5 and 1 + 3 = 4
   - B 1 + 4 = 5 and 3 + 2 = 5
   - C 2 + 2 = 4 and 4 + 1 = 4
   - (D) 3 + 1 = 4 and 1 + 3 = 4

3. Draw circles to show each number. What is the sum?

   0 + 6 = ____
   - A 60
   - (B) 6
   - C 3
   - D 0

4. Which is the sum?

   $6 + 2$
   - A 4
   - B 7
   - (C) 8
   - D 9

Go On

Form A • Multiple Choice AG99 Assessment Guide © Harcourt • Grade 1

Name ____________ CHAPTER 2 POSTTEST

Choose the correct answer.

5. Which is a way to make 8?
   - (A) 2 + 6
   - B 4 + 3
   - C 2 + 7
   - D 6 + 1

6. How many in all?

   2 4

   ☐ + ☐ = ☐

   part part whole
   - A 1 in all
   - B 4 in all
   - C 5 in all
   - (D) 6 in all

7. How many puppies in all?

   2 puppies 2 more puppies
   - A 2 puppies in all
   - B 3 puppies in all
   - (C) 4 puppies in all
   - D 5 puppies in all

8. Glenn sees 3 flowers on a plant. He sees the same number of flowers on another plant. How many flowers does Glenn see in all?
   - A 1 flower
   - (B) 6 flowers
   - C 7 flowers
   - D 8 flowers

Stop

Assessment Guide AG100 Form A • Multiple Choice © Harcourt • Grade 1

Name

CHAPTER 3 POSTTEST

Choose the correct answer.

1. What is the difference?

  7
− 4

A 2
(B) 3
C 4
D 5

2. What is the difference?

6 − 0 = ____

A 0
B 3
(C) 6
D 60

3. Which subtraction sentence is shown by the 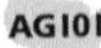?

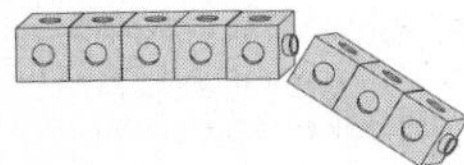

A 8 − 4 = 4
B 5 − 3 = 2
C 8 − 2 = 6
(D) 8 − 3 = 5

4. Which subtraction sentence does the picture show?

(A) 5 − 3 = 2
B 2 + 3 = 5
C 8 − 3 = 5
D 5 − 4 = 1

Go On

Form A • Multiple Choice AG101 Assessment Guide
© Harcourt • Grade 1

Name

CHAPTER 3 POSTTEST

Choose the correct answer.

5. How many fewer ?

(A) 5 fewer
B 4 fewer
C 3 fewer
D 2 fewer

6. Which number completes the subtraction sentence?

6 − 4 = ☐
whole part part

A 10
B 5
C 3
(D) 2

7. How many boys are left?

A 0 boys are left
(B) 1 boy is left
C 2 boys are left
D 3 boys are left

8. There are 6 gray birds and 3 white birds in a tree. How many fewer white birds are there?

A 1 fewer white bird
B 2 fewer white birds
(C) 3 fewer white birds
D 9 fewer white birds

Stop

Assessment Guide AG102 Form A • Multiple Choice
© Harcourt • Grade 1

Name

CHAPTER 4 POSTTEST

Choose the correct answer.

1. Which number sentences match the picture?

(A) 5 + 3 = 8
8 − 3 = 5

B 3 + 2 = 5
5 − 2 = 3

C 6 + 3 = 9
5 − 3 = 2

D 8 + 3 = 11
8 − 5 = 3

2. Which number sentence matches the picture?

A 2 + 2 = 4
(B) 8 − 4 = 4
C 8 − 3 = 5
D 4 + 4 = 8

3. Which is a related subtraction fact?

1 + 6 = 7

A 6 + 1 = 5
B 8 − 7 = 1
C 7 − 5 = 2
(D) 7 − 6 = 1

4. How many butterflies are there in all?

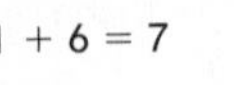

A 1
B 6
(C) 7
D 8

Go On

Form A • Multiple Choice AG103 Assessment Guide
© Harcourt • Grade 1

Name

CHAPTER 4 POSTTEST

Choose the correct answer.

5. Which is a related addition fact?

6 − 2 = 4

(A) 4 + 2 = 6
B 6 + 2 = 8
C 6 + 4 = 10
D 3 + 3 = 6

6. Which number sentence matches the picture?

A 4 + 3 = 7
B 7 − 3 = 4
C 5 − 2 = 3
(D) 2 + 5 = 7

7. How many birds fly away?

A 1 (B) 2 C 3 D 8

8. There are 6 markers. Carol brings 1 more marker. How many markers are there now?

A 5
(B) 7
C 8
D 9

9. There are 8 books. Jack takes 3 books away. How many books are left?

A 11
B 8
(C) 5
D 2

Stop

Assessment Guide AG104 Form A • Multiple Choice
© Harcourt • Grade 1

Name ____________________ UNIT 1 POSTTEST

Choose the correct answer.

1. Which shows the numbers in order from least to greatest?

A 13, 12, 7
(B) 7, 12, 13
C 12, 13, 7
D 7, 13, 12

2. Which is the difference?

8 − 0 = ____

A 0
B 4
(C) 8
D 88

3. Which addition sentences use the same addends?

(A) 2 + 6 = 8 and 6 + 2 = 8
B 6 + 2 = 8 and 6 + 3 = 9
C 2 + 3 = 5 and 1 + 4 = 5
D 4 + 2 = 6 and 3 + 3 = 6

4. There are 5 cars. 1 car leaves. Which number sentence matches the words?

(A) 5 − 1 = 4
B 6 − 1 = 5
C 5 + 1 = 6
D 6 + 1 = 7

5. Which is correct?

A 9 is less than 7.
B 18 is less than 8.
(C) 6 is greater than 5.
D 10 is greater than 13.

6. Which is a related subtraction fact?

4 + 5 = 9

A 5 − 2 = 3
B 9 − 3 = 6
C 5 − 4 = 1
(D) 9 − 5 = 4

Go On

Name ____________________ UNIT 1 POSTTEST

Choose the correct answer.

7. Use the 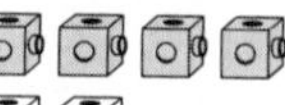 below. There are 6 beavers and 2 raccoons. How many fewer raccoons are there?

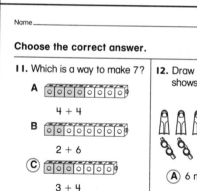

A 1 raccoon
B 2 raccoons
C 3 raccoons
(D) 4 raccoons

8. Which number sentence matches the picture?

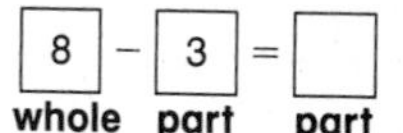

A 7 − 5 = 2
(B) 7 − 2 = 5
C 7 + 2 = 9
D 5 + 1 = 6

9. Draw circles to show each number. Which is the sum?

6 + 0 = ____

A 60
(B) 6
C 1
D 0

10. Which number completes the subtraction sentence?

8 − 3 = ☐
whole part part

(A) 5
B 4
C 3
D 2

Go On

Name ____________________ UNIT 1 POSTTEST

Choose the correct answer.

11. Which is a way to make 7?

A 4 + 4
B 2 + 6
(C) 3 + 4
D 1 + 3

12. Draw lines to match. Which shows how many more flippers?

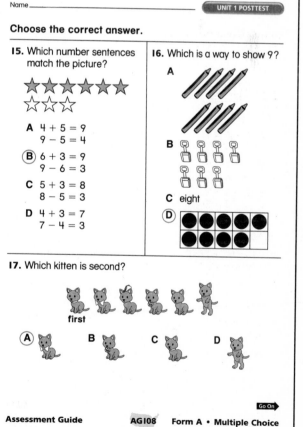

(A) 6 more
B 5 more
C 4 more
D 3 more

13. How many bats are left?

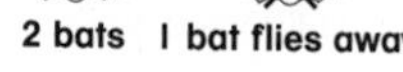

2 bats 1 bat flies away

(A) 1 bat is left
B 2 bats are left
C 3 bats are left
D 4 bats are left

14. Which addition sentence does the picture show?

A 4 + 1 = 5
B 5 + 2 = 7
C 3 + 1 = 4
(D) 3 + 2 = 5

Go On

Name ____________________ UNIT 1 POSTTEST

Choose the correct answer.

15. Which number sentences match the picture?

A 4 + 5 = 9
9 − 5 = 4
(B) 6 + 3 = 9
9 − 6 = 3
C 5 + 3 = 8
8 − 5 = 3
D 4 + 3 = 7
7 − 4 = 3

16. Which is a way to show 9?

A
B
C eight
(D)

17. Which kitten is second?

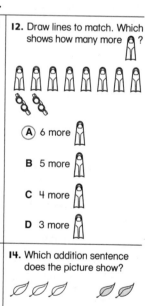

first

(A) 
B 

C 
D 

Go On

Name ______ UNIT 1 POSTTEST

Choose the correct answer.

18. How many mice are there in all?

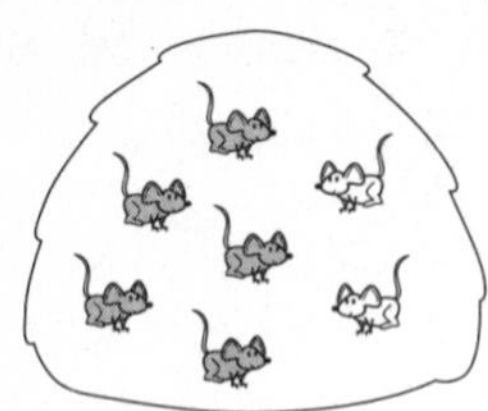

A 9
(B) 7
C 5
D 2

19. Which is the sum?

$$\begin{array}{r} 2 \\ -7 \\ \hline \end{array}$$

A 6
B 7
C 8
(D) 9

20. Which subtraction sentence is shown by the 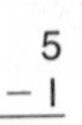?

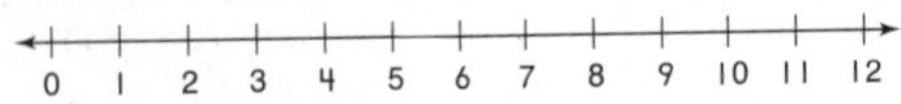

A $9 - 6 = 3$
B $8 - 5 = 3$
(C) $8 - 6 = 2$
D $7 - 6 = 1$

21. There are 2 children playing ball. The same number of children join them. How many children are there playing ball?

A 0 children
B 2 children
(C) 4 children
D 6 children

Go On

Name ______ UNIT 1 POSTTEST

Choose the correct answer.

22. Which is the difference?

$$\begin{array}{r} 5 \\ -1 \\ \hline \end{array}$$

A 1
B 2
C 3
(D) 4

23. Which tells how many?

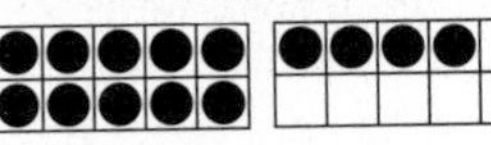

(A) fourteen
B fifteen
C eighteen
D nineteen

24. How many in all?

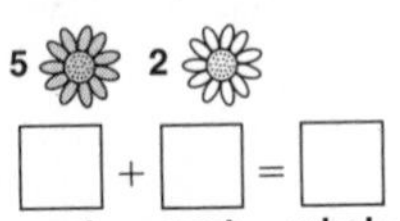

5 2

☐ + ☐ = ☐
part part whole

A 4 in all
B 5 in all
C 6 in all
(D) 7 in all

25. How many fewer?

$9 - 3 =$ ____

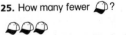

A 7 fewer
(B) 6 fewer
C 5 fewer
D 4 fewer

Stop

Name ______ CHAPTER 5 POSTTEST

Choose the correct answer.

Use the number line to answer questions 1 and 2.

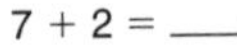

0 1 2 3 4 5 6 7 8 9 10 11 12

1. What is the sum?

$$\begin{array}{r} 6 \\ +3 \\ \hline \end{array}$$

A 3
B 8
(C) 9
D 10

2. What is the sum?

$$\begin{array}{r} 8 \\ +2 \\ \hline \end{array}$$

A 6
(B) 10
C 11
D 12

3. Which addition sentence shows the doubles fact?

(A) $3 + 3 = 6$
B $2 + 4 = 6$
C $4 + 4 = 8$
D $3 + 2 = 5$

4. Which addition sentence shows the doubles plus one fact?

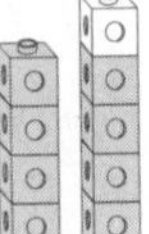

A $4 + 4 = 8$
B $3 + 4 = 7$
C $5 + 5 = 10$
(D) $4 + 5 = 9$

Go On

Name ______ CHAPTER 5 POSTTEST

Choose the correct answer.

5. Count on. What is the sum?

$$\begin{array}{r} 3 \\ +8 \\ \hline \end{array}$$

(A) 11
B 10
C 9
D 5

6. What is the sum?

$9 + 3 =$ ____

A 6
B 10
C 11
(D) 12

7. Count on. What is the sum?

$7 + 2 =$ ____

A 8 (B) 9 C 10 D 11

8. Draw a picture to solve. There are 10 turtles in all. 5 turtles are brown. The other turtles are green. How many turtles are green?

Check children's work.

(A) 5 turtles
B 7 turtles
C 8 turtles
D 15 turtles

9. Draw a picture to solve. There are 9 birds in all. 3 birds are blue. The other birds are red. How many birds are red?

Check children's work.

A 12 birds
B 8 birds
(C) 6 birds
D 4 birds

Stop

Name ______________________ CHAPTER 6 POSTTEST

Choose the correct answer.

Use the number line to answer questions 1 through 4.

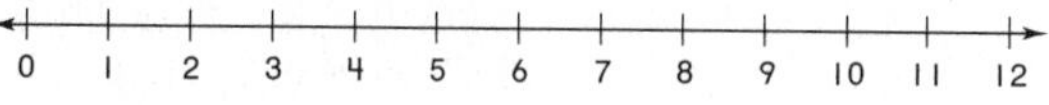

1. What is the difference?

$$\begin{array}{r} 9 \\ -2 \\ \hline \end{array}$$

(A) 7
B 8
C 9
D 12

2. What is the difference?

10 − 3 = ____

A 6
(B) 7
C 8
D 9

3. What is the difference?

____ = 12 − 3

A 14
B 11
C 10
(D) 9

4. What is the difference?

$$\begin{array}{r} 9 \\ -1 \\ \hline \end{array}$$

A 5
B 6
C 7
(D) 8

Go On

Name ______________________ CHAPTER 6 POSTTEST

Choose the correct answer.

5. What is the difference?

$$\begin{array}{r} 12 \\ -3 \\ \hline \end{array}$$

A 10 C 8
(B) 9 D 7

6. What is the difference?

$$\begin{array}{r} 7 \\ -3 \\ \hline \end{array}$$

A 6 (C) 4
B 5 D 3

7. Use [cube] and [cube] to add.

$$\begin{array}{r} 6 \\ +6 \\ \hline \end{array}$$

(A) 12 C 1
B 11 D 0

8. Use [cube] and [X] to subtract.

$$\begin{array}{r} 5 \\ -2 \\ \hline \end{array}$$

A 7 C 4
B 6 (D) 3

9. Which number sentence matches the story?

There are 9 seashells. 4 seashells are washed away. How many seashells are there now?

A 9 + 4 = 13
B 13 − 9 = 4
(C) 9 − 4 = 5
D 4 − 5 = 9

10. Which number sentence matches the story?

There are 11 fish. 3 fish swim away. How many fish are there now?

(A) 11 − 3 = 8
B 8 − 3 = 5
C 11 + 3 = 14
D 8 + 3 = 11

Stop

Name ______________________ CHAPTER 7 POSTTEST

Choose the correct answer.

1. Which numbers are in the fact family?

7 + 3 = 10   10 − 3 = 7
3 + 7 = 10   10 − 7 = 3

A 3, 4, 7
(B) 3, 7, 10
C 3, 10, 13
D 7, 10, 17

2. Which is a way to make 12?

(A) 8 + 4
B 12 − 1
C 10 − 2
D 9 + 2

3. Which shows the related addition fact?

$$\begin{array}{r} 6 \\ +3 \\ \hline \square \end{array}$$

A $\begin{array}{r} 2 \\ +7 \\ \hline 9 \end{array}$ C $\begin{array}{r} 5 \\ +4 \\ \hline 9 \end{array}$

B $\begin{array}{r} 3 \\ +3 \\ \hline 6 \end{array}$ (D) $\begin{array}{r} 3 \\ +6 \\ \hline 9 \end{array}$

4. Which number sentence shows how many bugs there are?

5 gray bugs
6 white bugs

A 5 + 1 = 6
B 6 − 5 = 1
(C) 5 + 6 = 11
D 11 − 6 = 5

Go On

Name ______________________ CHAPTER 7 POSTTEST

Choose the correct answer.

5. Which number completes the fact family?

4 + □ = 10   10 − □ = 4
□ + 4 = 10   10 − 4 = □

(A) 6 C 12
B 8 D 14

6. Follow the rule. Which number completes the table?

Subtract 3	
5	2
7	
9	6

A 3 (B) 4 C 5 D 10

7. Which shows a pair of related subtraction facts?

A $\begin{array}{r} 11 \\ -4 \\ \hline 7 \end{array}$ $\begin{array}{r} 11 \\ -5 \\ \hline 6 \end{array}$ B $\begin{array}{r} 10 \\ -4 \\ \hline 6 \end{array}$ $\begin{array}{r} 12 \\ -6 \\ \hline 6 \end{array}$ C $\begin{array}{r} 12 \\ -3 \\ \hline 9 \end{array}$ $\begin{array}{r} 12 \\ -5 \\ \hline 7 \end{array}$ (D) $\begin{array}{r} 10 \\ -6 \\ \hline 4 \end{array}$ $\begin{array}{r} 10 \\ -4 \\ \hline 6 \end{array}$

8. Draw a picture to solve. There are 11 owls. Some owls fly away. There are 6 owls left. How many owls flew away?

Check children's work.

A 3 owls (C) 5 owls
B 4 owls D 6 owls

9. Draw a picture to solve. There are 12 rabbits. Some rabbits hop away. There are 7 rabbits left. How many rabbits hopped away?

Check children's work.

A 6 rabbits C 4 rabbits
(B) 5 rabbits D 3 rabbits

Stop

Name__________ UNIT 2 POSTTEST

Choose the correct answer.

1. Which addition sentence shows the doubles fact?

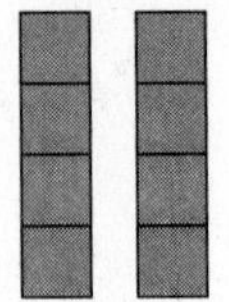

A 2 + 2 = 4
B 3 + 3 = 6
(C) 4 + 4 = 8
D 4 + 3 = 7

2. Draw a picture to solve. There are 6 zebras. Some zebras walk away. There are 4 zebras left. How many zebras walked away?

Check children's work.

(A) 2 zebras C 6 zebras
B 4 zebras D 8 zebras

3. Follow the rule. Which number completes the table?

Subtract 3	
10	7
9	
8	5

A 3 C 5
B 4 (D) 6

4. Which numbers are in the fact family?

7 + 3 = 10 10 − 3 = 7
3 + 7 = 10 10 − 7 = 3

A 3, 7, 13
B 3, 10, 13
(C) 3, 7, 10
D 3, 10, 17

Go On

Name__________ UNIT 2 POSTTEST

Choose the correct answer.

Use the number line to answer questions 5 and 6.

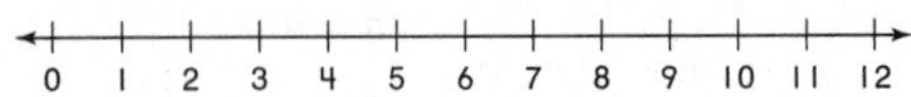

5. What is the sum?

$$\begin{array}{r} 9 \\ +1 \\ \hline \end{array}$$

A 8 (C) 10
B 9 D 11

6. What is the sum?

$$\begin{array}{r} 6 \\ +3 \\ \hline \end{array}$$

(A) 9 C 11
B 10 D 12

7. What is the difference?

$$\begin{array}{r} 12 \\ -4 \\ \hline \end{array}$$

A 5 C 7
B 6 (D) 8

8. Use 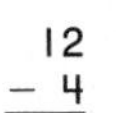 and to add.

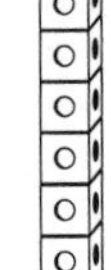

$$\begin{array}{r} 6 \\ +3 \\ \hline \end{array}$$

(A) 9 C 7
B 8 D 6

9. Which shows a pair of related subtraction facts?

A $\begin{array}{r} 9 \\ -2 \\ \hline 7 \end{array}$ $\begin{array}{r} 9 \\ -3 \\ \hline 6 \end{array}$ (B) $\begin{array}{r} 10 \\ -3 \\ \hline 7 \end{array}$ $\begin{array}{r} 10 \\ -7 \\ \hline 3 \end{array}$ C $\begin{array}{r} 5 \\ -3 \\ \hline 2 \end{array}$ $\begin{array}{r} 6 \\ -3 \\ \hline 3 \end{array}$ D $\begin{array}{r} 11 \\ -5 \\ \hline 6 \end{array}$ $\begin{array}{r} 11 \\ -7 \\ \hline 4 \end{array}$

Go On

Name__________ UNIT 2 POSTTEST

Choose the correct answer.

10. Count on. What is the sum?

7 + 1 = ____

(A) 8 B 9 C 18 D 71

11. Which number sentence matches the story?

There are 10 sheep.
There are 4 goats.
How many more sheep are there than goats?

(A) 10 − 4 = 6
B 10 + 6 = 16
C 10 − 5 = 5
D 4 + 5 = 9

12. Which shows the related addition fact?

$$\begin{array}{r} 6 \\ +3 \\ \hline \end{array}$$

A $\begin{array}{r} 6 \\ +2 \\ \hline 8 \end{array}$ C $\begin{array}{r} 3 \\ +3 \\ \hline 6 \end{array}$

B $\begin{array}{r} 3 \\ +4 \\ \hline 7 \end{array}$ (D) $\begin{array}{r} 3 \\ +6 \\ \hline 9 \end{array}$

13. Which is a way to make 8?

A 12 − 5
B 7 + 3
(C) 11 − 3
D 8 + 3

14. Count on. What is the sum?

$$\begin{array}{r} 7 \\ +2 \\ \hline \end{array}$$

A 10 C 8
(B) 9 D 7

Go On

Name__________ UNIT 2 POSTTEST

Choose the correct answer.

Use the number line to answer questions 15 and 16.

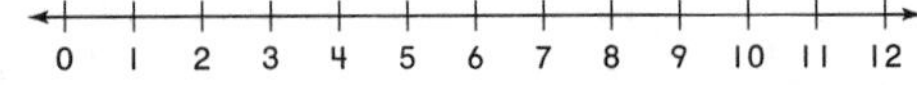

15. What is the difference?

$$\begin{array}{r} 7 \\ -2 \\ \hline \end{array}$$

A 7 (C) 5
B 6 D 4

16. What is the difference?

10 − 2 = ____

(A) 8 C 6
B 7 D 5

17. Follow the rule. Which number completes the table?

Subtract 3	
6	3
5	
4	1

(A) 2 C 4
B 3 D 5

18. Which addition sentence shows the doubles plus one fact?

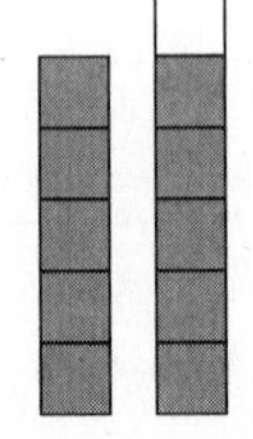

A 2+3=5 C 4+5=9
B 3+4=7 (D) 5+6=11

Go On

Name____________________ UNIT 2 POSTTEST

Choose the correct answer.

19. Which number completes the fact family?

4 + □ = 6   6 − □ = 4

□ + 4 = 6   6 − 4 = □

A 1
Ⓑ 2
C 3
D 4

20. What is the sum?

3 + 3 = ____

Ⓐ 6
B 7
C 8
D 9

21. Which number sentence shows how many ducks there are?

____ gray ducks

____ white ducks

A 11 − 3 = 8
B 12 − 3 = 9
Ⓒ 8 + 4 = 12
D 8 + 3 = 11

22. Which number sentence matches the story?

There are 9 horses.
5 horses trot away.
How many horses are there now?

A 9 + 5 = 14
B 9 − 3 = 6
Ⓒ 9 − 5 = 4
D 9 + 4 = 13

Go On

Name____________________ UNIT 2 POSTTEST

Choose the correct answer.

23. Use cubes and cubes to subtract.

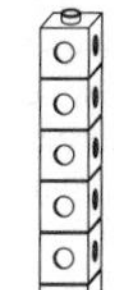

$$\begin{array}{r} 8 \\ -2 \\ \hline \end{array}$$

A 3
B 4
C 5
Ⓓ 6

24. Which numbers are in the fact family?

6 + 2 = 8   8 − 2 = 6

2 + 6 = 8   8 − 6 = 2

A 2, 6, 14
B 2, 8, 10
Ⓒ 2, 6, 8
D 6, 8, 14

25. There are 7 children. Some children walk away. There are 3 children left. How many children walked away?

A 1 children
B 2 children
C 3 children
Ⓓ 4 children

26. There are 6 hats in all. 3 hats are red. The other hats are blue. How many hats are blue?

Ⓐ 3 hats
B 4 hats
C 5 hats
D 6 hats

Stop

Name____________________ CHAPTER 8 POSTTEST

Choose the correct answer.

1. Which figure belongs in group B?

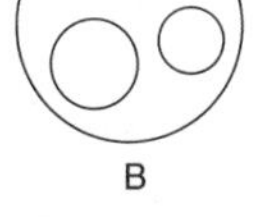

A   B   C

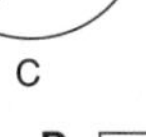
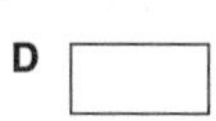

Ⓐ   B   C   D

2. How many more children chose dog than fish?

Animals We Like								
fish								
cat								
dog								

A 1 more child
Ⓑ 2 more children
C 3 more children
D 5 more children

Go On

Name____________________ CHAPTER 8 POSTTEST

Choose the correct answer.

3. Which bear belongs in the group?

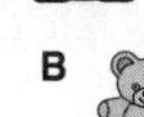

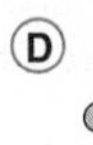

A   B   C   Ⓓ

Use the picture graph to answer questions 5 and 6.

Kinds of Sport Balls															
football															
soccer ball															
basketball															

4. How many footballs are there?

A 7 footballs
B 8 footballs
C 9 footballs
Ⓓ 11 footballs

5. How many fewer basketballs are there than soccer balls?

A 5 fewer basketballs
B 4 fewer basketballs
Ⓒ 3 fewer basketballs
D 2 fewer basketballs

Stop

Name ______________________ CHAPTER 9 POSTTEST

Choose the correct answer.

1. Which bear are you more likely to pull from the bowl?

(A) [bear]
B [black bear]
C [white bear]

2. Use the tally chart to answer the question.

Animals We Like	
fish	𝍸 IIII
turtle	II
gerbil	𝍸 I

How many children chose the gerbil?

A 5 children
(B) 6 children
C 7 children
D 9 children

3. From which box is it **impossible** to pull a white cube?

A 
B 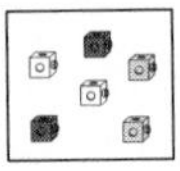
C 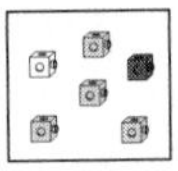
(D)

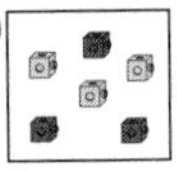

Go On

Name ______________________ CHAPTER 9 POSTTEST

Choose the correct answer.

Use the bar graph to answer questions 4 and 5.

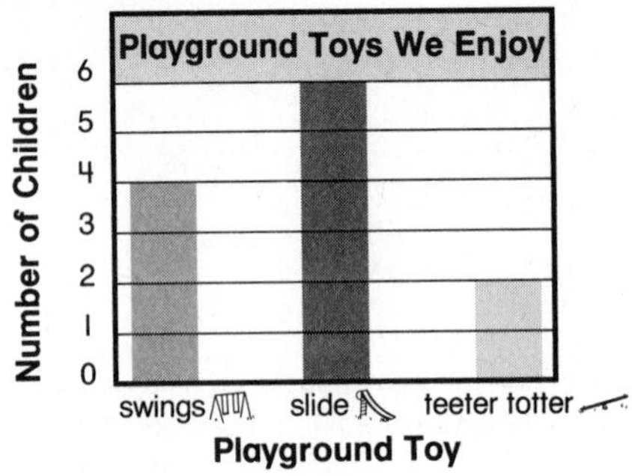

Playground Toys We Enjoy

Number of Children: 0 1 2 3 4 5 6

Playground Toy: swings, slide, teeter totter

4. How many children chose slide?

A 2 children
B 4 children
C 5 children
(D) 6 children

5. Which playground toy did the fewest children choose?

A [swings]
B [slide]
(C) [teeter totter]

6. There are 9 white cubes and 2 cubes in a bowl. Which color are you more likely to pull?

(A) [white cube]
B [cube]
C [black cube]

7. There are 3 black cubes and 6 white cubes in a bag. Which color are you more likely to pull?

A [cube]
(B) [white cube]
C [black cube]

Stop

Name ______________________ CHAPTER 10 POSTTEST

Choose the correct answer.

1. Count how many tens and ones. What is the number?

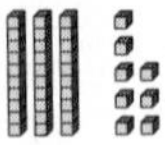

A 33
B 35
(C) 38
D 83

2. Count how many tens and ones. Which shows the number in a different way?

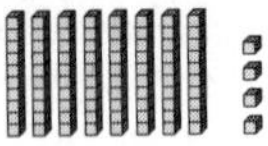

(A) 80 + 4
B 80 + 40
C 40 + 8
D 8 + 4

3. Count by tens. What number is shown?

6 tens

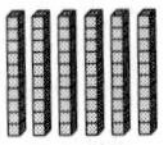

A 5
B 50
C 55
(D) 60

4. Which shows the number of tens and ones?

19 nineteen

A 0 tens 9 ones
B 10 tens 9 ones
C 9 tens 10 ones
(D) 1 ten 9 ones

Go On

Name ______________________ CHAPTER 10 POSTTEST

Choose the correct answer.

5. Count how many tens and ones. What is the number?

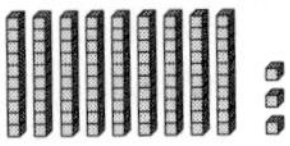

A 39
B 83
(C) 93
D 903

6. Count how many tens and ones. Which shows the number in a different way?

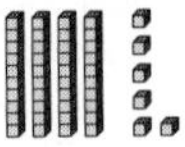

A 4 + 6
B 60 + 4
C 40 + 60
(D) 40 + 6

7. About how many paper clips can you hold in one hand?

A about 3
(B) about 30
C about 300

8. About how many books would cover your desk?

(A) about 6
B about 60
C about 600

Stop

Name ______________________ CHAPTER 11 POSTTEST

Choose the correct answer.

1. Which is true?

43 47

A 43 is greater than 47.
Ⓑ 47 is greater than 43.
C 47 is equal to 43.
D 47 is less than 43.

2. Which number is between 56 and 58?

56 ☐ 58

A 50
B 55
Ⓒ 57
D 59

3. Which symbol can you use to compare the numbers?

76 ◯ 67

Ⓐ >
B <
C =

4. Which shows the numbers in order from least to greatest?

48 29 25

A 48, 29, 25
B 29, 25, 48
C 25, 48, 29
Ⓓ 25, 29, 48

5. Which number is one less than 63?

A 53 Ⓑ 62 **C** 64 **D** 73

Go On

Name ______________________ CHAPTER 11 POSTTEST

Choose the correct answer.

6. Which is true?

74 68

A 74 is less than 68.
Ⓑ 68 is less than 74.
C 74 is equal to 68.
D 68 is greater than 74.

7. Which number is ten more than 54?

A 44
B 53
C 55
Ⓓ 64

Use the table to answer questions 8 and 9.

Season	Sunny Days
spring	81
summer	87
fall	71
winter	78

8. Which season had more sunny days?

Ⓐ spring
B fall

9. Which season had the least number of sunny days?

A spring
B summer
Ⓒ fall
D winter

Stop

Name ______________________ CHAPTER 12 POSTTEST

Choose the correct answer.

Use the hundred chart for questions 1 and 2.

1	2	3	4	5	6	7	8	9	10
11	12	13	14	15	16	17	18	19	20
21	22	23	24	25	26	27	28	29	30
31	32	33	34	35	36	37	38	39	40
41	42	43	44	45	46	47	48	49	50
51	52	53	54	55	56	57	58	59	60
61	62	63	64	65	66	67	68	69	70
71	72	73	74	75	76	77	78	79	80
81	82	83	84	85	86	87	88	89	90
91	92	93	94	95	96	97	98	99	100

1. Count by twos. Which number comes next?

36, 38, 40, 42, 44, ____

A 43
B 45
Ⓒ 46
D 50

2. Count by tens. Which numbers come next?

7, 17, 27, ____, ____, ____

A 30, 40, 50
Ⓑ 37, 47, 57
C 29, 31, 33
D 32, 37, 42

3. Skip count. How many fingers are there?

A 7 **B** 14 **C** 35 Ⓓ 70

Go On

Name ______________________ CHAPTER 12 POSTTEST

Choose the correct answer.

4. Count forward. Which numbers come next?

93, 94, 95, ____, ____, ____

A 100, 105, 110
Ⓑ 96, 97, 98
C 97, 98, 99
D 96, 98, 100

5. Find the pattern. What are the missing numbers?

48, 50, ____, 54, 56, ____

A 51, 53
B 58, 60
C 51, 52
Ⓓ 52, 58

6. Which number is even?

Ⓐ 12 **B** 13 **C** 15 **D** 17

7. There are 10 crayons in a box.
How many crayons are there in 7 boxes?

number of boxes	1	2	3	4	5	6	7
number of crayons	10	20					

A 14 crayons
B 25 crayons
C 35 crayons
Ⓓ 70 crayons

Stop

Name ____________________ UNIT 3 POSTTEST

Choose the correct answer.

1. Which number is between 42 and 44?

42 [ ] 44

A 34 (C) 43
B 40 D 45

2. Count by tens. What number is shown?

5 tens

A 20 C 40
B 30 (D) 50

3. Use the tally chart to answer the question.

Snacks We Like	
popcorn	IIII
fruit	~~IIII~~ I
cheese	~~IIII~~

How many children chose fruit?

A 4 children
B 5 children
(C) 6 children
D 7 children

4. Count how many tens and ones. Which shows the number in a different way?

A 5 + 6
(B) 50 + 6
C 56 + 6
D 50 + 60

Go On

Name ____________________ UNIT 3 POSTTEST

Choose the correct answer.

Use the hundred chart for questions 5 and 6.

1	2	3	4	5	6	7	8	9	10
11	12	13	14	15	16	17	18	19	20
21	22	23	24	25	26	27	28	29	30
31	32	33	34	35	36	37	38	39	40
41	42	43	44	45	46	47	48	49	50
51	52	53	54	55	56	57	58	59	60
61	62	63	64	65	66	67	68	69	70
71	72	73	74	75	76	77	78	79	80
81	82	83	84	85	86	87	88	89	90
91	92	93	94	95	96	97	98	99	100

5. Count by tens. Which number comes next?

40, 50, 60, 70, 80, ___

(A) 90
B 80
C 70
D 60

6. Count by twos. Which numbers come next?

22, 24, 26, ___, ___, ___

A 36, 46, 56
B 28, 29, 30
C 31, 36, 41
(D) 28, 30, 32

Go On

Name ____________________ UNIT 3 POSTTEST

Choose the correct answer.

7. Which [dog] belongs in the group?

A (B) C D

8. From which box is it **impossible** to pull a gray cube?

(A) 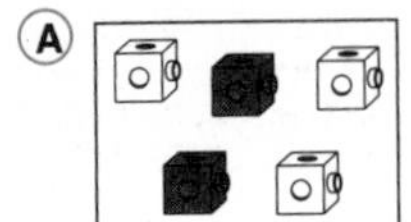

C 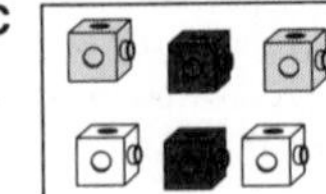

B 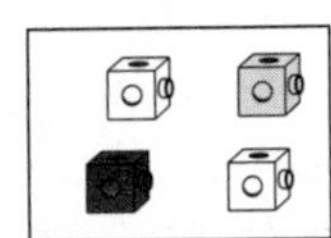

D 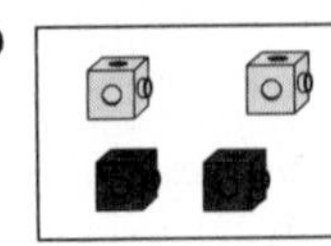

9. There are 10 oranges in a bag. How many oranges are there in 7 bags?

number of bags	1	2	3	4	5	6	7
number of oranges	10	20					

A 7 oranges (C) 70 oranges
B 8 oranges D 80 oranges

Go On

Name ____________________ UNIT 3 POSTTEST

Choose the correct answer.

10. Which is true?

A 36 is greater than 46.
(B) 36 is less than 46.
C 36 is equal to 46.
D 46 is less than 36.

11. There are 8 [black cubes] and 3 [white cubes] in a bag. Which color are you more likely to pull?

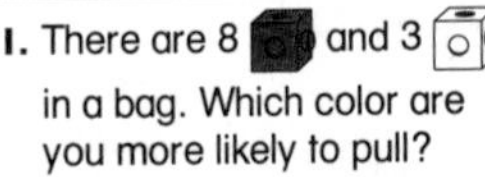

A  (C) 

B

Use the table to answer questions 12 and 13.

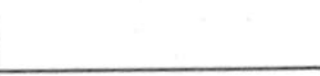

Month	Windy Days
December	12
January	15
February	10
March	16

12. Which month had the most number of windy days?

A December
B January
C February
(D) March

13. Which month had the least number of windy days?

A December
B January
(C) February
D March

Go On

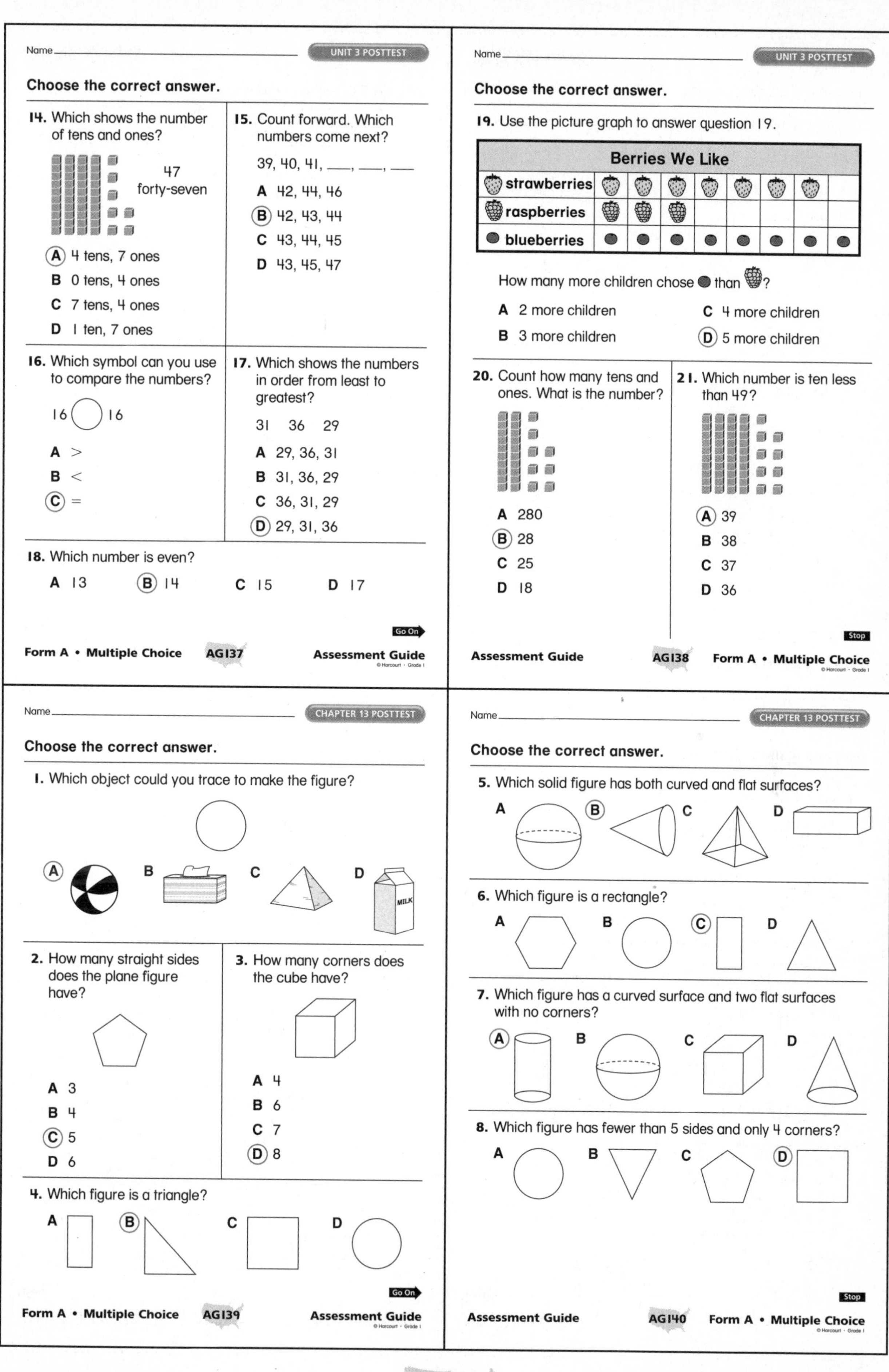

Name ____________ UNIT 3 POSTTEST

Choose the correct answer.

14. Which shows the number of tens and ones?

47 forty-seven

Ⓐ 4 tens, 7 ones
B 0 tens, 4 ones
C 7 tens, 4 ones
D 1 ten, 7 ones

15. Count forward. Which numbers come next?

39, 40, 41, ___, ___, ___

A 42, 44, 46
Ⓑ 42, 43, 44
C 43, 44, 45
D 43, 45, 47

16. Which symbol can you use to compare the numbers?

16 ◯ 16

A >
B <
Ⓒ =

17. Which shows the numbers in order from least to greatest?

31 36 29

A 29, 36, 31
B 31, 36, 29
C 36, 31, 29
Ⓓ 29, 31, 36

18. Which number is even?

A 13 Ⓑ 14 C 15 D 17

Go On

Form A • Multiple Choice AG137 Assessment Guide © Harcourt • Grade 1

Name ____________ UNIT 3 POSTTEST

Choose the correct answer.

19. Use the picture graph to answer question 19.

Berries We Like								
strawberries								
raspberries								
blueberries								

How many more children chose blueberries than raspberries?

A 2 more children
B 3 more children
C 4 more children
Ⓓ 5 more children

20. Count how many tens and ones. What is the number?

A 280
Ⓑ 28
C 25
D 18

21. Which number is ten less than 49?

Ⓐ 39
B 38
C 37
D 36

Stop

Assessment Guide AG138 Form A • Multiple Choice © Harcourt • Grade 1

Name ____________ CHAPTER 13 POSTTEST

Choose the correct answer.

1. Which object could you trace to make the figure?

Ⓐ B C D MILK

2. How many straight sides does the plane figure have?

A 3
B 4
Ⓒ 5
D 6

3. How many corners does the cube have?

A 4
B 6
C 7
Ⓓ 8

4. Which figure is a triangle?

A Ⓑ C D

Go On

Form A • Multiple Choice AG139 Assessment Guide © Harcourt • Grade 1

Name ____________ CHAPTER 13 POSTTEST

Choose the correct answer.

5. Which solid figure has both curved and flat surfaces?

A Ⓑ C D

6. Which figure is a rectangle?

A B Ⓒ D

7. Which figure has a curved surface and two flat surfaces with no corners?

Ⓐ B C D

8. Which figure has fewer than 5 sides and only 4 corners?

A B C Ⓓ

Stop

Assessment Guide AG140 Form A • Multiple Choice © Harcourt • Grade 1

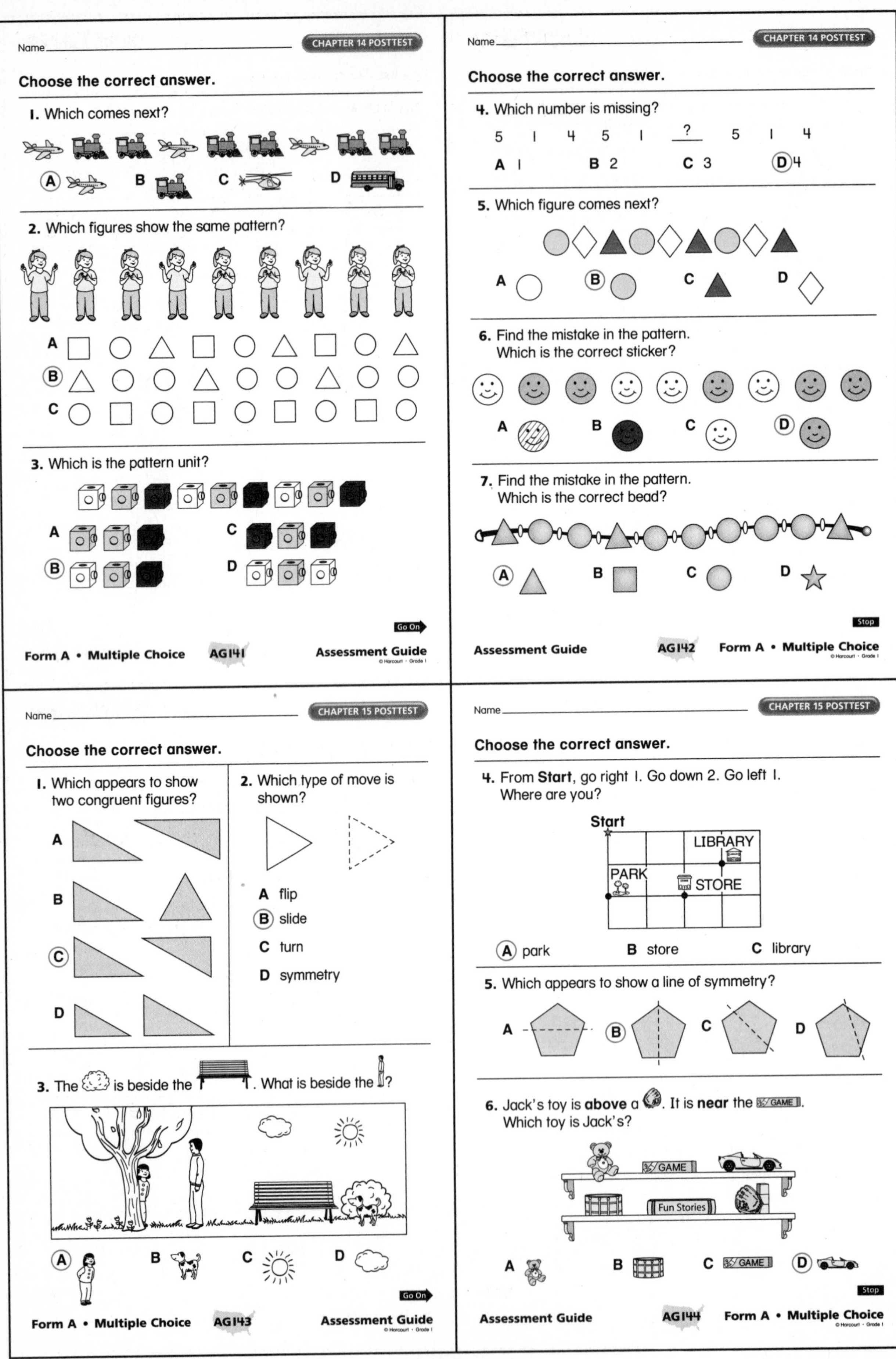

Name ____________________ CHAPTER 14 POSTTEST

Choose the correct answer.

1. Which comes next?

(A) B C D

2. Which figures show the same pattern?

A □ ○ △ □ ○ △ □ ○ △

(B) △ ○ ○ △ ○ ○ △ ○ ○

C ○ □ ○ □ ○ □ ○ □ ○

3. Which is the pattern unit?

A C

(B) D

Go On

Form A • Multiple Choice AG141 Assessment Guide © Harcourt • Grade 1

Name ____________________ CHAPTER 14 POSTTEST

Choose the correct answer.

4. Which number is missing?

5 1 4 5 1 __?__ 5 1 4

A 1 B 2 C 3 (D) 4

5. Which figure comes next?

A (B) C D

6. Find the mistake in the pattern. Which is the correct sticker?

A B C (D)

7. Find the mistake in the pattern. Which is the correct bead?

(A) B C D

Stop

Assessment Guide AG142 Form A • Multiple Choice © Harcourt • Grade 1

Name ____________________ CHAPTER 15 POSTTEST

Choose the correct answer.

1. Which appears to show two congruent figures?

A

B

(C)

D

2. Which type of move is shown?

A flip

(B) slide

C turn

D symmetry

3. The [cloud] is beside the [bench]. What is beside the [man]?

(A) B C D

Go On

Form A • Multiple Choice AG143 Assessment Guide © Harcourt • Grade 1

Name ____________________ CHAPTER 15 POSTTEST

Choose the correct answer.

4. From **Start**, go right 1. Go down 2. Go left 1. Where are you?

(A) park B store C library

5. Which appears to show a line of symmetry?

A (B) C D

6. Jack's toy is **above** a [mitt]. It is **near** the [GAME]. Which toy is Jack's?

A B C GAME (D)

Stop

Assessment Guide AG144 Form A • Multiple Choice © Harcourt • Grade 1

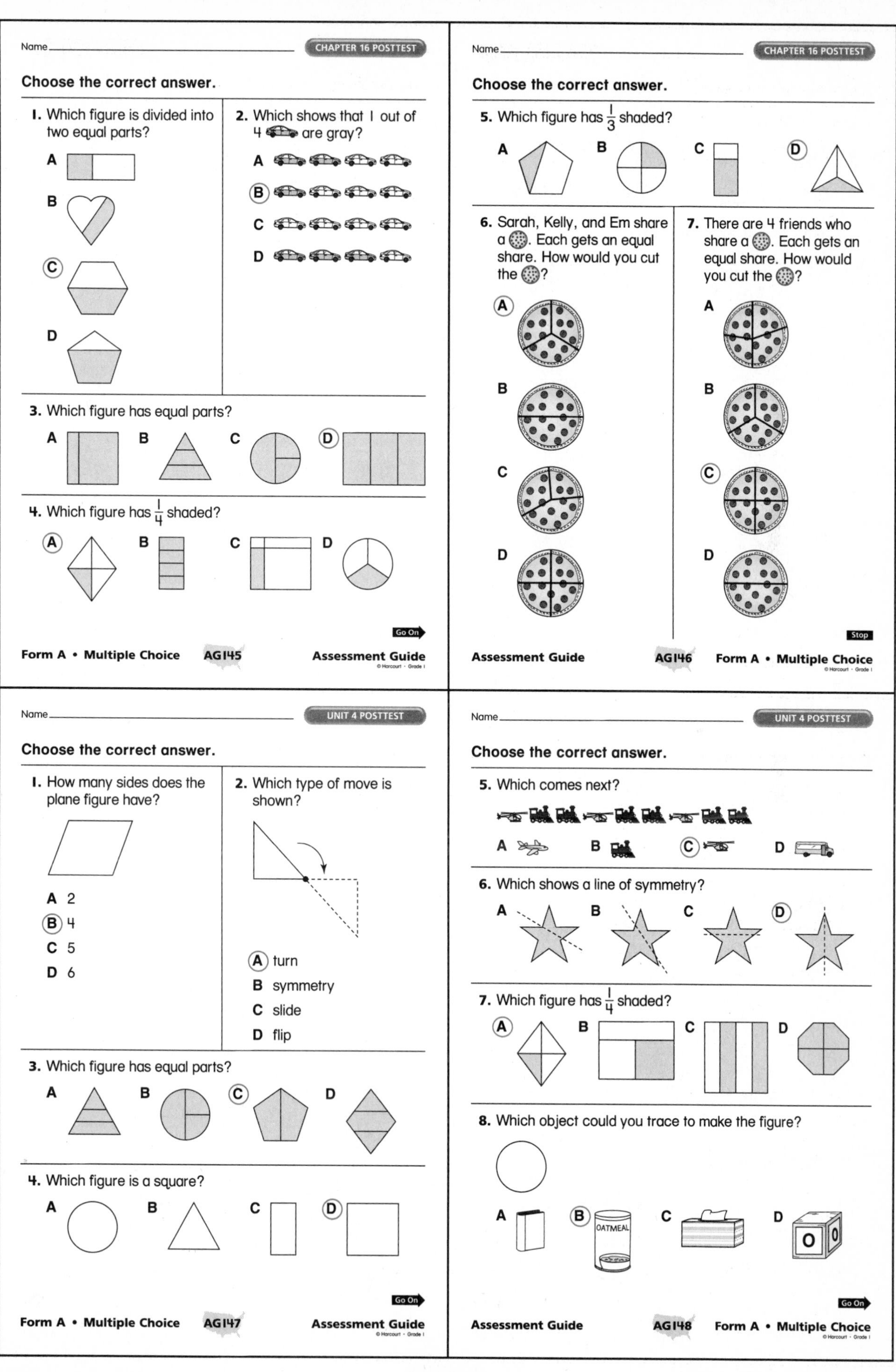

Name ______________________ CHAPTER 16 POSTTEST

Choose the correct answer.

1. Which figure is divided into two equal parts?

A B (C) D

2. Which shows that 1 out of 4 are gray?

A (B) C D

3. Which figure has equal parts?

A B C (D)

4. Which figure has $\frac{1}{4}$ shaded?

(A) B C D

Go On

Form A • Multiple Choice AG145 Assessment Guide
© Harcourt • Grade 1

Name ______________________ CHAPTER 16 POSTTEST

Choose the correct answer.

5. Which figure has $\frac{1}{3}$ shaded?

A B C (D)

6. Sarah, Kelly, and Em share a . Each gets an equal share. How would you cut the ?

(A) B C D

7. There are 4 friends who share a . Each gets an equal share. How would you cut the ?

A B (C) D

Stop

Assessment Guide AG146 Form A • Multiple Choice
© Harcourt • Grade 1

Name ______________________ UNIT 4 POSTTEST

Choose the correct answer.

1. How many sides does the plane figure have?

A 2
(B) 4
C 5
D 6

2. Which type of move is shown?

(A) turn
B symmetry
C slide
D flip

3. Which figure has equal parts?

A B (C) D

4. Which figure is a square?

A B C (D)

Go On

Form A • Multiple Choice AG147 Assessment Guide
© Harcourt • Grade 1

Name ______________________ UNIT 4 POSTTEST

Choose the correct answer.

5. Which comes next?

A B (C) D

6. Which shows a line of symmetry?

A B C (D)

7. Which figure has $\frac{1}{4}$ shaded?

(A) B C D

8. Which object could you trace to make the figure?

A (B) C D

Go On

Assessment Guide AG148 Form A • Multiple Choice
© Harcourt • Grade 1

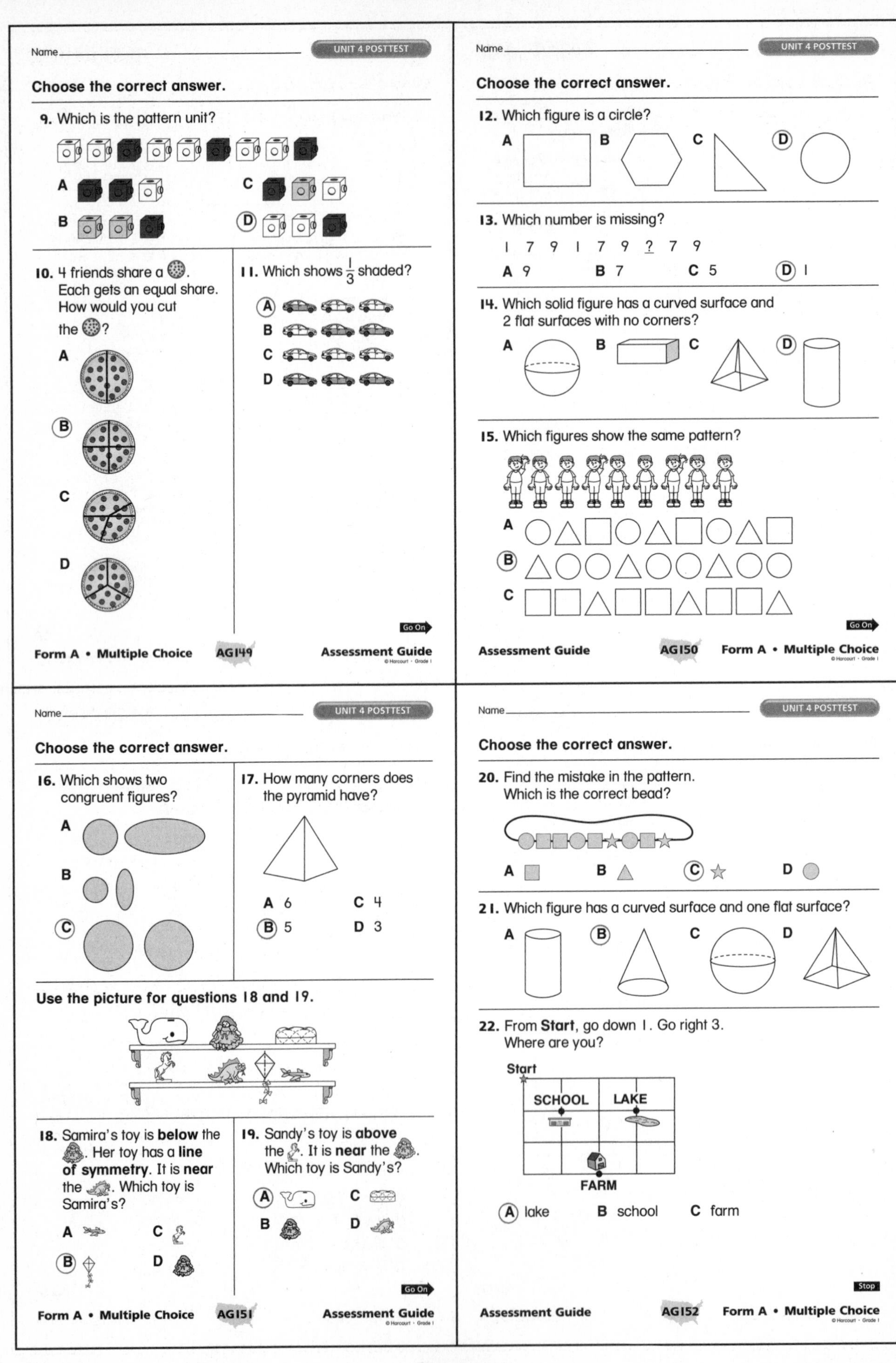

Name ______________________ UNIT 4 POSTTEST

Choose the correct answer.

9. Which is the pattern unit?

A

B

C

(D)

10. 4 friends share a pizza. Each gets an equal share. How would you cut the pizza?

A

(B)

C

D

11. Which shows $\frac{1}{3}$ shaded?

(A)

B

C

D

Go On

Form A • Multiple Choice AG149 Assessment Guide © Harcourt • Grade 1

Name ______________________ UNIT 4 POSTTEST

Choose the correct answer.

12. Which figure is a circle?

A B C (D)

13. Which number is missing?

1 7 9 1 7 9 ? 7 9

A 9 B 7 C 5 (D) 1

14. Which solid figure has a curved surface and 2 flat surfaces with no corners?

A B C (D)

15. Which figures show the same pattern?

A

(B)

C

Go On

Assessment Guide AG150 Form A • Multiple Choice © Harcourt • Grade 1

Name ______________________ UNIT 4 POSTTEST

Choose the correct answer.

16. Which shows two congruent figures?

A

B

(C)

17. How many corners does the pyramid have?

A 6 C 4

(B) 5 D 3

Use the picture for questions 18 and 19.

18. Samira's toy is **below** the doll. Her toy has a **line of symmetry**. It is **near** the dinosaur. Which toy is Samira's?

A C

(B) D

19. Sandy's toy is **above** the horse. It is **near** the doll. Which toy is Sandy's?

(A) C

B D

Go On

Form A • Multiple Choice AG151 Assessment Guide © Harcourt • Grade 1

Name ______________________ UNIT 4 POSTTEST

Choose the correct answer.

20. Find the mistake in the pattern. Which is the correct bead?

A B (C) D

21. Which figure has a curved surface and one flat surface?

A (B) C D

22. From **Start**, go down 1. Go right 3. Where are you?

Start

SCHOOL LAKE

FARM

(A) lake B school C farm

Stop

Assessment Guide AG152 Form A • Multiple Choice © Harcourt • Grade 1

Name ______________ CHAPTER 17 POSTTEST

Choose the correct answer.

1. What is the sum?

$$\begin{array}{r} 9 \\ +9 \\ \hline \end{array}$$

A 14
B 16
(C) 18
D 88

2. Make a ten and add. What is the sum?

$$\begin{array}{r} 6 \\ +5 \\ \hline \end{array}$$

A 3
(B) 11
C 14
D 15

3. What is the sum?

$$\begin{array}{r} 7 \\ +6 \\ \hline \end{array}$$

(A) 13
B 14
C 15
D 16

4. What is the sum?

$$\begin{array}{r} 3 \\ 6 \\ +3 \\ \hline \end{array}$$

A 6
B 9
(C) 12
D 15

Go On

Form A • Multiple Choice AG153 Assessment Guide

Name ______________ CHAPTER 17 POSTTEST

Choose the correct answer.

5. What is the sum?

$$\begin{array}{r} 10 \\ +4 \\ \hline \end{array}$$

A 104 (C) 14
B 41 D 4

6. Make a ten and add. What is the sum?

$$\begin{array}{r} 8 \\ +5 \\ \hline \end{array}$$

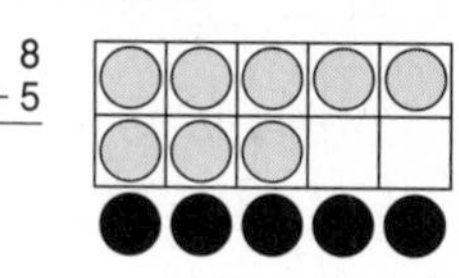

A 12 C 14
(B) 13 D 18

7. What is the sum?

10 + 10 = ____

A 1010 B 21 (C) 20 D 11

8. Which number sentence matches the story? 7 firefighters arrive at a fire. 5 more firefighters join them. How many firefighters are at the fire now?

(A) 7 + 5 = 12
B 7 − 5 = 2
C 2 + 5 = 7
D 12 − 7 = 5

9. Which number sentence matches the story? A town has 5 police cars. Then the town buys 6 more police cars. How many police cars does the town have altogether?

A 11 − 5 = 6
B 6 − 5 = 1
C 11 + 5 = 16
(D) 5 + 6 = 11

Stop

Assessment Guide AG154 Form A • Multiple Choice

Name ______________ CHAPTER 18 POSTTEST

Choose the correct answer.

Use the number line to answer questions 1 and 2.

0 1 2 3 4 5 6 7 8 9 10 11 12 13 14 15 16 17 18 19 20

1. What is the difference?

$$\begin{array}{r} 14 \\ -\ 5 \\ \hline \end{array}$$

A 7
B 8
(C) 9
D 19

2. What is the difference?

$$\begin{array}{r} 13 \\ -\ 7 \\ \hline \end{array}$$

A 8
(B) 6
C 5
D 4

3. How many more birds are there than nests?

$$\begin{array}{r} 12 \\ -\ 3 \\ \hline \end{array}$$

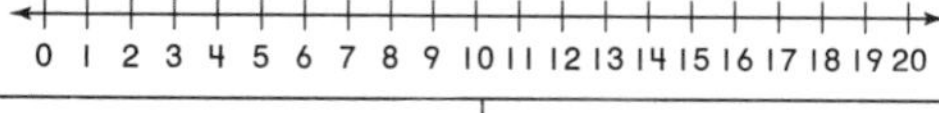

A 15 more birds
B 11 more birds
C 10 more birds
(D) 9 more birds

4. What is the difference?

14 − 8 = ____

(A) 6 B 7 C 9 D 22

Go On

Form A • Multiple Choice AG155 Assessment Guide

Name ______________ CHAPTER 18 POSTTEST

Choose the correct answer.

5. Use the addition fact to help you subtract. What is the difference?

$$\begin{array}{r} 7 \\ +9 \\ \hline \end{array} \qquad \begin{array}{r} 16 \\ -\ 9 \\ \hline \end{array}$$

(A) 7 C 13
B 8 D 25

6. What is the difference?

$$\begin{array}{r} 15 \\ -\ 6 \\ \hline \end{array}$$

A 7 (C) 9
B 8 D 11

7. How many more butterflies are there than flowers?

$$\begin{array}{r} 13 \\ -\ 8 \\ \hline \end{array}$$

A 21 more butterflies
B 7 more butterflies
C 6 more butterflies
(D) 5 more butterflies

8. There are 16 children playing on the playground. 8 children go home. How many children are now playing on the playground?

A 12 children
(B) 8 children
C 6 children
D 2 children

9. Sarah counted trees in her backyard. She counted 7 oak trees and 9 elm trees. How many trees did Sara count in all?

A 2 trees
B 12 trees
(C) 16 trees
D 79 trees

Stop

Assessment Guide AG156 Form A • Multiple Choice

Name ______________________ CHAPTER 19 POSTTEST

Choose the correct answer.

1. Which number is missing?

$$\begin{array}{r} 10 \\ + \square \\ \hline 20 \end{array} \qquad \begin{array}{r} 20 \\ -10 \\ \hline \square \end{array}$$

A 5 C 12
(B) 10 D 21

2. Which is a way to make 14?

A 18 − 5
B 8 + 8
C 15 − 2
(D) 3 + 7 + 4

3. Which number sentence shows how many kites there are?

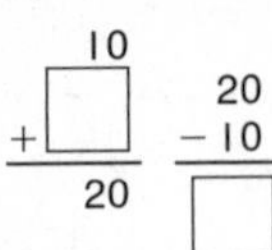

_____ gray kites

_____ white kites

(A) 7 + 8 = 15 C 8 − 7 = 1
B 15 − 7 = 8 D 9 + 6 = 15

4. Which number is missing?

$$\begin{array}{r} 6 \\ + \square \\ \hline 15 \end{array} \qquad \begin{array}{r} 15 \\ -6 \\ \hline \square \end{array}$$

A 7 B 8 (C) 9 D 11

Go On

Name ______________________ CHAPTER 19 POSTTEST

Choose the correct answer.

5. Which is a way to make 7?

A 1 + 5
B 16 − 7
(C) 15 − 8
D 2 + 2 + 4

6. Follow the rule. Which number completes the table?

Subtract 8	
12	4
14	
16	8
17	9

A 5 (B) 6 C 7 D 10

7. Which fact is part of the fact family?

$$\begin{array}{r} 6 \\ +7 \\ \hline 13 \end{array} \qquad \begin{array}{r} 7 \\ +6 \\ \hline 13 \end{array} \qquad \begin{array}{r} 13 \\ -6 \\ \hline 7 \end{array}$$

(A) $\begin{array}{r} 13 \\ -7 \\ \hline 6 \end{array}$ B $\begin{array}{r} 13 \\ +6 \\ \hline 19 \end{array}$ C $\begin{array}{r} 7 \\ -6 \\ \hline 1 \end{array}$ D $\begin{array}{r} 8 \\ +5 \\ \hline 13 \end{array}$

8. Michelle has 5 apples. Zack brings 9 more apples. How many apples are there now?

A 4 apples (C) 14 apples
B 13 apples D 15 apples

9. Andy buys 14 pears. He gives 6 pears away. How many pears does Andy have now?

A 20 pears C 9 pears
B 12 pears (D) 8 pears

Stop

Name ______________________ CHAPTER 20 POSTTEST

Choose the correct answer.

1. Which shows the amount of money in a different way?

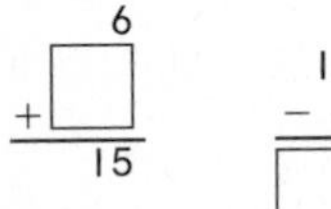

A 

B 

C 

(D) 

2. Which shows a way to make 1 dollar?

(A) 

B 

C 

D 

Go On

Name ______________________ CHAPTER 20 POSTTEST

Choose the correct answer.

3. Which symbol can you use to compare the amounts?

_____ ¢ ◯ _____ ¢

(A) < B > C =

4. Max buys a toy boat for 55¢. He uses

2 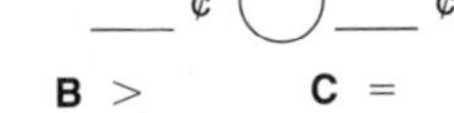 and 1 . Which shows the same amount in a different way?

A 

C 

(B) 

D 

Stop

Name ______________________________ CHAPTER 21 POSTTEST

Choose the correct answer.

1. What time does the clock show?

A 3:30

(B) 4:30

C 4:00

D 6:30

2. What time does the clock show?

(A) 8:00

B 12:00

C 8:30

D 9:00

3. Use the calendar. How many Mondays are in this month?

A 2

B 3

C 4

(D) 5

OCTOBER						
Sunday	Monday	Tuesday	Wednesday	Thursday	Friday	Saturday
	1	2	3	4	5	6
7	8	9	10	11	12	13
14	15	16	17	18	19	20
21	22	23	24	25	26	27
28	29	30	31			

Go On

Name ______________________________ CHAPTER 21 POSTTEST

Choose the correct answer.

4. Which clock matches the time shown?

7:30

A  B (C)  D

Use the table to answer questions 5 and 6.

Sports Camp		
Event	**Start**	**End**
tennis lessons		
soccer practice		
swim class		

5. Which event starts at 1:00?

(A) tennis lessons

B soccer practice

C swim class

6. Which event lasts the longest time?

A tennis lessons

(B) soccer practice

C swim class

Stop

Name ______________________________ UNIT 5 POSTTEST

Choose the correct answer.

1. Use the calendar. How many days are in this month?

October						
Sunday	Monday	Tuesday	Wednesday	Thursday	Friday	Saturday
	1	2	3	4	5	6
7	8	9	10	11	12	13
14	15	16	17	18	19	20
21	22	23	24	25	26	27
28	29	30	31			

A 7 C 21

B 17 (D) 31

2. Use the addition fact to help you subtract. What is the difference?

$$\begin{array}{r} 4 \\ +\,9 \\ \hline \end{array} \qquad \begin{array}{r} 13 \\ -\,9 \\ \hline \end{array}$$

A 16

B 9

C 6

(D) 4

3. What is the sum?

$$\begin{array}{r} 9 \\ +\,9 \\ \hline \end{array}$$

A 19

(B) 18

C 11

D 9

4. Follow the rule. Which number completes the table?

Add 6	
4	10
6	12
8	
9	15

A 13 C 17

(B) 14 D 19

Go On

Name ______________________________ UNIT 5 POSTTEST

Choose the correct answer.

5. How many fewer bees are there than flowers?

$$\begin{array}{r} 14 \\ -\,8 \\ \hline \end{array}$$

A 4 fewer bees C 8 fewer bees

(B) 6 fewer bees D 9 fewer bees

6. Which number sentence shows how many umbrellas are gray?

_____ umbrellas in all

_____ white umbrellas

(A) 12 − 5 = 7 C 7 + 5 = 12

B 12 − 6 = 6 D 12 − 7 = 5

7. What is the sum?

$$\begin{array}{r} 4 \\ 3 \\ +\,6 \\ \hline \end{array}$$

A 7 (C) 13

B 10 D 15

8. What is the time of day?

A morning

B afternoon

(C) evening

Go On

Name ____________________ UNIT 5 POSTTEST

Choose the correct answer.

9. Which shows the amount of money in a different way?

A

B

Ⓒ

D

10. Which shows a way to make 1 dollar?

Ⓐ

B

C

11. What is the difference?

$$\begin{array}{r} 18 \\ -\ 9 \\ \hline \end{array}$$

Ⓐ 9 C 11

B 10 D 12

Go On

Name ____________________ UNIT 5 POSTTEST

Choose the correct answer.

12. Which number sentence matches the story?

A man buys 6 daisies. Then he buys 4 roses. How many flowers does the man buy in all?

A 6 − 2 = 4

B 14 − 6 = 8

Ⓒ 6 + 4 = 10

D 16 + 4 = 20

13. Which number is missing?

$$\begin{array}{r} 9 \\ +\ \square \\ \hline 12 \end{array} \qquad \begin{array}{r} 12 \\ -\ 9 \\ \hline \square \end{array}$$

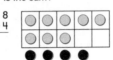

A 2 C 4

Ⓑ 3 D 5

14. Make a ten and add. What is the sum?

$$\begin{array}{r} 8 \\ +\ 4 \\ \hline \end{array}$$

A 10

Ⓑ 12

C 14

D 16

15. Albert has 16 oranges. He gives 7 oranges to his mother. How many oranges does Albert have now?

A 6 oranges

B 7 oranges

C 8 oranges

Ⓓ 9 oranges

Go On

Name ____________________ UNIT 5 POSTTEST

Choose the correct answer.

16. Which symbol can you use to compare the amounts?

40 ¢ ◯ 50 ¢

Ⓐ < B > C =

17. Which clock matches the time shown?

A

B

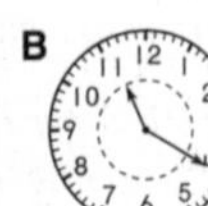

C

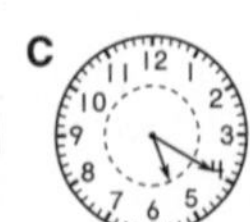

Ⓓ

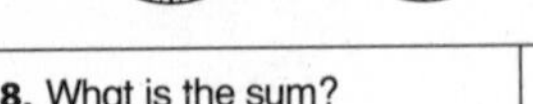

18. What is the sum?

5 + 6 = ____

A 7 C 16

Ⓑ 11 D 56

19. What is the difference?

12 − 3 = ____

A 7 C 9

Ⓑ 8 D 15

Go On

Name ____________________ UNIT 5 POSTTEST

Choose the correct answer.

Use the table to answer question 20.

Ms. Clark's Class		
Event	**Start**	**End**
rest time		
lunch		
recess		

20. Which event starts at 12:00?

A rest time Ⓑ lunch C recess

21. Which fact is part of the fact family?

$$\begin{array}{r} 8 \\ +\ 9 \\ \hline 17 \end{array} \qquad \begin{array}{r} 17 \\ -\ 9 \\ \hline 8 \end{array} \qquad \begin{array}{r} 17 \\ -\ 8 \\ \hline 9 \end{array}$$

A $\begin{array}{r} 17 \\ -\ 6 \\ \hline 11 \end{array}$ B $\begin{array}{r} 10 \\ +\ 7 \\ \hline 17 \end{array}$ Ⓒ $\begin{array}{r} 9 \\ +\ 8 \\ \hline 17 \end{array}$ D $\begin{array}{r} 20 \\ -\ 3 \\ \hline 17 \end{array}$

Stop

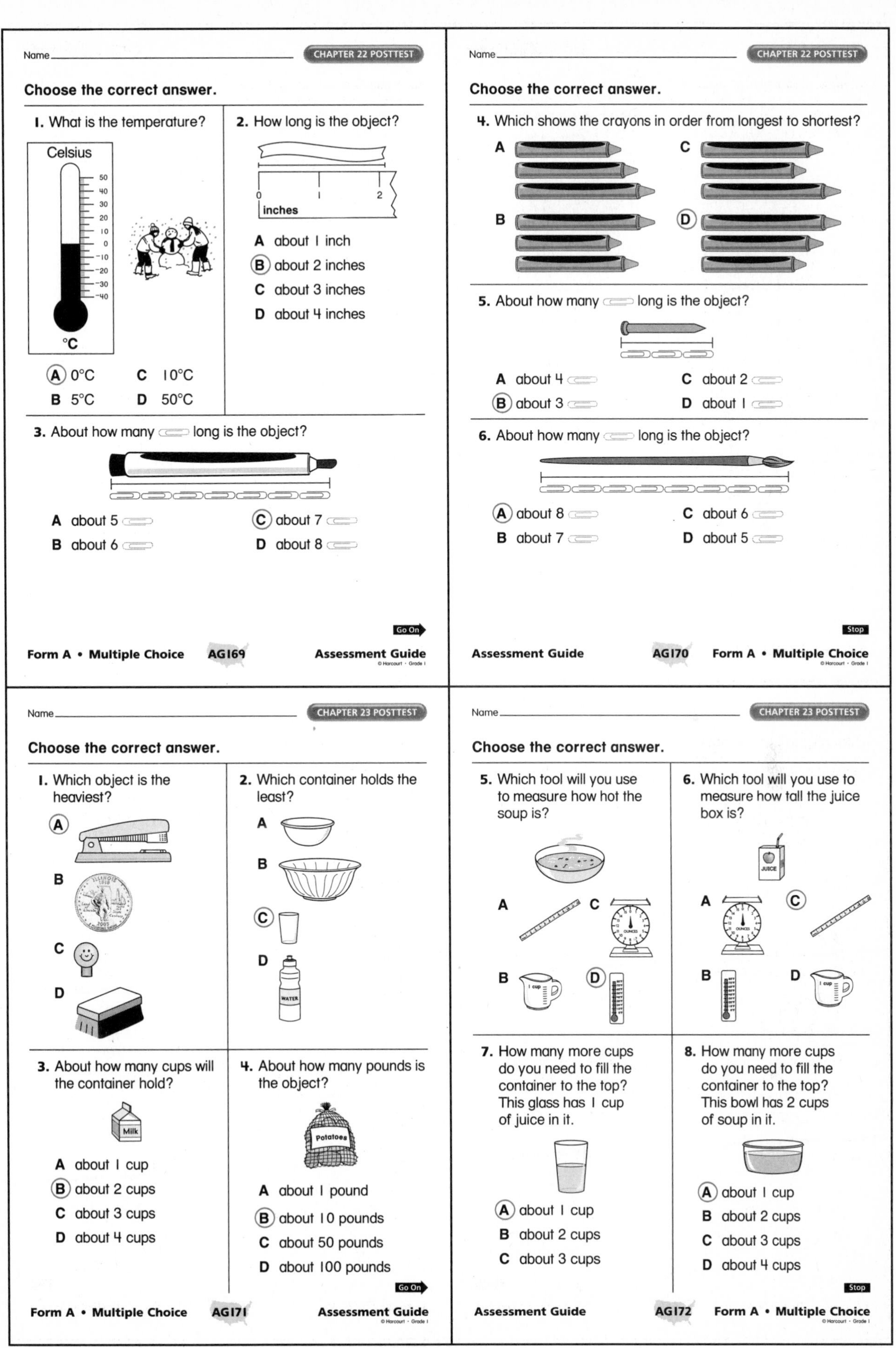

Name ______________________ CHAPTER 22 POSTTEST

Choose the correct answer.

1. What is the temperature?

(A) 0°C
B 5°C
C 10°C
D 50°C

2. How long is the object?

A about 1 inch
(B) about 2 inches
C about 3 inches
D about 4 inches

3. About how many ⊂⊃ long is the object?

A about 5 ⊂⊃
B about 6 ⊂⊃
(C) about 7 ⊂⊃
D about 8 ⊂⊃

Go On

Form A • Multiple Choice **AG169** **Assessment Guide**
© Harcourt • Grade 1

Name ______________________ CHAPTER 22 POSTTEST

Choose the correct answer.

4. Which shows the crayons in order from longest to shortest?

A
B
C
(D)

5. About how many ⊂⊃ long is the object?

A about 4 ⊂⊃
(B) about 3 ⊂⊃
C about 2 ⊂⊃
D about 1 ⊂⊃

6. About how many ⊂⊃ long is the object?

(A) about 8 ⊂⊃
B about 7 ⊂⊃
C about 6 ⊂⊃
D about 5 ⊂⊃

Stop

Assessment Guide **AG170** **Form A • Multiple Choice**
© Harcourt • Grade 1

Name ______________________ CHAPTER 23 POSTTEST

Choose the correct answer.

1. Which object is the heaviest?

(A)
B
C
D

2. Which container holds the least?

A
B
(C)
D

3. About how many cups will the container hold?

A about 1 cup
(B) about 2 cups
C about 3 cups
D about 4 cups

4. About how many pounds is the object?

A about 1 pound
(B) about 10 pounds
C about 50 pounds
D about 100 pounds

Go On

Form A • Multiple Choice **AG171** **Assessment Guide**
© Harcourt • Grade 1

Name ______________________ CHAPTER 23 POSTTEST

Choose the correct answer.

5. Which tool will you use to measure how hot the soup is?

A
B
C
(D)

6. Which tool will you use to measure how tall the juice box is?

A
B
(C)
D

7. How many more cups do you need to fill the container to the top? This glass has 1 cup of juice in it.

(A) about 1 cup
B about 2 cups
C about 3 cups

8. How many more cups do you need to fill the container to the top? This bowl has 2 cups of soup in it.

(A) about 1 cup
B about 2 cups
C about 3 cups
D about 4 cups

Stop

Assessment Guide **AG172** **Form A • Multiple Choice**
© Harcourt • Grade 1

Name ______________________ CHAPTER 24 POSTTEST

Choose the correct answer.

1. What is the difference?

80 − 30 = ____

A 30
B 40
(C) 50
D 60

2. What is the sum?

70 + 20 = ____

A 50
B 60
C 80
(D) 90

3. What is the difference?

	tens	ones
	2	8
−		3

Workmat: Tens | Ones

A 22
(B) 25
C 26
D 31

4. What is the sum?

	tens	ones
	3	4
+		5

Workmat: Tens | Ones

(A) 39
B 37
C 33
D 31

Go On

Name ______________________ CHAPTER 24 POSTTEST

Choose the correct answer.

5. What is the sum?

	tens	ones
	3	3
+	2	4

Workmat: Tens | Ones

A 17
B 51
(C) 57
D 67

6. What is the difference?

	tens	ones
	3	6
−	1	4

Workmat: Tens | Ones

A 42
(B) 22
C 20
D 12

8. There are 63 books on bugs. Julie checks out 8 of the books. About how many books are left?

A about 5 books
(B) about 50 books
C about 70 books
D about 500 books

9. Luke counts 56 birds. Then he counts 40 more birds. About how many birds does Luke count in all?

A about 1 bird
B about 10 birds
C about 20 birds
(D) about 100 birds

Stop

Name ______________________ UNIT 6 POSTTEST

Choose the correct answer.

1. What is the sum?

	tens	ones
	2	3
+		5

Workmat: tens | ones

A 29
(B) 28
C 27
D 22

2. Which container holds the most milk?

(A)
B
C
D

3. About how many (paper clips) long is the object?

A about 6
B about 7
(C) about 8
D about 9

Go On

Name ______________________ UNIT 6 POSTTEST

Choose the correct answer.

4. About how many pounds is the object?

Potatoes

A about 1 pound
(B) about 10 pounds
C about 20 pounds
D about 100 pounds

5. What is the temperature?

Celsius

50 40 30 20 10 0 −10 −20 −30 −40

°C

A 0°C
B 5°C
C 10°C
(D) 15°C

6. What is the difference?

90 − 40 = ____

A 70
B 60
(C) 50
D 40

7. About how many cups will the container hold?

MILK

(A) about 4 cups
B about 3 cups
C about 2 cups
D about 1 cup

Go On

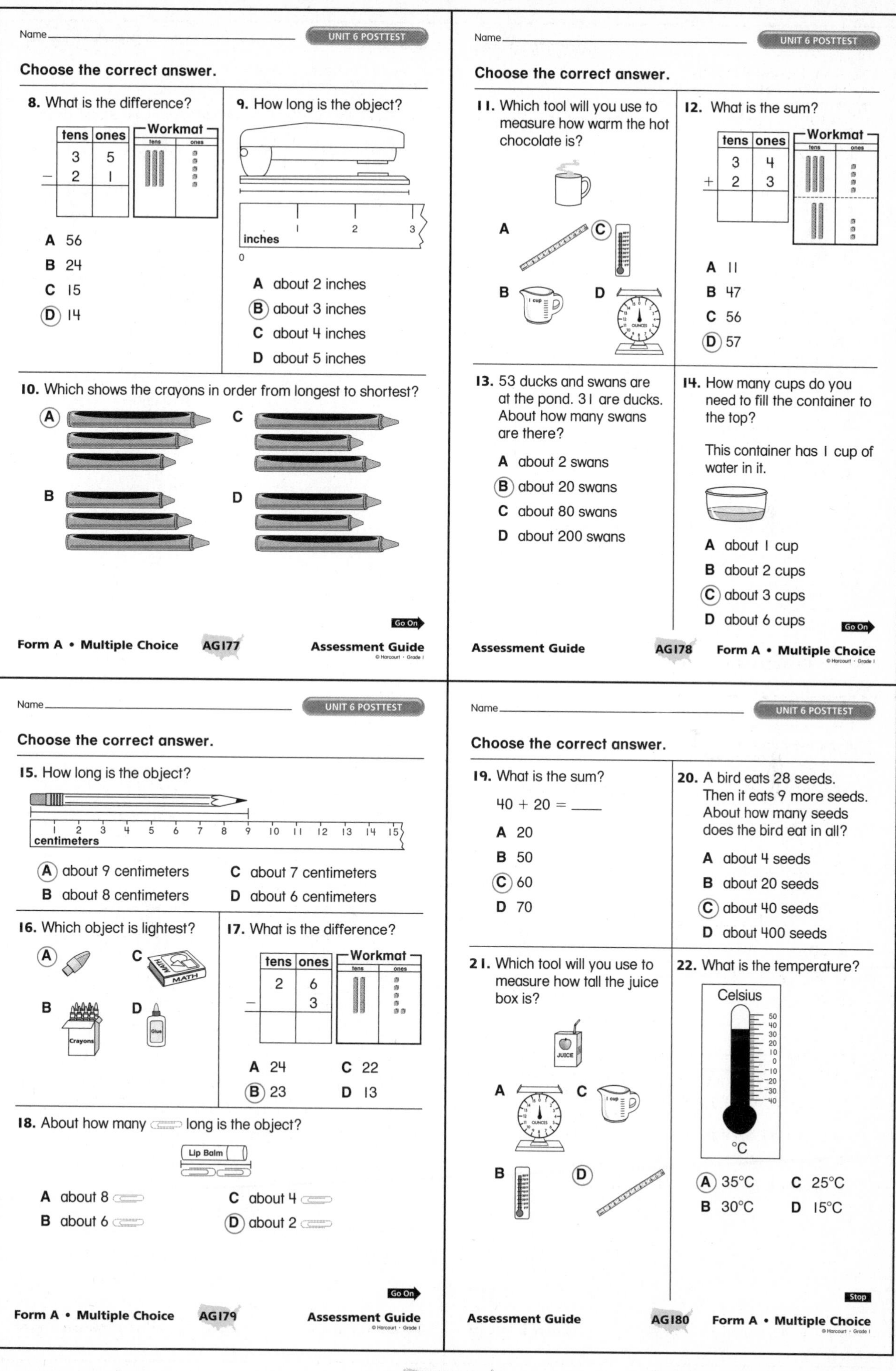

Name ______ UNIT 6 POSTTEST

Choose the correct answer.

8. What is the difference?

	tens	ones
	3	5
−	2	1

Workmat (tens, ones)

A 56
B 24
C 15
(D) 14

9. How long is the object?

inches 0 1 2 3

A about 2 inches
(B) about 3 inches
C about 4 inches
D about 5 inches

10. Which shows the crayons in order from longest to shortest?

(A) B C D

Go On

Form A • Multiple Choice AG177 Assessment Guide © Harcourt • Grade 1

Name ______ UNIT 6 POSTTEST

Choose the correct answer.

11. Which tool will you use to measure how warm the hot chocolate is?

A B (C) D

12. What is the sum?

	tens	ones
	3	4
+	2	3

Workmat (tens, ones)

A 11
B 47
C 56
(D) 57

13. 53 ducks and swans are at the pond. 31 are ducks. About how many swans are there?

A about 2 swans
(B) about 20 swans
C about 80 swans
D about 200 swans

14. How many cups do you need to fill the container to the top?

This container has 1 cup of water in it.

A about 1 cup
B about 2 cups
(C) about 3 cups
D about 6 cups

Go On

Assessment Guide AG178 Form A • Multiple Choice © Harcourt • Grade 1

Name ______ UNIT 6 POSTTEST

Choose the correct answer.

15. How long is the object?

1 2 3 4 5 6 7 8 9 10 11 12 13 14 15 centimeters

(A) about 9 centimeters
B about 8 centimeters
C about 7 centimeters
D about 6 centimeters

16. Which object is lightest?

(A) B C D

17. What is the difference?

	tens	ones
	2	6
−		3

Workmat (tens, ones)

A 24
(B) 23
C 22
D 13

18. About how many (paper clips) long is the object?

Lip Balm

A about 8
B about 6
C about 4
(D) about 2

Go On

Form A • Multiple Choice AG179 Assessment Guide © Harcourt • Grade 1

Name ______ UNIT 6 POSTTEST

Choose the correct answer.

19. What is the sum?

40 + 20 = ____

A 20
B 50
(C) 60
D 70

20. A bird eats 28 seeds. Then it eats 9 more seeds. About how many seeds does the bird eat in all?

A about 4 seeds
B about 20 seeds
(C) about 40 seeds
D about 400 seeds

21. Which tool will you use to measure how tall the juice box is?

A B C (D)

22. What is the temperature?

Celsius °C

(A) 35°C
B 30°C
C 25°C
D 15°C

Stop

Assessment Guide AG180 Form A • Multiple Choice © Harcourt • Grade 1

Name ______________________ END OF YEAR TEST

Choose the correct answer.

1. What is the temperature?

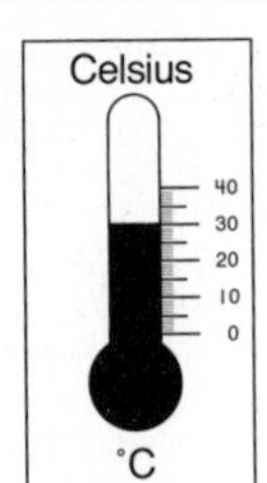

A 3°C　Ⓒ 30°C
B 13°C　**D** 35°C

2. How many flat surfaces does the solid figure have?

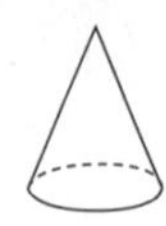

Ⓐ 1　**C** 3
B 2　**D** 4

3. Use the picture graph to answer question 3.

Sports We Like							
	baseball						
	soccer						
	football						

How many more children chose than ?

A 1 more child　Ⓒ 3 more children
B 2 more children　**D** 5 more children

Go On

Name ______________________ END OF YEAR TEST

Choose the correct answer.

4. Which belongs in the group?

A　**B**　**C**　Ⓓ

5. What is the sum?

60 + 20 = ____

A 40
B 70
Ⓒ 80
D 90

6. Which tells how many?

Ⓐ nineteen
B eighteen
C sixteen
D fourteen

7. Which shows a pair of related subtraction facts?

A $\begin{array}{r}12\\-4\\\hline 8\end{array}$ $\begin{array}{r}8\\-4\\\hline 4\end{array}$　Ⓑ $\begin{array}{r}11\\-3\\\hline 8\end{array}$ $\begin{array}{r}11\\-8\\\hline 3\end{array}$　**C** $\begin{array}{r}10\\-3\\\hline 7\end{array}$ $\begin{array}{r}11\\-4\\\hline 7\end{array}$　**D** $\begin{array}{r}12\\-5\\\hline 7\end{array}$ $\begin{array}{r}12\\-6\\\hline 6\end{array}$

Go On

Name ______________________ END OF YEAR TEST

Choose the correct answer.

8. Which type of move is shown?

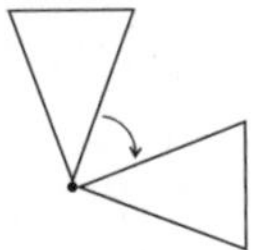

A flip
B slide
Ⓒ turn
D symmetry

9. Which tool will you use to measure how tall the can is?

Ⓐ

C

B

D

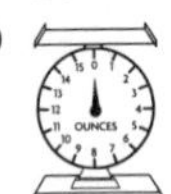

10. How many fewer bees are there than flowers?

$\begin{array}{r}11\\-4\\\hline\end{array}$

A 15 fewer bees　**C** 6 fewer bees
Ⓑ 7 fewer bees　**D** 4 fewer bees

Go On

Name ______________________ END OF YEAR TEST

Choose the correct answer.

11. Use the tally chart to answer the question.

Snacks We Like	
cheese	III
yogurt	卌 I
pretzels	卌 III

How many children chose yogurt?

A 3 children
Ⓑ 6 children
C 8 children
D 9 children

12. What time does the clock show?

Ⓐ 1:00
B 12:30
C 1:30
D 12:00

13. Which symbol can you use to compare the amounts?

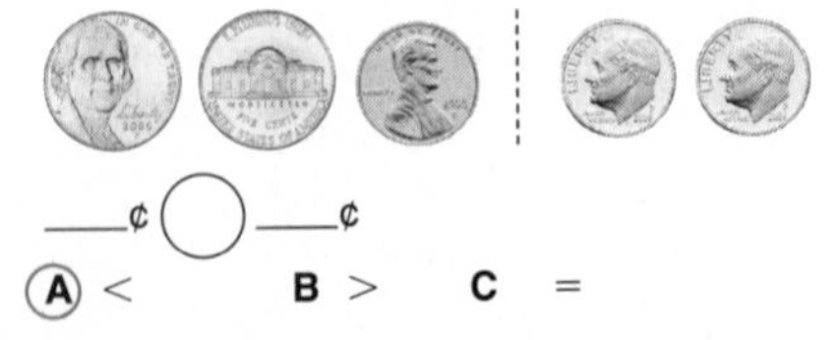

____¢ ◯ ____¢

Ⓐ $<$　**B** $>$　**C** $=$

Go On

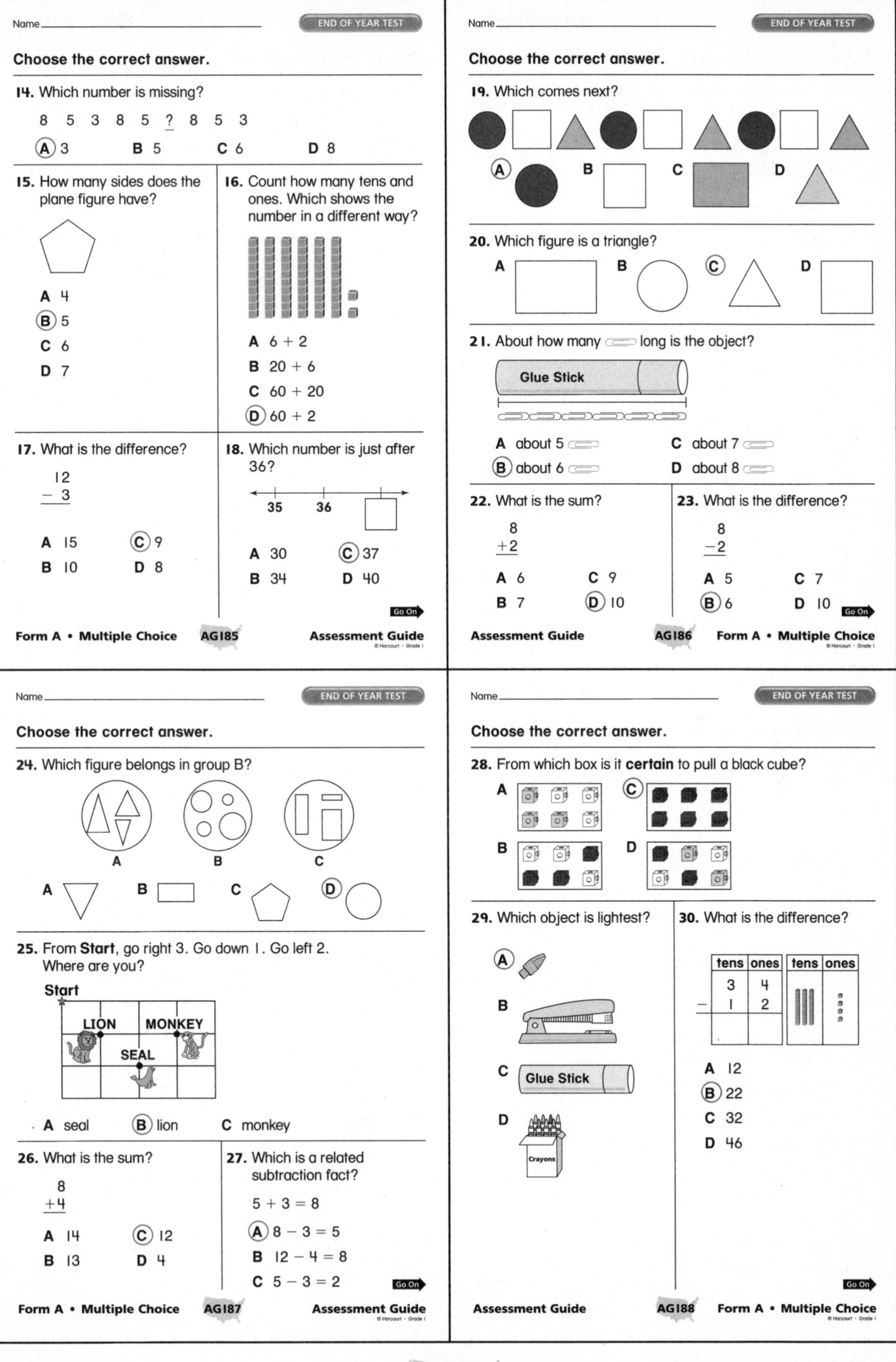

Name ______________________ END OF YEAR TEST

Choose the correct answer.

14. Which number is missing?

8 5 3 8 5 ? 8 5 3

(A) 3 B 5 C 6 D 8

15. How many sides does the plane figure have?

A 4
(B) 5
C 6
D 7

16. Count how many tens and ones. Which shows the number in a different way?

A 6 + 2
B 20 + 6
C 60 + 20
(D) 60 + 2

17. What is the difference?

$$\begin{array}{r} 12 \\ -\ 3 \\ \hline \end{array}$$

A 15 (C) 9
B 10 D 8

18. Which number is just after 36?

35 36 ☐

A 30 (C) 37
B 34 D 40

Go On

Form A • Multiple Choice AG185 **Assessment Guide**
© Harcourt • Grade 1

Name ______________________ END OF YEAR TEST

Choose the correct answer.

19. Which comes next?

(A) B C D

20. Which figure is a triangle?

A B (C) D

21. About how many long is the object?

Glue Stick

A about 5 C about 7
(B) about 6 D about 8

22. What is the sum?

$$\begin{array}{r} 8 \\ +2 \\ \hline \end{array}$$

A 6 C 9
B 7 (D) 10

23. What is the difference?

$$\begin{array}{r} 8 \\ -2 \\ \hline \end{array}$$

A 5 C 7
(B) 6 D 10

Go On

Assessment Guide AG186 **Form A • Multiple Choice**
© Harcourt • Grade 1

Name ______________________ END OF YEAR TEST

Choose the correct answer.

24. Which figure belongs in group B?

A B C

A B C (D)

25. From **Start**, go right 3. Go down 1. Go left 2. Where are you?

Start
LION MONKEY
SEAL

A seal (B) lion C monkey

26. What is the sum?

$$\begin{array}{r} 8 \\ +4 \\ \hline \end{array}$$

A 14 (C) 12
B 13 D 4

27. Which is a related subtraction fact?

5 + 3 = 8

(A) 8 − 3 = 5
B 12 − 4 = 8
C 5 − 3 = 2

Go On

Form A • Multiple Choice AG187 **Assessment Guide**
© Harcourt • Grade 1

Name ______________________ END OF YEAR TEST

Choose the correct answer.

28. From which box is it **certain** to pull a black cube?

A (C)
B D

29. Which object is lightest?

(A)
B
C Glue Stick
D Crayons

30. What is the difference?

	tens	ones
	3	4
−	1	2

A 12
(B) 22
C 32
D 46

Go On

Assessment Guide AG188 **Form A • Multiple Choice**
© Harcourt • Grade 1

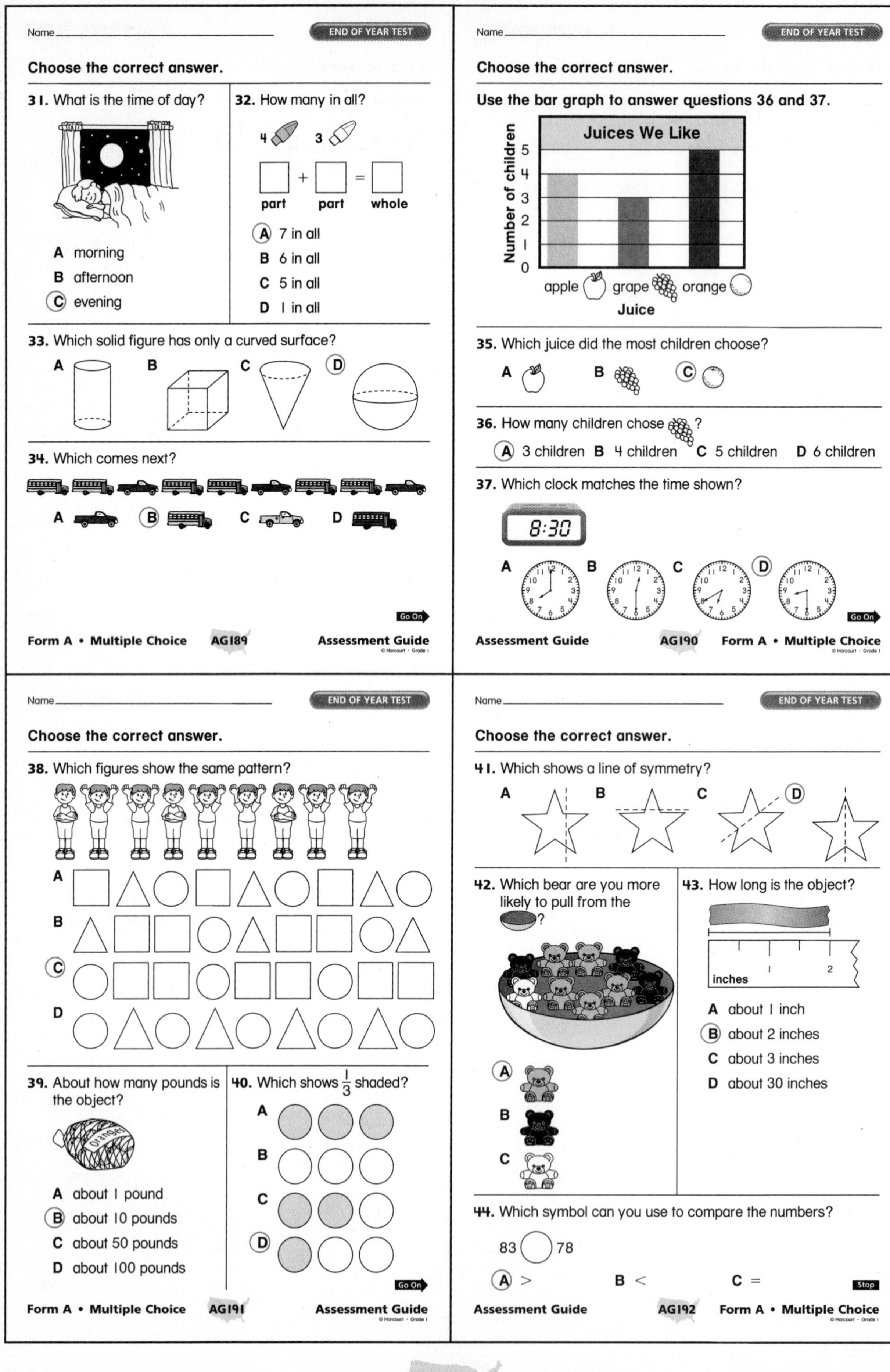
Name

END OF YEAR TEST

Choose the correct answer.

31. What is the time of day?

A morning
B afternoon
Ⓒ evening

32. How many in all?

4 3

☐ + ☐ = ☐
part part whole

Ⓐ 7 in all
B 6 in all
C 5 in all
D 1 in all

33. Which solid figure has only a curved surface?

A B C Ⓓ

34. Which comes next?

A Ⓑ C D

Go On

Form A • Multiple Choice AG189 Assessment Guide
© Harcourt • Grade 1

Name

END OF YEAR TEST

Choose the correct answer.

Use the bar graph to answer questions 36 and 37.

35. Which juice did the most children choose?

A B Ⓒ

36. How many children chose ?

Ⓐ 3 children B 4 children C 5 children D 6 children

37. Which clock matches the time shown?

8:30

A B C Ⓓ

Go On

Assessment Guide AG190 Form A • Multiple Choice
© Harcourt • Grade 1

Name

END OF YEAR TEST

Choose the correct answer.

38. Which figures show the same pattern?

A
B
Ⓒ
D

39. About how many pounds is the object?

A about 1 pound
Ⓑ about 10 pounds
C about 50 pounds
D about 100 pounds

40. Which shows $\frac{1}{3}$ shaded?

A
B
C
Ⓓ

Go On

Form A • Multiple Choice AG191 Assessment Guide
© Harcourt • Grade 1

Name

END OF YEAR TEST

Choose the correct answer.

41. Which shows a line of symmetry?

A B C Ⓓ

42. Which bear are you more likely to pull from the ?

Ⓐ
B
C

43. How long is the object?

A about 1 inch
Ⓑ about 2 inches
C about 3 inches
D about 30 inches

44. Which symbol can you use to compare the numbers?

83 ◯ 78

Ⓐ > B < C =

Stop

Assessment Guide AG192 Form A • Multiple Choice
© Harcourt • Grade 1

Name ____________ BEGINNING OF YEAR TEST

Write the correct answer.

1. Write the temperature.

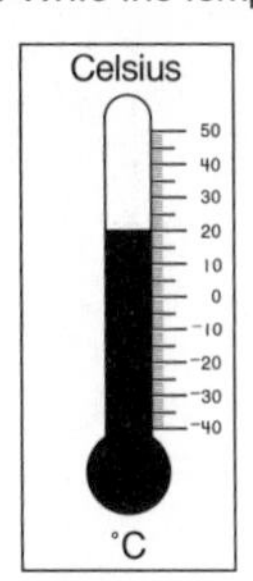

20 °C

2. Write how many corners the solid has.

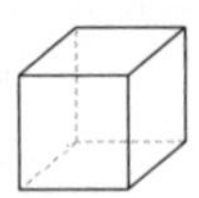

8 corners

3. Use the picture graph to answer question 3.

Snacks We Like								
pretzels	🥨	🥨	🥨	🥨				
yogurt	yogurt	yogurt	yogurt	yogurt	yogurt	yogurt	yogurt	yogurt
crackers	▦	▦	▦	▦	▦	▦		

Write how many more children chose yogurt than crackers.

2 more children

Go On

Name ____________ BEGINNING OF YEAR TEST

Write the correct answer.

4. Circle which belongs in the group.

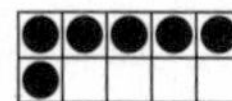

5. What is the sum?

50 + 30 = 80

6. Write the number word that tells how many.

sixteen

7. Circle the pair of related subtraction facts.

$10 - 3 = 7$, $11 - 4 = 7$ | ($11 - 7 = 4$, $11 - 4 = 7$) | $12 - 3 = 9$, $12 - 5 = 7$ | $10 - 4 = 6$, $6 - 4 = 2$

Go On

Name ____________ BEGINNING OF YEAR TEST

Write the correct answer.

8. Circle slide, flip, or turn to name the move.

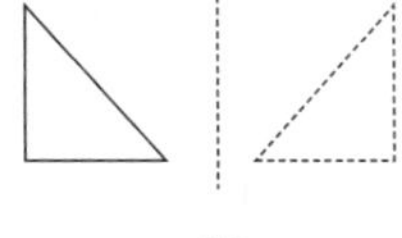

slide (flip) turn

9. Circle which tool you will use to measure how warm the water is.

10. Write how more leaves there are than birds.

$10 - 3$

7 more leaves

Go On

Name ____________ BEGINNING OF YEAR TEST

Write the correct answer.

11. Use the tally chart to answer the question.

Places We Like	
city	𝍸 ǁ
park	ǁǁ
mountains	𝍸

Write how many children chose the city.

7 children

12. Write the time.

13. Count. Compare the amounts. Write <, >, or =.

67 ¢ (>) 65 ¢

Go On

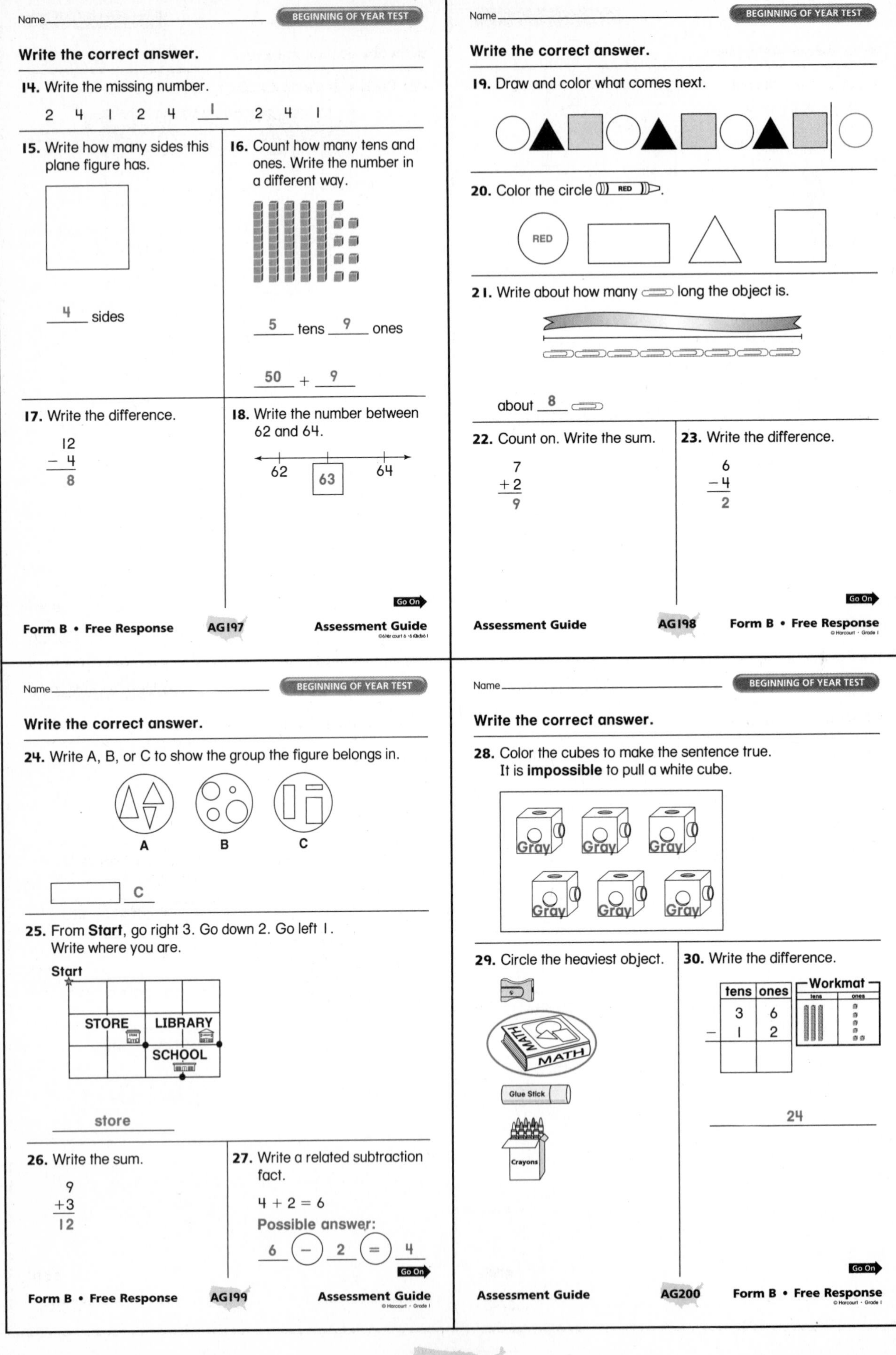

Name ______ BEGINNING OF YEAR TEST

Write the correct answer.

14. Write the missing number.

2 4 1 2 4 __1__ 2 4 1

15. Write how many sides this plane figure has.

__4__ sides

16. Count how many tens and ones. Write the number in a different way.

__5__ tens __9__ ones

__50__ + __9__

17. Write the difference.

$$\begin{array}{r} 12 \\ -\ 4 \\ \hline 8 \end{array}$$

18. Write the number between 62 and 64.

62 [63] 64

Go On

Name ______ BEGINNING OF YEAR TEST

Write the correct answer.

19. Draw and color what comes next.

20. Color the circle RED.

RED

21. Write about how many long the object is.

about __8__

22. Count on. Write the sum.

$$\begin{array}{r} 7 \\ +\ 2 \\ \hline 9 \end{array}$$

23. Write the difference.

$$\begin{array}{r} 6 \\ -\ 4 \\ \hline 2 \end{array}$$

Go On

Name ______ BEGINNING OF YEAR TEST

Write the correct answer.

24. Write A, B, or C to show the group the figure belongs in.

A B C

__C__

25. From **Start**, go right 3. Go down 2. Go left 1. Write where you are.

__store__

26. Write the sum.

$$\begin{array}{r} 9 \\ +3 \\ \hline 12 \end{array}$$

27. Write a related subtraction fact.

4 + 2 = 6

Possible answer:

__6__ (−) __2__ (=) __4__

Go On

Name ______ BEGINNING OF YEAR TEST

Write the correct answer.

28. Color the cubes to make the sentence true. It is **impossible** to pull a white cube.

29. Circle the heaviest object.

30. Write the difference.

	tens	ones
	3	6
−	1	2

Workmat (tens, ones)

__24__

Go On

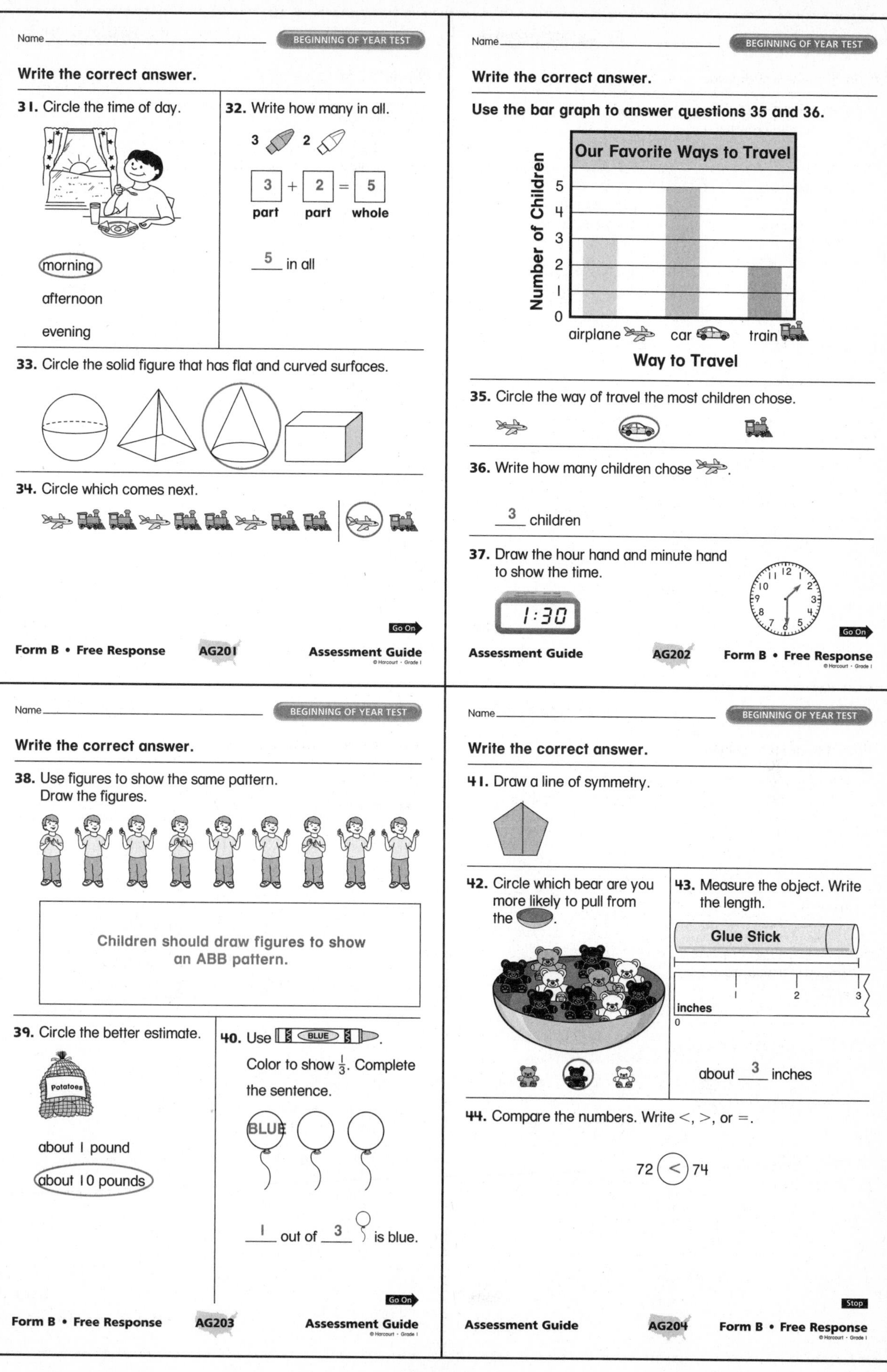

Name__________ BEGINNING OF YEAR TEST

Write the correct answer.

31. Circle the time of day.

(morning) — circled

afternoon

evening

32. Write how many in all.

3 2

3 + 2 = 5

part part whole

5 in all

33. Circle the solid figure that has flat and curved surfaces.

34. Circle which comes next.

Form B • Free Response AG201 Assessment Guide © Harcourt · Grade 1

Go On

Name__________ BEGINNING OF YEAR TEST

Write the correct answer.

Use the bar graph to answer questions 35 and 36.

Our Favorite Ways to Travel

Way to Travel	Number of Children
airplane	3
car	5
train	2

35. Circle the way of travel the most children chose.

36. Write how many children chose (airplane).

3 children

37. Draw the hour hand and minute hand to show the time.

1:30

Assessment Guide AG202 Form B • Free Response © Harcourt · Grade 1

Go On

Name__________ BEGINNING OF YEAR TEST

Write the correct answer.

38. Use figures to show the same pattern. Draw the figures.

Children should draw figures to show an ABB pattern.

39. Circle the better estimate.

Potatoes

about 1 pound

(about 10 pounds) — circled

40. Use (BLUE crayon). Color to show $\frac{1}{3}$. Complete the sentence.

BLUE

1 out of 3 is blue.

Form B • Free Response AG203 Assessment Guide © Harcourt · Grade 1

Go On

Name__________ BEGINNING OF YEAR TEST

Write the correct answer.

41. Draw a line of symmetry.

42. Circle which bear are you more likely to pull from the (bowl).

43. Measure the object. Write the length.

Glue Stick

inches 0 1 2 3

about 3 inches

44. Compare the numbers. Write <, >, or =.

72 (<) 74

Assessment Guide AG204 Form B • Free Response © Harcourt · Grade 1

Stop

Name ____________________ UNIT 1 PRETEST

Write the correct answer.

1. Write the numbers in order from least to greatest.

12, 10, 15

10 12 15

2. Write the difference.

8 − 0 = 8

3. Circle the addition sentences that use the same addends.

1 + 8 = 9

(5 + 4 = 9)

2 + 7 = 9

(4 + 5 = 9)

4. Write the number sentence.

There are 5 oranges. Casey takes 3 oranges away. How many oranges are left?

5 (−) 3 (=) 2

2 oranges

5. Write **is greater than** or **is less than** to make the sentence true.

12 is less than 13.

6. Circle the related subtraction fact.

3 + 4 = 7

6 + 2 = 8

(7 − 4 = 3)

9 − 3 = 6

Go On

Form B • Free Response AG205 Assessment Guide © Harcourt • Grade 1

Name ____________________ UNIT 1 PRETEST

Write the correct answer.

7. Use the cube below. Draw lines to match. There are 6 black cats and 3 white cats. How many fewer white cats are there?

3 white cats

8. Write a number sentence to match the picture.

7 (−) 2 (=) 5

9. Draw circles to show each number. Write the sum.

0 + 7 = 7

10. Complete the subtraction sentence.

9	−	3	=	6
whole		part		part

Go On

Assessment Guide AG206 Form B • Free Response © Harcourt • Grade 1

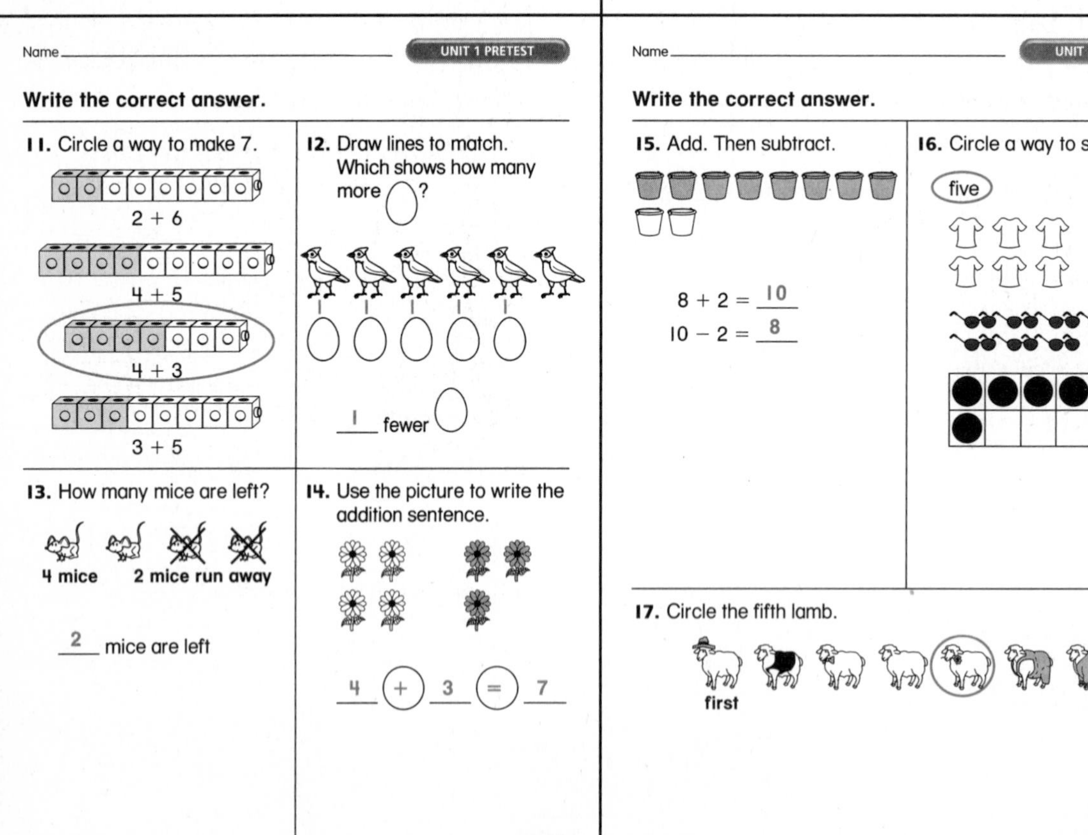

Name ____________________ UNIT 1 PRETEST

Write the correct answer.

11. Circle a way to make 7.

2 + 6

4 + 5

(4 + 3)

3 + 5

12. Draw lines to match. Which shows how many more ?

1 fewer

13. How many mice are left?

4 mice 2 mice run away

2 mice are left

14. Use the picture to write the addition sentence.

4 (+) 3 (=) 7

Go On

Form B • Free Response AG207 Assessment Guide © Harcourt • Grade 1

Name ____________________ UNIT 1 PRETEST

Write the correct answer.

15. Add. Then subtract.

8 + 2 = 10

10 − 2 = 8

16. Circle a way to show 5.

(five)

17. Circle the fifth lamb.

first

Go On

Assessment Guide AG208 Form B • Free Response © Harcourt • Grade 1

Name________________ UNIT 1 PRETEST

Write the correct answer.

18. How many birds are there in all?

6

19. Write the sum.

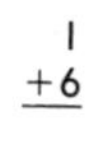

$$\begin{array}{r} 1 \\ +6 \\ \hline \end{array}$$

7

20. Use the cube below. Complete the subtraction sentence.

9 − 4 = 5

21. Write a number sentence.

Addie has 2 red crayons. She has the same number of green crayons. How many crayons does Addie have in all?

2 + 2 = 4

4 crayons

Go On

Name________________ UNIT 1 PRETEST

Write the correct answer.

22. Write the difference.

$$\begin{array}{r} 9 \\ -2 \\ \hline \end{array}$$

7

23. Circle the number word that tells how many.

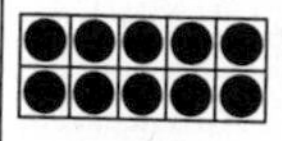

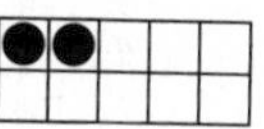

(twelve) thirteen

24. Write how many in all.

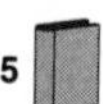

5 2

5	+	2	=	7
part		part		whole

7 in all

25. Draw lines to match. Write how many fewer ?

8 − 4 = 4

4 fewer

Stop

Name________________ UNIT 2 PRETEST

Write the correct answer.

1. Write the doubles fact.

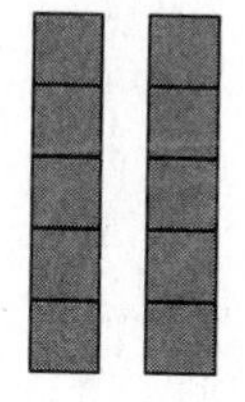

5 (+) 5 (=) 10

2. Draw a picture to solve. There are 7 prairie dogs. Some prairie dogs go underground. There are 3 prairie dogs left. How many prairie dogs went underground?

Check children's work.

4 prairie dogs

3. Follow the rule to complete the table.

Subtract 3	
8	5
7	4
6	3

4. Write the numbers in the fact family.

2 + 3 = 5   5 − 3 = 2

3 + 2 = 5   5 − 2 = 3

2	3	5

Go On

Name________________ UNIT 2 PRETEST

Write the correct answer.

Use the number line to answer questions 5 and 6.

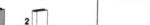

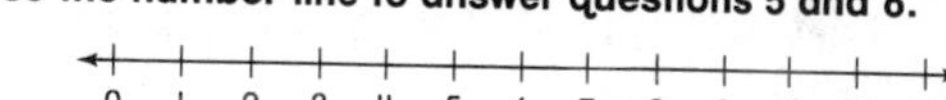

5. What is the sum?

$$\begin{array}{r} 5 \\ +3 \\ \hline 8 \end{array}$$

6. What is the sum?

$$\begin{array}{r} 7 \\ +2 \\ \hline 9 \end{array}$$

7. What is the difference?

$$\begin{array}{r} 11 \\ -7 \\ \hline 4 \end{array}$$

8. Use cubes and cubes to add.

$$\begin{array}{r} 4 \\ +5 \\ \hline 9 \end{array}$$

9. Circle the pair of related subtraction facts.

$$\begin{array}{r} 7 \\ -3 \\ \hline 4 \end{array} \quad \begin{array}{r} 7 \\ -5 \\ \hline 2 \end{array} \qquad \left(\begin{array}{r} 11 \\ -8 \\ \hline 3 \end{array} \quad \begin{array}{r} 11 \\ -3 \\ \hline 8 \end{array}\right) \qquad \begin{array}{r} 11 \\ -4 \\ \hline 7 \end{array} \quad \begin{array}{r} 11 \\ -5 \\ \hline 6 \end{array} \qquad \begin{array}{r} 8 \\ -4 \\ \hline 4 \end{array} \quad \begin{array}{r} 8 \\ -5 \\ \hline 3 \end{array}$$

Go On

Name

UNIT 2 PRETEST

Write the correct answer.

10. Count on. Write the sum.

7 + 2 = 9

11. Write a number sentence to match the story.

There are 12 black dogs. There are 5 white dogs. How many more black dogs are there than white dogs?

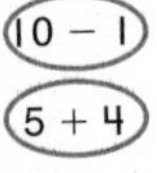

12 (−) 5 (=) 7

7 black dogs

12. Write the sum. Then write the related addition fact.

6	2
+2	+ 6
8	8

13. Circle the ways to make 9.

(10 − 1)

(5 + 4)

10 − 3

5 + 6

14. Count on. Write the sum.

8
+2
10

Go On

Name

UNIT 2 PRETEST

Write the correct answer.

Use the number line to answer questions 15 and 16.

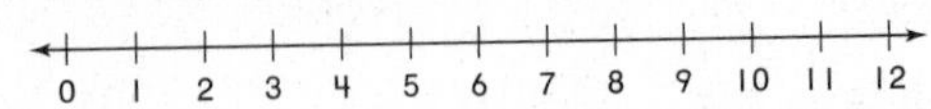

15. Write the difference.

9
−2
7

16. Write the difference.

5 − 3 = 2

17. Follow the rule to complete the table.

Subtract 2	
6	4
5	3
4	2

18. Write the doubles plus one fact.

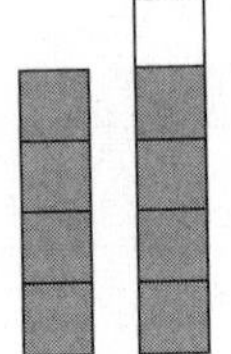

4 (+) 5 (=) 9

Go On

Name

UNIT 2 PRETEST

Write the correct answer.

19. Complete the fact family.

6 + 5 = 11

5 + 6 = 11

11 − 5 = 6

11 − 6 = 5

20. Write the sum.

9 + 1 = 10

21. Write the number sentence that shows how many buttons there are.

2 gray buttons

6 white buttons

2 (+) 6 (=) 8

22. Write the number sentence that matches the story.

There are 12 grasshoppers. 3 grasshoppers hop away. How many grasshoppers are there now?

12 (−) 3 (=) 9

9 grasshoppers

Go On

Name

UNIT 2 PRETEST

Write the correct answer.

23. Use cubes and cubes to subtract.

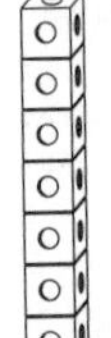

10
− 3
7

24. Write the numbers in the fact family.

9 + 2 = 11   11 − 2 = 9

2 + 9 = 11   11 − 9 = 2

2 9 11

25. There are 10 ants. Some ants walk away. There are 7 ants left. How many ants walked away?

3 ants

26. There are 8 mittens in all. 3 mittens are blue. The other mittens are yellow. How many mittens are yellow?

5 mittens

Stop

Name ____________________ **UNIT 3 PRETEST**

Write the correct answer.

1. Write the number that is between 38 and 40.

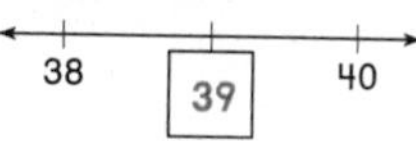

2. Count by tens. Write the number.

3 tens

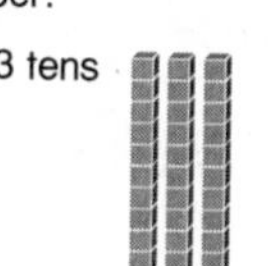

30

3. Use the tally chart to answer the question.

Drinks We Like	
milk	𝍸 I
juice	𝍸 III
water	IIII

Write how many children chose milk.

6 children

4. Count how many tens and ones. Write the number in a different way.

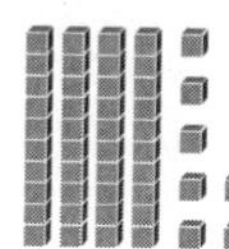

4 tens 7 ones

40 + 7

Go On

Name ____________________ **UNIT 3 PRETEST**

Write the correct answer.

Use the hundred chart for questions 5 and 6.

1	2	3	4	5	6	7	8	9	10
11	12	13	14	15	16	17	18	19	20
21	22	23	24	25	26	27	28	29	30
31	32	33	34	35	36	37	38	39	40
41	42	43	44	45	46	47	48	49	50
51	52	53	54	55	56	57	58	59	60
61	62	63	64	65	66	67	68	69	70
71	72	73	74	75	76	77	78	79	80
81	82	83	84	85	86	87	88	89	90
91	92	93	94	95	96	97	98	99	100

5. Count by twos. Write the number that comes next.

12, 14, 16, 18, 20, 22

6. Count by fives. Write the numbers that come next.

34, 39, 44, 49, 54, 59

Go On

Name ____________________ **UNIT 3 PRETEST**

Write the correct answer.

7. Circle which belongs in the group.

8. Color the cubes to make the sentence true. It is **impossible** to pull a white cube.

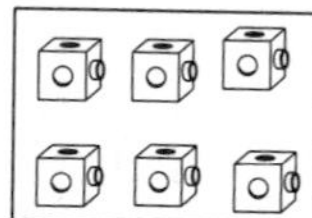

The drawing must not contain any white cubes.

9. There are 5 pencils in a box. Write how many pencils there are in 7 boxes.

number of boxes	1	2	3	4	5	6	7
number of pencils	5	10					

7 boxes have 35 pencils.

Go On

Name ____________________ **UNIT 3 PRETEST**

Write the correct answer.

10. Write the numbers.

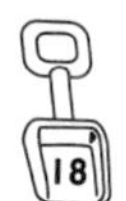

18 is less than 21.

18 < 21

11. There are 9 black cubes and 5 white cubes in a bag. Circle which color you are more likely to pull.

Use the table to answer questions 12 and 13.

Month	Rainy Days
May	12
June	15
July	10
August	11

12. Write the month that had more rainy days.

12 (<) 15
May **June**

June

13. Write the month that had the least number of rainy days.

15 12 11 10
greatest **least**

July

Go On

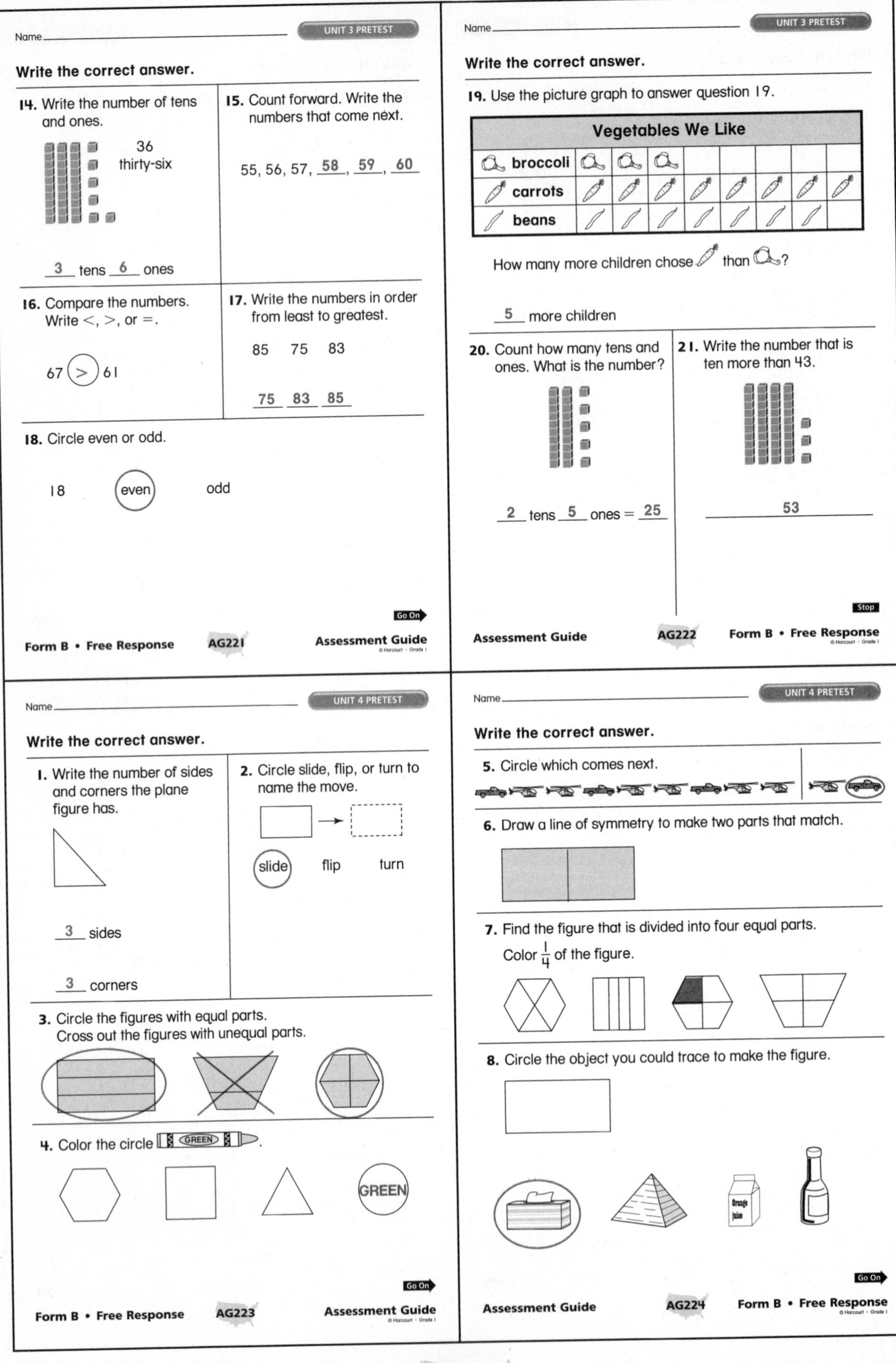

Name____________________ UNIT 3 PRETEST

Write the correct answer.

14. Write the number of tens and ones.

36
thirty-six

3 tens 6 ones

15. Count forward. Write the numbers that come next.

55, 56, 57, 58, 59, 60

16. Compare the numbers. Write <, >, or =.

67 (>) 61

17. Write the numbers in order from least to greatest.

85 75 83

75 83 85

18. Circle even or odd.

18 (even) odd

Go On

Form B • Free Response AG221 Assessment Guide © Harcourt • Grade 1

Name____________________ UNIT 3 PRETEST

Write the correct answer.

19. Use the picture graph to answer question 19.

Vegetables We Like								
broccoli								
carrots								
beans								

How many more children chose carrots than broccoli?

5 more children

20. Count how many tens and ones. What is the number?

2 tens 5 ones = 25

21. Write the number that is ten more than 43.

53

Stop

Assessment Guide AG222 Form B • Free Response © Harcourt • Grade 1

Name____________________ UNIT 4 PRETEST

Write the correct answer.

1. Write the number of sides and corners the plane figure has.

3 sides

3 corners

2. Circle slide, flip, or turn to name the move.

(slide) flip turn

3. Circle the figures with equal parts. Cross out the figures with unequal parts.

4. Color the circle GREEN.

GREEN

Go On

Form B • Free Response AG223 Assessment Guide © Harcourt • Grade 1

Name____________________ UNIT 4 PRETEST

Write the correct answer.

5. Circle which comes next.

6. Draw a line of symmetry to make two parts that match.

7. Find the figure that is divided into four equal parts. Color $\frac{1}{4}$ of the figure.

8. Circle the object you could trace to make the figure.

Orange juice

Go On

Assessment Guide AG224 Form B • Free Response © Harcourt • Grade 1

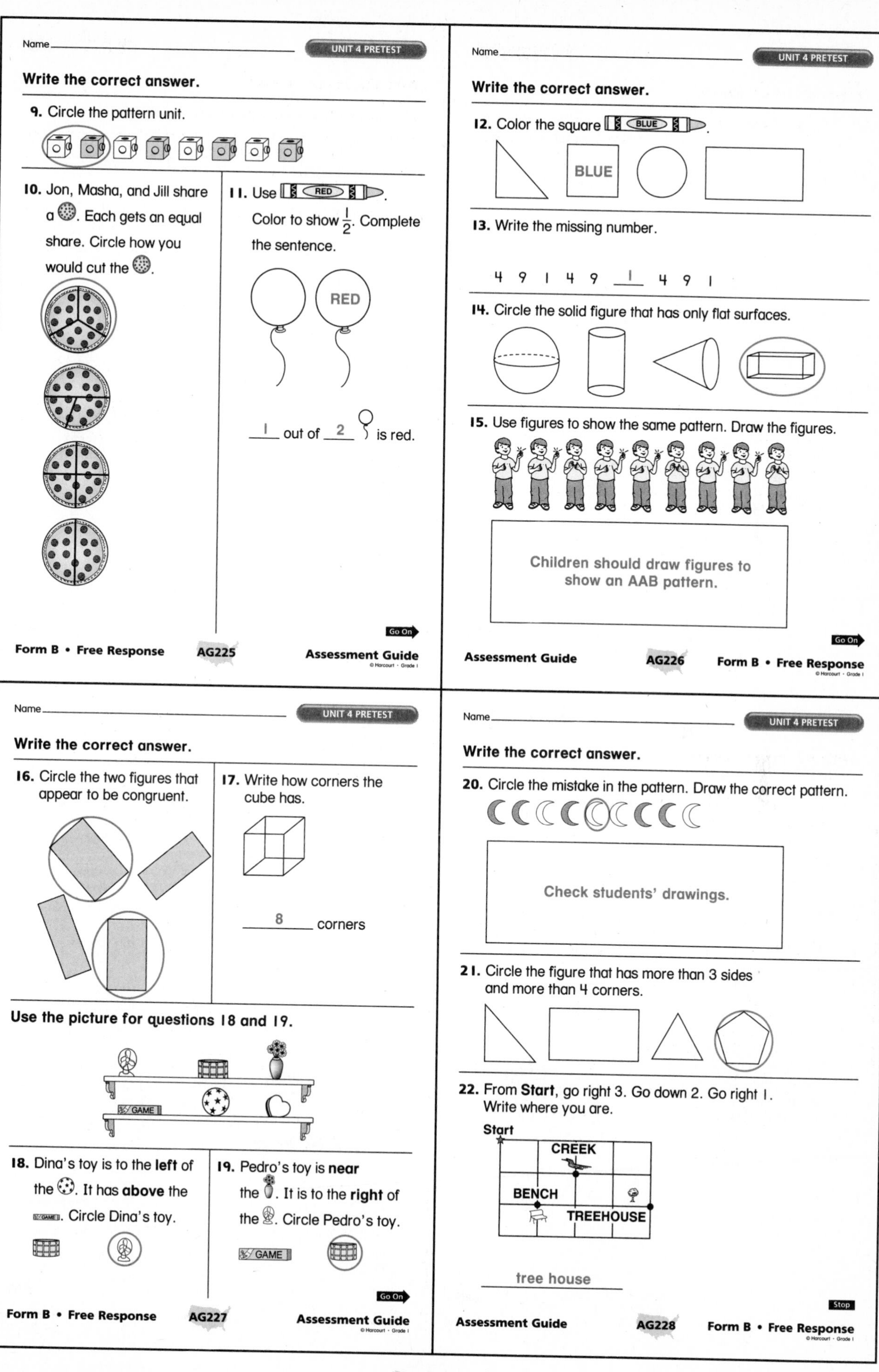

Name

UNIT 4 PRETEST

Write the correct answer.

9. Circle the pattern unit.

10. Jon, Masha, and Jill share a pizza. Each gets an equal share. Circle how you would cut the pizza.

11. Use RED. Color to show $\frac{1}{2}$. Complete the sentence.

RED

1 out of 2 balloons is red.

Go On

Form B • Free Response AG225 Assessment Guide © Harcourt • Grade 1

Name

UNIT 4 PRETEST

Write the correct answer.

12. Color the square BLUE.

BLUE

13. Write the missing number.

4 9 1 4 9 1 4 9 1

14. Circle the solid figure that has only flat surfaces.

15. Use figures to show the same pattern. Draw the figures.

Children should draw figures to show an AAB pattern.

Go On

Assessment Guide AG226 Form B • Free Response © Harcourt • Grade 1

Name

UNIT 4 PRETEST

Write the correct answer.

16. Circle the two figures that appear to be congruent.

17. Write how corners the cube has.

8 corners

Use the picture for questions 18 and 19.

GAME

18. Dina's toy is to the **left** of the ball. It has **above** the GAME. Circle Dina's toy.

19. Pedro's toy is **near** the vase. It is to the **right** of the fan. Circle Pedro's toy.

GAME

Go On

Form B • Free Response AG227 Assessment Guide © Harcourt • Grade 1

Name

UNIT 4 PRETEST

Write the correct answer.

20. Circle the mistake in the pattern. Draw the correct pattern.

Check students' drawings.

21. Circle the figure that has more than 3 sides and more than 4 corners.

22. From **Start**, go right 3. Go down 2. Go right 1. Write where you are.

Start

CREEK

BENCH

TREEHOUSE

tree house

Stop

Assessment Guide AG228 Form B • Free Response © Harcourt • Grade 1

Name ____________ UNIT 5 PRETEST

Write the correct answer.

1. Use the calendar. Write how many Mondays are in this month.

July						
Sunday	Monday	Tuesday	Wednesday	Thursday	Friday	Saturday
1	2	3	4	5	6	7
8	9	10	11	12	13	14
15	16	17	18	19	20	21
22	23	24	25	26	27	28
29	30	31				

5 Mondays

2. Use the addition fact to help you subtract. Write the sum. Then write the difference.

$$\begin{array}{r} 7 \\ +4 \\ \hline 11 \end{array} \qquad \begin{array}{r} 11 \\ -4 \\ \hline 7 \end{array}$$

3. Write the sum.

$$\begin{array}{r} 6 \\ +6 \\ \hline 12 \end{array}$$

4. Follow the rule. Write the number that completes the table.

Subtract 7	
12	5
14	7
16	9
17	10

Go On

Name ____________ UNIT 5 PRETEST

Write the correct answer.

5. Write how many more birds there are than nests.

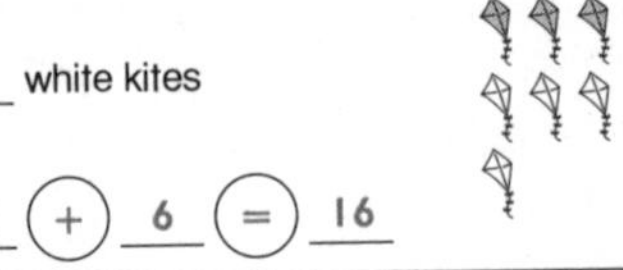

$$\begin{array}{r} 15 \\ -8 \\ \hline 7 \end{array}$$

6. Use the picture to write the numbers.
Write a number sentence to show how many kites there are.

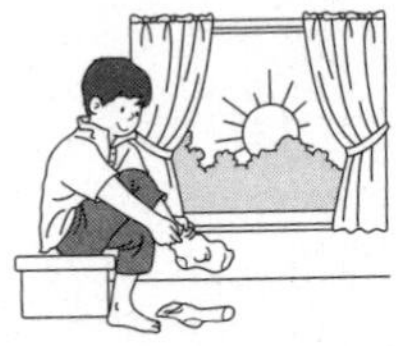

10 gray kites

6 white kites

10 + 6 = 16

7. Write the sum.

$$\begin{array}{r} 4 \\ 5 \\ +6 \\ \hline 15 \end{array}$$

8. Circle the time of day.

(morning) evening afternoon

Go On

Name ____________ UNIT 5 PRETEST

Write the correct answer.

9. Draw and label coins to show the amount a different way.

Check children's drawings. Possible answer: 7 dimes and 5 pennies.

10. Draw and label coins to show a way to make 1 dollar.
Use quarters and nickels.

Check children's drawings. Possible answer: 3 quarters and 5 nickels.

11. Write the difference.

$$\begin{array}{r} 14 \\ -5 \\ \hline 9 \end{array}$$

Go On

Name ____________ UNIT 5 PRETEST

Write the correct answer.

12. Write a number sentence to solve.

7 children are waiting for the bus. 6 more children join them. How many children are waiting for the bus now?

7 + 6 = 13

13 children

13. Write the missing numbers.

$$\begin{array}{r} 9 \\ +\boxed{8} \\ \hline 17 \end{array} \qquad \begin{array}{r} 17 \\ -9 \\ \hline \boxed{8} \end{array}$$

14. Make a ten and add. Write the sum.

$$\begin{array}{r} 4 \\ +9 \\ \hline 13 \end{array}$$

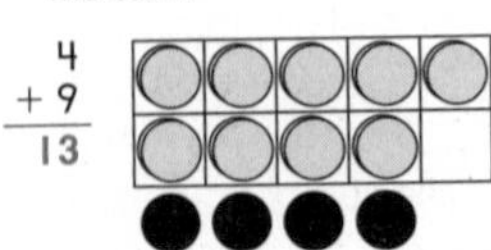

15. Write a number sentence to solve.

Daisy has 8 strawberries. Sally brings 4 more strawberries. How many strawberries are there in all?

8 + 4 = 12

12 strawberries

Go On

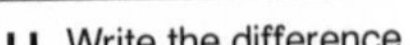
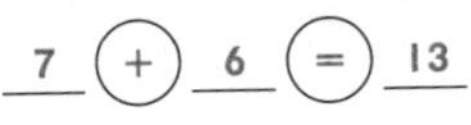
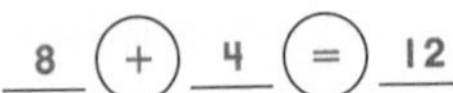

Name ______________________ UNIT 5 PRETEST

Write the correct answer.

16. Count. Compare the amounts. Write <, >, or =.

62 ¢ (>) 56 ¢

17. Draw the hour hand and minute hand to show the time.

18. Write the sum.

10 + 10 = 20

19. Write the difference.

16 − 8 = 8

Go On

Name ______________________ UNIT 5 PRETEST

Write the correct answer.

Use the table to answer question 20.

Festival Events		
Event	**Start**	**End**
picnic	12:00	7:00
music	2:00	8:00
fireworks	9:30	10:00

20. Which event starts at 9:30?

fireworks

21. Write each sum or difference.
Circle the facts in the same fact family.

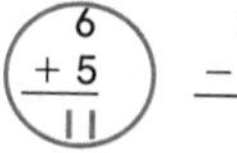

$\begin{array}{r} 6 \\ +5 \\ \hline 11 \end{array}$ (circled) $\begin{array}{r} 10 \\ -5 \\ \hline 5 \end{array}$  $\begin{array}{r} 11 \\ -6 \\ \hline 5 \end{array}$ (circled) 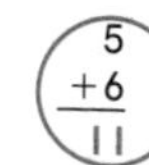 $\begin{array}{r} 5 \\ +6 \\ \hline 11 \end{array}$ (circled)  $\begin{array}{r} 11 \\ -5 \\ \hline 6 \end{array}$ (circled)

Stop

Name ______________________ UNIT 6 PRETEST

Write the correct answer.

1. Write the sum.

	tens	ones
	3	2
+		5
	3	7

Workmat (tens | ones)

2. Circle the container that holds the least amount of juice.

3. Write about how many ▭ long the object is.

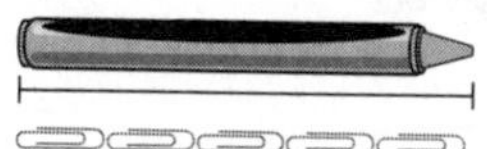

about 5 ▭

Go On

Name ______________________ UNIT 6 PRETEST

Write the correct answer.

4. Circle the better estimate.

about 1 pound

(about 10 pounds)

5. Write the temperature.

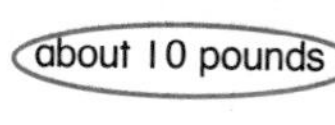

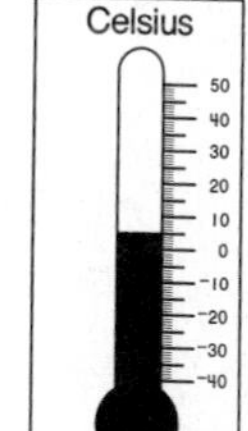

5 °C

6. Write the difference.

80 − 10 = 70

7. Circle the size of the container.

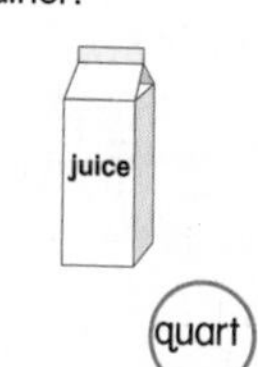

pint (quart)

Go On

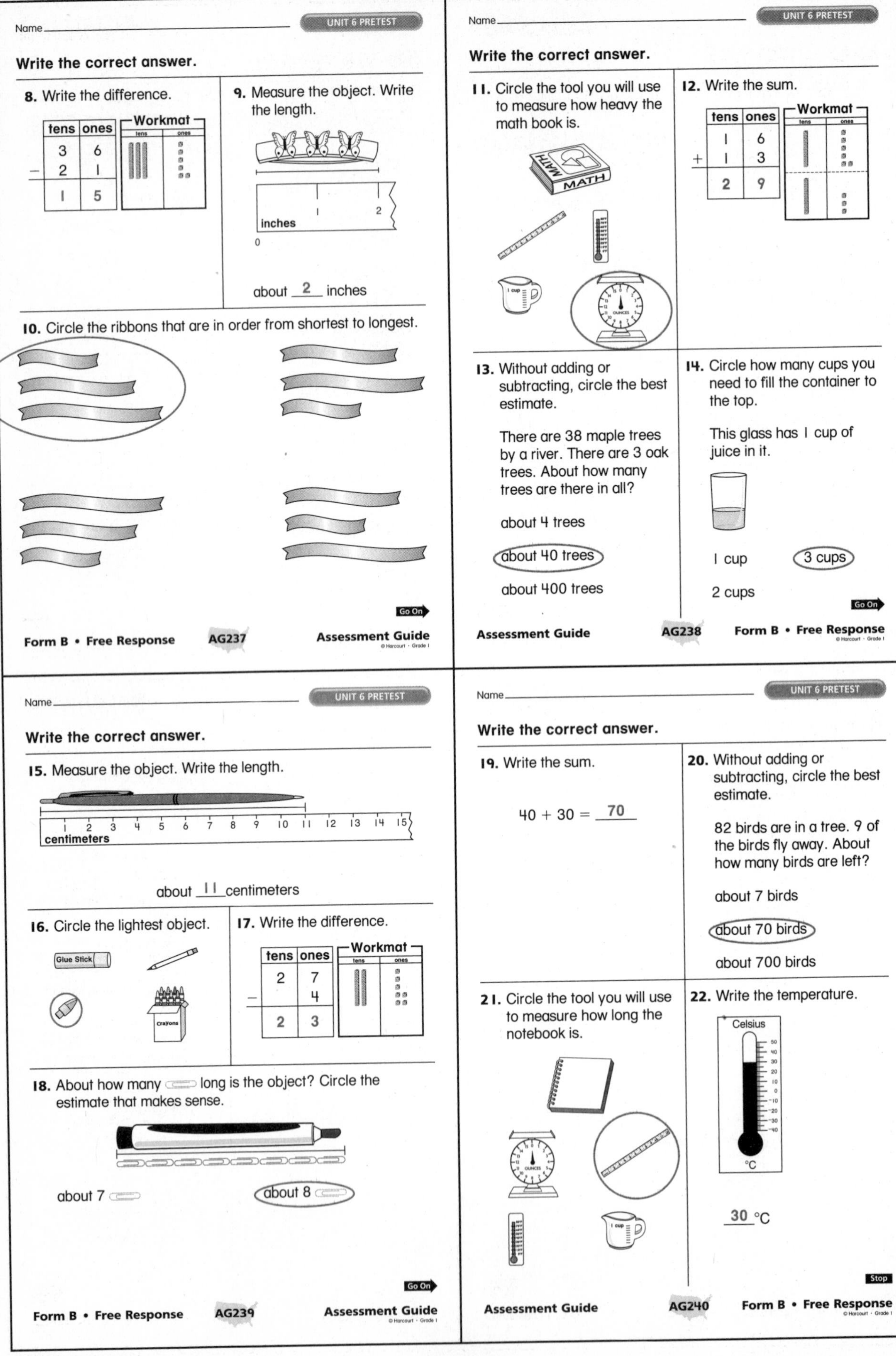
Name

UNIT 6 PRETEST

Write the correct answer.

8. Write the difference.

	tens	ones
	3	6
−	2	1
	1	5

Workmat (tens / ones)

9. Measure the object. Write the length.

inches 0 1 2

about 2 inches

10. Circle the ribbons that are in order from shortest to longest.

Go On

Form B • Free Response AG237 Assessment Guide © Harcourt • Grade 1

Name

UNIT 6 PRETEST

Write the correct answer.

11. Circle the tool you will use to measure how heavy the math book is.

MATH

1 cup

OUNCES

12. Write the sum.

	tens	ones
	1	6
+	1	3
	2	9

Workmat (tens / ones)

13. Without adding or subtracting, circle the best estimate.

There are 38 maple trees by a river. There are 3 oak trees. About how many trees are there in all?

about 4 trees

(about 40 trees) — circled

about 400 trees

14. Circle how many cups you need to fill the container to the top.

This glass has 1 cup of juice in it.

1 cup

(3 cups) — circled

2 cups

Go On

Assessment Guide AG238 Form B • Free Response © Harcourt • Grade 1

Name

UNIT 6 PRETEST

Write the correct answer.

15. Measure the object. Write the length.

1 2 3 4 5 6 7 8 9 10 11 12 13 14 15 centimeters

about 11 centimeters

16. Circle the lightest object.

Glue Stick

Crayons

17. Write the difference.

	tens	ones
	2	7
−		4
	2	3

Workmat (tens / ones)

18. About how many paper clips long is the object? Circle the estimate that makes sense.

about 7

(about 8) — circled

Go On

Form B • Free Response AG239 Assessment Guide © Harcourt • Grade 1

Name

UNIT 6 PRETEST

Write the correct answer.

19. Write the sum.

40 + 30 = 70

20. Without adding or subtracting, circle the best estimate.

82 birds are in a tree. 9 of the birds fly away. About how many birds are left?

about 7 birds

(about 70 birds) — circled

about 700 birds

21. Circle the tool you will use to measure how long the notebook is.

OUNCES

1 cup

22. Write the temperature.

Celsius 50 40 30 20 10 0 −10 −20 −30 −40 °C

30 °C

Stop

Assessment Guide AG240 Form B • Free Response © Harcourt • Grade 1

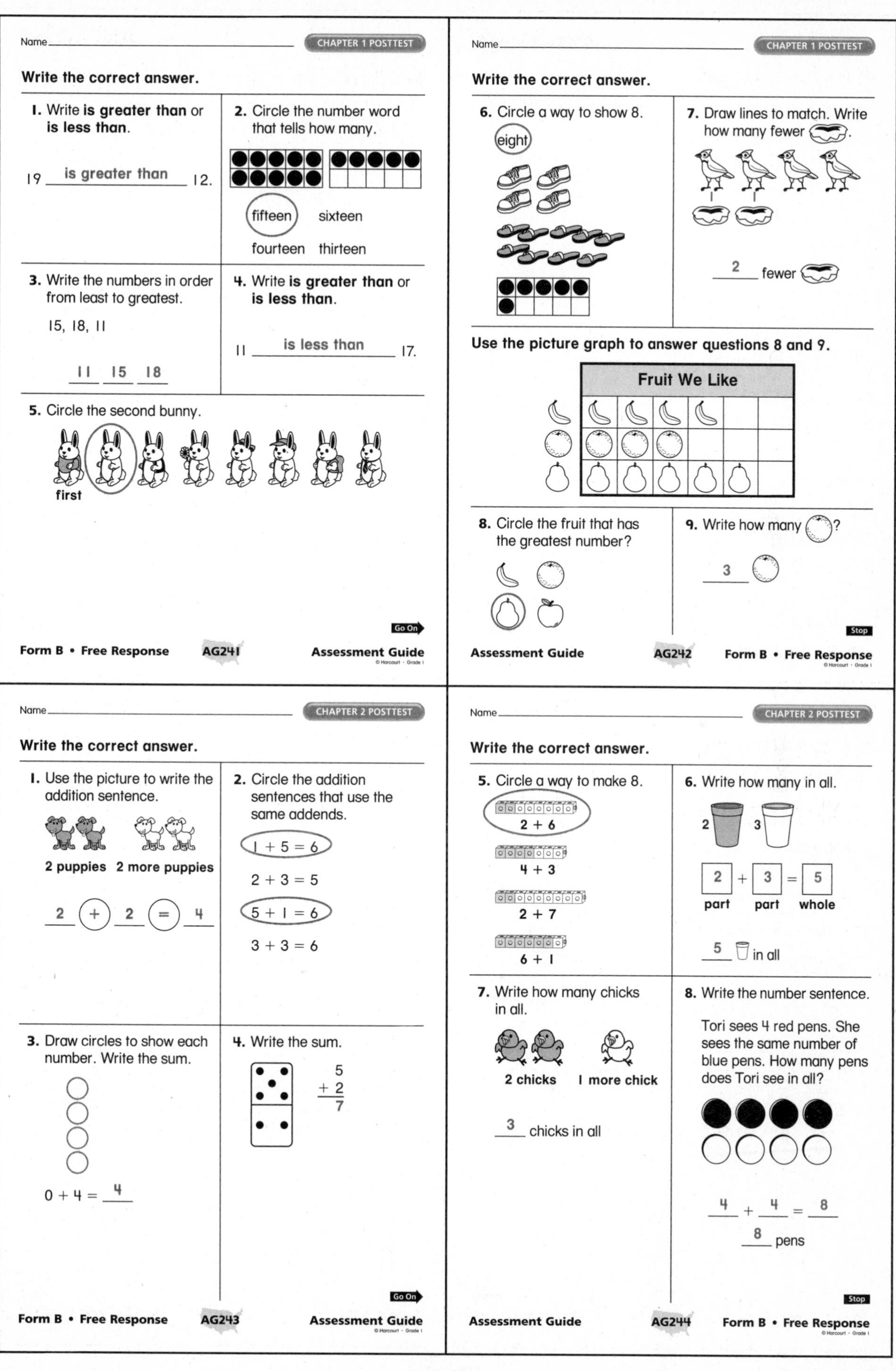

Name

CHAPTER 1 POSTTEST

Write the correct answer.

1. Write **is greater than** or **is less than**.

19 is greater than 12.

2. Circle the number word that tells how many.

fifteen (circled) sixteen

fourteen thirteen

3. Write the numbers in order from least to greatest.

15, 18, 11

11 15 18

4. Write **is greater than** or **is less than**.

11 is less than 17.

5. Circle the second bunny.

first

Go On

Form B • Free Response AG241 Assessment Guide

© Harcourt • Grade 1

Name

CHAPTER 1 POSTTEST

Write the correct answer.

6. Circle a way to show 8.

eight (circled)

7. Draw lines to match. Write how many fewer.

2 fewer

Use the picture graph to answer questions 8 and 9.

Fruit We Like

8. Circle the fruit that has the greatest number?

9. Write how many?

3

Stop

Assessment Guide AG242 Form B • Free Response

© Harcourt • Grade 1

Name

CHAPTER 2 POSTTEST

Write the correct answer.

1. Use the picture to write the addition sentence.

2 puppies **2 more puppies**

2 + 2 = 4

2. Circle the addition sentences that use the same addends.

1 + 5 = 6 (circled)

2 + 3 = 5

5 + 1 = 6 (circled)

3 + 3 = 6

3. Draw circles to show each number. Write the sum.

0 + 4 = 4

4. Write the sum.

5
+ 2
7

Go On

Form B • Free Response AG243 Assessment Guide

© Harcourt • Grade 1

Name

CHAPTER 2 POSTTEST

Write the correct answer.

5. Circle a way to make 8.

2 + 6 (circled)

4 + 3

2 + 7

6 + 1

6. Write how many in all.

2 3

2 + 3 = 5

part **part** **whole**

5 in all

7. Write how many chicks in all.

2 chicks **1 more chick**

3 chicks in all

8. Write the number sentence.

Tori sees 4 red pens. She sees the same number of blue pens. How many pens does Tori see in all?

4 + 4 = 8

8 pens

Stop

Assessment Guide AG244 Form B • Free Response

© Harcourt • Grade 1

Name

CHAPTER 3 POSTTEST

Write the correct answer.

1. Write the difference.

$$\begin{array}{r} 7 \\ -\ 3 \\ \hline 4 \end{array}$$

2. Write the difference.

3 − 0 = 3

3. Use the 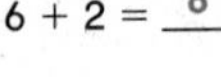 below. Complete the subtraction sentence.

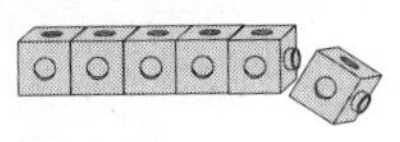

6 − 1 = 5

4. Use the picture. Write the subtraction sentence.

6 (−) 4 (=) 2

Name

CHAPTER 3 POSTTEST

Write the correct answer.

5. Draw lines to match. Write how many fewer.

1 fewer 

6. Complete the subtraction sentence.

7 − 3 = 4

whole part part

7. Write how many girls are left.

2 girls 1 girl walks away

1 girl is left

8. There are 5 brown bats and 2 fruit bats. How many fewer fruit bats are there?

3 fewer fruit bats

Name

CHAPTER 4 POSTTEST

Write the correct answer.

1. Add. Then subtract.

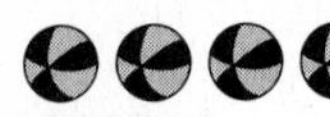

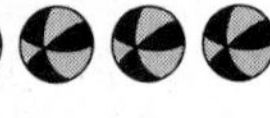

6 + 2 = 8

8 − 2 = 6

2. Write a number sentence to match the picture.

7 (−) 3 (=) 4

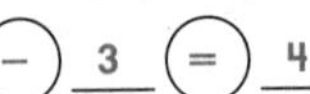

3. Circle the related subtraction fact.

6 + 3 = 9

6 + 3 = 9

(9 − 3 = 6)

8 − 6 = 2

8 − 4 = 4

4. How many ladybugs are there in all?

5

Name

CHAPTER 4 POSTTEST

Write the correct answer.

5. Circle the related addition fact.

2 − 0 = 2

4 − 0 = 4 0 + 3 = 3

(0 + 2 = 2) 2 + 2 = 4

6. Write a number sentence to match the picture.

3 (+) 4 (=) 7

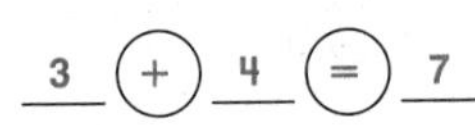

7. How many squirrels run away?

2

8. Write the number sentence. There are 7 erasers. Chante brings 2 more erasers. How many erasers are there now?

7 (+) 2 (=) 9

9 erasers

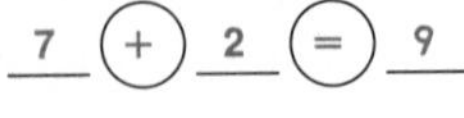

9. Write the number sentence. There are 6 blocks. Paige takes 2 blocks away. How many blocks are left?

6 (−) 2 (=) 4

4 blocks

Name

UNIT 1 POSTTEST

Write the correct answer.

1. Write the numbers in order from least to greatest.

9, 14, 11

9 11 14

2. Write the difference.

3 − 0 = 3

3. Circle the addition sentences that use the same addends.

(1 + 3 = 4)

4 + 1 = 5

2 + 3 = 5

(3 + 1 = 4)

4. Write the number sentence.

There are 8 grapes. Sadie takes 6 grapes away. How many grapes are left?

8 (−) 6 (=) 2

2 grapes

5. Write **is greater than** or **is less than** to make the sentence true.

17 is greater than 11.

6. Circle the related subtraction fact.

2 + 3 = 5

2 + 2 = 4

3 − 2 = 1

(5 − 3 = 2)

Go On

Name

UNIT 1 POSTTEST

Write the correct answer.

7. Use the 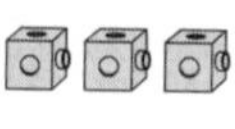 below.

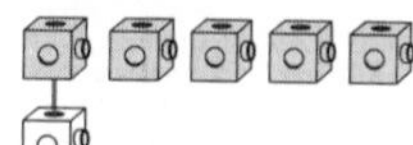

There are 5 gray blocks and 1 white block. How many fewer white blocks are there?

4 white blocks

8. Write a number sentence to match the picture.

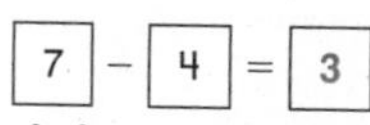

6 (−) 2 (=) 4

9. Draw circles to show each number. Write the sum.

0 + 3 = 3

10. Complete the subtraction sentence.

7	−	4	=	3
whole		part		part

Go On

Name

UNIT 1 POSTTEST

Write the correct answer.

11. Circle a way to make 5.

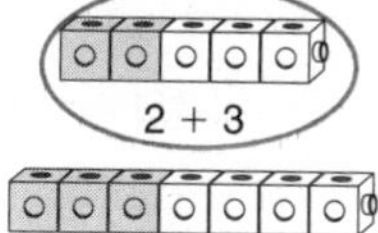

(2 + 3)

3 + 4

4 + 2

1 + 3

12. Draw lines to match. Which shows how many more leaves?

4 more

13. How many fish are left?

4 fish 1 fish swims away

3 fish are left

14. Use the picture to write the addition sentence.

3 (+) 2 (=) 5

Go On

Name

UNIT 1 POSTTEST

Write the correct answer.

15. Add. Then subtract.

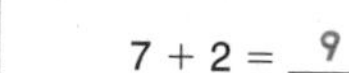

7 + 2 = 9

9 − 2 = 7

16. Circle a way to show 3.

four

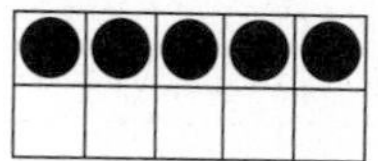

17. Circle the fourth puppy.

first

Go On

Name______ UNIT 1 POSTTEST

Write the correct answer.

18. How many hamsters are there in all?

8

19. Write the sum.

$$\begin{array}{r} 4 \\ +5 \\ \hline 9 \end{array}$$

20. Use the cube below. Complete the subtraction sentence.

5 − 2 = 3

21. Write a number sentence.

There are 4 children in a pool. The same number of children join them. How many children are there in all?

4 + 4 = 8

8 children

Go On

Name______ UNIT 1 POSTTEST

Write the correct answer.

22. Write the difference.

$$\begin{array}{r} 9 \\ -1 \\ \hline 8 \end{array}$$

23. Circle the number word that tells how many.

(fourteen) eighteen

24. Write how many in all.

2 butterflies 7 butterflies

2	+	7	=	9
part		part		whole

9 butterflies in all

25. Draw lines to match. Write how many fewer clothespins?

6 − 4 = 2

2 fewer

Stop

Name______ CHAPTER 5 POSTTEST

Write the correct answer.

Use the number line to answer questions 1 and 2.

0 1 2 3 4 5 6 7 8 9 10 11 12

1. What is the sum?

$$\begin{array}{r} 3 \\ +3 \\ \hline 6 \end{array}$$

2. What is the sum?

$$\begin{array}{r} 4 \\ +2 \\ \hline 6 \end{array}$$

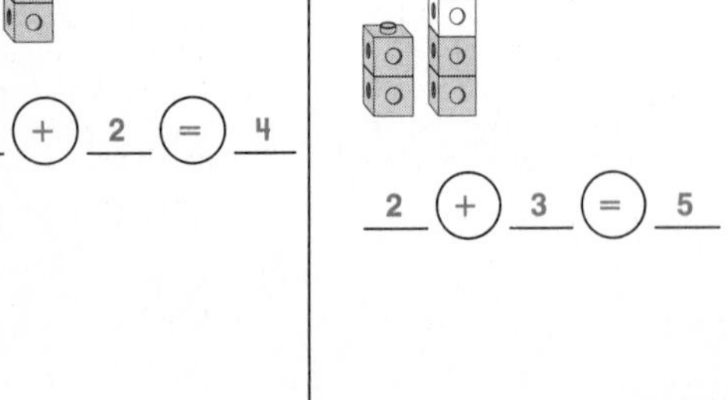

3. Write the doubles fact.

2 + 2 = 4

4. Write the double plus one fact.

2 + 3 = 5

Go On

Name______ CHAPTER 5 POSTTEST

Write the correct answer.

5. Count on. Write the sum.

$$\begin{array}{r} 2 \\ +9 \\ \hline 11 \end{array}$$

6. Write the sum.

6 + 3 = 9

7. Count on. Write the sum.

5 + 3 = 8

8. Draw a picture to solve. There are 9 flowers in all. 4 flowers are red. The other flowers are yellow. Write how many flowers are yellow.

Check children's work.

5 yellow flowers

9. Draw a picture to solve. There are 4 bananas in all. 2 bananas are yellow. The other bananas are green. Write how many bananas are green.

Check children's work.

2 green bananas

Stop

Name________________________ CHAPTER 6 POSTTEST

Write the correct answer.

Use the number line to answer questions 1 through 4.

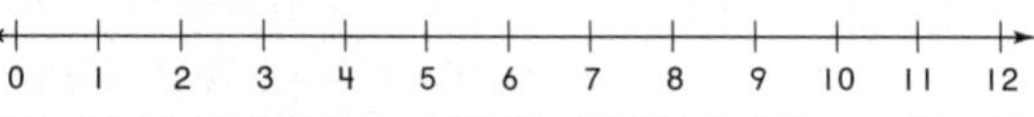

1. Write the difference.

$$\begin{array}{r} 10 \\ -\ 2 \\ \hline 8 \end{array}$$

2. Write the difference.

9 − 3 = __6__

3. Write the difference.

__8__ = 11 − 3

4. Write the difference.

$$\begin{array}{r} 8 \\ -\ 1 \\ \hline 7 \end{array}$$

Go On

Name________________________ CHAPTER 6 POSTTEST

Write the correct answer.

5. Write the difference.

$$\begin{array}{r} 12 \\ -\ 2 \\ \hline 10 \end{array}$$

6. Write the difference.

$$\begin{array}{r} 10 \\ -\ 3 \\ \hline 7 \end{array}$$

7. Use cubes and cubes to add.

$$\begin{array}{r} 5 \\ +5 \\ \hline 10 \end{array}$$

8. Use cubes and crossed-out cubes to subtract.

$$\begin{array}{r} 6 \\ -3 \\ \hline 3 \end{array}$$

9. Write a number sentence to match the story.

There are 11 seashells. 3 seashells are washed away. How many seashells are there now?

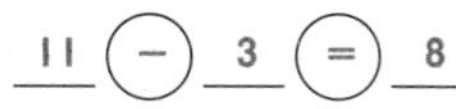

__11__ (−) __3__ (=) __8__

__8__ seashells

10. Write a number sentence to match the story.

There are 10 fish. 1 fish swims away. How many fish are there now?

__10__ (−) __1__ (=) __9__

__9__ fish

Stop

Name________________________ CHAPTER 7 POSTTEST

Write the correct answer.

1. Write the numbers in the fact family.

7 + 3 = 10 10 − 3 = 7

3 + 7 = 10 10 − 7 = 3

[3] [7] [10]

2. Circle the ways to make 11.

8 + 4

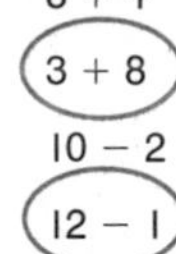

(3 + 8)

10 − 2

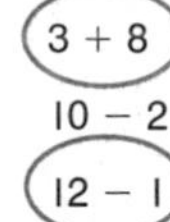

(12 − 1)

3. Write the sum. Then write the related addition fact.

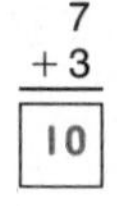

$$\begin{array}{r} 7 \\ +3 \\ \hline 10 \end{array}$$

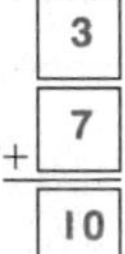

$$\begin{array}{r} 3 \\ +7 \\ \hline 10 \end{array}$$

4. Write the numbers and a number sentence to show how many flowers there are.

__4__ gray flowers

__6__ white flowers

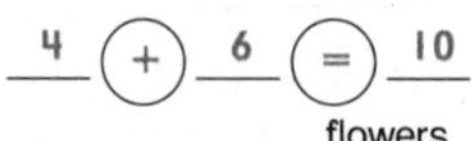

__4__ (+) __6__ (=) __10__ flowers

Go On

Name________________________ CHAPTER 7 POSTTEST

Write the correct answer.

5. Complete the fact family.

[7] + 5 = 12

5 + 7 = [12]

12 − [5] = 7

[12] − [7] = [5]

6. Follow the rule to complete the table.

Subtract 3	
11	8
10	7
8	5

7. Circle the pair of related subtraction facts?

$$\begin{array}{r} 11 \\ -\ 3 \\ \hline 8 \end{array} \quad \begin{array}{r} 11 \\ -\ 3 \\ \hline 7 \end{array} \quad \begin{array}{r} 12 \\ -\ 3 \\ \hline 6 \end{array} \quad \begin{array}{r} 12 \\ -\ 3 \\ \hline 6 \end{array} \quad \begin{array}{r} 10 \\ -\ 3 \\ \hline 7 \end{array} \quad \begin{array}{r} 10 \\ -\ 7 \\ \hline 3 \end{array} \quad \begin{array}{r} 12 \\ -\ 5 \\ \hline 7 \end{array} \quad \begin{array}{r} 11 \\ -\ 4 \\ \hline 7 \end{array}$$

(Circled: 10 − 3 = 7 and 10 − 7 = 3)

8. Draw a picture to solve.

There are 12 blue jays. Some blue jays fly away. There are 4 blue jays left. How many blue jays flew away?

Check children's work.

__8__ blue jays

9. Draw a picture to solve.

There are 11 frogs. Some frogs hop away. There are 5 frogs left. How many frogs hopped away?

Check children's work.

__6__ frogs

Stop

Name ______ UNIT 2 POSTTEST

Write the correct answer.

1. Write the doubles fact.

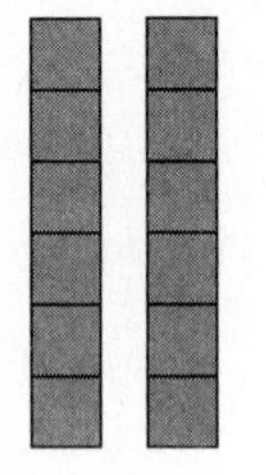

6 (+) 6 (=) 12

2. Draw a picture to solve. There are 7 dolphins. Some dolphins swim away. There are 4 dolphins left. How many dolphins swam away?

Check children's work.

3 dolphins

3. Follow the rule to complete the table.

Subtract 2	
10	8
11	9
12	10

4. Write the numbers in the fact family.

4 + 7 = 11 11 − 7 = 4

7 + 4 = 11 11 − 4 = 7

4 7 11

Go On

Name ______ UNIT 2 POSTTEST

Write the correct answer.

Use the number line to answer questions 5 and 6.

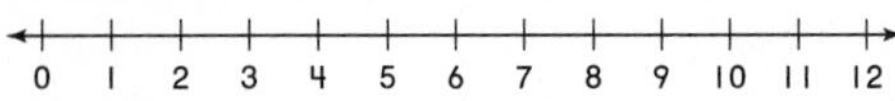

5. What is the sum?

$$\begin{array}{r} 9 \\ +3 \\ \hline 12 \end{array}$$

6. What is the sum?

$$\begin{array}{r} 5 \\ +1 \\ \hline 6 \end{array}$$

7. What is the difference?

$$\begin{array}{r} 9 \\ -4 \\ \hline 5 \end{array}$$

8. Use and to add.

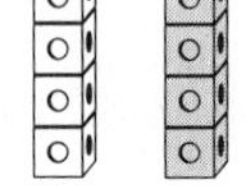

$$\begin{array}{r} 7 \\ -4 \\ \hline 11 \end{array}$$

9. Circle the pair of related subtraction facts.

(circled) 6 − 2 = 4, 6 + 4 = 2 | 10 − 6 = 4, 11 − 4 = 7 | 9 − 5 = 4, 9 − 6 = 3 | 7 − 3 = 4, 7 − 5 = 2

Go On

Name ______ UNIT 2 POSTTEST

Write the correct answer.

10. Count on. Write the sum.

5 + 1 = 6

11. Write a number sentence to match the story.

There are 10 green leaves. There are 6 orange leaves. How many more green leaves are there than orange leaves?

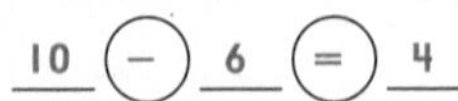

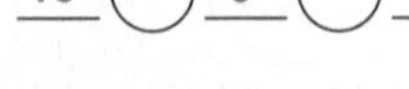

10 (−) 6 (=) 4

4 green leaves

12. Write the sum. Then write the related addition fact.

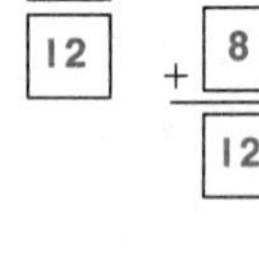

$$\begin{array}{r} 8 \\ +4 \\ \hline 12 \end{array} \qquad \begin{array}{r} 4 \\ +8 \\ \hline 12 \end{array}$$

13. Circle the ways to make 11.

(12 − 1)

5 + 5

11 − 1

(5 + 6)

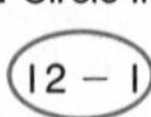

14. Count on. Write the sum.

$$\begin{array}{r} 4 \\ +3 \\ \hline 7 \end{array}$$

Go On

Name ______ UNIT 2 POSTTEST

Write the correct answer.

Use the number line to answer questions 15 and 16.

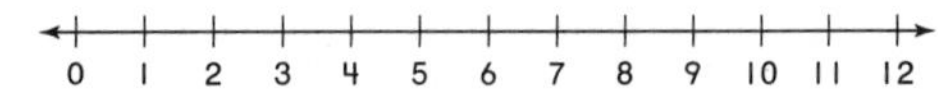

15. Write the difference.

$$\begin{array}{r} 11 \\ -1 \\ \hline 10 \end{array}$$

16. Write the difference.

9 − 3 = 6

17. Follow the rule to complete the table.

Subtract 3	
7	4
8	5
9	6

18. Write the doubles plus one fact.

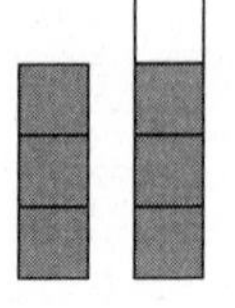

3 (+) 4 (=) 7

Go On

Name

UNIT 2 POSTTEST

Write the correct answer.

19. Complete the fact family.

[7] + 5 = 12

5 + 7 = [12]

12 − [5] = 7

[12] − [7] = [5]

20. Write the sum.

4 + 5 = 9

21. Write the number sentence that shows how many bears there are.

5 gray bears

6 white bears

5 (+) 6 (=) 11

22. Write the number sentence that matches the story.

There are 10 ladybugs. 3 ladybugs fly away. How many ladybugs are there now?

10 (−) 3 (=) 7

7 ladybugs

Go On

Name

UNIT 2 POSTTEST

Write the correct answer.

23. Use and to subtract.

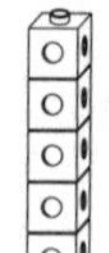

$$\begin{array}{r} 7 \\ -2 \\ \hline 5 \end{array}$$

24. Write the numbers in the fact family.

5 + 4 = 9 9 − 4 = 5

4 + 5 = 9 9 − 5 = 4

[4] [5] [9]

25. There are 8 seals. Some seals swim away. There are 6 seals left. How many seals swam away?

2 seals

26. There are 7 socks in all. 2 socks are green. The other socks are white. How many socks are white?

5 socks

Stop

Name

CHAPTER 8 POSTTEST

Write the correct answer.

1. Write A, B, or C to show the group the figure belongs in.

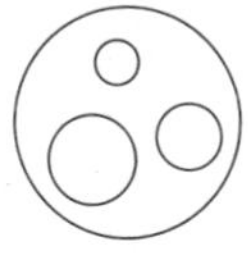
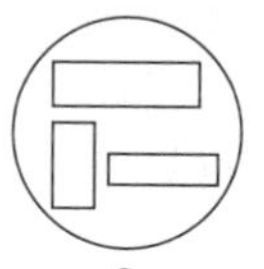

A B C

A

2. How many more children chose 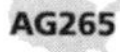 than ?

Animals We Like								
fish	🐟	🐟	🐟	🐟	🐟	🐟		
turtle	🐢	🐢	🐢	🐢				
cat	🐱	🐱	🐱	🐱	🐱	🐱	🐱	🐱

2 more children

Go On

Name

CHAPTER 8 POSTTEST

Write the correct answer.

3. Circle which belongs in the group.

Use the picture graph to answer questions 5 and 6.

Kinds of Birds											
hawk	🦅	🦅	🦅	🦅	🦅	🦅	🦅	🦅	🦅		
peacock	🦚	🦚	🦚	🦚	🦚	🦚					
blue bird	🐦	🐦	🐦	🐦	🐦	🐦	🐦	🐦	🐦	🐦	🐦

4. How many hawks are there?

9 hawks

5. How many fewer peacocks are there than blue birds?

5 fewer peacocks

Stop

Name ______ CHAPTER 9 POSTTEST

Write the correct answer.

1. Circle the bear you are more likely to pull from the bowl.

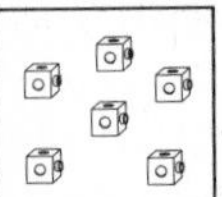

2. Use the tally chart to answer the question.

Pets We Like	
dog	𝍸 III
cat	III
fish	𝍸 II

Write how many children chose the fish.

7 children

3. Color the cubes to make the sentence true. It is **possible** to pull a gray cube.

The drawing must include at least 1 gray cube.

Form B • Free Response AG269 Assessment Guide © Harcourt • Grade 1

Name ______ CHAPTER 9 POSTTEST

Write the correct answer.

Use the bar graph to answer questions 4 and 5.

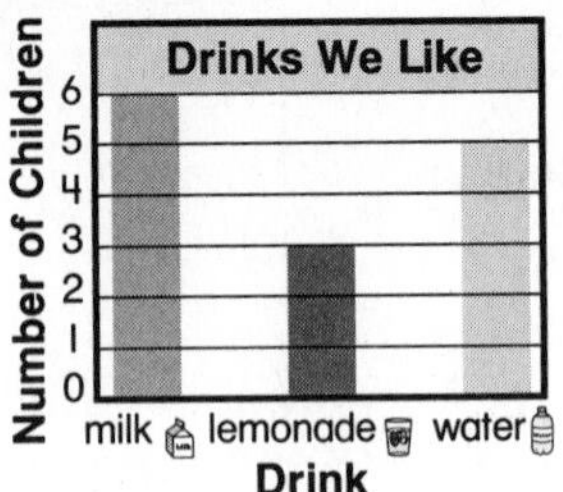

4. Write how many children chose water.

5 children

5. Circle which drink the most children chose.

6. There are 7 white cubes and 4 gray cubes in a bowl. Circle the color you are more likely to pull.

7. There are 6 black cubes and 1 white cube in a bag. Circle the color you are more likely to pull.

Stop

Assessment Guide AG270 Form B • Free Response © Harcourt • Grade 1

Name ______ CHAPTER 10 PRETEST

Write the correct answer.

1. Count how many tens and ones. Write the number.

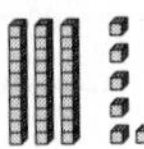

3 tens 6 ones

= 36

2. Count how many tens and ones. Write the number in a different way.

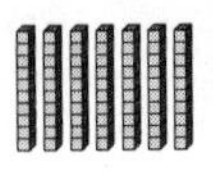

7 tens 9 ones

70 + 9

3. Count by tens. Write the number.

7 tens 

70

4. Write the number of tens and ones.

18 eighteen

1 tens 8 ones

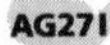

Form B • Free Response AG271 Assessment Guide © Harcourt • Grade 1

Name ______ CHAPTER 10 PRETEST

Write the correct answer.

5. Count how many tens and ones. Write the number.

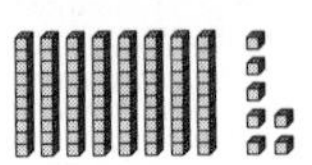

8 tens 7 ones

= 87

6. Count how many tens and ones. Write the number in a different way.

4 tens 2 ones

40 + 2

7. Circle the closest estimate.

About how many pennies can you hold in one hand?

about 9 

about 90 

about 900 

8. Circle the closest estimate.

About how many paper clips would fit in one cup?

about 3

about 30

about 300 (circled)

Stop

Assessment Guide AG272 Form B • Free Response © Harcourt • Grade 1

Name ______________________ CHAPTER 11 POSTTEST

Write the correct answer.

1. Write the numbers.

57 is greater than 49.

2. Write the number that is between 88 and 90.

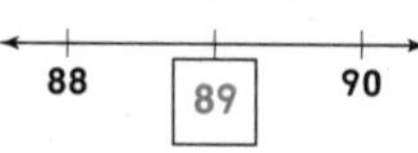

3. Compare the numbers. Write <, >, or =.

39 (>) 34

4. Write the numbers in order from least to greatest.

38 63 36

36 38 63

5. Write the number that is one less than 74.

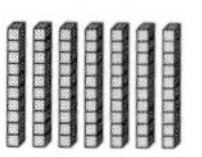

73

Go On

Name ______________________ CHAPTER 11 POSTTEST

Write the correct answer.

6. Write the numbers.

64 is less than 68.

7. Write the number that is ten more than 62.

72

Use the table to answer questions 8 and 9.

Month	Sunny Days
March	21
April	17
May	28
June	23

8. Compare the number of sunny days for the given months. Write the numbers.

21 (<) 23
March June

9. Write the number of sunny days in order from greatest to least.

28 23 21 17

Stop

Name ______________________ CHAPTER 12 POSTTEST

Write the correct answer.

Use the hundred chart for questions 1 and 2.

1	2	3	4	5	6	7	8	9	10
11	12	13	14	15	16	17	18	19	20
21	22	23	24	25	26	27	28	29	30
31	32	33	34	35	36	37	38	39	40
41	42	43	44	45	46	47	48	49	50
51	52	53	54	55	56	57	58	59	60
61	62	63	64	65	66	67	68	69	70
71	72	73	74	75	76	77	78	79	80
81	82	83	84	85	86	87	88	89	90
91	92	93	94	95	96	97	98	99	100

1. Count by twos. Write the number that comes next.

56, 58, 60, 62, 64, 64

2. Count by tens. Write the numbers that come next.

6, 16, 26, 36, 46, 56

3. Skip count. Write how many toes there are.

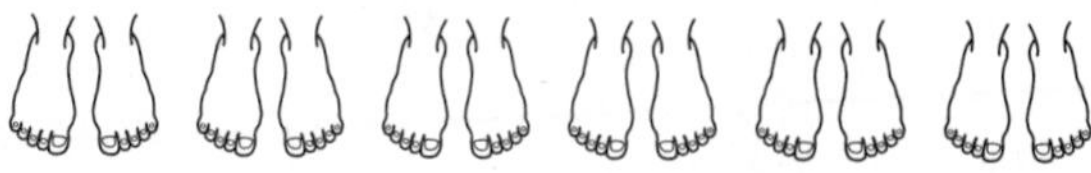

10 20 30 40 50 60 toes

Go On

Name ______________________ CHAPTER 12 POSTTEST

Write the correct answer.

4. Count forward. Write the numbers that come next.

82, 83, 84, 85, 86, 87

5. Find the pattern. Write the missing numbers.

34, 36, 38, 40, 42, 44

6. Is the number odd or even? Circle even or odd.

17 even (odd)

7. There are 2 wheels on a bicycle. Write how many wheels there are on 7 bicycles.

number of bicycles	1	2	3	4	5	6	7
number of wheels	2	4	6	8	10	12	14

14 wheels

Stop

Name ______________________ UNIT 3 POSTTEST

Write the correct answer.

1. Write the number that is between 71 and 73.

71 [72] 73

2. Count by tens. Write the number.

6 tens

60

3. Use the tally chart to answer the question.

Sports We Like	
soccer	𝍸 I
baseball	𝍸 III
swimming	𝍸 IIII

Write how many children chose swimming.

9 children

4. Count how many tens and ones. Write the number in a different way.

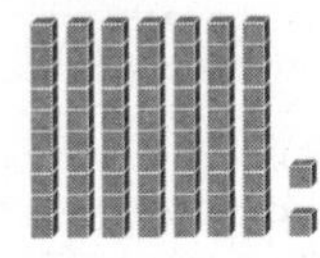

7 tens 2 ones

70 + 2

Go On

Name ______________________ UNIT 3 POSTTEST

Write the correct answer.

Use the hundred chart for questions 5 and 6.

1	2	3	4	5	6	7	8	9	10
11	12	13	14	15	16	17	18	19	20
21	22	23	24	25	26	27	28	29	30
31	32	33	34	35	36	37	38	39	40
41	42	43	44	45	46	47	48	49	50
51	52	53	54	55	56	57	58	59	60
61	62	63	64	65	66	67	68	69	70
71	72	73	74	75	76	77	78	79	80
81	82	83	84	85	86	87	88	89	90
91	92	93	94	95	96	97	98	99	100

5. Count by fives. Write the number that comes next.

35, 40, 45, 50, 55, 60

6. Count by tens. Write the numbers that come next.

21, 31, 41, 51, 61, 71

Go On

Name ______________________ UNIT 3 POSTTEST

Write the correct answer.

7. Circle which belongs in the group.

8. Color the cubes to make the sentence true. It is **possible** to pull a black cube.

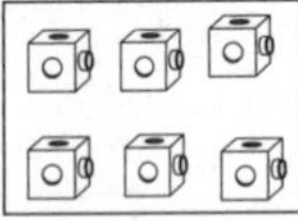

The drawing must contain at least one black cube.

9. There are 2 wheels on a scooter. Write how many wheels there are on 7 scooters.

number of scooters	1	2	3	4	5	6	7
number of wheels	2	4					

7 scooters have 14 wheels.

Go On

Name ______________________ UNIT 3 POSTTEST

Write the correct answer.

10. Write the numbers.

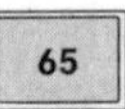

65 is less than 72.

65 < 72

11. There are 2 ▢ and 6 ▢ in a bag. Circle which color you are more likely to pull.

Use the table to answer questions 12 and 13.

Team	Points Scored
Jays	55
Wolves	65
Lions	49
Mammoths	63

12. Write the team that scored more points.

55 (<) 65

Jays Wolves

Wolves

13. Write the team that scored the least number of points.

65 63 55 49

greatest least

Lions

Go On

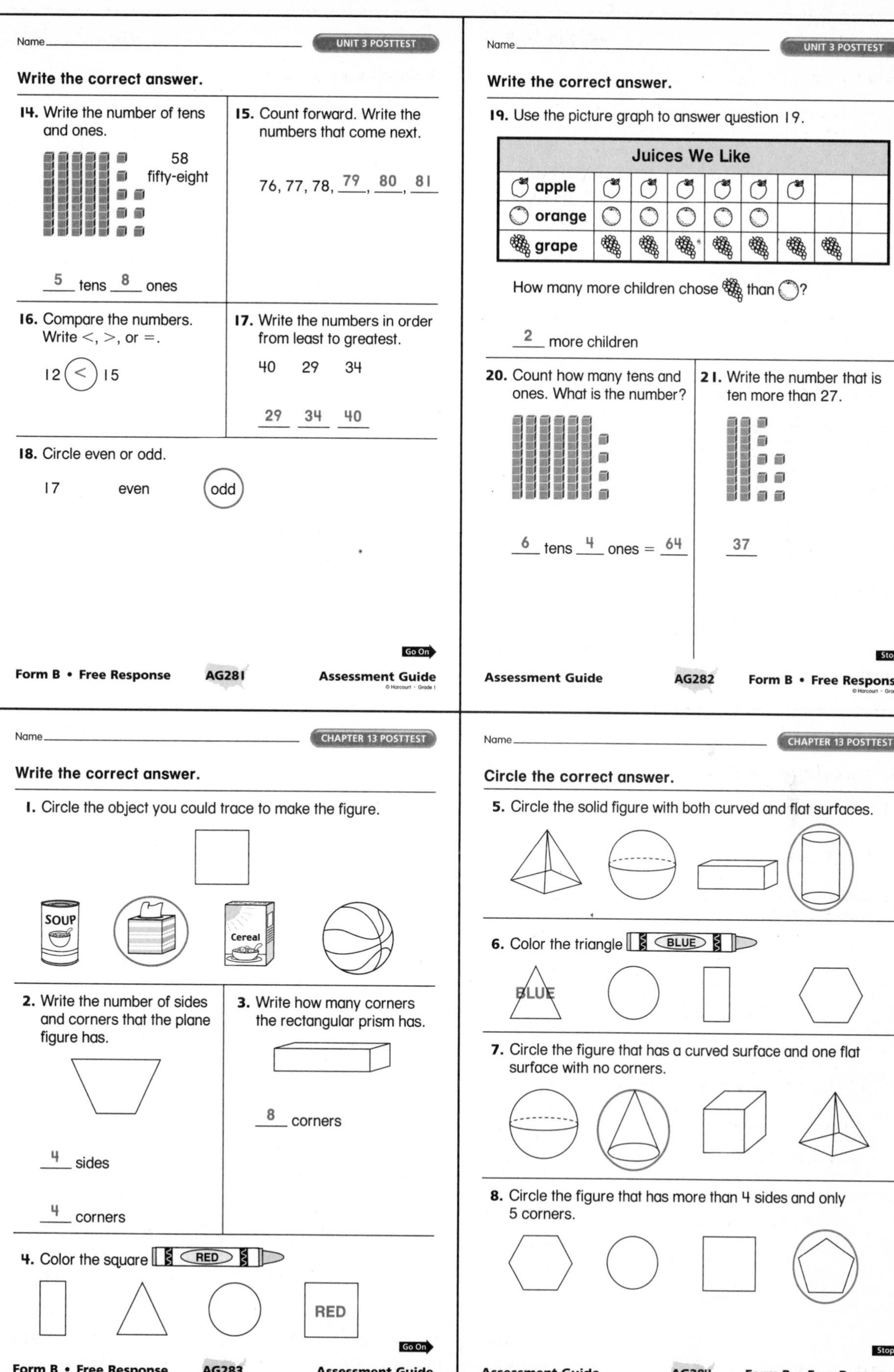

Name ______ UNIT 3 POSTTEST

Write the correct answer.

14. Write the number of tens and ones.

58
fifty-eight

5 tens 8 ones

15. Count forward. Write the numbers that come next.

76, 77, 78, 79, 80, 81

16. Compare the numbers. Write <, >, or =.

12 (<) 15

17. Write the numbers in order from least to greatest.

40 29 34

29 34 40

18. Circle even or odd.

17 even (odd)

Go On

Form B • Free Response AG281 Assessment Guide
© Harcourt • Grade 1

Name ______ UNIT 3 POSTTEST

Write the correct answer.

19. Use the picture graph to answer question 19.

Juices We Like								
apple	🍎	🍎	🍎	🍎	🍎	🍎		
orange	🍊	🍊	🍊	🍊	🍊			
grape	🍇	🍇	🍇	🍇	🍇	🍇	🍇	

How many more children chose grape than orange?

2 more children

20. Count how many tens and ones. What is the number?

6 tens 4 ones = 64

21. Write the number that is ten more than 27.

37

Stop

Assessment Guide AG282 Form B • Free Response
© Harcourt • Grade 1

Name ______ CHAPTER 13 POSTTEST

Write the correct answer.

1. Circle the object you could trace to make the figure.

SOUP
Cereal

2. Write the number of sides and corners that the plane figure has.

4 sides

4 corners

3. Write how many corners the rectangular prism has.

8 corners

4. Color the square RED

RED

Go On

Form B • Free Response AG283 Assessment Guide
© Harcourt • Grade 1

Name ______ CHAPTER 13 POSTTEST

Circle the correct answer.

5. Circle the solid figure with both curved and flat surfaces.

6. Color the triangle BLUE

BLUE

7. Circle the figure that has a curved surface and one flat surface with no corners.

8. Circle the figure that has more than 4 sides and only 5 corners.

Stop

Assessment Guide AG284 Form B • Free Response
© Harcourt • Grade 1

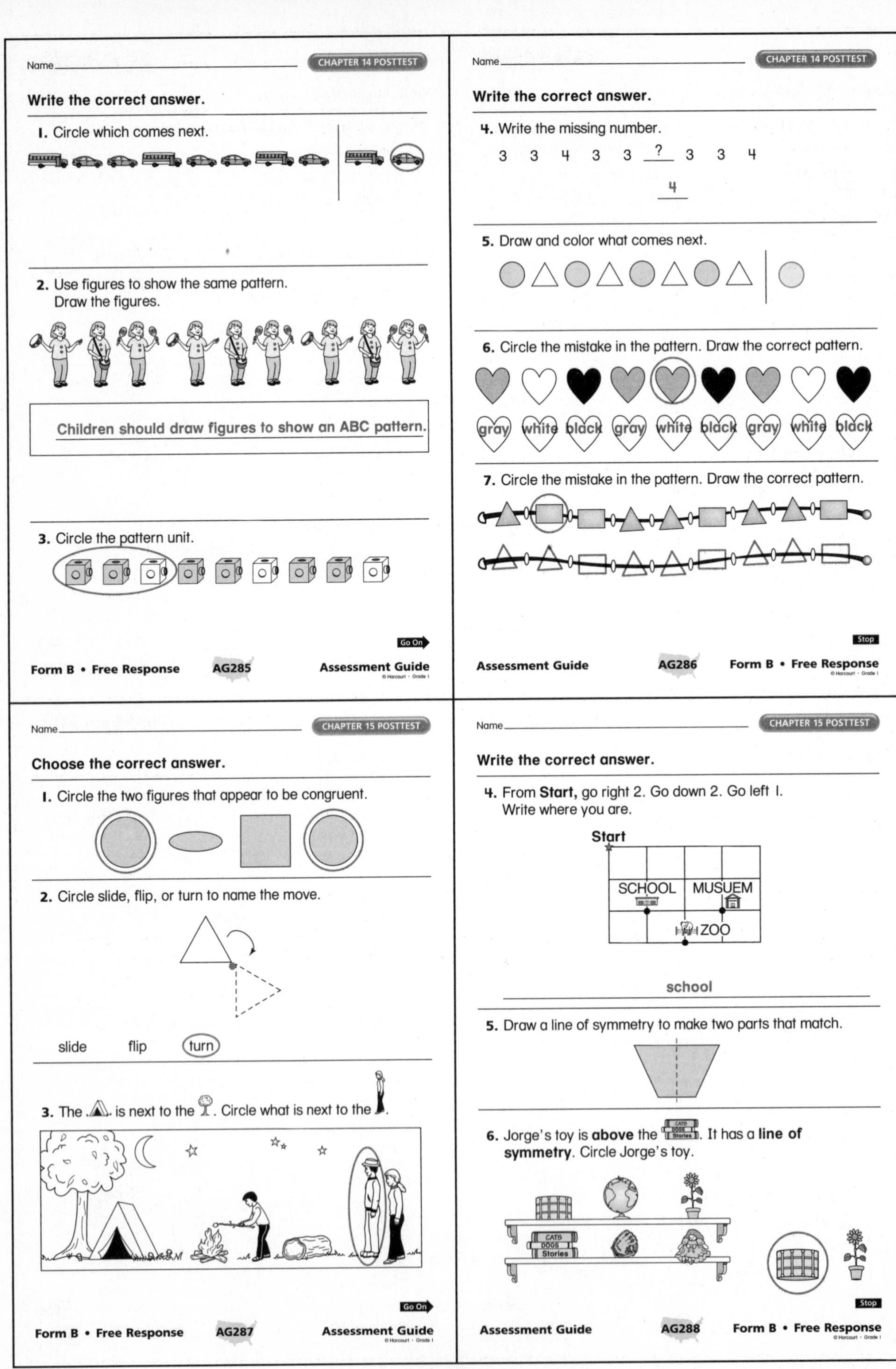

Name

CHAPTER 14 POSTTEST

Write the correct answer.

1. Circle which comes next.

2. Use figures to show the same pattern.
Draw the figures.

Children should draw figures to show an ABC pattern.

3. Circle the pattern unit.

Go On

Form B • Free Response AG285 Assessment Guide
© Harcourt • Grade 1

Name

CHAPTER 14 POSTTEST

Write the correct answer.

4. Write the missing number.

3 3 4 3 3 ? 3 3 4

4

5. Draw and color what comes next.

6. Circle the mistake in the pattern. Draw the correct pattern.

gray white black gray white black gray white black

7. Circle the mistake in the pattern. Draw the correct pattern.

Stop

Assessment Guide AG286 Form B • Free Response
© Harcourt • Grade 1

Name

CHAPTER 15 POSTTEST

Choose the correct answer.

1. Circle the two figures that appear to be congruent.

2. Circle slide, flip, or turn to name the move.

slide flip turn

3. The tent is next to the tree. Circle what is next to the person.

Go On

Form B • Free Response AG287 Assessment Guide
© Harcourt • Grade 1

Name

CHAPTER 15 POSTTEST

Write the correct answer.

4. From **Start,** go right 2. Go down 2. Go left 1.
Write where you are.

Start

SCHOOL MUSUEM

ZOO

school

5. Draw a line of symmetry to make two parts that match.

6. Jorge's toy is **above** the books. It has a **line of symmetry**. Circle Jorge's toy.

CATS
DOGS
Stories

Stop

Assessment Guide AG288 Form B • Free Response
© Harcourt • Grade 1

Name ______________________ CHAPTER 16 POSTTEST

Write the correct answer.

1. Find the figure that is divided into two equal parts. Color $\frac{1}{2}$ of the figure.

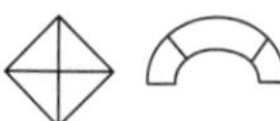

2. Use [BLUE crayon]. Color to show $\frac{1}{4}$. Complete the sentence.

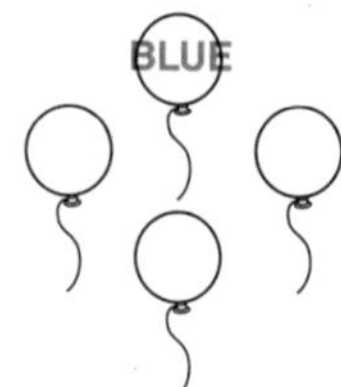

1 out of 4 balloons is blue.

3. Circle the figures with equal parts. Cross out the figures with unequal parts.

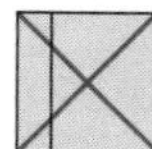
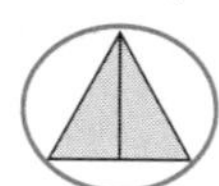
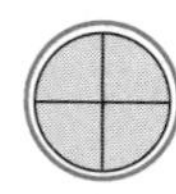

4. Find the figure that is divided into four equal parts. Color $\frac{1}{4}$ of the figure.

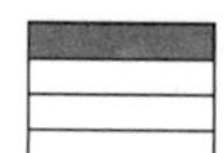

Go On

Name ______________________ CHAPTER 16 POSTTEST

Write the correct answer.

5. Find the figure that is divided into three equal parts. Color $\frac{1}{3}$ of the figure.

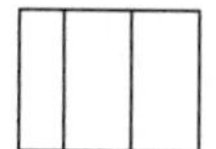
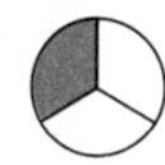

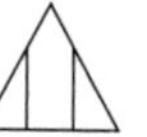
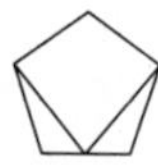

6. Jon and a friend share a pizza. Each gets an equal share. Circle how you would cut the pizza.

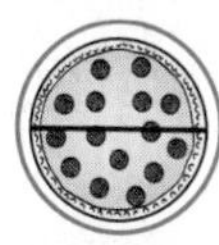
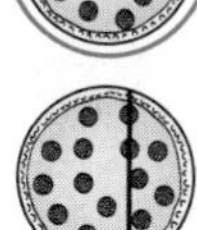

7. Ruby, Angie, and Sam share a pizza. Each gets an equal share. Circle how you would cut the pizza.

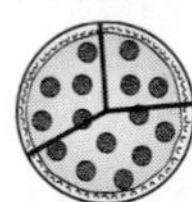

Stop

Name ______________________ UNIT 4 POSTTEST

Write the correct answer.

1. Write the number of sides and corners the plane figure has.

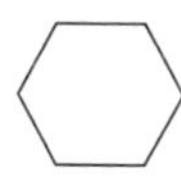

6 sides

6 corners

2. Circle slide, flip, or turn to name the move.

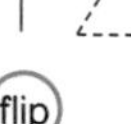

slide (flip) turn

3. Circle the figures with equal parts. Cross out the figures with unequal parts.

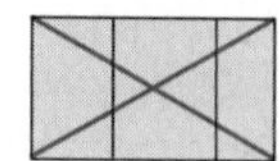
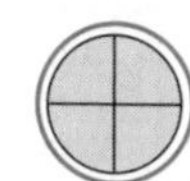
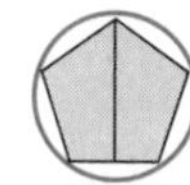

4. Color the triangle [RED crayon].

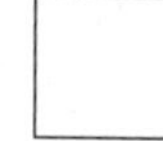

Go On

Name ______________________ UNIT 4 POSTTEST

Write the correct answer.

5. Circle which comes next.

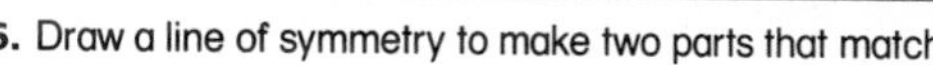

6. Draw a line of symmetry to make two parts that match.

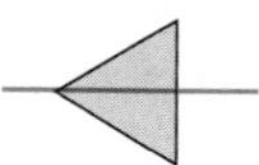

7. Find the figure that is divided into four equal parts. Color $\frac{1}{4}$ of the figure.

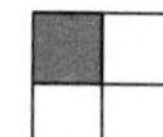
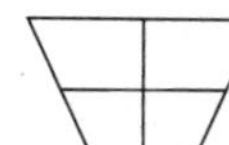

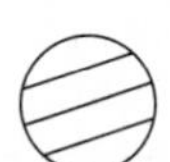

8. Circle the object you could trace to make the figure.

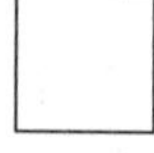

Go On

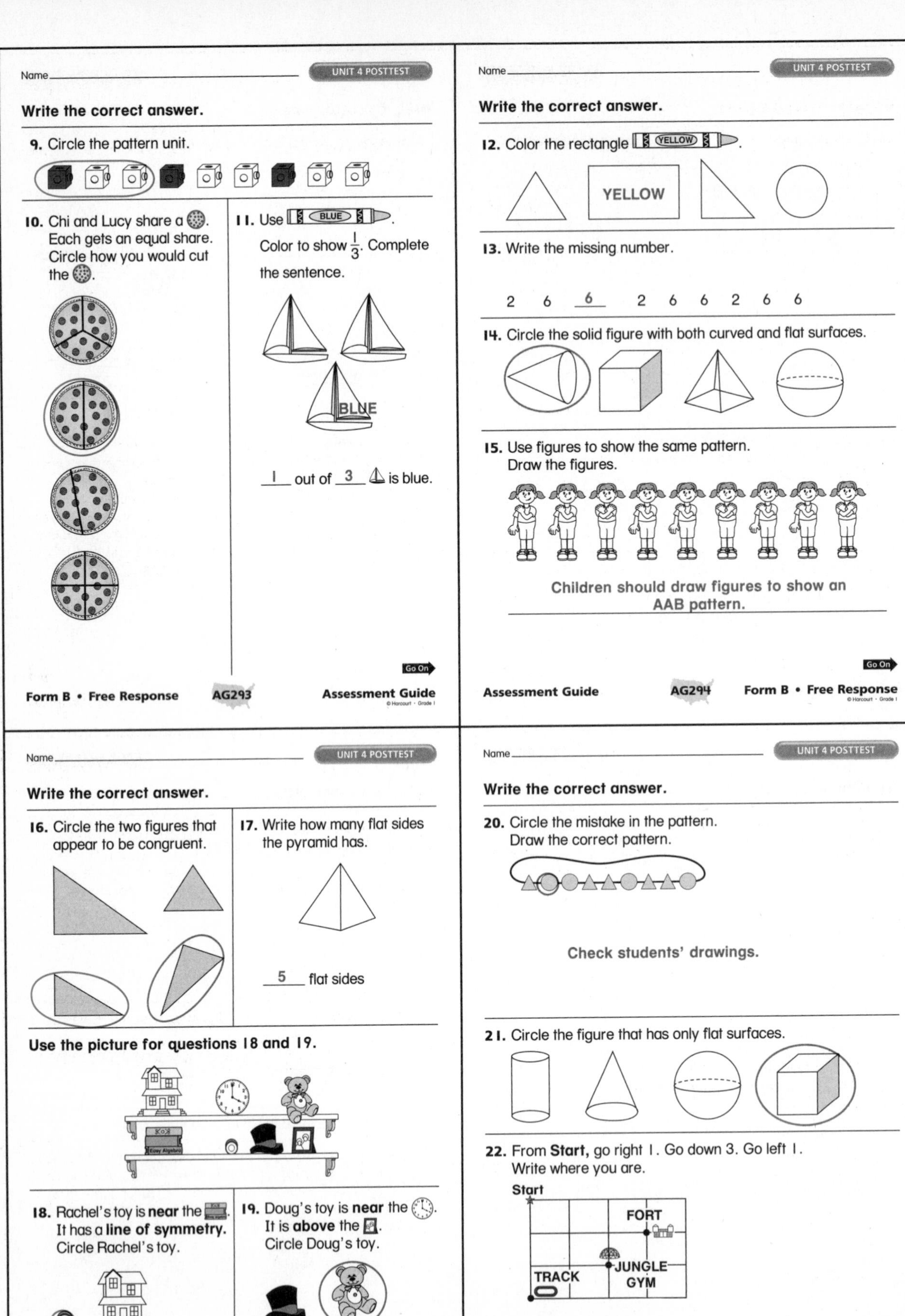

Name

UNIT 4 POSTTEST

Write the correct answer.

9. Circle the pattern unit.

10. Chi and Lucy share a pizza. Each gets an equal share. Circle how you would cut the pizza.

11. Use BLUE. Color to show $\frac{1}{3}$. Complete the sentence.

BLUE

1 out of 3 is blue.

Go On

Form B • Free Response AG293 Assessment Guide © Harcourt · Grade 1

Name

UNIT 4 POSTTEST

Write the correct answer.

12. Color the rectangle YELLOW.

YELLOW

13. Write the missing number.

2 6 6 2 6 6 2 6 6

14. Circle the solid figure with both curved and flat surfaces.

15. Use figures to show the same pattern. Draw the figures.

Children should draw figures to show an AAB pattern.

Go On

Assessment Guide AG294 Form B • Free Response © Harcourt · Grade 1

Name

UNIT 4 POSTTEST

Write the correct answer.

16. Circle the two figures that appear to be congruent.

17. Write how many flat sides the pyramid has.

5 flat sides

Use the picture for questions 18 and 19.

Easy Algebra

18. Rachel's toy is **near** the book. It has a **line of symmetry.** Circle Rachel's toy.

19. Doug's toy is **near** the clock. It is **above** the picture. Circle Doug's toy.

Go On

Form B • Free Response AG295 Assessment Guide © Harcourt · Grade 1

Name

UNIT 4 POSTTEST

Write the correct answer.

20. Circle the mistake in the pattern. Draw the correct pattern.

Check students' drawings.

21. Circle the figure that has only flat surfaces.

22. From **Start,** go right 1. Go down 3. Go left 1. Write where you are.

Start

FORT

JUNGLE GYM

TRACK

track

Stop

Assessment Guide AG296 Form B • Free Response © Harcourt · Grade 1

Name ______________________ CHAPTER 17 POSTTEST

Write the correct answer.

1. Write the sum.

$$\begin{array}{r} 7 \\ +7 \\ \hline \end{array}$$

14

2. Make a ten and add. Write the sum.

$$\begin{array}{r} 8 \\ +6 \\ \hline \end{array}$$

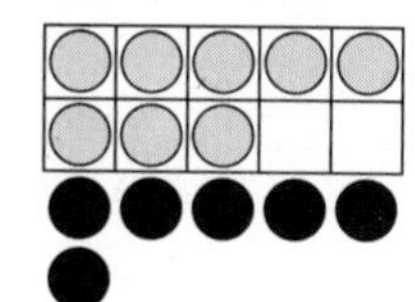

14

3. Write the sum.

$$\begin{array}{r} 8 \\ +9 \\ \hline \end{array}$$

17

4. Write the sum.

$$\begin{array}{r} 2 \\ 3 \\ +8 \\ \hline \end{array}$$

13

Go On

Name ______________________ CHAPTER 17 POSTTEST

Write the correct answer.

5. Write the sum.

$$\begin{array}{r} 10 \\ +5 \\ \hline \end{array}$$

15

6. Make a ten and add. Write the sum.

$$\begin{array}{r} 9 \\ +6 \\ \hline \end{array}$$

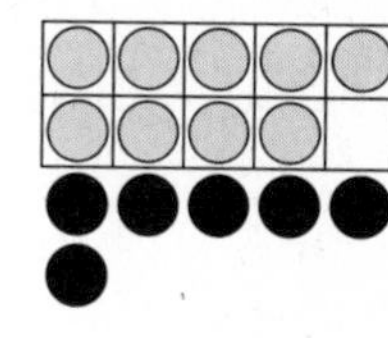

15

7. Write the sum.

8 + 8 = 16

8. Write a number sentence to solve.
8 firefighters arrive at a fire. 4 more firefighters join them. How many firefighters are at the fire now?

8 (+) 4 (=) 12

12 firefighters

9. Write a number sentence to solve.
A mail carrier delivers 7 letters. Then he delivers 6 more letters. How many letters does the mail carrier deliver in all?

7 (+) 6 (=) 13

13 letters

Stop

Name ______________________ CHAPTER 18 POSTTEST

Write the correct answer.

Use the number line to answer questions 1 and 2.

1. Write the difference.

$$\begin{array}{r} 15 \\ -\ 7 \\ \hline 8 \end{array}$$

2. Write the difference.

$$\begin{array}{r} 13 \\ -\ 6 \\ \hline 7 \end{array}$$

3. Write how many more birds there are than nests.

$$\begin{array}{r} 14 \\ -\ 7 \\ \hline 7 \end{array}$$

4. Write the difference.

17 − 8 = 9

Go On

Name ______________________ CHAPTER 18 POSTTEST

Write the correct answer.

5. Use the addition fact to help you subtract. Write the sum. Then write the difference.

$$\begin{array}{r} 9 \\ +6 \\ \hline 15 \end{array} \qquad \begin{array}{r} 15 \\ -\ 6 \\ \hline 9 \end{array}$$

6. Write the difference.

$$\begin{array}{r} 13 \\ -\ 8 \\ \hline 5 \end{array}$$

7. Write how many fewer butterflies there are than flowers.

$$\begin{array}{r} 14 \\ -\ 8 \\ \hline 6 \end{array}$$

8. There are 14 children playing on the playground. 6 children go home. Write how many children are playing on the playground now.

8 children

9. Peter counted birds at the park. He counted 8 wrens and 9 robins. Write how many birds Peter counted in all.

17 birds

Stop

Name

CHAPTER 19 POSTTEST

Write the correct answer.

1. Write the missing number.

$$\begin{array}{r} 7 \\ + \boxed{6} \\ \hline 13 \end{array} \qquad \begin{array}{r} 13 \\ - 7 \\ \hline \boxed{6} \end{array}$$

2. Write a way to make 15.

Possible answer:
4 + 6 + 5

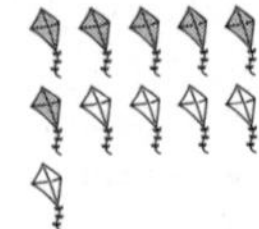

3. Use the picture to write the numbers. Write a number sentence to show how many kites there are.

6 gray kites

5 white kites

6 (+) 5 (=) 11

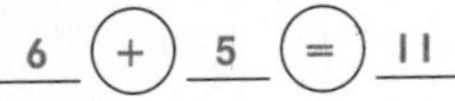

4. Write the missing numbers.

$$\begin{array}{r} 5 \\ + \boxed{7} \\ \hline \boxed{12} \end{array} \qquad \begin{array}{r} 12 \\ - 5 \\ \hline \boxed{7} \end{array}$$

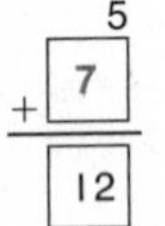

Go On

Name

CHAPTER 19 POSTTEST

Write the correct answer.

5. Write a way to make 9.

Possible answer:
14 – 5

6. Follow the rule. Write the number that completes the table.

Subtract 9	
12	3
14	5
16	7
17	8

7. Write each sum or difference. Circle the facts in the same fact family.

(8 + 7 = 15) (15 − 7 = 8) 13 − 7 = 6 (7 + 8 = 15) (15 − 8 = 7)

8. Write a number sentence to solve.
Jamie has 7 peppers. Aidan brings 7 more peppers. How many peppers are there in all?

7 (+) 7 (=) 14

14 peppers

9. Write a number sentence to solve.
A store has 15 watermelons. Gina buys 8 of them. How many watermelons are still at the store?

15 (−) 8 (=) 7

7 watermelons

Stop

Name

CHAPTER 20 POSTTEST

Write the correct answer.

1. Draw and label coins to show the amount in a different way.

Check children's drawings. Possible answer: 6 dimes.

2. Use quarters and dimes. Draw and label coins to show a way to make 1 dollar.

Check children's drawings. Drawings should show 2 quarters and 5 dimes.

Go On

Name

CHAPTER 20 POSTTEST

Write the correct answer.

3. Count. Compare the amounts. Write <, >, or =.

51 ¢ (<) 55 ¢

4. Charlie buys a teddy bear for 50¢. He uses 2 . Draw and label coins to show the same amount in a different way.

Check children's drawings. Possible answer: 5 dimes

Stop

Name ____________________ CHAPTER 21 POSTTEST

Write the correct answer.

1. Write the time.

2. Write the time.

5:00

3. Use the calendar. Write how many days are in this month.

JUNE						
Sunday	Monday	Tuesday	Wednesday	Thursday	Friday	Saturday
					1	2
3	4	5	6	7	8	9
10	11	12	13	14	15	16
17	18	19	20	21	22	23
24	25	26	27	28	29	30

30 days

Go On

Name ____________________ CHAPTER 21 POSTTEST

Write the correct answer.

4. Draw the hour hand and minute hand to show the time.

10:30

Use the table to answer questions 5 and 6.

Field Day		
Event	Start	End
sack race		
relay race		
tug-of-war		

5. Which event starts at 10:30?

relay race

6. Which event lasts the shortest time?

tug-of-war

Stop

Name ____________________ UNIT 5 POSTTEST

Write the correct answer.

1. Use the calendar. Write how many days are in this month.

March						
Sunday	Monday	Tuesday	Wednesday	Thursday	Friday	Saturday
						1
2	3	4	5	6	7	8
9	10	11	12	13	14	15
16	17	18	19	20	21	22
23	24	25	26	27	28	29
30	31					

31 days

2. Use the addition fact to help you subtract. Write the sum. Then write the difference.

$6 + 8 = 14$ $14 - 8 = 6$

3. Write the sum.

$8 + 8 = 16$

4. Follow the rule. Write the number that completes the table.

Add 5	
6	11
8	13
9	14
10	15

Go On

Name ____________________ UNIT 5 POSTTEST

Write the correct answer.

5. Write how many fewer birds are there than leaves.

$12 - 6 = 6$

6. Use the picture to write the numbers. Write a number sentence to show how many kites are white.

11 kites in all

4 gray kites

11 − 4 = 7

7. Write the sum.

$2 + 3 + 8 = 13$

8. Circle the time of day.

morning evening

afternoon (circled)

Go On

Name ______ UNIT 5 POSTTEST

Write the correct answer.

9. Draw and label coins to show the amount a different way.

Check children's drawings. Possible answer: 5 dimes and 4 nickels.

10. Draw and label coins to show a way to make 1 dollar. Use dimes and nickels.

Check children's drawings. Possible answer: 7 dimes and 6 nickels.

11. Write the difference.

$$\begin{array}{r} 17 \\ -\ 9 \\ \hline 8 \end{array}$$

Go On

Name ______ UNIT 5 POSTTEST

Write the correct answer.

12. Write a number sentence to solve.

A woman buys 3 books. Then she buys 9 more books. How many books does the woman buy in all?

3 (+) 9 (=) 12

12 books

13. Write the missing numbers.

$$\begin{array}{r} 6 \\ +\ \boxed{10} \\ \hline 16 \end{array} \qquad \begin{array}{r} 16 \\ -\ 6 \\ \hline \boxed{10} \end{array}$$

14. Make a ten and add. Write the sum.

$$\begin{array}{r} 8 \\ +\ 7 \\ \hline 15 \end{array}$$

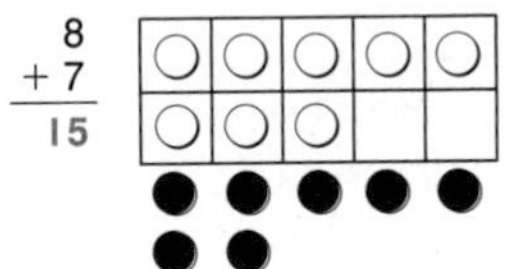

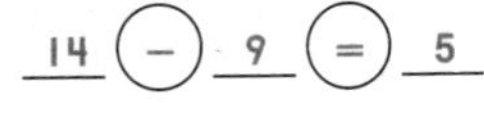

15. Write a number sentence to solve.

Pablo has 14 apples. He gives 9 apples away. How many apples does Pablo have now?

14 (−) 9 (=) 5

5 apples

Go On

Name ______ UNIT 5 POSTTEST

Write the correct answer.

16. Count. Compare the amounts. Write <, >, or =.

80 ¢ (=) 80 ¢

17. Draw the hour hand and minute hand to show the time.

18. Write the sum.

4 + 5 = 9

19. Write the difference.

10 − 8 = 2

Go On

Name ______ UNIT 5 POSTTEST

Write the correct answer.

Use the table to answer question 20.

Aquarium		
Event	Start	End
tour	(clock 10:00)	(clock 10:30)
feed turtles	(clock 11:00)	(clock 11:30)
dolphin show	(clock 2:00)	(clock 3:00)

20. Which event starts at 11:00?

feed turtles

21. Write each sum or difference. Circle the facts in the same fact family.

$$\begin{array}{r} 14 \\ -\ 5 \\ \hline 9 \end{array}$$

$$\begin{array}{r} 14 \\ -\ 9 \\ \hline 5 \end{array}$$

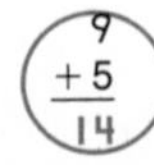

$$\begin{array}{r} 9 \\ +\ 5 \\ \hline 14 \end{array}$$

$$\begin{array}{r} 5 \\ +\ 9 \\ \hline 14 \end{array}$$

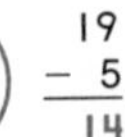

$$\begin{array}{r} 19 \\ -\ 5 \\ \hline 14 \end{array}$$

Stop

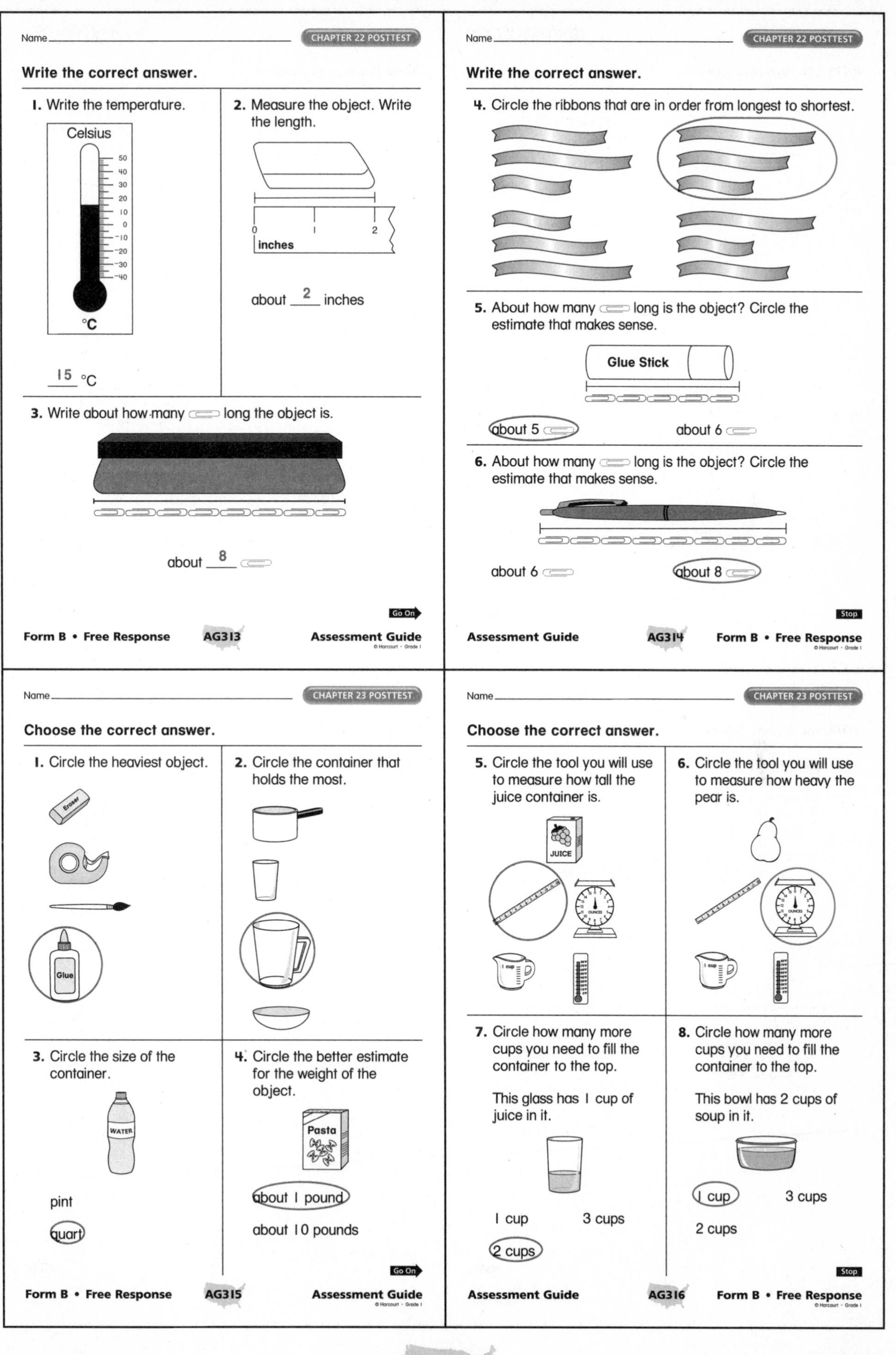

Name ______________________ CHAPTER 22 POSTTEST

Write the correct answer.

1. Write the temperature.

15 °C

2. Measure the object. Write the length.

about 2 inches

3. Write about how many long the object is.

about 8

Go On

Form B • Free Response AG313 Assessment Guide © Harcourt • Grade 1

Name ______________________ CHAPTER 22 POSTTEST

Write the correct answer.

4. Circle the ribbons that are in order from longest to shortest.

5. About how many long is the object? Circle the estimate that makes sense.

(about 5) about 6

6. About how many long is the object? Circle the estimate that makes sense.

about 6 (about 8)

Stop

Assessment Guide AG314 Form B • Free Response © Harcourt • Grade 1

Name ______________________ CHAPTER 23 POSTTEST

Choose the correct answer.

1. Circle the heaviest object.

2. Circle the container that holds the most.

3. Circle the size of the container.

pint

(quart)

4. Circle the better estimate for the weight of the object.

(about 1 pound)

about 10 pounds

Go On

Form B • Free Response AG315 Assessment Guide © Harcourt • Grade 1

Name ______________________ CHAPTER 23 POSTTEST

Choose the correct answer.

5. Circle the tool you will use to measure how tall the juice container is.

6. Circle the tool you will use to measure how heavy the pear is.

7. Circle how many more cups you need to fill the container to the top.

This glass has 1 cup of juice in it.

1 cup 3 cups

(2 cups)

8. Circle how many more cups you need to fill the container to the top.

This bowl has 2 cups of soup in it.

(1 cup) 3 cups

2 cups

Stop

Assessment Guide AG316 Form B • Free Response © Harcourt • Grade 1

Name ______________________ CHAPTER 24 POSTTEST

Write the correct answer.

1. Write the difference.

70 − 40 = 30

2. Write the sum.

30 + 50 = 80

3. Write the difference.

	tens	ones
	3	6
−		4
	3	2

Workmat (Tens, Ones)

4. Write the sum.

	tens	ones
	2	3
+		6
	2	9

Workmat (Tens, Ones)

Go On

Name ______________________ CHAPTER 24 POSTTEST

Write the correct answer.

5. Write the sum.

	tens	ones
	2	4
+	1	5
	3	9

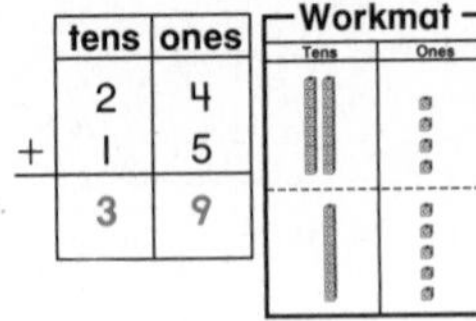

6. Write the difference.

	tens	ones
	2	7
−	1	4
	1	3

Workmat (Tens, Ones)

8. Circle the best estimate. There are 51 birds at the lake. 9 of the birds fly away. About how many birds are left?

about 4 birds

(about 40 birds) — circled

about 400 birds

9. Circle the best estimate. Brett has 41 stickers in his collection. Anna has 28 stickers in her collection. About how many stickers do they both have?

about 7 stickers

(about 70 stickers) — circled

about 700 stickers

Stop

Name ______________________ UNIT 6 POSTTEST

Write the correct answer.

1. Write the sum.

	tens	ones
	2	3
+		6

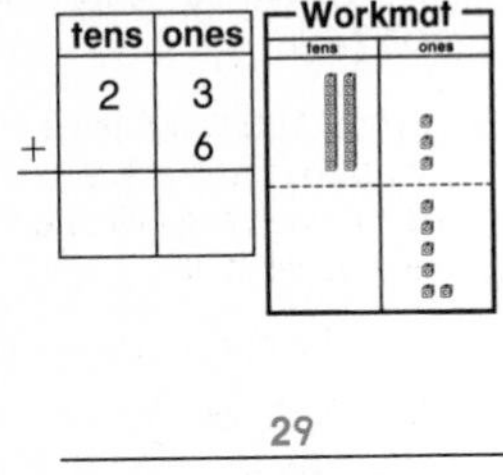

29

2. Circle the container that holds the most water.

3. Write about how many long the object is.

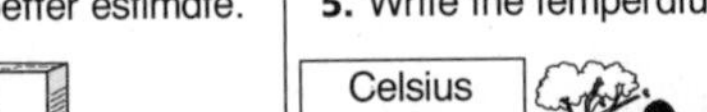

about 6

Go On

Name ______________________ UNIT 6 POSTTEST

Write the correct answer.

4. Circle the better estimate.

(about 1 pound) — circled

about 10 pounds

5. Write the temperature.

10 °C

6. Write the difference.

70 − 30 = 40

7. Circle the size of the container.

(pint) — circled quart

Go On

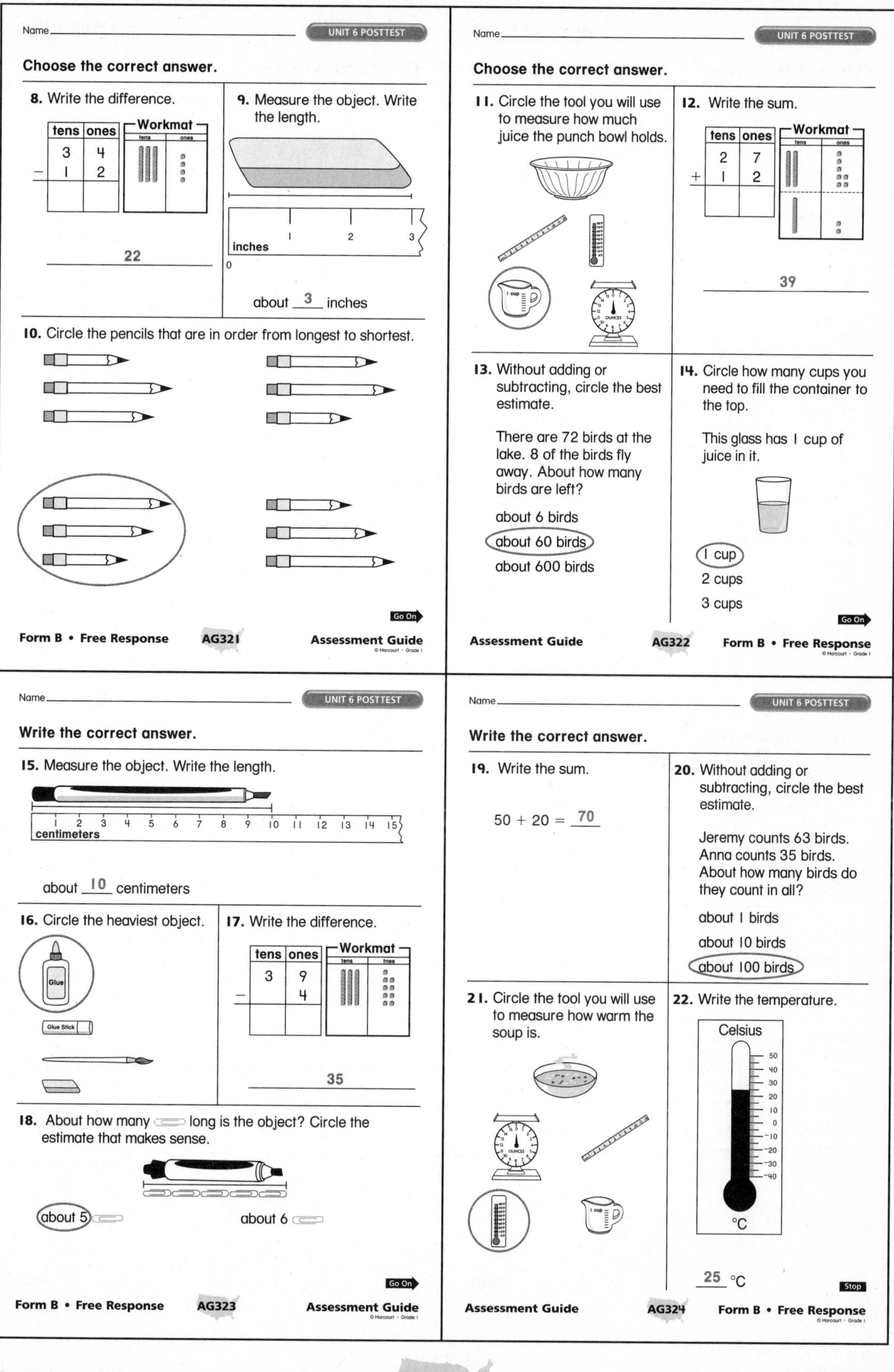

Name ______________________ UNIT 6 POSTTEST

Choose the correct answer.

8. Write the difference.

tens	ones
3	4
− 1	2

Workmat (tens, ones)

22

9. Measure the object. Write the length.

inches 0 1 2 3

about 3 inches

10. Circle the pencils that are in order from longest to shortest.

Go On

Form B • Free Response AG321 Assessment Guide © Harcourt • Grade 1

Name ______________________ UNIT 6 POSTTEST

Choose the correct answer.

11. Circle the tool you will use to measure how much juice the punch bowl holds.

12. Write the sum.

tens	ones
2	7
+ 1	2

Workmat (tens, ones)

39

13. Without adding or subtracting, circle the best estimate.

There are 72 birds at the lake. 8 of the birds fly away. About how many birds are left?

about 6 birds

(about 60 birds)

about 600 birds

14. Circle how many cups you need to fill the container to the top.

This glass has 1 cup of juice in it.

(1 cup)

2 cups

3 cups

Go On

Assessment Guide AG322 Form B • Free Response © Harcourt • Grade 1

Name ______________________ UNIT 6 POSTTEST

Write the correct answer.

15. Measure the object. Write the length.

1 2 3 4 5 6 7 8 9 10 11 12 13 14 15 centimeters

about 10 centimeters

16. Circle the heaviest object.

Glue Glue Stick

17. Write the difference.

tens	ones
3	9
−	4

Workmat (tens, ones)

35

18. About how many [paper clip] long is the object? Circle the estimate that makes sense.

(about 5 [paper clip]) about 6 [paper clip]

Go On

Form B • Free Response AG323 Assessment Guide © Harcourt • Grade 1

Name ______________________ UNIT 6 POSTTEST

Write the correct answer.

19. Write the sum.

50 + 20 = 70

20. Without adding or subtracting, circle the best estimate.

Jeremy counts 63 birds. Anna counts 35 birds. About how many birds do they count in all?

about 1 birds

about 10 birds

(about 100 birds)

21. Circle the tool you will use to measure how warm the soup is.

22. Write the temperature.

Celsius

50 40 30 20 10 0 −10 −20 −30 −40

°C

25 °C

Stop

Assessment Guide AG324 Form B • Free Response © Harcourt • Grade 1

Name______________________ END OF YEAR TEST

Write the correct answer.

1. Write the temperature.

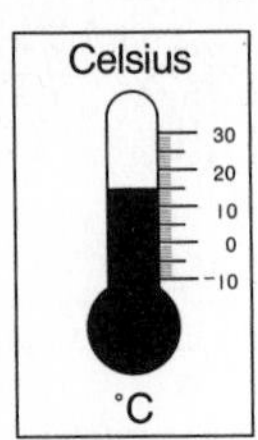

15 °C

2. Write how many flat surfaces the solid figure has.

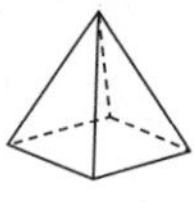

5 flat surfaces

3. Use the picture graph to answer question 3.

Special Classes We Like									
	music	●	●	●	●	●	●		
	art	●	●	●	●	●	●	●	
	gym	●	●	●	●				

Write how many more children chose [music] than [gym].

2 more children

Go On

Name______________________ END OF YEAR TEST

Write the correct answer.

4. Circle which belongs in the group.

5. Write the sum.

20 + 70 = 90

6. Write the number word that tells how many.

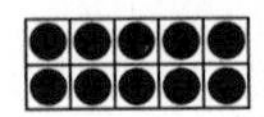
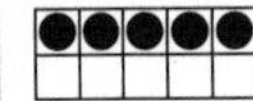

fifteen

7. Circle the pair of related subtraction facts.

(11 − 2 = 9, 11 − 9 = 2) [circled]   10 − 3 = 7, 11 − 4 = 7   12 − 4 = 8, 8 − 4 = 4   12 − 5 = 7, 12 − 3 = 9

Go On

Name______________________ END OF YEAR TEST

Write the correct answer.

8. Circle slide, flip, or turn to name the move.

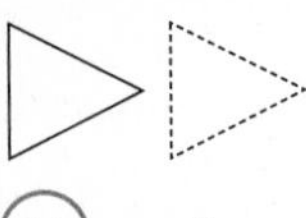

(slide) flip turn

9. Circle which tool you will use to measure how much water the bucket holds.

10. Write how more nests there are than birds.

12
− 3

9 more nests

Go On

Name______________________ END OF YEAR TEST

Write the correct answer.

11. Use the tally chart to answer the question.

Music We Like	
country	𝍸 I
pop	𝍸 IIII
classical	II

Write how many children chose country music.

6 children

12. Write the time.

13. Count. Compare the amounts. Write <, >, or =.

41 ¢ (=) ¢ 41

Go On

Name________________________ END OF YEAR TEST

Write the correct answer.

14. Write the missing number.

2 4 7 2 4 __7__ 2 4 7

15. Write how many corners the plane figure has.

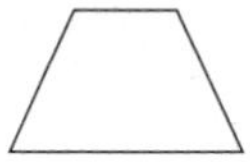

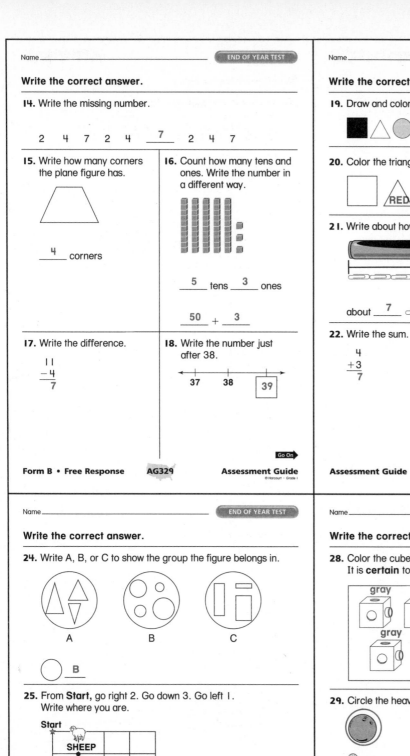

__4__ corners

16. Count how many tens and ones. Write the number in a different way.

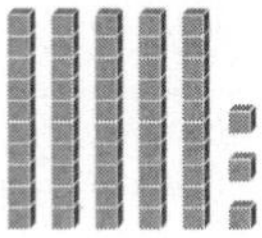

__5__ tens __3__ ones

__50__ + __3__

17. Write the difference.

$$\begin{array}{r} 11 \\ -\ 4 \\ \hline 7 \end{array}$$

18. Write the number just after 38.

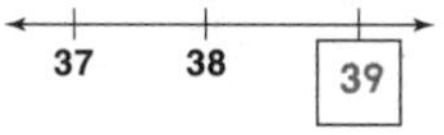

37 38 39

Go On

Name________________________ END OF YEAR TEST

Write the correct answer.

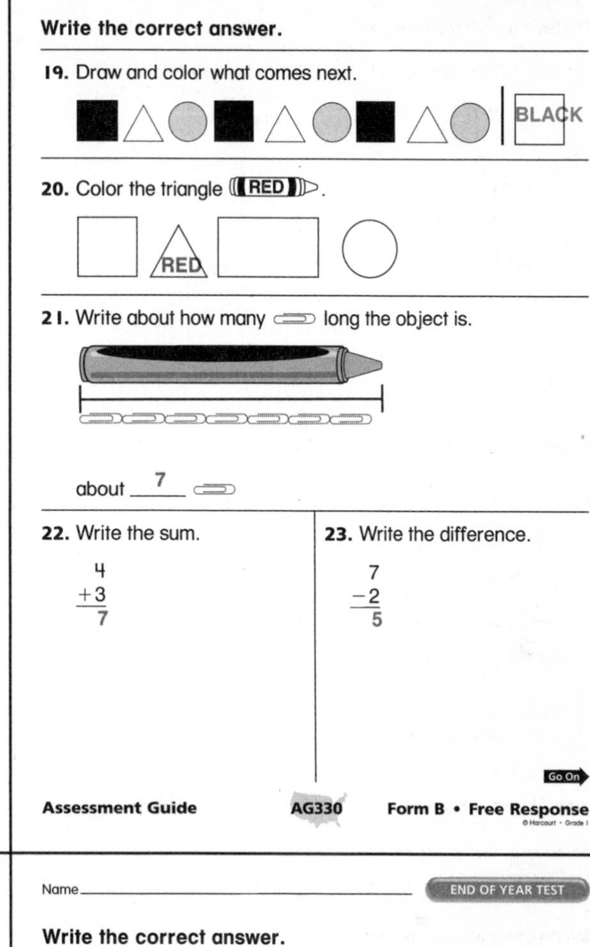

19. Draw and color what comes next.

BLACK

20. Color the triangle RED.

RED

21. Write about how many long the object is.

about __7__

22. Write the sum.

$$\begin{array}{r} 4 \\ +\ 3 \\ \hline 7 \end{array}$$

23. Write the difference.

$$\begin{array}{r} 7 \\ -\ 2 \\ \hline 5 \end{array}$$

Go On

Name________________________ END OF YEAR TEST

Write the correct answer.

24. Write A, B, or C to show the group the figure belongs in.

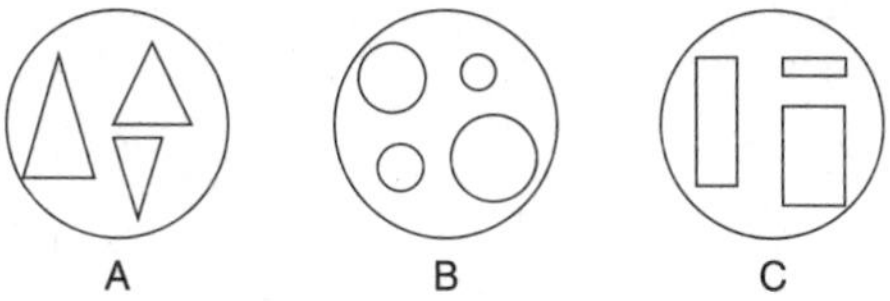

A B C

__B__

25. From **Start,** go right 2. Go down 3. Go left 1. Write where you are.

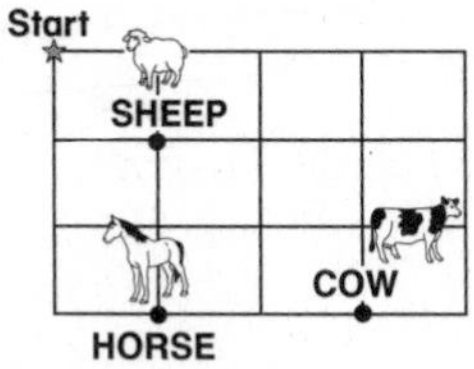

Start SHEEP COW HORSE

__horse__

26. Write the sum.

$$\begin{array}{r} 8 \\ +\ 3 \\ \hline 11 \end{array}$$

27. Write a related subtraction fact.

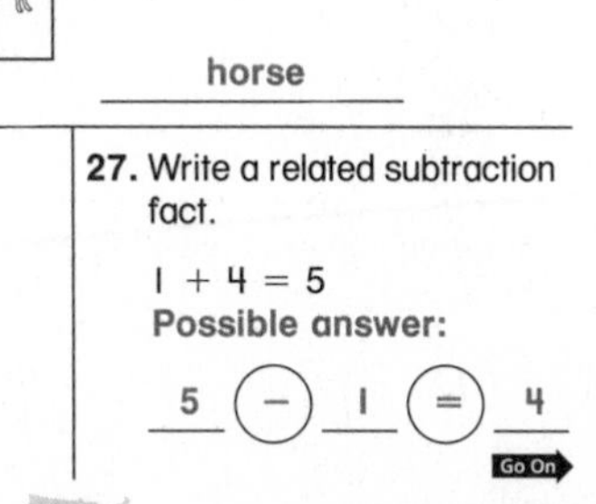

1 + 4 = 5

Possible answer:

__5__ − __1__ = __4__

Go On

Name________________________ END OF YEAR TEST

Write the correct answer.

28. Color the cubes to make the sentence true. It is **certain** to pull a gray cube.

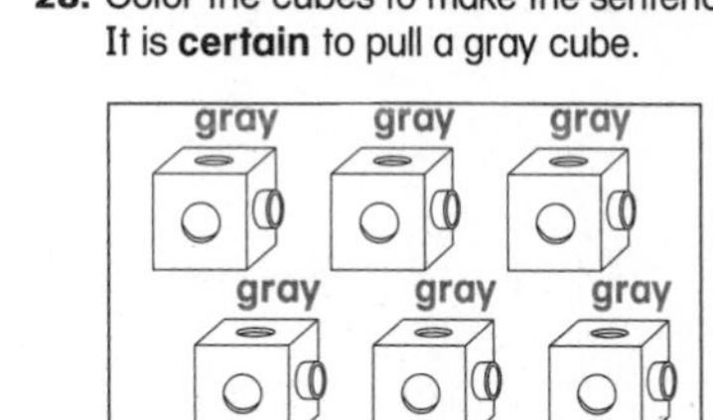

29. Circle the heaviest object.

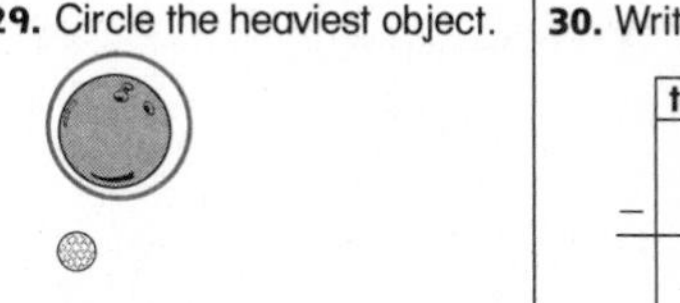

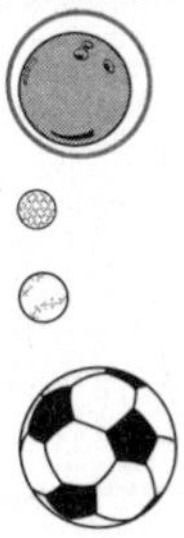

30. Write the difference.

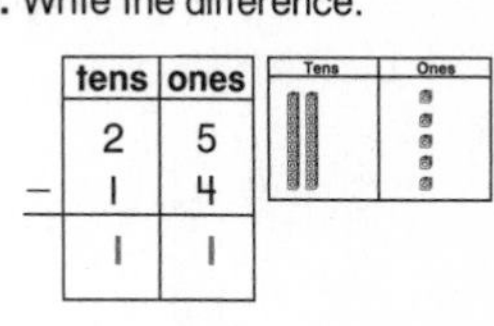

	tens	ones
	2	5
−	1	4
	1	1

Go On

Name________________________ END OF YEAR TEST

Write the correct answer.

31. Circle the time of day.

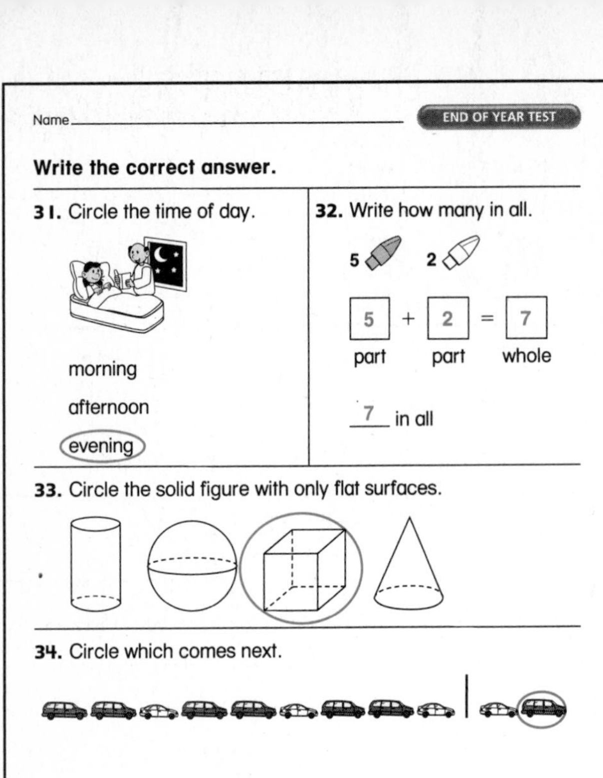

morning

afternoon

(evening)

32. Write how many in all.

5 2

[5] + [2] = [7]

part part whole

7 in all

33. Circle the solid figure with only flat surfaces.

34. Circle which comes next.

Go On

Name________________________ END OF YEAR TEST

Write the correct answer.

Use the bar graph to answer questions 35 and 36.

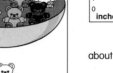

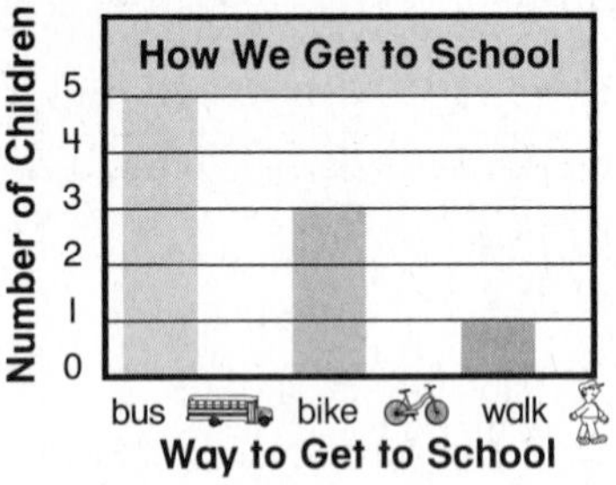

How We Get to School	Number of Children
bus	5
bike	3
walk	1

Way to Get to School

35. Circle the way of travel the fewest children chose.

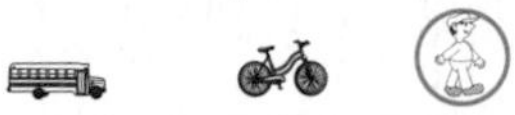

36. Write how many children chose (bus).

7 in all

37. Draw the hour hand and minute hand to show the time.

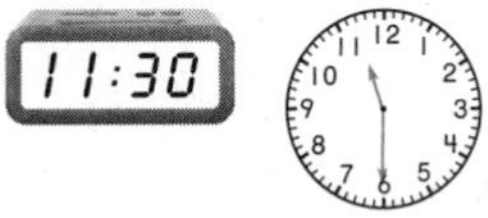

11:30

Go On

Name________________________ END OF YEAR TEST

Write the correct answer.

38. Use figures to show the same pattern.
Draw the figures.

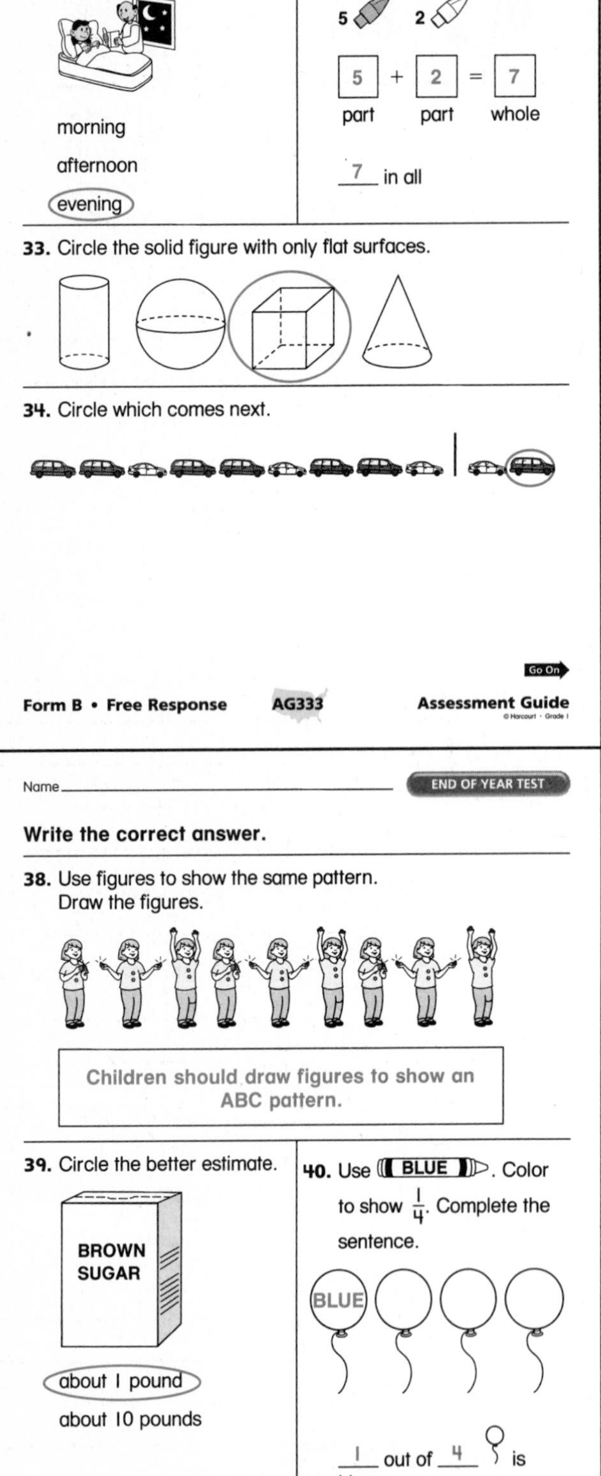

Children should draw figures to show an ABC pattern.

39. Circle the better estimate.

BROWN SUGAR

(about 1 pound)

about 10 pounds

40. Use (BLUE). Color to show $\frac{1}{4}$. Complete the sentence.

BLUE

1 out of 4 is blue.

Go On

Name________________________ END OF YEAR TEST

Write the correct answer.

41. Draw a line of symmetry to make two parts that match.

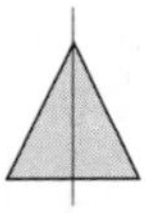

42. Circle the bear you are less likely to pull from the (bowl).

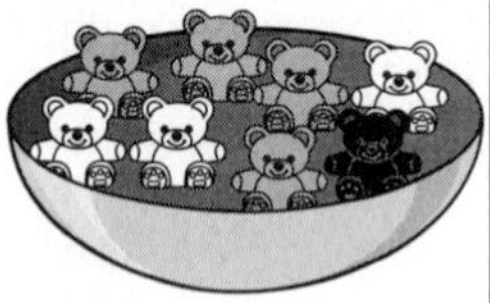

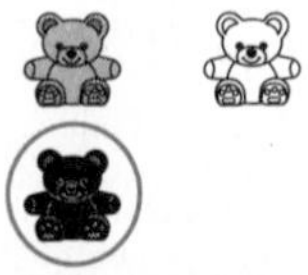

43. Measure the object. Write the length.

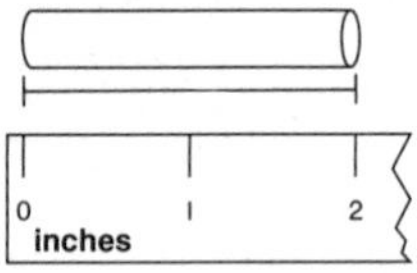

0 1 2
inches

about 2 inches

44. Compare the numbers. Write $<$, $>$, or $=$.

65 (>) 63

Stop

Class Record Form

INVENTORY TEST

School

Teacher

NAME	Date	Score

Class Record Form

CHAPTER PRETESTS/POSTTESTS

School

Teacher

STUDENT NAME	Date	Chapter 1 Pre	Chapter 1 Post	Chapter 2 Pre	Chapter 2 Post	Chapter 3 Pre	Chapter 3 Post	Chapter 4 Pre	Chapter 4 Post	Chapter 5 Pre	Chapter 5 Post	Chapter 6 Pre	Chapter 6 Post	Chapter 7 Pre	Chapter 7 Post	Chapter 8 Pre	Chapter 8 Post	Chapter 9 Pre	Chapter 9 Post	Chapter 10 Pre	Chapter 10 Post

Class Record Form

CHAPTER PRETESTS/POSTTESTS (continued)

Chapter 11 Pre	Chapter 11 Post	Chapter 12 Pre	Chapter 12 Post	Chapter 13 Pre	Chapter 13 Post	Chapter 14 Pre	Chapter 14 Post	Chapter 15 Pre	Chapter 15 Post	Chapter 16 Pre	Chapter 16 Post	Chapter 17 Pre	Chapter 17 Post	Chapter 18 Pre	Chapter 18 Post	Chapter 19 Pre	Chapter 19 Post	Chapter 20 Pre	Chapter 20 Post	Chapter 21 Pre	Chapter 21 Post	Chapter 22 Pre	Chapter 22 Post	Chapter 23 Pre	Chapter 23 Post	Chapter 24 Pre	Chapter 24 Post

Class Record Form

UNIT PRETESTS/POSTTESTS

School

Teacher

STUDENT NAME	Date	Unit 1 Pre	Unit 1 Post	Unit 2 Pre	Unit 2 Post	Unit 3 Pre	Unit 3 Post	Unit 4 Pre	Unit 4 Post	Unit 5 Pre	Unit 5 Post	Unit 6 Pre	Unit 6 Post

Class Record Form

BEGINNING OF YEAR/END OF YEAR TEST

School Teacher NAME	Date	Beginning of Year Test	End of Year Test

INDIVIDUAL RECORD FORM

Student's Name ______________________ Date ____________

Chapter/ Lesson	Lesson Objective	Items	Criterion Score	Student's Score	On-Level Intervention Skills	Prescriptions
1.1	Use one-to-one correspondence to compare groups.	7	1/1	__/1		**R, P, PS, RTE:** 1.1 **MM:** CCD/HC Level A
1.2	Count, read, and write numbers up to 10.	6	1/1	__/1	2	**R, P, PS, RTE:** 1.2 **MM:** CCD/CC Levels A, B
1.3	Count, read, and write numbers up to 20.	2	1/1	__/1	2	**R, P, PS, RTE:** 1.3 **MM:** CCD/CC Levels A, B, D
1.4	Compare numbers to 20.	1, 4	2/2	__/2	3	**R, P, PS, RTE:** 1.4 **MM:** CCD/CC Level D
1.5	Order numbers to 20.	3	1/1	__/1	3	**R, P, PS, RTE:** 1.5 **MM:** NBR/CN Levels A, B, C
1.6	Identify ordinal numbers.	5	1/1	__/1		**R, P, PS, RTE:** 1.6
1.7	Solve problems by using the skill *use data from a graph*.	8, 9	2/2	__/2		**R, P, PS, RTE:** 1.7 **MM:** CCD/WW Level C
2.1	Use the joining concept to model and solve addition problems with concrete objects.	7	1/1	__/1	5	**R, P, PS, RTE:** 2.1 **MM:** NBR/LL Level C
2.2	Use pictures and symbols to write addition sentences.	1	1/1	__/1	6	**R, P, PS, RTE:** 2.2 **MM:** CCD/BB Level C
2.3	Use the part-part-whole concept to model and solve addition problems with concrete objects.	6	1/1	__/1	8	**R, P, PS, RTE:** 2.3 **MM:** NBR/CS Levels A, F, K
2.4	Understand and apply the Zero Property for Addition.	3	1/1	__/1	7	**R, P, PS, RTE:** 2.4 **MM:** CCD/HC Level C
2.5	Explore the Order Properly for Addition.	2	1/1	__/1	9	**R, P, PS, RTE:** 2.5 **MM:** CCD/BB Level A
2.6	Write addition sentences to show different ways to make numbers to 8.	5	1/1	__/1	10	**R, P, PS, RTE:** 2.6 **MM:** CCD/BB Level A, NBR/CS Level A

Student's Name ______________________ Date ____________

Chapter/ Lesson	Lesson Objective	Items	Criterion Score	Student's Score	On-Level Intervention Skills	Prescriptions
2.7	Write vertical addition sentences.	4	1/1	__/1	11	**R, P, PS, RTE:** 2.7 **MM:** CCD/BB Level E
2.8	Solve problems by using the strategy *make a model*.	8	1/1	__/1	12	**R, P, PS, RTE:** 2.8 **MM:** NBR/LL Level C
3.1	Model and solve take-away problem situations using concrete objects.	7	1/1	__/1	13	**R, P, PS, RTE:** 3.1 **MM:** CCD/BB Level B, NBR/CS Level B
3.2	Use pictures to write subtraction sentences.	4	1/1	__/1	14	**R, P, PS, RTE:** 3.2 **MM:** CCD/BB Level F
3.3	Identify how many are left when subtracting all or 0.	2	1/1	__/1	15	**R, P, PS, RTE:** 3.3
3.4	Model and record ways to subtract from 7 and 8.	3	1/1	__/1	16	**R, P, PS, RTE:** 3.4 **MM:** CCD/BB Level B, NBR/CS Level B
3.5	Write vertical subtraction sentences.	1	1/1	__/1	17	**R, P, PS, RTE:** 3.5 **MM:** CCD/BB Level F
3.6	Use the part-part-whole concept of subtraction to model and solve problems with concrete objects.	6	1/1	__/1	18	**R, P, PS, RTE:** 3.6 **MM:** NBR/CS Levels B, L
3.7	Model and compare to show the meaning of subtraction.	5	1/1	__/1	19	**R, P, PS, RTE:** 3.7 **MM:** NBR/CS Level C
3.8	Solve problems by using the strategy *make a model*.	8	1/1	__/1	12	**R, P, PS, RTE:** 3.8 **MM:** NBR/LL Level D
4.1	Identify addition and subtraction problem situations.	4, 7	2/2	__/2	20	**R, P, PS, RTE:** 4.1 **MM:** NBR/CS Levels D, J
4.2	Explore how addition and subtraction are related.	1	1/1	__/1	20	**R, P, PS, RTE:** 4.2 **MM:** NBR/CS Level D, NBR/CN Level M

Key: Workbooks: R: Reteach Workbook **P:** Practice Workbook **PS:** Problem Solving and Reading Strategies Workbook **RTE:** Reteach (Teacher Edition) **MM:** Mega Math **CCD:** Country Countdown **BB:** Block Busters **CC:** Counting Critters **HC:** Harrison's Comparisons **CD:** Clock-a-Doodle-Doo **WW:** White Water Graphing **SA:** Shapes Ahoy! **SS:** Ship Shapes **3D:** Undersea 3D **SCS:** Sea Cave Sorting **MTM:** Made to Measure **NBR:** Numberopolis **LL:** LuLu's Lunch Counter **CS:** Carnival Stories **CN:** Cross Town Number Line **WS:** Wash 'n Spin **FA:** Fraction Action **FF:** Fraction Flare Up **LC:** Last Chance Canyon **TNG:** The Number Games **TT:** Tiny's Think Tank **AG:** ArachnaGraph **ISE:** Ice Station Exploration **AA:** Arctic Algebra **LL:** Linear Lab

Student's Name ______________________ Date ____________

Chapter/ Lesson	Lesson Objective	Items	Criterion Score	Student's Score	On-Level Intervention Skills	Prescriptions
4.3	Identify and write related facts.	3, 5	2/2	__/2	21	**R, P, PS, RTE:** 4.3 **MM:** CCD/CC Levels I, L, U
4.4	Write number sentences to represent addition and subtraction situations.	2, 6	2/2	__/2	21	**R, P, PS, RTE:** 4.4 **MM:** CCD/CC Levels I, L, U
4.5	Solve problems by using the skill *choose the operation*.	8, 9	2/2	__/2		**R, P, PS, RTE:** 4.5 **MM:** NBR/CS Level D
5.1	Count on 1 or 2 to find sums.	7	1/1	__/1	22	**R, P, PS, RTE:** 5.1 **MM:** NBR/CN Level D
5.2	Use a number line to count on using small numbers to find sums to 12.	1, 2	2/2	__/2	22	**R, P, PS, RTE:** 5.2 **MM:** NBR/CN Level D
5.3	Count on from the greater number.	5	1/1	__/1	22	**R, P, PS, RTE:** 5.3 **MM:** NBR/CN Levels D, E, I
5.4	Use doubles as a strategy to solve addition facts through 12.	3	1/1	__/1	23	**R, P, PS, RTE:** 5.4 **MM:** CCD/CC Level F
5.5	Use doubles and near doubles as strategies to find sums to 12.	4	1/1	__/1	24	**R, P, PS, RTE:** 5.5 **MM:** CCD/CC Level J
5.6	Use the strategies *count on, doubles,* and *near doubles* to practice facts to 12.	6	1/1	__/1	22, 23, 24	**R, P, PS, RTE:** 5.6 **MM:** CCD/CC Level S, NBR/CS Level F
5.7	Solve problems by using the strategy *draw a picture*.	8, 9	2/2	__/2	25	**R, P, PS, RTE:** 5.7 **MM:** NBR/CS Level E
6.1	Count back 1 or 2 to subtract from 12 or less.	1, 4	2/2	__/2	26	**R, P, PS, RTE:** 6.1 **MM:** NBR/CN Levels D, E, G, I
6.2	Subtract from 12 or less using a number line to count back.	2, 3	2/2	__/2	26	**R, P, PS, RTE:** 6.2 **MM:** NBR/CN Level E
6.3	Use addition as a strategy to subtract from 12 or less.	7, 8	2/2	__/2	27	**R, P, PS, RTE:** 6.3 **MM:** CCD/CC Level I

Student's Name ____________________ Date __________

Chapter/ Lesson	Lesson Objective	Items	Criterion Score	Student's Score	On-Level Intervention Skills	Prescriptions
6.4	Use the strategies *count back* and *think addition to subtract* to practice subtraction facts.	5, 6	2/2	__/2	26, 27	**R, P, PS, RTE:** 6.4 **MM:** CCD/CC Level I, NBR/CN Level G
6.5	Solve problems by using the strategy *write a number sentence.*	9, 10	2/2	__/2	28	**R, P, PS, RTE:** 6.5 **MM:** NBR/CS Level A
7.1	Identify related addition facts to 12.	3	1/1	__/1		**R, P, PS, RTE:** 7.1 **MM:** CCD/CC Level G
7.2	Identify related subtraction facts to 12.	7	1/1	__/1		**R, P, PS, RTE:** 7.2 **MM:** CCD/CC Level H
7.3	Identify fact families.	1	1/1	__/1	31	**R, P, PS, RTE:** 7.3 **MM:** CCD/CC Level I
7.4	Record fact families.	5	1/1	__/1	31	**R, P, PS, RTE:** 7.4 **MM:** CCD/CC Level I
7.5	Complete a table by using a rule.	6	1/1	__/1	32	**R, P, PS, RTE:** 7.5 **MM:** CCD/CC Level I
7.6	Represent equivalent forms of numbers to 12.	2	1/1	__/1	33	**R, P, PS, RTE:** 7.6 **MM:** NBR/CS Level J
7.7	Create addition and subtraction situations and write the corresponding number sentence.	4	1/1	__/1	34	**R, P, PS, RTE:** 7.7 **MM:** NBR/CS Levels D, J
7.8	Solve problems by using the strategy *draw a picture.*	8, 9	2/2	__/2	28	**R, P, PS, RTE:** 7.8 **MM:** NBR/CS Levls C, I
8.1	Use Venn diagrams to sort and classify objects by common attributes.	4	1/1	__/1	35	**R, P, PS, RTE:** 8.1 **MM:** SA/SCS Levels B, C, D
8.2	Sort and classify objects into three groups by common attributes.	1	1/1	__/1	35	**R, P, PS, RTE:** 8.2 **MM:** SA/SCS Levels A, C, G

Key: Workbooks: R: Reteach Workbook **P:** Practice Workbook **PS:** Problem Solving and Reading Strategies Workbook **RTE:** Reteach (Teacher Edition) **MM:** Mega Math **CCD:** Country Countdown **BB:** Block Busters **CC:** Counting Critters **HC:** Harrison's Comparisons **CD:** Clock-a-Doodle-Doo **WW:** White Water Graphing **SA:** Shapes Ahoy! **SS:** Ship Shapes **3D:** Undersea 3D **SCS:** Sea Cave Sorting **MTM:** Made to Measure **NBR:** Numberopolis **LL:** LuLu's Lunch Counter **CS:** Carnival Stories **CN:** Cross Town Number Line **WS:** Wash 'n Spin **FA:** Fraction Action **FF:** Fraction Flare Up **LC:** Last Chance Canyon **TNG:** The Number Games **TT:** Tiny's Think Tank **AG:** ArachnaGraph **ISE:** Ice Station Exploration **AA:** Arctic Algebra **LL:** Linear Lab

Student's Name ______________________ Date ____________

Chapter/ Lesson	Lesson Objective	Items	Criterion Score	Student's Score	On-Level Intervention Skills	Prescriptions
8.3	Make concrete graphs from organized data and use the data to make comparisons.	2	1/1	__/1	36	**R, P, PS, RTE:** 8.3 **MM:** CCD/CC Levels C, D, CCD/WW Level B
8.4	Read and compare data from a picture graph.	3	1/1	__/1	36	**R, P, PS, RTE:** 8.4 **MM:** CCD/WW Level A
8.5	Solve problems by using the skill *make and use a graph.*	5, 6	2/2	__/2		**R, P, PS, RTE:** 8.5 **MM:** CCD/WW Levels B, C, F
9.1	Read a tally chart and interpret the data.	2	1/1	__/1	37, 38	**R, P, PS, RTE:** 9.1 **MM:** CCD/WW Level D
9.2	Read a bar graph to compare data.	4, 5	2/2	__/2	39	**R, P, PS, RTE:** 9.2 **MM:** CCD/WW Level F
9.3	Determine if an event is possible or impossible.	3	1/1	__/1		**R, P, PS, RTE:** 9.3 **MM:** NBR/WS Level B, FA/LC Level A
9.4	Determine whether events are *more likely* or *less likely.*	1	1/1	__/1		**R, P, PS, RTE:** 9.4 **MM:** NBR/WS Level D
9.5	Solve problems by using the strategy *predict and test.*	6, 7	2/2	__/2		**R, P, PS, RTE:** 9.5 **MM:** NBR/WS Level I, FA/LC Level D
10.1	Count, group, and describe objects using tens and ones.	4	1/1	__/1	43	**R, P, PS, RTE:** 10.1 **MM:** CCD/CC Level P
10.2	Model and count groups of tens.	3	1/1	__/1	44	**R, P, PS, RTE:** 10.2 **MM:** CCD/BB Level G, NBR/CN Level P
10.3	Count and group objects to 50 as tens and ones.	1	1/1	__/1	45	**R, P, PS, RTE:** 10.3 **MM:** CCD/BB Level H
10.4	Count and group objects to 100 as tens and ones.	5	1/1	__/1	45	**R, P, PS, RTE:** 10.4 **MM:** CCD/BB Level H
10.5	Write 2-digit numbers in expanded forms.	2, 6	2/2	__/2	46	**R, P, PS, RTE:** 10.5 **MM:** CCD/BB Levels V, W

Student's Name ____________________ Date __________

Chapter/ Lesson	Lesson Objective	Items	Criterion Score	Student's Score	On-Level Intervention Skills	Prescriptions
10.6	Solve problems by using the skill *make reasonable estimates.*	7, 8	2/2	__/2		**R, P, PS, RTE:** 10.6 **MM:** CCD/CD Level C, SA/MTM Level D
11.1	Model and compare 2-digit numbers to determine which is greater.	1	1/1	__/1	47	**R, P, PS, RTE:** 11.1 **MM:** CCD/HC Level I, SA/SCS Levels G, O
11.2	Model and compare 2-digit numbers to determine which is less.	6	1/1	__/1	48	**R, P, PS, RTE:** 11.2 **MM:** CCD/HC Level I, SA/SCS Levels G, O
11.3	Use the symbols for *is less than* $<$, *is greater than* $>$, and *is equal to* $=$ to compare numbers.	3	1/1	__/1	49	**R, P, PS, RTE:** 11.3 **MM:** CCD/HC Level K, SA/SCS Level O
11.4	Identify one more than and one less than a given number.	5	1/1	__/1	50	**R, P, PS, RTE:** 11.4 **MM:** NBR/CN Levels D, M
11.5	Identify ten more than and ten less than a given number.	7	1/1	__/1	50	**R, P, PS, RTE:** 11.5 **MM:** NBR/CN Level P
11.6	Use a number line to determine *before, between,* and *after.*	2	1/1	__/1	51	**R, P, PS, RTE:** 11.6 **MM:** NBR/CN Level T
11.7	Order numbers from least to greatest or greatest to least.	4	1/1	__/1	51	**R, P, PS, RTE:** 11.7 **MM:** SA/MTM Level C, NBR/CN Level O
11.8	Solve problems by using the skill *use a table.*	8, 9	2/2	__/2		**R, P, PS, RTE:** 11.8
12.1	Count forward and backward to 100.	4	1/1	__/1		**R, P, PS, RTE:** 12.1 **MM:** NBR/CN Levels M, O, P

Key: Workbooks: R: Reteach Workbook **P:** Practice Workbook **PS:** Problem Solving and Reading Strategies Workbook **RTE:** Reteach (Teacher Edition) **MM:** Mega Math **CCD:** Country Countdown **BB:** Block Busters **CC:** Counting Critters **HC:** Harrison's Comparisons **CD:** Clock-a-Doodle-Doo **WW:** White Water Graphing **SA:** Shapes Ahoy! **SS:** Ship Shapes **3D:** Undersea 3D **SCS:** Sea Cave Sorting **MTM:** Made to Measure **NBR:** Numberopolis **LL:** LuLu's Lunch Counter **CS:** Carnival Stories **CN:** Cross Town Number Line **WS:** Wash 'n Spin **FA:** Fraction Action **FF:** Fraction Flare Up **LC:** Last Chance Canyon **TNG:** The Number Games **TT:** Tiny's Think Tank **AG:** ArachnaGraph **ISE:** Ice Station Exploration **AA:** Arctic Algebra **LL:** Linear Lab

Student's Name ______________________ Date ____________

Chapter/ Lesson	Lesson Objective	Items	Criterion Score	Student's Score	On-Level Intervention Skills	Prescriptions
12.2	Use pictures to skip count by twos, fives, and tens.	3	1/1	__/1	53	**R, P, PS, RTE:** 12.2 **MM:** NBR/CN Level Q
12.3	Use patterns on a hundred chart to skip count by twos, fives, and tens.	1	1/1	__/1	53	**R, P, PS, RTE:** 12.3
12.4	Use patterns on a hundred chart to count by tens from any number.	2	1/1	__/1	54	**R, P, PS, RTE:** 12.4
12.5	Use skip counting to identify, describe, and extend number patterns.	5	1/1	__/1	54	**R, P, PS, RTE:** 12.5 **MM:** TNG/TT Level K
12.6	Use patterns to classify numbers as even or odd.	6	1/1	__/1		**R, P, PS, RTE:** 12.6 **MM:** NBR/CN Level S, SA/SCS Level M
12.7	Solve problems by using the strategy *find a pattern*.	7, 8	2/2	__/2	56	**R, P, PS, RTE:** 12.7 **MM:** SA/SS Levels A, B, C
13.1	Identify and sort solid figures by their flat and curved surfaces.	5	1/1	__/1	57	**R, P, PS, RTE:** 13.1 **MM:** SA/SS Levels I, J
13.2	Classify solid figures by the number of flat surfaces and corners they have.	3	1/1	__/1	58	**R, P, PS, RTE:** 13.2 **MM:** SA/3D Level F
13.3	Identify plane figures on solids.	1	1/1	__/1	59	**R, P, PS, RTE:** 13.3 **MM:** SA/3D Level G
13.4	Identify and sort plane figures.	4, 6	2/2	__/2	60	**R, P, PS, RTE:** 13.4 **MM:** SA/SCS Level K
13.5	Classify plane figures by the number of sides and corners they have.	2	1/1	__/1	60	**R, P, PS, RTE:** 13.5 **MM:** SA/3D Level G
13.6	Solve problems by using the strategy *use logical reasoning*.	7, 8	2/2	__/2	61	**R, P, PS, RTE:** 13.6 **MM:** SA/SS Levels B, C, O
14.1	Identify and describe concrete repeating patterns.	3	1/1	__/1	62	**R, P, PS, RTE:** 14.1 **MM:** SA/SS Levels B, C

Student's Name ______________________ Date ____________

Chapter/ Lesson	Lesson Objective	Items	Criterion Score	Student's Score	On-Level Intervention Skills	Prescriptions
14.2	Predict and extend concrete repeating patterns.	5	1/1	__/1	63	**R, P, PS, RTE:** 14.2 **MM:** SA/SS Levels B, D, TNG/TT Level J
14.3	Predict and extend pictorial repeating patterns.	1	1/1	__/1		**R, P, PS, RTE:** 14.3 **MM:** SA/SS Level B
14.4	Identify and describe patterns with missing elements.	4	1/1	__/1	65	**R, P, PS, RTE:** 14.4 **MM:** SA/SS Level C, TNG/TT Level J
14.6	Transfer patterns from one representation to another.	2	1/1	__/1		**R, P, PS, RTE:** 14.6 **MM:** SA/SS Level F
14.7	Solve problems by using the strategy *find a pattern*.	6, 7	2/2	__/2	56	**R, P, PS, RTE:** 14.7 **MM:** SA/SS Level C
15.1	Identify and describe spatial relationships using position words.	3	1/1	__/1		**R, P, PS, RTE:** 15.1 **MM:** SA/SS Level A
15.2	Use position words to give and follow directions.	4	1/1	__/1		**R, P, PS, RTE:** 15.2 **MM:** SA/SS Level A, TNG/AG Level G
15.3	Identify and match congruent figures.	1	1/1	__/1		**R, P, PS, RTE:** 15.3 **MM:** SA/SS Level L
15.4	Make and identify shapes that have a line of symmetry.	5	1/1	__/1		**R, P, PS, RTE:** 15.4 **MM:** SA/SS Levels M, N
15.5	Identify and explore the effects of slides, flips, and turns.	2	1/1	__/1		**R, P, PS, RTE:** 15.5 **MM:** SA/SS Levels O, P
15.6	Solve problems by using the strategy *use logical reasoning*.	6	1/1	__/1	61	**R, P, PS, RTE:** 15.6

Key: Workbooks: R: Reteach Workbook **P:** Practice Workbook **PS:** Problem Solving and Reading Strategies Workbook **RTE:** Reteach (Teacher Edition) **MM:** Mega Math **CCD:** Country Countdown **BB:** Block Busters **CC:** Counting Critters **HC:** Harrison's Comparisons **CD:** Clock-a-Doodle-Doo **WW:** White Water Graphing **SA:** Shapes Ahoy! **SS:** Ship Shapes **3D:** Undersea 3D **SCS:** Sea Cave Sorting **MTM:** Made to Measure **NBR:** Numberopolis **LL:** LuLu's Lunch Counter **CS:** Carnival Stories **CN:** Cross Town Number Line **WS:** Wash 'n Spin **FA:** Fraction Action **FF:** Fraction Flare Up **LC:** Last Chance Canyon **TNG:** The Number Games **TT:** Tiny's Think Tank **AG:** ArachnaGraph **ISE:** Ice Station Exploration **AA:** Arctic Algebra **LL:** Linear Lab

Student's Name ____________________ Date __________

Chapter/ Lesson	Lesson Objective	Items	Criterion Score	Student's Score	On-Level Intervention Skills	Prescriptions
16.1	Identify equal and unequal parts of a whole.	3	1/1	__/1		**R, P, PS, RTE:** 16.1 **MM:** SA/SS Level Q
16.2	Identify, describe, and name halves.	1	1/1	__/1		**R, P, PS, RTE:** 16.2 **MM:** SA/SS Levels R, S
16.3	Identify, describe, and name fourths.	4	1/1	__/1		**R, P, PS, RTE:** 16.3 **MM:** SA/SS Levels R, S
16.4	Identify, describe, and name thirds.	5	1/1	__/1		**R, P, PS, RTE:** 16.4 **MM:** SA/SS Level S
16.5	Identify, describe, and name fractions as parts of a group.	2	1/1	__/1		**R, P, PS, RTE:** 16.5 **MM:** FA/FF Level C
16.6	Solve problems by using the strategy *use logical reasoning*.	6, 7	2/2	__/2		**R, P, PS, RTE:** 16.6
17.1	Add by using the strategies *doubles* and *near doubles*.	1	1/1	__/1	79	**R, P, PS, RTE:** 17.1 **MM:** CCD/CC Levels J, O
17.2	Use a ten frame to add 10 and a number less than 10.	5	1/1	__/1	80	**R, P, PS, RTE:** 17.2 **MM:** CCD/BB Levels J, K, CCD/CC Level P
17.3	Use the strategy *make-a-ten* to find sums.	2, 6	2/2	__/2	80	**R, P, PS, RTE:** 17.3 **MM:** CCD/CC Level Q
17.4	Use the Order Property and addition strategies to add three numbers.	4	1/1	__/1	81	**R, P, PS, RTE:** 17.4 **MM:** CCD/CC Level K
17.5	Practice addition facts to 20.	3, 7	2/2	__/2	79	**R, P, PS, RTE:** 17.5 **MM:** CCD/CC Levels O, U
17.6	Solve problems by using the strategy *write a number sentence*.	8, 9	2/2	__/2	28	**R, P, PS, RTE:** 17.6 **MM:** CCD/CC Level I
18.1	Subtract from 20 or less using a number line to count back.	1, 2	2/2	__/2	82	**R, P, PS, RTE:** 18.1 **MM:** NBR/CN Level I

Student's Name ______________________ Date ____________

Chapter/ Lesson	Lesson Objective	Items	Criterion Score	Student's Score	On-Level Intervention Skills	Prescriptions
18.2	Model and compare to show the meaning of subtraction.	3, 7	2/2	__/2	83	**R, P, PS, RTE:** 18.2 **MM:** NBR/CS Level C
18.3	Use think addition as a strategy to subtract numbers from 20 or less.	5	1/1	__/1	84	**R, P, PS, RTE:** 18.3 **MM:** CCD/CC Levels I, L, U
18.4	Practice subtraction facts from 20 or less.	4, 6	2/2	__/2	82, 84	**R, P, PS, RTE:** 18.4 **MM:** CCD/CC Levels T, U
18.5	Solve problems by using the skill *choose a method.*	8, 9	2/2	__/2		**R, P, PS, RTE:** 18.5 **MM:** NBR/CS Levels D, J
19.1	Use fact families to find sums and differences to 20.	7	1/1	__/1	107	**R, P, PS, RTE:** 19.1 **MM:** CCD/CC Level U
19.2	Identify a missing number in a number sentence.	1, 4	2/2	__/2	86	**R, P, PS, RTE:** 19.2 **MM:** NBR/CS Levels E, H, N
19.3	Represent numbers by using sums and differences to 20.	2, 5	2/2	__/2	87	**R, P, PS, RTE:** 19.3 **MM:** CCD/HC Level H
19.4	Complete a function table.	6	1/1	__/1	88	**R, P, PS, RTE:** 19.4 **MM:** ISE/AA Level J
19.5	Use pictures to create addition and subtraction problems.	3	1/1	__/1	89	**R, P, PS, RTE:** 19.5 **MM:** ISE/AA Level B
19.6	Solve problems by using the skill *choose the operation.*	8, 9	2/2	__/2		**R, P, PS, RTE:** 19.6 **MM:** NBR/CS Levels D, J
20.3	Identify the total value of a group of coins that includes pennies, nickels, and/or dimes.	3	1/1	__/1	92	**R, P, PS, RTE:** 20.3 **MM:** NBR/LL Level G
20.5	Show ways to make 100¢ with coins and dollars.	2	1/1	__/1		**R, P, PS, RTE:** 20.5 **MM:** NBR/LL Level I

Key: Workbooks: R: Reteach Workbook **P:** Practice Workbook **PS:** Problem Solving and Reading Strategies Workbook **RTE:** Reteach (Teacher Edition) **MM:** Mega Math **CCD:** Country Countdown **BB:** Block Busters **CC:** Counting Critters **HC:** Harrison's Comparisons **CD:** Clock-a-Doodle-Doo **WW:** White Water Graphing **SA:** Shapes Ahoy! **SS:** Ship Shapes **3D:** Undersea 3D **SCS:** Sea Cave Sorting **MTM:** Made to Measure **NBR:** Numberopolis **LL:** LuLu's Lunch Counter **CS:** Carnival Stories **CN:** Cross Town Number Line **WS:** Wash 'n Spin **FA:** Fraction Action **FF:** Fraction Flare Up **LC:** Last Chance Canyon **TNG:** The Number Games **TT:** Tiny's Think Tank **AG:** ArachnaGraph **ISE:** Ice Station Exploration **AA:** Arctic Algebra **LL:** Linear Lab

Student's Name ______________________ Date ______________

Chapter/ Lesson	Lesson Objective	Items	Criterion Score	Student's Score	On-Level Intervention Skills	Prescriptions
20.6	Identify and compare given money amounts.	4	1/1	__/1		**R, P, PS, RTE:** 20.6 **MM:** NBR/LL Level J
20.7	Identify different ways to make equal amounts using coins or one dollar.	1	1/1	__/1	96	**R, P, PS, RTE:** 20.7 **MM:** NBR/LL Levels J
20.8	Solve problems by using the strategy *act it out*.	5, 6	2/2	__/2	97	**R, P, PS, RTE:** 20.8 **MM:** NBR/LL Levels B, J, G
21.1	Tell and write time to the hour on analog and digital clocks.	2	1/1	__/1	98	**R, P, PS, RTE:** 21.1 **MM:** CCD/CD Level G
21.2	Tell and write time to the half hour on analog and digital clocks.	1	1/1	__/1	99	**R, P, PS, RTE:** 21.2 **MM:** CCD/CD Level H
21.3	Read and show time to the hour and half hour using analog and digital clocks.	5	1/1	__/1	98, 99	**R, P, PS, RTE:** 21.3 **MM:** CCD/CD Levels G, H
21.4	Read and use a calendar.	3	1/1	__/1		**R, P, PS, RTE:** 21.4 **MM:** CCD/CD Level E
21.5	Understand and order the sequence of events with respect to time.	4	1/1	__/1		**R, P, PS, RTE:** 21.5 **MM:** CCD/CD Level B
21.6	Solve problems by using the skill *use data from a table*.	6, 7	2/2	__/2		**R, P, PS, RTE:** 21.6 **MM:** TNG/TT Level E
22.1	Compare and order objects by length.	4	1/1	__/1	102	**R, P, PS, RTE:** 22.1 **MM:** SA/MTM Level A
22.3	Estimate and measure length by using nonstandard units.	3	1/1	__/1	103	**R, P, PS, RTE:** 22.3 **MM:** SA/MTM Levels D, E, ISE/LL Level A
22.4	Measure objects to the nearest inch using a ruler.	2	1/1	__/1		**R, P, PS, RTE:** 22.4 **MM:** SA/MTM Level G, ISE/LL Level D

Student's Name ______________________ Date ______________

Chapter/ Lesson	Lesson Objective	Items	Criterion Score	Student's Score	On-Level Intervention Skills	Prescriptions
22.6	Read temperature to the nearest degree from Fahrenheit and Celsius thermometers.	1	1/1	__/1		**R, P, PS, RTE:** 22.6 **MM:** TNG/TT Level P
22.7	Solve problems by using the skill *make reasonable estimates.*	5, 6	2/2	__/2		**R, P, PS, RTE:** 22.7 **MM:** CCD/CD Levels A, B, C
23.3	Measure, compare, and order weights of objects.	1	1/1	__/1	108	**R, P, PS, RTE:** 23.3 **MM:** CCD/HC Levels E, G
23.4	Estimate and measure the weight of objects using pounds.	4	1/1	__/1		**R, P, PS, RTE:** 23.4 **MM:** TNG/TT Level O
23.6	Measure, compare, and order capacity of containers.	2	1/1	__/1	111	**R, P, PS, RTE:** 23.6
23.7	Estimate and measure capacity to the nearest cup, pint, or quart.	3	1/1	__/1		**R, P, PS, RTE:** 23.7 **MM:** TNG/TT Level N
23.8	Choose the correct measuring tool.	5, 6	2/2	__/2		**R, P, PS, RTE:** 23.8
23.9	Solve problems by using the strategy *predict and test.*	7, 8	2/2	__/2		**R, P, PS, RTE:** 23.9
24.1	Use mental math to add tens and find sums.	2	1/1	__/1		**R, P, PS, RTE:** 24.1 **MM:** CCD/BB Level J
24.2	Add tens and ones to find sums.	4	1/1	__/1	116	**R, P, PS, RTE:** 24.2 **MM:** CCD/BB Level K
24.3	Add 2-digit numbers to find sums.	5	1/1	__/1	117	**R, P, PS, RTE:** 24.3 **MM:** CCD/BB Level K
24.4	Use mental math to subtract tens and find differences.	1	1/1	__/1	118	**R, P, PS, RTE:** 24.4 **MM:** CCD/BB Level O
24.5	Subtract tens and ones to find differences.	3	1/1	__/1	119	**R, P, PS, RTE:** 24.5 **MM:** CCD/BB Level P

Key: Workbooks: R: Reteach Workbook **P:** Practice Workbook **PS:** Problem Solving and Reading Strategies Workbook **RTE:** Reteach (Teacher Edition) **MM:** Mega Math **CCD:** Country Countdown **BB:** Block Busters **CC:** Counting Critters **HC:** Harrison's Comparisons **CD:** Clock-a-Doodle-Doo **WW:** White Water Graphing **SA:** Shapes Ahoy! **SS:** Ship Shapes **3D:** Undersea 3D **SCS:** Sea Cave Sorting **MTM:** Made to Measure **NBR:** Numberopolis **LL:** LuLu's Lunch Counter **CS:** Carnival Stories **CN:** Cross Town Number Line **WS:** Wash 'n Spin **FA:** Fraction Action **FF:** Fraction Flare Up **LC:** Last Chance Canyon **TNG:** The Number Games **TT:** Tiny's Think Tank **AG:** ArachnaGraph **ISE:** Ice Station Exploration **AA:** Arctic Algebra **LL:** Linear Lab

Student's Name ______________________ Date ____________

Chapter/ Lesson	Lesson Objective	Items	Criterion Score	Student's Score	On-Level Intervention Skills	Prescriptions
24.6	Subtract 2-digit numbers to find differences.	6	1/1	__/1	120	**R, P, PS, RTE:** 24.6 **MM:** CCD/BB Level R
24.7	Solve problems by using the skill *make reasonable estimates.*	7, 8	2/2	__/2		**R, P, PS, RTE:** 24.7

INDIVIDUAL RECORD FORM

Student's Name ______________________ Date ____________

Chapter/ Lesson	Lesson Objective	Items	Criterion Score	Student's Score	On-Level Intervention Skills	Prescriptions
Unit 1						
1.1	Use one-to-one correspondence to compare groups.	12	1/1	__/1		**R, P, PS, RTE:** 1.1 **MM:** CCD/HC Level A
1.2	Count, read, and write numbers up to 10.	16	1/1	__/1	2	**R, P, PS, RTE:** 1.2 **MM:** CCD/CC Levels A, B
1.3	Count, read, and write numbers up to 20.	23	1/1	__/1	2	**R, P, PS, RTE:** 1.3 **MM:** CCD/CC Levels A, B, D
1.4	Compare numbers to 20.	5	1/1	__/1	3	**R, P, PS, RTE:** 1.4 **MM:** CCD/CC Level D
1.5	Order numbers to 20.	1	1/1	__/1	3	**R, P, PS, RTE:** 1.5 **MM:** NBR/CN Levels A, B, C
1.6	Identify ordinal numbers.	17	1/1	__/1		**R, P, PS, RTE:** 1.6
2.2	Use pictures and symbols to write addition sentences.	14	1/1	__/1	6	**R, P, PS, RTE:** 2.2 **MM:** CCD/BB Level C
2.3	Use the part-part-whole concept to model and solve addition problems with concrete objects.	24	1/1	__/1	8	**R, P, PS, RTE:** 2.3 **MM:** NBR/CS Levels A, F, K
2.4	Understand and apply the Zero Property for Addition.	9	1/1	__/1	7	**R, P, PS, RTE:** 2.4 **MM:** CCD/HC Level C
2.5	Explore the Order Properly for Addition.	3	1/1	__/1	9	**R, P, PS, RTE:** 2.5 **MM:** CCD/BB Level A
2.6	Write addition sentences to show different ways to make numbers to 8.	11	1/1	__/1	10	**R, P, PS, RTE:** 2.6 **MM:** CCD/BB Level A, NBR/CS Level A

Key: Workbooks: R: Reteach Workbook **P:** Practice Workbook **PS:** Problem Solving and Reading Strategies Workbook **RTE:** Reteach (Teacher Edition) **MM:** Mega Math **CCD:** Country Countdown **BB:** Block Busters **CC:** Counting Critters **HC:** Harrison's Comparisons **CD:** Clock-a-Doodle-Doo **WW:** White Water Graphing **SA:** Shapes Ahoy! **SS:** Ship Shapes **3D:** Undersea 3D **SCS:** Sea Cave Sorting **MTM:** Made to Measure **NBR:** Numberopolis **LL:** LuLu's Lunch Counter **CS:** Carnival Stories **CN:** Cross Town Number Line **WS:** Wash 'n Spin **FA:** Fraction Action **FF:** Fraction Flare Up **LC:** Last Chance Canyon **TNG:** The Number Games **TT:** Tiny's Think Tank **AG:** ArachnaGraph **ISE:** Ice Station Exploration **AA:** Arctic Algebra **LL:** Linear Lab

Student's Name ____________________ Date __________

Chapter/ Lesson	Lesson Objective	Items	Criterion Score	Student's Score	On-Level Intervention Skills	Prescriptions
2.7	Write vertical addition sentences.	19	1/1	__/1	11	**R, P, PS, RTE:** 2.7 **MM:** CCD/BB Level E
2.8	Solve problems by using the strategy *make a model.*	21	1/1	__/1	12	**R, P, PS, RTE:** 2.8 **MM:** NBR/LL Level C
3.1	Model and solve take-away problem situations using concrete objects.	13	1/1	__/1	13	**R, P, PS, RTE:** 3.1 **MM:** CCD/BB Level B, NBR/CS Level B
3.3	Identify how many are left when subtracting all or 0.	2	1/1	__/1	15	**R, P, PS, RTE:** 3.3
3.4	Model and record ways to subtract from 7 and 8.	20	1/1	__/1	16	**R, P, PS, RTE:** 3.4 **MM:** CCD/BB Level B, NBR/CS Level B
3.5	Write vertical subtraction sentences.	22	1/1	__/1	17	**R, P, PS, RTE:** 3.5 **MM:** CCD/BB Level F
3.6	Use the part-part-whole concept of subtraction to model and solve problems with concrete objects.	10	1/1	__/1	18	**R, P, PS, RTE:** 3.6 **MM:** NBR/CS Levels B, L
3.7	Model and compare to show the meaning of subtraction.	25	1/1	__/1	19	**R, P, PS, RTE:** 3.7 **MM:** NBR/CS Level C
3.8	Solve problems by using the strategy *make a model.*	7	1/1	__/1	12	**R, P, PS, RTE:** 3.8 **MM:** NBR/LL Level D
4.1	Identify addition and subtraction problem situations.	18	1/1	__/1	20	**R, P, PS, RTE:** 4.1 **MM:** NBR/CS Levels D, J
4.2	Explore how addition and subtraction are related.	15	1/1	__/1	20	**R, P, PS, RTE:** 4.2 **MM:** NBR/CS Level D, NBR/CN Level M
4.3	Identify and write related facts.	6	1/1	__/1	21	**R, P, PS, RTE:** 4.3 **MM:** CCD/CC Levels I, L, U
4.4	Write number sentences to represent addition and subtraction situations.	8	1/1	__/1	21	**R, P, PS, RTE:** 4.4 **MM:** CCD/CC Levels I, L, U
4.5	Solve problems by using the skill *choose the operation.*	4	1/1	__/1		**R, P, PS, RTE:** 4.5 **MM:** NBR/CS Level D

Student's Name ________________ Date ________

Chapter/ Lesson	Lesson Objective	Items	Criterion Score	Student's Score	On-Level Intervention Skills	Prescriptions
Unit 2						
5.1	Count on 1 or 2 to find sums.	10	1/1	__/1	22	**R, P, PS, RTE:** 5.1 **MM:** NBR/CN Level D
5.2	Use a number line to count on using small numbers to find sums to 12.	5, 6	2/2	__/2	22	**R, P, PS, RTE:** 5.2 **MM:** NBR/CN Level D
5.3	Count on from the greater number.	14	1/1	__/1	22	**R, P, PS, RTE:** 5.3 **MM:** NBR/CN Levels D, E, I
5.4	Use doubles as a strategy to solve addition facts through 12.	1	1/1	__/1	23	**R, P, PS, RTE:** 5.4 **MM:** CCD/CC Level F
5.5	Use doubles and near doubles as strategies to find sums to 12.	18	1/1	__/1	24	**R, P, PS, RTE:** 5.5 **MM:** CCD/CC Level J
5.6	Use the strategies *count on, doubles,* and *near doubles* to practice facts to 12.	20	1/1	__/1	22, 23, 24	**R, P, PS, RTE:** 5.6 **MM:** CCD/CC Level S, NBR/CS Level F
5.7	Solve problems by using the strategy *draw a picture.*	26	1/1	__/1	25	**R, P, PS, RTE:** 5.7 **MM:** NBR/CS Level E
6.1	Count back 1 or 2 to subtract from 12 or less.	15	1/1	__/1	26	**R, P, PS, RTE:** 6.1 **MM:** NBR/CN Levels D, E, G, I
6.2	Subtract from 12 or less using a number line to count back.	16	1/1	__/1	26	**R, P, PS, RTE:** 6.2 **MM:** NBR/CN Level E
6.3	Use addition as a strategy to subtract from 12 or less.	7, 23	2/2	__/2	27	**R, P, PS, RTE:** 6.3 **MM:** CCD/CC Level I
6.4	Use the strategies *count back* and *think addition to subtract* to practice subtraction facts.	8	1/1	__/1	26, 27	**R, P, PS, RTE:** 6.4 **MM:** CCD/CC Level I, NBR/CN Level G

Key: Workbooks: R: Reteach Workbook **P:** Practice Workbook **PS:** Problem Solving and Reading Strategies Workbook **RTE:** Reteach (Teacher Edition) **MM:** Mega Math **CCD:** Country Countdown **BB:** Block Busters **CC:** Counting Critters **HC:** Harrison's Comparisons **CD:** Clock-a-Doodle-Doo **WW:** White Water Graphing **SA:** Shapes Ahoy! **SS:** Ship Shapes **3D:** Undersea 3D **SCS:** Sea Cave Sorting **MTM:** Made to Measure **NBR:** Numberopolis **LL:** LuLu's Lunch Counter **CS:** Carnival Stories **CN:** Cross Town Number Line **WS:** Wash 'n Spin **FA:** Fraction Action **FF:** Fraction Flare Up **LC:** Last Chance Canyon **TNG:** The Number Games **TT:** Tiny's Think Tank **AG:** ArachnaGraph **ISE:** Ice Station Exploration **AA:** Arctic Algebra **LL:** Linear Lab

Student's Name ______________________ Date ____________

Chapter/ Lesson	Lesson Objective	Items	Criterion Score	Student's Score	On-Level Intervention Skills	Prescriptions
6.5	Solve problems by using the strategy *write a number sentence.*	11, 12	2/2	__/2	28	**R, P, PS, RTE:** 6.5 **MM:** NBR/CS Level A
7.1	Identify related addition facts to 12.	12	1/1	__/1		**R, P, PS, RTE:** 7.1 **MM:** CCD/CC Level G
7.2	Identify related subtraction facts to 12.	9	1/1	__/1		**R, P, PS, RTE:** 7.2 **MM:** CCD/CC Level H
7.3	Identify fact families.	4, 24	2/2	__/2	31	**R, P, PS, RTE:** 7.3 **MM:** CCD/CC Level I
7.4	Record fact families.	19	1/1	__/1	31	**R, P, PS, RTE:** 7.4 **MM:** CCD/CC Level I
7.5	Complete a table by using a rule.	3, 17	2/2	__/2	32	**R, P, PS, RTE:** 7.5 **MM:** CCD/CC Level I
7.6	Represent equivalent forms of numbers to 12.	13	1/1	__/1	33	**R, P, PS, RTE:** 7.6 **MM:** NBR/CS Level J
7.7	Create addition and subtraction situations and write the corresponding number sentence.	21	1/1	__/1	34	**R, P, PS, RTE:** 7.7 **MM:** NBR/CS Levels D, J
7.8	Solve problems by using the strategy *draw a picture.*	2, 25	2/2	__/2	28	**R, P, PS, RTE:** 7.8 **MM:** NBR/CS Levels C, I
Unit 3						
8.1	Use Venn diagrams to sort and classify objects by common attributes.	7	1/1	__/1	35	**R, P, PS, RTE:** 8.1 **MM:** SA/SCS Levels B, C, D
8.4	Read and compare data from a picture graph.	19	1/1	__/1	36	**R, P, PS, RTE:** 8.4 **MM:** CCD/WW Level A
9.1	Read a tally chart and interpret the data.	3	1/1	__/1	37, 38	**R, P, PS, RTE:** 9.1 **MM:** CCD/WW Level D
9.3	Determine if an event is possible or impossible.	8	1/1	__/1		**R, P, PS, RTE:** 9.3 **MM:** NBR/WS Level B, FA/LC Level A

Student's Name ____________________ Date __________

Chapter/ Lesson	Lesson Objective	Items	Criterion Score	Student's Score	On-Level Intervention Skills	Prescriptions
9.5	Solve problems by using the strategy *predict and test.*	11	1/1	__/1		**R, P, PS, RTE:** 9.5 **MM:** NBR/WS Level I, FA/LC Level D
10.1	Count, group, and describe objects using tens and ones.	14	1/1	__/1	43	**R, P, PS, RTE:** 10.1 **MM:** CCD/CC Level P
10.2	Model and count groups of tens.	2	1/1	__/1	44	**R, P, PS, RTE:** 10.2 **MM:** CCD/BB Level G, NBR/CN Level P
10.4	Count and group objects to 100 as tens and ones.	20	1/1	__/1	45	**R, P, PS, RTE:** 10.4 **MM:** CCD/BB Level H
10.5	Write 2-digit numbers in expanded forms.	4	1/1	__/1	46	**R, P, PS, RTE:** 10.5 **MM:** CCD/BB Levels V, W
11.2	Model and compare 2-digit numbers to determine which is less.	10	1/1	__/1	48	**R, P, PS, RTE:** 11.2 **MM:** CCD/HC Level I, SA/SCS Levels G, O
11.3	Use the symbols for *is less than* $<$, *is greater than* $>$, and *is equal to* $=$ to compare numbers.	16	1/1	__/1	49	**R, P, PS, RTE:** 11.3 **MM:** CCD/HC Level K, SA/SCS Level O
11.5	Identify ten more than and ten less than a given number.	21	1/1	__/1	50	**R, P, PS, RTE:** 11.5 **MM:** NBR/CN Level P
11.6	Use a number line to determine *before, between,* and *after.*	1	1/1	__/1	51	**R, P, PS, RTE:** 11.6 **MM:** NBR/CN Level T
11.7	Order numbers from least to greatest or greatest to least.	17	1/1	__/1	51	**R, P, PS, RTE:** 11.7 **MM:** SA/MTM Level C, NBR/CN Level O
11.8	Solve problems by using the skill *use a table.*	12, 13	2/2	__/2		**R, P, PS, RTE:** 11.8

Key: Workbooks: R: Reteach Workbook **P:** Practice Workbook **PS:** Problem Solving and Reading Strategies Workbook **RTE:** Reteach (Teacher Edition) **MM:** Mega Math **CCD:** Country Countdown **BB:** Block Busters **CC:** Counting Critters **HC:** Harrison's Comparisons **CD:** Clock-a-Doodle-Doo **WW:** White Water Graphing **SA:** Shapes Ahoy! **SS:** Ship Shapes **3D:** Undersea 3D **SCS:** Sea Cave Sorting **MTM:** Made to Measure **NBR:** Numberopolis **LL:** LuLu's Lunch Counter **CS:** Carnival Stories **CN:** Cross Town Number Line **WS:** Wash 'n Spin **FA:** Fraction Action **FF:** Fraction Flare Up **LC:** Last Chance Canyon **TNG:** The Number Games **TT:** Tiny's Think Tank **AG:** ArachnaGraph **ISE:** Ice Station Exploration **AA:** Arctic Algebra **LL:** Linear Lab

Student's Name ______________________ Date ____________

Chapter/ Lesson	Lesson Objective	Items	Criterion Score	Student's Score	On-Level Intervention Skills	Prescriptions
12.1	Count forward and backward to 100.	15	1/1	__/1		**R, P, PS, RTE:** 12.1 **MM:** NBR/CN Levels M, O, P
12.3	Use patterns on a hundred chart to skip count by twos, fives, and tens.	5	1/1	__/1	53	**R, P, PS, RTE:** 12.3
12.4	Use patterns on a hundred chart to count by tens from any number.	6	1/1	__/1	54	**R, P, PS, RTE:** 12.4
12.6	Use patterns to classify numbers as even or odd.	18	1/1	__/1		**R, P, PS, RTE:** 12.6 **MM:** NBR/CN Level S, SA/SCS Level M
12.7	Solve problems by using the strategy *find a pattern.*	9	1/1	__/1	56	**R, P, PS, RTE:** 12.7 **MM:** SA/SS Levels A, B, C
Unit 4						
13.1	Identify and sort solid figures by their flat and curved surfaces.	14	1/1	__/1	57	**R, P, PS, RTE:** 13.1 **MM:** SA/SS Levels I, J
13.2	Classify solid figures by the number of flat surfaces and corners they have.	17	1/1	__/1	58	**R, P, PS, RTE:** 13.2 **MM:** SA/3D Level F
13.3	Identify plane figures on solids.	8	1/1	__/1	59	**R, P, PS, RTE:** 13.3 **MM:** SA/3D Level G
13.4	Identify and sort plane figures.	4, 12	2/2	__/2	60	**R, P, PS, RTE:** 13.4 **MM:** SA/SCS Level K
13.5	Classify plane figures by the number of sides and corners they have.	1	1/1	__/1	60	**R, P, PS, RTE:** 13.5 **MM:** SA/3D Level G
13.6	Solve problems by using the strategy *use logical reasoning.*	21	1/1	__/1	61	**R, P, PS, RTE:** 13.6 **MM:** SA/SS Levels B, C, O
14.1	Identify and describe concrete repeating patterns.	9	1/1	__/1	62	**R, P, PS, RTE:** 14.1 **MM:** SA/SS Levels B, C
14.3	Predict and extend pictorial repeating patterns.	5	1/1	__/1		**R, P, PS, RTE:** 14.3 **MM:** SA/SS Level B

Student's Name ______________________ Date ____________

Chapter/ Lesson	Lesson Objective	Items	Criterion Score	Student's Score	On-Level Intervention Skills	Prescriptions
14.4	Identify and describe patterns with missing elements.	13	1/1	__/1	65	**R, P, PS, RTE:** 14.4 **MM:** SA/SS Level C, TNG/TT Level J
14.6	Transfer patterns from one representation to another.	15	1/1	__/1		**R, P, PS, RTE:** 14.6 **MM:** SA/SS Level F
14.7	Solve problems by using the strategy *find a pattern.*	20	1/1	__/1	56	**R, P, PS, RTE:** 14.7 **MM:** SA/SS Level C
15.2	Use position words to give and follow directions.	22	1/1	__/1		**R, P, PS, RTE:** 15.2 **MM:** SA/SS Level A, TNG/AG Level G
15.3	Identify and match congruent figures.	16	1/1	__/1		**R, P, PS, RTE:** 15.3 **MM:** SA/SS Level L
15.4	Make and identify shapes that have a line of symmetry.	6	1/1	__/1		**R, P, PS, RTE:** 15.4 **MM:** SA/SS Levels M, N
15.5	Identify and explore the effects of slides, flips, and turns.	2	1/1	__/1		**R, P, PS, RTE:** 15.5 **MM:** SA/SS Levels O, P
15.6	Solve problems by using the strategy *use logical reasoning.*	18, 19	2/2	__/2	61	**R, P, PS, RTE:** 15.6
16.1	Identify equal and unequal parts of a whole.	3	1/1	__/1		**R, P, PS, RTE:** 16.1 **MM:** SA/SS Level Q
16.3	Identify, describe, and name fourths.	7	1/1	__/1		**R, P, PS, RTE:** 16.3 **MM:** SA/SS Levels R, S
16.5	Identify, describe, and name fractions as parts of a group.	11	1/1	__/1		**R, P, PS, RTE:** 16.5 **MM:** FA/FF Level C
16.6	Solve problems by using the strategy *use logical reasoning.*	10	1/1	__/1		**R, P, PS, RTE:** 16.6

Key: **Workbooks:** **R:** Reteach Workbook **P:** Practice Workbook **PS:** Problem Solving and Reading Strategies Workbook **RTE:** Reteach (Teacher Edition) **MM:** Mega Math **CCD:** Country Countdown **BB:** Block Busters **CC:** Counting Critters **HC:** Harrison's Comparisons **CD:** Clock-a-Doodle-Doo **WW:** White Water Graphing **SA:** Shapes Ahoy! **SS:** Ship Shapes **3D:** Undersea 3D **SCS:** Sea Cave Sorting **MTM:** Made to Measure **NBR:** Numberopolis **LL:** LuLu's Lunch Counter **CS:** Carnival Stories **CN:** Cross Town Number Line **WS:** Wash 'n Spin **FA:** Fraction Action **FF:** Fraction Flare Up **LC:** Last Chance Canyon **TNG:** The Number Games **TT:** Tiny's Think Tank **AG:** ArachnaGraph **ISE:** Ice Station Exploration **AA:** Arctic Algebra **LL:** Linear Lab

Student's Name ____________________ Date __________

Chapter/ Lesson	Lesson Objective	Items	Criterion Score	Student's Score	On-Level Intervention Skills	Prescriptions
Unit 5						
17.1	Add by using the strategies *doubles* and *near doubles.*	3	1/1	__/1	79	**R, P, PS, RTE:** 17.1 **MM:** CCD/CC Levels J, O
17.3	Use the strategy *make-a-ten* to find sums.	14	1/1	__/1	80	**R, P, PS, RTE:** 17.3 **MM:** CCD/CC Level Q
17.4	Use the Order Property and addition strategies to add three numbers.	7	1/1	__/1	81	**R, P, PS, RTE:** 17.4 **MM:** CCD/CC Level K
17.6	Solve problems by using the strategy *write a number sentence.*	12	1/1	__/1	28	**R, P, PS, RTE:** 17.6 **MM:** CCD/CC Level I
18.2	Model and compare to show the meaning of subtraction.	5	1/1	__/1	83	**R, P, PS, RTE:** 18.2 **MM:** NBR/CS Level C
18.3	Use think addition as a strategy to subtract numbers from 20 or less.	2	1/1	__/1	84	**R, P, PS, RTE:** 18.3 **MM:** CCD/CC Levels I, L, U
18.4	Practice subtraction facts from 20 or less.	11, 19	2/2	__/2	82, 84	**R, P, PS, RTE:** 18.4 **MM:** CCD/CC Levels T, U
19.1	Use fact families to find sums and differences to 20.	21	1/1	__/1	107	**R, P, PS, RTE:** 19.1 **MM:** CCD/CC Level U
19.2	Identify a missing number in a number sentence.	13	1/1	__/1	86	**R, P, PS, RTE:** 19.2 **MM:** NBR/CS Levels E, H, N
19.4	Complete a function table.	4	1/1	__/1	88	**R, P, PS, RTE:** 19.4 **MM:** ISE/AA Level J
19.5	Use pictures to create addition and subtraction problems.	6	1/1	__/1	89	**R, P, PS, RTE:** 19.5 **MM:** ISE/AA Level B
19.6	Solve problems by using the skill *choose the operation.*	15	1/1	__/1		**R, P, PS, RTE:** 19.6 **MM:** NBR/CS Levels D, J
20.5	Show ways to make 100¢ with coins and dollars.	10	1/1	__/1		**R, P, PS, RTE:** 20.5 **MM:** NBR/LL Level I

Student's Name ______________________ Date ____________

Chapter/ Lesson	Lesson Objective	Items	Criterion Score	Student's Score	On-Level Intervention Skills	Prescriptions
20.6	Identify and compare given money amounts.	16	1/1	__/1		**R, P, PS, RTE:** 20.6 **MM:** NBR/LL Level J
20.7	Identify different ways to make equal amounts using coins or one dollar.	9	1/1	__/1	96	**R, P, PS, RTE:** 20.7 **MM:** NBR/LL Level J
21.1	Tell and write time to the hour on analog and digital clocks.	18	1/1	__/1	98	**R, P, PS, RTE:** 21.1 **MM:** CCD/CD Level G
21.3	Read and show time to the hour and half hour using analog and digital clocks.	17	1/1	__/1	98, 99	**R, P, PS, RTE:** 21.3 **MM:** CCD/CD Levels G, H
21.4	Read and use a calendar.	1	1/1	__/1		**R, P, PS, RTE:** 21.4 **MM:** CCD/CD Level E
21.5	Understand and order the sequence of events with respect to time.	8	1/1	__/1		**R, P, PS, RTE:** 21.5 **MM:** CCD/CD Level B
21.6	Solve problems by using the skill *use data from a table.*	20	1/1	__/1		**R, P, PS, RTE:** 21.6 **MM:** TNG/TT Level E
Unit 6						
22.1	Compare and order objects by length.	10	1/1	__/1	102	**R, P, PS, RTE:** 22.1 **MM:** SA/MTM Level A
22.3	Estimate and measure length by using nonstandard units.	3	1/1	__/1	103	**R, P, PS, RTE:** 22.3 **MM:** SA/MTM Levels D, E, ISE/LL Level A
22.4	Measure objects to the nearest inch using a ruler.	9	1/1	__/1		**R, P, PS, RTE:** 22.4 **MM:** SA/MTM Level G, ISE/LL Level D
22.5	Measure objects to the nearest centimeter by using a centimeter ruler.	15	1/1	__/1		**R, P, PS, RTE:** 22.5 **MM:** SA/MTM Level H, ISE/LL Level H

Key: Workbooks: R: Reteach Workbook **P:** Practice Workbook **PS:** Problem Solving and Reading Strategies Workbook **RTE:** Reteach (Teacher Edition) **MM:** Mega Math **CCD:** Country Countdown **BB:** Block Busters **CC:** Counting Critters **HC:** Harrison's Comparisons **CD:** Clock-a-Doodle-Doo **WW:** White Water Graphing **SA:** Shapes Ahoy! **SS:** Ship Shapes **3D:** Undersea 3D **SCS:** Sea Cave Sorting **MTM:** Made to Measure **NBR:** Numberopolis **LL:** LuLu's Lunch Counter **CS:** Carnival Stories **CN:** Cross Town Number Line **WS:** Wash 'n Spin **FA:** Fraction Action **FF:** Fraction Flare Up **LC:** Last Chance Canyon **TNG:** The Number Games **TT:** Tiny's Think Tank **AG:** ArachnaGraph **ISE:** Ice Station Exploration **AA:** Arctic Algebra **LL:** Linear Lab

Student's Name ____________________ Date __________

Chapter/ Lesson	Lesson Objective	Items	Criterion Score	Student's Score	On-Level Intervention Skills	Prescriptions
22.6	Read temperature to the nearest degree from Fahrenheit and Celsius thermometers.	5, 22	2/2	__/2		**R, P, PS, RTE:** 22.6 **MM:** TNG/TT Level P
22.7	Solve problems by using the skill *make reasonable estimates.*	18	1/1	__/1		**R, P, PS, RTE:** 22.7 **MM:** CCD/CD Levels A, B, C
23.3	Measure, compare, and order weights of objects.	16	1/1	__/1	108	**R, P, PS, RTE:** 23.3 **MM:** CCD/HC Levels E, G
23.4	Estimate and measure the weight of objects using pounds.	4	1/1	__/1		**R, P, PS, RTE:** 23.4 **MM:** TNG/TT Level O
23.6	Measure, compare, and order capacity of containers.	2	1/1	__/1	111	**R, P, PS, RTE:** 23.6
23.7	Estimate and measure capacity to the nearest cup, pint, or quart.	7	1/1	__/1		**R, P, PS, RTE:** 23.7 **MM:** TNG/TT Level N
23.8	Choose the correct measuring tool.	11, 21	2/2	__/2		**R, P, PS, RTE:** 23.8
23.9	Solve problems by using the strategy *predict and test.*	14	1/1	__/1		**R, P, PS, RTE:** 23.9
24.1	Use mental math to add tens and find sums.	19	1/1	__/1		**R, P, PS, RTE:** 24.1 **MM:** CCD/BB Level J
24.2	Add tens and ones to find sums.	1	1/1	__/1	116	**R, P, PS, RTE:** 24.2 **MM:** CCD/BB Level K
24.3	Add 2-digit numbers to find sums.	12	1/1	__/1	117	**R, P, PS, RTE:** 24.3 **MM:** CCD/BB Level K
24.4	Use mental math to subtract tens and find differences.	6	1/1	__/1	118	**R, P, PS, RTE:** 24.4 **MM:** CCD/BB Level O
24.5	Subtract tens and ones to find differences.	17	1/1	__/1	119	**R, P, PS, RTE:** 24.5 **MM:** CCD/BB Level P
24.6	Subtract 2-digit numbers to find differences.	8	1/1	__/1	120	**R, P, PS, RTE:** 24.6 **MM:** CCD/BB Level R

Student's Name ______________________ Date ____________

Chapter/ Lesson	Lesson Objective	Items	Criterion Score	Student's Score	On-Level Intervention Skills	Prescriptions
24.7	Solve problems by using the skill *make reasonable estimates.*	13, 20	2/2	__/2		**R, P, PS, RTE:** 24.7

Key: Workbooks: R: Reteach Workbook **P:** Practice Workbook **PS:** Problem Solving and Reading Strategies Workbook **RTE:** Reteach (Teacher Edition) **MM:** Mega Math **CCD:** Country Countdown **BB:** Block Busters **CC:** Counting Critters **HC:** Harrison's Comparisons **CD:** Clock-a-Doodle-Doo **WW:** White Water Graphing **SA:** Shapes Ahoy! **SS:** Ship Shapes **3D:** Undersea 3D **SCS:** Sea Cave Sorting **MTM:** Made to Measure **NBR:** Numberopolis **LL:** LuLu's Lunch Counter **CS:** Carnival Stories **CN:** Cross Town Number Line **WS:** Wash 'n Spin **FA:** Fraction Action **FF:** Fraction Flare Up **LC:** Last Chance Canyon **TNG:** The Number Games **TT:** Tiny's Think Tank **AG:** ArachnaGraph **ISE:** Ice Station Exploration **AA:** Arctic Algebra **LL:** Linear Lab

INDIVIDUAL RECORD FORM

End of Year Test Form A/Form B

Student's Name ______________________ Date ____________

Chapter/ Lesson	Lesson Objective	Items	Criterion Score	Student's Score	On-Level Intervention Skills	Prescriptions
1.3	Count, read, and write numbers up to 20.	6	1/1	__/1	2	**R, P, PS, RTE:** 1.3 **MM:** CCD/CC Levels A, B, D
2.3	Use the part-part-whole concept to model and solve addition problems with concrete objects.	32	1/1	__/1	8	**R, P, PS, RTE:** 2.3 **MM:** NBR/CS Levels A, F, K
3.5	Write vertical subtraction sentences.	23	1/1	__/1	17	**R, P, PS, RTE:** 3.5 **MM:** CCD/BB Level F
4.3	Identify and write related facts.	27	1/1	__/1	21	**R, P, PS, RTE:** 4.3 **MM:** CCD/CC Levels I, L, U
5.3	Count on from the greater number.	22	1/1	__/1	22	**R, P, PS, RTE:** 5.3 **MM:** NBR/CN Levels D, E, I
6.4	Use the strategies *count back* and *think addition to subtract* to practice subtraction facts.	17	1/1	__/1	26, 27	**R, P, PS, RTE:** 6.4 **MM:** CCD/CC Level I, NBR/CN Level G
7.2	Identify related subtraction facts to 12.	7	1/1	__/1		**R, P, PS, RTE:** 7.2 **MM:** CCD/CC Level H
8.1	Use Venn diagrams to sort and classify objects by common attributes.	4	1/1	__/1	35	**R, P, PS, RTE:** 8.1 **MM:** SA/SCS Levels B, C, D
8.2	Sort and classify objects into three groups by common attributes.	24	1/1	__/1	35	**R, P, PS, RTE:** 8.2 **MM:** SA/SCS Levels A, C, G
8.3	Make concrete graphs from organized data and use the data to make comparisons.	3	1/1	__/1	36	**R, P, PS, RTE:** 8.3 **MM:** CCD/CC Levels C, D, CCD/WW Level B
9.1	Read a tally chart and interpret the data.	11	1/1	__/1	37, 38	**R, P, PS, RTE:** 9.1 **MM:** CCD/WW Level D
9.2	Read a bar graph to compare data.	35, 36	2/2	__/2	39	**R, P, PS, RTE:** 9.2 **MM:** CCD/WW Level F

Student's Name ____________________ Date __________

Chapter/ Lesson	Lesson Objective	Items	Criterion Score	Student's Score	On-Level Intervention Skills	Prescriptions
9.3	Determine if an event is possible or impossible.	28	1/1	__/1		**R, P, PS, RTE:** 9.3 **MM:** NBR/WS Level B, FA/LC Level A
9.4	Determine whether events are *more likely* or *less likely*.	42	1/1	__/1		**R, P, PS, RTE:** 9.4 **MM:** NBR/WS Level D
10.5	Write 2-digit numbers in expanded forms.	16	1/1	__/1	46	**R, P, PS, RTE:** 10.5 **MM:** CCD/BB Levels V, W
11.3	Use the symbols for *is less than* $<$, *is greater than* $>$, and *is equal to* $=$ to compare numbers.	44	1/1	__/1	49	**R, P, PS, RTE:** 11.3 **MM:** CCD/HC Level K, SA/SCS Level O
11.6	Use a number line to determine *before, between,* and *after.*	18	1/1	__/1	51	**R, P, PS, RTE:** 11.6 **MMP:** NBR/CN Level T
13.1	Identify and sort solid figures by their flat and curved surfaces.	33	1/1	__/1	57	**R, P, PS, RTE:** 13.1 **MM:** SA/SS Levels I, J
13.2	Classify solid figures by the number of flat surfaces and corners they have.	2	1/1	__/1	58	**R, P, PS, RTE:** 13.2 **MM:** SA/3D Level F
13.4	Identify and sort plane figures.	20	1/1	__/1	60	**R, P, PS, RTE:** 13.4 **MM:** SA/SCS Level K
13.5	Classify plane figures by the number of sides and corners they have.	15	1/1	__/1	60	**R, P, PS, RTE:** 13.5 **MM:** SA/3D Level G
14.2	Predict and extend concrete repeating patterns.	19	1/1	__/1	63	**R, P, PS, RTE:** 14.2 **MM:** SA/SS Levels B, D, TNG/TT Level J
14.3	Predict and extend pictorial repeating patterns.	34	1/1	__/1		**R, P, PS, RTE:** 14.3 **MM:** SA/SS Level B

Key: Workbooks: R: Reteach Workbook **P:** Practice Workbook **PS:** Problem Solving and Reading Strategies Workbook **RTE:** Reteach (Teacher Edition) **MM:** Mega Math **CCD:** Country Countdown **BB:** Block Busters **CC:** Counting Critters **HC:** Harrison's Comparisons **CD:** Clock-a-Doodle-Doo **WW:** White Water Graphing **SA:** Shapes Ahoy! **SS:** Ship Shapes **3D:** Undersea 3D **SCS:** Sea Cave Sorting **MTM:** Made to Measure **NBR:** Numberopolis **LL:** LuLu's Lunch Counter **CS:** Carnival Stories **CN:** Cross Town Number Line **WS:** Wash 'n Spin **FA:** Fraction Action **FF:** Fraction Flare Up **LC:** Last Chance Canyon **TNG:** The Number Games **TT:** Tiny's Think Tank **AG:** ArachnaGraph **ISE:** Ice Station Exploration **AA:** Arctic Algebra **LL:** Linear Lab

Student's Name ______________________ Date ____________

Chapter/ Lesson	Lesson Objective	Items	Criterion Score	Student's Score	On-Level Intervention Skills	Prescriptions
14.4	Identify and describe patterns with missing elements.	14	1/1	__/1	65	**R, P, PS, RTE:** 14.4 **MM:** SA/SS Level C, TNG/TT Level J
14.6	Transfer patterns from one representation to another.	38	1/1	__/1		**R, P, PS, RTE:** 14.6 **MM:** SA/SS Level F
15.2	Use position words to give and follow directions.	25	1/1	__/1		**R, P, PS, RTE:** 15.2 **MM:** SA/SS Level A, TNG/AG Level G
15.4	Make and identify shapes that have a line of symmetry.	41	1/1	__/1		**R, P, PS, RTE:** 15.4 **MM:** SA/SS Levels M, N
15.5	Identify and explore the effects of slides, flips, and turns.	8	1/1	__/1		**R, P, PS, RTE:** 15.5 **MM:** SA/SS Levels O, P
16.5	Identify, describe, and name fractions as parts of a group.	40	1/1	__/1		**R, P, PS, RTE:** 16.5 **MM:** FA/FF Level C
17.5	Practice addition facts to 20.	26	1/1	__/1	79	**R, P, PS, RTE:** 17.5 **MM:** CCD/CC Levels O, U
18.2	Model and compare to show the meaning of subtraction.	10	1/1	__/1	83	**R, P, PS, RTE:** 18.2 **MM:** NBR/CS Level C
20.6	Identify and compare given money amounts.	13	1/1	__/1		**R, P, PS, RTE:** 20.6 **MM:** NBR/LL Level J
21.1	Tell and write time to the hour on analog and digital clocks.	12	1/1	__/1	98	**R, P, PS, RTE:** 21.1 **MM:** CCD/CD Level G
21.3	Read and show time to the hour and half hour using analog and digital clocks.	37	1/1	__/1	98, 99	**R, P, PS, RTE:** 21.3 **MM:** CCD/CD Levels G, H
21.5	Understand and order the sequence of events with respect to time.	31	1/1	__/1		**R, P, PS, RTE:** 21.5 **MM:** CCD/CD Level B
22.2	Estimate and measure length by using nonstandard units.	21	1/1	__/1	103	**R, P, PS, RTE:** 22.2 **MM:** SA/MTM Level D

Student's Name ____________________ Date ____________

Chapter/ Lesson	Lesson Objective	Items	Criterion Score	Student's Score	On-Level Intervention Skills	Prescriptions
22.4	Measure objects to the nearest inch using a ruler.	43	1/1	__/1		**R, P, PS, RTE:** 22.4 **MM:** SA/MTM Level G, ISE/LL Level D
22.6	Read temperature to the nearest degree from Fahrenheit and Celsius thermometers.	1	1/1	__/1		**R, P, PS, RTE:** 22.6 **MM:** TNG/TT Level P
23.3	Measure, compare, and order weights of objects.	29	1/1	__/1	108	**R, P, PS, RTE:** 23.3 **MM:** CCD/HC Levels E, G
23.4	Estimate and measure the weight of objects using pounds.	39	1/1	__/1		**R, P, PS, RTE:** 23.4 **MM:** TNG/TT Level O
23.8	Choose the correct measuring tool.	9	1/1	__/1		**R, P, PS, RTE:** 23.8
24.1	Use mental math to add tens and find sums.	5	1/1	__/1		**R, P, PS, RTE:** 24.1 **MM:** CCD/BB Level J
24.6	Subtract 2-digit numbers to find differences.	30	1/1	__/1	120	**R, P, PS, RTE:** 24.6 **MM:** CCD/BB Level R

Key: **Workbooks:** **R:** Reteach Workbook **P:** Practice Workbook **PS:** Problem Solving and Reading Strategies Workbook **RTE:** Reteach (Teacher Edition) **MM:** Mega Math **CCD:** Country Countdown **BB:** Block Busters **CC:** Counting Critters **HC:** Harrison's Comparisons **CD:** Clock-a-Doodle-Doo **WW:** White Water Graphing **SA:** Shapes Ahoy! **SS:** Ship Shapes **3D:** Undersea 3D **SCS:** Sea Cave Sorting **MTM:** Made to Measure **NBR:** Numberopolis **LL:** LuLu's Lunch Counter **CS:** Carnival Stories **CN:** Cross Town Number Line **WS:** Wash 'n Spin **FA:** Fraction Action **FF:** Fraction Flare Up **LC:** Last Chance Canyon **TNG:** The Number Games **TT:** Tiny's Think Tank **AG:** ArachnaGraph **ISE:** Ice Station Exploration **AA:** Arctic Algebra **LL:** Linear Lab

CORRELATIONS

	Lesson Objective	Practice/Test Item Numbers
1.1	Use one-to-one correspondence to compare groups.	**Chapter 1 Posttest Form A/Form B:** 7 **Unit 1 Pretest/Posttest Form A/B:** 12
1.2	Count, read, and write numbers up to 10.	**Chapter 1 Posttest Form A/Form B:** 6 **Unit 1 Pretest/Posttest Form A/B:** 16
1.3	Count, read, and write numbers up to 20.	**Chapter 1 Posttest Form A/Form B:** 2 **Unit 1 Pretest/Posttest Form A/B:** 23 **Beginning/End of Year:** 6
1.4	Compare numbers to 20.	**Chapter 1 Posttest Form A/Form B:** 1, 4 **Unit 1 Pretest/Posttest Form A/B:** 5
1.5	Order numbers to 20.	**Chapter 1 Posttest Form A/Form B:** 3 **Unit 1 Pretest/Posttest Form A/B:** 1
1.6	Identify ordinal numbers.	**Chapter 1 Posttest Form A/Form B:** 5 **Unit 1 Pretest/Posttest Form A/B:** 17
1.7	Solve problems by using the skill *use data from a graph.*	**Chapter 1 Posttest Form A/Form B:** 8, 9
2.1	Use the joining concept to model and solve addition problems with concrete objects.	**Chapter 2 Posttest Form A/Form B:** 7
2.2	Use pictures and symbols to write addition sentences.	**Chapter 2 Posttest Form A/Form B:** 1 **Unit 1 Pretest/Posttest Form A/B:** 14
2.3	Use the part-part-whole concept to model and solve addition problems with concrete objects.	**Chapter 2 Posttest Form A/Form B:** 6 **Unit 1 Pretest/Posttest Form A/B:** 24 **Beginning/End of Year:** 32
2.4	Understand and apply the Zero Property for Addition.	**Chapter 2 Posttest Form A/Form B:** 3 **Unit 1 Pretest/Posttest Form A/B:** 9
2.5	Explore the Order Properly for Addition.	**Chapter 2 Posttest Form A/Form B:** 2 **Unit 1 Pretest/Posttest Form A/B:** 3
2.6	Write addition sentences to show different ways to make numbers to 8.	**Chapter 2 Posttest Form A/Form B:** 5 **Unit 1 Pretest/Posttest Form A/B:** 11
2.7	Write vertical addition sentences.	**Chapter 2 Posttest Form A/Form B:** 4 **Unit 1 Pretest/Posttest Form A/B:** 19
2.8	Solve problems by using the strategy *make a model.*	**Chapter 2 Posttest Form A/Form B:** 8 **Unit 1 Pretest/Posttest Form A/B:** 21
3.1	Model and solve take-away problem situations using concrete objects.	**Chapter 3 Posttest Form A/Form B:** 7 **Unit 1 Pretest/Posttest Form A/B:** 13
3.2	Use pictures to write subtraction sentences.	**Chapter 3 Posttest Form A/Form B:** 4
3.3	Identify how many are left when subtracting all or 0.	**Chapter 3 Posttest Form A/Form B:** 2 **Unit 1 Pretest/Posttest Form A/B:** 2
3.4	Model and record ways to subtract from 7 and 8.	**Chapter 3 Posttest Form A/Form B:** 3 **Unit 1 Pretest/Posttest Form A/B:** 20
3.5	Write vertical subtraction sentences.	**Chapter 3 Posttest Form A/Form B:** 1 **Unit 1 Pretest/Posttest Form A/B:** 22 **Beginning/End of Year:** 23

	Lesson Objective	Practice/Test Item Numbers
3.6	Use the part-part-whole concept of subtraction to model and solve problems with concrete objects.	**Chapter 3 Posttest Form A/Form B:** 6 **Unit 1 Pretest/Posttest Form A/B:** 10
3.7	Model and compare to show the meaning of subtraction.	**Chapter 3 Posttest Form A/Form B:** 5 **Unit 1 Pretest/Posttest Form A/B:** 25
3.8	Solve problems by using the strategy *make a model.*	**Chapter 3 Posttest Form A/Form B:** 8 **Unit 1 Pretest/Posttest Form A/B:** 7
4.1	Identify addition and subtraction problem situations.	**Chapter 4 Posttest Form A/Form B:** 4, 7 **Unit 1 Pretest/Posttest Form A/B:** 18
4.2	Explore how addition and subtraction are related.	**Chapter 4 Posttest Form A/Form B:** 1 **Unit 1 Pretest/Posttest Form A/B:** 15
4.3	Identify and write related facts.	**Chapter 4 Posttest Form A/Form B:** 3, 5 **Unit 1 Pretest/Posttest Form A/B:** 6 **Beginning/End of Year:** 27
4.4	Write number sentences to represent addition and subtraction situations.	**Chapter 4 Posttest Form A/Form B:** 2, 6 **Unit 1 Pretest/Posttest Form A/B:** 8
4.5	Solve problems by using the skill *choose the operation.*	**Chapter 4 Posttest Form A/Form B:** 8, 9 **Unit 1 Pretest/Posttest Form A/B:** 4
5.1	Count on 1 or 2 to find sums.	**Chapter 5 Posttest Form A/Form B:** 7 **Unit 2 Pretest/Posttest Form A/B:** 10
5.2	Use a number line to count on using small numbers to find sums to 12.	**Chapter 5 Posttest Form A/Form B:** 1, 2 **Unit 2 Pretest/Posttest Form A/B:** 5, 6
5.3	Count on from the greater number.	**Chapter 5 Posttest Form A/Form B:** 5 **Unit 2 Pretest/Posttest Form A/B:** 14 **Beginning/End of Year:** 22
5.4	Use doubles as a strategy to solve addition facts through 12.	**Chapter 5 Posttest Form A/Form B:** 3 **Unit 2 Pretest/Posttest Form A/B:** 1
5.5	Use doubles and near doubles as strategies to find sums to 12.	**Chapter 5 Posttest Form A/Form B:** 4 **Unit 2 Pretest/Posttest Form A/B:** 18
5.6	Use the strategies *count on, doubles,* and *near doubles* to practice facts to 12.	**Chapter 5 Posttest Form A/Form B:** 6 **Unit 2 Pretest/Posttest Form A/B:** 20
5.7	Solve problems by using the strategy *draw a picture.*	**Chapter 5 Posttest Form A/Form B:** 8, 9 **Unit 2 Pretest/Posttest Form A/B:** 26
6.1	Count back 1 or 2 to subtract from 12 or less.	**Chapter 6 Posttest Form A/Form B:** 1, 4 **Unit 2 Pretest/Posttest Form A/B:** 15
6.2	Subtract from 12 or less using a number line to count back.	**Chapter 6 Posttest Form A/Form B:** 2, 3 **Unit 2 Pretest/Posttest Form A/B:** 16
6.3	Use addition as a strategy to subtract from 12 or less.	**Chapter 6 Posttest Form A/Form B:** 7, 8 **Unit 2 Pretest/Posttest Form A/B:** 7, 23
6.4	Use the strategies *count back* and *think addition to subtract* to practice subtraction facts.	**Chapter 6 Posttest Form A/Form B:** 5, 6 **Unit 2 Pretest/Posttest Form A/B:** 8 **Beginning/End of Year:** 17
6.5	Solve problems by using the strategy *write a number sentence.*	**Chapter 6 Posttest Form A/Form B:** 9, 10 **Unit 2 Pretest/Posttest Form A/B:** 11, 22

	Lesson Objective	Practice/Test Item Numbers
7.1	Identify related addition facts to 12.	**Chapter 7 Posttest Form A/Form B:** 3 **Unit 2 Pretest/Posttest Form A/B:** 12
7.2	Identify related subtraction facts to 12.	**Chapter 7 Posttest Form A/Form B:** 7 **Unit 2 Pretest/Posttest Form A/B:** 9 **Beginning/End of Year:** 7
7.3	Identify fact families.	**Chapter 7 Posttest Form A/Form B:** 1 **Unit 2 Pretest/Posttest Form A/B:** 4, 24
7.4	Record fact families.	**Chapter 7 Posttest Form A/Form B:** 5 **Unit 2 Pretest/Posttest Form A/B:** 19
7.5	Complete a table by using a rule.	**Chapter 7 Posttest Form A/Form B:** 6 **Unit 2 Pretest/Posttest Form A/B:** 3, 17
7.6	Represent equivalent forms of numbers to 12.	**Chapter 7 Posttest Form A/Form B:** 2 **Unit 2 Pretest/Posttest Form A/B:** 13
7.7	Create addition and subtraction situations and write the corresponding number sentence.	**Chapter 7 Posttest Form A/Form B:** 4 **Unit 2 Pretest/Posttest Form A/B:** 21
7.8	Solve problems by using the strategy *draw a picture*.	**Chapter 7 Posttest Form A/Form B:** 8, 9 **Unit 2 Pretest/Posttest Form A/B:** 2, 25
8.1	Use Venn diagrams to sort and classify objects by common attributes.	**Chapter 8 Posttest Form A/Form B:** 4 **Unit 3 Pretest/Posttest Form A/B:** 7 **Beginning/End of Year:** 4
8.2	Sort and classify objects into three groups by common attributes.	**Chapter 8 Posttest Form A/Form B:** 1 **Beginning/End of Year:** 24
8.3	Make concrete graphs from organized data and use the data to make comparisons.	**Chapter 8 Posttest Form A/Form B:** 2 **Beginning/End of Year:** 3
8.4	Read and compare data from a picture graph.	**Chapter 8 Posttest Form A/Form B:** 3 **Unit 3 Pretest/Posttest Form A/B:** 19
8.5	Solve problems by using the skill *make and use a graph*.	**Chapter 8 Posttest Form A/Form B:** 5, 6
9.1	Read a tally chart and interpret the data.	**Chapter 9 Posttest Form A/Form B:** 2 **Unit 3 Pretest/Posttest Form A/B:** 3 **Beginning/End of Year:** 11
9.2	Read a bar graph to compare data.	**Chapter 9 Posttest Form A/Form B:** 4, 5 **Beginning/End of Year:** 35, 36
9.3	Determine if an event is possible or impossible.	**Chapter 9 Posttest Form A/Form B:** 3 **Unit 3 Pretest/Posttest Form A/B:** 8 **Beginning/End of Year:** 28
9.4	Determine whether events are *more likely or less likely*.	**Chapter 9 Posttest Form A/Form B:** 1 **Beginning/End of Year:** 42
9.5	Solve problems by using the strategy *predict and test*.	**Chapter 9 Posttest Form A/Form B:** 6, 7 **Unit 3 Pretest/Posttest Form A/B:** 11
10.1	Count, group, and describe objects using tens and ones.	**Chapter 10 Posttest Form A/Form B:** 4 **Unit 3 Pretest/Posttest Form A/B:** 14
10.2	Model and count groups of tens.	**Chapter 10 Posttest Form A/Form B:** 3 **Unit 3 Pretest/Posttest Form A/B:** 2

Lesson Objective		Practice/Test Item Numbers
10.3	Count and group objects to 50 as tens and ones.	**Chapter 10 Posttest Form A/Form B:** 1
10.4	Count and group objects to 100 as tens and ones.	**Chapter 10 Posttest Form A/Form B:** 5 **Unit 3 Pretest/Posttest Form A/B:** 20
10.5	Write 2-digit numbers in expanded forms.	**Chapter 10 Posttest Form A/Form B:** 2, 6 **Unit 3 Pretest/Posttest Form A/B:** 4 **Beginning/End of Year:** 16
10.6	Solve problems by using the skill *make reasonable estimates.*	**Chapter 10 Posttest Form A/Form B:** 7, 8
11.1	Model and compare 2-digit numbers to determine which is greater.	**Chapter 11 Posttest Form A/Form B:** 1
11.2	Model and compare 2-digit numbers to determine which is less.	**Chapter 11 Posttest Form A/Form B:** 6 **Unit 3 Pretest/Posttest Form A/B:** 10
11.3	Use the symbols for *is less than* $<$, *is greater than* $>$, and *is equal to* $=$ to compare numbers.	**Chapter 11 Posttest Form A/Form B:** 3 **Unit 3 Pretest/Posttest Form A/B:** 16 **Beginning/End of Year:** 44
11.4	Identify one more than and one less than a given number.	**Chapter 11 Posttest Form A/Form B:** 5
11.5	Identify ten more than and ten less than a given number.	**Chapter 11 Posttest Form A/Form B:** 7 **Unit 3 Pretest/Posttest Form A/B:** 21
11.6	Use a number line to determine *before, between,* and *after.*	**Chapter 11 Posttest Form A/Form B:** 2 **Unit 3 Pretest/Posttest Form A/B:** 1 **Beginning/End of Year:** 18
11.7	Order numbers from least to greatest or greatest to least.	**Chapter 11 Posttest Form A/Form B:** 4 **Unit 3 Pretest/Posttest Form A/B:** 17
11.8	Solve problems by using the skill *use a table.*	**Chapter 11 Posttest Form A/Form B:** 8, 9 **Unit 3 Pretest/Posttest Form A/B:** 12, 13
12.1	Count forward and backward to 100.	**Chapter 12 Posttest Form A/Form B:** 4 **Unit 3 Pretest/Posttest Form A/B:** 15
12.2	Use pictures to skip count by twos, fives, and tens.	**Chapter 12 Posttest Form A/Form B:** 3
12.3	Use patterns on a hundred chart to skip count by twos, fives, and tens.	**Chapter 12 Posttest Form A/Form B:** 1 **Unit 3 Pretest/Posttest Form A/B:** 5
12.4	Use patterns on a hundred chart to count by tens from any number.	**Chapter 12 Posttest Form A/Form B:** 2 **Unit 3 Pretest/Posttest Form A/B:** 6
12.5	Use skip counting to identify, describe, and extend number patterns.	**Chapter 12 Posttest Form A/Form B:** 5
12.6	Use patterns to classify numbers as even or odd.	**Chapter 12 Posttest Form A/Form B:** 6 **Unit 3 Pretest/Posttest Form A/B:** 18
12.7	Solve problems by using the strategy *find a pattern.*	**Chapter 12 Posttest Form A/Form B:** 7, 8 **Unit 3 Pretest/Posttest Form A/B:** 9
13.1	Identify and sort solid figures by their flat and curved surfaces.	**Chapter 13 Posttest Form A/Form B:** 5 **Unit 4 Pretest/Posttest Form A/B:** 14 **Beginning/End of Year:** 33

	Lesson Objective	Practice/Test Item Numbers
13.2	Classify solid figures by the number of flat surfaces and corners they have.	**Chapter 13 Posttest Form A/Form B:** 3 **Unit 4 Pretest/Posttest Form A/B:** 17 **Beginning/End of Year:** 2
13.3	Identify plane figures on solids.	**Chapter 13 Posttest Form A/Form B:** 1 **Unit 4 Pretest/Posttest Form A/B:** 8
13.4	Identify and sort plane figures.	**Chapter 13 Posttest Form A/Form B:** 4, 6 **Unit 4 Pretest/Posttest Form A/B:** 4, 12 **Beginning/End of Year:** 20
13.5	Classify plane figures by the number of sides and corners they have.	**Chapter 13 Posttest Form A/Form B:** 2 **Unit 4 Pretest/Posttest Form A/B:** 1 **Beginning/End of Year:** 15
13.6	Solve problems by using the strategy *use logical reasoning*.	**Chapter 13 Posttest Form A/Form B:** 7, 8 **Unit 4 Pretest/Posttest Form A/B:** 21
14.1	Identify and describe concrete repeating patterns.	**Chapter 14 Posttest Form A/Form B:** 3 **Unit 4 Pretest/Posttest Form A/B:** 9
14.2	Predict and extend concrete repeating patterns.	**Chapter 14 Posttest Form A/Form B:** 5 **Beginning/End of Year:** 19
14.3	Predict and extend pictorial repeating patterns.	**Chapter 14 Posttest Form A/Form B:** 1 **Unit 4 Pretest/Posttest Form A/B:** 5 **Beginning/End of Year:** 34
14.4	Identify and describe patterns with missing elements.	**Chapter 14 Posttest Form A/Form B:** 4 **Unit 4 Pretest/Posttest Form A/B:** 13 **Beginning/End of Year:** 14
14.6	Transfer patterns from one representation to another.	**Chapter 14 Posttest Form A/Form B:** 2 **Unit 4 Pretest/Posttest Form A/B:** 15 **Beginning/End of Year:** 38
14.7	Solve problems by using the strategy *find a pattern*.	**Chapter 14 Posttest Form A/Form B:** 6, 7 **Unit 4 Pretest/Posttest Form A/B:** 20
15.1	Identify and describe spatial relationships using position words.	**Chapter 15 Posttest Form A/Form B:** 3
15.2	Use position words to give and follow directions.	**Chapter 15 Posttest Form A/Form B:** 4 **Unit 4 Pretest/Posttest Form A/B:** 22 **Beginning/End of Year:** 25
15.3	Identify and match congruent figures.	**Chapter 15 Posttest Form A/Form B:** 1 **Unit 4 Pretest/Posttest Form A/B:** 16
15.4	Make and identify shapes that have a line of symmetry.	**Chapter 15 Posttest Form A/Form B:** 5 **Unit 4 Pretest/Posttest Form A/B:** 6 **Beginning/End of Year:** 41
15.5	Identify and explore the effects of slides, flips, and turns.	**Chapter 15 Posttest Form A/Form B:** 2 **Unit 4 Pretest/Posttest Form A/B:** 2 **Beginning/End of Year:** 8
15.6	Solve problems by using the strategy *use logical reasoning*.	**Chapter 15 Posttest Form A/Form B:** 6 **Unit 4 Pretest/Posttest Form A/B:** 18, 19
16.1	Identify equal and unequal parts of a whole.	**Chapter 16 Posttest Form A/Form B:** 3 **Unit 4 Pretest/Posttest Form A/B:** 3
16.2	Identify, describe, and name halves.	**Chapter 16 Posttest Form A/Form B:** 1

Lesson Objective		Practice/Test Item Numbers
16.3	Identify, describe, and name fourths.	**Chapter 16 Posttest Form A/Form B:** 4 **Unit 4 Pretest/Posttest Form A/B:** 7
16.4	Identify, describe, and name thirds.	**Chapter 16 Posttest Form A/Form B:** 5
16.5	Identify, describe, and name fractions as parts of a group.	**Chapter 16 Posttest Form A/Form B:** 2 **Unit 4 Pretest/Posttest Form A/B:** 11 **Beginning/End of Year:** 40
16.6	Solve problems by using the strategy *use logical reasoning*.	**Chapter 16 Posttest Form A/Form B:** 6, 7 **Unit 4 Pretest/Posttest Form A/B:** 10
17.1	Add by using the strategies *doubles* and *near doubles*.	**Chapter 17 Posttest Form A/Form B:** 1 **Unit 5 Pretest/Posttest Form A/B:** 3
17.2	Use a ten frame to add 10 and a number less than 10.	**Chapter 17 Posttest Form A/Form B:** 5
17.3	Use the strategy *make-a-ten* to find sums.	**Chapter 17 Posttest Form A/Form B:** 2, 6 **Unit 5 Pretest/Posttest Form A/B:** 14
17.4	Use the Order Property and addition strategies to add three numbers.	**Chapter 17 Posttest Form A/Form B:** 4 **Unit 5 Pretest/Posttest Form A/B:** 7
17.5	Practice addition facts to 20.	**Chapter 17 Posttest Form A/Form B:** 3, 7 **Beginning/End of Year:** 26
17.6	Solve problems by using the strategy *write a number sentence*.	**Chapter 17 Posttest Form A/Form B:** 8, 9 **Unit 5 Pretest/Posttest Form A/B:** 12
18.1	Subtract from 20 or less using a number line to count back.	**Chapter 18 Posttest Form A/Form B:** 1, 2
18.2	Model and compare to show the meaning of subtraction.	**Chapter 18 Posttest Form A/Form B:** 3, 7 **Unit 5 Pretest/Posttest Form A/B:** 5 **Beginning/End of Year:** 10
18.3	Use think addition as a strategy to subtract numbers from 20 or less.	**Chapter 18 Posttest Form A/Form B:** 5 **Unit 5 Pretest/Posttest Form A/B:** 2
18.4	Practice subtraction facts from 20 or less.	**Chapter 18 Posttest Form A/Form B:** 4, 6 **Unit 5 Pretest/Posttest Form A/B:** 11, 19
18.5	Solve problems by using the skill *choose a method*.	**Chapter 18 Posttest Form A/Form B:** 8, 9
19.1	Use fact families to find sums and differences to 20.	**Chapter 19 Posttest Form A/Form B:** 7 **Unit 5 Pretest/Posttest Form A/B:** 21
19.2	Identify a missing number in a number sentence.	**Chapter 19 Posttest Form A/Form B:** 1, 4 **Unit 5 Pretest/Posttest Form A/B:** 13
19.3	Represent numbers by using sums and differences to 20.	**Chapter 19 Posttest Form A/Form B:** 2, 5
19.4	Complete a function table.	**Chapter 19 Posttest Form A/Form B:** 6 **Unit 5 Pretest/Posttest Form A/B:** 4
19.5	Use pictures to create addition and subtraction problems.	**Chapter 19 Posttest Form A/Form B:** 3 **Unit 5 Pretest/Posttest Form A/B:** 6
19.6	Solve problems by using the skill *choose the operation*.	**Chapter 19 Posttest Form A/Form B:** 8, 9 **Unit 5 Pretest/Posttest Form A/B:** 15

	Lesson Objective	Practice/Test Item Numbers
20.3	Identify the total value of a group of coins that includes pennies, nickels, and/or dimes.	**Chapter 20 Posttest Form A/Form B:** 3
20.5	Show ways to make 100¢ with coins and dollars.	**Chapter 20 Posttest Form A/Form B:** 2 **Unit 5 Pretest/Posttest Form A/B:** 10
20.6	Identify and compare given money amounts.	**Chapter 20 Posttest Form A/Form B:** 4 **Unit 5 Pretest/Posttest Form A/B:** 16 **Beginning/End of Year:** 13
20.7	Identify different ways to make equal amounts using coins or one dollar.	**Chapter 20 Posttest Form A/Form B:** 1 **Unit 5 Pretest/Posttest Form A/B:** 9
20.8	Solve problems by using the strategy *act it out.*	**Chapter 20 Posttest Form A/Form B:** 5, 6
21.1	Tell and write time to the hour on analog and digital clocks.	**Chapter 21 Posttest Form A/Form B:** 2 **Unit 5 Pretest/Posttest Form A/B:** 18 **Beginning/End of Year:** 12
21.2	Tell and write time to the half hour on analog and digital clocks.	**Chapter 21 Posttest Form A/Form B:** 1
21.3	Read and show time to the hour and half hour using analog and digital clocks.	**Chapter 21 Posttest Form A/Form B:** 5 **Unit 5 Pretest/Posttest Form A/B:** 17 **Beginning/End of Year:** 37
21.4	Read and use a calendar.	**Chapter 21 Posttest Form A/Form B:** 3 **Unit 5 Pretest/Posttest Form A/B:** 1
21.5	Understand and order the sequence of events with respect to time.	**Chapter 21 Posttest Form A/Form B:** 4 **Unit 5 Pretest/Posttest Form A/B:** 8 **Beginning/End of Year:** 31
21.6	Solve problems by using the skill *use data from a table.*	**Chapter 21 Posttest Form A/Form B:** 6, 7 **Unit 5 Pretest/Posttest Form A/B:** 20
22.1	Compare and order objects by length.	**Chapter 22 Posttest Form A/Form B:** 4 **Unit 6 Pretest/Posttest Form A/B:** 10
22.2	Estimate and measure length by using nonstandard units.	**Beginning/End of Year:** 21
22.3	Estimate and measure length by using nonstandard units.	**Chapter 22 Posttest Form A/Form B:** 3 **Unit 6 Pretest/Posttest Form A/B:** 3
22.4	Measure objects to the nearest inch using a ruler.	**Chapter 22 Posttest Form A/Form B:** 2 **Unit 6 Pretest/Posttest Form A/B:** 9 **Beginning/End of Year:** 43
22.5	Measure objects to the nearest centimeter by using a centimeter ruler.	**Unit 6 Pretest/Posttest Form A/B:** 15
22.6	Read temperature to the nearest degree from Fahrenheit and Celsius thermometers.	**Chapter 22 Posttest Form A/Form B:** 1 **Unit 6 Pretest/Posttest Form A/B:** 5, 22 **Beginning/End of Year:** 1
22.7	Solve problems by using the skill *make reasonable estimates.*	**Chapter 22 Posttest Form A/Form B:** 5, 6 **Unit 6 Pretest/Posttest Form A/B:** 18
23.3	Measure, compare, and order weights of objects.	**Chapter 23 Posttest Form A/Form B:** 1 **Unit 6 Pretest/Posttest Form A/B:** 16 **Beginning/End of Year:** 29

	Lesson Objective	Practice/Test Item Numbers
23.4	Estimate and measure the weight of objects using pounds.	**Chapter 23 Posttest Form A/Form B:** 4 **Unit 6 Pretest/Posttest Form A/B:** 4 **Beginning/End of Year:** 39
23.6	Measure, compare, and order capacity of containers.	**Chapter 23 Posttest Form A/Form B:** 2 **Unit 6 Pretest/Posttest Form A/B:** 2
23.7	Estimate and measure capacity to the nearest cup, pint, or quart.	**Chapter 23 Posttest Form A/Form B:** 3 **Unit 6 Pretest/Posttest Form A/B:** 7
23.8	Choose the correct measuring tool.	**Chapter 23 Posttest Form A/Form B:** 5, 6 **Unit 6 Pretest/Posttest Form A/B:** 11, 21 **Beginning/End of Year:** 9
23.9	Solve problems by using the strategy *predict and test.*	**Chapter 23 Posttest Form A/Form B:** 7, 8 **Unit 6 Pretest/Posttest Form A/B:** 14
24.1	Use mental math to add tens and find sums.	**Chapter 24 Posttest Form A/Form B:** 2 **Unit 6 Pretest/Posttest Form A/B:** 19 **Beginning/End of Year:** 5
24.2	Add tens and ones to find sums.	**Chapter 24 Posttest Form A/Form B:** 4 **Unit 6 Pretest/Posttest Form A/B:** 1
24.3	Add 2-digit numbers to find sums.	**Chapter 24 Posttest Form A/Form B:** 5 **Unit 6 Pretest/Posttest Form A/B:** 12
24.4	Use mental math to subtract tens and find differences.	**Chapter 24 Posttest Form A/Form B:** 1 **Unit 6 Pretest/Posttest Form A/B:** 6
24.5	Subtract tens and ones to find differences.	**Chapter 24 Posttest Form A/Form B:** 3 **Unit 6 Pretest/Posttest Form A/B:** 17
24.6	Subtract 2-digit numbers to find differences.	**Chapter 24 Posttest Form A/Form B:** 6 **Unit 6 Pretest/Posttest Form A/B:** 8 **Beginning/End of Year:** 30
24.7	Solve problems by using the skill *make reasonable estimates.*	**Chapter 24 Posttest Form A/Form B:** 7, 8 **Unit 6 Pretest/Posttest Form A/B:** 13, 20